LEARNING AND HUMAN ABILITIES

EDUCATIONAL PSYCHOLOGY

Herbert J. Klausmeier

William Goodwin

SECOND EDITION

Harper & Row, Publishers NEW YORK AND LONDON

C1

Library of Congress Catalog Card Number: 66-12558

CONTENTS

PART I

Components of the Teaching-Learning Situation

Contents

Contents

PART II

Achieving Learning Outcomes Efficiently

Contents

Rapid and Accurate Movements — Coordination of Move-
ment and Responses   MODEL FOR IMPROVING SKILLS:
Analyze the Skill in Terms of the Learner's Abilities —
Demonstrate the Correct Response — Guide Initial Re-
sponses Verbally and Physically — Arrange for Appropriate
Practice — Provide Knowledge of Results and Correct In-
adequate Responses — Encourage Independent Evaluation
SUMMARY

PART III

Desirable Conditions for Learning

Contents

Contents

AUTOINSTRUCTION: *Skinner's Linear Programing — Crowder's Branching Programing — Pressey's Adjunct Programing — Problems to be Overcome — Computer-Based Teaching Machines* NEW ORGANIZATIONS FOR INSTRUCTION: *Instructional Teams — Noncertified Personnel in Teams — Interns in Teams* NONGRADED SCHOOLS SUMMARY

P A R T I V
Evaluation and Measurement

Contents

PREFACE

The main purpose of the second edition, essentially the same as the first, is to present material which will help students learn more efficiently as individuals and will also help them as professional workers in education, psychology, and related fields. In this, as in the previous edition, we have emphasized learning-teaching processes and have bridged the gap between learning and development as separate entities through the concept of emergent human abilities. The main variables affecting efficiency of learning in the classroom or in other group settings are treated in detail as are the conditions essential to efficient learning.

Many significant events have occurred since the writing of the first edition: More attention is being given nationally to human learning and abilities, and, a great deal of research has been completed in educational settings as a result of substantial financial support from private foundations and the federal government. Also, innovation has become popular in the schools.

Recently, more attention is being given to improving efficiency of learning and the related development of human abilities. Instead of attempting to develop comprehensive learning theories, scholars are now formulating subtheories that deal with more specific matters such as concept learning, problem solving, and motivation. Also, they are extending principles of laboratory learning to complex human behavior in ongoing daily situations. Generalizations drawn from many disciplines are being transformed into principles of instruction. We have included a substantial amount of this large body of new material in the second edition. In addition, we have pioneered in setting forth a functionalist theory of purposeful learning and in formulating nine models of instruction, each dealing with these more specific learning outcomes and phenomena: factual information, concepts, problem solving, creativity, psychomotor abilities and skills, attitudes and values, personality integration, motivation, retention and transfer.

The federal government and private agencies have invested large sums of money in educational research and are continuing to do so. Much of this research has been conducted in school settings with impressive results. We have participated in these research activities and are continuing to do so on a broad scale. Recent research which we felt would contribute materially to the improvement of teaching and learning is incorporated in this edition. Thus, this edition, as did the first, emphasizes learning in the schools and presents much empirical information from research. This is not, however, an unrelated mass of facts. It is organized and anchored firmly to a structure of classroom learning theory and models of instruction.

During the late 1950s, innovations were started in the schools. Foreign-language laboratories, instructional television, instructional teams, nongraded classes, production of textbooks and other instructional material by professional and scientific associations, multimedia instruction, and programed instruction were being talked about by school people. Today they are commonplace. We have incorporated some of these innovations in our own teaching of educational psychology. In the second edition, we have updated the material to take into account these fast-moving innovations, and we also encourage more research in order to evaluate innovations of all types.

In the first edition, the main emphasis was upon learning and the development of human abilities, including measurement and evaluation, with lesser attention given to traditional topics such as social development, physical development, emotional growth, mental hygiene, and counseling and guidance. We secured the reactions of about 100 of the many instructors who used the first edition to determine whether it gave about the proper amount of attention to learning and teaching, development, measurement and evaluation, and statistics. All instructors wanted as much or more attention given to learning and teaching, and most preferred about the same to the other topics; some indicated they did not include all the material on evaluation and statistics. With this in mind, along with the ideas presented in the previous paragraphs, we bolstered the learning-teaching part substantially and kept the other emphases at about the same level. Recognizing that instructors will want to emphasize these topics differently according to the needs of their students, we have organized the second edition for more flexible use. This edition provides the instructor considerable freedom in planning the material he will use and how he will use it. Immediately following the preface there are suggestions in "To the Instructor." Here three different courses for which the book might be used are outlined: a teaching-oriented course, a teaching and science oriented course, and a comprehensive course. The outlines presented are merely examples, and they may be adapted as the instructor chooses. We have found that the comprehensive course can be handled readily by upper division and beginning graduate students. At the sophomore level and in a quarter system with undergraduates, the comprehensive course would be strenuous.

An *Adjunct Program to Accompany Learning and Human Abilities* was prepared for the first edition. We are presenting a *Student Workbook* with the second edition. The *Student Workbook* has two main parts. One part consists of adjunct, objective questions which include revised material from the original adjunct program that will be of help to students in deciding the most important concepts in the second edition and in evaluating their own learning. The other part has questions and activities that are designed to facilitate productive thinking and evaluation, as well as comprehension and recall.

We prepared an *Instructor's Manual* with the first edition, comprised mainly of multiple-choice questions for each chapter. With this edition, we are presenting a *Student Evaluation Guide*. The items are multiple choice, and each question is indexed according to chapter, topic, and page of the text. Provision is made on each card for keeping a record of use.

In 1964, Professor Richard Ripple brought out *Readings in Learning and Human Abilities* in consultation with the senior author of this edition. This book of readings is organized according to the same plan as this edition and can be used advantageously to clarify and supplement the research material presented here. At the end of each chapter of the present edition, in "Suggestions for Further Reading," readings from the Ripple volume are included. Selections from other books of readings are also given.

We cannot properly register appreciation of the assistance of all the persons who contributed ideas to this edition. We have given the usual acknowledgement for ideas used from published sources. We are grateful to Mr. Ray Debus, Senior Lecturer in Education at the University of Sydney, who identified many of the references in English-speaking countries other than the U.S.A. We express appreciation to the many users of the first edition who responded in an interview about numerous facets of the first edition. Other users offered oral and written suggestions for improvement. The many hundreds of students in the classes of the senior author in a course, "Human Abilities and Learning," also gave helpful suggestions. Representing a variety of subject-matter interests and levels of schooling, these students identified some of the applications of psychological knowledge to educational practices. Recent graduated Ph.D. advisees responded with frank and helpful criticism. Included here are Ronald Ady, Chicago Teachers College; Joey Byers, University of California, Berkeley; John Check, University of Michigan, Flint College; Zackaria Ethnathios, Ministry of Education, United Arab Republic; John Feldhusen, Purdue University; William Franzen, University of Toledo; Gerald Gleason, University of Wisconsin—Milwaukee; Mrs. Elmira Layague Johnson, Syracuse University; Leo Loughlin, Northern Illinois University; Dean Meinke, Miami University; Ralph Pippert, University of Massachusetts; Richard Ripple, Cornell University; Mrs. Laila Russell, American University in Cairo, United Arab Republic; Terrence Snowden, Wisconsin State University—Stevens Point; Glenn Tagatz, Indiana State College. Current Ph.D. candidates in educational psychology who have made constructive suggestions include Robert Conry, Kent Davis, Wayne Fredrick, Patricia Kalish, Daniel Lynch, James Ramsay, and Dan Woolpert.

Small but important tasks connected with getting the manuscript in shape were performed by Mrs. Mary Davies and Mrs. Shelby Johnson, who also read the final draft and improved its readability. Mrs. Carolyn Sutton spent many hours at night and on weekends typing the manuscript as did Mrs. Herbert J. Klausmeier. The encouragement provided by our advisory editor, colleague, and dear friend, John Guy Fowlkes, is sincerely appreciated.

HERBERT J. KLAUSMEIER
WILLIAM GOODWIN

December, 1965

TO THE INSTRUCTOR

This book has been written and organized with the expectation that not all instructors will use the chapters in the exact same sequence. Also, some instructors may not assign the entire book for intensive study. Each instructor will decide these and other matters in the light of time available and the needs of the students. In the hope of making decisions easier, we suggest three types of emphases in a course: teaching oriented, teaching and science oriented, and comprehensive with measurement and statistics. Further, two different sequences are outlined for the comprehensive plan. Although all plans require some reading in each of the 18 chapters, the teaching-oriented plan is substantially shorter than the others. This plan might prove appropriate when the course is offered during a quarter, to lower-division students only, or to in-service teachers in one meeting per week.

TEACHING ORIENTED			TEACHING AND SCIENCE ORIENTED		
Chapter No.	Portion of Chapter	Title of Part or Chapter	Chapter No.	Portion of Chapter	Title of Part or Chapter
1.	pp. 1–10	Study of Human Learning	1.	All	The Scope of Educational Psychology
2.	All	Educational Objectives and Human Abilities	2.	All	Educational Objectives and Human Abilities
3.	pp. 60–70	Purposeful Learning	3.	All	Learning Processes and Theories
4.	All	Pupil Characteristics and Learning	4.	All	Pupil Characteristics and Learning
5.	All	Teacher Characteristics and Pupil Learning	5.	All	Teacher Characteristics and Pupil Learning

To the Instructor

To the Instructor

COMPREHENSIVE, INCLUDING EVALUATION AND STATISTICS

To the Instructor

It is apparent that the sequences of the Comprehensive Plans may be maintained while including only the teaching-oriented emphasis or the teaching and science emphasis, simply through omitting parts of chapters, as was done in the first two plans. Other sequences of chapters and of parts of chapters are also possible.

In no plan are there separate chapters dealing with development and learning. Only Chapters 5, 6, and 18 do not include some discussion of readiness for learning or developmental trends in learning. The development of human abilities through learning in educational settings is the central theme of the book, with far greater emphasis on teaching-learning processes than on the nonschool, nonlearning processes of physical, social, and emotional development. Students taking a course that focuses on these topics will not find much overlap with this book. However, with minor additions from outside reading, the educational implications of development are adequately covered by the present book.

In the "To The Student" section are listed 19 books of readings which became the primary sources for the "Suggestions for Further Reading" at the end of each chapter. Some books of readings were used much more extensively than others. This feature is incorporated to facilitate and encourage additional reading by the students in that pertinent materials are made more readily accessible to them.

TO THE STUDENT

Learning from a textbook is facilitated through developing and using an efficient strategy or plan for learning. We had in mind a plan for the student when we wrote this book and offer it here as our best suggestion for facilitating your learning. You may have already developed a more effective plan. Therefore, consider our plan only as a suggestion. Your instructor also may present additional suggestions.

First, study the titles of the four main parts of the book and the chapter titles. Doing this helps you learn the authors' organization of all the information. If the organization is meaningful to you, it will serve as your master organization for selecting, acquiring, retaining, and using the information presented.

Read and study Chapter 1. It presents an overview and is an advance organizer for the remainder of the book.

Select the chapter you are going to study. Study the Contents of the selected chapter until you can remember all the main topics and are familiar with the subtopics. Then read the advance material for that part of the book in which the chapter appears. Studying the advance material will help you acquire key concepts so that your subsequent study will be more meaningful. Also, the advance material serves as a transition between the previous material and that which is presented in the next chapters. The advance material does more than present an overview, however. It helps you to develop an organization so that new material can be compared with and discriminated better from what you already know.

After studying the advance material and learning as much as you can from it, read the entire chapter or any part of it, as may seem best to you. Some students find it helpful to change each main heading to a question and to answer it after completing the appropriate part of the chapter. As you read and study a chapter, think about possible uses of the information. Don't ask yourself merely: "What is important for me to learn and remember?" but also: "How can I *use* what the authors are reporting?" Do not stop with one application to your personal or professional life; think of several. Inasmuch as an instructor cannot point out all possible applications to the personal and professional lives of his students, you must make most of the applications yourself—and there are many to be made.

Some students do not give sufficient attention to the material in figures and tables. We have included figures and tables in this book because they present more information in less space than would any corresponding discussions. When you encounter a reference to a figure or table, read first the entire paragraph containing the reference. Then, turn to the figure or table and study it carefully. Much detailed information is included in tables from which important generalizations may be drawn. These generalizations are not always included in the corresponding discussion.

All behavioral sciences necessarily include some technical information, and educational psychology is no exception. Understanding the technical information in this book requires some understanding of measurement and statistics. Some instructors start the course by discussing statistical terminology as given in Chapter 18 and by making additional assignments to the student for reading the measurement chapters, namely 16 and 17. Other professors put this material in the last weeks of the course; some omit much of it. Regardless of when this material may be assigned, when you encounter a reference to a type of test or a statistical procedure that you do not understand, go first to the index or to the table of contents and then to the appropriate pages of Chapters 16 through 18. Do not hesitate to secure help from the instructor or other students.

There is a *Student Workbook* that you may purchase and use as an aid in your study. It has two main parts. One part consists of objective questions; the other part is essay questions and activities. Perhaps the main values of the objective questions are to let you know what the authors consider to be the key ideas in each chapter and also to inform you of how well you have learned the material. The essay questions and activities are designed to facilitate productive thinking and evaluation, as well as comprehension and recall.

New knowledge is produced by scholars, and we want you to know the name of every scholar whose ideas we have included. We have foregone mentioning the scholar and the date of his publication in the discussions within the chapters; rather, we have put a number inside parentheses to indicate the appropriate reference at the end of the chapter. In the reference section at the end of each chapter, the name of the author, the title of his work, and other bibliographical information are given. You may wish to read some of the references in their entirety.

At the end of each chapter there are also Questions and Activities and Suggestions for Further Reading. The Questions are intended to encourage you to review the important points of the chapter, to apply the information, and to think independently. The Suggestions for Further Reading have been selected with care and are intended to provide a source by which you may expand your knowledge about a topic. Since students often have difficulty locating the suggested readings, you will be pleased to know that the majority of the readings included are available in more than one source. In the Suggestions for Further Reading section, the reading is referenced by its original source as well as by current books of readings in which it appears. Nineteen books of readings were screened for this purpose; the books had to be pertinent, recent, and available when this book was in its latter stages of preparation. Your instructor may indicate that he desires you to obtain one or more of them, thus reducing the necessity for frequent trips to, and often futile searches in, the library.

To conserve space at the end of each chapter, the complete reference for the pertinent book of readings is not given. You will want to refer back to this section to obtain the complete bibliographical reference for any book of readings of interest to you.

Anderson, R. C. & D. P. Ausubel (Eds.). *Readings in the psychology of cognition.* New York: Holt, Rinehart and Winston, 1965.

Charters, W. W., Jr. & N. L. Gage (Eds.). *Readings in the social psychology of education.* Boston: Allyn & Bacon, 1963.

Cohen, J. (Ed.). *Readings in psychology.* London: Allen & Unwin, 1964.

Crow, L. D. & Alice Crow (Eds.). *Readings in human learning.* New York: Longmans, 1963.

DeCecco, J. P. (Ed.). *Human learning in the school: Readings in educational psychology.* New York: Holt, Rinehart and Winston, 1963.

DeCecco, J. P. (Ed.). *Educational technology: Readings in programmed instruction.* New York: Holt, Rinehart and Winston, 1964.

French, J. L. (Ed.). *Educating the gifted: A book of readings* (rev. ed.). New York: Holt, Rinehart and Winston, 1964.

Fullagar, W. A., H. G. Lewis, & C. F. Cumbee (Eds.). *Readings for educational psychology* (2nd ed.). New York: Crowell, 1964.

Gordon, I. J. (Ed.). *Human development: Readings in research.* Chicago: Scott, Foresman, 1965.

Grinder, R. E. (Ed.). *Studies in adolescence.* New York: Macmillan, 1963.

Harper, R. J. C., C. C. Anderson, C. M. Christenson, & S. M. Hunka (Eds.). *The cognitive processes: Readings.* Englewood Cliffs, N. J.: Prentice-Hall, 1964.

Kuhlen, R. G. & G. G. Thompson (Eds.). *Psychological studies of human development.* New York: Appleton-Century-Crofts, 1963.

Mussen, P. H., J. J. Conger, & J. Kagan (Eds.). *Readings in child development and personality.* New York: Harper & Row, 1965.

Page, E. B. (Ed.). *Readings for educational psychology.* New York: Harcourt, Brace, & World, 1964.

Ripple, R. E. (Ed.). *Readings in learning and human abilities: Educational psychology.* New York: Harper & Row, 1964.

Rosenblith, Judy F. & W. Allinsmith (Eds.). *The causes of behavior: Readings in child development and educational psychology.* Boston: Allyn & Bacon, 1962.

Russell, R. W. (Ed.). *Frontiers in psychology.* Chicago: Scott, Foresman, 1964.

Seidman, J. M. (Ed.). *Readings in educational psychology* (2nd ed.). Boston: Houghton Mifflin, 1965.

Staats, A. W. (Ed.). *Human learning: Studies extending conditioning principles to complex behavior.* New York: Holt, Rinehart and Winston, 1964.

It should go without saying that the authors do not endorse all the viewpoints expressed in the suggested readings. Many readings have been included primarily to introduce the student to varying points of view on the same topic.

LEARNING

AND

HUMAN

ABILITIES

CHAPTER 1

The Scope of
Educational Psychology

THIS BOOK is about learning in educational settings, from the stating of educational objectives through measuring and evaluating the results of instruction. It is concerned with human learning in all its richness and variations and with the processes of learning that change the helpless newborn into a thinking, doing, feeling adult of magnificent abilities—into an individual who can use machines to do much of his physical work, who can organize ideas that influence his life and the lives of others, who can create and perform in the fine arts, who can deftly remove a malignant tumor to restore health, and who has compassion and respect for his fellow man.

In this book we present a very positive picture of what the teacher and education generally can do for children and youth. This confidence derives from the findings of a vast accumulation of research which show clearly that the environment can be modified to facilitate learning. The teacher can get uninterested students to want to learn. Situations can be organized to nurture intellectual abilities of students, to facilitate their learning of psychomotor skills, to help them to master subject matter, to encourage favorable attitudes, and to develop buoyant personalities. Of course, not every teacher will be successful with every child, but this does not mean that a teacher cannot learn to teach or that a child cannot learn. No teaching or learning problem should be abandoned as hopeless until most recent knowledge has been brought to bear upon the situation. One should not accept the idea, for example, that half of all beginning sixth-graders are destined to read below the present level of beginning sixth-graders. On the contrary, it is entirely possible that in a decade or so nearly all beginning sixth-graders will read at or above the level of beginning sixth-graders of 1965 and that reading achievement will continue to improve. This can come about from new and improved research methods and more efficient methods of teaching.

The importance of scientific research to man's understanding of his world and of himself can be seen in many areas. For example, over 100 years of research in agriculture has resulted in a very sharp decrease in the actual number of farmers. Yet these few farmers are producing more than enough food for a sharply increasing population. Research connected with human learning and education cannot yet cite a similar dramatic advancement—although illiteracy has decreased sharply in the past century and the level of education has risen consistently. However, with increasing research efforts, bits of knowledge are accumulating which, when brought together, comprise a substantial body of information. Principles of instruction, based upon research in laboratories and schools, are now stated with the full assurance that, if properly applied, they will result in more efficient learning. And an increasing number of psychologists and educators are concerned with improving learning in formal and informal school settings.

This emphasis on the study of learning is stated by Hilgard: ". . . we believe that scientific psychology of learning has the obligation to go all the way from theory to practice, using criticized data in every step" (2). Not only American but also British (4) and Canadian (5) psychologists agree that the main concern of educational psychology should be with learning in school settings, and with both theory and practice.

THE STUDY OF HUMAN LEARNING

At age 5 you probably could not read, yet now you can. How did you learn to read your first word? Was it through seeing the word, hearing the teacher say the word, and imitating the teacher? Was it through looking at the printed word, accidentally saying it correctly, and having the teacher inform you that you had said it correctly? Was it some other way? As you think about how you learned to read your first word, try to recall your first teacher. What do you recall about her? Why don't you recall more of the details? Is it because the details have faded away with the passage of time? Is it because experiences with later teachers have interfered, causing you to forget? Did you *try* to forget her? What explanations might be offered to explain forgetting? Consider, too, what you have already learned in college. Can you apply it? How is it that some knowledge and some skills are useful in acquiring still more knowledge and skill? How is it that some is not useful?

Psychologists who study learning are interested in explaining initial acquisition, remembering, and transfer. They are also interested in finding out the effects of instructions, of practice schedules, of rewards or reinforcements, of meaningfulness of tasks, and of other variables in the efficiency of learning. Readiness for learning and the upper limits of learning are also exciting research problems. All of these problems can be pursued in laboratory experiments with carefully selected subjects. When, however, we move to a normal group situation wherein students are to attain many specified objectives, the situation becomes more complex and we must consider seven main groups of variables, as shown in Fig. 1.1, that affect efficiency of learning in a group situation. Notice that efficiency of learning is related to educational *objectives*. For example, if an objective is to have students learn to speak a second language fluently, we can listen to them speak to determine whether they are attaining this objective efficiently. If, on the other hand, the objective is to have students write a second language fluently, we can assess their efficiency in writing. There are numerous ways of stating objectives, but they should be clearly stated in terms of what the students are specifically to learn, the specific abilities they are to improve, and so forth. Ways of categorizing objectives are treated in Chapter 2.

Characteristics of Learners

In most situations, pupil characteristics is the most important variable in determining the efficiency of learning. Almost nothing can keep bright, healthy children from learning something. Put ten bright 6-year-olds in a room with appropriate reading and writing materials, and they will learn to read and write without much assistance from anyone. If put in a swimming pool, none will likely drown; rather, each will probably learn to swim. But with an excellent teacher, they learn more efficiently. On the other hand, put ten mentally retarded

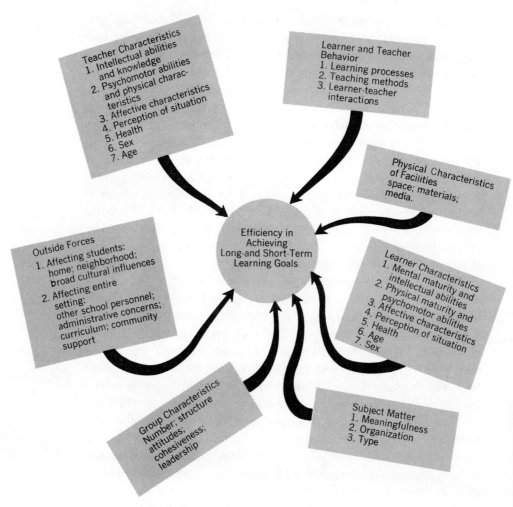

Fig. 1.1.   The behavioral setting for learning.

students of high school age in an algebra class, and even with the very best teacher and all other conditions favorable, none will probably acquire a concept of algebraic equations. In a shop class, however, they might learn wholesome attitudes toward self, others, and work, and many might acquire a salable vocational skill.

Let us now draw other sharp contrasts related to the characteristics of the learner. One 15-year-old has poor coordination, is completely uninterested in learning, does not accept himself or the teacher, has a chronic cold with a low fever, and perceives the learning activity as another in a long series of failures. The second 15-year-old has excellent coordination, is highly interested in learning, accepts himself and the teacher both as worthwhile persons, is in excellent health, and perceives the learning activity as potentially another in a long series of successes. The same teacher who will experience excellent results with the latter pupil will not be able to teach the first pupil very well unless each of the conditions can be changed. Chapter 4 treats characteristics of pupils in detail.

Characteristics of the Teacher

How important is the teacher? In most situations, the teacher exercises a great deal of influence on the personal lives of the learners as well as on what they learn. Consider the contrasting characteristics of two teachers. One knows music exceedingly well, sings excellently, has high interest in teaching children to sing, is in excellent health, accepts himself and the pupils as worthwhile persons, and perceives in this situation a challenging opportunity for helping learners develop their abilities and, in turn, for experiencing success as a teacher. The second teacher knows little music, sings poorly, and so on. Unless the pupils are unusually well behaved and have a burning desire to sing, they will not profit from instruction with the second teacher. Characteristics of the teacher, treated in more detail in Chapter 5, are thus of considerable influence.

Subject Matter

The same student does not always achieve equally well in different subject matters—for example, in mathematics, foreign language, music, and typing; and the older he gets the more specialized do his interests and achievements become. Also, after primary school, only a rare, exceptional teacher is found to be equally strong, or even competent, in all the different subject matters that children are to learn. Thus, the subject matter to be learned is an important variable associated with efficiency of learning.

The potential meaningfulness of the subject matter derives from the clarity with which the field is defined. Older disciplines have more clearly defined content than do the more recent ones—for example, chemistry in comparison with political science. Psychological meaningfulness is an individual matter, referring to how well the individual can form and retain associations among the parts or elements of a subject. Mathematics is not equally meaningful psychologically to all students. Meaningfulness is not synonymous with organization but the two are related. In general, better organization of the subject matter leads to more efficient learning, whether the material is to be memorized or fully comprehended. Subject matter could be equally well defined and potentially meaningful but vary in type, such as English grammar and federal government. Because of interaction among teachers, students, and subject matter, differences in efficiency of learning might occur among the same students. Our state of knowledge has progressed sufficiently that we recognize subject matter as a powerful variable; that is, we do not expect the same students to acquire all subject matter equally efficiently.

Learner and Teacher Behavior

The behavior of the learner includes the processes by which he learns. To some extent, the same processes are involved, regardless of the type of learning outcome—for example, cognizing environmental events. However, it appears that certain processes also vary according to the type of learning outcome—for example, learning to ride a bicycle and attitudes toward government. The attitudes are learned at a low level of awareness on the part of the learner through a process of imitation and with few repetitions, whereas learning to ride a bicycle well is accomplished with conscious purpose and many repetitions. Modern theories that are more relevant to certain outcomes than others are discussed in Chapter 3. Relevant elements of these theories are again presented in Chapters 7 through 15.

The behavior of the teacher includes his methods. Based on what we know about learning, it would seem that different methods would be used in achieving different objectives. In addition, these various methods should be based on principles, rather than being purely intuitive. Broudy gives an interesting account of historic exemplars of teaching methods, including the Socratic dialectic, scholasticism, and the method of nature by Comenius (1). A brief summary of modern methods is made by Wallen and Travers (3). We shall not give major attention to methods in this book; only a brief note is made on methods in Chapter 6. However, in Chapters 7 through 13, principles are stated in terms of possible actions of the teacher in directing the learning activities of students. Thus, in Chapter 3, some relevant theories are described; in the early parts of Chapters 7 through 13 empirical information about learning processes is presented; and in the sections devoted to principles, the knowledge and theory are combined into statements of generalizations and related principles of instruction.

From the interaction of the teacher and students, other conditions associated with efficient learning arise. Included here are motivation, the management of practice and review which in turn affect retention and transfer, and provisions for individual differences among students. The effects of the teacher's actions depend upon the students' reactions; therefore, the transactions between teacher and students, not merely the actions of the teacher or the interaction between the teacher and students, are significant. A more complete discussion of teacher and pupil behavior is presented in Chapter 5. Chapter 12 deals with motivation, Chapter 13 with retention and transfer, Chapter 14 with provisions for differences among students, and Chapter 15 includes media and organization for instruction.

Group Characteristics

The fifth main factor in Fig. 1.1 is designated "group characteristics." A group may be merely a collection of individuals. For example, if 25 or 30 college students who do not know one another meet for the first time in a classroom, the particular group at that point has no structure or cohesiveness and has not yet generated common group attitudes. These same students, however, may come to know one another well; and small groups may form within the larger group, in which case there will be a group structure. Further, if they consider themselves members in the sense that the players on a basketball or football team do, definite group attitudes and cohesiveness will emerge. If the teacher is at all concerned with helping students acquire social attitudes and skills, he may encourage this group formation so that it develops in a relatively short time.

Think now of two classroom groups. One is characterized by several cliques. That is, a class of 25 to 30 pupils is informally arranged into smaller groups, and each of these smaller groups operates independently of the others. Further, one of the cliques is a minority group. The majority group does not interact at all with the minority group. Another clique is composed of four or five students from wealthy homes; these associate only with one another and no one else. Still another clique is composed of four or five students with low economic status.

They, too, associate among themselves but not with other cliques. A contrasting classroom group would be one in which all the students know one another, accept one another, and associate freely with one another. The same teacher would have a very different problem in attempting to help each of these classroom groups develop social skills and a common background of attitudes and values.

Characteristics of Physical Facilities

A sixth main factor in the behavioral setting is the easiest to control if adequate monies are available. It is designated "physical characteristics." Although it is perfectly obvious that no one would try to teach students to play the piano without a piano, or to teach swimming without available water, there is a tendency to try to teach many concepts in science, mathematics, social studies, and English without the needed space, supplies, or equipment. Again consider two contrasts. In one foreign-language class there are booths with tape recorders, and each pupil may use the tape recorder to record his own voice and play it back or to listen to a recording of the teacher's voice. The tape recorders in this room are managed in such a way that the pupil can learn on his own and use the recorder to learn at a speed appropriate to him. The teacher may use his recording to point out specific pronunciation difficulties.

In the second class, no tape recorder is available. The only opportunity the student has to learn is in direct interaction with the teacher or in interaction with other learners. In the second situation it is impossible for each student to proceed at his own rate or even to hear himself. The possibility for efficient learning is less in the latter situation. Similarly, if a group of 30 pupils has only 20 typewriters the possibilities for efficient learning are much less than if 30 typewriters were available.

Outside Forces

The seventh factor shown in Fig. 1.1 is called "outside forces." Each of the forces included might readily be considered as a separate factor; however, for the sake of convenience they are all grouped under one main heading to present an overview. The home, neighborhood, and broader cultural influences brought to bear on the pupil are reflected in his personal characteristics and behavior in the classroom. These out-of-school forces often affect his attitude toward learning in school.

8

Some children come to school eager to learn; others are much less eager or are actually resistant.

Somewhat as the home and neighborhood affect the pupil, so also do other school personnel who work with the teacher or the pupils directly. If, for example, a school system has visiting teachers, psychologists, counselors, and curriculum supervisors who are available to help the teacher when necessary, many problems that the teacher might not be able to deal with effectively can be overcome.

The administrative organization of the school, too, may influence the behavioral setting. If the school day is divided into seven class periods and students attend seven different classes with instruction from seven different teachers, it is entirely possible that no teacher will know any student very well. On the other hand, if one teacher has a small group of 25 or 30 pupils in a multiple-period or homeroom class for two periods a day, at least that one teacher in the school can know and understand each pupil in the class quite well.

Curriculum requirements placed upon teachers vary widely among schools. In some schools teachers are required, regardless of the ability of their pupils, to complete a certain amount of material from the recommended textbook each day. In a larger school system, one ninth-grade class has students of low intelligence, whereas in another class there are students of exceptionally high intelligence. Yet, by a curriculum prescription, both classes are required to use the same textbook, and the teachers are expected to "cover" the textbook material at the same rate of speed. Such rigid curriculum prescriptions, of course, greatly impede the efficiency of pupil learning.

Communities also vary in expectations and support of the school. In some communities, most of the parents expect their children to behave decently and to work hard in school. In other communities the parents treat the school as a place to send their children to get them out of the way; they do not have high expectations for the school nor do they encourage their children to work hard or to acquire the idea that hard work and consistent effort in school are wise. These and other community attitudes impose some limitations upon what and how efficiently the students will learn.

When we say that outside forces such as the home, and that student characteristics such as intellectual abilities are variable, we are indicating that they can be studied in experiments. Consider home background. Assume that, in Community A, the home backgrounds of children can be divided, according to family relationships, into five

9

categories. We could draw samples of children from each of the five categories, instruct them in a given way, and determine the relationship of home background to achievement after instruction. Does this mean then that future children from the particular type of background associated with lowest achievement would be the lower achievers? Not at all. In line with our earlier discussion, we hypothesize that, provided time, personnel, and monies were available, parents and children could learn to change their home relationships and also their school achievements. Similarly, we do not accept the idea of intellectual ability as being a fixed and unchangeable characteristic. Research shows that intelligence test scores change markedly, especially in young children; and we are now getting knowledge that will very likely enable us to improve the intellectual abilities of children from impoverished educational backgrounds. While the intellectual ability and other characteristics of the teacher are relatively more stable than are similar characteristics in young children, we know that teachers are capable of varying their actions in the classroom. Thus, we consider most of the variables given in Fig. 1.1 to be of the type that can actually be changed to produce more efficient learning, not merely used as stratifying variables in experiments for the purpose of finding relationships that exist at the present time.

OTHER CONCERNS
OF EDUCATIONAL PSYCHOLOGY

The educational psychologist cannot get far in his study of learning in the school without taking into account the student, the teachers, the subject matter, the instructional media and materials, and the other important groups of variables discussed previously. Further, adding to knowledge requires careful observation and analysis, and these in turn demand knowledge of experimental design and statistics. Measurement is needed in order to determine how much learning occurs. Thus, the study of learning takes into account these variables, but this is not the same as the study of them. Human development, experimental design and statistics, and measurement and evaluation are important fields of study in their own right. In addition school psychology and counseling are career fields that require considerable preparation in educational psychology. Let us consider these further in order to clarify the relationship of learning to them and to outline the entire field of educational psychology, including graduate work. Many prospective teachers become graduate students in educational psychology.

Human Development and Exceptional Children

The study of human development is concerned with describing, understanding, and predicting the development of the individual from early childhood into adulthood. Also, control of behavior is increasingly being studied by those who consider development to be the product of both maturation and learning. Despite the fact that some psychologists accept this point of view, there still appears to be a substantial difference among the topics of learning and of development. Thus, we have a typical sequence of four courses in human development—infancy and early childhood, childhood, adolescence, and maturity—along with specialized advanced work.

Closely related to human development is the area of exceptional children. Up to the present time, most of the emphasis has been given to children with exceptionalities below normal, rather than above. The main areas of investigation have been related to mental retardation, handicaps of the various sensory modalities, orthopedic handicaps, emotional disturbance, and antisocial behavior and delinquency. Provisions for giftedness and creativity, however, have been making considerable headway since World War II.

Statistics and Experimental Design

As was noted previously the discovery of new knowledge depends primarily on making careful observations and analyzing the resulting data. Statistical procedures are often used in the analysis of data. Experimental design and statistics are related because many experimental designs are based on statistical methods, sampling, etc. Designs for experimentation in school have not been given much attention until recently and, in general, have been characterized by lack of imagination. Other difficulties in experimentation in the schools have included lack of cooperation from the schools in securing samples of children and the inability to secure teachers to carry out different instructional procedures. In addition, problems frequently stem from opposition of parents who do not want their children used as experimental subjects. In recent years, however, most of the problems with the schools have disappeared and bright, young graduate students are becoming proficient in experimental design.

We shall not at this point attempt to enumerate the statistical principles upon which educational psychology so heavily depends (see Chapter 18); it is enough to emphasize here the vast importance of statistics to the scientific method. The student of educational psychology should familiarize himself with statistics and experimental design if he is to observe and to understand the complexities of the learning situation and of learning behavior. Further, the test manuals which accompany standardized educational achievement and general intellectual ability tests used in schools include much statistical terminology, such as *mean, median, standard deviation, percentile, reliability,* and *validity.* Thus, knowledge of statistics at the level indicated in Chapter 18 is important to the student of this book.

Measurement and Evaluation

Determining the efficiency of learning requires measurement and evaluation. Also, learning is more efficient when readiness for learning is ascertained, when students are made aware of their progress, and when they are informed of correct responses and are helped to overcome incorrect responses. The administration and scoring of tests of any type is considered to be measurement. Interpreting scores, which involves judging performance or some other characteristic in relation to a standard, is evaluation. For example, administering and scoring a mathematics test is measurement. Evaluation is concerned with deciding how well each student is doing in relation to the teacher's expectations of him, to some prediction of his ability in mathematics, to the desirability of his continuing the study of mathematics, or to some other standard.

Measurement and evaluation are useful in making educational decisions of two main types: readiness of pupils for learning and amount of progress made. In connection with readiness, let us assume that there are wide differences in the present levels of achievement in reading among the 5000 second-grade pupils in a city. Proper measurement materially helps to define these differences and also to estimate where each child achieves in relation to others. Evaluation is necessary to determine what type of reading material might be best suited for individuals and groups of children among the 5000.

Amount of progress is not easy to assess, but learning is more efficient when a continuous record of achievement is kept by each student. Measurement and evaluation are essential for achieving this purpose. For example, if we wished to secure a reliable estimate of achievement in spelling, we sample from among all the possible new words that might be learned during the semester. By administering a test based on this sampling at the beginning and the end of the semester, we secure an estimate of the gain in achievement in spelling during the semester.

Evaluating how well students achieve is a complex task that requires objectives stated in such a way that they specify the behavior which should result from instruction. It also requires development or selection of instructional materials and activities which will produce this behavior, and then the construction of appropriate measuring instruments to determine the extent to which the behavior has been achieved. This task is of sufficient complexity that in most instances it is postponed until graduate study, with little or no instruction being given to prospective teachers.

School Psychology and Counseling

Both school psychology and counseling in the public schools have demonstrated remarkable growth and vitality in the last decades. School psychologists work mainly in the elementary schools; guidance and counseling personnel work in the high school. The preparation of both groups of professional personnel is concentrated at the graduate level.

School psychologists do a considerable amount of diagnostic and therapeutic work with individual children and their parents. They work with teachers in outlining programs of education appropriate for the children receiving diagnosis or treatment, and also participate in broader aspects of curriculum development and improvement of instruction. It is not uncommon in large cities for the chief school psychologist to hold a doctorate degree and to head the entire program of school testing and pupil guidance services, including those in the high schools.

Located most frequently in the senior high school, the counselor does less individual testing and more occupational guidance than does the school psychologist in the elementary school. Most high school counselors do less intensive diagnosis and psychotherapy, primarily because they have not been prepared for this type of work. It is not uncommon for each student to visit with a counselor twice during the school year; whereas many elementary school children are not seen at all by a school psychologist, but some are seen each week over an extended period of time.

Besides the usual program of graduate work in learning, development, exceptional children, measurement and evaluation, and statistics, both counselors and school psychologists have clinical experiences as interns in the schools.

EDUCATIONAL PSYCHOLOGY
AS A SCIENCE

As noted previously, the scientific study of learning and other human behavior with relevance to education is the principal concern of educational psychology. Thus, educational psychology may be thought of as a behavioral science with two main referents—human behavior and education. Human beings are the objects of investigation about whom generalizations are developed and knowledge is sought. The second important referent is education. Educational psychology is concerned with behavioral questions that are related to the objectives and practices of education. Let us consider further what is meant by behavior.

Although *behavior* as generally understood covers a broad area, by strict definition, the word refers only to activity that can be observed and recorded. Certain muscular movements, for example, and speaking and writing, are examples of observable behavior, while feelings, attitudes, and thought processes are not strictly classified as behaviors as they are not directly observable. Nevertheless, we can infer these important internal aspects from manifest behavior, and thus, in a less restricted sense, *behavior* refers to anything the individual does. In this way, feeling, thinking, and learning are behavior, and can be subjected to scientific investigation. Some psychologists even include cellular activity as behavior. However, educational psychology is not concerned with explaining cellular activity.

Other disciplines that are also concerned with human behavior include education, sociology, anthropology, economics, and political science. Each is properly a part of or based on the behavioral sciences. Indeed, knowledge from these and other behavioral sciences is often relevant to education, both to the institution and to the means of educating. However, psychology may be considered the primary behavioral science. The domain of psychology is very broad, ranging from the study of the behavior of single living cells of animals to the study of the collective behavior of human beings. The domain of educational psychology also is broad.

The Methods of Science

Recall your activities and behavior, of the past 24 hours. Your behavior was varied. You and other human beings are capable of a rich variety of behavior, ranging from simple acts connected with maintaining life to highly complex acts like communicating your thoughts to others, solving complex problems, engaging in skilled motor acts, and producing new knowledge. Because human behavior varies so much some people doubt that it can be studied scientifically. Though varied, much of one's behavior is also surprisingly consistent; it can be understood and predicted, even controlled. Here is the basis for the scientific study of behavior, inasmuch as the purposes of any science are to understand, to predict, and to control.

In order to understand behavior or any other phenomenon, it is necessary to observe it carefully. To fail to do so, or to form too quickly an opinion on the basis of what may seem like common sense, can lead to beliefs which are different from what is really the case. Predictions made on such beliefs will prove to be inaccurate. Because of this, scientific methods have been developed—and are still developing —which are increasingly precise and will therefore yield consistently reliable, repeatable results as long as the same methods are used to observe the same phenomena under the same conditions.

The methods of observing human behavior range from noting the behavior of an individual or individuals in a naturalistic setting, without any controls brought into the setting, through observation in a laboratory, where all elements of the situation are controlled so that one variable can be manipulated and its effects on other behavior noted. We are all familiar with careful observations as reported in descriptions of short duration and in descriptions of behavior covering long periods of time, such as incorporated in case studies. Developmental psychologists have observed and categorized the behavior of many children at various ages. These descriptions of typical behaviors become the age "norm" behaviors. Educators and test specialists observe the achievements of students in reading at the various age or grade levels. The typical achievement becomes the norm for the grade. The same persons observe the variations in reading achievement. These variations are also reported and supply some of our knowledge concerning individual differences. This type of observing and reporting yields descriptions of behavior but it does not explain why the behavior occurs.

We may, through careful observation, note that two things seem to occur simultaneously. For example, the same children are given an intelligence test in the fall and an achievement test in reading the following spring. It is noted that the children tend to score alike on the two tests. We properly conclude that intelligence and reading achievement, as measured by the tests, are positively related. If the relationship is high (and based on other knowledge about predicting) we may be able to predict, from the intelligence-test scores, how well the children will achieve in reading. This is very useful information to have, and many correlational studies are done in the study of human behavior. However, the fact that two behaviors are related does not explain them in terms of cause and effect. We cannot conclude that being able to read well results in higher intelligence or that higher intelligence results in higher reading.

Securing reliable information about cause-and-effect relationships (functional relationships) requires a special kind of observation, in which one event can be determined as resulting in another. For example, it is established that heating water to 212° F causes it to change from a liquid to a gaseous state. While this does not explain fully why heat causes water to vaporize, it does permit very effective control in the sense that we can control the liquid and gaseous states of water if we can control the heating process. In human behavior, we are interested in functional relationships that permit more accurate predictions and control as well as in describing and correlating.

If enough time is spent in accurate, repeatable observation of human behavior in its natural state, many cause-and-effect relations will be found. In order to save time and to improve the accuracy of observations and resulting conclusions, psychologists have developed certain methods of observation and of controlling situational factors that are loosely labeled *controlled experimentation*. In controlled experimentation in the laboratory, for example, certain conditions are varied or manipulated, while everything else about the experiment is controlled, in order to determine the effect of one variable (the independent variable) upon performance (the dependent variable). For example, an experiment is arranged to determine the effects on typing performance of five trials of 4 minutes each with a 1-minute rest interval (distributed practice) in comparison with one trial of 24 minutes (massed practice). If a significant difference in performance is observed, one would conclude that the improved performance was functionally related to the distribution of practice. Most psychologists prefer to say "functionally related to" or "a function of" rather than "caused by."

Although 20 different psychologists with 20 successive students get this result in the laboratory, we cannot be sure that 20 teachers, each with 30 students, will get the same results. So we also do controlled experimentation in the classrooms. Let us identify 50 teachers offering typing instruction to ninth-graders. Let us randomly divide them into two groups, one of which uses the distributed practice and the other the massed practice. We must make sure that the teachers use the same materials, methods, etc., except that one group follows the distributed practice and the other the massed procedure. After appropriate periods of time during a year, we determine how well the students type and observe the differences, if any. This outline of an unrefined classroom experiment shows the difficulties of controlled experimentation in the classroom, but it also emphasizes that generalizations drawn from the laboratory should not be applied directly to school situations without testing in the schools.

The Vocabulary of Science

Art, religion, philosophy—all have a specialized vocabulary, and science has also. From the immense vocabulary of science, consider only four terms: *generalization, principle, hypothesis,* and *theory.* We shall provide one or two applications of these terms to educational psychology as a further means of clarifying the scientific nature of educational psychology.

A *generalization* explicitly states or implies a relationship between two or more events. For example, *knowledge of results facilitates the learning of skills* is a generalization. In educational psychology we are concerned with the relationships among teachers, students, instructional materials, etc. More specifically we are interested in the stimulating events (causes)—for example, teacher actions, type of instructional material, class activities, etc.—upon the learner; and the *response* events (effects)—that is, how the learner responds. Of course, how the student responds (or doesn't respond) will, in turn, provide a stimulus for teacher behavior, class reaction, and so forth; so educational psychology is concerned with the generalizations which state functional (cause-and-effect) relationships among nonstatic variables.

We use the term *principle* to indicate a statement which implies action. For example:

GENERALIZATION	PRINCIPLE
Immediate knowledge of results facilitates the learning of skills.	(The teacher) Provides knowledge of results immediately (to students).
An observer acquires new behaviors through imitating a model.	(The teacher) Provides exemplary models (for students).

Notice the relationship implied in the first principle: "If the teacher provides knowledge of results immediately (informs students when their responses are correct or incorrect), students will acquire a series of responses more efficiently." Some scientists use the term *principle* as we have used *generalization*. We have differentiated the terms in order to make very clear that generalizations are conclusions derived from research and theory while principles indicate actions to be taken by teachers or other educational personnel.

If the relationship stated in a generalization has been empirically proved by reliable, repeatable methods, it is considered to be a factual relationship. However, if such a relationship is believed to exist but has not yet been proven empirically, the statement is called a *hypothesis*. Of course, if empirical research disproves the relationship hypothesized, the statement is dropped from the body of scientific knowledge.

Simultaneously with establishing functional relationships between independent and dependent variables, science is concerned with *theory* building. It should be noted here that some believe the word *theory* to mean the opposite of *practical*. This sort of definition leads to the notion that theory is misleading, dangerous, or at least too vague to merit serious consideration. For example, it is common to hear teachers disregard what they label "misty theory" by remarking that thinkers in "ivory towers" have no conception of what is occurring on the firing line. In part this results because the term *theory* has been used by some to indicate unsupported notions about how something should be done. Unfortunately, many persons have developed beliefs about how things should be done in schools and call the results "theories," instead of what they really are: opinions about educational practice. Much of what goes for educational theory today is derived from philosophical traditions, unrelated to empirical information or to principles based on empirical information. Theory, however, does serve several important purposes in science, and the word has a different meaning to scientists.

A scientific theory is comprised of a relatively small number of general explanatory statements and, thus, has one main purpose of summarizing relationships among a large amount of empirical information, concepts, and generalizations. However, the statements of relationships go beyond the empirical information itself and apply to more events. For example, many observations are summarized in the statement "an observer acquires new behavior through imitating a model." This statement, while based on research, is intended to explain many events in addition to those associated with the empirical information gathered. Thus, a theory summarizes a large amount of empirical information and concepts which are useful in prediction. Given a child as an observer and an adult as a model, we may predict that the child will make new responses—utter words, make gestures, etc.—that the adult makes, and that the child will pronounce words and incorporate usage patterned after the adult model.

A theory also is useful to scientists in formulating new hypotheses and carrying out further experimentation. In the early part of this century, Thorndike stated a theory of learning in which the main statements were summarized in a small number of generalizations that he called "laws." One of his laws was that a connection (an association between a stimulus and response) followed by a satisfying state of affairs will be strengthened, and a connection followed by an annoying state of affairs will be weakened. This law was the basis for much subsequent experimentation and the formation of other theories. At the present time, many experiments are being conducted with human beings to determine more precisely the nature and effects of reward and punishment on behavior.

Classification Systems in Science

Science is concerned not only with the generation of empirical information, generalizations, and theory, but also with classification schemes. Some classification schemes involve a hierarchy, such as the kingdom-to-subspecies arrangement of the animal and plant worlds. In educational psychology, the whole field of measurement can be hierarchically organized. Measurement itself would be the most complex concept, followed by the subconcepts of the different types of tests, such as objective and essay tests. The specific tests under each type would be lowest in the hierarchy. Other classification schemes may include concepts of equal value. For example, outcomes of learning such as psychomotor skills, concepts, and attitudes are not arranged in a hierarchy; one can start and end with any one of them.

The usefulness of a classification scheme depends on many factors. Most important is the quality of the observations and descriptions upon which the empirical information is based. If the observation is detailed and systematic and its verbal description is reliable, we could build useful classification schemes for understanding and predicting. For example, by knowing the attributes or characteristics of mammals, we can predict reliably that any animal classed as a mammal will suckle its young. Similarly, by knowing what an attitude is and the generalization that attitudes are acquired through imitation, we can understand why a young child acquires the attitudes of the other people in his environment. In biology and other sciences, observation, description, and classification rather than controlled experimentation, are the main activities of many scientists.

As already indicated, educational psychology uses the methods of science and has a substantial body of knowledge. This is not to say, however, that it is a complete science or that the entire body of knowledge is systematized adequately. Educational psychology has a specifiable scope of inquiry, uses the methods of science, has organized some of its knowledge in a reasonably systematic fashion, and includes some techniques for applying the knowledge to practical ends in educational settings.

SUMMARY

Educational psychology is a behavioral science which contributes methods, empirical information, principles, and theory to the improvement of learning and teaching.

Efficiency of learning in a classroom is associated with seven groups of variables: characteristics of the learners, characteristics of the teacher, the subject matter, the behavior of the teacher and learners, characteristics of the group, physical characteristics of the setting, and outside forces.

In this book we emphasize learning, instruction, emergent human abilities and other characteristics of students, achieving learning outcomes efficiently, desirable conditions for efficient learning, and the measurement and evaluation of abilities and progress in learning.

QUESTIONS AND ACTIVITIES

1. a. What are the seven main groups of variables that affect efficient learning in the classroom?
   b. Based on your experiences in classrooms, put the seven groups of variables in rank order of their effects on efficiency of learning, the first rank being most important. Indicate why you put them in the particular order.
   c. Examine all the variables listed under each of the seven main headings. Delete or add to the list and indicate your reasons for doing so.

2. a. Five areas of concentration in educational psychology, in addition to human learning, were described briefly. Which of these appeals most to you for intensive study?
   b. What additional information do you need about educational

psychology in order to determine whether you would pursue it in graduate study?

c. What seems to be the relationship among the six areas so that they are all included in a comprehensive program of graduate study in educational psychology?

3. Why is educational psychology classified as a behavioral science?

4. What are the relationships among empirical information, generalizations, hypotheses, and theory?

5. What is the relationship of educational psychology to the practice of teaching?

6. Why is it that knowledge in educaticnal psychology is more tentative than in physics or history?

7. What may the reader do in order to profit from study of this book?

SUGGESTIONS FOR FURTHER READING

Bieliauskas, V. J. Science, philosophy, and psychology. In F. L. Ruch (Ed.), *Psychology and life.* Chicago: Scott, Foresman, 1963, pp. 575–579. (In Russell, 1964, 1–6.)

Chaplin, J. P., & T. S. Krawiec. *Systems and theories of psychology.* New York: Holt, Rinehart and Winston, 1960. (Pp. 4–10 reprinted under the title "Psychology within the framework of science" in Russell, 1964, 6–9.)

Coladorci, A. P. The relevancy of educational psychology. *Educ. Leadership,* 1956, **13,** 489–492. (In Ripple, 1964, 38–42.)

Rogers, C. R. Implications of recent advances in prediction and control of behavior. *Teachers Coll. Rec.* 1956, **57,** 316–322.

Royce, J. R. Psychology, existentialism, and religion. *J. gen. Psychol.,* 1962, **66,** 3–16. (In Fullagar, *et al.,* 1964, 95–106.)

REFERENCES

1. Broudy, H. S. Historic exemplars of teaching method. In N. L. Gage (Ed.), *Handbook of research on teaching.* Chicago: Rand McNally, 1963, pp. 1–43.

2. Hilgard, E. R. Postscript: Twenty years of learning theory in relation to education. In E. R. Hilgard (Ed.), *Theories of learning and instruction.* Yearb. nat. Soc. Stud. Educ., 1964, 63, Part I., pp. 416–418.

3. Wallen, N. E., & R. M. W. Travers. Analysis and investigation of teaching methods. In N. L. Gage (Ed.), *Handbook of research on teaching.* Chicago: Rand McNally, 1963, pp. 448–505.

4. Wiseman, S. Trends in educational psychology. *Brit. J. educ. Psychol.,* 1959, **29,** 128–135.

5. Woodsworth, J. G. Some theoretical bases for a psychology of instruction. *Canad. Educ. Res. Dig.,* 1965, **5,** 14–26.

PART I

Components of the Teaching-Learning Situation

WHAT ARE your present abilities? Do you possess more and higher-level abilities than your ancestors of 5000 years ago? How much knowledge do you possess? Is it more or less than your ancestors of 100 years ago? What kind of a person are you? Are you happier and more productive than your parents? How has the school contributed to your present abilities, knowledge, and personality? What do we know about learning and teaching that will enable us to raise the level of human abilities, to add to knowledge and skills, to enable a person to understand himself and others better, and to behave accordingly? We shall consider the following key questions regarding the teaching-learning situation in the next chapters:

How are children's abilities, knowledge, and affective characteristics related to objectives of education?	Chapter 2. Educational Objectives and Human Abilities
How does knowledge of learning processes and theories contribute to more efficient learning and teaching?	Chapter 3. Learning Processes and Theories
How do characteristics of the learner affect his readiness to learn and efficiency of learning?	Chapter 4. Pupil Characteristics and Learning
How do characteristics of the teacher affect efficient pupil learning?	Chapter 5. Teacher Characteristics and Pupil Learning
How do the behaviors of the teacher and the student affect efficiency of learning?	Chapter 6. Classroom Interactions and Learning

As you read and study, try to relate the content to your previous experiences, to your present interests, and to your future commitments. Make the applications to yourself as a learner and as a teacher.

CHAPTER 2

Educational Objectives
and Human Abilities

Every teacher makes some judg-
ments, explicitly or implicitly, concerning the objectives of the schools.
When thinking about objectives we must consider a number of key
questions. To what extent should public-school education through the
twelfth grade be preparation for college attendance? for employment
of terminal students or dropouts? What kind of education is good preparation for college? What kind of education is good for employment
after high school? What is the role of the school in relation to personality development, to health and physical fitness, and to citizenship
education of each individual student? What moral values should students learn while in school? What is the role of the school in solving
social problems related to school dropouts, juvenile delinquency, poverty, and the living conditions of minority groups? The answers to
questions such as these determine the overall objectives of the school
and also have direct effects upon the activities of individual teachers.

After World War II, and until very recently, there has been a strong
concern about substantially increasing the content of education. Students have been expected to learn more subject matter in five main
fields—English-language arts, mathematics, foreign languages, science,
and social studies. The results of this emphasis have been seen in
curriculum-reform movements. In fact, many new approaches are still

being tried—instructional teams, using at least one teacher with more knowledge in the subject, have been instated at all school levels; more specialized teachers in foreign language or mathematics have been hired for the elementary grades; switches have been made to nongraded classes based on level of achievement rather than on age; special programs have been initiated for gifted students; the school day and year have been lengthened; and there has been greater use of recent technological advances, including instructional television, teaching machines, language laboratory equipment, and other audiovisual media. As attention increased on the five main subjects, the emphasis on the fine arts, vocational subjects, and personality development of the student decreased.

Recently, however, the problems of juvenile delinquency; emotional disturbance among youth; antisocial behavior with accompanying disrespect for self, law, and order; unemployment of youth under age 21; and other factors have led to a reexamination of the functions of education and to massive federal legislation designed to improve or to alleviate undesirable conditions. Some states have also attempted to work out procedures to improve educational opportunities for the non-college-bound student and for brighter students not highly interested in a college-preparatory program. The final effects of the many diverse social forces on the objectives of education are problematic. Therefore, the school's objectives must be sufficiently comprehensive to contribute to the development of the emergent cognitive and psychomotor abilities of all children and youth, and to their affective characteristics.

Regardless of how much individuals and groups disagree about what should be learned in school, the teacher must decide upon objectives if learning is to proceed efficiently (10, 11). In turn, these objectives must be incorporated into the goals of the students. In the absence of clearly defined goals, there is much aimless and unproductive activity. But how do we get objectives and how do students set their more immediate goals? Ideas about these matters will be clarified as we study a few broad statements of objectives at each school level, as we consider the development of emergent human abilities as objectives, and as we examine some immediate teaching-learning goals.

GENERAL OBJECTIVES

In most states, the local school system has the responsibility for deciding the general objectives of education in its schools. This includes the selection of textbooks and other instructional materials and activities.

The usual procedure for developing comprehensive objectives of education is through a committee of teachers, administrators, and curriculum workers who call in scholars, parents, and others for assistance. In turn, smaller groups within the school system, the state, or the region frequently look toward large national committees for assistance. Many committees at the state and national level—representing a broad sample of persons, including civic leaders and scholars—have been engaged in formulating general objectives of education at every school level. Unlike the situation in many other countries, no agency of our federal government has either the responsibility or the authority to set the objectives of education for state or local school systems. In most respects, we feel this is in harmony with democratic government.

A quick survey of some statements and discussion of objectives for the elementary school and the high school will give the flavor of general objectives.

Elementary Education

One of the best statements of objectives of elementary education was prepared by the Mid-Century Committee on Outcomes in Elementary Education (9). Figure 2.1 shows the objectives as organized in a three-dimensional framework. The first dimension is a growth scale dividing the nine years of elementary school into three equal time

Fig. 2.1. The behavioral continuum, showing broad curriculum areas intersecting major behavior categories. (From N. C. Kearney. *Elementary school objectives.* New York: Russell Sage Foundation, 1953, p. 38.)

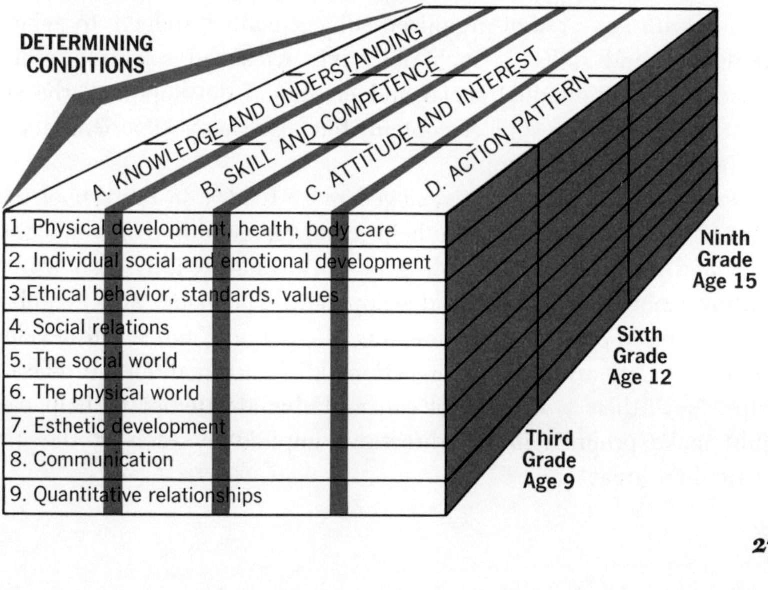

DETERMINING CONDITIONS

A. KNOWLEDGE AND UNDERSTANDING
B. SKILL AND COMPETENCE
C. ATTITUDE AND INTEREST
D. ACTION PATTERN

1. Physical development, health, body care
2. Individual social and emotional development
3. Ethical behavior, standards, values
4. Social relations
5. The social world
6. The physical world
7. Esthetic development
8. Communication
9. Quantitative relationships

Ninth Grade Age 15

Sixth Grade Age 12

Third Grade Age 9

units. Although the detailed objectives for each time unit are not shown in Fig. 2.1, the Committee did propose objectives which might reasonably be attained by most pupils toward the end of the third, sixth, and ninth grades. The second dimension includes the broad areas of elementary learning which are represented by the nine horizontal rows: Physical Development, Health, Body Care; Individual, Social, and Emotional Development; Ethical Behavior, Standards, Values; Social Relations; the Social World; the Physical World; Esthetic Development; Communication; and Quantitative Relationships.

The third dimension gives the type of behavioral changes expected: A. Knowledge and Understanding, B. Skill and Competence, C. Attitude and Interest, and D. Action Pattern. The Determining Conditions cannot properly be called "outcomes" in the same sense as knowledge, understanding, skill, and competence. Instead, determining conditions refer to the biological and sociological context in which children, teachers, and others in the school interact. It is possible that over a long period of time, perhaps two or three generations, these determining conditions might change because of more efficient pupil learning; that is, the nature of the students and of the environment itself might change.

When parents, other laymen, and subject-matter specialists first encounter these objectives, they are often perplexed because the objectives do not seem to fit neatly into separate subject fields. The communication area can readily be associated with reading, spelling, and English; quantitative relationships with arithmetic or mathematics; the physical world with science and geography; and so on. The Committee did not specify that the objectives had to be achieved in connection with any area of organized subject matter. Indeed, to achieve knowledge and skills in such objectives as social relations, ethical behavior, and individual social and emotional development, the student needs not only subject content, but also many experiences with the teacher and other pupils.

Certain objectives can be achieved more readily in the school than others; for example, we can help children acquire communication skills and knowledge of the physical world more readily than we can healthy emotional and social development. The home and neighborhood are more powerful determinants of emotional and social development than they are of communication skills and quantitative relationships. Nevertheless, the school can and should attempt to help each child make progress in the directions implied by each of the nine curriculum areas.

Secondary Education

The idea that every child should attend elementary school has long been accepted in the United States. Although there now is considerable agreement that every boy and girl should attend high school to age 18 or graduation, the idea is new in broad historical perspective. As yet, some teachers are doubtful about requiring uninterested or mentally slow students to remain in high school. This is especially true where teaching conditions and curriculum arrangements are not satisfactorily worked out to help these students actually profit from school. The extent to which high school education should be devoted to preparing students for college, or for jobs immediately after high school graduation, or to giving students a general education is indicated in brief excerpts from two statements of objectives of secondary education. Of these statements, the most widely publicized during the 1950s was that of James B. Conant, who with his associates studied a number of comprehensive high schools in the United States and made many recommendations which tended to become objectives. Conant stated:

> . . . the three main objectives of a comprehensive high school are: first, to provide a general education for all the future citizens; second, to provide good elective programs for those who wish to use their acquired skills immediately on graduation; third, to provide satisfactory programs for those whose vocations will depend on their subsequent education in a college or university (2,17).

Conant made 21 recommendations for improving public secondary education. All should be studied, although not necessarily accepted, by anyone interested in education from kindergarten through graduate school. Few besides Conant would agree with all 21 recommendations. He has been criticized properly for stating the objectives of general education simply as the number of years or semesters in various subjects required of all students for graduation. He did not state what students of varying intellectual abilities were to achieve through taking the subjects, and he did not give his value system which led to this and other recommendations. These criticisms are more apparent after studying the following two recommendations:

RECOMMENDATION 7: DIVERSIFIED PROGRAMS FOR THE DEVELOPMENT OF MARKETABLE SKILLS[1]

Programs should be available for girls interested in developing skills in typing, stenography, the use of clerical machines, home economics, or a spe-

[1] J. B. Conant. *The American high school today.* New York: McGraw-Hill, 1959. By permission of Dr. James B. Conant.

cialized branch of home economics which through further work in college might lead to the profession of dietitian. Distributive education should be available if the retail shops in the community can be persuaded to provide suitable openings. If the community is rural, vocational agriculture should be included. For boys, depending on the community, trade and industrial programs should be available. Half a day is required in the eleventh and twelfth grades for this vocational work. In each specialized trade, there should be an advisory committee composed of representatives of management and labor. Federal money is available for these programs.

The school administration should constantly assess the employment situation in those trades included in the vocational programs. When opportunities for employment in a given trade no longer exist within the community, the training program in that field should be dropped. The administration should be ready to introduce new vocational programs as opportunities open in the community or area. In some communities, advanced programs of a technical nature should be developed; these programs often involve more mathematics than is usually required for the building trades or auto mechanics programs.

. . . the students enrolled in programs which develop marketable skills should also be enrolled in English, social studies, and other courses required for graduation. Furthermore, efforts should be made to prevent isolation from the other students. Homerooms may be effective means to this end . . . (2,52).

RECOMMENDATION 9: THE PROGRAMS OF THE ACADEMICALLY TALENTED

A policy in regard to the elective programs of academically talented boys and girls should be adopted by the school to serve as a guide to the counselors. In the type of school I am discussing the following program should be strongly recommended as a minimum:

Four years of mathematics, four years of one foreign language, three years of science, in addition to the required four years of English and three years of social studies; a total of eighteen courses with homework to be taken in four years. This program will require at least fifteen hours of homework each week.

Many academically talented pupils may wish to study a second foreign language or an additional course in social studies. Since such students are capable of handling twenty or more courses with homework, these additional academic courses may be added to the recommended minimum program. If the school is organized on a seven- or eight-period day (Recommendation 12), at least one additional course without homework (for example, art or music) may also be scheduled each year.

If as school policy a minimum academic program including both mathematics and a foreign language is recommended to the academically talented pupils and their parents, the counselors will have the problem of identifying as early as possible the members of the group. It may well be that, in the next lower 10 or 20 per cent of the boys and girls in terms of scholastic aptitude on a national basis, there are a number who ought to be guided into similar but less rigorous programs (2, 57).

Although Recommendation 9 is dogmatic, another recommendation provides for individualized programs for each pupil, including the opportunity for academically talented students to take some work in the fine arts. Conant would not classify pupils according to various curricula or tracks, such as college preparatory, vocational, or commercial. In addition, if a talented girl had no interest in mathematics and disliked it strongly, she would not be required to take four years of mathematics. Likewise, Conant would not require an uninterested girl or boy to take the third year of science.

In a later volume, Conant pointed out that the problems of education in the slums and suburbs are very different from those in small independent cities which are not part of a metropolitan complex:

> The task with which the school people in the slum must struggle is, on the one hand, to prepare a student for getting and keeping a job as soon as he leaves school, and, on the other hand, to encourage those who have academic talent to aim at a profession through higher education. . . . In the suburban high school from which 80 per cent or more of the graduates enter some sort of college, the most important problem from the parents' point of view is to ensure the admission of their children to prestige colleges. . . . From the educator's point of view, however, the most vexing problem is to adjust the family's ambitions to the boy's or girl's abilities (3, 1–2).

According to Conant, neither the suburban nor the slum schools are comprehensive, although a far greater problem exists in the latter; in the slum schools we are allowing "social dynamite" to accumulate.

In a very different manner from that of Conant, a large committee of the National Education Association made 33 recommendations regarding what to teach, plans and organization of teaching, and education in a changing society. All of these recommendations need to be studied in order to understand their scope; however, 7 of the 33 describe part of the content of education, and indicate for whom it is intended:

RECOMMENDATION 9

The instructional program should provide: (a) opportunities for developing the individual potentialities represented in the wide range of differences among people; (b) a common fund of knowledge, values, and skills vital to the welfare of the individual and the nation.

To achieve these objectives, the instructional program cannot be the same for all. Provision for individual differences should be made by qualified teaching personnel through diagnosis of learning needs and through appropriate variety of content, resources for learning, and instructional methods.

RECOMMENDATION 10

Priorities for the school are the teaching of skills in reading, composition, listening, speaking (both native and foreign languages), and computation . . . ways of creative and disciplined thinking, including methods of inquiry and application of knowledge . . . competence in self-instruction and independent learning . . . fundamental understanding of the humanities and the arts, the social sciences and natural sciences, and mathematics . . . appreciation of and discriminating taste in literature, music, and the visual arts . . . instruction in health education and physical education.

Responsibilities best met by joint efforts of the school and other social agencies include: development of values and ideals . . . social and civic competence . . . vocational preparation.

The decision to include or exclude particular school subjects or outside-of-class activities should be based on: (a) the priorities assigned to the school and to other agencies; (b) data about learners and society, and developments in the academic disciplines; (c) the human and material resources available in the school and community.

RECOMMENDATION 11

The schools can help to combat such serious national problems as youth unemployment and juvenile delinquency by: (a) evaluating the intellectual and creative potential of *all* children and youth in the schools; (b) identifying early the potential dropout and delinquent; (c) developing positive programs to challenge these young people to educational endeavor; (d) participating in cooperative programs with parents and with community groups and organizations—business and industry, labor, service groups, government agencies, and the many youth-serving agencies.

RECOMMENDATION 12

Rational discussion of controversial issues should be an important part of the school program. The teacher should help students identify relevant information, learn the techniques of critical analysis, make independent judgments, and be prepared to present and support them. The teacher should also help students become sensitive to the continuing need for objective reexamination of issues in the light of new information and changing conditions in society.

RECOMMENDATION 13

To help the student think critically about current issues, the curriculum should provide opportunities for adequate instruction concerning social forces and trends. Attention commensurate with their significance in modern society should be given to issues such as international relations, economic growth, urbanization, population growth, science and technology, and mass media.

RECOMMENDATION 14

The school curriculum should include a study of political and social ideologies focusing upon communism. The methods of rational inquiry should be stressed. The study should be set in the perspective of the modern world and be incorporated into the instructional program at appropriate points. If a special unit on communism is deemed desirable in the secondary school, it should supplement and complement earlier study of these topics.

As with other areas of the curriculum, decisions about *what to teach* and *how to teach* about these topics should be based upon policies developed by school administrators and teachers of the local school system. In the formulation and implementation of such policies, school personnel should utilize the resources of scholarship and be supported in their decisions by the school board and by an informed community opinion.

RECOMMENDATION 15

The school can provide and maintain a curriculum appropriately balanced for each student by offering a comprehensive program of studies, making early and continuous assessment of individual potentialities and achievements, and providing individualized programs based on careful counseling.

To avoid the imbalance that can result from limiting financial support to certain selected subjects and services, general financial support should be provided for the total program. This applies to local, state, and federal support (15, 125–129).

ABILITIES AND AFFECTIVE OUTCOMES AS OBJECTIVES

As noted previously, objectives may be formulated in terms of broad areas of curriculum content, such as quantitative relationships or communications. They also may be stated as outcomes of learning, or, in the words of Kearney, as "behavioral changes: i.e. knowledge and understanding, attitude and interest," etc. (9). Another way of expressing objectives which has recently come to the fore is through the use of processes, such as critical thinking and creativity as shown in *Schools for the Sixties* (15). Still another way to state objectives is as abilities, an ability being a union of a content and a process; for example, performing mathematical operations efficiently might be called computational ability. Educational psychology has much to say about the nature of mental processes and intellectual abilities, probably more than does any other discipline.

If we accept the ability concept, which will be described more explicitly later, we may think of the main objective of education as helping students to develop and improve their emerging abilities, abilities which previous generations required thousands of years to generate. How long did it take mankind to develop the alphabet which children now master in kindergarten and the first grade? to develop the number system which many children in the third grade understand and use quite well in solving immediate problems? to use the printing press, combustible engines, atomic power? to invent the Salk vaccine and antibiotics in preventing and curing disease? In view of the properly increasing tendency to state objectives in terms of processes and abilities, let us examine the status of knowledge concerning abilities.

What is an ability? An ability is the "actual power to perform an act, physical or mental, whether or not (the power is) attained by training and education. . . . Ability implies that the task can be performed *now*, if the necessary external circumstances are present; no further training is needed" (4). Accepting this definition of ability, we properly infer that human abilities change with age—the 10-year-old has many abilities which the infant does not. Similarly, a highly intelligent and physically strong 10-year-old demonstrates more or higher-level abilities than does a 10-year-old of low intelligence and low coordination.

What is the relationship between capacity and ability? Tests are designed to measure abilities—what the test respondent actually performs.[2] On the basis of certain measured abilities, we can infer capacity or what the individual might be able to do some time hence with further maturation and education. In this sense, the items in an intelligence-test sample present abilities from which future performance or abilities are inferred. To clarify the relationship between capacity and ability, imagine two quart-sized milk bottles side by side. We see that each has the capacity for holding a quart of milk. One bottle is half full, the other entirely full. The present *ability* of the two bottles to provide milk is unequal, although both have the same *capacity*. This analogy may serve to clarify the terms, but there it stops, for our means of measuring present abilities are much less adequate in the field of human learning than in the physical world of liquid, linear, and other measures.

What is the relationship between abilities and learning? One set of definitions of learning is made by English and English:

A highly general term for the relatively enduring change, in response to a task-demand, that is induced directly by experience; or the process or processes whereby such change is brought about. Not included under learning are changes due to bodily injury or surgery, disease, fatigue, sensory adaptation . . . Learning is manifested by performance, and all performance is dependent in part on learning, but the two are not identical (4).

All human abilities are the product of maturation and learning; no ability would be manifested without some learning. Furthermore, the

[2] Various types of tests are discussed in Chapter 16. It will be helpful to refer to the index and then to pages of Chapter 16 when new information about testing is encountered throughout the earlier chapters.

learning of certain abilities makes possible the learning of other abilities. For example, speech normally precedes the ability to read, and reading normally precedes spelling ability.

Let us use an example in order to understand the proper relationship between the three key terms—*ability, capacity,* and *learning.* When a healthy infant is born, we properly infer that he has the capacity, transmitted through heredity, to learn all the basic abilities characteristic of the human species. When sufficiently mature, the infant will smile, crawl, walk upright, run, hop, skip, talk, sing, and so on. Some of these abilities will be acquired with little if any instruction and with relatively little learning. Through instruction at home or in school he will acquire other abilities that people without instruction do not— the ability to read, to spell, to write, to count, to play a musical instrument, to drive an automobile, and many others.

At present, abilities have been identified which vary from the very general to the highly specific. A general mental ability, as measured by certain intelligence tests, correlates positively and highly, but far from perfectly, with achievements in subject fields such as English, mathematics, science, and social studies. A more specific ability, such as numerical reasoning, correlates much higher with achievements in mathematics than in English. However, we are still in the early stages of systematically identifying and categorizing human abilities, but have made more progress in this direction since 1900 than during the previous recorded history of mankind.

Cognitive Abilities as Objectives

Figure 2.2 indicates 120 possible human abilities in the cognitive domain (8). Let us consider these abilities in more detail. An ability is a combination of an operation or process, a content, and a product. Each of the five operations, in combination with one of the four contents and with one of six products, comprises an ability. Guilford calls each of these an intellectual factor. Specifically, each of the operations, contents, and products are:

OPERATIONS	Major kinds of intellectual activities or processes; things that the organism does with the raw materials of information.[3]
Cognition	Immediate discovery, awareness, rediscovery, or recognition of information in various forms; comprehension or understanding.

[3] *Information* is defined as "that which the organism discriminates."

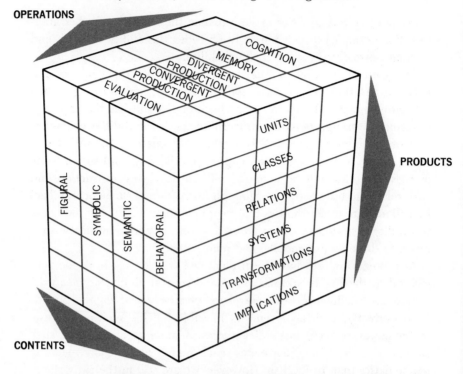

Fig. 2.2. Model of the structure of the intellect. (Adapted from J. P. Guilford & R. Hoepfner. Current summary of structure-of-intellect factors and suggested tests. *Rep. psychol. Lab.*, No. 30. Los Angeles: Univer. of Southern California, 1963, p. 2.)

Memory	Retention or storage, with some degree of availability, of information in the same form in which it was committed to storage and in response to the same cues in connection with which it was learned.
Divergent production	Generation of information from given information, where the emphasis is upon variety and quantity of output from the same source. Likely to involve what has been called transfer.
Convergent production	Generation of information from given information, where the emphasis is upon achieving unique or conventionally accepted best outcomes. It is likely that the given (cue) information fully determines the response.
Evaluation	Reaching decisions or making judgments concerning the goodness (correctness, suitability, adequacy, desirability, etc.) of information in terms of criteria of identity, consistency, and goal satisfaction.

CONTENTS
Broad classes of information.

Figural content
Information in concrete form, as perceived or as recalled in the form of images. The term "figural" implies some degree of organization or structuring. Different sense modalities may be involved, e.g., visual, auditory, kinesthetic.

Symbolic content
Information in the form of signs, having no significance in and of themselves, such as letters, numbers, musical notations, and other "code" elements.

Semantic content
Information in the form of meanings to which words commonly become attached, hence most notable in verbal thinking and in verbal communication.

Behavioral content
Information, essentially non-verbal, involved in human interactions, where awareness of the attitudes, needs, desires, moods, intentions, perceptions, thoughts, etc., of other persons and of ourselves is important.

PRODUCTS
Forms that information takes in the organism's processing of it.

Units
Relatively segregated or circumscribed items of information having "thing" character. May be close to Gestalt psychology's "figure on a ground."

Classes
Recognized sets of items of information grouped by virtue of their common properties.

Relations
Recognized connections between units of information based upon variables or points of contact that apply to them.

Systems
Organized or structured aggregates of items of information; complexes of interrelated or interacting parts.

Transformations
Changes of various kinds of existing or known information or in its use.

Implications
Extrapolations of information, in the form of expectancies, predictions, known or suspected antecedents, concomitants, or consequences (8).

A few definitions and examples are needed to clarify the processes, contents, and products. Let us start with the contents. You will find it profitable to slow your reading and think of examples other than those given.

Figural content is information in concrete form as experienced directly through seeing, touching, hearing, etc. The information does not represent anything but itself (information refers to anything that is sensed and discriminated). Think of walking on campus. Everything you see, hear, feel, smell, etc. that is not embodied in signs or words is figural content. *Symbolic content* is information in the form of signs which have no significance in and of themselves. Such information includes the letters of the alphabet, numerals, musical notations, and any other elements used in coding systems. Observe these letters— *x, b, u, f, s*—and these numerals—3, 8, 4, 0. You are observing symbolic content. *Semantic content* is information in the form of meanings attached to words and is thus most important in verbal communication and thinking. Reread and think about the last sentence. You are dealing with semantic content. *Behavioral content* is essentially nonverbal information inherent in interactions with human beings, where awareness of the attitudes, moods, desires, intentions, perceptions, etc. of others and of oneself is important. The identification of abilities involving this type of content has not proceeded to an appreciable degree up to the present and the precise nature of the abilities is problematic.

Now let us move to the six products by which information in each of the four content areas may be classified. A *unit* is an entity, a relatively segregated or circumscribed item of information. For example, 2 is a symbolic unit, and baseball is a semantic unit. *Classes* are sets of items of information grouped by virtue of their common properties. Some concepts embody classes; for example, *birds* and *mammals* embody a large number of units, classified according to their common properties. *Relations* involve recognized connections or associations between units of information. For example, we state that meat and bread make a sandwich and that the number set represented by 4 is larger than that represented by 2. We are expressing relations between semantic units in the first part of the sentence and between symbolic units in the second part. The category, *systems,* is the most inclusive of the four—units, classes, relations, and systems—and implies organ-. ized aggregates of information. The laws regarding the arabic numbers comprise a symbolic system. The laws or rules regarding the transmission of information in sentences, rules of syntax, clarify our language system, in this case a semantic system. Now consider an example of units, classes, relations, and systems in symbolic content: 3 and 8 are *units;* uneven numbers and even numbers represent *classes;* "3 is to 6 as 5 is to 10" indicates a *relationship;* and the associative and commutative laws are parts of a *system.*

Transformations and implications are not a continuation of the hierarchy from units through systems. *Transformations* involve making changes of various kinds in existing or known information or in usages of this information. For example, changing 65 in base 10 to 145 in base 6 involves *transformation*. Changing "the boy was hit by a man" to "the man hit the boy" also requires transformation. Writing a plot for a story requires transformation of the given information into something else. *Implications* take the form of predictions, statements of expectancy, known or suspected antecedents of events, consequences of certain actions, and other extrapolations of the given information. For example, identifying questions, the answers to which should help reach a decision in a conflict situation, implies implications from known information. Adding the detailed operations needed to make a briefly outlined plan succeed also illustrates implications with semantic content.

We are now ready to consider the last set of the triad—processes. *Cognition* refers to immediate discovery, awareness, rediscovery, or recognition of information that has been discriminated; synonyms for cognition are comprehension and understanding. If one could not distinguish figural, symbolic, semantic, or behavioral information, one could not cognize it. Memory means the retention or storage of information in the same form in which it was initially learned, and also the capacity for recalling or reproducing it. Tests of memory are such that if the individual cannot recognize, recall, or reproduce what he has learned, we assume that he no longer has the information in storage; he has forgotten it. *Divergent production* refers to the generation of new information from given information, where the emphasis is upon variety and quantity of output. Divergent thinking leads in different directions to responses that cannot be scored as correct or incorrect. For example, giving clever titles to a story plot leads to responses that cannot be scored as right or wrong. The solutions or ideas produced through divergent thinking are novel to the producer, not necessarily to others. *Convergent thinking* implies the generation of new information from given information, where the emphasis is upon achieving unique or conventionally accepted best outcomes. The given information determines the response to be accepted as correct. For example, "$2 - 2 = ?$" requires convergent thinking. *Evaluation* means reaching decisions or making judgments concerning the goodness, correctness, suitability, adequacy, or desirability of information in terms of criteria. The criteria might be consistency and goal satisfactions.

We have now dealt with processes, contents, and products. Table

Components of the Teaching-Learning Situation

2.1 shows certain tasks; the combinations of process, content, and product involved; and the names of the factors. Examples are given of each task that is thought to be difficult. Study the material carefully and think of other examples.

TABLE 2.1.

Illustrative Tasks, Processes, Contents, Products, and Abilities

Task	Process	Content	Product	Ability
Finding correct synonym for word	Cognition	Semantic	Unit	Verbal comprehension
Selecting word in a set that does not belong to the class	Cognition	Semantic	Class	Conceptual classification
Selecting word to complete meaningful relationship	Cognition	Semantic	Relation	Semantic relations
Solving problems with minimal arithmetic computation, maximum reasoning	Cognition	Semantic	System	General reasoning
Writing words containing a specified letter; e.g., *r*	Divergent production	Symbolic	Unit	Word fluency
Listing classes of uses for an object	Divergent production	Semantic	Class	Spontaneous semantic flexibility
Listing steps in appropriate order for completing a project (e.g., building a birdhouse)	Convergent production	Semantic	System	Semantic ordering
Naming an object that could be made by combining two given objects; e.g., a coil spring and a beach ball to make a punching bag	Convergent production	Semantic	Transformation	Semantic redefinition
Indicating each digit in a row of 30 digits that is like the first one in the row	Evaluation	Symbolic	Unit	Symbolic identification
Judging whether symbolic conclusions are true or false based upon given premises.	Evaluation	Symbolic	Relation	Symbolic manipulation

Source: Based on J. P. Guilford, & R. Hoepfner. Current summary of structure-of-intellect factors and suggested tests. *Rep. psychol. Lab.*, No. 30. Los Angeles: Univer. Southern Calif., 1963.

Three types of intelligence not directly related to objectives are associated with the various contents by Guilford. *Concrete intelligence* involves the abilities connected with figural content. Mechanics, operators of machines, artists, and musicians depend heavily on these abilities. *Abstract intelligence* pertains to abilities concerned with symbolic and semantic content. Learning to recognize words, to spell, and to operate with numbers involves abilities with symbolic content. Abilities with semantic content are required for understanding verbal concepts and ideas of all types. Present-day intelligence tests are heavily loaded with test items requiring the use of abstract abilities. *Social intelligence* is concerned with behavioral content, with understanding the behavior of others and oneself. Teachers, lawyers, social workers, politicians, and leaders are hypothesized to be high in social intelligence.

Substantial evidence is accumulating which indicates that specific abilities can be identified in children, youth, and adults. For example, the same six divergent-thinking abilities with semantic content that were discovered in ninth-graders and young adults (5), were also identified in sixth-graders (13). However, the chronological age at which the separate abilities become differentiated is not clear. Abilities markedly different from those of the sixth-graders were found in children of ages 4 to 6 (14). The semantic abilities are not yet clearly differentiated at age 4 to 6. It is interesting to note that British psychologists find fewer abilities than American psychologists. This is in part because of differences in theoretical orientation and in part because of the statistical procedures used (17).

In relation to the objectives of education, the concept of abilities is most meaningful when combined with outcomes of learning and broad subject-matter fields. In Fig. 2.3 the abilities connected with each type of content are related to outcomes and curriculum areas. For example, the ability to think productively with figural material is associated with performance in art and music and with certain aspects of the applied arts such as home economics, agriculture, and industrial arts. An example of abilities involving symbolic and semantic content is productive thinking which leads to learning factual information, concepts, problem-solving skills, and to developing creativity in the English-language arts, social studies, science, mathematics, and other subject fields. Abilities with behavioral content are less clearly defined but include understanding oneself and others and interacting in a group. Later in this chapter we shall see that objectives may be stated as the improvement of abilities.

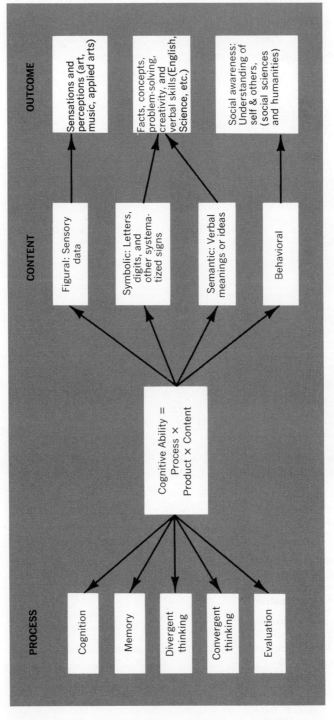

Fig. 2.3. Schematic arrangement of cognitive abilities and learning outcomes. (Based on data from J. P. Guilford. Three faces of intellect. *Amer. Psychologist*, 1959, **14**, 469–479.)

A *Taxonomy of Objectives in the Cognitive Domain*

An attempt to develop a statement of educational objectives in terms of processes resulted in a taxonomy of objectives in the cognitive domain (1). The goal was to organize learner behavior into a relatively small number of classes which could be applied to all subject fields at all school levels.

The principal part of this taxonomy deals with five processes, called intellectual abilities or skills. This terminology varies from that of Guilford. Table 2.2 lists the processes in the two classification schemes. Bloom proposed a continuum ranging from simple to complex, from concrete to abstract. Each process would be essential for the appearance of the next. Guilford, on the other hand, did not indicate a continuum.

TABLE 2.2.

Parallel Processes from Guilford and Bloom

Guilford	Bloom
Cognition—discovery, rediscovery or recognition	Comprehension—understanding of communicated material without relating it to other material
Memory—retention of what is cognized	(Memory is subsumed but not stated as an intellectual process.)
Convergent thinking—arriving at one right answer or at a recognized best or conventional answer from known and remembered information	Application—using methods, concepts, principles, and theories in new situations
Divergent thinking—arriving at variety of unique responses not completely determined by known and remembered information	Analysis—breaking down a communication into its constituent elements Synthesis—putting together constituent elements or parts to form a whole
Evaluation—arriving at decisions as to goodness, correctness, suitability, or adequacy of what we know, what we remember, and what we produce in productive thinking	Evaluation—judging the value of materials and methods for given purposes; applying standards and criteria

Sources: Based on J. P. Guilford. Three faces of intellect. *Amer. Psychologist,* 1959, **14,** and B. S. Bloom (Ed.), *Taxonomy of educational objectives. Handbook I: Cognitive domain.* New York: McKay, 1956.

Let us examine the parallel terminology of Guilford and Bloom. *Cognition* and *comprehension* have the same meaning—becoming aware of and understanding something. Guilford proposed a process of memory, whereas Bloom did not list memory as an intellectual ability. He did, however, assume that memory is essential to the other processes. Guilford indicated two kinds of productive thinking—convergent and divergent, whereas Bloom proposed three processes without reference to the outcome produced. Nevertheless, the application and synthesis of information may lead to different and novel responses of the type resulting from Guilford's divergent thinking involving transformations. Similarly, the application and analysis of information leads to the production of responses that may be judged as correct or incorrect, thus being similar to convergent thinking. In both systems, problem solving is considered to be a highly complex activity, dependent upon a combination of many abilities.

How may schools move from these abstract statements of abilities and processes to objectives, and more important, to educational practices designed to develop these abilities in students? A good example is provided by the work of Sanders in the Manitowoc, Wisconsin, Public Schools (16). Besides teaching social-studies classes, Sanders works with teachers in improving their use of questions, problem activities, and projects so that students of the teachers will achieve more of the higher-level abilities. His main approach is through a systematic consideration of teacher activities which require students not simply to remember information, concepts, and theories but to use them. This in no way denies the importance of acquiring and remembering factual information but properly stresses that this is only one objective in any field.

In his early work with teachers, Sanders clarified the terminology related to objectives with these examples:

1. *Memory:* The student recalls or recognizes information. . . .
4. *Application:* The student solves a lifelike problem that requires the identification of the issue and the selection and use of appropriate generalizations and skills.
5. *Analysis:* The student solves a problem in the light of conscious knowledge of the parts and forms of thinking.
6. *Synthesis:* The student solves a problem that requires original, creative thinking.
7. *Evaluation:* The student makes a judgment of good or bad, right or wrong, according to standards he designates (16, 3).

These objectives are properly stated in terms of student behavior. As teachers arrange activities to achieve the objectives, they move from having students memorize information to having them use it in a variety of situations. In the process, they improve higher-level abilities. A possible procedure that a teacher might use for each process shows the relationship between the processes and the teaching-learning activities:

Memory: What is meant by "gerrymandering"? (The student is asked to recall the definition given to him earlier.) . . .

Application: The mayor recently appointed a committee to study the fairness of the boundaries of the election districts in our community. Gather information about the present districts and the population in each. Determine whether the present city election districts are adequate. (The student is expected to apply principles of democracy studied in class to this new problem.)

Analysis: Analyze the reasoning in this quotation: "Human beings lack the ability to be fair when their own interests are involved. Party X controls the legislature and now it has taken upon itself the responsibility of redrawing the boundaries of the legislative election districts. We know in advance that our party will suffer."

Synthesis: (This question must follow the preceding application question.) If current election districts in our community are inadequate, suggest how they might be redrawn.

Evaluation: Would you favor having your political party engage in gerrymandering if it had the opportunity (**16**, 3–5)?

It is easy to observe that the activities and questions after "memory" involve thought processes different from mere recall or recognition. In this connection, let us examine an additional example of an activity intended to encourage synthesis of information. Here is an initial suggestion to teachers about how to get started:

However, students who are less creative or less motivated would find it difficult to get a foothold. To get them started, the following list of questions involving production is presented:

Directions: Which in this list do you believe are legitimate questions for collective bargaining?
  A. How much should workers of various skills be paid?
  B. How much should managers be paid?
  C. How much vacation should workers have?
  D. How fast should the assembly line move?
  E. Is a particular worker incompetent and deserving of being discharged?
  F. For what price should the products be offered for sale?
  G. Who should be selected as officers of a company?
  H. Should a new plant be constructed to expand production?
  I. How much should be paid the owners of the company in dividends?
  J. What new products should be produced?
  K. How many laborers are required to do a certain job? . . .

. . . After studying this list, students are presented with this synthesis problem: *What principles or standards can you devise that would be helpful in determining which of the above questions should be decided by collective bargaining (16, 132–133)?*

Sanders notes that the synthesis problem could be presented for individual study or for group discussion. The following ideas resulted from a class discussion:

A. Workers should have the right to bargain on questions that immediately and directly affect wages, hours, and working conditions. Current law gives them this right.
B. Managers should make decisions in which there is little or no conflict of interests with workers.
C. Manager and workers should participate in those decisions in which they have a special competency that the other side does not possess or possesses to a lesser degree.
D. A principle of capitalism gives owners a right to initiate and operate a business. Under laissez-faire capitalism this right was almost absolute, but it has been limited to an indefinite degree (16, 133).

The ideas of the students were not first read or heard by them. Instead, the ideas resulted from their synthesis of other information. Sanders does not indicate how much previous experience is needed to secure these responses. He cites many other examples of questions and activities that teachers in many subject fields and school levels, from primary through high school, use to facilitate the development of the higher-level abilities.

Psychomotor Abilities as Objectives

With the great attention given to interscholastic athletics and professional sports, it is easy to underestimate the importance of psychomotor abilities and physical fitness in the development of man and in the daily lives of individuals. There is a tendency to think of the great literature, the great advances in architecture, medicine, and science almost exclusively in terms of cognitive abilities. Nevertheless, the musical composer, the painter, and the author use psychomotor abilities to develop their products. The great advances made recently in surgery of the brain and heart also require the highest level of psychomotor abilities. Furthermore, each of us maintains better health and intellectual productivity through keeping physically fit. Millions of people still make a living primarily through physical activity. We must banish the notion that the development of psychomotor abilities should be limited to only a small portion of the school population or confined only to physical education classes. Every growing child has the potentiality of becoming a more effective individual through developing his psychomotor abilities.

Guilford made a systematic and comprehensive survey of research completed in the field of psychomotor abilities and subsequently identified six psychomotor factors which he believed to be involved in many kinds of motor performances (6). These processes, combined with parts of the body, may be called psychomotor abilities. The factors identified by Guilford are shown in Fig. 2.4. While some of the terms are self-explanatory, others need defining. *Impulsion* pertains to the rate at which movements are initiated from stationary positions, thus distinguishing it from *speed*, which pertains to the rate of movements after they have started. The deer's bounding from a stationary position illustrates impulsion and its running thereafter exemplifies speed. *Precision* has to do with the accuracy with which bodily positions can be held and with precision of directed movements once started. The tightrope walker moves with precision. *Flexibility* is suggested as pertaining to the extent to which a part of the body is free to bend or to the scope of movement pertaining to a particular joint. The contortionist and the acrobat are flexible. In addition to these six major processes, muscular endurance, circulatory-respiratory endurance, and perhaps other psychomotor factors are thought to be basic to vocal activities such as singing and speaking.

In the many perceptual motor skills taught in the schools—drawing, handwriting, typewriting, shorthand, the making of maps in social studies, and the manipulating of objects in home economics, agriculture, industrial arts, and other classes—a combination of several of the psychomotor abilities is used. The same is true in many motor performances in physical education. A perceptual motor task, such as shorthand or playing a musical instrument, requires not only the physical movements but also the perception of words or musical notes that direct the physical movements. Here a combination of cognitive and psychomotor abilities is involved.

Other outcomes of learning in the psychomotor domain are motor sets. When an individual gets ready to hit a golf ball, to bat, to type, or to start playing a musical instrument, he has a feeling within himself about the stance and proper body attitude to assume. From observation of an individual's performances and from the individual's own verbalization of how he thinks as he prepares to do something, we have some knowledge of motor set; but it is relatively difficult, if not impossible, for an individual to verbalize accurately the motor set. The

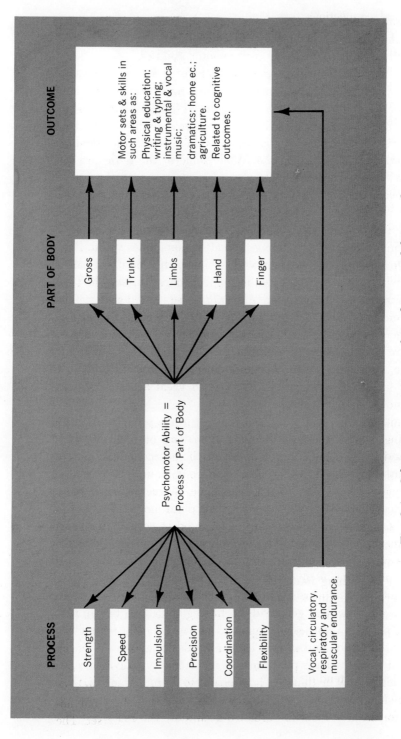

Fig. 2.4. Schematic arrangement of psychomotor abilities and learning outcomes. (Based on data from J. P. Guilford. A system of the psychomotor abilities. *Amer. J. Psychol.*, 1958, **71**, 161–174.)

many neural connections from the brain to the muscles and joints, although felt, cannot be described accurately. Just as cognitive abilities are improved through purposefully learning how to read, to solve problems, and the like, so the psychomotor abilities are also brought to higher levels through engaging in appropriate physical activities.

Classifying objectives and abilities as *cognitive* or *psychomotor* does not indicate the relationship between abilities that exists in many school learning tasks. Two examples may clarify this. The main abilities involved in a child's learning to read are cognitive—the five processes combined with symbolic and semantic content. However, psychomotor abilities are also involved in opening the book properly, sitting properly, and focusing on the printed page in a left-to-right and top-to-bottom sequence. Playing a musical instrument involves speed, flexibility, precision, and coordination in combination with hands, fingers, and limbs. The reading of musical notes to guide the motor movements requires the development of cognitive abilities, but once note-reading is mastered, further improvement in performance results primarily from improvement of the psychomotor abilities. Similarly, once the motor aspects of reading become habitual, further improvement in reading requires development of the cognitive abilities.

Affective Processes and Outcomes as Objectives

Affect refers to the feeling aspect of behavior. The arts are concerned with the feeling components of behavior. Unfortunately, affect has come under scientific scrutiny only recently; however, a number of classification schemes have already been proposed. One with clear implications for objectives of education was developed recently by a national committee (**12**).

When developing the classification scheme, the authors tried to order and relate the different kinds of affective behavior and finally used the concept *internalization*. Internalization is the process of incorporating something into one's behavior as one's own, not merely conforming or accepting the values of others. Internalization has more than the dimension of external to internal; it also has dimensions of simple to complex, and concrete to abstract as may be noted in the order of headings from top to bottom:

1.0. Receiving (Attending)
    1.1. Awareness; e.g., the person is aware of the feelings of others whose activities are of little interest to him.

    1.2. Willingness to Receive; e.g., the person listens to others with respect.

    1.3. Controlled or Selected Attention; e.g., alertness toward human values and judgments on life as they are recorded in history.

2.0. Responding

    2.1. Acquiescence in Responding; e.g., obedience to the playground regulations.

    2.2. Willingness to Respond; e.g., the person practices the rules of safety on the playground.

    2.3. Satisfaction in Response; e.g., the person enjoys participating in activities and plays according to the rules.

3.0. Valuing

    3.1. Acceptance of a Value; e.g., the person accepts the importance of social goals in a free society.

    3.2. Preference for a Value; e.g., the person assumes an active role in clarifying the social goals in a free society.

    3.3. Commitment; e.g., the person is loyal to the social goals of a free society.

4.0. Organizing

    4.1. Conceptualization of a Value; e.g., the person judges the responsibility of society for conserving human resources.

    4.2. Organization of a Value System; e.g., the person develops a plan for conserving human resources.

5.0. Characterization by a Value or Value Complex

    5.1. Generalized Set; e.g., the person faces facts and conclusions that can be logically drawn from them with a consistent value orientation.

    5.2. Characterization; e.g., the person develops a philosophy of life (**12**).

The process of internalization begins with awareness of some phenomenon in the individual's environment. After becoming aware of something, he is willing to give it his attention; and, in selected attention, he actually seeks the stimuli. For example, a person is aware of the feelings of others, next, he is willing to listen to others with respect, and then he gives selective attention to discussions of human values. This is the lowest level in the hierarchy, namely receiving. Acquiescence in responding is close to selected attention in that the individual merely complies with the expectations of someone else. Then he willingly responds from inner motivation. At the third level of responding, satisfaction is experienced. This sequence is illustrated by acquiescence to playground regulations, overt practice of them, and then satisfaction from following them. The next level, valuing, implies increasing internalization. Acceptance of a value, for example, the importance of social goals, does not involve preference. However, preference for a value followed by commitment is exemplified by actively clarifying social goals and becoming loyal to them because one cannot live comfortably with oneself otherwise. Illustrative of the latter level of valuing is the behavior of the dedicated Peace Corps volunteers, religious missionaries, and students who participate in the registration of voters.

As values become more internalized and more abstract, they also embrace more facets of experience. Organization is needed. Before there can be organization, however, conceptualization is required. Values ordinarily are put into words so that they can be manipulated readily in thought. Subsequent to this level of conceptualization and organization, the individual's behavior is characterized by a value complex, the highest level in the hierarchy. The first behavioral step here is indicated by a generalized set; that is, the individual meets a large number of different situations in his daily life with a fairly consistent method of analyzing and responding to them. For example, when he hears diverse opinions and emotional appeals, he is willing to face facts and draw conclusions logically from them. As groups of organized values are internalized, they form the individual's philosophy of life.

In this brief examination of processes in the affective domain, relationships between the cognitive and affective domains are evident. For example, cognizing any type of content is a necessary condition for receiving, responding, and valuing. Productive thinking with semantic content is essential for verbalizing a value and for organizing a value system. Although the relationship between the cognitive and the affective is close, the principal outcomes in the affective domain are not solely or even primarily cognitive. The outcomes are interests, attitudes, values, and personality integration, as shown in Fig. 2.5. All are heavily loaded with the feeling component.

In addition to being based on the feeling component, outcomes as indicated in Figure 2.5 are applicable to many areas of human experience. For example, five of the most pervasive influences in our lives are family, education, work, religion, and government. One has not only factual information and concepts regarding these, he also has preferences, attitudes, and values. In turn, living by a value system and

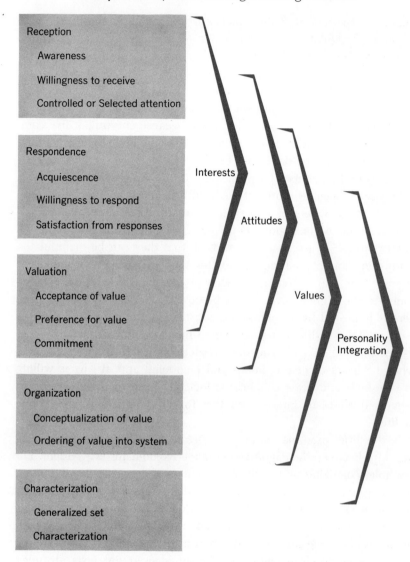

Fig. 2.5. Schematic arrangement of affective processes and related outcomes. (Based on data from D. R. Krathwohl, B. S. Bloom, & B. B. Masia. *Taxonomy of objectives: The classification of educational goals; Handbook II: Affective domain.* New York: McKay, 1964.)

achieving goals in correspondence with it is a principal motivational force in adult life. Some teachers may choose to give little attention to the affective components of education and may try to concentrate exclusively on the cognitive and psychomotor. Although this may be the case, the maturing student is acquiring preferences, attitudes, and values throughout his school years; these vitally affect the efficiency of his initial learning and also the use of any cognitive and psycho-motor abilities that he may develop.

IMMEDIATE TEACHING-LEARNING GOALS

There are many ways of stating objectives. One that is widely used is to indicate what the teacher will do. We often encounter statements such as:

1. Stimulate the students to acquire knowledge.
2. Impart information to the students.
3. Transmit the cultural heritage.

A better way to state objectives is in terms of what the students will do or learn, in other words, in behavioral terms. The latter has many advantages, including the possibility that students may read the objectives themselves and understand the behaviors that are desired. The following set of objectives was drawn up by five different teachers for classes attended by the same girl, and indicate more clearly the advantages of stating objectives in behavioral terms:

Typewriting
1. Understands rules for syllabication of words and rules for spelling.
2. Improves in using the hyphen, the shift-lock key, and carbon paper with letters.
3. Uses the proper forms and terms in addressing envelopes.
4. Wants to be neat in handling and using carbon paper.
5. Wants to use time and materials efficiently.

U.S. History
1. Understands cause-and-effect relationships applied to historical events.
2. Improves in obtaining information from maps.
3. Becomes more proficient in reading for specific information.
4. Uses information about history in analyzing our current problems, policies, and institutions.
5. Develops understanding and appreciation of Washington's role and his policies in this country's early history and its present problems.

English (focused on speech improvement)
1. Understands the mechanics of producing classroom plays on the radio.

2. Understands the significance of background music and timing in class-produced radio plays.
3. Improves in interpreting ideas and feelings.
4. Elicits the desired audience response better.
5. Improves in using the body and voice to convey intended meanings.

Home Economics

1. Understands such terms as dart, tuck, pleat, seam allowance, alteration marking, straight-of-goods marking, ease allowance, and stay-stitching.
2. Improves in laying out a pattern, marking it, and cutting it out.
3. Increases skill in stitching, pressing, fitting, and altering; and putting in zippers, waistbands, buttonholes, snaps, hooks and eyes.
4. Wants to use time efficiently in order to complete garment.
5. Appreciates value of careful marking, cutting, and assembling.

Spanish

1. Increases understanding of written and spoken Spanish.
2. Increases ability to think directly in Spanish, rather than in English and then translating.
3. Speaks Spanish more fluently, with correct pronunciation and meaningful expression.
4. Writes Spanish correctly with greater facility, noting spelling, accent marks, and word endings.
5. Appreciates the value of using Spanish well, both written and spoken.

Even these objectives in behavioral terms do not assure efficient pupil learning. Though the teachers want the girl to achieve them, efficient learning starts only when the girl also wants to achieve. Similarly, the instructor in educational psychology sets a goal of having each student learn the characteristics of an efficient teaching-learning situation, but it is only when each student sets the same personal goal that he will benefit most. Realistic goal setting is something each individual must learn. For a teacher to manage a classroom so that each learner sets realistic goals is one of the most important tasks of teaching. Chapter 12 treats goal setting in the classroom in considerably more detail.

SUMMARY

Long-term and more immediate objectives are needed in order to decide what students should learn, and to a lesser extent, how they will learn it. Many local, state, and national groups formulate objectives of education. Eventually each teacher and each student must also decide what is important to learn. Learning is efficient only when the student knows what is to be learned and tries to learn it well.

An exciting development is underway in the identification and stating of objectives. For a long time objectives were thought of only in relation to specific subject-matter fields. Now the schools are trying to improve abilities and other characteristics of children and youth. An ability is a combination of a process, content, and product. Abilities in the cognitive and psychomotor domains are being identified and subsequently nurtured through instruction. Also, attention is given to pupil characteristics in the affective domain, including interests, attitudes, values, and personality integration. Objectives which focus on abilities promise to vitalize instruction. When attempting to nurture emerging human abilities, teachers deal with processes and content simultaneously.

QUESTIONS AND ACTIVITIES

1. How are the objectives of education related to what students learn?
2. Select one of the broad statements of objectives given for the elementary or secondary school and discuss its relevance to modern times.
3. a. What is an ability? a general ability? a specific ability?
   b. What are the relationships between learning and abilities?
4. a. Define and give examples of each of the four contents specified by Guilford.
   b. Related to your major subject-matter interest, indicate the content that is most and least important.
5. a. Define and give examples of each of the six products specified by Guilford.
   b. How are units, classes, relations, and systems alike? different?
   c. How do transformations and implications differ from the preceding four products?
6. a. Define and give examples of the five intellectual processes specified by Guilford.
   b. Based on your educational experiences, identify the process which has received most and least attention in your education thus far. Why do you think this has occurred?
7. What is the relationship between abilities and outcomes of learning in the cognitive domain?
8. a. State the subject-matter field and level of schooling with which you are most concerned.
   b. For this situation and related to a unit of instruction, give five to eight objectives in the cognitive domain to be achieved by pupils in terms of abilities or in terms of Bloom's taxonomy. Use about one paragraph per objective to clarify its nature and indicate its importance.
   c. Indicate a question or activity

55

for the pupil which when acted on would contribute toward his achieving the objective.

9. a. What are the main abilities and outcomes of learning in the psychomotor domain?
   b. Which psychomotor abilities have you developed most fully? least fully?
   c. Are your abilities more fully developed in the cognitive or psychomotor domain? why?

10. a. How is the concept of internalization related to affective processes?
    b. Indicate what you consider to be the role of the school in promoting learning in the affective domain.

11. Compare the usefulness of stating immediate goals in terms of teacher and student behavior.

SUGGESTIONS FOR FURTHER READING

Bloom, B. S. (Ed.) *Taxonomy of educational objectives. Handbook I: Cognitive domain.* New York: McKay, 1956.

Conant, J. B. *Slums and suburbs.* New York: McGraw–Hill, 1961.

Krathwohl, D. R., B. S. Bloom, & B. B. Masia. *Taxonomy of objectives: The classification of educational goals. Handbook II: Affective domain.* New York: McKay, 1964.

National Education Association. *Schools for the sixties.* New York: McGraw–Hill, 1963.

Parsons, T. The school class as a social system: Some of its functions in American society. *Harv. educ. Rev.,* 1959, **29**, 297–318. (In Grinder, 1963, 28–49.)

Sanders, N. M. *Classroom questions: What kinds?* New York: Harper & Row, 1965.

REFERENCES

1. Bloom, B. S. (Ed.) *Taxonomy of educational objectives. Handbook I: Cognitive domain.* New York: McKay, 1956.

2. Conant, J. B. *The American high school today.* New York: McGraw–Hill, 1959.

3. Conant, J. B. *Slums and suburbs.* New York: McGraw-Hill, 1961.

4. English, H. B., & Ava C. English. *A comprehensive dictionary of psychological and psychoanalytical terms.* New York: Longmans, 1958.

5. Gershon, A., J. P. Guilford, & P. R. Merrifield. Figural and symbolic divergent-production abilities in adolescent and adult populations. *Rep. psychol. Lab.,* No. 29. Los Angeles: Univer. Southern Calif., 1963.

6. Guilford, J. P. A system of the psychomotor abilities. *Amer. J. Psychol.,* 1958, **71**, 161–174.

7. Guilford, J. P. Three faces of intellect. *Amer. Psychologist,* 1959, **14**, 469–479.

8. Guilford, J. P., & R. Hoepfner. Current summary of structure-of-intellect factors and suggested tests. *Rep. psychol. Lab.,* No. 30. Los Angeles: Univer. Southern Calif., 1963.

9. Kearney, N. C. *Elementary school objectives.* New York: Russell Sage, 1953.

10. Klausmeier, H. J. *Teaching in the secondary school.* (2nd ed.) New York: Harper & Row, 1958.

11. Klausmeier, H. J., & Katharine Dresden. *Teaching in the elementary school.* (2nd ed.) New York: Harper & Row, 1962.

12. Krathwohl, D. R., B. S. Bloom, &

B. B. Masia. *Taxonomy of objectives: The classification of educational goals. Handbook II: Affective domain.* New York: McKay, 1964.

13. Merrifield, P. R., J. P. Guilford, & A. Gershon. The differentiation of divergent-production abilities at the sixth-grade level. *Rep. psychol. Lab.*, No. 27. Los Angeles: Univer. Southern Calif., 1963.

14. Meyers, C. E., & H. F. Dingman. The structure of abilities at the preschool ages: Hypothesized domains. *Psychol. Bull.*, 1960, **57**, 514–532.

15. National Education Association. *Schools for the sixties.* New York: McGraw–Hill, 1963.

16. Sanders, N. M. *Classroom questions: What kinds?* New York: Harper & Row, 1965.

17. Vernon, P. E. *The structure of human abilities.* New York: Wiley, 1950.

CHAPTER 3

Learning Processes
and Theories

WHAT GOES ON inside the human being as he learns? What external conditions result in improved performance by an individual? These questions are of great interest to many people. Psychologists have developed theories in an attempt to explain internal processes and to identify conditions that are related to efficiency of learning.

During the first decade of this century many educators and some psychologists were hopeful that a comprehensive learning theory would emerge and, in turn, would contribute to the improvement of student learning in the schools. Although several comprehensive theories were formulated, they were based almost exclusively on experimentation in animal laboratories, and their application to school practice did not produce revolutionary changes in the learning efficiency of students.

Few psychologists are attempting to formulate comprehensive learning theories at the present time. Many are, however, attempting to clarify principles that may be applied to improvement of learning in the schools. Instead of formulating comprehensive theories, they are studying in greater depth a single phenomenon such as cognitive processes or the learning of outcomes—factual information, attitudes, concepts, and personality development. Another recent trend is to extend principles formulated in laboratories to school situations. The final validation of laboratory principles is to be carried out through experimentation with human beings in nonlaboratory settings. A third approach is to derive principles from empirical research in educational settings and then classify these principles around some organizing center, such as outcomes of learning.

Four theories with relevance to school learning are described briefly in this chapter. Each theory is not comprehensive, and it might appropriately be termed a *subtheory*. Only a small part of the empirical research is presented about each theory, and the experimental methodology is not described because our purpose is to indicate only the main substance of each theory.

In the first part of this chapter, the authors' ideas are presented about purposeful learning as a function of variables, the same variables mentioned earlier in Chapter 1. Purposeful learning is especially applicable to the learning of concepts, problem-solving skills, creative thinking, and verbal and motor skills. Other theories are more applicable to other outcomes.

Conditioning theory as outlined by Staats and Staats is included in this chapter (11). Conditioning theory has value in explaining how behavior may be changed with no intention on the learner's part to modify his behavior. Principles initially derived from conditioning experiments are being applied to programed instruction. This type of teaching is widely used in the school and will be discussed more fully in a later chapter. Also, Staats and Staats and many others are engaged in ascertaining how principles of conditioning, first developed in animal laboratories, can be applied to human learning.

The main concern of Bandura and Walters is social learning and personality development (6). The bulk of the experimentation underlying this theory has been with young children. Imitative learning is central in this theory, although principles of conditioning are also quite prominent. Imitative learning is prevalent during the school years and is applicable to a large class of behaviors.

Ausubel's subsumption theory was developed directly as an explanatory system for a large class of outcomes dealing with subject-matter knowledge that is presented to students in books, by teachers, and through audiovisual media of various types (2). A main class of outcomes not dealt with in subsumption theory includes concepts acquired by inductive methods, solutions to problems acquired independently, and others. The main principles of this subsumption theory are concerned with explaining internal events in the learner.

In each of these four theories the attempt is made to explain learning processes, to show the relationship among variables, or to indicate conditions conducive to learning. Learning itself is not directly observable; it is inferred from the performances of the individual. Learning, as we have defined it, is a process whereby a change in behavior results from some form of experience—activity, training, observation, and the like. Changes in behavior which result from bodily injury, disease, fatigue, or use of drugs are not considered learning. This definition is probably acceptable in each of the four theories. However, the interpretations of how learning occurs vary markedly.

PURPOSEFUL LEARNING

Think momentarily about what you have learned with deliberate intent to learn in contrast to what you have learned through imitating someone else, to having been conditioned by someone else, or to having learned material that someone else has provided and told you to learn. Learning that occurs with intent is called *purposeful learning*. Much human learning is purposeful. At times it is controlled solely by the individual without instruction or guidance. At other times someone else is available to instruct the individual. We shall first describe a sequence in purposeful learning without relating the sequence to variables. Then, purposeful learning in a group situation will be related to a number of variables, including those associated with instruction. The latter might be seen as a theory of classroom learning or as a theory of instruction.

Purposeful Learning by an Individual

Some outcomes of learning are acquired by individuals without receiving instruction. Figure 3.1 shows a sequence in purposeful learning without instruction. This sequence describes how individuals acquire many of their intellectual and psychomotor abilities. To clarify the sequence, we shall consider two situations which exemplify this process. In analyzing the examples which follow, you might profitably think about your present repertoire of learned behaviors and attempt to decide the extent to which the sequence in Fig. 3.1 applies.

An individual at some stage in his maturation is motivated to reach

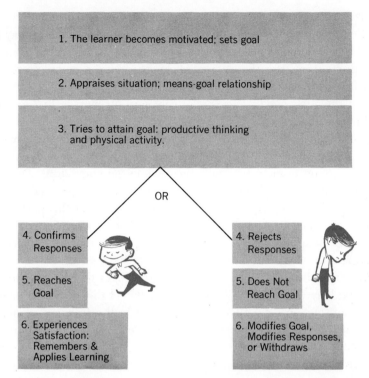

Fig. 3.1. Sequence in purposeful learning without instruction.

a goal. For example, he may be hungry or thirsty and desire to satisfy these biological needs. He may see a bright object and want to know what it is; this leads to exploratory behavior. He may desire approval from an age-mate or adult, or he may seek another form of social satisfaction. He may have a printed page in front of him and want to know what the printed page says. There are many sources of motivation, as will be shown in Chapter 12.

Let us assume that a young child, Bill, already rides a tricycle well. After receiving a bicycle, he is highly motivated to learn to ride it and sets as his goal (not using the word *goal*, of course) to ride it as well as his friend can ride his bicycle. He has now experienced the first phase outlined in Fig. 3.1—becoming motivated and setting a goal.

Bill now appraises the situation—the bicycle, himself, and his relationship to the bicycle. He makes preliminary trials almost immediately as part of the appraisal of the situation. Some delayed imitation may be involved; that is, imitating the actions of his friend (model) whom he has previously observed riding a bicycle. These early trials, much like a person's early tries at automobile driving, are usually characterized by lack of such psychomotor abilities as precision, coordination, and flexibility. Bill at first may not get on the bicycle properly and may not put his foot pedal in proper position to start off. After several trials he will probably master the skills of starting, making a complete revolution first with one pedal, and then continuing on to make the revolution of the other pedal. This is relatively easy for most 5- to 7-year-old children with proper-sized bicycles. The next big task is to maintain and shift the body balance while returning to the pedal from which the ride started. Falls frequently occur at this point because the bicycle must continue to move at a fair speed while the body shifts. Depending upon his size and other characteristics, Bill may proceed quickly at this point, or he may try every day for weeks to get this part of the skill accomplished. After mastering this, Bill continues his trials. He drops the inappropriate responses and improves the ones which he interprets as useful.

As soon as Bill feels that he is making progress or that he can actually ride the bicycle as well as he had originally set out to do, he experiences satisfaction—the affective component in the learning sequence. This component first entered when he originally wanted to learn and continues throughout the entire learning sequence. Bill is learning likes and dislikes and experiencing feelings of satisfaction and dissatisfaction in all his trying.

Suppose that with his best and continued efforts, Bill is not able to ride the bicycle as well as he would like or perhaps cannot ride it at all. After repeated trials and feelings of failure, he may engage in a variety of behaviors. The behavior which might be most appropriate and lead to future success would be to try to improve his performance with further effort. If he has no basis for making improvements, he may simply continue to try as he has in the past with the possibility that such trying will lead to success. Bill may, however, quit. It is not uncommon for individuals to quit after experiencing repeated failure with their best efforts. In the case of bicycle riding, most children do not quit; they continue trying. Rather than quitting or trying the same or new responses, an individual without guidance may substitute a different goal if he is convinced that the present goal is unattainable. If Bill cannot learn to ride the bicycle, he may return to his tricycle and attempt to perfect skills in riding it.

Learning to ride a bicycle takes many tries. In contrast, consider an example of verbal learning which is purposeful, without instruction, and which may be accomplished in few trials and in a short time. Suppose that Mary, a fifth-grader, is reading about a basketball game in her school. She wants to understand the account fully; she is motivated. Suppose that Mary encounters the following sentence and finds an unfamiliar word, *crucial:*

John scored his lone point at a *crucial* moment.

Referring again to the sequence in purposeful learning in Fig. 3.1, examine how the sequence applies. Mary appraises the situation—directs her attention toward the unknown word and studies it in relation to the other words in the sentence in order to get an estimate of its possible meaning from the context. Her preliminary trials to pronounce the word occur almost simultaneously with the initial appraisal. In trying to get the pronunciation, Mary may look at the various letters in the word and try to sound them out. Or, she may try to divide the word into syllables and pronounce the syllables. If Mary has had good previous instruction in reading she will probably attempt all three—getting the meaning of the word from the context, phonetic analysis, and structural analysis. Eventually she will come forth with some pronunciation of the word, correct or incorrect, or may simply give up.

Uninstructed, Mary accepts the pronunciation that makes most sense to her, and the one that best completes the meaning and her appraisal of its pronunciation. It is possible that from the context the word might be *critical* rather than *crucial.* Regardless of whether Mary pronounces the word as *critical* or *crucial,* she has reached her goal and experiences satisfaction. This is a difficult word for fifth-graders. It is possible that Mary may realize that she cannot read it. In this case, she does not reach the goal of getting full meaning, but she may have sufficient understanding of the word and quit without further effort. The frustration resulting from not knowing this one word may not be sufficiently high that she tries again or sets a substitute or modified goal.

Purposeful Learning in a Classroom Setting

In mathematics we say that $y = (f)x;$ or verbally, that y is a function of x. We call x a variable. When the value of x changes, the value of y does also. Purposeful learning in the classroom or in other group situations is a function of a large number of variables. When a variable changes, the efficiency of learning does also. Although the relationships among variables cannot yet be stated in precise mathematical terms, it is possible that they may at some time in the future.

Figure 3.2 shows the now familiar sequence in purposeful learning, instructional processes, and the seven groups of variables in a class-

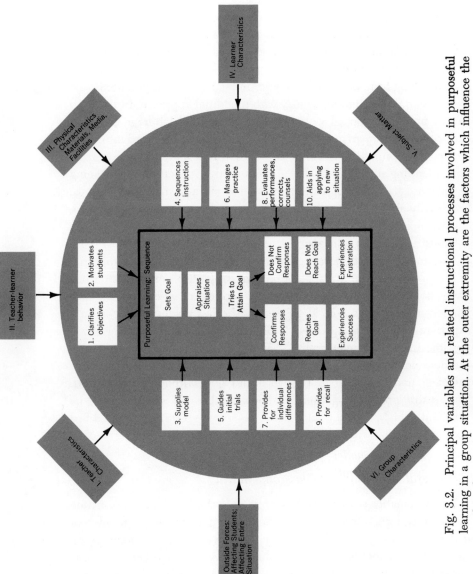

Fig. 3.2. Principal variables and related instructional processes involved in purposeful learning in a group situation. At the outer extremity are the factors which influence the teaching-learning process; the middle ring represents the instructional processes which impinge on the learner. At the core of the learning process is the sequence through which

room setting as associated with how well an individual learns in a group situation. Since we are dealing with learning under instruction, we have identified 10 instructional processes most directly related to three teaching variables: teacher characteristics, teaching actions and interactions with the students, and physical characteristics of the setting, including instructional materials and media.

Let us now examine 10 major generalizations that relate the sequence in purposeful learning to the 10 instructional processes. Only one of several possible generalizations will be given for each process, and only a brief explanatory statement will follow each generalization. The supporting evidence for each generalization and further implications for practice are given in later chapters.

1. *Clarifying objectives* of instruction facilitates goal setting by the student. Realistic goal setting by the student encourages learning. Because education is prescriptive—that is, because society through the school and the teacher indicates what students should learn—realistic goal setting by the student is possible only as instructional objectives are clear to the student. This clarification of objectives should specify the type of performance expected of the student so that he has sufficient knowledge to appraise the situation, including means-goals relationships.

2. *Motivating students* is essential for securing consistent pupil effort. The teacher may engage in four broad categories of behaviors to get students activated: manipulating materials and activities to arouse curiosity and interest; engaging in goal setting procedures with the students; manipulating rewards and punishments, and competition and cooperation; and providing knowledge of progress. Motivation that is too intense may be accompanied by disruptive emotional states which impede learning.

3. *Supplying a model*—actual persons, verbal descriptions of procedures, and representations by audio-visual means—facilitates the learning of responses that are new to the learner, responses he has not yet made. For example, the child who has not written the word *man* nor any of the letters in it, profits not only from seeing the word but also from watching someone write it. By observing a model, many incorrect preliminary trials of the student are eliminated.

4. *Sequencing of the subject matter* properly enables the student to cognize information initially, think productively about it, remember it, and use it in new situations. Logical organization of subject matter results in a hierarchical, topical sequence. Psychological organization is based upon conditions under which material is learned efficiently.

65

These two types of organization may be identical; however, the sequencing of subject matter has not been studied intensively until very recently. The student's lack of knowledge about the sequence and organization makes difficult his appraisal of means-goals relationships and initial trials.

5. *Guiding initial trials* is essential to the establishment of correct responses and the avoidance of habitual errors. Guidance may be given by words, physical contact, or demonstration. Early guidance directs the learner's attention to more adequate skills or knowledge, aids the learner in understanding the nature of a successful performance, provides encouragement to continue, and relieves possible anxiety that may appear if the learner is uncertain about his ability to perform the task.

6. *Managing practice effectively,* not merely repeating the same activity, is essential to goal attainment in the psychomotor and cognitive domains, to improved performance in most subject fields. Effective practice usually requires both productive thinking and physical activity. A teacher can manipulate whole-part relationships, the length and spacing of practice sessions, reinforcements, knowledge of progress, and other conditions to make practice effective.

7. *Providing for individual differences* through making available materials and activities suited to the individual permits each to reach his goal and to learn efficiently in the process. Two practices which facilitate individualization are becoming increasingly common in the schools: grouping students to secure greater homogeneity in relation to learning tasks, and improving materials and physical arrangements for independent study. In some schools pupils are being arranged into instructional groups which are independent of age and grade level, a common practice for many years in music and athletic activities. Also in some schools, individual study booths are provided wherein each student has available a variety of instructional materials suited to his rate of learning.

8. *Evaluating student performance* can help in reinforcing desirable learning. Informing students of their progress and aiding them to overcome errors facilitates learning because it provides encouragement to continue and eliminates inadequate or incorrect responses. The greatest possibility for the improvement of human abilities occurs in connection with this generalization. Lack of progress and simultaneous failure in reaching goals is a principal contributor to a student's losing his zest for learning and his interest in subject matter and schooling.

9. *Providing for recall* and long-term retention through systematic review of verbal material and spaced practice of skills is essential. One means of providing review and practice is to elicit from students the necessary information and skills that are needed to perform a novel task. The novel tasks may be arranged on a daily basis so that there is cumulative improvement. This procedure produces more permanent learning than does holding one review or practice session immediately prior to a monthly examination.

10. *Helping students apply* knowledge and skills in new situations facilitates both long-term retention and use. Verbal description of applications is less effective than actual situations in which new knowledge and skills can be put to use. The great loss in learning from one year to the next and the inability to cross from one subject to another and from the school situation to outside the school results from lack of knowledge and of opportunities to apply it.

Although the three primary variables related to teaching are most directly associated with the instructional processes as we have indicated, the other four groups of variables shown in Fig. 3.2 are also related to purposeful learning and to instructional processes. Another way of stating this is that purposeful learning in a group situation is a function of these seven variables also. Obviously not all the generalizations related to these last four variables can be enumerated at this time; therefore we shall indicate five that are especially important and readily understood. Generalizations 11, 12, and 13 pertain to variables IV, V, and VI, respectively, while 14 and 15 pertain to variable VII, outside forces.

11. *Characteristics of the learner* affect his readiness to learn any subject matter and the efficiency with which he subsequently proceeds with the task. Characteristics of individuals that are closely associated with efficiency of learning are general intellectual ability, specific abilities required to perform the task, previous achievements related to the task, and strength of motivation. Modern assessment techniques and computer technology may make this essential information about students quickly available to teachers; the computer itself eventually may be used to monitor the learning activities of students.

12. *Subject matter* of high meaningfulness is acquired, remembered, and used more efficiently than is material of low meaningfulness. Certain material, for example, the word *bird* in comparison with the syllable *dax* is potentially more meaningful to people of roughly equivalent English-speaking backgrounds. Two ways of making semantic mate-

rial more meaningful are to relate new material to what the student already knows and to provide experience with the referents, including objects and processes, for which the words stand.

13. *Group characteristics* have a strong effect on the efficiency of individual learning. For example, individuals in cohesive groups learn subject matter more effectively than do fragmented collections of individuals. A fragmented group, characterized by dissension among cliques and individuals, results in the development of unwholesome rivalries, unfavorable attitudes among individuals, and low efficiency in learning subject matter.

14. *Outside forces that impinge upon the child* affect his learning in school. The lower the socioeconomic and social class status of the family, the lesser utilization does the child make of schooling. When well conducted, the school makes possible upward mobility of the children of lower social class and at the same time engenders harmonious relations among children of all social classes. Many factors contribute to the lack of efficient learning of children from lower social classes. Perhaps the most critical factor is the heavy emphasis given in schools to preparation for further education, including college, and the lesser emphasis given to preparation for occupations and living. One large discrepancy between the outlook of high school students and the traditional high school is that the majority of the students view the primary role of high school as occupational training rather than general or liberal education.

15. *Outside forces reflected through the teacher* are related to efficient pupil learning. Administrative support of the educational program facilitates learning by providing necessary material and human resources. Adequate instructional facilities, materials, and equipment are essential to modern education. Furthermore, teachers need assistance with a variety of instructional problems, including students who do not learn efficiently. The lack of trained personnel to assist teachers continues to be a critical problem of education.

The sequence in purposeful learning and the instructional processes were discussed in the same order as given in Figs. 3.1 and 3.2 in order to facilitate study of them. However, we should not think of the order as being fixed and unchangeable. For example, productive thinking is undertaken not only when trying to achieve a goal, but also when setting a goal. Furthermore, some provision for individual differences is often made before the teacher meets a classroom group. On the basis of previous teacher grades and ratings, scores on an achievement test in the subject, and scores on a general intellectual ability test, students are placed in classroom groups by guidance personnel long before the teacher sees the class.

Just as the order of the processes and variables is not fixed, neither is the exact number of processes. A five-step sequence in purposeful learning is indicated in Fig. 3.2, starting with setting a goal and concluding with reaching or not reaching the goal. A similar three-step sequence has been identified and validated as being appropriate for problem solving—preparation, production, and judgment (8). Preparation includes what is given in Fig. 3.2 as goal setting and appraisal of the situation; production corresponds to trying to attain the goal through productive thinking and physical activity; and judgment corresponds to confirming or rejecting responses.

In Chapter 2, we saw that Guilford identified and named five internal processes—cognition, memory, convergent thinking, divergent thinking, and evaluation. In the sequence of purposeful learning, we have included the same terms with the exception of cognition, which we may assume is essential to appraising a situation. This functionalist framework is also comprehensive enough to incorporate the terms *assimilation* and *accommodation,* generally attributed to Piaget (**10**), but also applied to inquiry learning:

> Inquiry is a fundamental form of learning. . . . In analyzing the act of inquiry it is helpful to think in terms of two basic processes. The first of these consists of taking in and incorporating what we perceive in terms of what we know and understand. We process data in terms of our conceptual systems. A child sees an object that has a wooden handle and a long metal blade attached to it. It looks to him very much like a knife. We can say that the child has *assimilated* his perception of the object in terms of a well established conceptual system related to knives. . . . This process of reshaping and reorganizing conceptual structures until they fit and account for perceived events is known as *accommodation.* Inquiry involves both assimilation and accommodation in complementary roles. . . . When the mode of learning is inquiry, however, the process of data gathering, analysis, and experimentation is under the control of the learner himself. He is free to reach out in whatever direction he chooses for data and to gather this information in whatever sequence is most meaningful to him. Through inquiry, the learner influences and actually programs his own learning in terms of his own cognitive needs as dictated by his style of learning and his informational needs of the moment (**12**, 59–61).

It thus might appear that inquiry learning proceeds without instruction of any type and is thus similar to the sequence in purposeful learning without instruction. This is only partly true. When he has no assistance, the individual does proceed by inquiry. This is, however, a very slow process, especially for school children. Therefore, the situation is carefully arranged by the teacher in order that the student may utilize the inquiry process productively rather than proceeding randomly and inefficiently.

CONDITIONING

A young child strokes a furry pet, apparently without fear. Later, an adult strikes a bell sharply immediately behind the child. The child cries in fright, an unconditioned response to the harsh sound. Now each time the pet is presented, the adult strikes the bell harshly. After this is repeated a number of times, the pet is presented by itself, and the child cries. The child, by another person's manipulation of the two stimuli events—the presentation of the pet and of the harsh sound of the bell—has acquired a conditioned response of crying to a previously nonfeared stimulus. Other furry pets of similar color are now presented to the child. He responds with crying to these also. The conditioned response of crying has now generalized to other stimuli of the same class.

A toddler avoids a hot stove after touching it when hot (avoidance learning) and seeks milk as food after having drunk milk when hungry (approach learning). Here the child has learned to suppress or continue responses on the basis of the effects of these responses. Through manipulating a system of rewards and punishments, some parents shape the religious, political, and other attitudes of children. These examples are typical of extensions of principles of conditioning to human learning.

Principles of conditioning are reasonably well established and are being extended from animal studies to a wide class of human behaviors. Not everyone agrees completely with the applications or extensions. However, the principles themselves should be understood. A clear presentation of the principles and samples of extensions to a wide range of human behaviors are given by Staats and Staats (11). Although many ideas of Staats and Staats are based on the prior work of many psychologists, their statements are followed closely in this section in an attempt to present a concise overview of the principles.

Classical Conditioning

Figure 3.3 schematizes first-order and higher-order classical conditioning. As noted in first-order conditioning, a neutral stimulus, in this

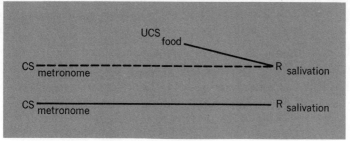

Learning Processes and Theories

A First Order Conditioning

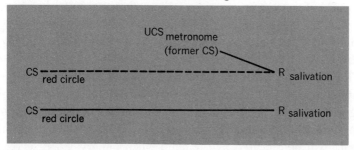

B Higher Order Conditioning

Fig. 3.3. Schematic arrangement of classical conditioning. (Adapted from A. W. Staats & Carolyn K. Staats. *Complex human behavior: A systematic extension of learning principles.* New York: Holt, Rinehart and Winston, Inc. 1963.)

case the sound of a bell, is presented almost simultaneously with the unconditioned stimulus, food. The sight of food leads to the response of salivation in a hungry organism. By presenting both again repeatedly and withdrawing the food gradually, the sound of the bell alone eventually elicits the response of salivation. The bell sound is now the conditioned stimulus, and salivation is the conditioned response.

In higher-order conditioning, the sound of the bell produces the response of salivation and now serves the same function as did the previous unconditioned stimulus, food. When a new neutral stimulus, a red circle, is presented immediately preceding the sound of the bell, and through repetition, subtraction, and substitution as above, the sight of the red circle elicits the response of salivation. The stimuli do not produce the response directly. They lead to internal cues or movements which subsequently lead to the response of salivation. We shall not treat the internal events in more detail inasmuch as the results are the same, independent of what happens internally.

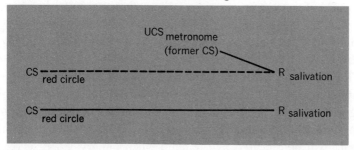

These principles of classical conditioning may be stated more formally. Whenever a stimulus which elicits a response occurs in close time proximity with a stimulus which does not, there results a tendency for the new stimulus to elicit the response. Further, when a conditioned stimulus elicits the conditioned response, it may be manipulated with another neutral stimulus and result in bringing the response under the control of the previously neutral stimulus.

Operant Conditioning

In laboratory experiments, a clear distinction can be made between classical and operant conditioning. When extended to human learning, however, the distinction is not clear, especially since close temporal contiguity is involved in operant conditioning. Let us examine operant conditioning.

When the behavior of an individual is followed by a reinforcer, there is a tendency for the behavior to be repeated again. For example, a hungry child says "Please" and is given food by a parent or teacher. Each time this is done the probability is strengthened that saying "Please" will be repeated by the child when hungry. Food serves as a positive reinforcer of the "Please" response.

Children are often presented with aversive stimuli, such as punishment. Let us assume that a child is being punished by having to sit in the front of the class. When the child makes a certain response, namely apologizes, the punishment stops and the child is permitted to return to his seat. In this case, the removal of the aversive stimulus increases the probability that the response leading up to it, namely, apologizing, will be made the next time the child is in the same situation in order to avoid the aversive stimulus. Removal of an aversive stimulus serves as a reinforcer of the response, apologizing.

There is little doubt that providing a positive reinforcement following a response increases the probability that the response will be made again. Also, the removal of an aversive stimulus strengthens the response that leads to its removal. This is different, however, from punishing. The effects of punishment immediately following a response cannot be predicted reliably. When an adult punishes a child for an act and the child knows that he is being punished for having committed the act, there is a tendency for the child not to commit the act again. Punishment has a suppressing effect on the act in the presence of the punisher. However, the child may repeat the act later in the absence of the punisher, particularly if the child has not developed another action to replace the punished one. In addition, the presence of the punisher may become an aversive stimulus through higher-order conditioning. Our main purpose here is to treat the nature of negative reinforcers, not to discuss punishment. We shall give more attention to punishment later.

In the prior discussion of classical conditioning we showed that higher-order conditioning is possible. The same is true in operant conditioning. For example, when discussing positive reinforcers, we indicated that presenting food to a hungry child who says "Please" increases the probability of the child's continuing to say "Please." One could pair words, for example, "good boy," with the presentation of the food. After a number of presentations, the words "good boy" would have the same effect as the presentation of the food in maintaining the strength of the "Please" response.

Positive reinforcers and punishments are used in the schools on many occasions. Teachers use such words as *good, fine, excellent,* and *nice* to encourage the continuation of the behavior which preceded it. Also, giving high grades in school subjects, commenting favorably on written work, and similar techniques are used to encourage types of behavior desired by the teacher. However, these may not work as positive reinforcers with all children. For example, some students may not desire high grades or favorable teacher comments if these are also associated with losing the friendship of a peer. Punishments are employed frequently to suppress behavior that the teacher considers undesirable. We merely state that punishments are used frequently in the school; we do not advocate their widespread use.

We will now summarize the main generalizations concerning operant conditioning. A reinforcement, when following closely a certain behavior, increases the probability that the behavior will occur again in the future. The removal of negative reinforcers, closely following a certain behavior, also increases the probability of the behavior occurring again. Higher-order conditioning occurs in operant conditioning. A neutral stimulus which is paired with a conditioned reinforcing stimulus will, through repeated pairings, acquire reinforcing value itself. Secondary reinforcers are usually social. Among the positive social reinforcers are complimentary words spoken to another; physical or verbal responses of endearment; tokens, such as money, honors, and good grades; and approval of the group, in the form of applause, group laughter, or attention. Negative reinforcers and conditioned aversive stimuli include disapproval by words or actions; threats and harsh tones; low grades; and group disapproval in the form of silence, booing, and the like.

Schedules of Reinforcement

If all the responses that are made are reinforced, the schedule of reinforcement is 100 percent. Many other schedules are possible and have been shown to have a pronounced effect upon behavior in experimental situations with animals. The effects are more clearly defined in laboratory experiments, where controls are more rigorously applied, than in school classrooms where the controls cannot be so rigorous. Four main types of scheduling have been demonstrated in the laboratory.

In a *fixed-ratio* schedule, there is regular reinforcement of a certain proportion of the same response, such as every third, sixth, tenth, hundredth, and so on. *Variable-ratio* reinforcement provides for reinforcement of a certain proportion of the responses, but not on a systematic basis. A variable-ratio schedule tends to produce rapid responding in a hungry animal.

In a *fixed-interval* schedule, reinforcement is given at a set time interval, such as every 15 seconds, 30 seconds, and so on. In a *variable-interval* schedule, the reinforcement does not come at regular intervals; often the interval is established on a random basis. Variable-interval reinforcement produces a consistent, stable rate of responding in animals. Schedules of reinforcement in teaching-learning situations are usually not carefully controlled. There is, instead, intermittent reinforcement of socially approved responses.

Stimulus Generalization and Response Discrimination

Stimulus generalization and response discrimination are equally applicable to classical and operant conditioning. A response is conditioned to a specific reinforcing stimulus. In classical conditioning, what happens if a slight change is made in the stimulus complex? Within limits, the same response will be made to stimuli of the same class. In this case we say that stimulus generalization has occurred. For example, children received 16 reinforced trials of pulling a lever during a presentation of a one-colored visual stimulus (15). A marble was used for the reinforcement. Later, the same experimental situation without the marbles was presented and the visual stimuli differed in hue, brightness, or both. The children responded to the varied visual stimuli with the lever-pressing response, although with less frequency than to the original stimulus. Stimulus generalization had occurred.

A young child may at first call his father and all other men *daddy*. Later, he calls only his father *daddy* and refers to other men by appropriate titles, such as Mister, Uncle, and Grandfather. He has learned to *discriminate* among the objects so that he makes only the appropriate response to certain stimuli. Go back to the first sentence in this paragraph. You make a different response to each word. You are discriminating the stimuli and making a different response to each. Reading involves discrimination of responses whereby the appropriate pronunciation is given only to a certain word.

Successive Approximation

In the preceding examples a response is made and in turn is reinforced. How does one go about getting the response to be made in the first place? An attempt is made to shape the behavior through a series of successive approximations. For example, human subjects were given score points as reinforcers in order to shape a variety of behaviors, such as scratching the ear, smiling, and saying certain classes of words (14). At first, the experimenter reinforced any movement of the subject. This strengthened the movement response. The next step was to reinforce another movement, such as of the arms. Then movement of the hand toward the head, and finally scratching movements were reinforced. This is a rough sketch of how the final scratching response was shaped by successive approximations.

In another experiment, college students were conditioned to make statements of opinion beginning with "I think . . .," "I believe . . .," "It seems to me . . .," and the like (13). In the first 10 minutes the students were engaged in conversation and *primed* to talk with questions. The number of their opinion statements was merely recorded. In the second 10 minutes, two reinforcement procedures were used. In the first the opinion statements were reinforced with agreement by saying "You're right," "I agree," "That's so," nodding the head, or smiling. The second reinforcement procedure was to repeat back to the student in paraphrase what he had said. Each student at some time during the experiment also had his opinion statements ignored or disagreed with. The conversations were carried out on a variety of topics; however, the students were unaware that they were in an experiment. Every student increased his rate of stating opinions when reinforced by paraphrase or agreement; however, the number of opinions stated varied widely among the students. Nonreinforcement resulted in fewer opinion statements.

Forgetting and Conditioning

Psychologists who use conditioning principles as the explanation of learning do not speak of *forgetting*. They refer to weakening of the response as *extinction*. Previously we pointed out that a response followed with a positive reinforcer is strengthened. Behavior acquired through conditioning may be weakened through nonreinforcement. For example, children who pull a lever in response to a red stimulus will eventually cease doing so if reinforcement is not given after the lever pulling. Extinction of responses that have first become strong through reinforcement is relatively slow.

Motivation and Conditioning

Some psychological scientists, such as Staats and Staats, define terms as relationships between two events. Furthermore, they talk of drives instead of motivation. A number of relationships are involved in the concept of drive. First, deprivation of something, such as food, has the effect of making the organism more active, up to the point when further deprivation results in a lessening of activity as starvation is approached. Deprivation of water has the same activating effect. A second effect is that deprivation makes presentation of the deprived stimulus reinforcing. For example, deprivation of food makes food a reinforcer. The hunger drive is what we infer from the relationship between deprivation of food and its activating and reinforcing effects. Aversive stimuli also produce increased general activity.

Primary drives do not depend on learning; they are associated with the maintenance of life. The possibility also exists that individuals may be deprived of secondary reinforcers, which were discussed earlier. Deprivation of secondary reinforcers may have the same effects as the deprivation of primary stimuli, such as food and water.

Applicability to School Learning

In Chapter 2, reference was made to three domains under which to organize objectives of education and outcomes of learning. These were the cognitive, psychomotor, and affective. Conditioning principles probably have most applicability to the affective domain, less to the psychomotor and to the cognitive.

Preferences, attitudes, values, and interests all have an affective connotation, positive or negative. So do beliefs. None of these necessarily requires a substantial cognitive or intellectual base. One can have a negative attitude toward a professor but have little or no information about him. One can have a positive attitude toward a religious group with little or no information. Behavior in the affective domain can be shaped in a young child through judicious use of operant-conditioning principles without including informational content in the training (7). This is not to say that conditioning should be used or that it is the only means of influencing behavior in the affective domain.

It is possible that motor skills are partly learned in accordance with the principles of temporal contiguity, repetition or practice, and reinforcement, when the definition of reinforcement is sufficiently broad to include the results of activities themselves serving as reinforcers (11). In learning to type, for example, there is a certain number of keys in a certain number of combinations, and an association has to be formed between each key, each combination, and the related correct response or movement. Each time an individual strikes a correct key, he makes a correct association. Repetition or practice in typing tends to integrate many such relatively discrete associations. Reinforcement, including knowledge that the intended key has been struck, tends to strengthen the probability that the correct response will be made again. At this point, it is important to recognize that we are discussing three principles—contiguity of two stimuli or a stimulus and response, repetition or practice, and reinforcement of responses. These principles can be identified through empirical research on typing, independent of a stimulus-response or conditioning theory. Nevertheless, the principles of contiguity, repetition, and reinforcement are central in the Staats' outline of conditioning and also in the statements of earlier and contemporary S-R conditioning psychologists (11).

Up to the present time, the greatest impact of operant conditioning in school learning has been through programed instruction, which will be discussed more fully in a later chapter. All of the principles of conditioning discussed in this section and other more detailed principles have been applied to programed instruction of the linear type.

IMITATION AND
OBSERVATIONAL LEARNING

A child for the first time observes his father hug his mother when the father comes home in the evening. His mother and father appear happier. The next time the child comes into the house he too hugs his mother. An adolescent for the first time observes a singer engage in certain bodily movements when singing. The adolescent when singing tries to repeat the same motions. The first time a tenth-grader hears a phrase in a foreign language he tries to pronounce it exactly as the teacher. Are these examples of learning through conditioning or through imitation? According to Bandura and Walters, new responses made after observing a model are learned through imitation (6). These psychologists think that enough laboratory experimentation and field study, including research in schools, has been done to warrant a reasonably adequate description of learning through the observation and imitation of models. In the next few pages the most fundamental concepts and principles of Bandura and Walters related to imitation are discussed without reference to specific research or to specific pages of the book by the two authors.

Prevalence of Imitative Learning

Young children especially, but also older children, including adolescents, often do what they see adults do. Further, the patterns of behavior acquired through imitation are typically large units in their entirety, rather than small bits accumulated through a slow, gradual accretion by differential reinforcement.

The models whom children observe and imitate may be classified as real-life and symbolic. At home real-life models for younger children are parents and relatives. Teachers constitute the real-life models for many school children, as do other persons in the child's community. There are many other models in this category. Symbolic models are presented to children through oral or written instructions and pictures, or through a combination of verbal and pictorial devices. The models presented in books and the other printed material are important; however, those presented by audiovisual means, particularly television, are highly influential. So strong are these symbolic models that parents are in danger of becoming less influential in the lives of their children.

In the schools and in many homes much attention is given to exemplary models, models who demonstrate social norms or behavior that are considered desirable by the adults responsible for the education of the children. This social aspect of learning is probably more critical than is generally assumed. In the socialization of the human being, it is difficult to estimate how much of his behavior is acquired through imitation, but it is probably more than we have generally thought.

The Process of Imitation

From one point of view, imitative learning occurs when a subject who is motivated matches the responses of a model and is positively reinforced for doing so (9). The subject must be motivated, and his initial random, trial-and-error responses must be differentially reinforced in order for a matching response to be learned. Bandura and Walters do not accept this point of view and state that the initial acquisition of imitative responses results primarily from the contiguity of sensory events. However, the strength and continued use of imitative responses is dependent upon reinforcement. That is, the observer learns behavior through imitation; whether and how frequently he uses the behavior is related to the consequences of the learned behavior. Further, the anticipation of positive or negative reinforcement may augment or reduce the probability of the occurrence of observing, which is essential to imitation.

The major processes involved, then, in imitative learning are observing a model and patterning one's behavior after that of the model. The relationships become more clear through considering three different effects of observation and imitation.

One effect is for the observer to match the behavior of the model with responses that are new to the observer, responses made for the first time. In order for this to occur, the model must, of course, demonstrate behavior which is novel to the observer, but which the observer is capable of executing. As shown in Fig. 3.4, children observed a model who performed various aggressive acts which the children had not previously exhibited. Subsequently, without reinforcement in any form, the young preschoolers demonstrated the same behaviors (5).

The observation and imitation of a model may also strengthen or weaken inhibitory responses which the observer already has in his repertoire. Aggressive behavior is generally disapproved and, to some extent, inhibited. Observation of a model displaying aggressive behavior tends to result not only in an expression of this particular aggressive behavior, but also in the release of other aggressive behavior which was previously inhibited. This is termed a *disinhibitory effect,* the strengthening of a whole class of behavior that is usually inhibited. Other forms of deviant behavior have also been shown to be disinhibited in individuals who have observed models displaying the behavior freely.

Inhibition of behavior in the observer's repertoire is most likely to occur under two circumstances. The model may be subjected to painful

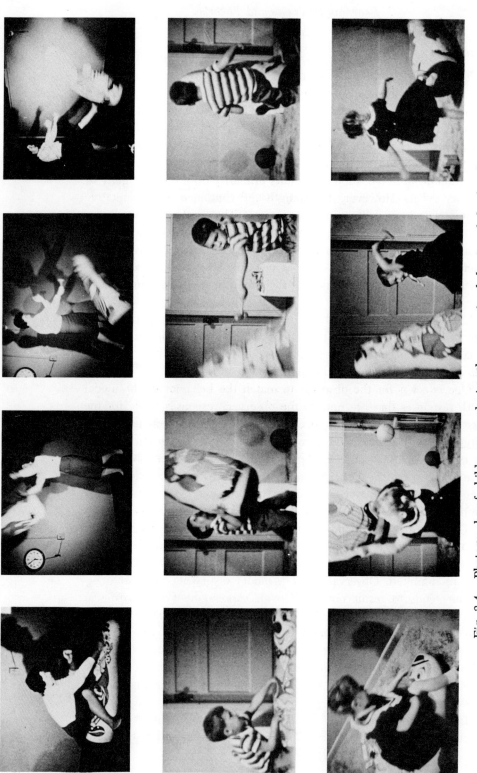

Fig. 3.4. Photographs of children reproducing the aggressive behavior of the female model they had observed on film. (A. Bandura, Dorothea Ross, & Sheila A. Ross. Imitation of film-mediated aggressive models. *J. abnorm. soc. Psychol.*, 1963, **66**, 10.)

consequences as a result of his behavior. The observer inhibits behavior which he perceives to be associated with the fearful reactions. Undoubtedly, this is related to the tendency of children to be fearful of some of the same events as their mothers.

A final effect that can be demonstrated experimentally, but which one can infer only if he knows the history of the observer, is the eliciting of behavior already in the observer's repertoire. Volunteering services or monetary contributions, pledging oneself to a course of action, and eating foods not ordinarily selected is behavior that can be elicited through the presentation of appropriate models. A final note of relationship among these three effects is in order:

> Modeling effects are possible only if the model exhibits responses that the observer has not yet learned to make, while disinhibitory effects can occur only if inhibitions have already been set up. However, in many cases of deviant behavior the model acts in ways which are both novel for the observer and socially disapproved; in such cases it is possible for the modeling, disinhibitory, and eliciting effects to occur simultaneously, and it is therefore virtually impossible to identify their relative contributions to the genesis of deviation (6, 81).

Some Factors Affecting Imitation

Many factors may be associated with imitation. One of these is the consequences of the responses to the model and to the observer. Another is the characteristics of the observer. We may think of the consequences of the responses in terms of rewards and punishments.

Imitation is facilitated when the model receives rewards for his behavior and is hindered when the model is punished. Further, if the observer knows that the model receives either rewards or punishments, even though he cannot observe them, the same tendencies toward imitation and nonimitation occur; however, the effect of punishment is not as predictable as that of rewards. Rewards and punishments have the same effects on the observer's responses as they do on the model's responses.

Characteristics of the observer are also related to imitative behavior. The more imitative persons are those who lack self-esteem and competence because they have experienced insufficient rewards thus far, who have been previously rewarded for exhibiting matching behavior, or who have been frequently rewarded for conforming behavior and have thus become dependent. Others who believe themselves to be similar to the models in some attributes rather than dissimilar also are more imitative. Transient emotional states also seem to be related to imitation. Being emotionally aroused probably increases the likelihood of imitation. Such arousal can come through the stress of external situations or the use of drugs.

Forgetting of Imitative Responses

Exposure to models and reinforcement of socially approved behavior strengthens behavior acquired through imitation. Certain responses become more firmly established than others primarily through the joint operation of differential modeling cues which elicit the responses and reinforcement of only these responses. Antisocial behavior is also strengthened and becomes persistent from intermittent, positive reinforcement. Similarly, the persistence of anxiety-motivated avoidance behavior is accounted for in terms of intermittent reinforcement through reduction of anxiety.

Although the above statements account for the strengthening of responses learned by imitation, they do not account for the weakening, forgetting, or extinction of them. Bandura and Walters are concerned primarily with the extinction of behavior disapproved by someone or in some way harmful to the individual rather than with the weakening of behavior that is socially approved (6). Some means of extinguishing responses are: nonreward of responses, removal of a positive reinforcer through the deprivation of a privilege or possession that has previously served as a reinforcer, the use of an aversive stimulus such as physical or verbal punishment, and counterconditioning by means of classical-conditioning procedures. The effects of these, however, may vary a great deal.

Nonreward is not effective when there is a strong dominant response to be extinguished. The individual gains so much satisfaction from the activity that he continues it even though it is not rewarded. Removal of a positive reinforcer and the use of an aversive stimulus are both forms of punishment. Punishment is often used to inhibit antisocial responses. Punishment may accomplish this, particularly in the presence of the punisher, but it also may lead to other conditioned emotional responses, such as fear of the punisher. Also, the punished individual may independently learn other responses which enable him to avoid the unpleasant or aversive stimulus.

Counter-conditioning techniques involve the use of procedures of classical conditioning. For example, in counter-conditioning of fear, a stimulus that produces the fear response is gradually introduced into the situation with a stimulus that does not elicit fear. Eventually the stimulus that produced the fear gets conditioned to the nonfear response. Positive reinforcement of responses that are incompatible with the undesired response serves also as a counter-conditioning effect. For example, positive reinforcement can follow accomplishing homework, and doing the homework is incompatible with conversing with one's friends at the same time. Although difficult to arrange, counter-conditioning procedures appear to be more effective than attempts at eliminating undesired responses through punishment, for the use of punishment often has many undesirable side effects.

Motivation and Imitative Learning

The terms *motivation* and *drive* do not appear in the index of Bandura's and Walters's book, suggesting that little attention has been given to motivation (6). The principle which may be inferred most clearly is that individuals engage in behavior which results in rewarding consequences, including self-reward.

Self-control is also exhibited in the *postponement of culturally approved immediate reinforcements in favor of some potentially more rewarding long-term goal.* Professional status can often be achieved only through long hours of arduous study and training; similarly, the attainment of some valued possession, such as a home, may entail the sacrifice of many day-to-day pleasures. Self-control of this kind occurs in the life-histories of most individuals. ... (6, 171–172).

Applicability to School Learning

The role of the schools in providing models for students to imitate is critical, according to the principles and concepts of imitative learning set forth in the previous pages. There must be models for students of varying backgrounds, not just for those who are college bound. Although the importance of imitation in connection with personality development and socialization was stressed in the preceding discussion, imitation is important in other aspects of education also.

Imitative learning is probably most prevalent in the affective domain. Through imitation children and adolescents acquire most of the behavior involved in living with other human beings, including behavior indicative of stable personality integration as well as that of an antisocial nature. Aggressive and dependency behaviors, warmth, methods of expressing affection, the development of self-control, and moral behavior are illustrative of the type of outcomes acquired partially through imitation. Although teachers may not engage in the modification of deviant behavior, the idea of developing prosocial responses that are incompatible with deviant behavior, and therefore are substitutes, holds much promise for school psychologists and other educational workers.

Imitation plays an important role in the learning of psychomotor activities. The extent to which walking, the motor aspects of talking, and the execution of movements in vocational and avocational skills are learned through imitation is not known. However, we generally assume that real-life and symbolic models who demonstrate psychomotor skills play an important role in the learning of skills.

In the cognitive domain, the learning of language by a younger child or the learning of a second language is facilitated by the presence of a model to imitate. As Bandura and Walters indicate, the principle of contiguity of sensory events or stimuli and the principle of reinforcement of response may contribute to the learning of language. However, these principles do not account satisfactorily for the emergence of novel responses during the model-observer sequence. Moreover, language learning ordinarily does not start with a model's or teacher's matching a response of the learner or reinforcing an appropriate response that the learner happens to make. On the contrary, a proficient model is selected for the student to imitate.

MEANINGFUL RECEPTION LEARNING

Textbooks and similar expository materials are used extensively in the schools. Let us assume that students read and study the material of these books, without memorizing the content. In the process they learn some information and concepts. Can the teacher do anything that might help them learn more efficiently? According to a subsumption theory of learning set forth by Ausubel, this question is answered in the affirmative (2). In the following pages, clarification of the concepts in subsumption theory is attempted, using Ausubel's ideas without continuous reference to pages of his book. Subsequently, further comments are made about the applicability of the theory to school learning.

Meaningful Reception and Other Learning

Subsumption theory is concerned with reception learning. Reception learning may be rote or meaningful. The critical feature of reception learning is that the entire content of what is to be learned is presented to the learner in final form. The only requirement is to internalize the material so that it is available and reproducible at some later date. A very large amount of the subject matter of each discipline is presented by the teacher in textbooks and other printed material, and by a variety of audiovisual means.

How do rote and meaningful reception learning differ? The process of meaningful reception learning, by definition, requires the learner to use a meaningful set. Also, the material to be learned must be potentially meaningful. If anything is committed to memory verbatim, the process is rote, not meaningful. Also, no matter how meaningful the learner's set may be, neither the process nor the outcome can be meaningful if the learning task consists of purely arbitrary associations; for example, Russian words encountered for the first time by an English-speaking child. Rote learning involves verbatim memory, meaningless material, or both.

A distinction is also necessary between reception and discovery learning, such as is involved in inductive concept formation and problem solving. In discovery learning, what is to be learned is not given, but must be identified by the learner independently before he can internalize it. For example, attaining a concept by discerning the common attribute in a number of diverse stimuli or getting the solution to a verbal or nonverbal problem involves discovery by the learner. Even though concepts may be acquired by induction, they also can be understood by means of meaningful reception learning. One does not have to discover all concepts independently.

Learning set was introduced earlier in the discussion of meaningful reception learning. Set most nearly denotes a disposition that orients the learner to proceed in one way, rather than another. For example, in meaningful reception learning the individual tries to assimilate new content into his already existing knowledge. At this point let us clarify the meaning of cognitive structure and some related terms.

"Cognitive structure" refers solely to the stability, clarity, and organization of a learner's subject matter knowledge in a given discipline. The actual ideas and information embodied in this knowledge are "cognitive content." "Cognitive style" refers to the self-consistent inter-individual differences and idiosyncratic trends in cognitive organization and functioning (2, 76).

The Subsumption Process

In Ausubel's meaningful reception learning, the principle of subsumption is the primary one for explaining the process of learning.

The model of cognitive organization proposed for the learning and retention of meaningful materials assumes the existence of a cognitive structure that is hierarchically organized in terms of highly inclusive conceptual traces under which are subsumed traces of less inclusive subconcepts as well as traces of specific informational data (2, 24).

The hierarchy is conceived as in Fig. 3.5. *Trace* is used simply to account for the representation of prior experience in the nervous system which, in turn, comprises the present cognitive structure. Other psychologists use terms such as *connections* and *information* to indicate what remains internally from a learning experience.

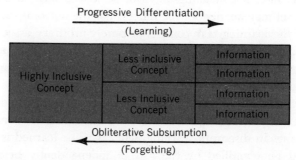

Fig. 3.5. Schematic organization of the trace system and the direction of subsumption in learning and forgetting. (Based on D. P. Ausubel. *The psychology of meaningful verbal learning.* New York: Grune & Stratton, 1963. By permission of Grune & Stratton, Inc.)

Let us turn to the subsumption principle again. It implies a progressive differentiation of the trace system from the regions of greater to lesser inclusiveness, the region and differentiation being linked to the next higher order in the hierarchy through a process of subsumption learning. The new outcome is incorporated into the existing trace system through progressive differentiation. This gives the existing cognitive structure—one's present organization, stability, and clarity of knowledge related to the particular subject—central importance in initial learning and also in retention. For, as new material is cognized, it interacts with and is appropriately subsumed under a relevant and more inclusive conceptual system already acquired by the learner. Subsumption of the trace of the current learning task by an already established ideational system, or cognitive structure, provides anchorage for the new material, thus also providing means of retaining it as part of the conceptual trace system. Any material that is subsumable is, by definition, relatable to the stable elements in the cognitive structure and this accounts for its meaningfulness and makes possible insightful relationships among the various elements of the subject matter.

The initial effects of subsumption of new material into an already organized cognitive structure facilitate both initial learning and retention. At first, only orienting, relational, and cataloguing operations are involved; that is, the new material is oriented and related to the existing structure and then somehow is classified and stored according to the primary principle of subsumption. This constitutes the initial learning. At the same time, anchorage for the new material is provided, thus providing an orderly way for retaining it for future reproducibility. For a variable period of time the recently catalogued subconcepts and information can be dissociated or kept separate from their subsuming concepts and are reproducible as individually identifiable entities.

So long as the material maintains its identifiable identity, it is readily reproduced. However, the new material, paradoxically, is subject to the erosive influence of the conceptualizing trend, as shown in Fig. 3.5. This is because a larger more inclusive concept is more economical to retain than subconcepts and specific information. When the obliterative stage of subsumption begins, the specific items become progressively less dissociable as entities until they are no longer reproducible and can be said to be forgotten.

Variables in Meaningful Verbal Learning

Initial learning and the subsequent retention of new material are related to the availability of relevant subsuming concepts in the cognitive structure; that is, to what one already knows about the subject matter. When appropriate subsumers are not present, the learner uses the most relevant ones available. Often these do not provide optimal anchorage. Therefore, appropriate subsumers in the form of *advance organizers* should be introduced before the learner encounters the new material. The advance organizers are not topical outlines of the new material presented. Rather, they are short expository passages that perform three main functions—provide a general overview of the material, provide organizing elements, such as subconcepts, and point out how previously learned related concepts are basically different from or similar to the new ideas to be presented. Thus, an important variable in efficiency of learning and retention is the use of appropriate advance organizers.

Another variable influencing meaningful reception learning is the discriminability of the new material from the already established conceptual systems that subsume it. If the new material is not clearly discriminable from the stable subsuming concepts and principles, it becomes incorporated in the latter and does not persist. Information provided to the learners in advance of a new material which indicates similarities and differences between it and the presumed subsumers facilitates initial learning and retention. New material that is not discriminable from what is already known is forgotten quickly.

The stability and clarity of the subsumers of new meaningful material comprise a third variable related to forgetting. Ambiguous and unstable subsumers, in comparison with ones that are clear and stable, do not permit ready discrimination or the finding of relationships. In other words, concepts and principles that are well understood and related to other knowledge provide clear and stable subsumers for subsequent material.

Practice also is a principal variable in meaningful reception learning. By practice is meant the repeated presentations of the same learning material. Practice influences and modifies the existing cognitive structure. It also increases the stability and clarity of newly learned materials in the cognitive structure and hence enhances dissociability strength and retention. However, the effect of repetition on meaningful learning is not established clearly through empirical research. In general, distributing practice facilitates retention of large amounts of meaningful learning. Massed practice appears to be more effective for the immediate retention of smaller amounts of meaningful learning materials.

Motivation and Meaningful Reception Learning

Cognitive variables are directly implicated in the cognitive interactional processes during meaningful reception learning and retention. Motivational variables are not directly involved in the cognitive processes. However, a meaningful learning set which implies a disposition to incorporate new material into the cognitive structure is, by definition, essential to meaningful reception learning. Also, motivation is related to meaningful reception learning and retention in other ways. During the initial phase of meaningful reception learning, all or selected components of the learning field may be energized through such mechanisms as mobilization of effort and concentration of attention. The net result is more clearly differentiated knowledge that is more resistant to forgetting. In addition to its energizing aspect, motivation also mobilizes the individual's immediate readiness for meaningful reception learning by lowering the thresholds of those general kinds of perceptions and responses that are customarily implicated in this type of learning. As a result of all types of facilitating motivational mechanisms, clearer and more stable meanings are acquired and retained. In turn, these meanings facilitate the sequential type of learning involved in the mastery of subject matter.

Retention of meaningful material is influenced more by intention to learn (a motivational mechanism) than intention to remember after learning has been accomplished. Further evidence of this is indicated by the fact that retention is better when practice is accomplished with intent to learn than when learning takes place incidentally. One possible explanation of this is that intention to remember, in line with other principles of meaningful retention learning, does not influence the dissociability strength of the learned material, and thereby resistance to forgetting after the material has already been learned. Presumably, it does increase dissociability strength during initial learning.

The great importance of cognitive structure and the relative lesser importance of motivation in meaningful reception learning is indicated by the fact that motivation is not an indispensable condition of meaningful learning:

> . . . it is unnecessary to postpone learning activities until appropriate interests and motivations have been developed. Frequently the best way of teaching an unmotivated student is to ignore his motivational state for the time being, and to concentrate on teaching him as effectively as possible. Much to his surprise and his teacher's, he will learn despite his lack of motivation; and from the satisfaction of learning he will hopefully develop the motivation to learn more. Paradoxically, therefore, we may discover that the most effective method of developing intrinsic motivation to learn is to focus on the cognitive rather than on the motivational aspects of learning, and to rely on the motivation that is developed retroactively from successful educational achievement (2, 226).

Applicability to School Learning

A considerable amount of experimentation with human beings using potentially meaningful learning material provides a substantial, though incomplete, empirical foundation for the subsumption theory. Unfamiliar scientific information in a 2500 word passage dealing with the metallurgical properties of plain carbon steel was learned initially and retained better for 48 hours when introduced with an expository advance organizer of about 500 words. The main effect of the advance organizing material was to provide subconcepts that increased the

familiarity and meaningfulness of the new material (1). An advance
organizer had the same effect on learning unfamiliar material dealing
with endocrinology (4). Advance organizers can also serve as transitional material by bridging the gap between novel and familiar material in order to help the learner discriminate between what he already
knows and what he is about to learn. Expository advance material
relating concepts of Christianity (familiar material) to those of Buddhism (new material) facilitated initial learning and retention of the
new material incorporated in a passage about Buddhism (3). One may
also instruct students to note similarities, differences, or both, between
the new material to be studied and what they already know (16).
Instructions of this type serve as a set; they do not provide an advance
organizer. However, they do result in better initial acquisition and in
subsequent retention than do instructions which merely tell the student
to try to understand and remember the new material.

The present authors have included this theory and some of the related experimentation because of its usefulness in explaining the learning of information presented to students. More important, the formulation of advance organizers is a promising activity not only for teachers,
but also for those who prepare programed instruction and textbooks. In
all forms of meaningful reception learning the attempt can be made
to identify and develop advance organizers instead of presenting sequential topics or assigning material to be memorized by whatever
trial-and-error procedures the student can devise.

SUMMARY

The purposes of a theory are to explain, to predict, and to control.
Traditionally theories of learning have been formulated to explain
all processes and outcomes of learning in all organisms. Modern theories described in this book are less ambitious.

The functionalist theory that we have set forth attempts to explain
learning in terms of functional relationships among independent variables in school settings—teacher characteristics, teacher actions and
interactions with students, instructional material and media, subject
matter, characteristics of the learner, characteristics of the group, and
outside forces. The dependent variable is efficiency of learning, which,
in turn, is dependent upon the educational objectives. The intervening
processes include cognition, memory, convergent thinking, divergent
thinking, evaluation, and others. These intervening processes are set

forth as a sequence in purposeful learning: setting a goal, appraising the situation, trying to attain a goal through productive thinking and physical activity, confirming or rejecting responses, reaching or not reaching a goal, and experiencing feelings of success or failure.

Conditioning theory as delimited by Staats and Staats includes principles of classical and operant conditioning. These principles have been refined in animal laboratories and are now being extended to complex human behavior. The applicability of these principles to high-level mental processes, such as convergent and divergent thinking, is less well established than to lower-level processes such as associating simple stimulus-response events. Other principles might also be more applicable to associative learning, such as involved in a young child's learning to speak the language of his parents. For example, Bandura and Walters offer learning by observing and imitating as a better explanation.

Meaningful reception learning is based on subsumption theory and is proposed by Ausubel as an explanation of the learning of most material that is presented to students in a final form in textbooks and by other means. Ausubel offers subsumption theory as an explanation for only this one type of learning, not as a substitute for functionalist, conditioning, or imitation theory.

Despite the theoretical framework, each theory offers principles that have been derived or refined in experimental settings unrelated to the particular theory. Some of these principles will be found in later chapters that deal with outcomes of learning and desirable conditions for learning.

QUESTIONS AND ACTIVITIES

1. a. What is the main purpose of learning theory?
   b. What are the main directions in modern learning theory?
2. Give an example of purposeful learning by an individual without instruction. By a group in a classroom setting.
3. Which 5 of the 15 generalizations regarding purposeful learning do you think are most closely associated with efficient learning in the schools? why?
4. a. Outline the characteristics and principles of classical conditioning.
   b. Outline the characteristics and principles of operant conditioning.
   c. Give examples of behavior you have developed through being conditioned.
5. a. Under what circumstances would you attempt to condition another human being without his being aware that you are conditioning him?
   b. Do teachers, directly or indi-

rectly, shape the behavior of their students? by what procedures?

6. a. Discuss the characteristics of imitation and observational learning.
   b. Discuss and give examples of each of the three effects of observational learning.
   c. How are novel responses that are acquired through observational learning strengthened?
7. According to Ausubel, how do the following differ: rote reception learning, meaningful reception learning, discovery learning?
8. Discuss and give examples of how the subsumption process facilitates initial learning and subsequent retention.

9. How are motivation and forgetting explained in each theory: purposeful learning, conditioning, imitation, and subsumption?
10. a. Related to your interest in subject matter and level of schooling, give examples of outcomes of learning that you have acquired through purposeful learning, conditioning, imitation, and meaningful reception learning.
    b. Discuss the principles from all of the theories that you will try to implement in improving your own learning efficiency.
    c. Discuss the principles from all of the theories that you will try to implement in improving the learning of others.

SUGGESTIONS FOR FURTHER READING

Ausubel, D. P. The use of advance organizers in the learning and retention of meaningful verbal material. *J. educ. Psychol.*, 1960, **51**, 267–272. (In Ripple, 1964, 420–427; and abridged in Rosenblith & Allinsmith, 1962, 463–466.)

Ausubel, D. P. In defense of verbal learning. *Educ. Theory*, 1961, **11**, 15–25. (In Anderson & Ausubel, 1965, 87–102.)

Ausubel, D. P. Cognitive structure and the facilitation of meaningful verbal learning. *J. teacher Educ.*, 1963, **14**, 217–222. (In Anderson & Ausubel, 1965, 103–115.)

Ausubel, D. P., & D. Fitzgerald. Organizer, general background, and antecedent learning variables in sequential verbal learning. *J. educ. Psychol.*, 1962, **53**, 243–249. (In Anderson & Ausubel, 1965, 290–302.)

Bandura, A., & Aletha C. Huston. Identification as a process of incidental learning. *J. abnorm. soc. Psychol.*, 1961, **63**, 311–318. (In Mussen, Conger, & Kagan, 1965, 247–262.)

Bandura, A., & F. J. McDonald. Influence of social reinforcement and the behavior of models in shaping children's moral judgments. *J. abnorm. soc. Psychol.*, 1963, **67**, 274–281. (In Seidman, 1965, 264–282.)

Bruner, J. S. Learning and thinking. *Harv. educ. Rev.*, 1959, **29**, 184–192. (In Anderson & Ausubel, 1965, 76–86; and Rosenblith & Allinsmith, 1962, 446–450.)

Bruner, J. S. The act of discovery. *Harv. educ. Rev.*, 1961, **31**, 21–32. (In Anderson & Ausubel, 1965, 606–620; Crow & Crow, 1963, 423–435; DeCecco, 1963, 254–270; Gordon, 1965, 67–74; and Ripple, 1964, 236–248.)

Hartup, W. W. Social behavior of children. *Rev. educ. Res.*, 1965, **35**, 122–129.

Hebb, D. O. The American Revolution. *Amer. Psychologist*, 1960, **15**, 735–745. (In Harper, *et al.*, 1964, 1–16.)

Rosenblith, Judy F. Imitative color choices in kindergarten children. *Child Develpm.*, 1961, **32**, 211–223. (In Rosenblith & Allinsmith, 1962, 120–126.)

Staats, Carolyn K., & A. W. Staats. Meaning established by classical conditioning. *J. exp. Psychol.*, 1957, **54**, 74–80. (In Anderson & Ausubel, 1965, 230–240.)

REFERENCES

1. Ausubel, D. P. The use of advance organizers in the learning and retention of meaningful verbal learning. *J. educ. Psychol.*, 1960, **51**, 267–272.
2. Ausubel, D. P. *The psychology of meaningful verbal learning.* New York: Grune & Stratton, 1963.
3. Ausubel, D. P., & D. Fitzgerald. The role of discriminability in meaningful verbal learning and retention. *J. educ. Psychol.*, 1961, **52**, 266–274.
4. Ausubel, D. P., & D. Fitzgerald. Organizer, general background, and antecedent learning variables in sequential verbal learning. *J. educ. Psychol.*, 1962, **53**, 243–249.
5. Bandura, A., Dorothea Ross, & Sheila A. Ross. Imitation of film-mediated aggressive models *J. abnorm. soc. Psychol.*, 1963, **66**, 3–11.
6. Bandura, A., & R. H. Walters. *Social learning and personality development.* New York: Holt, Rinehart and Winston, 1963.
7. Eysenck, H. J. Symposium: The development of moral values in children: VII. The contribution of learning theory. *Brit. J. educ. Psychol.*, 1960, **30**, 11–21.
8. Johnson, D. M., & J. W. Jennings. Serial analysis of three problem-solving processes. *J. Psychol.*, 1963, **56**, 43–52.

9. Miller, N. E., & J. Dollard. *Social learning and imitation.* New Haven: Yale, 1941.
10. Piaget, J. *The origins of intelligence in children.* New York: Int. Univer. Press, 1952.
11. Staats, A. W., & Carolyn K. Staats. *Complex human behavior: A systematic extension of learning principles.* New York: Holt, Rinehart and Winston, 1963.
12. Suchman, J. R. The child and the inquiry process. In A. H. Passow (Ed.), *Intellectual development: Another look.* Washington, D.C.: Association for Supervision and Curriculum Development, 1964, pp. 59–77.
13. Verplanck, W. S. The control of content of conversation: Reinforcement of statements of opinion. *J. abnorm. soc. Psychol.*, 1955, **51**, 668–676.
14. Verplanck, W. S. The operant conditioning of human motor behavior. *Psychol. Bull.*, 1956, **53**, 70–83.
15. White, S. H. Generalization of an instrumental response with variations in two attributes of the CS. *J. exp. Psychol.*, 1958, **56**, 339–343.
16. Wittrock, M. C. Effects of certain sets upon complex verbal learning. *J. educ. Psychol.*, 1963, **54**, 85–88.

CHAPTER 4

Pupil Characteristics and Learning

WHEN GIVEN the same amount of time to practice or study, students do not achieve equally well. There are also differences among students in the amount that is remembered. Furthermore, when the situation is changed, students do not use equally well what they have learned. Efficiency of learning is inferred from performances immediately after initial instruction or practice, at a later time, and in different situations. Some of the criteria used to determine efficiency of learning are accuracy, appropriateness, speed, form, and style. At this point we are concerned only with clarifying what is meant by efficiency of learning, not with its measurement, for measurement and evaluation are treated in the last section of this book.

Efficiency of learning varies among students of the same age or grade level. In part, this is because students are not equally ready to engage successfully in such tasks as reading, swimming, playing the violin, understanding the meaning of an equation, writing a short story, or speaking a second language. Figure 4.1 shows the six main pupil characteristics which strongly affect an individual pupil's learning. The age and sex of the individual have the least effect upon his readiness for, or progress in, learning and, for most school tasks, his cognitive

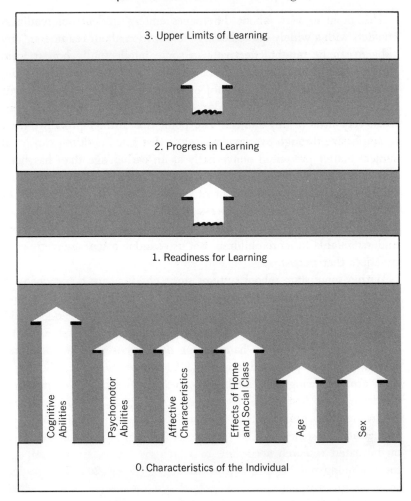

Fig. 4.1.   The primary variable in learning: Pupil characteristics.

abilities and intellectual characteristics play the strongest role. However, the relative influence of these six variables will differ according to the specific learning task involved. Readiness for learning and learning progress is also associated with teacher behavior, instructional materials, and other variables that were mentioned in Chapter 1. Readiness is thus not a singular condition comprised of a generalizable characteristic which can be assumed for all or most learning tasks. Further, no single criterion, such as intelligence, is a reliable predictor of readiness for even one activity, such as beginning reading, much less for a number of activities. Instead, readiness is a composite of many characteristics and varies from one learning activity to another.

This point of view about differences among students in readiness conflicts with a widely quoted overgeneralization about readiness: "any subject can be taught effectively in some intellectually honest form to any child at any stage of development" (7, 33). Of course, young infants cannot be taught any subject matter which depends on words for the transmission of ideas. Also, mentally deficient individuals can learn very little of any subject. The point that Bruner probably tried to emphasize through overgeneralizing is that some children can learn subject matter presented nonverbally at an earlier age than has been generally assumed. Few persons disagree with this point of view. During the past decade, much content has been moved from higher- to lower-grade levels, and the process is still underway. In addition, we need more ingenuity in translating subject matter into a form more understandable to more children. Let us examine a few unimaginative practices that persist.

Within some state school systems some children are being changed from the manuscript to the cursive form of handwriting in the second grade; in other schools the change is made in the third grade; in still others it is not made until the fourth grade. Each school system seems to justify its procedure in handwriting on the basis of outmoded research and ideas proposed long ago (10). Unwisely, some school systems are still using only intelligence tests as the basis for grouping children in the first grade. Here one groups starts with a first-grade reader, another group gets a readiness book, and a third group has conversation instruction. This practice of grouping is apparently based on outdated research according to which the necessary mental age for beginning reading is given as about 6½ years (20). The graded sequence in arithmetic in many school systems also follows an obsolescent study (71). Anyone who has recently studied arithmetic achievement in the elementary grades knows that many fourth-grade children of average abilities can perform arithmetic tasks which are taught in some schools in the fifth and sixth grades. Excellent information about spelling readiness is available (53). Although facts about differences in spelling readiness among first-graders were clearly indicated, many schools still give all pupils from the first through the eighth grades the same list of spelling words included in any of several textbooks for the particular grade level. Many children can learn to spell at a much more rapid rate than that provided by the textbook, whereas many other children are known to make little progress in spelling because the graded list is too long or too difficult for them.

In addition to the problem of readiness, certain characteristics of students lead to differences in the amount they learn, even though initially they are equally ready. For example, at some point in time two youngsters run at exactly the same speed. Thereafter, one improves more rapidly than the other and with the passage of time, they draw farther apart in running speed. This same condition prevails for other learning activities. As far as we know at present, the same characteristics that affect readiness also affect subsequent efficiency of learning. In connection with most school learning, differences among pupils in cognitive abilities and intellectual characteristics are of primary importance.

COGNITIVE ABILITIES AND INTELLECTUAL CHARACTERISTICS

Several factors in the cognitive domain affect efficiency of learning. Three of the more important of these are general intellectual ability, specific intellectual abilities, and previous experience related to the task. Even now the nature of all of these is being revised.

General Intellectual Ability

General intellectual ability, also referred to as mental ability or intelligence by some writers, is a composite of many abilities that are useful in performing a large number of tasks. Intelligence and general intellectual ability are used interchangeably in this section. Most clearly, high intelligence is associated with high performance in English, mathematics, science, and social studies—any activity where ideas are incorporated in symbols. General intellectual ability is measured by tests administered individually or to groups. An inexperienced person cannot infer what a test measures simply from examining the items in it. Many people confuse intelligence and educational achievement tests. Although there is some likeness of items, the purposes of the tests are quite different.

Two assumptions about intelligence, critical to the present discussion of efficiency of learning, have prevailed from the early part of the twentieth century through World War II and still are found among some people. One assumption is that intelligence is fixed and unchangeable; the other is that the individual's potentiality for all types of activity is determined by heredity. According to the first assumption, the individual's IQ remains constant from birth throughout life. The second assumption implies that the individual has inherited the potentiality for all his behavior and that the environment merely provides triggering mechanisms for the potentialities to unfold. Evidence from physiology and psychology may be interpreted to support or refute both assumptions. Evidence tending to refute the assumptions has been disregarded in the United States until recently, but the tendency now is to place greater emphasis upon environmental influences, especially during the early years of life (33). In fact, "it might be feasible to discover ways to govern the environments, especially during the early years of their development, to achieve a substantially faster rate of intellectual development and a substantially higher adult level of intellectual capacity" (33, 363).

An impoverished environment in childhood might retard development of the individual which he could not subsequently make up, and an enriched environment might accelerate his development (5). The early years are most critical, as shown in Table 4.1. The information

TABLE 4.1.

Hypothetical Effects of Different Environments on the Development of Intelligence in Three Selected Age Periods

| Age Period | Percent of Mature Intelligence | Variation from Normal Growth in I.Q. Units | | | |
		Deprived	Normal	Abundant	Abundant-Deprived
Birth–4	50	−5	0	+5	10
4–8	30	−3	0	+3	6
8–17	20	−2	0	+2	4
Total	100	−10	0	+10	20

SOURCE: B. S. Bloom. *Stability and change in human characteristics.* New York: Wiley, 1964, p. 72.

in Table 4.1 is based on the assumption that 100 percent of mature intelligence is achieved by age 17. Based on this assumption, Bloom estimated that 50 percent of mature intelligence is achieved by age 4 and that a deprived and an abundant environment can result in differences in intelligence scores of at least 10 points until age 4. Similarly, with 80 percent of mature intelligence being achieved at age 8, the difference resulting from the extreme environments can be at least 16 points; and at age 17 the difference can amount to 20 IQ points. In interpreting the change in IQ due to environment, we assume an average IQ of 100 with about two-thirds of all individuals having IQs between 84 and 116. Thus, a change of 20 IQ points is considerable. For example, two individuals at age 17 might have IQs of 120 and 100, the difference being due to an enriched and an impoverished environment. The individual with the IQ of 100 would not be expected to complete the baccalaureate whereas the one with 120 IQ would be expected to complete the baccalaureate and also graduate work in some fields. Bloom considered the 20 IQ points associated with environment to be a conservative estimate; we think the difference may be substantially larger.

Age 17 was used by Bloom for convenience as the age of full intellectual maturity. However, intellectual growth continues after age 17 as indicated in a few representative longitudinal studies. A significant increase has been noted from age 18 to 21 (**34, 66**). More specifically bright adults manifested a small increase in IQ from age 30 to 42 (**63**), and another group showed an increase of 11 IQ points from adolescence into adulthood (**6**). Intellectual growth is assumed to increase until age 50 (**2**).

The preceding estimate of an IQ change of 20 points from infancy to adulthood is conservative (**60**). The personality, familial, and physical correlates of the changes in intelligence from ages 3 to 12 were ascertained in a group of 140 children. The Revised Stanford-Binet Scale was used to measure intelligence. Each child was rated on 14 personality dimensions, and anatomical measures were also secured. Variations in IQ from one year to the next were found, with the highest degree of stability from ages 4 to 6 and again from ages 6 to 10. The median change throughout the study was 17.9 points, and 52 percent of the children had changes of 15 or more. Children showing a high need for achievement, competitive striving, and curiosity gained more in IQ than did children not showing these characteristics. Those who gained in IQ also showed high independence rather than emotional dependence on parents, aggressiveness rather than withdrawal behavior, and competitive inclinations. Rate of physical growth and rate of mental growth were found not to be related; that is, there was no relationship between how rapidly the children grew physically and how rapidly they grew mentally.

Let us accept the judgment that IQ is markedly influenced by environmental factors, exactly how much not being finally established. How does this compare with the total range in IQs found in the population? In the standardization of the Revised Stanford-Binet Scales, one of the two most widely used individual intelligence tests, a range in IQ from below 35 to above 175 was reported as shown in Fig. 4.2 (62). The majority of the standardization group had IQs between 85 and 114 with slightly over 66 percent of the total group in this IQ range, and approximately 17 percent above 114 and 17 percent below 85.

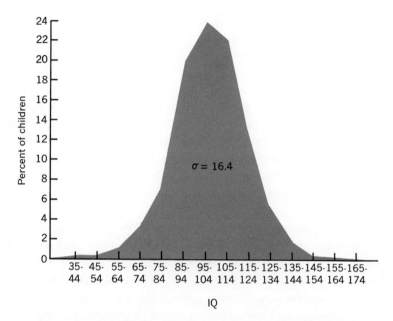

Fig. 4.2. Distribution of composite form L–M (Revised Stanford–Binet Intelligence Scale), IQs of standardization group, ages 2 to 18 (N: 2904). (Adapted from L. M. Terman & Maud A. Merrill. *Measuring intelligence.* Boston: Houghton Mifflin, 1937, p. 37.)

Suppose that in a community all the children of school age were tested during a certain month and their IQs were distributed much the same as those in Fig. 4.2. Would knowing the IQ of each child provide any useful information to the school in connection with readiness for learning and efficiency of learning? The IQ of each child, along with other information, might be used for short-term prediction of achievement in the academic subjects—mathematics, language arts, science, social studies, and to a lesser extent in foreign language. It would not be useful in predicting achievements in typing, art, music, physical education, and other activities requiring heavy use of psychomotor abilities.

Let us consider the extreme cases, that is, the 2 to 3 percent who have IQs below 70 and the same percent with IQs over 130. Let us consider these comparisons for the same year in which the IQ testing was done. We would expect children with IQs below 70 who come from enriched homes and neighborhood environments not to perform well in the academic subjects. Further, those below 55 from enriched environments will probably not do well in any school tasks, including most of those heavily based on psychomotor abilities. We would anticipate that the children with IQs of 35 and below would require much help throughout life with the simplest tasks of eating, dressing, keeping clean, and the like. Note that these comments do not apply to children from environments whose IQs might change markedly even in a year. At the top end of the scale, from 145 and higher, we should expect superior performance in all types of academic work. Those in the 130 to 145 range also could be predicted to do quite well. Occasionally, however, we get relatively mediocre performance from students with IQs in the 130 to 145 range. About 14 percent of the IQ group is shown in Fig. 4.2 to be in the 71 to 84 range and another 14 percent is in the 116 to 129 range. In some academic work, a few in the lower group might achieve higher than a few in the higher IQ group and vice versa. In the range of 85 to 115 we would expect much overlap.

The variation in IQ and achievement is sufficient that information in addition to IQ is needed in identifying talented students (1). For example, 9 percent of high school seniors in the bottom 10 percent in science achievement were in the upper 50 percent in IQ. This variation is in line with much other research at all school levels which shows that correlations between IQ and achievement in the academic subjects range from about .50 to .80. These correlations are not sufficiently high to predict achievement for individuals. They are sufficiently high that if, for example, only students with IQs above 115 were selected for college education, one would be fairly sure of having included in that group a large proportion of the highest achievers. Some high achievers, however, also would have been eliminated.

As may be inferred from the discussion thus far, much information in addition to IQ scores of students is available to school people and should be used in determining pupil readiness for learning. Misuse of the IQ comes from assuming that it is unchangeable, or that there is a perfect relationship between achievement in any school subject and IQ, or that an intelligence test is equally accurate and valid for measuring intelligence of students from all types of homes and neighborhood backgrounds. Categorizing children and youth as slow learners or as mentally retarded on the basis of IQ alone and then not providing them with an enriched educational environment is probably the most serious misuse that can be made of intelligence testing.

Specific Intellectual Abilities

Specific or specialized abilities may be contrasted with general intellectual ability in that a specific ability underlies performance of a limited range of tasks rather than a broad range. Specific abilities, like general intellectual ability, are usually inferred from test results. You may recall that Guilford hypothesized many specific abilities rather than a general intellectual ability. We shall not enumerate the many special abilities here and will give only brief consideration to their applicability in the schools.

The specific abilities are not as well understood as is general intellectual ability. Less longitudinal research has been done regarding specific abilities, and the relationships of the many specific abilities to achievements in the various school subjects are not established clearly. Tests of specific abilities have not yet proved more effective than general intellectual ability in predicting the efficiency of learning in different tasks in school, including secretarial work, handwriting, English, mathematics, and others. For example, composite general intellectual-ability scores are as useful in predicting mathematics achievement as are scores from a combination of special-abilities tests that purport to measure various mathematical abilities (**51**). More special abilities are found to underlie achievement in algebra than in general mathematics and by adding special-abilities tests to general intellectual-ability tests there is an increase in the accuracy of prediction. However, many tests must be administered to secure a small gain in prediction.

Guidance counselors and others need information that is more useful than IQ in predicting readiness to profit from instruction in fields in which the student has not had prior experience. Project TALENT, a study dealing with the identification, development, and utilization of human talents, may prove valuable in this regard (**19**). As part of Project TALENT, a two-day battery of tests and questionnaires was administered to about 440,000 students in grades 9 through 12 in the spring of 1960. The students were enrolled in 1353 different schools in all parts of the country and comprised about 5 percent of the total high school population of the United States at that time. Project TALENT hopes to produce:

1. An inventory of human resources;
2. A set of standards for educational and psychological measurement;
3. A comprehensive counseling guide identifying patterns of aptitude and ability that are predictive of success in various careers;
4. A better understanding of how young people choose their life work;
5. A better understanding of the educational experiences that prepare students for their life work (**19**, 1–4).

Followup studies have been carried out each year and others are planned through 1983, thus providing a continuous record of each student's activities for 20 years. Although a massive amount of information is now available about high school students, the nature of specific abilities of the type outlined in this section and their relationships to specific learning tasks await further analysis of the information. Many releases of information from Project TALENT have been made in professional journals and also in the popular press. Teachers and others interested in education will find Project TALENT of much importance during the next years.

Previous Related Experience

Accurate information about how well a student has performed thus far in any subject is the most useful type of information for predicting how he will do in the future in the same subject. In addition, when tasks are analyzed in relation to what is needed in order to perform them, various means of assessment may be used to determine whether the student has the background requisite to proceed successfully.

The most systematic information about the relationships between present and future achievements is drawn from longitudinal studies in which standardized educational achievement tests are used. This information is valuable in judging the extent to which the individual's level of achievement at one point in time is useful in predicting achievement at later times. In this connection, we point out that when a test is used to assess performance in a subject field at the present time, it is properly called an educational achievement test. When the same test is used to predict future performance, it is called an aptitude test.

Figure 4.3 indicates the correlations between achievement at each grade level and achievement at grade 12. The correlations reported by Traxler are based on his administering a reading comprehension

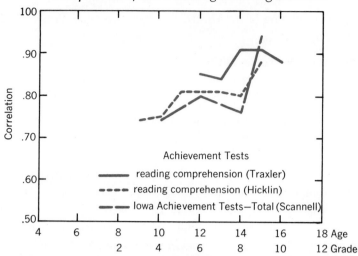

Fig. 4.3. Correlations between achievement at each grade and achievement at grade 12 (corrected for attenuation). (Adapted from B. S. Bloom. *Stability and change in human characteristics.* New York: Wiley, 1964, p. 101.)

test in the seventh through the twelfth grades (**67**). Hicklin secured his information by means of two different reading tests, one in grades 4 and 5, and the other in grades 6 to 10 (**30**). Scannell gave a test battery to students in the fourth, sixth, and eighth grades and another battery to the same students when they were in the ninth and twelfth grades (**54**). The correlations in Fig. 4.3 between an earlier grade and the twelfth grade range from about .65 in the second grade and .75 in the fourth grade to above .90 in the eighth grade. These correlations are high, indicating that achievement is stable over a long period of schooling. (For a more precise interpretation of correlation coefficients, see Chapter 18.)

Although the level of achievement in a subject field is a good indication of how the individual will achieve in the future, this is not to be interpreted to mean that achievement is fixed by heredity. On the contrary:

> . . . we would hypothesize that nursery school and kindergarten could have far reaching consequences on the child's general learning pattern . . . the first period of elementary school (grades 1 to 3) is probably the most crucial period available to the public schools for the development of general learning patterns (**5**, 110).

Inasmuch as the present level of achievement is a good indicator of future achievement, it is interesting to note the extent to which

103 students, enrolled in three seventh-grade classes, differed in reading and in arithmetic achievement, as shown in Fig. 4.4. The student lowest in reading achieved at a level of 3.7, the midpoint between 3.5 and 3.9, while the highest achiever was at 11.2. The scores are equivalent to grade levels. For example, a seventh-grader scoring 3.7 is achieving at the level of the average of third-graders in the seventh month of the school year; one scoring at 11.2 is at the average of eleventh-graders in the second month of the school year. The range among the students in arithmetic achievement was not so wide, namely, from 4.7 to 9.7; however, the difference in range may be partly due to the tests used. Allowing for some unreliability of an achievement

Average Arithmetic Grade Placement

Average Reading Grade Placement	4.5-4.9	5.0-5.4	5.5-5.9	6.0-6.4	6.5-6.9	7.0-7.4	7.5-7.9	8.0-8.4	8.5-8.9	9.0-9.4	9.5-9.9	No. of Cases
11.0-11.4								2	1			
10.5-10.9							2					
10.0-10.4					1		3	1	1	1		
9.5-9.9							1	2				36
9.0-9.4						1	1	2	3	1	1	
8.5-8.9			1			4	1	1	3	2		
8.0-8.4				1	2	3		1		1		
7.5-7.9			2		2	3	3	2	2	1		35
7.0-7.4					3	2	5	2				
6.5-6.9			1	2	1	2	2				1	
6.0-6.4	1		1	2	3		1	2	1			
5.5-5.9				2	1	4	1					
5.0-5.4												32
4.5-4.9		1	1									
4.0-4.4			1									
3.5-3.9					1							
No. of Cases	30					39				34		103

Fig. 4.4. Scatter-diagram of achievement (grade placement) in reading and arithmetic, Stanford Achievement Test, Advanced, Form J, for pupils in grade 7 in a school with average achievement. (Adapted from W. G. Findley. Purposes of school testing programs and their efficient development. In W. G. Findley (Ed.), *The impact and improvement of school testing programs.* Yearb. nat. Soc. Stud. Educ., 1963, **62**, Part II., 18.)

test, we can still assume that the differences in reading and arithmetic, represented by these students, are related to their future achievement. Those with reading achievement below 7.0, with few if any exceptions unless instruction is changed, will not achieve as high during the next semester as will those with achievement scores above 8.4. With few exceptions that a teacher might note in the early weeks of instruction, those with reading achievement below 7.0 will profit from using lower-level reading material than will those with achievements above 8.4.

The information in Fig. 4.4 is also interesting for comparing the achievements of the same students in reading and arithmetic. Note that Fig. 4.4 divides the students roughly into thirds in each subject. Of the 103 children, 21 are in the upper third (approximately) in both reading and arithmetic, 16 are in the middle third in both, and 18 are in the lower third in both. Fifty-five, slightly over half, are in the same third in both subjects; the other 48 are not. Six students are in the top third in one subject and in the bottom third in the other. Four who are in the top third in arithmetic are in the bottom third in reading; two who are in the top third in reading are in the bottom third in arithmetic. Cases such as these six provide good evidence for not using IQ alone either in predicting the achievements of children or in assigning them to sections, such as high, middle, and low in all subjects.

A further indication of the range of achievement is shown in Fig. 4.5. We determined achievement levels in arithmetic that would constitute appropriate new learning tasks for children of low, average, and high intelligence (16). On the basis of IQ, pupils averaging 117 months in age were divided into three groups each containing 20 boys and 20 girls. IQ was based on the Wechsler Intelligence Scale for Children (WISC), an individual intelligence test. We found the level at which each child could count without error and then found the level at which he could not count (the new learning-task level). Figure 4.5 shows that three low-IQ children could not count by 1s and that one high IQ child could count by all numbers through 22 and had as a new learning task counting by 23s. Although there is this large difference between the lowest and highest performance, it is surprising to note the extent to which the three distributions in the figure overlap, for example, one high-IQ child achieved at the same level (counting by 3s) as eight low-IQ children. Again, this points to the importance of using the child's present level of achievement related to the task at hand, rather than the IQ alone, in determining readiness.

We conclude that the present level of achievement is most useful in predicting subsequent achievement in the same subject or skill.

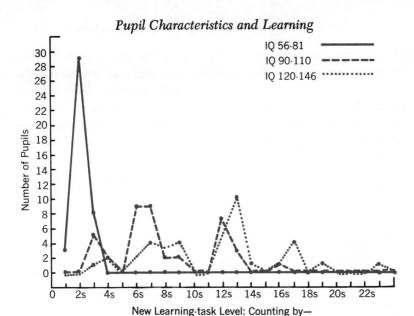

Fig. 4.5. Distribution of appropriate new learning-task levels. (Based on J. F. Feldhusen & H. J. Klausmeier. Achievement in counting and addition. *Elem. Sch. J.*, 1959, **59**, 391.)

General intellectual ability may be combined with the achievement level to improve the prediction over a short period of time. The most useful information from an intelligence test is the location of children whose IQs are considerably higher or lower than their achievement level. Further study of these children, including the use of another intelligence test, is warranted in planning an instructional program for them. The identification of special abilities and aptitudes is proceeding rapidly. However, knowledge of specific abilities does not add much to the combined use of present level of achievement in each subject and general intellectual ability.

PSYCHOMOTOR ABILITIES
AND PHYSICAL CHARACTERISTICS

Six factors, or processes, in the psychomotor area are strength, impulsion, speed, precision, coordination, and flexibility. These factors, combined with parts of the body are classed as psychomotor abilities. These abilities in various combinations are essential to excellent performance in many activities, such as in instrumental music, handwriting, typewriting, shorthand, the making of maps in social studies, and the making of objects in home economics, agriculture, industrial arts, and other classes. Individual and group sports also require the use of psychomotor abilities as do talking, singing, and dramatics. The wide range of performance in motor skills and the differences in physical characteristics found among students of about the same chronological age are shown in a few representative studies; and some relationships among physical, cognitive, and affective variables are indicated.

The range and the average, or mean, in six measures of 40 boys and 40 girls with IQs ranging from 62 to 146 are shown in Table 4.2. The

TABLE 4.2.

Means, Standard Deviations, and Ranges for Six Measurements[a]

Measure	Boys			Girls		
	Mean	S.D.	Range	Mean	S.D.	Range
Height in inches	55.10	2.80	47.9– 60.8	55.24	2.41	50.8– 60.0
Weight in pounds	77.22	16.23	49.3–113.3	75.36	13.78	55.0–115.5
Grip in kilograms	20.90	3.47	13.0– 28.5	17.70	3.28	9.4– 23.7
Permanent teeth	15.05	4.37	11.0– 28.0	16.45	4.53	11.0– 27.0
Carpal age in months	120.65	13.77	89.0–153.0	124.80	9.52	101.0–156.0
Handwriting speed in letters per minute	43.60	21.90	5.4– 98.0	47.20	20.70	9.2– 82.0

[a] Based on the measurements of 40 boys and 40 girls, normally distributed according to IQs (WISC) at 125 months of age.

SOURCE: H. J. Klausmeier, J. Feldhusen, & J. Check. *An analysis of learning efficiency in arithmetic of mentally retarded children in comparison with children of average and high intelligence.* U.S. Office of Education Cooperative Research Project No. 153. Madison: Univer. of Wisconsin, 1959, p. 86.

chronological age ranges from 119 to 132 months, and the mean age is 125 months. The difference in strength of grip, which is a good indicator of vitality, between the strongest and weakest boy is 15.5 kilograms. This measure of strength is obtained by giving the student a hand dynamometer which he squeezes as hard as he can. The strongest boy scored about three times higher than the weakest girl. Carpal age in months is the best indicator of skeletal maturity currently available. Carpal age is secured by X-raying the hand and wrist and then comparing the X-ray obtained with norms already established. Experienced radiologists do this reliably. The principal criterion of carpal age is ossification of the bone. The range in skeletal maturity ranges from

89 to 156 months—7 years, 5 months to 13 years. Handwriting speed of these children varied greatly, from 5.4 to 98 letters written per minute. It is obvious, of course, that at the time of these measurements, the children were not equally ready to engage in any lesson or activity that required the same amount of material to be written.

We correlated the measures above with achievement in reading, arithmetic, and language. Strength of grip and handwriting speed were found to be positively correlated with achievement in all subjects; however, four other physical measures were not, namely, carpal age, height, weight, and number of permanent teeth. Here skeletal development as inferred from carpal age was not positively related to rate of mental development, the same conclusion that was reported previously by Sontag and associates (**60**). This conclusion of Sontag and his associates and of the Wisconsin study differ sharply with the concept of organismic age. Proponents of organismic age consistently suggest that the teacher should examine the child's rate of growth in height, weight, number of permanent teeth, strength of grip, and carpal age in order to understand better his rate of growth in reading, arithmetic, language, and other school subjects (**46, 49, 50**). Further judgments that such physical characteristics as height, weight, number of permanent teeth, and carpal age should be given no attention in predicting the achievements of elementary school children in reading, arithmetic and language is provided by several authors (**4, 15, 21, 40, 68**). Those of us who do not accept the usefulness of organismic age in predicting achievement in no way deny that a child's size and his ability to perform various motor tasks may affect his feelings toward himself and others or that differences in age of reaching pubescence affect social and emotional behavior.

At pubescence, marked changes often occur in attitudes and values, suggesting a positive relationship between levels of maturation and affective characteristics. The age at which boys and girls reach puberty varies widely. Some normally developing girls, for example, reach menarche as early as age 9, whereas others do not until age 15. Some early maturing boys are in pubescence at age 11; others, not until age 16 or 17. Among 1000 girls of the same age, the postmenarcheal demonstrated considerably greater heterosexual interests, more interest in clothing and adornment, less interest in games or activities requiring rigorous or strenuous activity, and more daydreaming than did the premenarcheal (**61**). Socially rejected boys and socially rejected girls of junior high school age have several traits in common: unattractiveness, untidiness, restlessness, talkativeness, and unpopularity (**23**).

A longitudinal study, started with infants in the early 1930s at the University of California, provides much information about the relationship between skeletal development during adolescence and other facets of development. From the larger study, 16 early- and 16 late-maturing boys were identified, with level of maturity based on skeletal age, determined primarily from X-rays of the hand and wrist. In their early teens, the boys more advanced in maturity showed higher interest in matters of personal grooming such as cleanliness, neatness of clothing, care of hair and nails, and the like; they were more relaxed and friendly, more animated and eager; and they demonstrated better relationships with age-mates. Later, students who were mentioned frequently and infrequently in the school newspaper were compared. The infrequently mentioned students had lower carpal maturity than did the frequently mentioned (38).

Let us consider the range of differences among individuals in one more activity. As part of a physical fitness project, a nationwide survey was made of 8500 boys and girls in grades 5 through 12. The results were reported for many performances (32). Table 4.3 gives selected

TABLE 4.3.

Selected Percentile Norms in the 50-Yard Dash (Seconds)
for Boys and Girls at Selected Ages

Percentile[a]	Age 10		Age 13		Age 16	
	Boys	Girls	Boys	Girls	Boys	Girls
100th	6.5	6.9	5.8	6.0	5.4	6.0
95th	7.6	8.0	6.5	7.4	6.1	7.1
75th	8.3	8.6	7.3	8.0	6.5	7.9
50th	8.8	9.1	7.8	8.5	7.0	8.4
25th	9.4	9.8	8.3	9.0	7.3	9.0
5th	10.8	10.8	9.3	10.5	8.0	10.9
0th	13.5	15.1	12.5	13.0	9.7	12.3

[a] The general procedure is to report percentile scores from 1–99; in Chapter 18 a procedure for computing percentiles 1–99 is given.
SOURCE: Adapted from P. A. Hunsicker. *Youth fitness test manual.* Washington, D.C.: American Association for Health, Physical Education, and Recreation, National Education Association, 1958, pp. 19, 26.

percentile norms in the 50-yard dash for boys and girls at ages 10, 13, and 16. In the report other percentile scores are given also for each age from 10 through 17. The range in running the 50-yard dash at age

10 is from 6.5 seconds for boys to 15.1 seconds for girls, at age 13 from 5.8 to 13.0 seconds, and at age 16 from 5.4 to 12.3 seconds. At every age, the fastest time is for boys and the slowest for girls. Half of the boys and girls, by definition, are between the twenty-fifth and seventy-fifth percentile score. At age 10, this middle half of the boys (the twenty-fifth to the seventy-fifth percentiles) run the dash in from 8.3 to 9.4 seconds. It is interesting to note, also, that the top half of the boys at age 10 run the dash in 8.8 seconds or less, whereas at age 16, 25 percent of the girls yet require 9.0 or more seconds. For both sexes at all age levels (with the exception of 16-year-old boys) the fastest child runs the 50-yard dash in less than half the time of the slowest.

The large differences reported in this section in strength, handwriting speed, and running are representative of differences found by other researchers for the same and other performances. The main conclusions that might be drawn from all the information is that large differences exist among students of about the same age in all types of psychomotor abilities and physical characteristics. Large differences in performance up to the present time indicate varying degrees of readiness to continue the same activities. Physical measures such as height, weight, number of permanent teeth, and carpal age are not related to achievement in the academic subjects; the relationships among achievement in the academic subjects and strength and handwriting, though positive, are not of sufficient magnitude to add much to IQ and prior achievement. Skeletal maturity is related to a broad range of behavior in the affective domain, particularly during the period of puberty. Early-maturing individuals, who tend also to be stronger, taller, and heavier than the slow maturers, demonstrate more behavior that is considered socially acceptable.

AFFECTIVE CHARACTERISTICS

A bright, high-achieving child may do well in one subject but not in another because he is not interested or because he has a negative attitude toward the teacher or subject matter. A college student may not learn well in a required course because the content seems completely unrelated to achieving goals that he values. For another student emotional disturbances may result in low learning efficiency. Common to these three examples is low efficiency of learning resulting from characteristics of the student in the affective domain.

Interests

The great variation in the likes and dislikes of children and youth for sports and games, television programs, radio programs, school subjects, school activities, and eventually vocations point to the environmental influences upon interests. Prior to the days of television, jet airplanes, and atomic energy, children and youth showed interest in other aspects of their environment. Today at all school levels and in almost every classroom, it is possible to find pupil interest in the specific subject matter ranging from very low to very high.

The interests of 2248 first- to twelfth-graders in the Midwest, in the South, and around New York City show clear-cut patterns (36). Table 4.4 shows the pattern of pupil responses to various categories of things

TABLE 4.4.

School Activities Liked Best by Pupils at Various Grade Levels

Activity	Percent of Boys Grades				Percent of Girls Grades			
	1–3	4–6	7–9	10–12	1–3	4–6	7–9	10–12
Sports, gym, physical education	13	16	35	32	10	10	31	30
Arithmetic, mathematics	33	31	27	13	25	28	18	7
English usage, reading, etc.	38	24	11	10	43	30	19	25
Nature study, science	0	4	8	19	1	4	8	8
Local and world affairs, social studies	1	11	8	7	1	12	9	5
Art, music, dramatics, etc.	15	14	11	15	20	16	15	12
Self-improvement, vocations	0	0	0	4	0	0	0	13
Total percent	100	100	100	100	100	100	100	100

SOURCE: Adapted from A. T. Jersild, & Ruth Tasch. *Children's interests and what they suggest for education.* New York: Bureau of Publications, Teachers College, Columbia Univer., 1949, pp. 138–139.

liked best in school. For both boys and girls, sports, gym, and physical education were liked more at successive school levels, primary through senior high school. From this it is inferred that there is higher interest in sports and gym at successive school levels. Expressed interest in arithmetic and mathematics dropped off for girls especially from junior to senior high school. This cultural female bias has been the concern of those educators hoping to maximize the development of this nation's brainpower. English usage, reading, and other language arts showed a sharp drop for boys after the primary grade. Boys showed a sharp increase in a liking for science from junior to senior high school, whereas, for girls, the interest remained the same. After the first three grades, interest in local and world affairs remained fairly stable. Perhaps surprising to some, art, music, and dramatics—which remained fairly stable throughout the grades—were liked more than local and world affairs by both boys and girls at all school levels.

The trends in school interests from primary grades to senior high school are summarized as follows:

The typical first or second grader is interested in school and what the school represents. More likely than not he likes his teacher, too. The life of a scholar appeals to him. He is challenged by what there is to learn. He may say, as one child in this study said, that one of the happiest days in his life was the day he learned "to take away." When he tells what he likes about school he mentions things that distinctly belong to school much more frequently than he mentions things that school shares with life outside, such as games and outdoor play.

The young child's friendly feeling about school appears not only when he talks about school as such but also when he happens to mention school in describing his likes and wishes. When describing what he dislikes most in life outside school, the young child is likely to make very few unfavorable references to any burdens or discomforts which the school had placed on his out-of-school life.

As the average child moves up through the grades he seems to become less eager about things that distinctly belong to school and scholarliness, more inclined to complain, more interested in things that go along with school rather than with work in the classroom. He becomes relatively more interested in recess periods than in class periods. He mentions play and sports more often. There is a greater hiatus between his wishes and what the school offers. This is particularly marked, as we have seen, in connection with his wishes for self-improvement and for vocational competence, on the one hand, and what the school offers to further his aspiration (36, 41–42).

Whether similar patterns of interest would be found today is difficult to ascertain. The impact of television and the volatile world situation may have changed interest patterns. Many recent events have led to increased emphasis on instruction in science, mathematics, and foreign language. Higher interest in these areas has been generated for high school students of both sexes, and the peer status of students excelling in academic performance has increased. The role of the teacher in building interests in pupils and helping them to establish goals is treated in considerable detail in Chapter 12.

Attitudes and Values

Attitudes and values, like interests, are highly dependent upon environmental factors such as the home, the neighborhood, the school, the church, and many other agencies. Attitudes and values become more stable in later adolescence than prior to that age. The teaching of attitudes and values is considered sufficiently important that Chapter 10 is devoted to it entirely; however, the range among students in some specific behaviors indicative of attitudes and values is now described. The honesty of children was studied under the title of the Character Education Inquiry (25). Tests were devised and administered in which pupils were confronted with temptation or with a conflict between their own pleasure and the good of others. Among the tests was one in which the pupil was asked to do as well as he could on an impossible task, such as putting dots in small circles while blindfolded. The task is obviously so difficult that any pupil who succeeded in it certainly did so by removing or looking around his blindfold. In another test, the child was given a box of coins and had the opportunity to take some of the coins before returning them to the front of the room. The investigators could check whether or not the child actually took any coins.

The distribution of ratio scores for cheating, i.e., the number of times in ten opportunities to cheat in a large number of situations, is shown in Fig. 4.6. About 7 percent of the pupils had near perfect ratio scores (did not cheat at all) and about 4 percent cheated at every opportunity. However, since the high percent of cases fall between the high and the low ends, the tendency is for individuals to be honest in some situations and not honest in other situations. This distribution is not greatly dissimilar from the distribution of intelligence scores based on the Stanford-Binet, as previously shown in this chapter.

Besides indicating that character traits are distributed in the child population somewhat as IQ, the researchers drew some conclusions about the relationship of cheating to other characteristics:

The concomitants of deceit are, in order of their importance, (1) classroom association; (2) general personal handicaps, such as relatively low IQ, poor resistance to suggestion, and emotional instability; (3) cultural and social limitations in the home background; and (4) such other miscellaneous facts as are loosely associated with deception (25, 412).

More recently, elementary school children operated a "ray-gun" shooting gallery individually and were tempted to falsify their scores, which they recorded themselves, in order to win an attractive badge

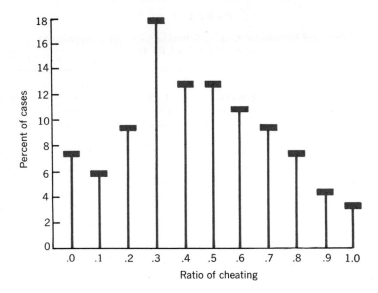

Fig. 4.6. Distribution of cheating ratios for children. (Adapted from H. Hartshorne & M. A. May. *Studies in the nature of character: I. Studies in deceit.* New York: Macmillan, 1928, p. 386.)

(22). The study confirms the hypothesis that resistance to temptation at age 11 or 12 can be successfully forecasted from reports by mothers of their children's feelings of guilt in early childhood (age 5 or 6); a capacity to experience guilt at the earlier age appeared to allow development of resistance to temptation by age 12.

Values and attitudes toward school have been inferred from interviews with 440 boys and girls, ages 14 to 19, who had quit school while still in the grades or in high school (37). Table 4.5 shows the principal reasons these dropouts gave as the basis for leaving school. Dissatisfaction with school was given as the reason in nearly half the cases. Though not shown, dissatisfaction was found to be associated with failing grades, courses, dislike of teachers, teaching methods, social relations in the school, and a few other miscellaneous reasons. It should be noted that the reasons for leaving school do not always reside in the individual student alone but in the situation. Some students in our high schools today, especially with the increased emphasis on high achievement in academic subjects, are being failed even though they do their best, and because of failures must either repeat many courses or drop out of school.

The dropout problem has received increasing attention in recent

TABLE 4.5.

Principal Reasons for Leaving School as Given by Nongraduates from High School, by Age

Reasons for Leaving School	Percent of Total	Age		
		14–15 Years	16–17 Years	18–19 Years
Dissatisfaction with school	47.7	42.5	53.3	42.6
Economic need	19.4	21.2	19.1	18.3
Lure of job	11.7	8.0	11.4	15.6
Marriage or pregnancy	6.6	17.7	1.4	5.2
Other reasons	14.6	10.6	14.8	18.3
Number of cases	440	113	211	116

SOURCE: Adapted from Elizabeth S. Johnson, & Caroline E. Legg. Why young people leave school. *Bull. Nat. Ass. Sec. Sch. Principals*, 1948, **32**, 17.

years. The current situation finds about one-third of all children dropping out at some point; only two-thirds of our pupils finish high school. Delinquency is much higher for dropouts than for graduates (**48**). Estimates are that 7,500,000 students will drop out of school during the decade of the 1960s, a third of them with less than eight years of formal education (**57**). The problem is even more acute when one considers the rapidly decreasing demand for unskilled labor; unskilled laborers comprised 59 percent of the U. S. labor force in 1900 and 28.9 percent in 1950 with estimates of 24.4 percent and 22.1 percent for 1965 and 1975, respectively (**48**). The extent to which school dropout is related to unfavorable attitudes toward teachers and subject matter has not been determined. It is clear that dropouts find much dissatisfaction with school.

Personality Integration

Some people are full of zest for life, show high enthusiasm for the future, a high acceptance of self, accept objective reality, and are well adjusted emotionally. At the other extreme, a small percent of the adult population is in public and private hospitals as incurable, psychotic individuals. Also, very young children are now being referred to child guidance centers and to private psychiatrists for emotional disturbances, and the incidence of emotional disturbance is quite high for pupils of elementary and high school age.

Figure 4.7 shows the incidence of emotionally disturbed children by grade (8). A sharp rise is seen in the incidence from kindergarten to first grade. The percent of disturbed children is about the same from first through seventh grade, with a rise again at the eighth grade. The

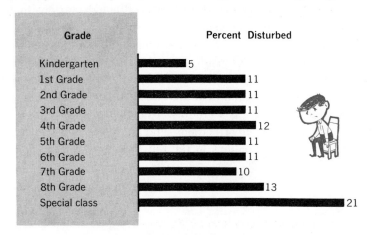

Fig. 4.7. Incidence of emotionally disturbed children by grade. (Adapted from Nora Clancy & Faith Smitter. A study of emotionally disturbed children in Santa Barbara county schools. *Calif. J. educ. Res.*, 1953, **4**, 212.)

ungraded special classes for mentally retarded children show a much higher percent than do the regular classes through eighth grade. Figure 4.8 shows the incidence of emotionally disturbed children by home

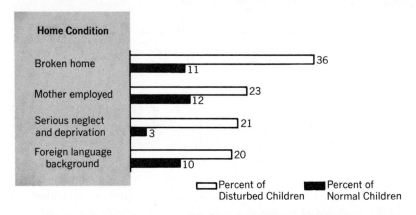

Fig. 4.8. Incidence of emotionally disturbed children by home conditions. (Adapted from Nora Clancy & Faith Smitter. A study of emotionally disturbed children in Santa Barbara county schools. *Calif. J. educ. Res.*, 1953, **4**, 214.)

condition. Emotionally disturbed, more frequently than normal children, come from broken homes, from homes where the mother is employed full time, from homes where there is serious neglect and deprivation of the child, and from homes in which a foreign language is spoken. Anxiety accompanies disturbance, although anxiety to some degree is exhibited by everyone.

We found that anxiety, to be discussed more fully in Chapter 11, was related to achievement in reading, arithmetic, and language (**17**). Independent of achievement, children of low IQs (56–81) were significantly higher in anxiety than children of average (90–110) and high (120–146) IQs. The girls as a group were higher in anxiety than boys. Table 4.6 shows the intercorrelations among anxiety and the achievement scores. (The correlations in the top three rows of the table are

TABLE 4.6.

*Correlations of Anxiety With Intelligence and Achievement Scores
for Fifth-Grade Children*

| Group | N | WISC IQ | Correlation of Anxiety with | | |
			Reading	Arithmetic	Language
IQ— 56 to 81	40	−.28	−.13	−.49**	−.27
IQ— 90 to 110	40	−.35*	−.31*	−.20	−.33*
IQ—120 to 146	40	−.07	+.15	−.02	+.12
Boys	60	−.47**	−.48**	−.47**	−.49**
Girls	60	−.40**	−.38**	−.40**	−.43**

NOTE: A single asterisk indicates an *r* significantly different from zero at or beyond the .05 level; a double asterisk at or beyond the .01 level.
SOURCE: J. F. Feldhusen, & H. J. Klausmeier. Anxiety, intelligence, and achievement in children of low, average, and high intelligence. *Child Develpm.*, 1962, **33**, 407.

low because of the restricted range of IQ in each group of 40, while those in the last two rows are somewhat high because of the relatively large number of children with high and low IQs in relation to the number in the average IQ group.) The pattern of negative correlations in Table 4.6 indicates that high achievement was accompanied with low anxiety scores, or vice versa. Apparently children of higher IQs are less anxious than are those of lower IQs, and lower anxiety and higher IQs are both associated with higher achievement. Possibly the more anxious children feel less free to respond to the teacher, to the learning material, and to the learning situation in general.

The same groups of children with low, average, and high IQs rated themselves in achievement (52). The self-ratings were made at intervals during a two-year period. The children with low IQs had less realistic and less reliable estimates of their actual achievements than the bright children with average IQs and tended to overestimate their achievements. Thus, higher anxiety and less reliable estimates of achievement characterize children with low IQs.

To summarize this discussion of efficiency of learning and characteristics in the affective domain, we may conclude that interests, as well as attitudes, are related to readiness and subsequent performance. Both interest and attitudes are directly related to environmental variables. Further, severe emotional disturbance is one of the most critical social problems of our time. At every school level, primary through higher education, some individuals do not learn efficiently because of severe emotional problems and related personality disorganization.

AGE

Large differences are found in any human characteristic at any chronological age (CA). So strong is the evidence about differences among children of the same CA that many persons favor the abandonment of CA as a basis for placing children in grades, kindergarten through grade 12. Only the most gross estimates can be made about a child's achievement from knowing his CA.

One significant attempt to relate the developmental characteristics of broad age groups to learning is incorporated in the concept of developmental tasks (26). Developmental tasks have been identified for six periods in human development: infancy and early childhood, middle childhood, adolescence, early adulthood, middle age, and later maturity. Developmental tasks are defined as follows:

The tasks the individual must learn—*the developmental tasks of life*—are those things that constitute healthy and satisfactory growth in our society. They are the things a person must learn if he is to be judged and to judge himself to be a reasonably happy and successful person. *A developmental task is a task which arises at or about a certain period in the life of the individual, successful achievement of which leads to his happiness and to success with later tasks, while failure leads to unhappiness in the individual, disapproval by the society, and difficulty with later tasks* (26, 2).

The developmental tasks of adolescence are now given. Space does not permit the inclusion of the tasks for all six age levels.

1. Achieving new and more mature relations with age-mates of both sexes. . . .
2. Achieving a masculine or feminine social role. . . .
3. Accepting one's physique and using the body effectively. . . .
4. Achieving emotional independence of parents and other adults. . . .
5. Achieving assurance of economic independence. . . .
6. Selecting and preparing for an occupation. . . .
7. Preparing for marriage and family life. . . .
8. Developing intellectual skills and concepts necessary for civic competence. . . .
9. Desiring and achieving socially responsible behavior. . . .
10. Acquiring a set of values and an ethical system as a guide to behavior. . . . (26, 111–147).

An intensive longitudinal study of 15 boys and 15 girls provides evidence of the utility of the concept of developmental tasks (56). Good achievement on a developmental task at one broad age level was followed by good achievement on the same task at subsequent age levels, and in addition, was generally associated with good achievement on other tasks at the same age level. In a few cases, good achievement on one developmental task was used by the individual to compensate for poor achievement on other tasks. In order for an adolescent to accomplish successfully the developmental tasks required in his society, he must master his impulsivity and accept himself. In this way, he can mobilize his energy to deal effectively with the social and cultural forces which impinge upon him (55). This suggests that learning efficiency of the usual school subject matter is related to emotional behavior and social adjustment. The emotionally disturbed or antisocial individual usually does not acquire knowledge and related cognitive skills as efficiently as does the one who is not disturbed or antisocial. A second conclusion is that within broad age limits, boys and girls must acquire some learning outcomes efficiently. If they do not achieve most of the tasks required of adolescence, they are likely to experience difficulties in young adulthood.

SEX

A major conclusion in one of the best summaries of sex differences within our country is that differences between the sexes become more pronounced from early infancy into adolescence (64). Both cultural and biological factors produce differences between the sexes, and those differences that might result from biological factors become more pronounced because society ascribes definite sex roles to males and females. Other conclusions about sex differences are now given in capsule form (**64**).

Several differences are found between the sexes in physical characteristics. Boys are taller and heavier than girls except at ages 11 to 15 when there is little difference because of the more rapid rate of maturation in girls. Girls precede boys by 12 to 20 months in reaching puberty. Boys have higher vital capacity than girls and are stronger than girls. There appears, however, to be a somewhat higher incidence of various defects of all sorts in males than in females. The death rate for males is higher at all ages (**47**). Despite the ratio of 105 boys to 100 girls born, the members of the two sexes are equal at the time an age group reaches the early 20s (**69**).

Differences in intelligence are not usually found between boys and girls because the widely used individual intelligence tests—the Revised Stanford-Binet Scale and the Wechsler Intelligence Scale for Children—have been constructed to eliminate sex differences. However, girls typically score higher on verbal items, boys on quantitative and spatial items in both intelligence and achievement tests. Girls receive higher grades in school than boys; however, after about the fifth grade, boys score as high or higher than do girls on achievement tests, particularly in science and mathematics.

In preference for play, games, and other activities, differences become apparent in early childhood and increase with successive age levels into adolescence. Girls, for example, prefer and actually do more reading on their own at all school levels than do boys. At all school levels boys engage in more active games. Large differences appear in vocational interests at the senior high school age. In this respect, certain occupations such as teaching in the primary grades and nursing will probably continue to be heavily preferred by females; whereas other occupations, especially those involving hard manual labor, will continue to attract males. Whether or not the great differences in the number of males and females in science, mathematics, engineering, and medicine will continue is not known. Apparently the Russians are educating many females for professional fields and occupations which are yet dominated by males in the United States.

Males show a higher degree of aggressive and dominant behavior than females, with more boys than girls apprehended as delinquents, and a much higher incidence of adult male criminals. Because of both biological and cultural forces, females apparently are more cooperative than males. In school, girls tend to comply with the teacher's wishes more frequently than do boys. However, daydreaming is more common in adolescent girls than in adolescent boys, and in adulthood, females show higher incidence of neuroticism than do males. The differences between the sexes in personality structure, emotional expression, sociability, character integration, and the like are much less clear than are the differences in physical characteristics, school achievements, and vocational interests.

These differences between groups of males and females should not be permitted to overshadow the large overlapping between the sexes in all the measures nor the large differences within the same sex. The average differences between the sexes and also the overlapping in six measures that we observed for boys and girls at a mean age of 125 months are shown in Fig. 4.9 (**41**). The range in IQ of the boys is from

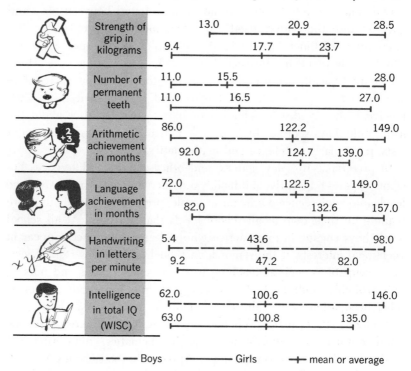

— — — Boys ——— Girls —+— mean or average

Fig. 4.9. Range and mean score for strength of grip, number of permanent teeth, arithmetic and language achievement, handwriting speed and IQ. 60 boys and 60 girls; mean age: 125 months. (Adapted from H. J. Klausmeier, J. F. Feldhusen, & J. Check. *An analysis in learning efficiency in arithmetic of mentally retarded children in comparison with children of average and high intelligence.* U.S. Office of Education Cooperative Research Project No. 153. Madison: School of Education, Univer. of Wisconsin, 1959.)

62 to 146 and of the girls from 63 to 135 with the mean IQ for boys 100.6 and for girls 100.8. These boys and girls are much alike in intelligence; we selected them to be of the same IQ and CA in our study. In strength of grip, however, the boys' mean score is 20.9 and the girls' is 17.7. Though this average difference is quite large, there is a great deal of overlap in strength of grip between boys and girls. The girls have, on the average, 16.5 permanent teeth and the boys 15.5; however, there is also a large amount of overlap, and the only child having a full set of 28 permanent teeth is a boy. We did not find the higher achievement generally found and predicted for boys in arithmetic; the girls had a slightly higher mean score. In language and in handwriting speed, the average achievements are higher for girls than for boys, as expected. In all areas except language, a boy had the highest score, and in all areas the overlapping between boys and girls is extensive. This overlap in achievements is of far more significance for learning efficiency than is the small difference between the mean scores of the boys and girls. For example, although the girls as a group have lower strength, there are many girls who can outperform a large number of boys on a variety of tasks where strength is needed. Also, although girls as a group are higher in language, a large number are far below the highest boy.

More recently, we compared the performances of boys and girls on divergent-thinking tests (**43**). One hundred sixty fifth-graders and 160 seventh-graders, all with IQs above 115, were given tests of both divergent thinking and convergent thinking which included educational achievements in different subject fields and special tests of current events, problem solving, and others. The girls scored higher than the boys on tests of divergent thinking, whereas the boys were significantly higher than the girls on tests requiring convergent thinking. Similar sex differences in divergent thinking were noted at the elementary level (**65**) and in the eleventh grade (**42**).

What do sex differences such as those reported mean with respect to separating boys and girls for educational purposes? Boys and girls can probably remain together for all instruction through at least the fourth grade. However, at the time of menarche in early-developing girls it is probably wise to have boys and girls separated for any strenuous activities. Further, at the time the male voice begins to change, boys should be separated from girls for instruction in vocal music, unless our music teachers can somehow provide better instruction in mixed groups to boys whose voices are changing. At present, vocal music is strongly disliked by many boys after grade 5 and into high school. It is possible also that some music teachers, unaware of the demands they are placing on maturing boys, are doing severe damage to the vocal abilities of boys. In elective courses at the high school level we need to have as many high-level courses in subject fields that are as interesting to girls as to boys. Many boys, and a considerable number of girls, are interested in science and mathematics and can achieve highly. We should have such high-level science and mathematics classes for boys and girls who like them and can do well. Girls are known to exhibit interest in music, art, and business education. High-level classes in music, art, literature, home economics, and business education are needed for the girls who want such courses, just as are the courses in physics, trigonometry, and mechanical drawing for the interested and able boys.

HOME BACKGROUND AND SOCIAL CLASS

All of the abilities and characteristics discussed thus far can be appraised through tests or observations of the child in the school situation. There are other forces continuously at work which also affect efficiency of learning. The family, not the school, provides the early education of the child. During kindergarten the child is in school from two to three hours a day. In the elementary grades and high school he is in school from five to seven hours a day. The school week is generally five days and the school year ranges from about 34 to 40 weeks.

As noted previously, many children having emotional disturbances come from broken homes, from homes where the mother is employed full time, from homes where there is neglect or deprivation of the child, and from homes in which a foreign language is spoken (8). However, some emotionally disturbed children also come from homes possessing the opposite characteristics.

Much has been written about a democratic family life in which decision making is shared by all members of the family, including the children. Some believe that this produces more self-reliant and well-adjusted children than does a home environment characterized by strife or by decision making by one person, usually the father or the mother. There is much confusion as to the characteristics of a democratic home life, just as there is about a democratic classroom. Additionally, many persons now question the desirability of giving a child of school age the same weight in decision making as the father or the mother. Family life can be harmonious when children accept either or both parents as responsible individuals who, because of experience and the responsibilities of parenthood, must make independent decisions affecting the welfare of the children. Furthermore, family life can be harmonious when children, as early as they are willing and able to accept responsibility for their decisions, share in making decisions.

High achievers in reading tend to come from homes in which there is parental agreement on methods of control (**59**). When the parents disagree on methods of raising the child, particularly in the presence of the child, the home situation may be a poor one. Also, homes in which the parents value intellectual mastery are associated with higher IQs at the preschool age and higher achievement in school (**39**). Parents who have more education apparently serve as models for their children, and these parents also reward academic achievement of their children more regularly. The attitudes of the parents of adolescents in Sydney, Australia, are found to be positively correlated with the adolescents' knowledge of science (**45**).

There are two opposing points of view with respect to the role of parents and the related effects upon children. One point of view is that if the child is allowed too much freedom he will remain at the mercy of the pleasure principle; a second is that parental restraint upon the child will result in his becoming anxious and lacking independence and creativity. High- and low-achieving junior high school students with IQs above 130, and high- and low-achieving students with IQs ranging from 93 to 120 were identified (**14**). The mothers of high achievers were more authoritarian and restrictive in the treatment of their children than were the mothers of the low achievers. The mothers of the high-achieving children of both high and average IQs seemed to have, in addition, the more punitive attitudes with respect to child-rearing practices. The question as to whether the more restricted and less permissive home environment resulted in any loss in creativity or independence on the part of the pupil was not answered. However, as achievement was assessed by teachers, the more restrictive and less permissive home environment was associated with higher achievement in children of both high and average IQs.

Patterns of home and family life have been related to social-class structure since the 1930s. The basic pattern for categorizing people residing in a community into social classes is shown in Fig. 4.10. The three main social classes are upper, middle, and lower, and within each of the three there is an upper and a lower, giving a total of six social classes. The relationship of social class and schooling provides an interesting study of American life (**27, 28, 35**). Different test batteries were administered to all the 10- and 16-year-old children in a community

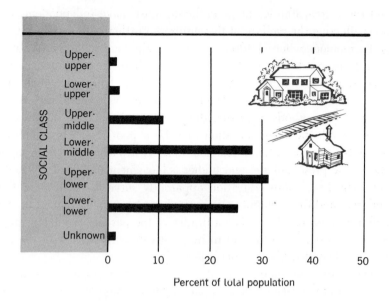

Fig. 4.10. Distribution of the population of "Yankee City" by social class. (Adapted from W. L. Warner & P. S. Lunt. *Social life of a modern community.* New Haven: Yale Univer. Press, 1941, p. 203.)

area of 10,000 population; the community was given the hypothetical name of Midwest. The 10-year-olds were retested three years later. The differences favoring the upper social class, already present at 10 years of age, were more apparent as age increased. Considerable overlapping of scores among children from the different social classes was also found.

Similar information about a different group of children in "River City" is shown in Fig. 4.11. Here all the children from the upper-upper, lower-upper, and upper-middle classes are combined into one group. Interest in church, amount of education, and socioeconomic rating as a young adult were lowest for the lower-lower social-class group, whereas the tendency of girls to marry under age and delinquency of boys was highest in the lower-lower social class. This and other evidence make it clear that the opportunities and rewards in life are unequally distributed, more good things going to the children of higher-status families. Although this is the case, a large minority of the children from the lower social class do very well in school and in the community; they make good use of the opportunities they find and

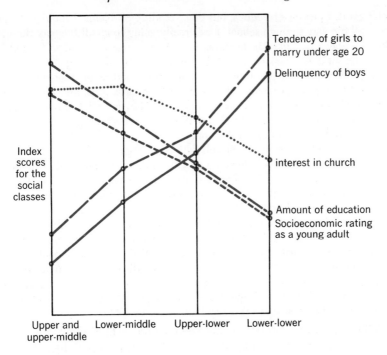

Fig. 4.11. Social class and facts about youth in River City. (R. J. Havighurst, *et al. Growing up in River City.* New York: Wiley, 1962, p. 13.)

many of them rise above the social-class level of their parents.

The following story of a girl dropout reveals some of the animosities in school related to social-class membership and also some of the difficulties a student from the lower strata may encounter:

Bernice is living with her mother-in-law. I scaled a fifteen-foot muddy embankment up to this little run-down house. Apparently there is a more accessible route from the rear. Bernice required very little explanation. I asked her how long she had been out of school.

"I quit two weeks before the end of school a year ago. I was only fifteen at the time but I talked to Mr. McCoy (principal). He said that they wouldn't come get me because I would be sixteen before fall. I just didn't take the exams. I knew I wouldn't pass anyway because I didn't do any work except in typing. I really loved typing. It seems I didn't like all of my teachers. I got kicked out of English six times. Me and the teacher couldn't get along. I don't think half the kids liked her. She talked about the same thing for about a week and you didn't learn anything. Then she would spend the whole period with one kid. I took a dislike to her the first two days. I guess I could have gotten along with her but after that I didn't try. And then I just didn't understand general math I suppose because I don't understand arithmetic. I love it but I don't get it. I just love fractions, but those reading problems, I could never get those all the way through school. I was really going to go all the way through Home Ec because I liked it, but then my schedule was changed so I could be in a different gym class. They said they wanted to break up a gang of us girls because we were beating all the other teams and smarting off a lot. Then I got changed to a gym class with a lot of these high class girls, as we call them. They think they are better than everyone else. They got a lot of money. They don't like us and we don't like them. When my class was changed, I didn't even dress for gym. So I failed that too."

"Bernice, what seems to be the rub with those high class kids?"

"Well, they seem to look down on us kids in this neighborhood. You know, they think we are scabs. You know, those kids always hung out on the east side of the building and us kids were always on the west side. Then in class, the rich kids always had their lessons. They never came without their lessons. Then if us kids didn't have ours, and we usually didn't, they would look at us. There were only two girls, Sally Clancy and Georgia Lane that I could get along with out of that bunch. I guess it's a good thing I quit school because whenever there was any trouble, I was in the middle of it, street fights or anything else. It seems like it has been that way all my life. My temper gets me into trouble. I slap and ask questions later. That's the way my Mother and Dad were and I guess that's the way I am" (**29**, 13–14).

A high positive correlation between school achievement and social class is found in Sao Paulo, Brazil, in the elementary school but not in the secondary school (**44**). The secondary schools of Brazil enroll students primarily from the upper social class. The home life of the children in Sao Paulo may vary from that in the United States, but the relations with intelligence and achievement in the elementary school seem to be much the same. In Scotland, a high correlation also is noted between occupational class and school achievement (**58**).

The effects of social class continue into higher education. A high proportion of students from families of the upper social class attend college, and a relatively small number of those from the lower social class do (**11**). Already in the ninth grade there is a substantial correlation between the social class of parents and the attitudes of ninth-grade pupils toward higher education. The higher the social class, the more favorable is the attitude toward higher education (**31**). In the British Isles, more grammar-school boys of the middle class desire to continue their education than do boys of the lower social class (**3**).

A strong protest is now being raised against currently used intelligence tests on the grounds that they discriminate against children from the lower socioeconomic classes. The same protest has been made before (**12**). After stating that a large majority of the teachers are from the middle class, Davis noted that the values of the American public school system are middle-class oriented. He lamented the verbal emphasis in intelligence tests and criticized homogeneous grouping:

. . . What proportion of the *basic mental problems* met by children (and by adults for that matter) in their daily life can be solved by having a large standard vocabulary, or skill in reading, or skill in arithmetic processes?

. . . Segregated from each other, unable therefore either to stimulate or to imitate each other, each group fails to learn well those problem-solving activities and insights in which the other group excels. Both groups lose more than they gain (12, 96, 98).

In order to permit the lower class a fair chance on intelligence tests, the Davis-Eells Games were developed which require reasoning but deal with everyday problems (13). Although the test does not predict academic performance under current teaching methods as well as other intelligence tests that rely more heavily on words and other symbols, it is designed to locate pupils for whom different teaching approaches are indicated. The task of devising a "culture fair" intelligence test is not easy, and it is entirely possible that adequate measures of general intellectual ability cannot be obtained merely by revising existing intelligence tests to remove their middle-class bias (24). The basic criticism that Davis raises is parried, but not belittled, by Cronbach:

. . . Fundamental as this argument is, it has limited practical significance at this moment, because neither Davis nor anyone else has suggested what educational methods should be used with the lower class. When and if new methods for this purpose are found, the tests that predict success may be different from those now used by schools (9, 242).

Davis does not confine his comments to testing alone but directs them at the middle-class bias of the public schools. In a recent and highly related discussion, the "philosophy of immediate gratification" is presented as the basic motivational pattern of lower-class children (47). The lower-class child does not have a predictable nor financially secure future; he has less opportunity to learn how to sacrifice immediate goals in favor of long-range goals that may be more rewarding. Teachers often fail to take this into account in dealing with lower-class pupils; you cannot eat a gold star.

In effect, the discussion above points up the difficult time that is forecast for the lower-class child in our educational system. As is shown in Fig. 4.12, the child who is either low in academic ability or from the lower socioeconomic class has barriers to hurdle in order to achieve happiness and progress in school. The child who is low in both

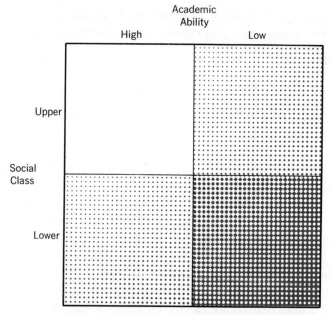

Fig. 4.12   Difficulty in adjusting to and succeeding in middle-class oriented schools. (Difficulty indicated by shading.)

academic ability and social class falls in the "cell of double jeopardy,"
and his attainment of success and contentment in school is exceptionally difficult.

Recapitulating, we find that home and neighborhood background,
reflected in the concept of social class, are powerful forces affecting
learning efficiency, as schools and educational practices are now organized. Children who come from family situations characterized by
low income, low educational attainment, low interest in schooling, and
unfavorable attitudes toward education find schooling less profitable
than do other children. Their low achievement and other educational
problems should no longer be rationalized away with terms such as
lazy, emotionally immature, of *low intellectual ability,* and *antisocial.*

SUMMARY

Our conceptions of readiness for learning and upper limits of learning
have changed markedly in recent years. We now recognize that subject matter can be organized and presented in such a manner that many
children can learn important concepts and skills at younger ages than
previously assumed. Also, environmental influences, including school-

ing, are being given increasing emphasis in comparison with heredity. No longer do we accept the notion that how well children achieve is determined at conception. The home, neighborhood, and school environments markedly influence what children learn and are closely associated with whether the students' abilities are developed fully.

No matter how the environment is manipulated, however, readiness among children of the same age for particular learning tasks varies markedly because of differences among children in the cognitive, psychomotor, and affective domains. The principal differences among pupils in the cognitive domain are in general intellectual ability, specific intellectual abilities, and previous experience related to the task. Likewise, pupils differ in the level of psychomotor abilities and physical characteristics. Interests, attitudes, values, and personality integration are important variables in the affective domain. These characteristics of students and other factors including sex, home background, and social class are associated not only with readiness for learning, but also with efficiency of learning after students have started a task. Even when a group of students starts at about the same level of achievement, marked differences subsequently occur in how well they learn. One of the most important tasks of teaching is to arrange instruction in line with the students' abilities and other characteristics.

QUESTIONS AND ACTIVITIES

1. a. What is meant by readiness for learning?
   b. Discuss some practices that violate knowledge about readiness for learning.
   c. How is efficiency of learning related to readiness for learning?

2. a. To what extent is efficiency of learning influenced by these factors in the cognitive domain: general intellectual ability, specific intellectual abilities, and previous experience or achievement, related to the task?
   b. To what extent are each of the above factors influenced by environment?

3. a. How have ideas regarding general intellectual ability changed in recent times?
   b. How stable are IQ and achievement from childhood into adulthood?

4. a. How variable are individuals of the same chronological age in psychomotor abilities and physical characteristics?
   b. What is the relationship between physical characteristics and school achievement in childhood?
   c. Discuss the relationships among skeletal development and social-emotional development during adolescence.

5. a. How variable are individuals

of the same chronological age in affective characteristics?

b. Which variable in the affective domain seems most closely associated with readiness for learning? efficiency of learning over a long period of time? Discuss your choices.

6. a. Related to your interest in subject matter and level of school, rank from highest to lowest the following variables from the standpoint of their importance in determining readiness for learning of a specific task that you designate: general intellectual ability, specific intellectual abilities, previous achievement, physical characteristics, psychomotor abilities, interests, attitudes, values, and personality integration.

b. Indicate why you selected the top and bottom variable.

7. What are the main implications of developmental tasks for educational practices?

8. a. Discuss briefly the characteristics and performances in which boys and girls on the average are most different.

b. How do the differences between the average scores of boys and girls compare in magnitude with the differences between individuals of the same sex?

c. Assume that students are to be grouped on the basis of similarity of reading achievement. To what extent will boys and girls be placed in the same groups? Explain.

9. List and discuss briefly three generalizations about the relationship among home background, social class, and education.

10. a. To what extent is the teacher limited in promoting efficient learning by the home and social-class background of the student?

b. If given the choice, in what kind of community would you prefer to teach? Why?

SUGGESTIONS FOR FURTHER READING

Bayley, Nancy. On the growth of intelligence. *Amer. Psychologist*, 1955, **10**, 805–818. (In DeCecco, 1963, 456–478.)

Bronfenbrenner, U. The changing American child: A speculative analysis. *J. soc. Issues*, 1961, **17**, 6–18. (In Seidman, 1965, 15–23.)

Canning, R. R. Does an honor system reduce classroom cheating? An experimental answer. *J. exp. Educ.*, 1956, **24**, 291–296. (In Page, 1964, 391–397.)

Charters, W. W., Jr. Social class and intelligence tests. In W. W. Charters, Jr., & N. L. Gage (Eds.). *Readings in the social psychology of education.* Boston: Allyn & Bacon, 1963, pp. 12–21.

Coleman, J. S. Social climates in high schools. *Coop. Res. Monogr.*, No. 4.

Washington, D. C.: U. S. Office of Education, 1961. Portions reprinted under the title "The adolescent culture"; in Gordon, 1965, 351–363; in Seidman, 1965, 30–41.)

Feldhusen, J. F., & H. J. Klausmeier. Anxiety, intelligence, and achievement in children of low, average, and high intelligence. *Child Develpm.*, 1962, **33**, 403–409. (In Ripple, 1964, 83–89.)

Guilford, J. P. Three faces of intellect. *Amer. Psychologist*, 1959, **14**, 469–479. (In Anderson & Ausubel, 1965, 194–214; Crow & Crow, 1963, 270–287; DeCecco, 1963, 435–456; Gordon, 1965, 23–33; and Ripple, 1964, 46–64.)

Harlow, H. F. The nature of love. *Amer. Psychologist*, 1958, **13**, 673–685. (In Gordon, 1965, 140–150.)

Harris, D. B. Sex differences in the life problems and interests of adolescents, 1935 and 1957. *Child Develpm.*, 1959, **30**, 453–459. (In Grinder, 1963, 219–226; and Ripple, 1964, 128–134.)

Harsh, R. Intelligence: Its nature and measurement. *Nat. elem. Principal*, 1961, **41** (1), 23–28. (In Crow & Crow, 1963, 252–261.)

Kohn, M. L. Social class and parental values. *Amer. J. Sociol.*, 1959, **64**, 337–351. (In Grinder, 1963, 187–207; and Mussen, Conger, & Kagan, 1965, 345–366.)

Lehmann, I. J. Changes in critical thinking, attitudes, and values from freshman to senior years. *J. educ. Psychol.*, 1963, **54**, 305–315. (In Seidman, 1965, 282–291.)

Mussen, P. H., & Mary C. Jones. Self-conceptions, motivations, and inter-personal attitudes of late—and early—maturing boys. *Child Develpm.*, 1957, **28**, (2), 243–256. (In Gordon, 1965, 325–333; Mussen, Conger, & Kagan, 1965, 419–434; under the title "Late and early maturing boys" in Page, 1964, 70–82; and in Rosenblith & Allinsmith, 1962, 43–51.)

Rarick, G. L., & W. Reddan. Youth fitness and health. *Rev. educ. Res.*, 1962, **32**, 515–529.

Remmers, H. H., & R. D. Franklin. Sweet land of liberty. *Phi Delta Kappan*, 1962, **44**, 22–27. (In Seidman, 1965, 243–249.)

REFERENCES

1. Anderson, K. E., T. C. Page, & H. A. Smith. A study of the variability of exceptional high school seniors in science and other academic areas. *Sci. Educ.*, 1958, **42**, 42–59.

2. Bayley, Nancy. On the growth of intelligence. *Amer. Psychologist*, 1955, **10**, 805–818.

3. Bene, Eva. Some differences between working class and middle class grammar school boys in their attitudes toward education. *Brit. J. Sociol.*, 1959, **10**, 148–152.

4. Blommers, P., Lotus M. Knief, & J. B. Stroud. The organismic age concept, *J. educ. Psychol.*, 1955, **46**, 142–150.

5. Bloom, B. S. *Stability and change in human characteristics.* New York: Wiley, 1964.

6. Bradway, Katherine P., & Clare W. Thompson. Intelligence at adulthood: A twenty-five year follow-up. *J. educ. Psychol.*, 1962, **53**, 1–14.

7. Bruner, J. S. *The process of education.* Cambridge: Harvard, 1961.

8. Clancy, Nora, & Faith Smitter. A study of emotionally disturbed children in Santa Barbara county schools. *Calif. J. educ. Res.*, 1953, **4**, 209–222.

9. Cronbach, L. J. *Essentials of psychological testing.* (2nd ed.) New York: Harper & Row, 1960.

10. Cutright, Prudence. Script-print and beginning reading and spelling. *Elem. Engl. Rev.*, 1936, **13**, 139–141.

11. Davie, J. S. Social class factors and school attendance. *Harv. educ. Rev.*, 1953, **23**, 175–185.

12. Davis, A. *Social-class influences upon learning.* Cambridge: Harvard, 1948.

13. Davis, A., & K. Eells. *Davis-Eells Games.* New York: Harcourt, Brace & World, 1953.

14. Drews, Elizabeth M., & J. E. Teahan. Parental attitudes and academic achievement. *J. clin. Psychol.*, 1957, **13**, 328–332.

15. Enos, F. A study of the relationships between physical status, emotional adjustment, and friendship choices of fourth-grade children. Unpublished doctoral dissertation, Univer. Wisconsin, 1958.

16. Feldhusen, J. F., & H. J. Klaus-

meier. Achievement in counting and addition. *Elem. Sch. J.,* 1959, **59**, 388–393.

17. Feldhusen, J. F., & H. J. Klausmeier. Anxiety, intelligence, and achievement in children of low, average, and high intelligence. *Child Develpm.,* 1962, **33**, 403–409.

18. Findley, W. G. Purposes of school testing programs and their efficient development. In W. G. Findley (Ed.), *The impact and improvement of school testing programs.* Yearb. nat. Soc. Stud. Educ., 1963, **62**, Part II., pp. 1–27.

19. Flanagan, J. C., *et al. Project TALENT: The identification, development, and utilization of human talents: The American high school student.* Pittsburgh: The Univer. of Pittsburgh Press, 1964.

20. Gates, A. I. The necessary mental age for beginning reading. *Elem. Sch. J.,* 1937, **37**, 497–508.

21. Gleason, G. T., & H. J. Klausmeier. The relationship between variability in physical growth and academic achievement among third- and fifth-grade children. *J. educ. Res.,* 1958, **51**, 521–527.

22. Grinder, R. E. Parental childbearing practices, conscience, and resistance to temptation of sixth-grade children. *Child Develpm.,* 1962, **33**, 803–820.

23. Gronlund, N. E., & L. Anderson. Personality characteristics of socially accepted, socially neglected, and socially rejected junior high school pupils. *Educ. Admin. Supervis.,* 1957, **43**, 329–338.

24. Haggard, E. A. Social-status and intelligence: An experimental study of certain cultural determinants of measured intelligence. *Genet. Psychol. Monogr.,* 1954, **49**, 141–186.

25. Hartshorne, H., & M. A. May. *Studies in the nature of character: I. Studies in deceit.* New York: Macmillan, 1928.

26. Havighurst, R. J. *Human development and education.* New York: Longmans, 1953.

27. Havighurst, R. J., & Fay H. Breese. Relations between ability and social status in a midwestern community: III. Primary mental abilities. *J. educ. Psychol.,* 1947, **38**, 241–247.

28. Havighurst, R. J., & Leota L. Janke. Relations between ability and social status in a midwestern community. I. Ten-year-old children. *J. educ. Psychol.,* 1944, **35**, 357–368.

29. Havighurst, R. J., *et al. Growing up in River City.* New York: Wiley, 1962.

30. Hicklin, W. J. A study of long-range techniques for predicting patterns of scholastic behavior. Unpublished doctoral dissertation, Univer. Chicago, 1962.

31. Hieronymus, A. N. A study of social class motivation: Relationships between anxiety for education and certain socio-economic and intellectual variables. *J. educ. Psychol.,* 1951, **42**, 193–205.

32. Hunsicker, P. A. *Youth fitness test manual.* Washington, D.C.: American Association for Health, Physical Education, and Recreation, National Education Association, 1958.

33. Hunt, J. M. *Intelligence and experience.* New York: Ronald, 1961.

34. Hunter, E. C. Changes in scores of college students on the American Council Psychological Examination at yearly intervals during the college course. *J. educ. Res.,* 1942, **36**, 284–291.

35. Janke, Leota L., & R. J. Havighurst. Relations between ability and social status in a midwestern community: II. Sixteen-year-old boys and girls. *J. educ. Psychol.,* 1945, **36**, 499–509.

36. Jersild, A. T., & Ruth Tasch. *Children's interests and what they suggest for education.* New York: Bureau of Publications, Teachers

College, Columbia Univer., 1949.

37. Johnson, Elizabeth S., & Caroline E. Legg. Why young people leave school. *Bull. Nat. Ass. Sec. Sch. Principals*, 1948, **32**, 14–24.

38. Jones, Mary C. A study of socialization patterns at the high school level. *J. genet. Psychol.*, 1958, **93**, 87–111.

39. Kagan, J., & M. Freeman. Relation of childhood intelligence, maternal behaviors, and social class to behavior during adolescence. *Child Develpm.*, 1963, **34**, 899–911.

40. Klausmeier, H. J., A. Beeman, & I. J. Lehmann. Comparison of organismic age and regression equations in predicting achievements in elementary school. *J. educ. Psychol.*, 1958, **49**, 182–186.

41. Klausmeier, H. J., J. Feldhusen, & J. Check. *An analysis of learning efficiency in arithmetic of mentally retarded children in comparison with children of average and high intelligence.* U. S. Office of Education Cooperative Research Project No. 153. Madison: Univer. Wisconsin, 1959.

42. Klausmeier, H. J., C. W. Harris, & Z. Ethnathios. Relationships between divergent thinking abilities and teacher ratings of high school students. *J. educ. Psychol.*, 1962, **53**, 72–75.

43. Klausmeier, H. J., & W. Wiersma. Relationship of sex, grade level, and locale to performance of high IQ students on divergent thinking tests. *J. educ. Psychol.*, 1964, **55**, 114–119.

44. Lindgren, H. C., & Hilda Guedes. Social status, intelligence, and educational achievement among elementary and secondary students in Sao Paulo, Brazil. *J. soc. Psychol.*, 1963, **60**, 9–14.

45. Meyer, G. R. Factors related to scientific attitudes within the secondary schools of an Australian city. *Aust. J. Educ.*, 1963, **7**, 21–40.

46. Millard, C. V. *Child growth and development.* Boston: Heath, 1951.

47. Mussen, P. H., J. J. Conger, & J. Kagan. *Child development and personality.* (2nd ed.) New York: Harper & Row, 1963.

48. National Education Association. High-school drop-outs. *NEA Res. Bull.*, 1960, **38**, 11–14.

49. Olson, W. C. *Child development.* Boston: Heath, 1949.

50. Olson, W. C., & B. Hughes. Growth of the child as a whole. In R. G. Barker (Ed.), *Child behavior and development.* New York: McGraw-Hill, 1943, pp. 199–208.

51. Petersen, H., J. P. Guilford, R. Hoepfner, & P. R. Merrifield. Determination of "structure-of-intellect" abilities involved in ninth-grade algebra and general mathematics. *Rep. psychol. Lab.*, No. 31. Los Angeles: Univer. Southern Calif., 1963.

52. Ringness, T. A. Self concept of children of low, average, and high intelligence. *Amer. J. ment. Def.*, 1961, **65**, 453–461.

53. Russell, D. H. A diagnostic study of spelling readiness. *J. educ. Res.*, 1943, **37**, 276–283.

54. Scannell, D. P. Differential prediction of academic success from achievement test scores. Unpublished doctoral dissertation, State Univer. Iowa, 1958.

55. Schoeppe, Aileen, E. A. Haggard, & R. J. Havighurst. Some factors affecting sixteen-year olds' success in five developmental tasks. *J. abnorm. soc. Psychol.*, 1953, **48**, 42–52.

56. Schoeppe, Aileen, & R. J. Havighurst. A validation of development and adjustment hypotheses of adolescence. *J. educ. Psychol.*, 1952, **43**, 339–353.

57. Schreiber, D. The dropout and the delinquent: Promising practices gleaned from a year of study. *Phi Delta Kappan*, 1963, **44**, 215–221.

135

58. Scottish Council for Research in Education. *Social implications of the 1947 Scottish mental survey.* London: Univer. London Press, Ltd., 1953.

59. Sheldon, W. D., & W. C. Cutts. Relation of parents, home, and certain developmental characteristics to children's reading ability: II. *Elem. Sch. J.,* 1953, **53**, 517–521.

60. Sontag, L. W., C. T. Baker, & Virginia L. Nelson. Mental growth and personality development: A longitudinal study. *Monogr. Soc. Res. Child Develpm.,* 1958, **23**, 1–143.

61. Stone, C. P., & R. G. Barker. The attitudes and interests of pre-menarcheal and post-menarcheal girls. *J. genet. Psychol.,* 1939, **54**, 27–71.

62. Terman, L. M., & Maud A. Merrill. *Measuring intelligence.* Boston: Houghton Mifflin, 1937.

63. Terman, L. M., & Melita H. Oden. *The gifted group at mid-life.* Stanford: Stanford, 1959.

64. Terman, L. M., & Leona E. Tyler. Psychological sex differences. In L. Carmichael (Ed.), *Manual of child psychology.* New York: Wiley, 1954, pp. 1064–1114.

65. Torrance, E. P. Factors affecting creative thinking in children: An interim research report. *Merrill-Palmer Quart.,* 1961, **7**, 171–180.

66. Tozer, A. H. D., & H. J. C. Larwood. The changes in intelligence test scores of students between the beginning and end of their university courses. *Brit. J. educ. Psychol.,* 1958, **28**, 120–128.

67. Traxler, A. E. Reading growth of secondary–school pupils during a five–year period. Achievement Testing Program in Independent Schools and Supplementary Studies. *Educ. Records Bull.,* 1950, **54**, 96–107.

68. Tyler, F. T. Concepts of organismic growth: A critique. *J. educ. Psychol.,* 1953, **44**, 321–342.

69. United States Bureau of the Census. *Statistical abstract of the United States.* (84th ed.) Washington, D.C.: U.S. Government Printing Office, 1963.

70. Warner, W. L., & P. S. Lunt. *Social life of a modern community.* New Haven: Yale, 1941.

71. Washburne, C. Mental age and the arithmetic curriculum: A summary of the Committee of Seven Grade-Placement Investigations to date. *J. educ. Res.,* 1931, **23**, 210–231.

CHAPTER 5

Teacher Characteristics and Pupil Learning

TEACHERS are not and should not be identical personalities. They represent a wide variety of personal and professional characteristics. In spite of this, anyone who continues to act as a teacher should be effective with students and should help them learn efficiently. This poses the question of how the effectiveness of teaching is determined. Until recently, many people have assumed that a teacher is uniformly good in all teaching activities with all children. For example, if a teacher does well with slow learners, it is assumed that he will also do well with gifted learners. Too, some assume that the same characteristics associated with success in teaching home economics will also be related to success in teaching chemistry or physics. These assumptions have undoubtedly arisen in connection with the evaluation of poor teachers; if a teacher is sufficiently poor in one activity or characteristic, no matter how good he may be in others, he loses his job and is classified as poor. Nevertheless, we are now recognizing that different patterns of characteristics may be associated, for example, with teaching in the primary school and in the senior high school. Further, the same teacher may not be equally good in organizing subject matter, maintaining discipline, and counseling students.

Substantial agreement has not yet been reached concerning the criteria of successful teaching. At the present, three main types of criteria are used as shown in Table 5.1 (**29**). One of these is the *product*, or what is learned. Persons who prefer this criterion think that the best test of teacher effectiveness is in terms of how much and how well students learn. This includes student learning in all domains—cognitive, psychomotor, and affective—in accordance with the objectives of education. A second set of criteria deals with *processes*. Judgments about the teacher's effectiveness are made in terms of what the teacher does, what the students do, the interactions between teacher and student, or all three. Some judge effectiveness in terms of teacher behavior, not in terms of student achievement. To use process criteria, observations must be made in the classroom. The final set of criteria is called *presage* and is indirect. Judgments are made about the teacher's effectiveness on the basis of his intellectual ability, grades made in college, personal appearance, and many other characteristics.

TABLE 5.1.

Criteria of Success in Teaching

Criterion	Examples	How Assessed
Product	Student gain in subject matter knowledge and related abilities Student gain in psychomotor skills and related abilities Student gain in interests, attitudes, personality integration, and other affective characteristics	Directly with tests and performance ratings before, during, and after instruction
Process	Teacher behaviors, such as explaining, questioning, leading a discussion, counseling, evaluating Student behaviors, such as courtesy, industriousness, attentiveness, conducting an experiment, leading a discussion Student-teaching interactions, such as teacher-directed and student-directed exchanges, information exchange, warmth	Directly through observations of the teacher and students during instruction in the classroom
Presage	Intellectual abilities of the teacher, amount of college work completed in the teaching major, grade-point average in college, personal characteristics, and others	Indirectly from college records, tests, ratings outside the classroom

Source: Based on H. E. Mitzel. Teacher effectiveness. In C. W. Harris (Ed.), *Encyclopedia of educational research.* New York: Macmillan, 1960.

The most widely used means of assessing teacher effectiveness are rating the teacher on the presage and process criteria and securing product information through testing the students (1). Examination of some presage criteria in the cognitive domain in relation to general teaching effectiveness will reveal some specific characteristics associated with successful teaching. Some patterns related to school levels and subject fields also will be given.

COGNITIVE ABILITIES
AND INTELLECTUAL CHARACTERISTICS

Three decades ago, teachers who were rated excellent, even distinguished, had higher general intellectual ability than did those who were rated average or failing. The superior group had a higher grade-point average while in college. No difference was noted between the average and failing group (39). Very recently, academic grade-point average and the grade in student teaching were related positively and significantly to administrators' rating of teachers on two criteria—preparation of subject matter and discipline. Faculty rating of the prospective teacher's appearance (noncognitive characteristic, of course) was also correlated significantly with three subsequent ratings by the administrator of the teachers' ability—preparation of subject matter, discipline, and tact with students (41). These two studies are typical of many which report a low but positive relationship between teaching effectiveness and general intellectual ability, academic grade-point average, and student-teaching grade.

Another variable in the cognitive domain which is frequently associated with teaching success is preparation in the major subject field. To learn more about this, principals were invited to nominate only highly superior and exceedingly poor teachers (32). The principals nominated 43 superior and 27 poor elementary teachers, 85 superior and 70 poor English and social-studies teachers, and 82 superior and 71 poor mathematics and science teachers. The elementary teachers represented 30 states; the English and social-studies teachers 32 states; and the mathematics and science teachers, 38 states. In no case did a principal suggest that a poor teacher had too much subject-matter preparation. On the contrary, 36 percent of the poor English and social-studies teachers were judged poor because of lack of subject-matter teaching ability, and 61 percent of the superior mathematics and science teachers were said to possess ability to teach subject matter as their outstanding characteristic.

What effect does the teacher's knowledge of the students have on their achievement and attitudes? Eighth-grade teachers of English, mathematics, and social studies were put into three groups and a different treatment was carried out with each group (18). One group was given no information about the pupils. The second group was given only the results of an intelligence test for each pupil and achievement test results in English, social studies, and mathematics. The third group was given all the test information plus a pupil information blank and was encouraged to discover all it could of significance about each pupil. Further, Hoyt helped the last two groups in understanding the information. No difference resulted in student achievement in any subject; however, the teacher's increased knowledge of the pupils resulted in improved attitudes of the pupils toward the teachers.

Slightly different results were obtained when teachers were given no information and much information about the pupils (30). Considerable information about each pupil was given to the experimental group of teachers, and the investigator assisted the teachers in understanding the information. Students in the experimental group made a significantly greater academic gain than did the students in the control group—those whose teachers were not given information. Further, the pupils in the experimental group showed better attitudes toward school and better general adjustment to school and to their classmates than did those in the control group. The teachers' knowledge of the pupils resulted in more effective guidance of academic learning and in better personality development in the pupil.

Although the interaction between the teacher and student is discussed in Chapter 6, we will consider interaction as well as teacher characteristics briefly at this point. The relationship between mathematical achievement of high school pupils and certain factors relating to the teacher, the teaching process, the pupils, and the school were ascertained for 3919 pupils in 102 elementary algebra classes and in 94 geometry classes (37). From this large sample were secured achievement measures of the pupils and other characteristics, characteristics of their teachers, the teaching practices employed, and the school in which the pupils were enrolled. A synthesis of the conclusions merits close attention:

1. Sex of pupils was not related to achievement in algebra, but it was in geometry, where boys achieved higher than girls.
2. Higher achievement was found in the schools with enrollments of 100 to 500 than in smaller or larger schools.

3. Higher achievement in algebra was found in classes of 20 to 30 pupils than in larger classes.
4. Algebra classes taught by teachers with more than eight years of experience achieved significantly higher than classes taught by teachers with less than eight years of experience.
5. Algebra classes taught by teachers who were graduates of state universities or privately operated schools achieved significantly higher than classes taught by graduates of state teachers colleges.
6. Algebra classes in which differentiated assignments for pupils were used achieved significantly higher than classes where they were seldom or never used.
7. Algebra classes in which life applications of mathematics were regularly studied achieved significantly higher than those where life applications were not studied.
8. Supervised study of 20 to 30 minutes per class period in both algebra and geometry resulted in higher pupil achievement than did less supervised study.

Equally interesting were some factors not associated with algebra achievement: sex of pupil, previous education in rural or urban schools, type of secondary school, and amount of the teachers' education in mathematics. In geometry also, a number of factors, including years of previous teaching experience, the amount of the teachers' education in mathematics, and the type of institution from which the teacher was graduated, were not related to pupil achievement.

Intellectual ability, total grade-point average in college, subject-matter preparation, information of a professional nature about child development and learning, and student-teaching grade are related to teaching effectiveness. However, the correlations between teaching success and these cognitive abilities and characteristics are quite low and are useful primarily in an actuarial sense of predicting the effectiveness of groups but not of individuals.

Why are high intelligence, good preparation while in college, and high achievement not more highly correlated with later teaching success? First, most prospective teachers who are graduated have above average intelligence, average or above-average achievement while in college, and fairly good preparation in one or more subject-matter fields. The low-ability and low-achieving students are eliminated before college graduation. Therefore, the relationship between IQ and teaching success is low since only those of higher ability teach. Second, the criteria of teaching success are often not well established in the varying situations in which teachers work. For example, supervisors or principals do not use the same criteria in judging teaching success. Third, it is possible that somehow our educational arrangements have become so institutionalized that the very bright and high-achieving students in college do not accept a first position, do not teach for an extended number of years, or do not subsequently find challenges in a teaching position. A large number of highly intelligent, high-achieving teachers are found in classrooms from kindergarten through twelfth grade. One would expect that a considerable amount of children's literature, literature for adolescents, musical compositions suitable for children, and art objects would be produced by these intelligent, high-achieving teachers. This is not the case at present. Apparently, the teachers who show considerable creativity and produce literature, art, or music do not remain long in the classroom but go into other fields. Further, neither society generally nor teachers themselves appear to accept productivity in music, art, literature, or other fields as desirable activity in addition to teaching.

PSYCHOMOTOR ABILITIES

An important objective of education is to help learners acquire skill in such activities as handwriting, shorthand, typing, and mechanical drawing; in dance, the fine arts, and instrumental and vocal music; in manipulating such materials as wood, metals, fabrics, and chemicals; in using tools and measuring and recording devices in the sciences, arts, and other fields. To perform motor activities efficiently, strength, speed, precision, coordination, and flexibility are required; still other skills may be required in superior vocal performances. To what extent should the teacher be highly skilled in the perceptual motor skills that the learners should acquire?

An important instructional principle related to perceptual motor learning is that the teacher should understand the nature of the skill to be taught and should be able to demonstrate it. It is assumed, for example, that, if children are to acquire efficiency in handwriting, the teacher must understand the nature of handwriting, provide a good model, and be able to help children overcome errors. In foreign language instruction also, the teacher must speak the language well if children are to learn efficiently from imitating the teacher. Similarly, in music, art, home economics, agriculture, and other fields, it is considered desirable for the teacher to be able to demonstrate the skills to be learned. The general recommendation for guiding experimentation by pupils in science is that the teacher should first have conducted the experiment himself and be able to demonstrate it. Good psychomotor abilities and related physical characteristics are probably as essential in some fields of teaching as are verbal or mathematical abilities in other fields.

AFFECTIVE CHARACTERISTICS

The range of differences among teachers in interests, attitudes, values, and personality integration is greater than that in general intellectual ability and other variables in the cognitive domain, or in physical characteristics. Also, for effective teaching in most subjects, the affective characteristics are more important than those in the psychomotor domain (Fig. 5.1). In addition to observations of teachers a number of tests have been used to assess affective characteristics. Among the tests are the Minnesota Teacher Attitude Inventory, the Allport-Vernon-Lindzey Study of Values, the Strong Vocational Interest Blank, the Minnesota Multiphasic Personality Inventory, and the Guilford-Zimmerman Temperament Survey. These are all written inventories and are adminis-

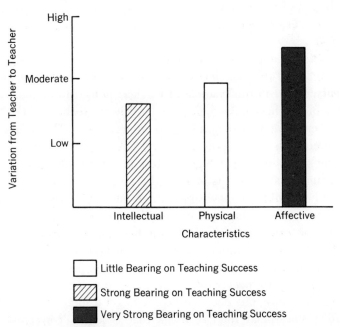

Fig. 5.1.   Teachers vary in the characteristics associated with teaching success.

tered according to standardized procedures that are given in the manuals accompanying the tests. Some projective techniques are also used in assessing teacher characteristics and personality, including the Rorschach Ink Blot Test and the Thematic Apperception Test. In projective testing, the test administrator usually presents stimulus material to which the respondent gives oral responses. The tester, usually a clinical psychologist, develops a protocol (based on these responses) from which he makes inferences about the respondent's personality. More information is given about tests in the affective domain in Chapter 16. A quick survey of these tests may prove helpful prior to reading the material on interests, attitudes, values, and personality integration of teachers.

Interests

A person's interests are assessed by knowing his favorite activities. The most and least successful student teachers were administered an appropriate form of the Strong Vocational Interest Blank. The most successful group showed higher social-service and intellectual interests than did the least successful group. Working with things, working by themselves, and working with people in a manipulative capacity for purposes of personal gain were of higher interest to the least successful group (36).

Ryans has done considerable work in the area of teacher characteristics (33, 34). Table 5.2 shows interests and other characteristics, to be discussed later in this chapter, of teachers judged to be more effective and of teachers judged to be relatively ineffective (34). These teachers represent various grades and subject fields. The information was secured with a self-report inventory. The better elementary teachers in the group indicated high interest in reading, literary matters, music, painting, and the arts in general. The less effective teachers, on the other hand, did not show similar high interests in these areas.

In the preceding paragraph, we noted a difference among teachers in interests as expressed directly by the teachers in response to questions. The Strong Vocational Interest Blank and other standardized interest inventories are constructed on the assumption that interests differ according to occupations, including different specialities in teaching. Therefore, one does not expect to get a total test score from the Strong Vocational Interest Blank that is highly correlated with teaching effectiveness generally. However, when part scores are examined, differences are sometimes found (36).

Attitudes and Values

Attitudes toward the behavior problems of students continue to be of interest to many people, apparently on the assumption that teachers who hold unfavorable attitudes do not work effectively with the problem students. Further, because certain behavior is rewarded and other behavior is punished, the behavior which teachers regard as serious is likely to be punished. Many years ago, Wickman observed marked differences between teachers' and clinicians' judgments about what constitutes serious behavior problems in children (**47**). Teachers in Wickman's study rated as most serious aggressive behaviors such as stealing, truancy, cheating, and impertinence. Experts, on the other hand, rated withdrawing and unhappy behaviors such as shyness, fearfulness, and suspiciousness as most serious. Ellis and Miller found somewhat the same pattern, as shown in Fig. 5.1, with mental hygienists judging as most serious such behaviors as withdrawing, suspiciousness, unhappiness, resentfulness, fearfulness, cruelty, being easily discouraged, suggestibility, overcriticalness, and sensitiveness (**11**). Teachers judged forms of behavior such as stealing, heterosexual activity, unreliableness, and untruthfulness as most serious. However, as shown in Fig. 5.2, the Denver teachers were more like the experts than were Wickman's teachers.

Somewhat like Ellis and Miller, Stouffer concluded that high school teachers had changed their attitudes somewhat but that clinicians or mental health experts had changed very little since 1927 (**42**). Apparently because of the role high school teachers must assume, they still rated extrovertive actions of the pupils such as impatience, destroying school property, disobedience, interest in the opposite sex, and profanity and inquisitiveness as most serious. The mental hygienists still rated withdrawing behaviors as being most serious.

All research since 1927, which has followed the pattern of the Wickman study, was summarized with these conclusions:

1. Differences existed in 1927 between the attitudes of teachers and clinicians toward the behavior problems of children. This seems to have been true in spite of the methodological limitations of the Wickman study.
2. Since 1927 there has been a shift in the hierarchy of teachers' attitudes to approximate more closely those of clinicians. This shift is not due to an artifact of research methodology. Those studies which incorporate adequate controls and consistent instructions show even greater congruence between the attitudes of the two groups.
3. There has been some change in the attitude of clinicians although this is based upon the conclusions of one study.

TABLE 5.2.

Personal Qualities Which Appear to Distinguish Teachers Selected to be "High" and "Low" with Respect to Overall Classroom Behavior

Characteristics of "High" Group Teachers

Elementary Teachers	Secondary Teachers	Elementary-Secondary Teachers Combined
A. "High" group members more frequently (than "low"):	A. "High" group members more frequently (than "low"):	A. "High" group members more frequently (than "low"):
1. Manifest extreme generosity in appraisals of the behavior and motives of other persons; express friendly feelings for others.	1. Manifest extreme generosity in appraisals of the behavior and motives of other persons; express friendly feelings for others.	1. Manifest extreme generosity in appraisals of the behavior and motives of other persons; express friendly feelings for others.
2. Indicate strong interest in reading and in literary matters.	2. Indicate strong interest in reading and in literary matters.	2. Indicate strong interest in reading and in literary matters.
3. Indicate interest in music, painting, and the arts in general.	3. Indicate interest in music, painting, and the arts in general.	3. Indicate interest in music, painting, and the arts in general.
4. Report participation in high school and college social groups.	4. Report participation in high school and college social groups.	4. Report participation in high school and college social groups.
5. Manifest prominent social service ideals.	5. Judge selves high in ambition and initiative.	5. Judge selves high in ambition and initiative.
6. Indicate preferences for activities which involve contact with people.	6. Report teaching experience of 4–9 years.	
7. Indicate interest in science and scientific matters.	7. Report teaching-type activities during childhood and adolescence.	
8. Report liking for outdoor activities.	8. Indicate preference for student-centered learning situations.	
9. Are young, or middle-aged.	9. Manifest independence, though not aggressiveness.	
10. Are married.		
11. Report that parental homes provided above-average cultural advantages.		
B. "High" group (compared with "low" group):	B. "High" group (compared with "low" group):	B. "High" group (compared with "low" group):
1. Indicates greater enjoyment of pupil relationships (i.e., more favorable pupil opinions).	1. Indicates greater enjoyment of pupil relationships (i.e., more favorable pupil opinions).	1. Indicates greater enjoyment of pupil relationships (i.e., more favorable pupil opinions).

2. Indicates greater preference for non-directive classroom procedures.
3. Is superior in verbal intelligence (I_{co} scores).
4. Is more satisfactory with regard to emotional adjustment (S_{co} scores).

A. "Low" group members more frequently (than "high"):
   1. Are from older age groups.
   2. Are restricted and critical in appraisals of the behavior and motives of other persons.
   3. Are unmarried.
   4. Indicate preferences for activities which do not involve close contacts with people.

B. "Low" group (compared with "high" group):
   1. Is less favorable in expressed opinions of pupils.
   2. Is less high with regard to verbal intelligence (I_{co} scores).
   3. Is less satisfactory with regard to emotional adjustment (S_{co} scores).

Characteristics of "Low" Group Teachers

A. "Low" group members more frequently (than "high"):
   1. Are from older age groups.
   2. Are restricted and critical in appraisals of the behavior and motives of other persons.
   3. Indicate preference for teacher-directed learning situations.
   4. Value exactness, orderliness, and "practical" things.
   5. Indicate preferences for activities which do not involve close contacts with people.

B. "Low" group (compared with "high" group):
   1. Is less favorable in expressed opinions of pupils.
   2. Is less high with regard to verbal intelligence (I_{co} scores).
   3. Is less satisfactory with regard to emotional adjustment (S_{co} scores).

2. Indicates greater preference for non-directive classroom procedures.
3. Is superior in verbal intelligence (I_{co} scores).
4. Is more satisfactory with regard to emotional adjustment (S_{co} scores).

A. "Low" group members more frequently (than "high"):
   1. Are from older age groups.
   2. Are restricted and critical in appraisals of the behavior and motives of other persons.
   3. Value exactness, orderliness, and "practical" things.
   4. Indicate preferences for activities which do not involve close contacts with people.

B. "Low" group (compared with "high" group):
   1. Is less favorable in expressed opinions of pupils.
   2. Is less high with regard to verbal intelligence (I_{co} scores).
   3. Is less satisfactory with regard to emotional adjustment (S_{co} scores).

Source: D. G. Ryans. *Characteristics of teachers: Their description, comparison, and appraisal.* Washington, D.C.: American Council on Education, 1960, pp. 360–361.

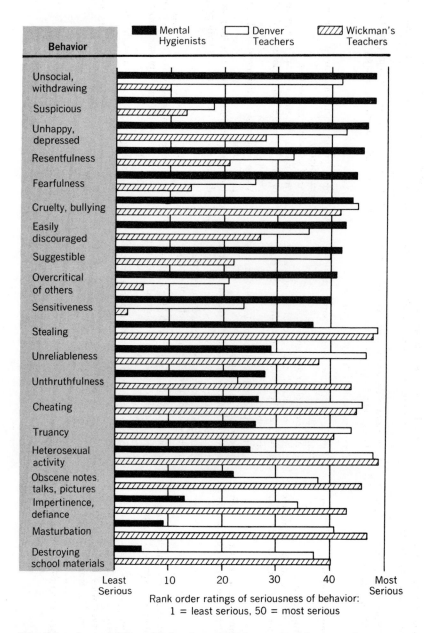

Fig. 5.2. A partial list of behavior problems as rated by mental hygienists and teachers. (Adapted from D. B. Ellis & L. W. Miller. Teachers' attitudes and child behavior problems. *J. educ. Psychol.*, 1936, **27**, 505.)

4. Criteria employed in evaluating the behavior problems of children differ for elementary and secondary school teachers.
5. More boys are identified as maladjusted than girls and the criteria of maladjustment (and adjustment) differ in part for each sex.
6. The sex of the teacher affects, in part, attitudes toward children's problems.
7. Studies of the relationships of socioeconomic factors to the evaluation of children's behavior problems are inadequately dealt with in the literature.

Differences in attitudes between teachers and clinicians are interpreted in the framework of role theory. The attitudinal hierarchies of teachers and clinicians are seen as reflecting their respective roles and the ways these roles influence the organization of their respective experiences. Wickman's findings of 1927 are interpreted as indicative of the role of the teacher in that era. The role expectations of teachers have changed. Replications of the Wickman study indicate these changes have resulted in greater congruence between teachers' and clinicians' attitudes. It is suggested by virtue of the teachers' essential task-orientation and the clinicians' adjustment-orientation that complete or nearly complete congruence is not likely to be achieved (3, 22).

Beilin does not expect teachers and clinical psychologists to rate pupil behavior identically. By the nature of their responsibilities, classroom teachers must be concerned about boisterous, aggressive behavior which disturbs the class and interferes with an orderly work situation. Clinicians typically work with one child at a time. They want the child to respond freely to them. Further, the clinician, because of his role, is less concerned about the child's immediate aggressive behavior and more concerned about his long-term adjustment. Withdrawal behavior indicates that the disturbed child has given up the fight against frustrating circumstances; the aggressive child is still fighting back to achieve a better feeling toward himself and is therefore considered to be less seriously maladjusted. The conclusions of Beilin seem to hold in other English-speaking countries also (13).

Attitudes may be reflected in punitiveness, especially in connection with what the teacher regards as essential to maintaining discipline. Punitiveness on the part of the teacher, in comparison with nonpunitiveness, affects how the child perceives misbehavior (22). Elementary school children who had punitive teachers, compared with those having nonpunitive teachers, manifested more aggression in their misconducts, were less concerned with learning and school situations, and also were unsettled and in conflict about misconduct. It is possible that children who have punitive teachers do not acquire as much trust of school as do those with nonpunitive teachers.

Some persons infer attitudes from test scores, rather than from observation. The Minnesota Teacher Attitude Inventory (MTAI), developed by Cook, Leeds, and Callis, purports to measure favorable attitudes toward students, toward a child-centered teaching-learning situation, and toward teaching in general (8). Over a short period of time in an instructional setting, the scores of the teachers and other educational personnel rise, as in the case of a two-week guidance workshop (40), and during student teaching (35). Further, large differences are noted among different school personnel. The order from the highest scores, indicating the most favorable attitudes, to the lowest are (1) guidance counselors, (2) elementary school teachers, (3) high school teachers, and (4) school administrators (2, 40). The relationship of the scores made by teachers and their subsequent teaching effectiveness has not been fully established, although there is a tendency for teachers with high scores to be liked better by students who have strong affective values toward teachers. If the students express strong cognitive values, the MTAI score of the teacher will make less difference (10).

The values held by teachers differ according to sex and to subject field (25). A number of interesting comparisons were drawn about 1700 teaching candidates to whom the Allport-Vernon-Lindzey Scale of Values was administered. Men preparing for teaching were lower in economic and higher in social values than were men in general. Women in education also scored lower on economic values than women generally. Women primary teachers were higher in aesthetic and social values and lower in economic values than women preparing to teach home economics. A main conclusion was that the differences in values among groups of education students according to school level and subject field was greater than was the difference between the entire group of education students and the population in general.

In another setting, the value scores of students while in college correlated significantly with their subsequent success in teaching two and four years after graduation (38). The two values associated with teaching success were economic and aesthetic. Teachers judged high in effectiveness scored low on the economic and high on the aesthetic value scales.

Personality Organization

The assessment of personality is complex; the establishment of relationships between teaching effectiveness and personality is even more complex. The use of the Minnesota Multiphasic Personality Inventory by Gowan (14) and the Guilford-Zimmerman Temperament Survey by Gowan and Gowan (15) present the teacher and the student in education as demonstrating psychologically favorable traits—sociable, emotionally stable, responsible, controlled, friendly, and secure. Prospective elementary and secondary teachers also perceive teachers as demonstrating five, socially approved traits, including a generally favorable evaluation characterized by such terms as *confident, good, cheerful, strong,* and *sociable;* restraint characterized by being reserved, restrained, and controlled; tenacity typified by stubbornness and control; predictability as identified with terms such as *sober, frank, polite, understanding,* and *admired;* and stability characterized by terms such as *calm, objective, unemotional, trusting,* and *quiet* (19).

A much discussed trait in all areas of human endeavor is enthusiasm. It is not identified as a separate trait on published scales or inventories, but in 19 of 20 classes in ten schools, teacher enthusiasm resulted in higher student achievement (26). In addition, the students were more favorable toward the enthusiastic teacher and to enthusiastically presented material. The differences in student achievement and in attitudes were large and consistent. This suggests that perhaps enthusiasm is a more powerful characteristic than many of those we have been discussing. A teacher's enthusiasm can obviously be impaired if he is dissatisfied. Some sources of dissatisfaction among a group of teachers in England were low salaries, poor human relations among staff, and a high teaching load (31). These are also mentioned frequently by American teachers.

Projective tests are more useful than are inventories in understanding personality integration and organization. Superior personality organization, good judgment and reasoning, the capacity to relate to others, and low aggression are the marks of effective teachers, according to Symonds and Dudek, who used the Rorschach Ink Plot Test to assess personality (43). These ratings of personality agree substantially with the traits previously mentioned as being characteristic of education students and effective teachers. Using a completely different method of gathering information, Ryans found emotional adjustment, favorable attitudes to students, generosity in appraisals of the behavior and motives of other persons, and participation in social and community affairs to be characteristic of more effective teachers (See Table 5.2).

AGE

Relatively little is known about the effectiveness of teachers of various ages. Superintendents of schools and other hiring officials recognize, however, that it is not wise to have a school staff comprised of teachers almost exclusively above or below age 45. Officials of large colleges, universities, and public school systems recognize that unmarried female teachers in the age range of 40 to 55 often experience rather severe emotional problems. At the same time, the present tendency is to reexamine compulsory retirement for men and women teachers at age 65 with a view of extending it to age 70 or beyond. While there are differences among younger, middle-aged, and older teachers as groups, some older individuals are exceedingly good teachers. Others, of course, are exceedingly poor, but the same holds for the middle and younger groups. Nevertheless, as shown in Table 5.2, older elementary and secondary teachers, in comparison with the younger and the middle-aged, are less effective in the classroom. Let us consider some of the effects of aging upon abilities in the cognitive and psychomotor domain. Why are older teachers as a group less effective than middle-aged teachers?

General intellectual ability more frequently than not has been shown to achieve its peak prior to age 30 (7), although as reported previously in Chapter 4, Bayley indicated increase until age 60. During the age span of 25 to 69, verbal abilities show less decline than the nonverbal abilities measured by the Wechsler Adult Intelligence Scale (46). However, verbal abilities show some decline. The special abilities underlying broad intellectual performances change from the 20s to over 65 years of age, with fewer abilities being present in persons above age 65 (16). Intelligence tests are usually timed and older people do not perform similar tasks as quickly as they did when they were younger.

Novel situations are especially troublesome to older persons, much more so than tasks with which they are familiar. Younger individuals between the ages of 22 and 33 and three older groups between the ages of 65 to 74, 75 to 84, and above 85 were given three tasks to perform which varied in degree of novelty (21). The tasks consisted of familiar word pairs, nonsense equations, and false equations. The results were quite clear:

Both groups performed best on the word-associate tasks, but there was little difference between the learning of nonsense and false equations within either group. On all three procedures the old group was significantly poorer, but they were proportionately more deficient in the learning of materials in which the facilitative effects of prior experience are minimized, i.e., the two forms of equations. However, they had no greater difficulty with the interference than with the nonsense material. The older person thus seems to be less capable in dealing with novel material which can not be readily integrated with earlier experience.

Older and younger Ss were also found to differ in their behavior during learning. Younger Ss are more likely to offer hypotheses, whether correct or incorrect, and through learning to have an increasing proportion of their errors responses which though correct elsewhere in the series are incorrect for the particular stimulus. By contrast, the old Ss respond correctly or not at all, and the proportion of "no response" errors remains high through learning. Three factors are discussed as joint reminders of this behavior: older persons are more cautious; they require more time to integrate response; and their learning may consist mainly of discrete stimulus-response associations, not preceded by more general learning. These factors are conceived as related parts of the total aging process (21, 69).

In part, the difficulty in coping with novel tasks may increase with age because of the loss of perceptual abilities. Of two age groups— 19 to 36, and 61 to 91—the latter consistently did not perform as well as the younger group (6). As the difficulty of the perceptual task increased, the older group required a longer response time. The same conclusions regarding loss in visual perception, along with other information, is noted in Table 5.3, which shows the average performance of different age groups in visual perception, four motor skills, and in comparison and judgment (28). The decline in visual perception is sharp after age 30 to 49, declining from 93 to 76 percent. The various motor skills hold up quite well through age 50 to 69, but then the drop is considerable. Fortunately for those in teaching, comparison and judgment is very good through age 49 and shows only a modest drop from 100 to 87 percent, ages 30–49 to 50–69. It is interesting to note the consistent drop in all abilities after age 49. Substantial decreases in

TABLE 5.3.

Average Performance of Different Age Groups on Various Tests[a]

Performance	Age in Years				
	10–17	18–29	30–49	50–69	70–89
Visual perception	100	95	93	76	46
Motor skills					
Rotary	90	100	97	89	72
Reach and grasp	92	100	98	88	70
Finger extension	87	100	98	99	71
Foot reaction	85	100	96	94	71
Comparison and					
judgment	72	100	100	87	69

[a] 100 indicates highest group average. Others are stated as percentages of this.
SOURCE: Based on W. R. Miles. Age and human ability. *Psychol. Rev.*, 1933, **40**, 112–116.

performance requiring coordination and speed of hand movements also occur among groups—students in their 20s, middle-aged persons of age 40 to 63, and veterans of the Spanish-American War, aged 76 to 89 (44).

The peak in body strength occurs during the 20s, with a gradual decline thereafter until age 60 when the average strength is about 16.5 percent less than at age 20 (12). The difference between those of 20 and 30 years of age in performing a serial task involving the turning out of lights by pressing telegraph keys in serial order was primarily a matter of speed, with the 30-year-olds showing the loss; the difference between the 30-year-olds and 40-year-olds was more a matter of accuracy (20). After age 50, a marked decline occurred in both speed and accuracy.

There is little difference from one country to another or from one historical period to another in the age of outstanding performances (24). Generally, best production in games and sports is achieved prior to age 29; in science, prior to age 35; and in literature, medicine, and philosophy, prior to age 40. Though the high incidence of outstanding performances is in early life, eminent achievements have been made by persons up to age 80 and even beyond, in such fields as literature, medicine, music, philosophy, government, and science.

What the general decline in most abilities after about age 45 to 50 means for the teaching profession is not clear. We still have much to learn about the psychological and sociological factors of aging, especially as applied to the interaction between pupils of varying ages from kindergarten through college and teachers of varying ages from about 20 to 70. A recent review of research on aging and psychological adjustment suggests that a high frequency of major personal adjustments required by changes in the environment, in health, and in interpersonal relations makes old age a very dynamic period (5).

It is entirely possible for a teacher to work up to age 65 or 70 if good physical and mental health can be maintained, if the daily interactions with pupils do not become a source of irritation or anxiety, if the teacher throughout professional life keeps up with the subject matter, and if the teacher accepts becoming older and approaching retirement with equanimity. The early years of teaching for the younger group (ages 20 to 25), for the middle-aged, especially women teachers, and for those above 60 appear to be the periods in which most difficulties are experienced.

SEX

Sex differences in interests, attitudes, and values are revealed in the choice of level of teaching. Teachers in the nursery school, kindergarten, and primary grades are almost exclusively female, with the percent of male teachers rising progressively through the intermediate grades, junior and senior high school, and college teaching. The large number of superintendents of schools are male, and a large percent of high school and elementary principals are also. Teaching fields such as science and mathematics are heavily dominated by males, whereas other teaching fields such as business education and English have many females. Agriculture teachers are male and home economics teachers are female. Both biological factors inherent in the male and female and cultural factors which delimit appropriate roles for each contribute to the choice of teaching level and subject field.

An excellent summary of sex differences in the population is made by Tyler (45). Males tend to be higher in mathematical reasoning, spatial judgment, and science, whereas females average higher in verbal fluency, rote memory, perceptual speed, and dexterity. These are averages and often small differences; the differences between the average scores of males and females in verbal fluency, for example, is not nearly so large as the differences within each sex. Much larger differences exist between males and females in interests, attitudes, and personality characteristics, although there is considerable overlapping between the sexes in these characteristics. Men show high interest in mechanical and scientific activities, physically strenuous and adventuresome activities; legal, political, and army occupations; selling activities; certain forms of entertainment such as chess; and miscellaneous activities such as working out-of-doors and for oneself. Women show high interests in musical and literary activities, artistic endeavors, social affairs, clerical work, teaching, social work, window-shopping, and other miscellaneous activities. Men tend to value theoretical, economic, and political values highly, whereas women tend to value aesthetic, social, and religious values highly.

Differences between men and women high school teachers in the use of criteria of adjustment have been noted (4). Each teacher was asked to nominate the three best-adjusted and the three least-adjusted students in the school regardless of sex. The male and female teachers used much the same criteria of adjustment in their nominations; however, the men teachers were more inclined to value maturity, good judgment, dependability, and trustworthiness and also tended to characterize the best-adjusted students as secure and self-confident. The women teachers placed greater emphasis on character traits in students such as humility and modesty and more often stressed student negativism, hostility to the teacher, discipline problems, and getting into trouble in school as criteria for poor adjustment.

When different criteria of adjustment are used by teachers, one also expects differences in teacher approval and disapproval of the behavior of boys and girls. Three classrooms with women teachers were observed (27). The boys received more disapproval from the teachers than did girls. Students of both sexes also said that boys received disapproval from the teacher more frequently than girls. The observations, corroborated by judgment of the pupils, led to relating the teacher's behavior to a theory of aggression. Boys are more aggressive than girls. Women teachers attempt to socialize boys by means of dominative counter-aggressive behavior. Since boys are more aggressive toward their teachers than are girls, the teachers tend to counteract with a higher degree of aggressiveness toward the boys. In turn, the boys become yet more aggressive and the vicious cycle continues. Women teachers could, however, improve the situation:

> We feel that the consistent trends in our findings imply that teachers' negative attitudes towards their male pupils arise from a lack of appreciation for the term "normal" male child. In our culture, aggressive outgoing behavior is as normal in the male as quiescent nonassertive behavior is in the female. The teacher who attempts to thwart this behavior by means of threats and punishment can only meet with frustration since the boy is confronted with a conflicting social code. A more reasonable plan to follow would seem to be one in which the excess energy and tensions of the male child could be discharged on some constructive activity. Planned physical education classes will do much to dissipate aggressive needs in a socially acceptable manner. Perhaps most important of all, however, is the knowledge that some degree of aggressive behavior is a normal part of development in both boys and girls and should be treated not as a personal threat to the teacher but as a sign of "normal" social and personality development (27, 393).

A small sex difference was noted between students who completed a program of teacher education and those who dropped out before completing the requirements (23). For the women students, the only difference was in valuing service to society. Forty-two percent of those who finished the program indicated they wanted to teach because they could serve society, whereas only 22 percent of those who dropped out gave the same reason. The differences between those men who persisted and those who quit were in desire to work in their major field and in perceiving teaching as a stepping stone to another occupation, with the persisters being higher in both areas.

Perhaps the most important implication of sex differences for men and women teachers is that teachers should examine their own attitudes toward self and sex role, abilities related to the particular level of teaching, and interests in and attitudes toward pupils of the same and opposite sex. Growing boys need some masculine males as exemplary models just as growing girls need feminine females. Women teachers generally appear to relate less well to boys in their classes than do male teachers to either boys or girls.

SOCIAL CLASS

Most teachers, and the schools generally, encourage the development of middle-class social attitudes and values. Many prospective teachers originally come from homes of lower social-class background, however, an increasingly larger number are coming from homes where the father is engaged in a profession or business. Although prospective teachers are drawn from various social-class backgrounds, it is probable that the interests, attitudes, and values which attract these students to teaching are much the same, and that, regardless of their social-class backgrounds, teachers are as homogeneous in attitudes, values, and goals as are members of other professions such as medicine and law. Persons in education, in turn, receive relatively high social status in the community. For example, school superintendents and teachers were given as high status in 1947 as in 1925. In both these years, superintendents were rated fourth and elementary teachers eighth in a group of 25 occupations. Physicians, lawyers, and bankers were rated higher in social status than the superintendents of schools (9).

It is important for teachers to recognize their own attitudes and values and those of their pupils, so that they do not discriminate inadvertently against a child whose attitudes and values are different from their own. A positive correlation was noted between achievement and social-class status of pupils (17). Also, the teachers had more contacts with the higher-status and higher-achieving pupils than with the lower-status and lower-achieving pupils. Although these teachers may not have discriminated against lower-status pupils, it could be that the children of lower social status who are not much interested in schoolwork, and whose parents are not, profit much less from attending school than do other children.

Emotionally accepting each child as he comes to school does not mean accepting antisocial conduct or permitting the highly withdrawn child to remain unattended. Regardless of the child's attitudes and values which he may have learned in the home, the teacher cannot permit fist fighting, cursing, stealing, vulgar language, destruction of property, and open rebellion against the rules and regulations needed to operate a school or classroom. The teacher can, although sometimes with difficulty, demonstrate affection and sympathy for a student and at the same time not permit him to violate generally accepted codes of conduct. If pupils of lower social class are going to profit from education as it is presently conceived, they must somehow internalize generally accepted attitudes and values and yet not destroy themselves through violent conflicts with their parents, neighborhood groups, or the school. Research is not clear as to whether teachers from upper, middle, or lower social-class backgrounds can be most helpful to the many boys and girls of lower social-class background. Apparently, the social-class background of a teacher is not nearly as important as his present attitudes, values, and skills. Because of community pressures and personal values, teachers and the schools generally cannot abandon such middle-class principles as respect for the rights of others, for good care of property, for wise use of time, and for making progress; but they can attempt to understand the way of life followed in the homes of their students.

SUMMARY

In the previous chapter we noted characteristics of the students that affect efficiency of learning. The characteristics of the pupils in the cognitive domain, for example, are more highly correlated with achievement in the academic subjects than are the characteristics of the teacher. This results in part because teachers are a selected group, whereas all pupils are required to attend school. Efficiency of pupil learning, however, is enhanced when guided by a teacher who is intelligent, well prepared in the subject matter, a high achiever while in college, and well educated. We in the United States would do well to make a more serious effort to get a larger number of the most able young people to prepare for a life career in teaching.

Teachers vary a great deal in affective characteristics. High interest in students and subject matter, favorable attitudes toward students and subject matter, and a stable personality are associated with successful teaching. Other characteristics also are important. For example, teachers above age 60 experience more difficulties than do younger teachers. Male teachers seem to get along better with boys than do female teachers. Although middle-class teachers may secure better results with children from the middle social class, we have not found out which teachers work well with children from the lower social class. The social-class background of the teacher's parents is probably not as important in determining his effectiveness as are his own interests and attitudes.

QUESTIONS AND ACTIVITIES

1. Think of the four of five teachers you know best. Are they uniformly good or poor in all teaching activities? Discuss fully.
2. a. Discuss the relationship between teacher characteristics in the cognitive domain and teaching success.
   b. Why are the correlations between characteristics in the cognitive domain and teaching success relatively low, rather than high?
3. Discuss the relationship between teaching success and characteristics in the affective domain: interests, attitudes, values, and personality organization.
4. a. Outline the effects of aging in the adult population generally.
   b. Discuss Ryan's conclusions about age and teaching effectiveness.
   c. Give your opinion as to whether all teachers should be permitted to teach up to age 70.
5. a. State and discuss the conclu-

sions from the research dealing with differences between male and female teachers.
   b. At which school level are boys provided least satisfactory models in their teachers? What might be done to improve this situation?
6. a. In which social class do you place your parents? Yourself?
   b. Describe the type of community in which you most prefer to work. Least prefer to work.
   c. Identify classroom behavior of children which you find difficult to tolerate. Easy to praise or reward.
7. Rate yourself on the personal qualities given in Table 5.2 by checking those in which you are above, below, or at the level of most teachers you know. Do you find you are equally high or low on all of them? You may find it useful to have someone who knows you well to rate you and discuss the ratings with you.

SUGGESTIONS FOR FURTHER READING

Boozer, H. R. External examinations as predictors of competence. *J. teacher Educ.*, 1965, **16**, 210–214.

Bradway, Katherine P., & Clare W. Thompson. Intelligence at adulthood: A twenty-five year follow up. *J. educ. Psychol.*, 1962, **53**, 1–14. (In Gordon, 1965, 403–413; and Ripple, 1964, 65–82.)

Bryan, R. C. *Reactions to teachers by students, parents and administrators.* Kalamazoo: Western Michigan Univer., 1963. (Portion reprinted under the title "Student reactions improve teacher effectiveness" in Seidman, 1965, 403–418.)

Getzels, J. W., & P. W. Jackson. The teacher's personality and characteristics. In N. L. Gage (Ed.), *Handbook of research on teaching*. Chicago: Rand McNally, 1963, pp. 506–582.

Horn, J. L., & W. L. Morrison. Dimensions of teacher attitudes. *J. educ. Psychol.*, 1965, **56**, 118–125.

Husek, T. R., & M. C. Wittrock. The dimensions of attitudes toward teachers as measured by the Semantic Differential. *J. educ. Psychol.*, 1962, **53**, 209–213.

Mitzel, H. E. Teacher effectiveness. In C. W. Harris (Ed.), *Encyclopedia of educational research*. New York: Macmillan, 1960, pp. 1481–1486.

Rocchio, P. D., & N. C. Kearney. Teacher-pupil attitudes as related to nonpromotion of secondary school pupils. *Educ. psychol. Measmt*, 1956, **16**, 244–252. (In Charters & Gage, 1963, 287–290.)

Rugg, E. U. Who shall be educated for teaching? *J. teacher Educ.*, 1965, **16**, 221–225.

Simpson, W. M. A parent looks at teaching. *J. secondary Educ.*, 1963, **38**, 175–181. (In Fullager, et al., 1964, 550–555.)

Simun, Patricia B., & J. W. Asher. The relationship of variables in undergraduate school and school administrators' ratings of first-year teachers. *J. teacher Educ.*, 1964, **15**, 293–302.

REFERENCES

1. Barr, A. S., *et al*. Wisconsin studies of the measurement and prediction of teacher effectiveness: A summary of investigations. *J. exp. Educ.*, 1961, **30**, 1–156.

2. Beamer, G. C., & Elaine W. Ledbetter. The correlation between teacher attitudes and the social service interest. *J. educ. Res.*, 1957, **50**, 655–666.

3. Beilin, H. Teachers' and clinicians' attitudes toward the behavior problems of children: A reappraisal. *Child Develpm.*, 1959, **30**, 9–25.

4. Beilin, H., & Emmy Werner. Sex differences among teachers in the use of criteria of adjustment. *J. educ. Psychol.*, 1957, **48**, 426–436.

5. Birren, J. E. Aging and psychological adjustment. *Rev. educ. Res.*, 1958, **28**, 475–490.

6. Birren, J. E., & J. Botwinick. Speed of response as a function of perceptual difficulty and age. *J. Geront.*, 1955, **10**, 433–436.

7. Bloom, B. S. *Stability and change in human characteristics*. New York: Wiley, 1964.

8. Cook, W. W., C. H. Leeds, & R. Callis. *Manual for the Minnesota Teacher Attitude Inventory, Form A*. New York: Psychological Corporation, 1950.

9. Deeg, M. E., & D. G. Paterson. Changes in social status of occupations. *Occupations*, 1947, **25**, 205–208.

10. Della Piana, G. M., and N. L. Gage. Pupils' values and the validity of the Minnesota Teacher Attitude Inventory. *J. educ. Psychol.*, 1955, **46**, 167–178.

11. Ellis, D. B., & L. W. Miller. Teachers' attitudes and child behavior problems. *J. educ. Psychol.*, 1936, **27**, 501–511.

12. Fisher, M. B., & J. E. Birren. Age and strength. *J. appl. Psychol.*, 1947, **31**, 490–497.

13. Gabriel, J. *An analysis of the emotional problems of the teacher in the classroom*. Melbourne, Australia: F. W. Cheshire, 1957.

14. Gowan, J. C. Relation of the "K" scale of the MMPI to the teaching personality. *Calif. J. educ. Res.*, 1955, **6**, 208–212.

15. Gowan, J. C., & May S. Gowan.

The Guilford-Zimmerman and the California Psychological Inventory in the measurement of teaching candidates. *Calif. J. educ. Res.*, 1955, **6**, 35–37.

16. Green, R. F., & B. Berkowitz. Changes in intellect with age: II. Factorial analysis of Wechsler-Bellevue scores. *J. genet. Psychol.*, 1964, **104**, 3–18.

17. Hoehn, A. J. A study of social status differentiation in the classroom behavior of nineteen third-grade teachers. *J. soc. Psychol.*, 1954, **39**, 269–292.

18. Hoyt, K. B. A study of the effects of teacher knowledge of pupil characteristics on pupil achievement and attitudes towards classwork. *J. educ. Psychol.*, 1955, **46**, 302–310.

19. Husek, T. R., & M. C. Wittrock. The dimensions of attitudes toward teachers as measured by the Semantic Differential. *J. educ. Psychol.*, 1962, **53**, 209–213.

20. Kay, H. Learning of a serial task by different age groups. *Quart. J. exp. Psychol.*, 1951, **3**, 166–183.

21. Korchin, S. J., & H. Basowitz. Age differences in verbal learning. *J. abnorm. soc. Psychol.*, 1957, **54**, 64–69.

22. Kounin, J. S., & P. V. Gump. The comparative influence of punitive and nonpunitive teachers upon childrens' concepts of school misconduct. *J. educ. Psychol.*, 1961, **52**, 44–49.

23. Labue, A. C. A study of motivation of "persistent" vs. "non-persistent" students in teacher education. *J. teacher Educ.*, 1954, **5**, 242–243.

24. Lehman, H. C. Men's creative productive rate at different ages and in different countries. *Scient. mon.*, 1954, **78**, 321–326.

25. MacLean, M. S., May S. Gowan, & J. C. Gowan. A teacher selection and counseling service. *J. educ. Res.*, 1955, **48**, 669–677.

26. Mastin, V. E. Teacher enthusiasm. *J. educ. Res.*, 1963, **56**, 385–386.

27. Meyer, W. J., & G. G. Thompson. Sex differences in the distribution of teacher approval and disapproval among sixth-grade children. *J. educ. Psychol.*, 1956, **47**, 385–396.

28. Miles, W. R. Age and human ability. *Psychol. Rev.*, 1933, **40**, 99–123.

29. Mitzel, H. E. Teacher effectiveness. In C. W. Harris (Ed.), *Encyclopedia of educational research.* New York: Macmillan, 1960, pp. 1481–1486.

30. Ojemann, R. H., & F. R. Wilkinson. The effect on pupil growth of an increase in teachers' understanding of pupil behavior. *J. exp. Educ.*, 1939, **8**, 143–147.

31. Rudd, W. G. A., & S. Wiseman. Sources of dissatisfaction among a group of teachers. *Brit. J. educ. Psychol.*, 1962, **32**, 275–291.

32. Ryans, D. G. Some validity extension data from empirically derived predictors of teacher behavior. *Educ. psychol. Measmt*, 1958, **18**, 355–370.

33. Ryans, D. G. Some correlates of teacher behavior. *Educ. psychol. Measmt*, 1959, **19**, 3–12.

34. Ryans, D. G. *Characteristics of teachers: Their description, comparison and appraisal.* Washington, D.C.: American Council on Education, 1960.

35. Sandgren, D. L., & L. G. Schmidt. Does practice teaching change attitudes toward teaching? *J. educ. Res.*, 1956, **49**, 673–680.

36. Schultz, R. E., & M. M. Ohlsen. Interest patterns of best and poorest student teachers. *J. educ. Sociol.*, 1955, **29**, 108–112.

37. Schunert, J. The association of mathematical achievement with certain factors resident in the teacher, in the teaching, in the pupil, and in the school. *J. exp. Educ.*, 1951, **19**, 219–238.

38. Seagoe, May V. Prediction of in-service success in teaching. *J. educ. Res.*, 1946, **39**, 658–663.

39. Shannon, J. R. A comparison of highly successful teachers, failing teachers, and average teachers at the time of their graduation from Indiana State Teachers College. *Educ. Admin. Supervis.*, 1940, **26**, 43–51.

40. Shaw, J., H. J. Klausmeier, A. H. Luker, & H. T. Reid. Changes occurring in teacher-pupil attitudes during a two-week workshop. *J. appl. Psychol.*, 1952, **36**, 304–306.

41. Simun, Patricia, & J. W. Asher. The relationship of variables in undergraduate school and school administrators' ratings of first-year teachers. *J. teacher Educ.*, 1964, **15**, 293–302.

42. Stouffer, G. A. W., Jr. The attitudes of secondary school teachers toward certain behavior problems of children. *Sch. Rev.*, 1956, **64**, 358–362.

43. Symonds, P. M., & Stephanie Dudek. Use of the Rorschach in the diagnosis of teacher effectiveness. *J. proj. Tech.*, 1956, **20**, 227–234.

44. Talland, G. A. The effect of age on speed of simple manual skill. *J. genet. Psychol.*, 1962, **100**, 69–76.

45. Tyler, Leona E. *The psychology of human differences.* (2nd ed.) New York: Appleton-Century-Crofts, 1956.

46. Wechsler, D. Intellectual changes with age. *Mental health in later maturity.* Supplement No. 168 to Public Health Report, Federal Security Agency, U. S. Public Health Service. Washington, D. C.: U. S. Government Printing Office, 1942, pp. 43–52.

47. Wickman, E. K. *Children's behavior and teachers' attitudes.* New York: Commonwealth Fund, 1928.

CHAPTER 6

Classroom Interactions and Learning

$$I$$N THE previous two chapters, cognitive, psychomotor, and affective characteristics of the learner and of the teacher were shown to be related to efficiency of learning. The more immediate interaction between the teacher and the pupils and among the pupils also is related to learning efficiency. It is in classroom or other behavioral settings that the characteristics of pupils and teachers are brought together. In these settings interaction takes place and desired behavioral changes can occur through efficient teaching-learning processes, as will be shown in a more complete discussion of teacher-pupil interaction, general teacher behavior, leadership behavior of the teacher, the teacher as a helpful person, and pupil-pupil interaction.

TEACHER—PUPIL INTERACTIONS

As shown in Chapter 1, the classroom setting is comprised of pupils, a teacher, a room, a group. All have unique characteristics. In addition to these features, we also have the behavior of teacher and pupils. Behavior includes not only overt physical activity such as talking and doing, but also cognitive processes like cognizing, thinking, and evaluating. In the classroom and the school, the teacher is to help bring about desirable changes in pupil behavior. Through the teacher's interaction with students and the students' interaction with one another, many desired interests, motives, social skills, and many outcomes in the cognitive and the psychomotor domains are acquired more efficiently than if there were no or partial interaction. Four facets of classroom interaction are now treated.

The Stimulus Nature of Pupils and Teachers

The most stimulating aspect of the environment is the person himself. The second most stimulating factor is usually other individuals. In most group situations there is continuous stimulation among members.

Pupils in a classroom group vary in many respects. Some speak freely, loudly, and often; others speak scarcely at all. Some are highly intelligent and learn easily; others are of low intelligence and learn with difficulty. These pupils stimulate teacher behavior. The observant teachers wonders why many arrive at school with soiled clothing and uncombed hair. Why does Johnny have such a strong need for attention? Why is he scuffling with others, talking loudly, and making himself a general nuisance? How is it that Bill already knows everything that other pupils are now struggling with? The university professor wants to know why several students enrolled in his course when they appear to be so uninterested and not inclined to take any initiative to learn. He also considers what might be the top limits of learning of several of the highly intelligent students. A well-dressed, well-mannered group of high-achieving pupils produces different teacher responses and feelings than does a group of mentally retarded, crippled, or emotionally disturbed children. The characteristics and behavior of pupils stimulate most teachers to treat them as human beings, not simply as a collection of objects to be molded or changed.

The teacher, too, serves as a stimulus for the learners. They are aware not only of the teacher's personal appearance, but also of his speech and actions. If the teacher is strongly admired, the pupil will attempt to pattern his behavior after the teacher. Similarly, if the teacher attempts to meet the minor aggressive reactions of a pupil with aggressive acts against him, the pupil's behavior in turn is likely to become even more aggressive. Students attending the same school for a year or two expect to behave somewhat differently in various classes because of the generally established reputation of the teacher. College students, for example, enroll in one class with the expectation of sitting quietly and taking notes from the lecturer throughout the entire semester. They enroll in another class expecting the instructor to help them identify significant problems and to provide the needed guidance for them to find some reasonable solution to these problems through laboratory work, library study, and discussions. Inasmuch as the teacher has the responsibility for instruction in the classroom, and because there are usually many pupils to one teacher, the teacher's total stimulus effect on the pupils is generally higher than that of an individual pupil on the teacher.

Social-Emotional Need Satisfactions

To live comfortably with themselves, most human beings need to give and to receive affection, to receive approval, to maintain self-respect and a feeling of well-being toward themselves, and to achieve success. Most of us satisfy these needs in a social setting through interacting and living with one another. For satisfaction of these needs, university and high school students rely upon immediate contacts in the classroom less than do children in the elementary grades. However, older students generally want respect, approval, and sometimes affection from their classmates. If given the opportunity, they attempt to seek emotional satisfactions in the classroom. In the elementary grades and high school, being liked by one or more members of the class is the strongest need many individuals experience. They rely heavily on their associations in the school as a means of satisfying emotional needs and building social skills.

The teacher who is happily committed to a lifetime career in teaching also relies upon the interaction with students for satisfaction of many of his social-emotional needs. To attain self-realization and to maintain a fairly well-integrated personality, the teacher must find satisfaction rather than dissatisfaction in his many daily contacts. The professional teacher must be assured that the students are learning under his direction. A person committed to a lifetime career in teaching cannot achieve any reasonable measure of self-realization when he knows that he is disliked by the students and that they are not learning as well as they might with a different teacher.

Reinforcement and Confirmation of Behaviors

During a single class period, much of the immediate behavior of the pupils can be reinforced or corrected, confirmed or denied. The behavior can be oral, as in discussions and question-and-answer periods; written, as in mathematics or social studies; or physical, as in music, and typing. For example, members of smaller groups within a class discuss what each person is going to do to complete a project. As the five or six members of each group discuss the project, large amounts of information can be exchanged. Also, if all the members discuss freely, many agreements and disagreements are encountered in planning activities and assigning responsibilities. When the discussions of the project start, Susan may immediately outline what each member is to do. The others being assigned duties respond negatively. Thus, Susan learns immediately that her proposal is unacceptable—she finds her behavior unconfirmed or even denied. Joyce now proposes that each member suggest what he would like to do. The others accept this proposition. Joyce's behavior is confirmed, and if Susan can profit from experience, her behavior is corrected. Many social skills are developed in this way.

Why does short question-and-answer recitation work? It is in part because students may study harder, but also, in part, because the pupil's answers are immediately reinforced or corrected by the teacher or classmates. Board work, too, is sometimes effective because it gives the teacher the opportunity to see the results of a number of students' work, to reinforce whatever is correct, and to help them identify and overcome immediately errors or difficulties.

How does a teacher judge the effectiveness of instructional materials or procedures? This judging is not done primarily through administering tests at the end of a week, month, or semester. A test given a month or two after learning has supposedly occurred is too late for the teacher to ascertain the extent to which the more immediate materials and procedures were successful. If oral or written instructions for making an outline map are given, the teacher should not wait a day or week to determine whether the pupils learned from the instructions. He needs to observe immediately whether the pupils are carrying out the instructions properly.

Successful teachers are generally observant of the behavior of students. They try to help the students do well and are guided in this effort by responding to the students' questions and reactions. Depending on how well the students respond, they continue some successful procedures but change them if any assignment, instructional activity, or teaching procedure appears not to be effective. The teacher thus confirms or corrects methods largely on the basis of the students' more immediate responses.

Interaction Patterns

The teacher's most direct means of interacting with pupils is through speaking, writing, and making actual physical contact with the pupil. Most of this behavior is manifested in good classroom demonstrations. For example, in demonstrating the solution of a problem, the teacher may write portions or all of it on the chalkboard, speak about it, and gesture while speaking and writing. The music teacher also may sing a song the first time with appropriate gestures and movements to convey the mood as well as the words and melody.

Less directly, a teacher interacts with the student through the use of instructional materials and equipment. The books made available to the students, television, teaching machines, and tape recorders are indirect means of interacting. Even less directly, a teacher interacts through personal appearance and through the appearance of the room. Without words, the personal appearance of the teacher conveys some ideas and feelings. A sloppily dressed and poorly groomed teacher gives the impression of having a low degree of self respect, or at least a value system different from that of most teachers.

Students have some of the same means of interacting with the teacher as does the teacher with them. Most of the interaction between teacher and students is by means of oral and written language. Inasmuch as the speech of students and the teacher can be observed and recorded, oral utterances in determining patterns of interaction in the classroom are used in assessing teacher-pupil interaction.

A widely used and sophisticated system for analysis of the interaction that occurs in the classroom is described, with suggestions for use by the teacher himself, by Amidon and Flanders (1). This system, referred to as the Flanders' system, is concerned only with verbal behavior on the assumption that the verbal behavior of the teacher and students is an adequate sample of their total behavior. Also, verbal behavior, or talk, can be observed with higher reliability than can nonverbal behavior. In this interaction analysis system, all teacher talk is first classified as direct or indirect, thus giving primary attention to the amount of freedom the teacher gives the students. Direct actions by the teacher minimize the opportunity for the students to initiate talk and respond; indirect actions maximize student opportunity. The student talk also is classified into two categories— responding to the teacher and initiating talk. A third classification, designated silence or confusion, is included in order to account for time spent that cannot be classified as teacher talk or student talk.

Components of the Teaching-Learning Situation

As shown in Table 6.1, teacher talk that demonstrates indirect influence is further classified into four categories—accepts feelings, praises or encourages, accepts or uses ideas of student, and asks questions. The categories of direct influence are lecturing, giving directions, and criticizing or justifying authority. The main behavior regarding

TABLE 6.1.

Summary of Categories for Interaction Analysis

TEACHER TALK	INDIRECT INFLUENCE	1. *Accepts feeling:* accepts and clarifies the feeling tone of the students in a nonthreatening manner. Feelings may be positive or negative. Predicting and recalling feelings are included.
		2. *Praises or encourages:* praises or encourages student action or behavior. Jokes that release tension, not at the expense of another individual, nodding head or saying "um hm?" or "go on" are included.
		3. *Accepts or uses ideas of student:* clarifying, building, or developing ideas or suggestions by a student. (As teacher brings more of his own ideas into play, shift to category five.)
		4. *Asks questions:* asking a question about content or procedure with the intent that a student answer.
	DIRECT INFLUENCE	5. *Lecturing:* giving facts or opinions about content or procedure; expressing his own idea; asking rhetorical questions.
		6. *Giving directions:* directions, commands, or orders with which a student is expected to comply.
		7. *Criticizing or justifying authority:* statements intended to change student behavior from nonacceptable to acceptable pattern; bawling someone out; stating why the teacher is doing what he is doing, extreme self-reference.
STUDENT TALK		8. *Student talk—response:* talk by students in response to teacher. Teacher initiates the contract or solicits student statement.
		9. *Student talk—initiation:* talk by students, which they initiate. If "calling on" student is only to indicate who may talk next, observer must decide whether student wanted to talk. If he did, use this category.
		10. *Silence or confusion:* pauses, short periods of silence, and periods of confusion in which communication cannot be understood by the observer.

SOURCE: E. J. Amidon, & N. A. Flanders. *The role of the teacher in the classroom: A manual for understanding and improving teachers' classroom behavior.* Minneapolis: Paul S. Amidon, 1963, p. 12.

each of the categories also is given. The intention of Amidon and Flanders was to provide enough information in a manual so that a teacher might rate himself; for example, consider all the information regarding Category 7, criticizing or justifying authority:

Category 7, Criticizing or Justifying Authority. A statement of criticism is one that is designed to change student behavior from nonacceptable to acceptable. The teacher is saying, in effect, "I don't like what you are doing. Do something else." Another group of statements included in this category are those that might be called statements of defense or self-justification. These statements are particularly difficult to detect when a teacher appears to be explaining a lesson or the reasons for doing a lesson to the class. If the teacher is explaining himself or his authority, defending himself against the student, or justifying himself, the statement falls in this category. Other kinds of statements that fall in this category are those of extreme self-reference or those in which the teacher is constantly asking the children to do something as a special favor to the teacher (1, 9).

Recall that only verbal behavior is categorized. If the teacher is talking (Categories 1 through 7), it is assumed that the students are listening. On the other hand, if the pupils are talking (Categories 8 and 9), the teacher is assumed to be listening.

Although this system of analyzing a classroom situation may seem complicated, it is really quite useable. A tape recorder may be used to record a classroom period for later analysis; however, a trained observer in the classroom would be able to analyze the interaction more efficiently. Every three seconds the observer must make a judgment as to what type of interaction just occurred. Thus, for every minute of instruction he will record 20 category numbers. A short time interval may be recorded in the observer's notebook as 10-9-3-3-3-4-8-10. Here the student proposed a new way to prove a geometric theorem (9), the teacher developed the student's idea at some length (3-3-3), the teacher asked a question applying the idea (4), and a student responded (8). The arbitrary addition of the 10 is always necessary to make a series of observations complete, for the series must begin and end with the same number.

To give an overall picture of the interaction and to help the teacher analyze what occurred, these observation numbers are rerecorded on a 10×10 matrix. To do this, a tally is made for each *pair* of numbers generated by proceeding through the series of observations one number at a time. In the above example, the pairs of numbers are (a) 10–9, (b) 9–3, (c) 3–3, (d) 3–3, (e) 3–4, (f) 4–8, and (g) 8–10. The first number of each pair is the row index, and the second number is the column index. Thus, to record pair (a), one enters a tally in the cell at the intersection of row 10 and column 9, pair (b) is recorded in the cell at the intersection of row 9 and column 3, etc. This series of observations would be recorded as shown in Fig. 6.1; the letters of the interaction pairs corresponding to those above are included in the figure for demonstration purposes and would not normally be used. In addition, it is well to remember that several hundred interaction pairs are normally tabulated on a single matrix rather than the seven used here for illustrative purposes.

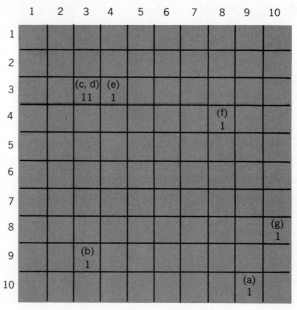

Fig. 6.1. Flanders' matrix showing classroom inter-action sequence. (Adapted from E. J. Amidon & N. A. Flanders. *The role of the teacher in the classroom: A manual for understanding and improving teachers' classroom behavior.* Minneapolis: Paul S. Amidon, 1963, p. 27.)

Large frequencies within a single cell sometimes result. Consider the situation in which a teacher lectures to the class for 15 minutes without interruption. The observer would record a 10 before starting, 300 fives (15 minutes × 20 judgments per minute), and a final 10. When re-recorded on the 10 × 10 matrix, the cell at the intersection of row 5 and column 5 would contain 300 tallies. Similarly, a student panel report lasting 10 minutes would result in 200 tallies in the 9–9 cell on the matrix.

Note that the data once in matrix form can be treated in two inter-related ways: *statistically* by comparing category frequencies (summing across rows or columns gives identical results), and *descriptively* by considering block areas of the matrix. The descriptive analysis is of particular interest because it tends to preserve the sequence of events that occurred in the classroom. Obviously total indirect teacher influence can be computed by summing the first four rows (or columns) that correspond to the four indirect categories; while the fifth, sixth, and seventh rows (or columns) are summed to arrive at total direct teacher influence. A ratio of teacher talk (rows 1 through 7) to student talk (rows 8 and 9) can also be computed. Other aspects of the descriptive analysis are not so obvious. For example, consider the diagram in Fig. 6.2. The shaded areas making up the diagram have been superimposed on the 10 × 10 matrix to facilitate the description of patterns of interaction occurring in the classroom. The five areas diagrammed and designated A through E may be explained quite readily

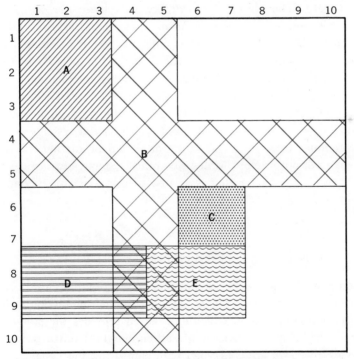

Fig. 6.2. Flanders' matrix shaded to show descriptive analysis areas. (Adapted from E. J. Amidon & N. A. Flanders. *The role of the teacher in the classroom: A manual for understanding and improving teachers' classroom behavior.* Minneapolis: Paul S. Amidon, 1963, pp. 31–37.)

(note that two small sections of Area B overlap with sections of Areas D and E):

A. Constructive Integration: teacher uses indirect influence to motivate students and uses their ideas constructively.
B. Content Cross: teacher emphasizes subject matter.
C. Vicious Cycle: teacher disciplines students and gives them direction.
D. Interested Acceptance: teacher is genuinely concerned with hearing and using student ideas.
E. Indifferent Acceptance: teacher ignores student participation and doesn't use their ideas.

This instrument for measuring classroom interaction is not a finished product. However, one can see the possibilities of using the model to obtain quantitative measures of classroom interaction, including differences among teachers. Interestingly, this system could be used as a basis for determining merit pay, inasmuch as Amidon and Flanders suggest that teachers of greater flexibility make the better pedagogues; that is, teachers equally at ease using indirect teacher influence, in addition to the usual direct teacher influence, were considered more effective (1). Some minor modifications of the Flanders' system have been recommended in connection with studying interaction in team-teaching classrooms (30).

Many other bases for observing and classifying social interactions in the classroom have been used (36, 51). The better systems are relatively complex because of the nature of classroom interaction. Therefore, we shall not attempt to describe other systems, but instead shall discuss teacher behavior that is related to classroom interaction and student learning.

GENERAL TEACHER BEHAVIOR

As noted in the preceding discussion, interaction implies behavior between or among human beings. Teacher-student interaction involves behavioral transactions in which one person provides the stimulating event for the behavior of another. In attempting to describe interaction processes, then, we are concerned with comparing the behavior of at least two persons. As in Flanders' system, there are two sets of information to take into account—one pertaining to the teacher and one pertaining to students. Interaction between these two sets of information are then studied. In this section when discussing general teacher behavior and in the next section when discussing leadership behavior of teachers, we shall not limit ourselves to a rigorous definition of interaction in which the conclusions are arrived at by comparing specified actions of the teacher and of the students. We shall be concerned with some effects of teacher behavior upon various aspects of student performance, not necessarily to the interaction only.

Teacher behavior has been described most extensively by Ryans (44). Some of the more immediate objectives of his research were to identify patterns of teacher behavior, to develop written instruments for estimating teacher behavior and personal qualities, and to compare various groups of teachers in relation to their behavior and other characteristics. These intermediate objectives were to lead to a more practical goal eventually:

> The Teacher Characteristics Study was conducted with two possible uses of the results in mind: first, by school systems as an aid in identifying teachers who, at the time of selection for employment or perhaps in connection with promotion, have characteristics similar to those deemed important and desirable by the particular school system and the culture it represents; and, second, by teacher education institutions as an aid to a better understanding of teacher characteristics and associated conditions, which would contribute to improved procedures for selecting teacher candidates and to the improvement of professional courses and curricula (44, 11).

During a period of six years, more than 6000 teachers in 1700 schools and about 450 school systems participated in the main study. From analysis of the behavior of teachers as observed by trained observers, from the use of written instruments, and from ratings by principals and supervisors, a fairly complete description of teacher behavior and characteristics emerged. In some instances the behavior and characteristics were related to effectiveness of teaching. The main concern was not to determine effectiveness but to determine whether the behavior was related to variables such as school level, sex of the teacher, subject field, and community. Some of the characteristics have already been noted in the previous chapter. Three main patterns of behavior were:

TCS Pattern X_o: warm, understanding, friendly *vs.* aloof, egocentric, restricted teacher behavior

TCS Pattern Y_o: responsible, businesslike, systematic *vs.* evading, unplanned, slipshod teacher behavior

TCS Pattern Z_o: stimulating, imaginative, surgent or enthusiastic, *vs.* dull, routine teacher behavior (44, 77).

The differences in behavior according to such variables as teaching level, subject field, and sex are worth careful consideration. These three patterns of behavior were highly intercorrelated among elementary teachers, suggesting that those high in one pattern were also high in the others. In other words warm, understanding and friendly behavior went along with responsible, businesslike, and systematic behavior and also stimulating, imaginative, and surgent behavior. The comparisons for high school teachers included only the subject fields of English, social studies, science, and mathematics. The correlations were not as high for high school as elementary teachers. Among the high school teachers, men and women social-studies teachers, and women English teachers were high in Pattern X_o. Women mathematics teachers were highest on Pattern Y_o, and women social studies and science teachers surpassed other groups on Pattern Z_o. Teachers over 55 years of age were lower than younger teachers on Pattern X_o, and lower on Pattern Z_o. Unmarried mathematics and science teachers received higher assessments on all three patterns than did those who were married; single English and social-studies teachers were higher than married teachers on Y_o, but somewhat lower on X_o and Z_o.

Teachers who were warm and understanding and more stimulating possessed more favorable attitudes toward pupils and also more favorable attitudes toward administrators. Those judged to be warm and understanding in their classroom behavior—and, to a lesser extent, stimulating and imaginative—expressed more permissive viewpoints toward education. Teachers more businesslike and systematic showed a slight tendency toward more traditional viewpoints about education. Elementary teachers who demonstrated warm and understanding classroom behavior—and, to a lesser extent, stimulating imaginative behavior—also manifested superior emotional adjustment. In general, teachers who demonstrated friendly and warm, organized and businesslike, and stimulating and surgent behavior were judged to be more effective teachers (**43**).

Behavior patterns of college instructors are somewhat different from those Ryans identified in elementary and high school teachers. College students rated their instructors on a large number of items drawn from many inventories (**22**). Six patterns, or factors, were identified. The names assigned to them and a few instances of the referent behavior indicate dimensions of the behavior of college instructors:

1. Skill—instructor puts material across in an interesting way, stimulates intellectual curiosity of the students, explains things clearly, observes student reaction skillfully.
2. Overload—instructor assigns difficult reading, asks for more than students can do, assigns a great deal of reading.

3. Structure—instructor decides in detail what should be done and how to do it, follows an outline closely, everything goes according to schedule, activities are planned in detail.
4. Feedback—instructor tells students when they have done a particularly good job, compliments students in front of others, criticizes poor work.
5. Interaction—students in the class are friendly, feel free to express opinions, frequently volunteer their own opinions.
6. Rapport—instructor listens attentively to students, is friendly, is permissive and flexible, explains reasons for criticism.

Isaacson, *et al.*, did not attempt to relate this behavior to instructor effectiveness in terms of how well the students learned or how they reacted to instructors. You may find it interesting to go back and mentally check which instructor behavior would probably result in higher achievement for you and in more favorable attitudes toward the instructor. Comparing your judgments with others will help to determine the extent of agreement.

A less sophisticated comparison was made of teacher behavior and other characteristics liked and disliked by elementary pupils at two different times, 1946 and 1951 (31). Table 6.2 shows the pupils' responses toward undesirable behavior of ten teachers most liked and ten teachers most disliked in each of the studies. All the characteristics and behavior listed in Table 6.2 are undesirable. In 1946, 10 percent of the pupils checked "Failure to praise" as being undesirable behavior in the upper ten teachers, while 49 percent checked this as undesirable behavior in the ten most disliked teachers. The mean percentages of total responses for 1946 and 1951 are 7.3 and 5.7 for the best-liked teachers, and 50.5 and 29.5 for the least-liked teachers. Though the lower ten teachers in both years generally received more disapproval, it is interesting to note that the upper ten teachers also were disliked by a large portion of the pupils for having pets among the class, for scolding a pupil in front of others, for being easily annoyed or bothered, and for detaining pupils during recess or after school. Though there are some fairly sharp differences on a few items between the teachers in 1951 and in 1946, pupils rated undesirable behaviors of best-liked and least-liked teachers with surprising consistency. Further, the 1946 and 1951 studies were done in different states.

From Table 6.2 it is seen that the behavior traits which differentiated most noticeably between the better and poorer teachers were: scolding pupils, usually cross, often bossy, talking too much, fussing at the pupils, becoming angry at pupil's failure to understand, and often

TABLE 6.2.

Frequency of Pupil Reaction Toward Undesirable Behavior of the
Ten Teachers Taken from Each End of the Distribution of
Pupils' Ratings (1946 and 1951 Studies)

| | | Percent of Pupil Reaction | | | |
| | | Upper Ten Teachers | | Lower Ten Teachers | |
Item Number	Undesirable Teacher Behavior	1946 (N:281)	1951 (N:257)	1946 (N:265)	1951 (N:261)
3	Failure to praise	10	5	49	15
4	Scolds pupils a lot	4	7	71	50
5	Usually cross	3	4	59	20
6	Doesn't explain school work	0	2	19	6
7	Doesn't speak to pupil on street	0	1	20	6
8	Unable to keep order	5	7	30	48
9	Does not make school work interesting	1	1	39	21
10	Often "bossy"	2	4	58	32
11	Difficult to approach with problems	5	6	56	26
12	Forces ideas on pupils	12	8	44	24
13	Not usually kind to pupil	2	0	37	10
14	Does not keep promises	2	0	25	19
15	Does not participate in children's games	9	17	64	64
16	Thinks she is always right and pupil wrong	7	2	51	31
17	Has "pets" among the children	27	16	54	57
18	Scolds a pupil in front of other pupils	44	23	91	80
19	Difficult to please	7	4	64	33
20	Talks too much	5	3	63	40
21	Easily annoyed or bothered	17	11	70	61
22	Unfair with pupils	3	2	39	18
23	Always "fussing at" the pupils	6	2	58	31
24	Failure to acknowledge pupil's hand	5	4	48	34
25	Detention during recess or after school	16	30	69	87
26	Makes fun of pupils	6	3	38	15
27	Disliked by most pupils	2	1	68	30
28	Doesn't laugh with pupils at amusing incidents	11	10	44	20
29	Unfair in grading	3	2	33	9
30	Talks too loudly	1	1	43	21
31	Does not give everyone a chance to recite	2	5	40	29
32	Failure to explain school work	1	0	28	9
33	Becomes angry at pupil's failure to understand	5	3	59	33

TABLE 6.2. *(Continued)*

| Item Number | Undesirable Teacher Behavior | Percent of Pupil Reaction | | | |
| | | Upper Ten Teachers | | Lower Ten Teachers | |
		1946 (N:281)	1951 (N:257)	1946 (N:265)	1951 (N:261)
34	Unwilling to help with school work	2	2	38	15
35	Doesn't seem to like children	1	0	42	16
36	Punishes whole class for 1 or 2 offenders	12	8	71	41
37	Scolds pupils for mistakes	4	2	55	22
38	Does not give opportunity for questions	0	3	34	21
39	Lowers grades for helping others	19	20	57	20
40	Will not permit making up work failed	13	9	54	18
41	Often becomes angry with pupils	7	4	74	61
42	Pupil afraid to ask for help	6	4	42	20
43	Assigns "lots" of homework	5	8	54	55
44	Punishes in front of other pupils	20	14	86	61
45	Unwilling to give extra help	1	2	31	10
46	Does not see things as children do	3	5	52	37
47	Uninterested in pupil's activities outside of school	33	9	63	39
48	Does not explain lessons clearly	1	1	31	11
49	Disliked by individual pupil	1	0	53	28
50	Disliked by other pupils	1	1	58	20
	Total average per item	7.3	5.7	50.5	29.5

SOURCE: C. H. Leeds. Teacher behavior liked and disliked by pupils. *Education*, 1954, **75**, 31–32.

becoming angry with pupils. The reasons the pupils gave for liking their teacher, not shown in Table 6.2, are as revealing as the dislikes. As you read the following list, check each one that you can recall as characteristic of one of your best teachers.

Reasons for Liking Teacher:

"Because she is always friendly to the pupils."
"She is very patient and kind."
"I like this teacher because she is kind and not a boss."
"I like her because she is interested in my hobby which is building airplanes, boats, and other models."
"She considers herself one of us."

"Because she is helpful. I can take problems to her. She understands. She is pretty (that helps out a lot)."

"Because when I came to this school she was kind to me."

"Because when I ask her questions she gives me a chance to tell her."

"I like my teacher because she is interested in children."

"She tries to be very understanding. I think she is grand to put up with us."

"She is kind and not like most other teachers."

"Because she keeps her promises and takes us on trips and lets us ask questions without getting mad at us."

"She is kind and helpful and explains things carefully and listens to what you say."

"I like this teacher because she is fair and I feel free to ask her anything."

"She isn't cranky. She doesn't get angry when you don't get everything right."

"Because she'll stop and help anybody who needs help when she has important work to do."

"Because she is helpful and understanding in my work. And she is like a mother to all the children."

"Because she lets you laugh when something is funny and she has fun with the children."

"I like this teacher because she's easy to get along with and I'm always at ease when I'm in her room."

"I like this teacher because she does not get angry. She does not embarrass us in front of the class."

"I like her for she is very nice, talks low, not too low, and she explains your lessons clearly."

"Because she likes all the children and not one or two."

"She goes skating like boys and girls and likes basketball and laughs when we do."

"Because she is humorous and laughs with the class and it makes school more fun" (**31**, **34**).[1]

The above information does not tell us whether pupils learned the usual subject matter more or less efficiently under the best- or least-liked teachers. We infer, however, that, if a teacher desires her pupils to like her, then certain behavior is appropriate and other behavior is inappropriate. Further, we know that teachers serve as real-life models for students to imitate.

Do all pupils respond in the same manner to teacher behavior? The effects of the teachers' use of praise or blame on the subsequent achievement of withdrawing or introverted pupils and of outgoing or extroverted pupils was determined (**47**). Six short tests over a short time period were administered to the pupils. Figure 6.3 shows the results. On the first three tests, before much praise or blame was given, the differences among the groups were very small. However, on the

[1] Reprinted from the September, 1954, issue of *Education* by permission of the publishers, The Bobbs-Merrill Company, Inc., Indianapolis, Ind.

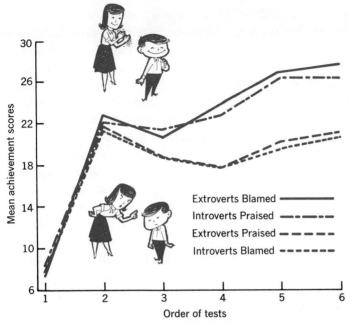

Fig. 6.3. Effects of praise and blame on extroverts and introverts. (Adapted from G. G. Thompson & C. W. Hunnicutt. The effect of repeated praise or blame on the work achievement of "introverts" and "extroverts." *J. educ. Psychol.*, 1944, **35**, 264.)

last three tests, moderate differences appeared. At the end of the study, the extroverts who were blamed scored highest, and the introverts who were praised were nearly as high; but the extroverts who were praised and the introverts who were blamed were considerably lower. Though not shown, either praise or blame was more effective than no external incentive in increasing the work output, and praise and blame were equally effective in motivating the pupils if the introverts and extroverts were not differentiated. In this study, each testing period was for only 30 seconds. Also, test items, involving cancellation, could be performed very quickly. Further, the praising consisted of the teacher's placing a "G" for good on the test paper after it was handed in, and the blaming consisted of placing a "P" for poor on a test paper. Subsequently and privately when returning the papers to each child, the teacher said that the "P" stood for poor work and the "G" for good work. One should not generalize from this study to the use of other forms of praise and blame or to often repeated use of the above forms over an extended period of time.

The use of praise and blame produces different results in introverted and extroverted students. Other behavior intended to get the student to carry out the teacher's wishes also is related to students' responses (41). The effects of five main sources of influence or power by the teacher were studied in relation to the student's setting his aspirations or goals. These five sources require further clarification. *Rewards* in the classroom are things given or promised for behavior which is in accord with the wishes of the teacher. *Coercion*, based upon the ability to punish, is exercised or threatened for behavior which is not in line with the wishes of the teachers; low grades, exclusion from the group, assignments, report to parents or authorities, etc. are used. Rewards and coercion may be used discriminately or indiscriminately. *Legitimate power* in the classroom is derived from the perception that the teacher is behaving in accord with the values of the students being influenced. *Expert power* in the classroom is based on the perceived reliability of the teacher's information. The more the teacher is seen as knowing what he is talking about, the more he is likely to influence the students. The teacher can exercise *referent power* to the extent that the students desire to be like him.

Responses of high school students to the five forms of power were ascertained. Indiscriminate, coercive influences by the teacher led to ignoring or opposition to the teacher's wishes; reward, and legitimate, referent, and expert power were accompanied with acceptance of the teacher's wishes. The teacher's disapproval of inadequate performance had no effect on aspirations or future performance of students; however, disapproval when performance was as good as the student felt he could do had a negative effect on future aspirations and performance. The teacher's influence was accepted when rewards were given for adequate performance but was lessened under indiscriminate reward. The positive and negative accompaniments of the various forms of power were related to the favorableness or negativeness of student attitudes toward teachers and course content. In summary, indiscriminate use of reward and coercion negatively affects how well students learn the subject matter and also how they feel toward the teacher and the subject matter.

LEADERSHIP BEHAVIOR OF THE TEACHER

In the preceding sections of this chapter, we have indicated four of many studies of teacher behavior. In each of them, leadership was either discussed directly or was implied. Table 6.3 shows some relationships among the behavior indicated in the four studies. This behavior is to be considered parallel, rather than identical. For example, Flanders, Ryans, and Isaacson all indicate a pattern of behavior of the warm, understanding type, clarified in such terms as praising and encouraging, accepting ideas of the students, asking questions, feedback—informing students of their good work, and encouraging student participation. All four also indicate a parallel teacher-behavior pattern

TABLE 6.3.

Parallel Relationships of Teacher Behavior as Specified in Four Studies

Amidon and Flanders[a]	Ryans[b]	Isaacson, et al.[c]	Rosenfeld and Zander[d]
Accepts feelings Praises or encourages Accepts or uses ideas of students Asks questions	Pattern X_o—Warm, understanding, friendly	Rapport Interaction Feedback	
Lectures Gives direction Criticizes or justifies authority	Aloof, restricted	Structure Overload	Discriminate use of power Indiscriminate use of rewards and punishments
	Pattern Y_o—Responsible, businesslike	Skill	

[a] E. J. Amidon & N. A. Flanders. *The role of the teacher in the classroom: A manual for understanding and improving teachers' classroom behavior.* Minneapolis: Paul S. Amidon, 1963.
[b] D. G. Ryans. *Characteristics of teachers: Their description, comparison, and appraisal.* Washington, D.C.: American Council on Education, 1960.
[c] R. L. Isaacson *et al.* Dimensions of student evaluations of teaching. *J. educ. Psychol.,* 1964, **55,** 344–351.
[d] H. Rosenfeld & A. Zander. The influence of teachers on aspirations of students. *J. educ. Psychol.,* 1961, **52,** 1–11.

characterized by criticizing or justifying authority, being aloof and restricted, overloading (assigning more than students can accomplish), and indiscriminately using rewards and punishments. Ryans' description of responsible, businesslike behavior corresponds to the skill, or teaching ability, of Isaacson *et al.;* there are not parallel categories by Flanders or by Rosenfeld and Zander for this pattern of behavior.

There is substantial agreement that certain types of behavior are related to the more efficient achievement of specific educational objectives. For example, warm and understanding behavior, accompanied with a greater amount of participation in activities by students, is more effective in securing better attitudes toward subject matter and the teacher; in developing favorable interpersonal attitudes, group cohesiveness, and social skills; and in securing higher achievement in the subject matter than are those associated with aloofness, restricted patterns, indiscriminate use of rewards and punishments, and justifying authority. The responsible, businesslike behavior and teaching ability also may produce generally excellent results. After surveying some direct studies of leadership, we shall be able to draw further generalizations about teacher behavior and the attainment of various school objectives.

A few definitions connected with leadership may be helpful in establishing a common understanding. Teacher behavior which affects the instructional group is synonymous with teacher leadership. The teacher has certain authority, delegated through a channel—the building principal, the superintendent, the school board, the local community. Authority may be defined as the power to make decisions which affect other people. The teacher has the authority to make decisions which affect the students (24). The manner in which the leader demonstrates his power and authority produces different results, as will now be shown.

Authoritarian, Democratic, and Laissez-Faire Leadership

Lewin and his associates, Lippitt and White, conducted a series of experiments to ascertain the effects of various forms of leadership upon the individual and group behavior of 11-year-old boys in a club situation. The report of their procedures and results are given in many articles and films. The best summary of all the results and procedures was reported by Lippitt and White (32). Three forms of leadership were experimentally arranged—authoritarian, democratic, and laissez-faire—and two atmospheres were found under autocratic leadership, designated as aggressive autocracy and apathetic autocracy. The situations were so arranged that the groups of boys experienced each type of leadership, making possible comparison of the leadership effects on the same boys. Now follow descriptions of the three leadership roles:

Plan for Authoritarian Leadership Role. Practically all policies as regards club activities and procedures should be determined by the leader. The techniques and activity steps should be communicated by the authority, one unit at a time, so that future steps are in the dark to a large degree. The adult should take considerable responsibility for assigning the activity tasks and companions of each group member. The dominator should keep his standards of praise and criticism to himself in evaluating individual and group activities. He should also remain fairly aloof from active group participation except in demonstrating.

Plan for the Democratic Leadership Role. Wherever possible, policies should be a matter of group decision and discussion with active encouragement and assistance by the adult leader. The leader should attempt to see that activity perspective emerges during the discussion period with the general steps to the group goal becoming clarified. Wherever technical advice is needed, the leader should try to suggest two or more alternative procedures from which choice can be made by the group members. Everyone should be free to work with whomever he chooses, and the divisions of responsibility should be left up to the group. The leader should attempt to communicate in an objective, fact-minded way the bases for his praise and criticism of individual and group activities. He should try to be a regular group member in spirit but not do much of the work (so that comparisons of group productivity can be made between the groups).

Plan for Laissez-Faire Leadership Role. In this situation, the adult should play a rather passive role in social participation and leave complete freedom for group or individual decisions in relation to activity and group procedure. The leader should make clear the various materials which are available and be sure it is understood that he will supply information and help when asked. He should do a minimum of taking the initiative in making suggestions. He should make no attempt to evaluate negatively or positively the behavior or productions of the individuals or the group as a group, although he should be friendly rather than "stand-offish" at all times (32, 498).

Figure 6.4 shows the behaviors of the leaders as actually carried out in the club situation. The authoritarian leader gave many more orders, disrupting commands, and nonconstructive criticisms. Guiding suggestions, extending knowledge, and stimulating self-guidance were much less frequent under authoritarian than under democratic and laissez-faire leadership. Praise and approval were engaged in most by the authoritarian leader, being jovial, self-confident, and matter of fact most by the democratic leader. Extending knowledge was the only behavior engaged in most by the laissez-faire leader. Thus with clearly planned procedures for producing differences in the leader behaviors, there were marked differences but also some overlapping of behaviors among the leaders.

Figure 6.5 gives the four patterns of reaction of the boys' groups to the three different styles of leadership. The boys' dependent actions upon the leader were much higher under authoritarian leadership than democratic or laissez-faire; critical discontent and demands for atten-

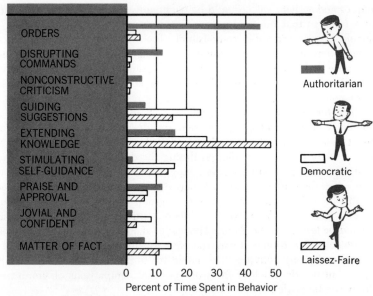

ORDERS
DISRUPTING COMMANDS
NONCONSTRUCTIVE CRITICISM
GUIDING SUGGESTIONS
EXTENDING KNOWLEDGE
STIMULATING SELF-GUIDANCE
PRAISE AND APPROVAL
JOVIAL AND CONFIDENT
MATTER OF FACT

Authoritarian
Democratic
Laissez-Faire

0   10   20   30   40   50
Percent of Time Spent in Behavior

Fig. 6.4. Percent of time given by authoritarian, democratic, and laissez-faire leaders to various behaviors. (Adapted from R. Lippitt & R. K. White. An experimental study of leadership and group life. In E. E. Maccoby, T. M. Newcomb, & E. E. Hartley (Eds.), *Readings in social psychology.* New York: Henry Holt, 1958, p. 499.)

tion also were higher under authoritarian leadership. Friendly and confiding behavior and group-minded suggestions were highest with democratic leadership, as were out-of-club-field conversations and work-minded conversations. The asking of information was highest under laissez-faire leadership; 37 percent of all the boys' behavior toward the laissez-faire leader consisted of asking for information. It is interesting that about as much work-minded conversation took place in the apathetic authoritarian situation as in the democratic.

Figure 6.6 shows the percent of time spent in high activity involvement. In aggressive autocracy, for example, the boys were highly active for about 53 percent of the time when the leader was present, about 17 percent of the time when the leader left the group; this figure moved up to nearly 60 percent immediately when the aggressive autocratic leader returned. The ratios are about the same in apathetic autocracy; however, the percent of time spent in high activity is much higher. Under democratic leadership work activity was about 50 percent when the leader was present; however, it did not drop off much when the leader left, and when he came back, it did not immediately pick up.

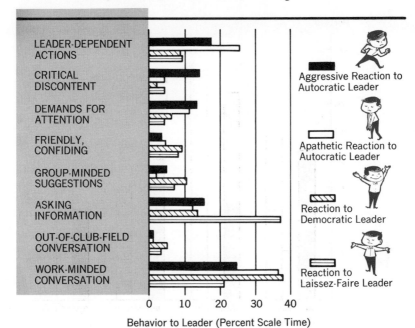

LEADER-DEPENDENT
ACTIONS

CRITICAL
DISCONTENT

DEMANDS FOR
ATTENTION

FRIENDLY,
CONFIDING

GROUP-MINDED
SUGGESTIONS

ASKING
INFORMATION

OUT-OF-CLUB-FIELD
CONVERSATION

WORK-MINDED
CONVERSATION

Aggressive Reaction to
Autocratic Leader

Apathetic Reaction to
Autocratic Leader

Reaction to
Democratic Leader

Reaction to
Laissez-Faire Leader

0   10   20   30   40

Behavior to Leader (Percent Scale Time)

Fig. 6.5. Four patterns of group reaction to the three different types of leadership. (Adapted from R. Lippitt & R. K. White. An experimental study of leadership and group life. In E. E. Maccoby, T. M. Newcomb, & E. E. Hartley (Eds.), *Readings in social psychology.* New York: Henry Holt, 1958, p. 502.)

With laissez-faire leadership the percent of time in high activity involvement by the boys was lowest among the various forms of leadership when the leader was present. However, it was also the highest when the leader was out. Thus, when the adult leader left, other leaders from within the boys' group emerged to take over activities, and as a group they were sufficiently interested in the activity to go ahead on their own. It is especially significant that under autocratic leadership, activity was much lower when the leader was out, but under democratic and laissez-faire leadership high activity involvement of the boys continued even though the adult leader left. With autocratic leadership, the boys did not know how to go ahead on their own and apparently did not want to go ahead.

Some of the more important conclusions reached by Lippitt and White other than those which may be inferred from the previous paragraphs are as follows:

The adult-leader role was found to be a very strong determiner of the pattern of social interaction and emotional development of the group. Four clear-

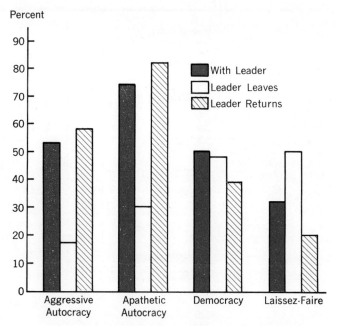

Fig. 6.6. Percent of time spent in high activity involvement. (Adapted from R. Lippitt & R. K. White. An experimental study of leadership and group life. In E. E. Maccoby, T. M. Newcomb, & E. E. Hartley (Eds.), *Readings in social psychology*. New York: Henry Holt, 1958, p. 503.)

cut types of social atmosphere emerged, in spite of great member differences in social expectation and reaction tendency due to previous adult-leader (parent, teacher) relationships.

It was clear that previous group history (i.e., preceding social climates) had an important effect in determining the social perception of leader behavior and reaction to it by club members. A club which had passively accepted an authoritarian leader in the beginning of its club history, for example, was much more frustrated and resistive to a second authoritarian leader after it had experienced a democratic leader than a club without such a history. There seems to be some suggestive implications here for educational practice (32, 510–511).

Though this study of leadership is one of the best from the standpoint of controlled experimentation, the authoritarian leadership was quite harsh and atypical of teacher leadership. One would not expect to find classrooms managed exclusively in an authoritarian or laissez-faire manner, as described in this experiment, except perhaps by beginning teachers or by experienced teachers in unusual situations.

Dominative and Integrative Leadership

Anderson measured three types of teacher-dominative and teacher-integrative behavior in the classroom (2). After computing a mental health quotient for the two classrooms he found that domination by the teacher was accompanied by evidence of conflict between the teacher and pupils and tended to produce a low mental health quotient. Integrative behavior, on the other hand, was accompanied by evidence of teacher and pupils working together and produced a good mental health situation. Short examples of both dominative and integrative teacher behavior are now presented to illustrate the meaning of dominative and integrative behavior:

Domination with Evidence of Conflict:

1. Teacher arbitrarily prescribes some activity: "Don't do it that way. I'll tell you what to do."
2. Teacher answers "No" when pupil asks if he can do something.
3. Teacher tells a child to go to another part of the room.
4. Teacher postpones something without giving any reason or setting a future date: "We can't do that now."
5. Teacher uses disapproval, blame, shame, obstruction, or interruption to secure different behavior from a pupil.
6. Teacher uses warning, threats, conditional promises: "If you can't do what you're supposed to do, you'll have to go out in the hall."
7. Teacher calls to attention: "Jimmy, face this way, won't you?"
8. Teacher deprives children of specific materials, activities, rights, or privileges, sometimes practices corporal punishment, sending a pupil out of the room, keeping him after school, and sending him to the principal's office.

Integration with Evidence of Working Together:

1. Teacher helps student to define, redefine, or make progress with the problem. The problem must have been stated and accepted by the pupil.
2. Teacher agrees with, approves of, or accepts the student's contribution. This is a response to spontaneous or self-initiated behavior; approval of the pupil's selection is given when several answers or new answers are possible.
3. Teacher extends invitation to go ahead in response to the pupil's wish, suggestion, or expression of need.
4. Teacher asks questions regarding the student's expressed interest or activity.
5. Teacher comments on such interest or activity.
6. Teacher accepts the responsibility for action by a child that is inconvenient, unjust, or unfair to another child; he also admits his own ignorance or incapacity (2, 465–468).

The effects of different teacher leadership behavior upon different types of students also have been determined (20). Three teacher styles were identified: Type A, characterized as turbulent, impulsive, and variable; Type B, self-controlling, orderly, and work oriented; and Type C, fearful, anxious, and unsure of herself. The greatest difference was between Types B and C. Type B teacher was warm and empathic with others; in contrast with Type C, she was not as fearful about how others felt toward her. The B teacher was self-severe; she set standards for herself and her pupils and then saw that they achieved these standards. Type C teacher was lower in organizing and leading others, either directly or indirectly, and lower in social interests, but much higher in hostility and aggression.

Students gained most under Type B teachers, least under Type C, with Type A falling in between. Type B teachers were especially successful with children who seemed to be unsure of themselves. Type A teachers—turbulent, impulsive, and variable—obtained different results with different kinds of children. Uncertain children achieved low with Type A teachers; however, the children as a total group gained well in the subjects in which these teachers were interested. Type C teacher was not successful with any children.

What relationships would be predicted between type of teacher and pupils' feelings toward self and authority? Teacher Type B, goal setting and work oriented, was particularly effective with negative, and hostile children. Toward the end of the school year, these children demonstrated more positive feelings toward authority, and their anxiety lessened. Apparently, the more hostile children develop better in an orderly, work-oriented environment than in a permissive environment. This latter conclusion has not always been reached in other studies.

Finally, the different types of teacher were reflected in the children's feelings toward each other. Children under Type B teachers became markedly more friendly toward each other than did children with either of the other two types of teachers. Apparently, the structuring and orderly tendencies of the Type B teacher developed a greater sense of security on the part of the children.

Leadership and Instructional Procedures

Our purpose here is not to present a lengthy discussion of teaching methods since many other books deal with methods. Only enough information is presented about methods to clarify some relationships with leadership patterns. In this connection, teaching methods, such as lecturing and project work, do not produce as large differences in student performance as do brief instructions in a controlled experiment. For example, in a concept-learning experiment, we administered instructions that varied in purpose. One type of instruction gave a minimal amount of information, just enough for the students to proceed with the task. A second set of instructions described the organization of the material. A third set described the organization of the material and also explained a strategy for arriving at the correct concept. Half of the students receiving each of the three different sets of instructions also were given a principle that would supposedly help them derive information more effectively. The results were exactly as anticipated. Those receiving information about the principle performed significantly better than did those not receiving it; also, the rank order of efficiency of the other three sets of instructions was as anticipated—strategy highest, structure next, and minimal lowest (28).

LECTURE AND GROUP DISCUSSION

At the college level, lecturing has been compared frequently with group discussion but less frequently at lower school levels. What is lecturing? As people who use the term indicate, *lecturing* runs the gamut from spending the entire period presenting information to using most of the time talking with students. Many lecturers stop to raise questions intermittently and also use part of an instructional period on group discussion. Group discussion, similarly, varies in the amount of control vested in the group to decide its topics and procedures. There may be completely unstructured groups in which the instructor acts primarily as an observer or is not present at all. He merely indicates to the students that they have a certain period of time to use for group discussion. On the other hand, an instructor may specify the topics, monitor the discussion so that it remains on the topic, and lead the group in decisionmaking.

Since a primary purpose of lecturing is to present information, we should expect it to yield as high initial acquisition of information as does group discussion. In a variety of college settings and subject fields, one method proved as effective as the other (3, 7, 13, 25, 35). Occasionally, the lecture has resulted in higher initial acquisition of information (38, 42). However, lower achievement has occasionally resulted (14). Perhaps more important than initial acquisition of information is retention. Group discussion resulted in better retention than lecture for one group (39); however, students of higher academic ability retained better under a discussion method while those of lower ability remembered better under lecturing (50).

The discussion method may not properly be expected to result in higher gain in information than the lecture method. However, in a well-managed group activity we might anticipate social skills, favorable attitudes, and lower anxiety. As described by McKeachie, a "Pyramid plan" of group activities in psychology was highly effective (34). Each group consisted of six freshmen, six sophomores, two juniors serving as assistant discussion leaders, and a senior who was the leader. The leaders, in turn, worked with faculty members in determining objectives, discussion procedures, and the like. Each group met weekly for two one-hour periods to discuss many topics of interest, including personal and professional goals, issues in higher education, and the main concepts in psychology. There were two other groups. One received no special attention, and the other received special attention by being given lectures, films, and demonstrations equal to the time spent in discussion by the pyramid groups. The performances in the pyramid groups were surprising. These groups were superior to both of the others in many important objectives—attitudes toward psychology, knowledge of psychology, scientific thinking, use of the library for reading the psychological literature, and resourcefulness in problem solving. In addition, a higher percent of the pyramid students continued as majors in psychology. The details of this program make interesting reading (10, 11, 12).

In general, instructor-centered classes are of the lecture type and student-centered classes involve group discussion or other activity besides listening to a lecture. When an instructor-centered approach and a student-centered approach were used, no difference was observed in amount learned initially as measured by an objective test; however, in contrast to students in the instructor-centered sections, those in the student-centered sections estimated that they had learned more of practical value and that more behavorial changes would take place as a result of the course. Six months later, there was no difference in retention of course content, but the student-centered group felt that the course had influenced a change in their behavior (37).

A more exciting adventure with the two forms of instruction involves two variations of instructor-centered classes and a client- or student-centered class (15). One type of instructor-centered class was characterized by the imparting of facts and information. A student summarized the method as follows: "It was, of course, filled with facts and information of both a theoretical and practical nature—and it was interestingly taught. Now and then we would ask questions of the instructor, but on the whole there wasn't very much general discussion. We just listened."

The second instructor-centered class was administered by a dynamic lecturer whose chief concern was with the content. A self-acceptant individual, he was popular among students and at times was permissive with them. One student described fairly well the general feeling of the students in the class:

Mr. ——————— did a lot of clowning in class and sometimes I felt that what he said was to get a laugh instead of being informative, but he had a way of talking about behavior and the way people feel, in such a natural and matter-of-fact way, that he made you feel normal and natural, even though he did all of the talking. He would sometimes express his own feelings and experiences as natural events and it made you feel, . . . "Hell, if he can accept his own feelings so easily and comfortably, why then I can accept these feelings about myself."

The sections taught by the client-centered or permissive method were also characterized by a student:

You feel pretty free in here. For example, things really had gone wrong with me today. It started out by my running out of gas coming to school and I was late to an exam; and then in History class I said the wrong thing and felt like a fool. But then in this class the professor really accepted my contribution. He seemed to understand exactly what I meant and, . . . Gee, I felt better than I had all day. It seemed like I got through to someone. You don't have to pretend in here. On the other hand you get as much information as in other classes (**15**, 138–139).

After having experienced the three methods of instruction, the students were put in a stress situation. The experimental stress situation was created by first assuring the student that all examinations would be announced in advance. However, without any advance announcement the students were given a "pop" quiz and verbally assured that this was an important test insofar as their total mark for the course was concerned. Further, they were given a limited amount of time to complete the test, and when they were about three-fourths finished, time was called to hand in the papers. Immediately after time was called, a word association test was used to measure the effects of stress upon them. Again, these papers were called in before sufficient time had elapsed for completion. At this point, the experimental situation was explained to the students, and it was pointed out that it was an experiment and that grades would not be recorded. The students were then invited to write their reactions from the first of the period up to the present time. These written comments were subsequently analyzed by two psychologists independently. Finally, the students responded to an opinion type of test to indicate the extent of their anxiety. Analysis of the information showed that the students who had experienced the permissive teaching showed less stress than did those who had experienced instructor-centered teaching; anxiety was highest in the instructor-centered classes and lowest in the permissive or client-centered classes.

LABORATORY AND PROJECT METHODS

The preceding discussion has been limited to lecture and discussion methods of teaching under warm and rigid teachers. Methods which encourage individual activity, rather than group activity or individual listening to a teacher's talk, include laboratory and project methods. The laboratory method proved superior to demonstration in a science class, not only in learning laboratory techniques but also in solving problems (29). In the same subject, the laboratory method was superior to traditional use of laboratory manuals in applying principles and also in interpreting information (5). While laboratory methods which emphasize the students' securing better understanding of concepts have proved effective, the project method—by which each student identifies and works on his own project—has not shown particularly promising results in high school or college classes (34).

A principal reason for results that are not clear-cut is the tendency to use either standardized achievement tests or teacher-made objective tests in evaluating student performance rather than other procedures designed to measure objectives of project methods, such as attitudes toward the subject matter, improved understanding of concepts, better application of information to new situations, improved problem-solving techniques, and motivation to continue independent study.

Comparison of Leadership Behavior and Outcomes

We may now try to relate the various methods of instruction to teacher leadership behavior as discussed throughout this chapter. Table 6.4 shows three aspects of teacher leadership behavior around which are organized various patterns; also, instructional procedures, subject-matter achievement of the students, and emotional security related to the various patterns are given. The dimensions that the authors have selected are warmth, planning and execution of classroom behavior, and approach to student behavior and subject matter. As with other

TABLE 6.4.

TABLE 6.4.

Comparisons of Teacher Leadership Behavior and Learning Outcomes

TEACHER BEHAVIOR

Warmth

Sentimental Personal identification with students	Warm, understanding, self-controlling Listens attentively Accepts feelings Accepts students' ideas Observes students' reactions skillfully Asks questions Praises and encourages	Aloof, egocentric Fearful, anxious

Planning and Execution of Classroom Behavior

Unplanned, slipshod	Responsible, business-like Systematic Flexible Integrative Orderly, work-oriented Explains things clearly Rewards fairly Explains reasons for criticism	Dominative Prescribes arbitrarily Uses power and coercion indiscriminately Asks for more than students can do Uses nonconstructive criticism

Approach to Student Behavior and Subject Matter

Impulsive, turbulent, variable	Stimulating, imaginative, surgent	Dull, routine

Related Instructional Procedures

May handle one type reasonably well, perhaps independent study best	Effective with group discussion, lectures, recitation, and independent activities	May handle one type well, perhaps lecturing best

STUDENT BEHAVIOR

Related Subject-Matter Achievement of Students

Inconsistent, varying with interest and ability of the students, insecure students do not learn well	High and consistent when procedures are selected in terms of objectives and student characteristics	May be high in outcomes emphasized by the teacher; rebellious students do not learn well

Related Emotional Security

Low for already unhappy children; might be high for a child who identifies with the teacher	High, when balance of direction and freedom is maintained in various activities	Low for most children

matters, we see teacher behavior on a continuum, rather than as a discontinuous and clearly delimited type. Ryans' patterns show up as one component in each dimension; however, Ryans' system presents only two polar expressions. Other patterns have been identified which seem to make it possible to arrange a continuum along three, rather than two, main points. Thus, the dimension of warmth extends from sentimental, personal identification with students through warm, understanding behavior to aloof and egocentric behavior. The planning and execution of classroom behavior extends from the unplanned and slipshod type through dominative. The approach of the teacher extends from impulsive and turbulent through dull and routine.

Teachers whose behavior patterns are toward the middle are capable of using a variety of instructional procedures. That is, teachers who are warm and understanding, responsible and businesslike, stimulating and imaginative, or who manifest parallel behavior as indicated in Table 6.4, use a variety of procedures rather than only one. They do not always lecture or use question-and-answer recitation, group activities, or independent work. The aloof, egocentric, and dominative teachers probably give information to students in lectures or by means of assignments more frequently than they organize the class into smaller instructional groups. Teachers characterized by sentimentality and personal identification with students, whose classroom behavior is unplanned and slipshod, and whose approach to students is impulsive and variable probably handle independent activities better than whole-class or group activities.

In securing high subject-matter achievement, teachers characterized by behavior toward the middle of the continuum are highest, because they are capable of selecting procedures in terms of objectives and student characteristics. Teachers characterized by the dominative and parallel patterns secure reasonably adequate achievement in the outcomes emphasized by the teacher, except with rebellious students. Further, when the dominative teacher remains aloof and uses power and coercion indiscriminately, there is much rebelliousness on the part of students. Unplanned, slipshod behavior produces inconsistent achievement, varying with the interests and abilities of the students. Insecure students and those of low ability should not be expected to accomplish much with teachers who manifest this behavior.

Emotional security is highest with warm, understanding teachers who are also businesslike. In varied activities they are capable of maintaining a balance of direction and freedom. On the other hand, the teacher who remains aloof from the students but who is also dominative produces low emotional security. Similarly, the sentimental, impulsive teacher, by focusing on some children and ignoring others, may produce low emotional security for most children, but provide an adequate emotional outlet for those who receive her attention and who identify with her. Children rejected at home but accepted wholeheartedly and impulsively by the teacher might find an emotional haven in the classroom.

The preceding generalizations were prefaced with the statement that the behavior patterns are not pure types; instead, any teacher is likely to be toward one or the other pole on any dimension. Ryans, you will recall, found the patterns highly correlated among elementary teachers but not among high school teachers. Despite the tentative nature of many of the conclusions regarding teacher behavior and efficiency of student learning in the cognitive, psychomotor, and affective domains, we have made remarkable progress during the past decade in identifying behavior on which teachers differ. Also, we now accept the idea that teachers have strengths and weaknesses, perform some functions better than others, and affect students differently.

THE TEACHER AS A HELPFUL PERSON

Regardless of the form of leadership, the teacher must be helpful to the learners in acquiring intellectual and related cognitive skills, psychomotor skills, and other learning in the affective domain. The learner experiences no satisfaction or success in a classroom unless he is helped to achieve one or more of these outcomes, and preferably all three. All of these outcomes should be achieved because the classroom is a planned learning environment (18). The school board or another regulating agency indicates generally what is to be learned, who is to do the learning, and who is to exercise leadership and assume responsibility for the conduct of the classroom. The teacher is responsible to school officials and, less directly, to the school board and community for interpreting these demands to the students. Though students can and do learn through interacting with one another in the classroom, it is the teacher who can be most helpful to the students as individuals and as a group (Fig. 6.7). The means of helping students are manifold (48). The teacher not only guides the more formal instructional activities, but also works in and out of school to improve learning opportunities for the students.

Further, students seek help from a respected and admired teacher in

> 1. The helpful teacher doesn't let the student sit in bewilderment;

> 2. . . . she considers the student's problem important . . .

> 3. and maintains communication with the student . . .

> 4. . . . on many topics.

> 5. The helpful teacher reduces the student's tension or discomfort.

Fig. 6.7. The teacher should be helpful.

solving a variety of problems originating in the home, neighborhood, and school. They need guidance in becoming reasonably effective and happy individuals and in contributing to the welfare of other members of the class. For example, the withdrawing child is assisted in becoming better adjusted to the group and the highly aggressive child in finding some constructive means for releasing his aggressive feelings.

What is the behavior of a helpful person? The person perceived as helpful considers the student's problem as important, shows willingness to maintain communication with the student, and is willing to communicate with the student about a broad variety of topics. Students judge that a helpful person is not only sensitive to the student's possible tension in an initial interview, but that he also wants to help reduce that tension or discomfort. Finally, the helpful person does not allow the student under tension simply to sit or to express ideas about anything. The helpful person structures the interview or other meeting with the student in such way that it is more readily possible for the student and the helper to gain insights into the nature of the problem and to find solutions to it (**46**).

While behavior of the helpful person as described above may seem to result from common-sense observations, it is surprising to find the large number of teachers who make no attempt to be helpful to the student in overcoming learning difficulties directly connected with the subject matter. Further, some teachers seem to think that their only responsibility is to impart information via lectures and to tell students what information to learn and the sources of it. Much teacher leadership still is confined to knowing the subject matter moderately well and then telling students what to learn and when to have it learned.

INTERACTION AMONG PUPILS

When given the opportunity, pupils communicate and otherwise interact with one another in the classroom. If not given this opportunity they interact in all types of informal meetings at school, going to and from school, and in the neighborhood. Interaction among pupils in the classroom can be guided to achieve useful ends. The class may become cohesive and leadership may be developed in many students. In turn, attitudes and values may be reinforced and social skills may be learned.

Group Cohesiveness

The goal to be sought in most classrooms is a highly cohesive group. A cohesive group is one in which all of the members wish to stay in that group; in other words, the members are sufficiently attracted to one another or to the group activity that they wish to stay in that particular classroom. Figure 6.8 shows a classroom group that is not highly cohesive. The circles at the far left represent four girls who gave mutual choices. When asked to list their five best friends in the class, these girls chose one another but, though given the opportunity, chose no one outside the group of four. In turn, only two girls from the entire

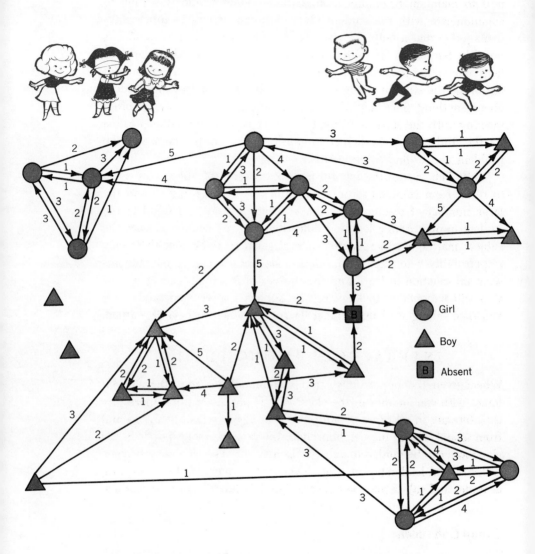

Fig. 6.8. Sociometric diagram of a classroom group. (Adapted from H. J. Klausmeier. *Teaching in the secondary school.* (2nd ed.) New York: Harper & Row, 1958, p. 54.)

class chose one of them as a friend and that as a fourth or fifth choice. The circles at the lower right of the diagram represent another clique, in which two of the three girls chose a boy (triangle) outside the group. The two boys at the left of the diagram are isolated from the class. They neither listed another member of this high school class as a friend nor did they receive any choice as a friend from any member of the class. The sociometric test on which Fig. 6.8 is based was administered on the West Coast in a large high school shortly after World War II. Both isolated boys were of Japanese descent and had only recently come back to this school after having been previously transferred outside the state during World War II. Thus, this class was characterized by some cliquishness, a majority-minority pattern with resulting isolation, and one strong male leader as shown toward the center of the diagram. It was not a cohesive group.

Consider now the effects of different bases of cohesiveness: personal attraction, performance of a task, and maintenance of group prestige (4). Each group was composed of two students. When cohesiveness was based on personal attraction, the group members tended to transform their work activity into a long, pleasant conversation. When cohesiveness was based on getting a job done, the members tried to get the job done quickly and efficiently, spending little time in conversation unrelated to the task. When cohesiveness was based on group prestige, the two members risked as little as possible to endanger their prestige status and acted cautiously, concentrating on their own actions and adjusting as best as possible to the partner.

Along similar lines, a larger class was divided into groups of five people of the same sex. The group members who were congenial with one another were more accurate in perceiving the behavior appropriate to the task than were members of noncongenial groups. Highly cohesive groups of elementary school children communicated more effectively with one another and also conformed more readily to the dominant group opinion than did less cohesive groups (33). Here group cohesiveness was considered to be a group property inferred from the number and strength of mutual positive attitudes among members of the group. In a different situation, children were given different amounts of rewards in the presence of others. Those who received the greatest rewards expressed more mutual positive attitudes toward one another (23). Praise has the same effect on students as rewards. The teacher's giving praise to individual students, rather than to groups of students, also results in the praised students receiving more sociometric choices from other students (16).

199

Second-graders in cohesive groups learned to spell more efficiently than did other children in low-cohesive groups. They also were more friendly and cooperative (**45**). These same conclusions have been drawn for older students in laboratory settings (**6**), Air Force bomber crews (**40**), and industrial groups (**49**).

Social status rose for all members of the classroom group when they experienced success in a common small group activity (**19**). However, the social status was lowered if the group experienced failure. The effect of the group's experiencing success lasted over a period of time, whereas experiencing failure was not permanent. This suggests that, in the elementary grades, group cohesiveness is increased by some form of group activity in which all members of the group feel successful in their accomplishments.

To establish cohesiveness within smaller groups, teachers may divide the whole class by putting friends together in the same group, putting learners together who have an interest in the same activity or a common goal, or putting congenial individuals together in the same group. Also, the task or activity can be arranged so that the members experience success feelings or secure prestige through doing the job well. Working with individuals and smaller groups within the class so that each member experiences a feeling of success is one of the most difficult tasks a teacher can set for himself.

Pupil Leadership

Leadership characteristics emerge in children's groups in the primary grades. With teacher guidance, group activities can be arranged in which most children develop some leadership ability. This in no way denies that all children should acquire excellent independent study habits and many individual skills. As emphasized earlier, certain objectives are achieved through group activities, and two of these are social skills and related leadership abilities.

One criterion of judging leadership is acceptance by others. Behavior most common to highly accepted young children is conforming more to classroom requirements and expectations, abiding more by the teacher's definition of appropriate behavior in the situation, smiling more frequently, engaging more frequently in some form of cooperative voluntary group activity, making more voluntary contributions to the group, and spending less time alone during free play or activity periods (**8**). Highly accepted adolescents more frequently demonstrate ability to perform such social skills as dancing, carrying on a conversation, singing, playing cards, playing a musical instrument, swimming, playing tennis, and skating. Further, in five of the skills, more girls than boys possessed a higher degree of skill, according to their own estimates (9).

Achievement in arithmetic is related to selection of a work partner and less, but significantly, related to general social acceptance (21). Also, elementary school children of higher intelligence and higher achievement tend to be somewhat more accepted than those of lower intelligence and achievement (17). However, living close together in the neighborhood is an important factor in choosing friends and is quite independent of intelligence. Similarly, being together in curricular activities and informal meetings or attending various school events is more important as the basis of friendship for all high school students than is attending the same classes (27).

We have seen that children and youth form groups on a variety of bases. Leadership in such groups is partly based upon being known favorably and also being helpful to the members. Children elect as class president a classmate who is well known and who the pupils think will be helpful to them. The high school football team elects a captain who they think will carry out his role efficiently and will be of mutual benefit to all. The prom queen selected in the high school or college is usually well known to both males and females, is attractive to them, and handles herself in such a manner that the majority feel that in this capacity she will be an excellent representative of the group. Leadership attitudes and skills developed in school transfer to life outside the school and are thus important objectives of schooling.

SUMMARY

The interaction between the teacher and students and among students are related to efficiency of learning. The students and teacher serve as stimuli for one another, social-emotional need gratifications may be sought and found by the students and teacher, and immediate reinforcement and confirmation of many responses directly connected with learning tasks may occur. Warm and understanding, responsible and businesslike, stimulating and imaginative teacher behavior is associated with effective instructional methods, high and consistent achievement of most students, and high emotional security of most students. Sentimental, unplanned and slipshod, impulsive and variable teacher behavior is associated with effectiveness of only some instructional methods, inconsistent student achievement depending on the nature of the students, and low emotional security except for children who might identify with the teacher. Aloof and egocentric, dominative and arbitrary, dull and routine teacher behavior is associated with effectiveness of only some instructional methods, high achievement in the subject matter by nonrebellious students, and low emotional security for most students. Clearly there is an interaction between teacher behavior and student behavior and learning. Most teachers are not effective with all children or all methods of instruction. However, some are far better than others.

Regardless of leadership and other behavior, the teacher must be perceived by the students as a helpful person in order for them to make progress toward significant educational objectives in the cognitive, psychomotor, and affective domains. Students perceive a helpful person as one who considers the problems of the student important, communicates with the student on a variety of topics, and helps the student with his problems. The helpful teacher, who also has developed some skills in pupil stimulation and control, quickly gets a group cohesive and working constructively. In this kind of environment, leadership and other attitudes and skills of students associated with productive group activity emerge. In the next sections of this book, Chapters 7 through 15, we deal more precisely with behavior of the teacher in achieving outcomes of learning in all domains and in securing desirable conditions for learning.

QUESTIONS AND ACTIVITIES

1. Describe briefly and give examples of how the classroom serves
   a. as a stimulating environment
   b. to satisfy social-emotional needs
   c. to provide for reinforcement and confirmation of behavior.
2. Observe a classroom and try to ascertain the interaction patterns, using the system of Amidon and Flanders. Compare your results with someone else who is observing simultaneously.
3. Discuss the three patterns of teacher behavior which Ryans found to characterize successful teachers.
4. a. Check the 10 items in the

Leeds' study which you consider to be the most undesirable teacher behaviors.
   b. How might this undesirable behavior be eliminated?
5. State and discuss briefly three generalizations from the Lippitt and White studies which you accept as applicable to yourself as a leader.
6. Based upon your own experiences as a student, describe
   a. a situation characterized by dominative leadership
   b. a situation characterized by integrative leadership.
7. a. Referring as necessary to the complete article, write a brief

Classroom Interactions and Learning

summary of one of the studies cited in the section on leadership and instructional procedures.

    b. Why is it difficult to design and execute a study to ascertain the relationship between leadership of instructors and outcomes in the cognitive and affective domains acquired by students?

8. Discuss possible restrictions upon teacher leadership which might be most difficult for a teacher to modify or change.

9. Describe the behavior of the teacher who has been most helpful to you.

10.   a. What conditions are associated with group cohesiveness?

    b. Under what conditions might group cohesiveness constitute a problem for the teacher?

11. What types of learning activities are needed to develop student leaders?

12. Make a careful analysis of your strengths and weaknesses as an educational leader.

SUGGESTIONS FOR FURTHER READING

Amidon, E., & Anita Simon. Teacher-pupil interaction. *Rev. educ. Res.*, 1965, **35**, 130–139.

Bales, R. F., & F. L. Strodtbeck. Phases in group problem-solving. *J. abnorm. soc. Psychol.*, 1951, **46**, 485–495.

Christensen, C. M. Relationships between pupil achievements, pupil affect-need, teacher warmth, and teacher permissiveness. *J. educ. Psychol.*, 1960, **51**, 169–174. (In Ripple, 1964, 199–206.)

Flanders, N. A. Teacher influence, pupil attitudes, and achievement. *Cooperative Res. Monogr.*, No. 12. Washington, D. C.: U. S. Office of Education, 1965.

Flanders, N. A., & S. Havumaki. Group compliance to dominative teacher influence. *Hum. Relat.*, 1960, **13**, 67–82. (In Charters & Gage, 1963, 162–172; and Ripple, 1964, 207–224.)

Gage, N. L., P. J. Runkel, & B. B. Chatterjee. Equilibrium theory and behavior change: An experiment in feedback from pupils to teachers. Urbana: Bur. educ. Res., Univer. of Ill., 1960. (Abridged and adapted under the title "Changing teacher behavior through feedback from pupils: An application of equilibrium theory" in Charters & Gage, 1963, pp. 173–181.)

Lewin, K. Experiments on autocratic and democratic atmospheres. *Soc.*

Frontier, 1938, **4**, 316–319. (In Fullagar, *et al.*, 1964, 459–465.)

Lippitt, R., & M. Gold. Classroom social structure as a mental health problem. *J. soc. Issues*, 1959, **15**, 40–49. (In Fullagar, *et al.*, 1964, 449–458; abridged in Rosenblith & Allinsmith, 1962, 334–339.)

McKeachie, W. J. Research on teaching at the college and university level. In N. L. Gage (Ed.), *Handbook of research on teaching*. Chicago: Rand McNally, 1963, pp. 1118–1172.

Medley, D. M., & H. E. Mitzel. Measuring classroom behavior by systematic observation. In N. L. Gage (Ed.), *Handbook of research on teaching*. Chicago: Rand McNally, 1963, pp. 247–328.

Ryans, D. G. Some relationships between pupil behavior and certain teacher characteristics. *J. educ. Psychol.*, 1961, **52**, 82–90. (In Ripple, 1964, 152–163.)

Wallen, N. E., & R. M. W. Travers. Analysis and investigation of teaching methods. In N. L. Gage (Ed.), *Handbook of research on teaching*. Chicago: Rand McNally, 1963, pp. 448–505.

Withall, J., & W. W. Lewis. Social interaction in the classroom. In N. L. Gage (Ed.), *Handbook of research on teaching*. Chicago: Rand McNally, 1963, pp. 683–714.

REFERENCES

1. Amidon, E. J., & N. A. Flanders. *The role of the teacher in the classroom: A manual for understanding and improving teachers' classroom behavior.* Minneapolis: Paul S. Amidon, 1963.

2. Anderson, H. H. Domination and socially integrative behavior. In R. G. Barker (Ed.), *Child behavior and development.* New York: McGraw-Hill, 1943, pp. 457–483.

3. Asch, M. J. Nondirective teaching in psychology: An experimental study. *Psychol. Monogr.*, 1951, **65**, No. 4 (Whole No. 321).

4. Back, K. W. Influence through social communication. *J. abnorm. soc. Psychol.*, 1951, **46**, 9–23.

5. Bainter, Monica E. A study of the outcomes of two types of laboratory techniques used in a course in general college physics for students planning to be teachers in the elementary grades. Unpublished doctoral dissertation, Univer. Wisconsin, 1955.

6. Berkowitz, L. Group standards, cohesiveness, and productivity. *Hum. Relat.*, 1954, **7**, 509–519.

7. Bills, R. E. An investigation of student centered teaching. *J. educ. Res.*, 1952, **46**, 313–319.

8. Bonney, M. E., & J. Powell. Difference in social behavior between sociometrically high and sociometrically low children. *J. educ. Res.*, 1953, **46**, 481–495.

9. Bretsch, H. S. Social skills and activities of socially accepted and unaccepted adolescents. *J. educ. Psychol.*, 1952, **43**, 449–458.

10. Carpenter, C. R. *The Penn State Pyramid Plan: Interdependent student work study groupings for increasing motivation for academic development.* Paper read at the 14th Nat. Conf. on Higher Educ., Chicago, March, 1959.

11. Davage, R. H. *The Pyramid Plan for the systematic involvement of university students in teaching-learning functions.* University Park, Pa.: Division of Academic Res. and Services, Penn. State Univer., 1958.

12. Davage, R. H. *Recent data on the Pyramid project in psychology.* University Park, Pa.: Division of Academic Res. and Services, Penn. State Univer., 1959.

13. Eglash, A. A group discussion method of teaching psychology. *J. educ. Psychol.*, 1954, **45**, 247–267.

14. Faw, V. A psychotherapeutic method of teaching psychology. *Amer. Psychologist*, 1949, **4**, 104–109.

15. Faw, V. Learning to deal with stress situations. *J. educ. Psychol.*, 1957, **48**, 135–144.

16. Flanders, N. A., & S. Havumaki. The effect of teacher-pupil contacts involving praise on the sociometric choices of students. *J. educ. Psychol.*, 1960, **51**, 65–68.

17. Gallagher, J. J. Social status of children related to intelligence, propinquity, and social perception. *Elem. Sch. J.*, 1958, **58**, 225–231.

18. Getzels, J. W., & H. A. Thelen. The classroom as a unique social system. In N. B. Henry (Ed.), *The dynamics of instructional groups.* Yearb. nat. Soc. Stud. Educ., 1960, **59**, Part II., pp. 53–82.

19. Heber, R., & Mary E. Heber. The effect of group failure and success on social status. *J. educ. Psychol.*, 1957, **48**, 129–134.

20. Heil, L. M., & C. Washburne. Brooklyn College research in teacher effectiveness. *J. educ. Res.*, 1962, **55**, 347–351.

21. Hudgins, B. B., L. M. Smith, & T. J. Johnson. The child's perception of his classmates. *J. genet. Psychol.*, 1962, **101**, 401–405.

22. Isaacson, R. L., *et al.* Dimensions

of student evaluations of teaching. *J. educ. Psychol.*, 1964, **55**, 344–351.

23. James, G., & A. J. Lott. Reward frequency and the formation of positive attitudes toward group members. *J. soc. Psychol.*, 1964, **62**, 111–115.

24. Jenkins, D. H. Characteristics and functions of leadership in instructional groups. In N. B. Henry (Ed.), *The dynamics of instructional groups.* Yearb. nat. Soc. Stud. Educ., 1960, **59**, Part II., pp. 164–184.

25. Johnson, D. M., & H. C. Smith. Democratic leadership in the college classroom. *Psychol. Monogr.*, 1953, **67**, No. 11 (Whole No. 361).

26. Klausmeier, H. J. *Teaching in the secondary school.* (2nd ed.) New York: Harper & Row, 1958.

27. Klausmeier, H. J., H. Wakefield, & J. M. Mulhern. High school students evaluate sectioning. *Educ. Leadership,* 1960, **17**, 221–225.

28. Klausmeier, H. J., C. W. Harris, & W. Wiersma. *Strategies of learning and efficiency of concept attainment by individuals and groups.* U.S. Office of Education Cooperative Research Project No. 1442. Madison: Univer. of Wisconsin, 1964.

29. Kruglak, H. Experimental outcomes of laboratory instruction in elementary college physics. *Amer. J. Physics,* 1952, **20**, 136–141.

30. Lambert, P., W. Wiersma, W. L. Goodwin, & R. F. Roberts. *Classroom interaction, pupil achievement and adjustment in team teaching as compared with the self-contained classroom.* U.S. Office of Education Cooperative Research Project No. 1391. Madison: Univer. of Wisconsin, 1964.

31. Leeds, C. H. Teacher behavior liked and disliked by pupils. *Education,* 1954, **75**, 29–36.

32. Lippitt, R., & R. K. White. An experimental study of leadership and group life. In E. E. Maccoby, T. M. Newcomb, & E. E. Hartley (Eds.), *Readings in social psychology.* New York: Holt, Rinehart & Winston, 1958, pp. 496–511.

33. Lott, A. J., & Bernice E. Lott. Group cohesiveness, communication level, and conformity. *J. abnorm. soc. Psychol.*, 1961, **62**, 408–412.

34. McKeachie, W. J. Research on teaching at the college and university level. In N. L. Gage (Ed.), *Handbook of research on teaching.* Chicago: Rand McNally, 1963, pp. 1118–1172.

35. Maloney, R. M. Group learning through group discussion: A group discussion implementation analysis. *J. soc. Psychol.*, 1956, **43**, 3–9.

36. Medley, D. M., & H. E. Mitzel. Measuring classroom behavior by systematic observation. In N. L. Gage (Ed.), *Handbook of research on teaching.* Chicago: Rand McNally, 1963, pp. 247–328.

37. Rasmussen, G. R. An evaluation of a student-centered and instructor-centered method of conducting a graduate course in education. *J. educ. Psychol.*, 1956, **47**, 449–461.

38. Remmers, H. H. Learning, effort and attitudes as affected by three methods of instruction in elementary psychology. *Purdue Univer. Stud. higher Educ.*, 1933, No. 21.

39. Rickard, P. B. An experimental study of the effectiveness of group discussion in the teaching of factual content. *Summaries of doctoral dissertations.* Evanston, Ill.: Northwestern Univer., 1946, **14**, 72–77.

40. Roby, T. B. *Sociometric index measures as predictors of medium-bomber crew performance.* Research Report AFPTRC-TN-56-46. Lackland Air Force Base, Texas: Air Force Personnel and Training Research Center, 1956.

41. Rosenfeld, H., & A. Zander. The

influence of teachers on aspirations of students. *J. educ. Psychol.*, 1961, **52**, 1–11.

42. Ruja, H. Outcomes of lecture and discussion procedures in three college courses. *J. exp. Educ.*, 1954, **22**, 385–394.

43. Ryans, D. G. Some correlates of teacher behavior. *Educ. psychol. Measmt*, 1959, **19**, 3–12.

44. Ryans, D. G. *Characteristics of teachers: Their description, comparison, and appraisal*. Washington, D.C.: American Council on Education, 1960.

45. Shaw, M. E., & Lilly M. Shaw. Some effects of sociometric grouping upon learning in a second grade classroom. *J. soc. Psychol.*, 1902, **57**, 453 158.

46. Thomas, E., N. Polansky, & J. Kounin. The expected behavior of a potentially helpful person. *Hum. Relat.*, 1955, **8**, 165–174.

47. Thompson, G. G., & C. W. Hun-nicutt. The effect of repeated praise or blame on the work achievement of "introverts" and "extroverts." *J. educ. Psychol.*, 1944, **35**, 257–266.

48. Trow, W. C. Role functions of the teacher in the instructional group. In N. B. Henry (Ed.), *The dynamics of instructional groups*. Yearb. nat. Soc. Stud. Educ., 1960, **59**, Part II., pp. 30–50.

49. Van Zelst, R. H. Validation of a sociometric regrouping procedure. *J. abnorm. soc. Psychol.*, 1952, **47**, 299–301.

50. Ward, J. N. Group vs. lecture-demonstration method in physical science instruction for general education college students. *J. exp. Educ.*, 1956, **24**, 197–210.

51. Withall, J., & W. W. Lewis. Social interaction in the classroom. In N. L. Gage (Ed.), *Handbook of research on teaching*. Chicago: Rand McNally, 1963, pp. 683–714.

PART II

PART II

Achieving
Learning Outcomes
Efficiently

*I*N CHAPTER 2 we indicated that we want students to learn subject matter efficiently, to develop their emerging cognitive and psychomotor abilities fully, and to develop personality integration. Recall now the useful ideas that each of four subtheories of learning—purposeful, conditioning, imitation, and subsumption—offer for understanding and improving classroom learning. Answer this question, too: How are the characteristics of the students (Chapter 4), the characteristics of the teacher (Chapter 5), and student-teacher interactions (Chapter 6) related to efficient learning? First try to collect your knowledge about these matters and then use it in studying this part of the book. Consider the following six key questions for *each* outcome of learning:

How is this outcome defined?	Chapter 7. Factual Information and Concepts
What does this outcome include related to my interest in subject matter and level of teaching?	Chapter 8. Problem Solving and Creativity
What generalizations can be made about the learning of this outcome?	Chapter 9. Psychomotor Abilities and Skills
What principles guide the teaching of this outcome?	Chapter 10. Attitude and values
How can I apply the generalizations and principles to my personal and professional life? In what respects is this outcome alike and different from the others?	Chapter 11. Personality Integration

To assume mastery of these materials, it is essential that you clearly differentiate among the various outcomes and find examples of them. For example, once you have studied the terms *factual information* and *concepts*, examples should come to your mind immediately when the terms are next encountered. An inability to differentiate the outcomes, or to relate them to your own interests and experiences, will almost surely result in inadequate understanding of the instructional model for each outcome. By following the suggestions given here you will improve your own learning and also develop some of your own dormant cognitive abilities.

CHAPTER 7

Factual Information
and Concepts

TRY TO RECALL the name of your first-grade teacher, the capital city of Nigeria, and the Vice President of the United States. What conditions are associated with the initial learning and subsequent retention of these bits of factual information?

Think now of what your concept of space was 20 years ago and what it is today. How do we first acquire our concepts and what leads to their increasing inclusiveness, generality, and abstractness? Our answers to these questions are not as complete as the agreement that the learning of factual information and concepts is an important educational objective. Children manifest these outcomes when they read with meaning, solve problems in mathematics, and understand and use the symbols and vocabulary of science, social studies, and other subject fields. Further, a considerable amount of what they are to learn is comprised of these outcomes and the related intellectual abilities that are simultaneously improved when learning the outcomes.

Figure 7.1 outlines a developmental and hierarchical sequence of cognitive outcomes. The arrangement is hierarchical in that the outcomes from the left to the right go in the direction of increasing inclusiveness, generality, and abstractness. Developmentally in his life span, a human being acquires preverbal percepts before he develops language in which to express his percepts. With the development of lan-

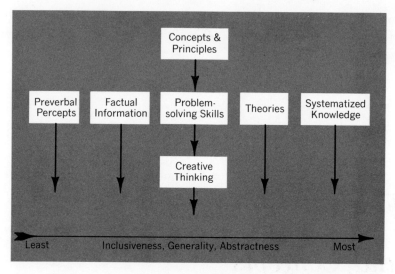

Fig. 7.1.   Summary of outcomes in the cognitive domain.

guage he acquires factual information more readily. This is followed with the learning of concepts and principles. The sequence is not direct at this point, for concept learning and creative thinking may be treated as special types of problem solving. They are sufficiently different, however, that each should receive special emphasis. Factual information, concepts and principles, problem solving and creative thinking eventually get organized into the systematized knowledge comprising a discipline. In most disciplines there are also theories.

Although an ontogenetic sequence is outlined in Fig. 7.1, we do not imply that only the successively higher outcomes are learned at successive maturational levels. For example, we acquire percepts and factual information throughout our lives, not just in childhood. Further, the sequence does not indicate that the learning of subject matter should proceed from the specific to the general. Often we move from the general to the specific and back again to the general when organizing knowledge systematically. The ensuing discussion in this chapter concerning factual information and concepts will clarify these and other points.

FACTUAL INFORMATION

A *fact* refers to something that has happened, an event, an actual state of affairs. One type of factual information is comprised of the association of the name or label with the object or event for which it stands.

For example, what you are reading is called a "book." Another type of factual information is the description of an object or event which stands by itself, unrelated to a larger pattern. It is a fact that right now you are reading a book, not a newspaper, not a magazine. These two types of factual information are not confined to any subject field or school level. Figure 7.2 will help to clarify the relationship among percepts, factual information embodied in words, and the least inclusive form of class concepts.

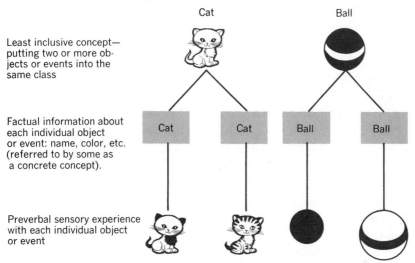

Least inclusive concept—putting two or more objects or events into the same class

Factual information about each individual object or event: name, color, etc. (referred to by some as a concrete concept).

Preverbal sensory experience with each individual object or event

Fig. 7.2. Relationships among preverbal knowledge, factual information, and subordinate concepts.

An individual has a sensory experience with each of two cats, each of two dogs, etc., and he acquires a percept, or mental image, of each. Each of the animals has a name, and properly associating the name with each animal exemplifies the acquisition of factual information. Some psychologists refer to this as associative learning. Each of the animals may be described on a number of different attributes, such as four legged, hairy, and vertebrate. Associating the labels with these attributes also represents acquiring factual information. However, when the individual perceives that two objects or events can be put into the same class such as cat, dog, cow, etc., we know that he has acquired a concept of low inclusiveness. When the attributes common to all the objects—cats, dogs, cow, etc.—are perceived and the child calls all exemplars *animals* he has a concept of higher inclusiveness and generality.

Once an individual has developed language and concepts, he may

213

use these to state factual information about objects and events. If he knows the concepts—*flag, red, white,* and *blue*—he may say, "That flag is red, white, and blue." If another person has these same concepts, he will know what the first is talking about. Eventually factual information such as this may be organized systematically into related patterns. Words embodying concepts are used to communicate about objects and events, and the resulting patterns are organized as factual information.

Consider the English-language arts. The correct spelling of each word, even when considered part of a system rather than independently, is a bit of accepted factual information. We must have dictionaries to check the accuracy of spelling. Rather than explaining to a child why *threw* and *through* are spelled the way they are, it is better simply to teach the child that these are the correct spellings. The names given to each part of speech, to the parts of a sentence, to punctuation marks, and to diacritical marks are likewise accepted facts. All the names or the labels given to objects and events in any language —ours or others—are accepted by children as fact when they are learning the language.

The mere association of names with objects and events is only the beginning of language learning. Associating meanings with the objects and events, and the names that embody them, is the beginning of concept learning. Once subject, predicate, and sentence are developed as concepts, they are used to express a state of affairs or a relationship, namely, that a sentence is comprised of a subject and predicate. You have developed many concepts and the words for these concepts aid you in learning other concepts. Thus, the study of this book may be approached from the standpoint of meaningful reception learning of factual information, factual in the sense that the two authors have stated certain things. In the process of learning factual information, you also will acquire some concepts that you do not yet have and will greatly extend the inclusiveness and generality of other concepts.

From this discussion, as well as from your study of Fig. 7.2, it should be apparent that there is not a sharp distinction between factual information and concepts. Factual information ranges from associations involved with naming one object or event to statements that describe an event or state of affairs. Concepts range in inclusiveness from two units in a class to millions of units arranged in a hierarchy of classes. In addition, there is the identity concept represented in only one of a kind. For example, there is only one person that is you. Others have a concept of you which includes you as the only exemplar.

CONCEPTS

As more is learned about concepts, the terminology used to describe the learning process becomes more varied. At the same time the role of concepts in school learning becomes more significant. Let us examine the attributes of concepts, in other words, the properties that make something a concept.

Psychological Meaningfulness

Consider a concept from the individual or psychological point of view. An individual's concept of anything is the organized inferences —meaningful associations—that he has formed of objects or events. These inferences enable him to categorize objects as belonging to the same class and to associate relevant observable and unobservable class attributes to them (35). A concept is not a word; however, some words stand for concepts, and some psychologists state that verbalizing correctly is essential in concept learning (3). An individual's concept of anything is a product of thought. It is a construct, unique to each individual. For example, one's concept of food is his own private construct; it does not inhere in food. Since concepts have an individual connotation, we cannot communicate concepts to one another directly. We can, however, organize verbal descriptions and visual representations of concepts that materially aid another person in acquiring a concept.

Note again that psychologically a concept is the organized inferences or meaningful associations one makes rather than merely the attributes or the responses that are common to otherwise dissimilar objects or events. Some concept learning is accomplished by abstracting the common elements of objects. For example, noting the attributes common to man and monkey leads to the response that they both are primates. Other concepts can be arrived at logically without observing common attributes. For example, it may be reasoned that all animals having backbones, the common attribute, are vertebrates and all not having backbones are invertebrates. Although the attributes of the concept *invertebrate* are not specified, the word serves to put all nonvertebrates into the same class.

Intrinsic, Functional, and Formal Properties

Many properties of objects can be experienced directly through the sensory organs; others can be experienced with instruments of various types. Observable properties which allow otherwise dissimilar objects or events to be put into one category might be called intrinsic properties. For example, all animals having backbones belong to the subphylum vertebrata. Similarly, animals that are warm-blooded, have mammary glands, and have hair are mammals. A liquid possessing certain properties is called water, regardless of where it is found. In the physical world these intrinsic properties of objects provide one basis for categorizing and relating. These are the so-called *common* elements or qualities, abstracted from the exemplars, which comprise the concept.

Figure 7.3 shows the classification scheme for certain animals, including man, all of which have intrinsic properties. These intrinsic properties form the attributes. Knowing the attributes of genus and species, family, order, class, and subphylum is the same as having a network of inferences about them, or a concept of them. A biologist

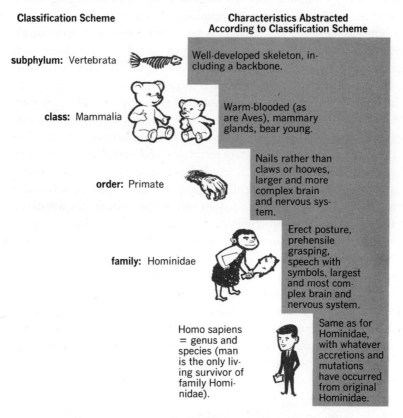

Classification Scheme

Characteristics Abstracted According to Classification Scheme

subphylum: Vertebrata — Well-developed skeleton, including a backbone.

class: Mammalia — Warm-blooded (as are Aves), mammary glands, bear young.

order: Primate — Nails rather than claws or hooves, larger and more complex brain and nervous system.

family: Hominidae — Erect posture, prehensile grasping, speech with symbols, largest and most complex brain and nervous system.

Homo sapiens = genus and species (man is the only living survivor of family Hominidae). — Same as for Hominidae, with whatever accretions and mutations have occurred from original Hominidae.

Fig. 7.3. Abstraction and classification scheme of animal kingdom applied to man.

might give a simplified description of man in terms of his attributes thus:

Man is of the genus and species, *Homo sapiens;* of the family, Hominidae; of the order, Primate; of the class, Mammalia; and of the subphylum, Vertebrata. Man is different from other animals in that he has erect posture, prehensile grasping, speech with symbols, and the largest and most complex brain and nervous system of all animals. But he is like some other primates in having nails rather than claws or hooves. Like other animals of the mammal class, man is warm blooded, has mammary glands at which the young suckle, and bears offspring; in these respects, man as a mammal is also different from all other classes of animals. Like other animals of the subphylum Vertebrata, man has a backbone; this also distinguishes him and other animals of this phylum from all animals in 16 other phyla.

Man invents many means of classifying things as similar. For example, strawberries, bread, and ice cream are all called food. Although they do not have perceptually common properties, they serve a similar function. (The intrinsic properties of each, of course, can be specified.) A nail, a metal clamp, and a piece of cord can be used to hold two pieces of wood together. Basing the classification of objects on the function or use of the objects is widespread.

Man has, however, invented systems (having no intrinsic properties), such as the number system and the alphabet. Both the Arabic and the binary system have properties, but these are the products of man's inventiveness. Yet the concepts in the Arabic number system do have formal properties that are agreed upon by mathematicians. As a matter of fact, there is probably more agreement concerning the properties of concepts in mathematics than there is in botany or zoology. These manmade formal properties are as useable as intrinsic properties in determining class inclusion.

At this point, it is apparent that there is some overlap between the attribute of psychological meaningfulness and the attribute of intrinsic, functional, or formal properties. The primary distinction is this: The latter can be defined by individuals who know most about the concept. We have a clearly defined concept to the extent that the men who know most about something can agree on its properties. Others who know very little about the specific properties do have a concept, but it is incomplete and inadequate in terms of expert knowledge. The properties, then, are objective while meaningfulness is subjective.

In connection with the intrinsic, functional, and formal properties of concepts, we can observe that nouns in the English language represent concepts. In mathematics, for example, nouns such as one, two, number, fraction, addition, and multiplication represent concepts. Many adjectives also embody concepts. In general, the adjectives related to the various sensory modalities embody concepts. Green, yellow, noisy, musical, bitter, sweet, hot, cold, rough, and smooth represent adjectival concepts. Concepts are also embodied in other parts of speech including some verbs, prepositions, and pronouns.

Abstractness, Inclusiveness, and Generality

Three related attributes of concepts are abstractness, inclusiveness, and generality. The continuum of abstractness ranges from sensory experiences with actual objects or events through purely verbal representations of objects and events, completely removed from the actual objects and events. Consider four concepts on a continuum of abstractness, starting with concrete: *berry*—many concrete instances with observable intrinsic properties; *food*—many concrete instances but instances are alike on the basis of function, not observable properties, e.g. strawberries and bread; *fearful*—instances may or may not be observable and what makes an object or event fearful is often unique to the individual, based on prior emotional experiences; *heaven*—no observable instances and no generally agreed upon function.

Concepts range in inclusiveness from one member to an unspecified number of members or exemplars. The identity concept includes one exemplar only. Each person is an identity concept in that there is only one of each of us. There are a few continents, many nations, an infinite number of stars. Concepts range in generality from applicability to members within the same lowest-order class to applicability to an unspecified number of members of the highest supraordinate class. For example, the concept of dog is applicable to members of the dog category only whereas the concept of vertebrate applies to many lower-order categories.

Structure

In addition to the attributes of abstractness, inclusiveness, and generality, concepts have an attribute of structure or organization, which is unique to concepts and not to other learning outcomes. According to structure, concepts may be conjunctive, disjunctive, and relational. Synonyms for conjunctive are *joining* and *connective*. A conjunctive concept is one in which all the attributes are present at the same time. For example, a sentence has a subject and a predicate. If either is missing, the group of words is not a sentence. Similarly, the attributes of mammal are warm blooded, having mammary glands, and bearing live offspring. If any one of these is not present in an animal, it is not a mammal. Many concepts which constitute classification or categorizing schemes are of the conjunctive type.

Disjunction implies separation, not joined. A disjunctive concept is one in which the attributes are not present in all the exemplars. For example, a strike in the game of baseball is a type of disjunctive concept because it can occur in a number of different ways, yet each is called a strike. A strike may be a ball thrown in the strike zone and called by the umpire. It may be a foul tip, or it may be a ball swung at but missed by the batter. At a more abstract level, Hindus, Moslems, Jews, and Christians are included in the concept *religious* although they differ markedly in their conceptions of the deity, worship, and other matters pertaining to religion.

Relational concepts, the third type, involve dependencies and are embodied in words such as *taller, older, wider, between,* and *down.* For example, a person at age 40 is older than another at 30 but younger than one of 50. Relational concepts also include if-then statements. If there is high humidity, precipitation is likely to occur. Geographic concepts such as south and north are relational. Relational concepts are difficult to acquire in part because the intrinsic attributes cannot be specified independently. We cannot give the attributes of south and younger except in terms of north and older. We can, however, specify the attributes of plants and of animals, and they are different from one another.

We shall see later in this chapter another attempt to classify concepts according to structure. When discussing a developmental sequence in concept learning, we shall note the work of Piaget.

Function

Concepts serve two main functions in human behavior: as responses to objects and events by which they are classified or categorized and as mediators between stimulating events and subsequent behavior. In this section thus far, we have been concerned with specifying the attributes of concepts, mainly to clarify the response function. Now let us consider the mediation function of concepts.

Assume that one has already developed a number of concepts; they are his responses to events and objects encountered thus far. Having the concepts enables the individual to deal with the physical and social world more effectively by simplifying it. For example, if one has the concept *book* then one treats all objects which fit his concept of book as belonging to the same category or set. All other objects may be treated as nonbook. This simplifies the environment in that one no longer has to treat each book object as a specific new entity. Instead, we are able to deal with classes of objects, events, and their relationships. In other words, the concepts we have serve to mediate between stimulating events and subsequent behaviors.

Concepts mediate in other ways. Knowing the attributes of a class facilitates recognizing other exemplars of the same class when they are encountered for the first time. For example, if you know the attributes of a noun and have specified some exemplars of nouns, you will have little difficulty in properly classifying words in this sentence as nouns or not nouns. Possessing concepts thus enables you to learn more efficiently.

In another way, concepts serve as mediators. Some concepts involve values and thus influence our behavior toward the exemplars of the concept. For example, murderer and thief have at least one attribute involving a value, namely, a disregard for the laws of society. Our understanding of these concepts affects our behavior, specifically our reactions to those who fit the category. For example, when we know that a murderer is at large, we do not pick up a hitchhiker.

These few examples show how concepts make the world less complex, enable us to learn more efficiently, and affect our behavior regarding values. As pointed to earlier in Chapter 3, concepts of varying levels of abstractness, inclusiveness, and generality are the principal content of the cognitive structure of the individual. In Chapter 3 we saw that concepts facilitate retention as well as the initial acquisition of new material.

Other Attributes

The preceding discussion is an attempt to define concepts in terms of specified attributes. To the best of our knowledge, no other person has made this attempt. Because this is the case, the attributes we have indicated must be considered tentative. There have been many attempts made by others to state definitions of concepts and also to organize and classify concepts according to subject matter. For example, one system puts all concepts into five large content classifications—events, processes, and behaviors; people; sensory substances;

dimensions and spatial and quantitative relationships; and personal feelings within persons (**46**). Another system of organizing discrete information into classes is contained in a thesaurus (**9**). The eight main classes here are abstract relations, space, physics, matter, sensation, intellect, volition, and affections. You may wish to study either of these classifications further. We do not have a better classification of content. We are certain that if one were developed, related to the subject matter learned in school, many persons would use it.

DEVELOPMENTAL TRENDS IN CONCEPT LEARNING

As stated earlier, we are becoming increasingly aware that abilities change with learning and maturation, rather than being inherited and unchanging. The precise changes in abilities and knowledge are not yet clearly defined. Because the field is being pursued with great vigor we shall consider three promising approaches to this problem.

Piaget's Conceptions

For a long time the ideas of Piaget concerning ontogenetic development of intellectual abilities were ignored in the United States. This was partly due to the type of observations that he conducted and the difficulties that were involved in arriving at final conclusions regarding a more complete system. Piaget's early methods were characterized by presenting certain material to an unspecified number of children, asking them to respond without an attempt to standardize the questioning procedures, and intertwining results with theory in reports. In general, no attempt was made to ascertain whether instruction would produce marked changes in the naturalistic type of development. Despite limitations in methodology, Piaget's ideas are now of widespread interest. Flavell has translated and summarized some of his many publications (**24**). The ideas which follow are drawn primarily from Flavell. Only the highpoints in the development of intellectual processes and related outcomes will be indicated.

There are four main periods in the development of intelligent behavior: sensorimotor, birth to 2 years; preoperational thought, 2 to 7 years; concrete operations, 7 to 11 years; and formal operations, 11 to 14 years. The years, which are further divided into phases or stages, are only rough approximations and vary among persons and cultures. Although there are these variations, each child is thought to go through the same stages. The characteristics of each period merit careful thought.

THE SENSORIMOTOR PERIOD (BIRTH TO 2 YEARS)

Birth marks the beginning of this period, and talking coherently, the end. Let us examine the characteristics in more detail from the standpoint of the change from purely motor to mental activity. The sequence may be telescoped thus: At first only reflexes are manifested; these reflexes undergo separate modifications with experience; actions are started that are oriented toward objects and events external to the child; intentionality emerges and the child learns and uses some means-ends sequences in exploring new objects presented to him; novelty is pursued in objects and experiments to find new ways of using objects; and lastly, new means are invented in goal-oriented activity. These means are mental-activity combinations that have developed from physical-activity combinations.

During the sensorimotor period the child develops a functional understanding of imitation, play, causality, objects, space, and time. The trend in all of these is from the almost purely motor activity of the newborn to higher-level sensory experiences and related mental activity. For example, at the beginning of this period, the functional equivalent of play is in the form of sucking. Toward the end of the period the child truly pretends to do things like eating, sleeping, washing himself —activities that he sees others doing.

THE PERIOD OF PREOPERATIONAL THOUGHT (2 TO 7 YEARS)

There is a gradual evolution of intellectual structure throughout the preoperational period that probably has its basis in imitation during the sensorimotor period. Preoperational thought has several important characteristics. One is egocentricism. The child is not able to take the viewpoint of another person. He feels neither the need to justify his reasonings nor the need to look for contradictions in his logic. The child thinks but cannot think about his own thinking. Toward the end of this period, egocentricism tends to be replaced by social interaction.

Another characteristic of preoperational thought is centration, the tendency to center attention upon the most striking feature of an object or occurrence. When a child sees his mother pour milk from a short glass to a tall, thin glass, he will say that there is now more liquid than there was before. Towards the end of preoperational thought when the child begins to decenter, he will take into account the compensating factors, such as the thinness of the glass.

During the first half of this period the child also tends to see action sequences as a series of not-too-well-related static states. It is very difficult for him to visualize the series of positions a bar takes in falling from upright to flat, but he can easily think of and demonstrate the beginning and end positions. Towards the end of the period he cognizes the transformations taking place between a beginning and an end state as a continuity and can easily picture a transformation at any given point.

Too, there is a noticeable lack of equilibrium between assimilation —incorporating material into the existing cognitive structure through structuring of environmental events—and accommodation—adjusting to the environment. The child has unstable, unenduring, moment-to-moment cognitive organization. His thinking is in the form of replicas of noticed action sequences and events. "Things are what they appear to be in immediate, egocentric perception . . ." (24, 159). He is unable to go back to an original premise in discourse and is unable to think in terms of inverses.

Preconcepts that are formed are action ridden, imagistic, and concrete, rather than schematic and abstract. They are imagistic in the sense that the child has a specific image of a given object when he talks about that type of object. For example, when he talks about a ball, he will be thinking specifically about his own ball. Early in preoperational thought, he has difficulty in considering members of a class as being distinct. For example, when a child sees a grasshopper, he will refer to it as "the grasshopper," as if only one grasshopper existed. On the other hand, things and persons that are familiar to the child of this age will be classified as totally different if their environment is changed. The toy under a chair is thought of as being different from the same toy when it is in bed. During this period a child seems to feel that everything has a directly observable cause, and he will immediately give a cause for almost anything if he is asked. He also cannot understand chance or probability, and might explain a flip of a coin by: "It fell on that side because it wanted to."

Preoperational thought is animistic and artificialistic. It is animistic in that the child attributes to inanimate objects the powers of humans, such as thinking, desiring, and feeling with emotion. The child might say, "The fire burns because it wants to. It likes to make us warm." Preoperational thought is artificialistic in the sense that if asked for a reason for something happening, the child will give some coincidently occurring characteristic or event as the reason. When asked why the sun sets, he may respond that it is because people go to bed. Concepts of morality and justice are primitive. The child cannot cope intellectually with problems concerning time, causality, space, measurement, number, quantity, movement, and velocity, although he understands what each of these things is by itself in concrete situations.

Here is an experiment that illustrates a child's inability to work effectively with numbers: Eight cups, each with an egg in it, are placed on a table in front of the child. The eggs are taken from the cups and placed in a line stretching across the table. The cups are now grouped together. When asked whether there are more cups or more eggs, the child will respond that there are more eggs than cups although he saw the eggs in the cups at the beginning of the experiment.

During the period of preoperational thought, conservation of mass, weight, and volume are not understood. Conservation of mass, weight, and volume means the permanency of these characteristics in objects and, more generally, in substances. For example, if a piece of clay is changed in shape, it still contains the same amount of clay (mass), it still weighs the same, and it still takes up the same amount of space. If a clay ball is changed in shape before his eyes, the child of 5 will readily assert that it is now bigger, heavier, or has more clay than it had before. The opposite will be asserted if he thinks the shape transformation has made the piece of clay smaller. The understanding of conservation of mass, weight, and volume appears sequentially during the period of concrete operations; at about age 7 the child learns conservation of mass, at about 9, conservation of weight, and at about 11, conservation of volume.

THE PERIOD OF CONCRETE OPERATIONS (7 TO 11 YEARS)

Concrete operations are characterized by the ability to solve concrete problems. The child steadily increases in this ability and toward the end of the period is able to attack abstract problems. The ability to solve real problems is accompanied with mental operations that the child could not previously perform. Piaget discusses these intellectual operations in terms of mathematics and logic. He defines operations as "interiorized actions whose efferent impulses do not develop into external movements" (24, 82).

Nine groupings of operations characterize the period of concrete operations. The first four deal with classes and the remainder with relations that may exist among elements of classes or among classes.

Each grouping is characterized briefly with an indication of the abilities related to it. The nine groupings are:

I. Primary Addition Classes
II. Secondary Addition Classes
III. Bi-univocal Multiplication of Classes
IV. Co-univocal Multiplication of Classes
V. Addition of Asymmetrical Relations
VI. Addition of Symmetrical Relations
VII. Bi-univocal Multiplication of Relations
VIII. Co-univocal Multiplication of Relations
IX. Preliminary Groupings of Equalities

In primary addition classes, intellectual operations involve putting together two classes to make a supraordinate class. An example is joining the class *spaniels* with the class *all dogs except spaniels* to get the class *all dogs*. Grouping I also refers to the breaking down of classes into lesser classes by the reverse procedure. The child at this stage can compose and decompose classes in a hierarchy but cannot destroy a classification scheme in order to impose a new one. An example of the former is seen in the child's ability to think of *collies* as part of the class *all dogs* and of *all dogs* as part of the class of *animals*. He also can go in the opposite direction to arrive at the class *collies*. Here is an example of the inability to destroy a classification scheme in a young child. A 6-year-old is presented with 20 wooden beads of which 2 are white and 18 are brown. He is then asked whether there are more brown or wooden beads. He answers that there are more brown than wooden beads even though he sees that all the beads are made of wood and 2 of them are not brown. This child is being forced into using two classification schemes (*color* and *material*) at once. He cannot use them because he cannot think in terms of alternate classification schemes. He cannot mentally destroy or remove one classification scheme to impose a new one. He can only think in terms of one scheme, and when presented with two, he becomes confused. The older child will have no trouble in mentally building alternative classification schemes, and he will have no trouble comparing them.

While Primary Addition is mainly concerned with the ordering of hierarchies of classes, Secondary Addition is concerned with operations involving the use of equivalent classes. The addition of *collies* to the class *all dogs except collies* produces an equation equivalent to that given previously using spaniels, namely, joining *spaniels* to *all dogs except spaniels*. Parts of the one example may be substituted for the other. Involved are operations such as those contained in the tautology: *Spaniels, plus all dogs not spaniels,* equal *collies plus all dogs not collies.*

Grouping III refers to the fact that a given class may be divided into multiple classes of the same rank. An example of this is the division of the class *dogs* into the following subclasses which are all of equivalent rank: *Airedales, beagles, terriers, spaniels, collies, shepherds, huskies, greyhounds,* etc. *Purebred* would be a class which would be of a different rank because it would include and exclude some of all categories mentioned. The other classes (*Airedales,* etc.) are all mutually exclusive. Grouping III also refers to the intersection of two classes to produce a third class. An example is the intersection of the class *green houses* with the class *two-story houses.*

Grouping IV is inserted by Piaget as a logical necessity although its actual presence has not been empirically verified.

Grouping V is concerned with all operations involving the ordering of elements or classes according to differences in sizes, rank, height, importance, etc., for instance, classifying cars into the categories *big, medium,* and *small.* Here is an example of a serial ordering not according to size but to importance: "A dollar is worth more than a half-dollar which is worth more than a quarter which is worth more than a dime which is worth more than a nickel which is worth more than a penny." Before about the age of 7, a child cannot rank order a given set of elements according to varying degrees of criteria such as size, importance, cost, etc.

Grouping VI is best explained with an example of a set of symmetrical relations. "Y is a cousin of *z*" expresses a symmetrical relation because its reverse is automatically true. If we are also given the fact that "*x* is a brother of *y*," we can perform an operation to arrive at the fact that "*x* is a cousin of *z*." In the preoperational period this ability was not present, but it now is at this level of concrete operations.

Grouping VII involves the setting up of a matrix of intersecting asymmetrical relations. Take deduction, for instance. A piece of lead is equal in size but heavier than a piece of iron. The iron is smaller than but weighs the same as a piece of wood. Consequently, we conclude that the piece of lead is both smaller and heavier than the piece of wood. The ability to deal similarly with the conservation of weight, mass, and volume is manifested at this level.

Grouping VIII serves a purpose concerning relations that is similar to the purpose that Grouping IV serves for classes. Groupings IV and VIII "were clearly invented because they describe *logically possible* cognitive structures, not empirically discovered (as yet, at least) logical structures" (**24**, 189).

Grouping IX involves the addition of equalities. An example of an operation in this category is the deduction $A = C$ from the given facts that $A = B$ and $B = C$. Grouping IX is said to exist in disguised form in all of the previous eight groupings. The child at this level understands equality relations, uses arithmetic and measurement, and understands the concept of number. He also realizes that other people see things differently from the way he does. "Through repeated and often frustrating interchanges with his peers, the child has to come to cognitive grips with other viewpoints and perspectives which differ from his own" (**24**, 201). The necessity of maintaining an original premise in an argument also is characteristic of this period.

Piaget states that the value system and social interaction of children also fit into the nine groupings, and he stresses that a child must interact socially in order to grow intellectually.

FORMAL OPERATIONS (11 TO 14 YEARS)

The primary difference here from the preceding is that the individual can manipulate ideas abstractly in the absence of the concrete or observable. Characteristic of formal operations is thinking in abstract terms, envisioning a variety of possible outcomes from a given situation, and forming logical procedures for the solution of a problem before it is dealt with in concrete form. A specific example of the distinction between concrete and logical operations is seen in the following problem.

The child is presented with four flasks containing colorless liquids. The experimenter takes a special material (x) and adds it to another flask also containing a colorless liquid, making this liquid turn yellow. He then asks the child to produce the same color using the four liquids in front of him. The child in concrete operations will not go beyond simple combinations; for example, x with flask 1, x with 2, x with 3, x with 4. If encouraged to try mixing the contents of more than one flask together before adding x, he will do some random mixing and may or may not come up with the color. He will not be able to think of all possible combinations and will have difficulty duplicating his actions if by chance he does produce the color. After first trying the simple combinations, the child who has reached formal operations will, without help, systematically try more complicated combinations until he solves the problem and then will continue to check the other possible combinations to see if there are other solutions.

The child who has reached the age of formal operations still possesses the nine groupings of concrete operational thought, but now they are better integrated, more fully developed, more flexible, and handled with much greater facility. The operations that the adolescent performs upon the propositions or hypotheses he is now able to generate may be changed by using the following four transformations.

1. Identity (I):   This is the null transformation of a proposition because it results in no change.
2. Negation (N):   This changes everything in the proposition to its logical opposite.
3. Reciprocal (R):   The reciprocal of a proposition changes what is stated without changing the conjunctions or disjunctions joining the parts of the proposition.
4. Correlative (C):   This changes the conjunctions or disjunctions between parts of a proposition without changing the remainder.

An example of a proposition is: "We can go to the show or go bowling tonight." If we attempt to change this proposition using only (I), it remains the same statement. If we use only (N), it is changed to: "We cannot go to the show and we cannot go bowling tonight." If we use only (R), it becomes: "Either we cannot go to the show or we cannot go bowling tonight." If we use only (C), we have: "We can go to a show and go bowling tonight."

All combinations of *INRC* transformations result in a transformation that is identical to one of the four possible transformations. If the transformations N, R, and C are sequentially performed on a proposition, the result will be (I) or the original proposition. Another example is that the Negative (N) of the Reciprocal (R) of a proposition will result in the Correlative (C) of that proposition. Piaget considers the *INRC* group an important part in the logical operations an adolescent is able to perform, especially with regard to operations upon hypotheses.

Piaget characterizes the adolescent as living in both the present and nonpresent. Besides his obvious interest in the present, he characteristically has great plans for the future of himself and society. He seems to be filled with theories about himself and about life. He is interested in distant events and places. These characteristics seem to be the result of his ability to generate orders of possibilities. The concrete operational child on the other hand is concerned with the immediate and the real, not with things that are theoretical, geographically remote, or in the future.

EVALUATION OF PIAGET'S IDEAS

A primary contribution of Piaget is his detailed outline of the changes in cognitive abilities which occur with age, only the briefest sketch of which is given in the preceding pages. Although the stage concept has some weaknesses when correlated directly with chronological age, verification of many of the developmental trends has occurred in replication studies in the United States and other countries. A sample of the generalizations similar to those of Piaget is revealing. Conservation of mass is easiest to learn, conservation of weight is intermediate, and conservation of volume is most difficult (18). Success on tasks of conservation increases with age (19). More junior and senior high school students have attained abstract concepts of mass and weight than of volume (20); the same is true of college students (22). The child's conception of brother and sister goes through the same basic stages as proposed by Piaget (21); the same is true in the development of conceptions of right and left (17). The abilities of discriminating, seriating, and enumerating size develop in three age-related phases (23). Considerable likeness has been observed in English children with respect to the growth of mathematical concepts (38), and logical thinking (37). Smedslund has reported replications of Piaget's work in European journals and now also is reporting confirmation and extension of Piaget's work in American journals (39). Support for Piaget's ideas also is found in Australian publications (16).

Bruner's Conceptions

The growing human being has three means of acting upon his environment: through direct action, through imagery, and through language (11). Individuals not only act upon the environment through these means, but have appropriate internal counterparts in the central nervous system for representing sensory-motor acts, percepts, and thoughts. These internal representational schemes are designated *enactive, iconic,* and *symbolic.* In early life the child proceeds in this sequence. He apparently first acts upon objects, or manipulates them (enactive representation) before developing a mental image (iconic) of them, and then later he associates names with the objects (symbolic). Although this sequence is typical of early life, one does not stop transacting with the environment through action and imagery. These continue throughout life; however, with the development of language, one increasingly deals with his environment at the symbolic level.

Enactive and iconic representation are characterized by immediacy. Objects and events in the immediate environment are represented in the cognitive structure. With language development comes the ability to translate experiences into words. This in turn releases one from immediate transactions with the environment. Language also permits combinatorial mental operations in the absence of what is represented. Thus, higher-order productive thinking is possible and enables one to interconnect and organize experiences into increasingly inclusive and abstract hierarchies. According to Bruner, man has inner capacities for language and imagery. However, growth of intellectual abilities is dependent primarily upon a specialized environment, not upon the innate capacities, to nurture and guide their emergence.

Recent experimentation under Bruner's direction includes replication and clarification of Piaget's work. Whether his terminology of enactive, iconic, and symbolic will prove more useful than that of Piaget—sensorimotor, preoperational, concrete, and formal—is questionable. However, the translation and refinement of Piaget's ideas and the fresh approach to the problem of intellectual development may eventually result in a major contribution. The most significant aspect of Bruner's approach is his attempt to determine how instruction affects the transition from iconic to symbolic representation and also how it affects the emergence of increasingly higher-level abilities associated with language.

Age Trends in Concept Development

Although Piaget and Bruner have provided valuable information regarding intellectual development, we still have little evidence concerning the difficulty of specific concepts in any subject matter. The size of vocabulary of children at various ages is a rough indication of the increasing difficulty of concepts. Figure 7.4 shows the average number of basic words for children at each of the 12 grade levels; quartiles also are given (**40**). Quartile 1 is the point below which 25 percent of the total cases fell; the median indicates the point below which 50 percent scored; and quartile 3 the point below which the lowest 75 percent scored. As shown in Fig. 7.4 the mean number of basic words for quartile 1 in grade 1 was about 13,000; for the median about 16,000, and for quartile 3 about 20,000. By grade 12 the corresponding number of words was 42,000, 47,000, and 51,000.

Specific changes concerning the concepts related to time are quite

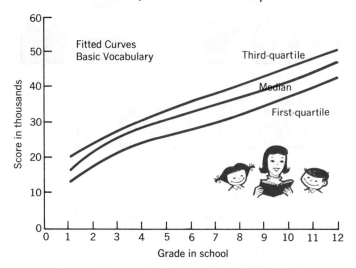

Fig. 7.4. Average number of basic words for children of various grade levels and at three levels within grades. (Adapted from Mary K. Smith. Measurement of the size of the general English vocabulary through the elementary grades and high school. *Genet. Psychol. Monogr.*, 1941, **24**, 338.)

marked from age 2½ to 8 years (1). Table 7.1 gives the percent of children answering correctly questions dealing with days, hours, months, seasons, and year. All questions were such that, if the child responded correctly, it was assumed he had a satisfactory concept of such terms as morning, Tuesday, and January. At 2½ years no child responded correctly as to whether it was morning or afternoon, whereas 100 percent did so at age 7. Not until 8 years of age did all the children answer correctly concerning the day of the week. At 7 years of age, all could tell time as measured by the clock. Not even at 8 years of age did all the children correctly identify the month of the year. Half of the 7-year-olds knew how many minutes in an hour, and about two-thirds of the 8-year-olds did. Half of the 7- and 8-year-olds correctly identified the season of the year. As shown in Table 7.1, only 50 percent of the 8-year-olds gave an adequate explanation of time as an abstraction.

An analysis of arithmetic textbooks and curriculum guides shows that pupils are expected to acquire concepts about liquid measurement as shown in Fig. 7.5 (34, 333). In the early primary grades they learn to identify correctly pint, quart, and gallon and recognize the different sizes. Informally, in grades 2 and 3, they learn how to change the meas-

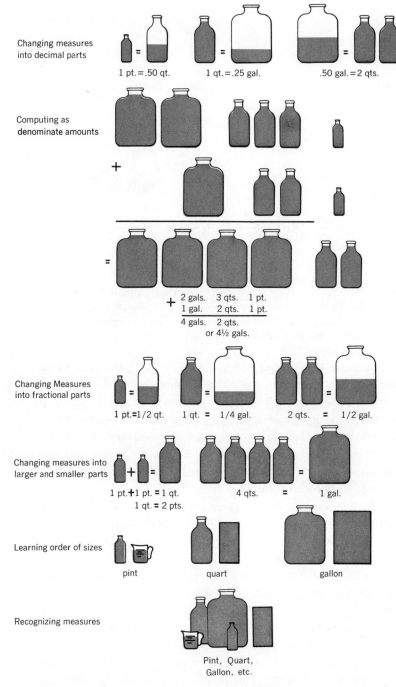

Changing measures into decimal parts

1 pt. = .50 qt.   1 qt. = .25 gal.   .50 gal. = 2 qts.

Computing as denominate amounts

+

=

+
2 gals.	3 qts.	1 pt.
1 gal.	2 qts.	1 pt.
4 gals.	2 qts.	

or 4½ gals.

Changing Measures into fractional parts

1 pt. = 1/2 qt.   1 qt. = 1/4 gal.   2 qts. = 1/2 gal.

Changing measures into larger and smaller parts

1 pt. + 1 pt. = 1 qt.   4 qts. = 1 gal.
1 qt. = 2 pts.

Learning order of sizes

pint   quart   gallon

Recognizing measures

Pint, Quart,
Gallon, etc.

Fig. 7.5. Developmental sequence, liquid measurement. (Adapted from H. J. Klausmeier & Katharine Dresden. *Teaching in the elementary school.* (2nd ed.) New York: Harper & Row, 1962, p. 333.)

TABLE 7.1.

Percentage of Children Correctly Answering Questions Dealing with Time

Question	2½ Yrs.	3 Yrs.	3½ Yrs.	4 Yrs.	5 Yrs.	6 Yrs.	7 Yrs.	8 Yrs.
Is it morning or afternoon?	0	40	15	71	90	84	100	100
What day is today?	10	5	5	26	70	48	84	100
What time is it?	0	0	0	7	0	32	100	100
What month is it?					30	33	84	66
How many minutes in an hour?					0	0	50	66
What season is it?					0	16	50	50
What year is it?					30	16	33	84
What day of the month?					0	0	0	66
What does time mean?					20	0	16	50

SOURCE: Adapted from Louise B. Ames. The development of the sense of time in the young child. *J. genet. Psychol.*, 1946, **68**, 104.

ures into larger and smaller parts; for example, 2 pints make 1 quart and 4 quarts make 1 gallon. Depending upon the particular school system and the textbook used in the third or fourth grade, children learn that 1 pint is the same as one-half quart and that 1 quart is one-fourth gallon. Not until about fifth or sixth grade do they learn the meaning of a decimal fraction or the concept of adding liquid measures as denominate numbers. Unless children are taught specifically the meaning of decimal fractions and denominate numbers, most seem not to learn it independently in home and neighborhood activities. Thus in acquiring mathematical concepts, the child's intelligence, his home environment, and instruction in school are very important.

Reading ability is closely related to the development of concepts when the attributes of the concepts are embodied in words (10). Figure 7.6 shows the curves of concept-formation scores for children whose reading achievement was considerably above that expected in relation to their intelligence test scores (overachievers), for underachievers, and for those whose achievement was close to that expected in comparison with their IQs (normals). Scores on the concept-formation test increased for all groups at each successive grade level—third, fifth, and seventh. However, the differences within each grade according to the levels of reading achievement were very large. For example, the difference within the third grade according to reading achievement—

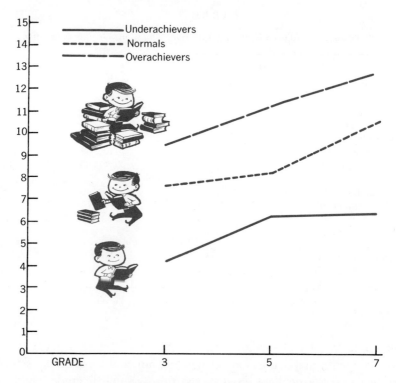

Fig. 7.6. Curves of means of underachievers, normals, and over-achievers on concept formation test from grade level to grade level. (Jean S. Braun. Relation between concept formation ability and reading achievement at three developmental levels. *Child Develpm.*, 1963, **34**, 680.)

overachiever, normal, underachiever—was larger than between the third and seventh grade for underachievers in reading.

In summary, a large body of information is accumulating concerning developmental trends in concept learning. The information, however, is not highly systematized. Urgently needed are two related types of information. One is the determination of whether concepts in various subject fields can be identified and placed in a relatively economical group of categories. The second job is to determine how school instruction may be manipulated so that the concepts are learned efficiently. In the next section of this chapter, models for teaching factual information and for teaching concepts are presented. The authors give their estimate of the best knowledge available at this time concerning how the teacher may proceed.

MODEL FOR TEACHING
FACTUAL INFORMATION

As indicated previously, factual information includes arbitrary associations and statements about objects and events of the type contained in textbooks. In this section generalizations derived from empirical research and theory, and instructional principles related to them will be discussed. Motivation, retention, transfer, provisions for individual differences, and instructional media and material will be mentioned only incidentally for they are included in later chapters. The learning of factual information will be approached from the standpoint of meaningful reception learning, while concept learning will be approached from the viewpoint of purposeful discovery learning, both of which were outlined in Chapter 3. The model for teaching factual information is composed of sequential, parallel generalizations and principles as follows:

GENERALIZATION	PRINCIPLE
1. Learners of varying characteristics acquire unequal amounts of factual information during any given time period.	1. Organize material appropriate for the individual.
2. Relating new material to an already existing cognitive structure facilitates the acquisition of the new material.	2. Use advance organizers.
3. Cognizing and organizing sequential components is essential to the mastery of complex material.	3. Provide for proper sequencing of material.
4. Practice increases the stability and clarity of the individual's organized knowledge and thereby reduces forgetting and facilitates the relearning of the same material and the learning of new material.	4. Arrange for appropriate practice.
5. Evaluation of one's own performance is essential for independence in learning.	5. Encourage independent evaluation.

Organize Material for the Individual[1]

Suppose that a high school student wants to learn the names of the bones of the body. How difficult is this task for him? How much time will be required for the learning? Stated differently, what is the length of the learning task? Can this task be organized so that only several portions of related facts in the total group can be mastered efficiently and then combined? Difficulty, length, and relationships among parts of a larger body of factual material are three dimensions to consider when organizing factual material into appropriate learning units.

The names given to the some 200 bones of the body are not easy to learn and are not encountered frequently in normal conversation or reading. If the high school student were simply presented an alphabetized list of the bone names, he would probably find this an exceedingly difficult learning task. But several relationships can be found for grouping the bone names. For example, the bones of the head, neck, and trunk can comprise one group or three related groups. The bones of the arms and hands can comprise another group, and those of the legs and feet, another. Inasmuch as 64 of the bones are in the hands and arms alone and have a relatively small number of names, such a grouping of related facts makes the total learning task easier than does the alphabetized list.

Though it may appear trite or common sense to suggest that related groupings of facts facilitate acquisition, many alphabetized lists are presented to pupils at every grade level. The following is an actual vocabulary list presented to sixth-grade children as one part of many units for the year in social studies: adapt, archeologist, domesticate, flint, glacier, government, Ice Age, Lake Dwellers, metals, nomad, pottery, property, Stone Age, tools, and tribe. In another single assignment to be accomplished in two short study periods in school and with homework, the same sixth-grade children were supposed to learn all the names of the countries of the Near East, the capital of each country, and the main seaport of countries which had seaports. No organizational scheme was presented by the teacher to help the pupils acquire these facts. Those pupils who acquired them did so through rote memory of facts, not through making meaningful associations among facts.

Figure 7.7 shows curves of learning for tasks of increasing difficulty. All of the easy items are learned in fewer trials than are the difficult items. The easy items show a rapid increase from first to third trial,

[1] This same principle applies to all learning outcomes and will not be discussed in the remaining chapters.

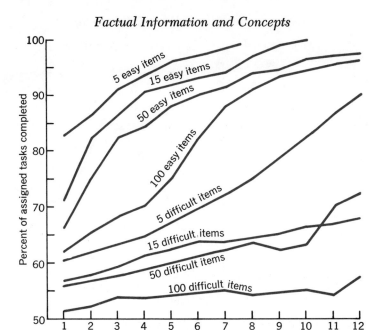

Fig. 7.7. Curves of learning for tasks of increasing difficulty. (Adapted from W. C. F. Krueger. Rate of progress as related to difficulty of assignment. *J. educ. Psychol.*, 1946, **37**, 248.)

and then less rapid. The learning of difficult items is very slow at first, gradually accelerating.

Analysis of the errors made in spelling clarifies the difficulty of one type of potentially meaningful material (**28**). Figure 7.8 shows the letter position at which errors were made in 7-letter words by eighth-graders and in 11-letter words by junior college freshmen. The peak error rate is at the fifth letter in 7-letter words and at the seventh letter in 11-letter words. Incidentally, no easy solution to eliminating the errors is apparent. When the missed letters (difficult parts of the word) are emphasized, fewer errors are made with them, but there is an increase in errors on the letters not emphasized. Thus, it appears not to be helpful to pick out the difficult part of the word for special attention when the student is first learning to spell the word.

Use Advance Organizers

Assume that a person has little or no knowledge about a field and is to learn new material. What can be done to facilitate the process? Studying material of higher generality and inclusiveness than the new material secures an organizational framework for the new material and

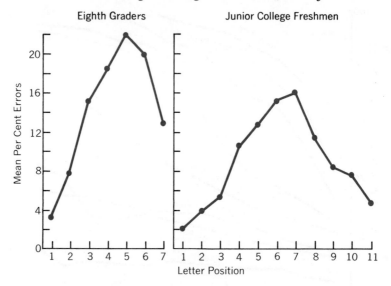

Fig. 7.8. Serial-position curves for errors in 7- and 11-letter words. (A. Jensen. Spelling errors and the serial-position effect. *J. educ. Psychol.*, 1962, **53**, 107.)

facilitates learning (**5**). For example, two specially prepared, sequentially related passages dealing with the endocrinology of pubescence were to be learned by college students who did not know this subject matter (**7**). A control group was given a 500-word introductory passage dealing with uniformity and variability among different cultures in the *behavioral* aspects of pubescence. This material supposedly would not serve as an advance organizer. The experimental group was given an expository organizer (advance organizer) of 500 words which provided an organizational framework for the first passage in terms of the different kinds of uniformity and variability prevailing among the primary and secondary sex characteristics. This organizing material was pitched at a higher level of abstraction, generality, and inclusiveness than the subsequent new material. As predicted, the experimental group receiving the appropriate advance organizer learned the new material better.

The preceding example shows how an advance organizer works when the learner has little previous knowledge about the new material. The advance organizer functions also as transitional material to relate new material to old (**6**). A comparative type of organizer was used that delineated clearly and precisely the main similarities and differences between new material to be learned (about Buddhism) and existing knowledge (about Christianity). The students who studied the comparative material, couched at a high level of abstractness and generality, learned and remembered the new material on Buddhism better than did students who studied a historical introduction to Buddhism. The learning and retention of the unfamiliar verbal material was facilitated when the unfamiliar material was discriminated from previously learned material.

The substantive content of an organizer is selected on the basis of its suitability for interrelating the material it precedes with what has already been learned. The content of the organizer is also more abstract and more general than that which it precedes or follows. In this way, the advance organizer provides the learner with a general overview of the more detailed material which follows. It also provides more inclusive organizing elements which take into account the particular content of the material to be learned. There is no final answer as to how frequently advance organizers of this type should be used. However, if one thinks of a body of material for a semester or year as being organized into a series of related units, one would probably start the instruction with an organizer for the total material and also would start each unit with a comparative organizer that would enable the student to differentiate and compare ideas between the unit just completed and the one to be studied (4).

Provide for Proper Sequencing of Material

Sequencing of material has proceeded on an intuitive basis until recently. The preceding analysis of advance organizers indicates a more systematic and psychological way to consider the large elements of a sequence. The advent in the 1950s of programed instruction also has led to more careful examination of the sequence in which specific material is presented to the learner. Both the advance-organizer concept and the programed material are properly concerned with arranging instruction so that new material is cognized and organized into a more complete total pattern.

Three general problems in sequencing subject matter revolve around the regularity of the structure of the material, the responses available to the learner, and the similarity and dissimilarity of different stimuli (25). Regularity of structure refers to the precision with which the concepts of the subject matter are differentiated. For example, the differentiation of animals according to specified attributes is reasonably concise. Differentiation of geometric forms is even more precise. However, in the behavioral and social sciences the attributes of many important concepts are not clearly specified. Social-studies teachers, for example, have difficulty in deciding the attributes or dimensions by which to compare various forms of government. Furthermore, there are many relational concepts in the social sciences for which the attributes are difficult to identify and to communicate.

Response availability is another important consideration in the sequencing of any material. This means that the individual must be able to make the responses required. This idea is central in the work of Piaget. If children are incapable of logical thinking until a certain age, instructional tasks which require logical thinking should not be undertaken. A more common example is found in connection with the use of the textbooks at different grade levels. If the students cannot read the material with meaning, the main job of the teacher becomes not teaching the content but teaching the children to read. Much current instruction calls for responses which the student is incapable of making.

The amount of similar and dissimilar material introduced into the sequence of instruction also is important. Discrimination of dissimilar material is made more readily than of similar material, whether this be letters, words, symbols, or forms of any type. Instruction should start with a lesser amount of maximally discriminable material and should gradually proceed in the direction of a greater amount of more similar material. Here the discrimination is more difficult to make but is essential to learning the subject matter. On an elementary level for instance, there is a greater and more obvious distinction between the colors brown and white than there is between beige and cream. In music we can readily make the distinction between a symphony and an opera, but what is the discrimination between an opera and an operetta?

Arrange for Appropriate Practice

The primary effect of practice in meaningful reception learning is the increase of stability and clarity of material that has been learned initially. This prevents forgetting. When retention is better, further learning of new material is facilitated because there is a more stable cognitive structure into which to assimilate or subsume the new material. Practice with factual material that has been learned initially involves not mere repetition of the same material, but also the use of it in a subsequent situation. For example, to practice recently learned spelling words the child should use these words in actual writing activities. This is much more meaningful than reviewing the same spelling list.

As will be indicated in the subsequent discussion of retention in Chapter 13, meaningful material is not subject to forgetting as rapidly as is meaningless. Although this is the case, we also have indicated previously that meaningfulness exists on a continuum of very low to very high. Therefore, we may be certain that material which students are to learn will vary in meaningfulness, even though the teacher makes a deliberate intent to make it meaningful. We state the following sub-principles in connection with arranging for appropriate practice tasks of meaningful material.

1. Establish a learning set (sometimes called a "strategy") so that the student attempts to secure meaning from the material that he studies. This is usually accomplished through discussing with students procedures for studying so that they can secure meaning from the material to be learned.

2. Provide for systematic use and review of verbal material. Utilize and review the material to aid in establishing the clarity and organization of it so that it is less subject to forgetting.

3. Distribute rather than mass practice. We assume that the subject matter of any field is comprehensive and will not be learned during any one year of schooling. This then requires that the material be organized into smaller units of some type and that this material be studied every week, rather than during one week only. Any daily practice session or learning period should be long enough for students to learn something well; if it is too short and they do not learn well, the material will be forgotten quickly. At the same time, the session should not be so long that it produces low motivation, fatigue, and other conditions which result in inefficiency. The length and spacing of instructional periods varies with the type of subject matter and the characteristics of the learners. In verbal tasks of short duration, where the longest interval between trials is about three minutes, distributed practice does not achieve better results than massed practice except under certain critical conditions (43).

4. Provide for reinforcement, including confirmation, of correct responses. The teacher cannot always and need not give students reinforcement, provided they themselves have means of determining if their responses are correct or appropriate. Some printed material is now being written in which confirmation by the student himself is possible. In meaningful reception learning, making progress on the learning task is all that many students require in order to continue with enthusiasm and vigor. Some students, however, require concrete rewards or other types of reinforcement. Feedback or knowledge of

results of some type is essential. One of the main jobs of teaching is to help students overcome errors. Awareness of the errors that students are making is essential to helping them overcome these errors.

Encourage Independent Evaluation

Again turn to classroom learning of factual information such as the correct spelling of words, the correct pronunciation of words, specific information about various objects and phenomena, and the location and size of cities and countries. A principal role of the teacher is to help the learner develop methods for evaluating his own responses. No person of average or above-average intelligence should be totally dependent on some other person either for reinforcement of correct responses or for arranging practice schedules for him. Nor should a child, even as early as the first grade, be totally dependent on a teacher, or teacher and machine combinations, to decide all the factual materials that are important for him to learn. As soon as children in the intermediate grades can use a dictionary, they themselves can check the correctness of the pronunciation of words; unless the word is spelled nonphonetically, 10- to 12-year-old children can learn to use the dictionary to check correctness of their spelling. Encyclopedias, atlases, and maps can be made available for securing and checking factual information. The high school graduate should already have developed the abilities required to locate and check sources of facts. He also should have considerable independence in deciding which facts are important for him to learn.

MODEL FOR AIDING CONCEPT LEARNING

Concepts are indispensable for transmitting man's previous experiences, interpreting present situations, and projecting plans into the future. Some concepts are acquired through meaningful reception learning, as described in the preceding section. Even though this is called meaningful reception learning, there is an element of discovery when an individual cognizes what the author means by the words he speaks or writes. Thus, meaningful reception and discovery learning merge into one another; however, at the extremes the two are quite different.

By discovery learning we mean learning in which the student, without being told by someone else, achieves an answer to a problem, a concept, or a principle. The main criterion of discovery learning is that the outcome is achieved without the individual being told what it is. This does not mean that there is no guidance of the learner or no arrangement of the situation to help the learner arrive independently at the solution. In fact, the vast increase in knowledge with each passing generation results mainly because we instruct the young, rather than letting them learn everything themselves. In our schools we need a fine balance between meaningful reception learning and discovery learning. The following six generalizations and related principles are intended to provide a framework for securing this balance:

GENERALIZATION	PRINCIPLE
1. Cognizing likenesses and differences among objects and events is essential to subsequently classifying them.	1. Emphasize the attributes of the concept.
2. Transforming perceptual experiences into communicable knowledge requires verbalizing the name of the concept and its attributes.	2. Establish correct language for the concept.
3. Concepts acquire stable organization through one's productive experiences with instances of the concept.	3. Provide for proper sequencing of instances.
4. The inclusiveness, generality, and abstractness of one's concepts are increased through active searching and productive thinking.	4. Encourage and guide student discovery.
5. The inclusiveness, generality, and abstractness of one's concepts are extended through use of concepts in new situations; also possessing relevant concepts facilitates learning in new situations.	5. Provide for application of the concept.
6. Evaluation of the adequacy of one's concepts is essential for independence in concept learning.	6. Encourage independent evaluation.

Emphasize the Attributes of the Concept

Suppose that one wishes to have children acquire concepts of triangles and squares. One could present three instances or examples of equilateral triangles of the same size and three instances of squares of identical size. Children at a certain developmental level would readily put the three identical triangles in the same pile and the three squares into another pile. How effective would this be in helping the children to identify the critical attribute, number of sides, in the concept of triangle and square? One cannot be certain. However, a different procedure might work better. One could present three equilateral triangles of different sizes and three squares of different sizes. The attribute of number of sides would be more obvious since it does not get confused with the equal length of sides. In the first situation number of sides may not be noted as the critical attribute.

Little disagreement has existed in the past concerning the usefulness of arranging instructional activities so that students can directly observe instances of the concept. For example, field trips are taken to the turkey farm, the evergreen forest, and the museum. Specimens are brought into the laboratories. These realistic experiences with instances or specific examples of a class have been shown to be helpful in concept learning. However, we have recently gone beyond this elementary level of thinking. We now try to identify the attributes by which things are classified. Rather than going to a turkey farm to see hundreds of turkeys, only one class of domesticated fowls, we instead show pictures of two turkeys, two hens, two geese, and two ducks. The latter provides better opportunity for cognizing likenesses and differences among members of the same class and of the four classes.

In another regard we have moved beyond merely providing direct experiences with the actual objects or even pictures of them. Actual objects and pictures often include details that are distracting, that prevent cognizing the attributes which are the basis of differences and likenesses. If you brought a live snake and a snail into the class for the purpose of discriminating between reptiles and mollusks, the distractions would keep many students from learning the differentiating attributes. Drawings or animated moving pictures in which only the differentiating attributes are clearly shown are more helpful in establishing the desired concept. Considerable evidence is mounting that too much detail in audiovisual material is distracting and hinders efficient learning (42).

For many concepts instructional activities can be arranged in which the attributes stand out clearly. Perceptual experiences with instances of the concept are especially helpful to younger children, because they lend reality to the words in which the concepts are subsequently expressed. Even with concepts embodied in numerals, the parts of speech, and the like, we would do well to arrange situations in which the attributes stand out (drawings, diagrams, etc.) rather than merely to present instances of the concept. Knowing the attributes of democracy and of numbers, not only being able to give examples of them, is the mark of meaningful concept learning.

Establish Correct Language for the Concept

We do not know how long man experienced many phenomena without developing language to communicate his experiences. It is known, however, that children as well as adults can have perceptual experiences with other human beings without developing a good concept of man. Similarly, vacationers see many plants and animals but form only a hazy concept of tree or grass. It is not enough in the teaching-learning situation for children to encounter instances and attributes of the concept. The teacher must go beyond this to the relevant names associated with the concept and the attributes. This is true not only for specific and less inclusive concepts but also for more inclusive and abstract generalizations and principles. It does not seem particularly difficult for children to learn the names associated with objects in their immediate environment. However, the observing and stating of relationships among events is more difficult.

In school learning, a lack of vocabulary has always been recognized as a deterrent to achievement in most subjects. For many years, we have associated lack of vocabulary with lack of direct experiences with objects and events. At present, this is still regarded as a serious problem in improving the educational achievements of millions of children in city slums and in poor rural areas. We also recognize, however, that children in these areas often have extensive nonverbal experiences outside of school but do not put into words what they are experiencing. Recently it has been hypothesized that children in culturally and economically disadvantaged areas are more deprived of verbal than of perceptual experiences.

Provide for Proper Sequencing of Instances

This principle has been stated previously in connection with the learning of factual information where applications to factual learning

245

were outlined. At this point we shall consider some applications to concept learning. The information regarding sequencing of concept material is drawn mainly from laboratory experiments; therefore, caution is justified in extrapolating to classroom situations:

1. The greater amount of irrelevant information presented along with relevant information, the more difficult it is to attain the concept (2, 26). An analogy to the classification scheme in zoology may again be appropriate. In teaching the concept of mammals, a teacher could present instances of vertebrates, including small numbers of mammals and larger numbers of nonmammals. These instances would have at least one characteristic of mammals, namely backbones, but the students would not learn very efficiently just what a mammal is. The picture of a chicken compared to one of a bear would only be confusing. The presentation of a larger number of instances of mammals would be more appropriate and efficient.

2. Concepts of high dominance and concepts embedded in instances of high dominance are attained more readily than are those of low dominance (14, 44). A high dominant attribute stands out clearly from those of low dominance; it is discriminated more readily. On this page, for example, the small lower case letters are probably more dominant for most people than is any word on the page. Similarly, the number of sides of a geometric figure is probably more dominant than is the number of angles.

3. A combination of positive and negative instances of the concept, rather than all positive or all negative instances, produces more efficient learning (27). For example, in teaching children the concept of equilateral triangle, it would probably be better to present mostly instances of equilateral triangles (positive instances) and a lesser number of right triangles (negative instances). The exact proportion of positive and negative instances is not known and may vary for individuals as well as for concepts.

4. A simultaneous presentation of instances of the concept is more effective than a successive presentation of instances (12, 30). Presenting several instances of the concept simultaneously permits discrimination of the attributes more readily and also reduces the memory load. If a child is presented three triangles, a square, and a pentagon simultaneously, he can compare them better than if he dealt with each of them one at a time. Obviously, the ability to discriminate and to recall are associated with previous learning. One who already has acquired the concept of triangle could readily remember and discriminate among the instances, even when presented successively.

Encourage and Guide Student Discovery

In recent years there has been a marked trend away from rote learning in favor of so-called "discovery learning." The University of Illinois Committee on School Mathematics (8), the School Mathematics Study Group (47), and the Chemical Education Material Study (13) have all given emphasis to the preparation of textbooks, films, and other instructional material in which the attempt is made to have students discover generalizations and concepts. Millions of dollars are going into the preparation of instructional materials and methods which supposedly will assist students in discovery. These programs, however, in no sense intend for the student to proceed without instruction. At least three features are usually incorporated into these and other programs: (1) Bringing to the students a problem that is real and meaningful, (2) encouraging and guiding students in gathering information, and (3) providing a responsive environment in which students get accurate feedback promptly so they can ascertain the adequacy of their responses (41). Further, the attempt is made to sequence the printed instructional material so that students are guided into arriving at the correct concept or generalization.

When these procedures are carried out, the instructional environment is perhaps as highly controlled as it is under meaningful reception learning and the principal attempt is to get the student to learn what mankind already knows about the discipline. The main difference is that in meaningful reception learning the answer is given before the student has had an opportunity to find it himself. It is entirely possible that encouraging the student to raise questions and to find his own answers increases temporary motivation for learning, facilitates initial learning, retention, and subsequent use of concepts, and also results in a permanent attitude of inquiry toward learning.

Let us clarify what is meant by guiding independent activity, or the discovery process. Does giving students some information about the structure of the subject matter, about a strategy or a principle to use in securing information facilitate concept learning? The answer to these questions is *yes* (35). Receiving information about a principle improved performance. The rank order of efficiency of the three other sets of instructions from most to least efficient was information about the strategy, information about the organization of the subject matter, and minimal information. Giving students information about a principle for arriving at answers to problems and for understanding material has had a uniform history of securing better initial learning than having the students proceed completely independently (**15, 29, 31, 33**).

The varying degrees of direction result in more efficient initial learning, retention, and subsequent use under certain conditions, but these require more study. The previous knowledge of the student, his previous strategies or methods of learning, his attitudes toward independent learning, the subject-matter field, the general climate for learning in the school, and the methods of the teacher all are related to the extent to which freedom for independent discovery operates effectively (**45**).

The teacher's encouragement of a questioning or searching attitude on the part of students is conducive to their acquiring new concepts and to broadening partially developed concepts. A final balance is required between giving too much information and direction, and giving too much freedom and responsibility. How much to help, when to help, and in what way to help require decision making by the teacher in the immediate situation.

Provide for Applications of the Concept

A number of principles have already been stated for facilitating the learning of facts and of concepts. These principles are themselves a complex form of concepts that can serve as guides to behavior in teaching-learning situations. On the pages of this book they are merely batches of ink. If presented orally by an instructor to students, they are merely puffs of air. The reader can memorize them without getting the meaning intended. Teachers with experience can probably read both the principles and the examples, think about them, and discover where the principles would have applied in previous teaching–learning situations or where they might be applied in future situations. The students without as much experience as teachers will probably have more difficulty at first in getting the intended meanings and then in attempting to find applications to future teaching situations. The student without teaching experience can draw on his many experiences as a student. But an instructor can take some definite steps to help prospective teachers in finding applications. Opportunities for observation of at least two different classroom settings while enrolled in a course in educational psychology might be arranged. Sound motion pictures and closed-circuit television offer many opportunities for helping the prospective teacher discover where the principles might apply.

A second example of application takes on a broader aspect:

What does it mean *to live* anything that is to be learned? What does it mean for example, *to live persistence?* Can we not agree that actually to *live* persistence in any instance means (1) that one faces a life situation which itself calls for persistence; and (2) that one does then in his own heart accept the idea of persisting; and (3) accordingly does indeed so persist? When all these three things concur, then one has on that occasion *lived* persistence. If with this positive instance we contrast a negative one, the meaning may come clearer.

Certain pupils were asked to write out the words of their morning flag salute. Among the various replies received the following were noted: I perjur legens; I plaig alegin; I pledge a legion; to the Republicans; one country invisable; one country inavisable; with liberty and jesters.

Is it not at once clear that these pupils did not adequately *live* the meaning of the words used in the salute? Whatever else they may or may not have lived, it stands clear that they did not in any full or adequate degree *live* the meanings which the words were supposed to carry.

It may be added that we can live things in many different degrees. Take feelings, for example; some we may live so slightly that we hardly think of them at the time, and soon forget all about them. Others we live so deeply and poignantly that we can hardly banish them to give due attention elsewhere needed (**32**, 535).

Now refer again to one of the principles for facilitating the learning of concepts: "Encourage and guide searching behavior." In terms of Kilpatrick's analysis, what does it mean to have fully understood and learned this principle? The person who has understood and fully learned this principle actually lives it in teaching–learning situations in which he finds himself: (1) he faces the situation by encouraging and guiding the pupils in the class to seek and search for better meanings and more accurate meanings than they presently have; (2) in his own heart he accepts the idea of searching for better meanings; and (3) his personal and teaching behavior patterns are characterized by searching behavior.

Encourage Independent Evaluation

This principle carries the identical meaning that it did previously when proposed for facilitating the learning of facts. It is also applicable to other learning outcomes which will be treated in subsequent chapters.

Self-evaluation of the adequacy of one's concepts is one of the most important attitudinal and cognitive learnings which individuals can acquire. Many individuals seem to develop an attitude of inquiry quite incidentally; others do not. As yet we have not found specific environmental influences whereby we can generalize precisely why it is that some individuals are continually seeking to evaluate not only their concepts but also their methods for acquiring them. It is quite certain, however, that when concepts are taught as facts to be memorized, opportunities to encourage self-evaluation are lost. Creating an attitude of seeking and searching as discussed previously, along with aiding learners to find means and sources for evaluating their concepts, is essential.

SUMMARY

Factual information, concepts, and related intellectual abilities are important outcomes of learning from kindergarten through graduate school. Many of man's experiences are organized into systems such as the alphabet and numbers. The names ascribed to these symbols are facts to be learned by children in school. Similarly, many events and states of affairs, current and past, are generally accepted and are to be learned as factual information rather than to be discovered. For example, the average annual rainfall in Tokyo, the name of the current Prime Minister of Canada, the latitude and longitude of New Delhi, and similar information are to be accepted as factual information. Factual learning proceeds most efficiently according to principles of meaningful reception learning: (1) organize material for the individual, (2) use advance organizers, (3) provide for proper sequencing of material, (4) arrange for appropriate practice, (5) encourage independent evaluation.

Much of man's experience is embodied in concepts, most of which are expressed in words. When thinking of a concept, one is concerned with the attributes of concepts that make them alike and different from other learning outcomes. One attribute of concepts is psychological meaningfulness. An individual's concept of anything is his organized inferences or meaningful associations that he has formed of objects or events that enable him to classify objects or events as belonging to the same class. Another set of attributes of concepts are objective, that is, people who have most knowledge about the concepts agree on the attributes. The objective attributes of concepts include the intrinsic properties of the objects or events; abstractness, inclusiveness, and generality; structure; and functions. Other attributes may be identified, perhaps content is one.

Concepts are learned through meaningful reception learning and purposeful discovery learning. No critical experiment has been conducted to determine which learning procedure results in more efficient acquisition; however, it appears that retention and transfer may be more effective when the learner participates in discovering the nature of the concept and its applications. Instructional principles of concept learning that embody primarily ideas of purposeful discovery learning are: (1) Emphasize the attributes of the concept, (2) establish correct language for the concept, (3) provide for proper sequencing of instances, (4) encourage and guide student discovery, (5) provide for application of the concept, and (6) encourage independent evaluation. Obviously, these principles do not imply that students should be left completely on their own initiative in concept learning. Instead, situations must be arranged so that students can arrive independently at concepts and their applications. Discovery may involve primarily the latter.

QUESTIONS AND ACTIVITIES

1. a. Define *factual information*.
   b. Give five examples of factual information, drawn from the subject matter and school level in which you are most interested.
   c. Discuss why it is difficult to determine whether something is properly classified as factual information.
2. a. Define *concept*.
   b. Give five examples of concepts drawn from the subject matter and school level in which you are most interested.
   c. Which of the attributes of concepts seem to apply best to the concepts in the subject field in which you are most interested? Explain.
3. For the age level in which you are most interested, write a brief summary of developmental trends as indicated by Piaget. Secure more information as necessary from Flavell or other sources.
4. Select any three references that deal with Piaget's work and summarize the extent to which Piaget's ideas are supported or rejected.
5. Compare the ideas and contributions of Bruner and Piaget regarding enactive, iconic, and symbolic representation.
6. Give the three main generalizations that you draw from the research on age trends in concept development.
7. a. Rank, from highest to lowest on the basis of their importance in learning factual information, the five principles of factual information.
   b. Should these principles be learned as factual information or as concepts? Why?
   c. What difference would this make in how to go about learning the principles?
8. Which of the principles for facilitating the learning of factual information are in harmony with the following subtheories presented in Chapter 3: purposeful learning, conditioning, imitation, and subsumption?

9.　a.　The generalizations and related principles comprise an instructional model for factual information. What should happen to the principles as more knowledge about learning is developed and incorporated into generalizations?

　　b.　Some authors present only empirical information or generalizations. Should a student be expected to infer the principles? Why or why not?

　　c.　Is application of principles to one's own personal or professional life a creative act? Explain.

10.　Evaluate the judgment of the authors in treating the learning of factual information primarily as meaningful reception learning and the learning of concepts as discovery learning.

11.　Discuss the adequacy of the instructional model for concepts.

SUGGESTIONS FOR FURTHER READING

Ausubel, D. P. Can children learn anything that adults can—and more efficiently? *Elem. Sch. J.*, 1962, **62**, 270–272. (In Seidman, 1965, 90–92.)

Berlyne, D. E. Recent developments in Piaget's work. *Brit. J. educ. Psychol.*, 1957, **27**, 1–12. (In Anderson & Ausubel, 1965, 173–193; and Harper, et al., 1964, 311–323.)

Brown, R. How shall a thing be called? *Psychol. Rev.*, 1958, **65**, 14–21. (In Harper, *et al.*, 1964, 647–654; Kuhlen & Thompson, 1963, 391–400; and Mussen, Conger, & Kagan, 1965, 267–276.)

Bruner, J. S., & Rose R. Olver. Development of equivalence transformations in children. *Monogr. Soc. Res. Child Develpm.*, 1963, 28 (Whole No. 86), 125–141. (In Anderson & Ausubel, 1965, 415–434.)

Fowler, W. Cognitive learning in infancy and early childhood. *Psychol. Bull.*, 1962, **59**, 116–152. (Excerpts in Staats, 1964, 6–20.)

Gagné, R. M. The acquisition of knowledge. *Psychol. Rev.*, 1962, **69**, 355–365. (In Anderson & Ausubel, 1965, 116–132; and DeCecco, 1964, 115–131.)

Huttenlocher, Janellen. Children's intellectual development. *Rev. educ. Res.*, 1965, **35**, 114–121.

Inhelder, Bärbel. Criteria of the stages of mental development. In J. M. Tanner & Bärbel Inhelder (Eds.), *Dis-cussions on child development: A consideration of the biological, psychological, and cultural approaches to the understanding of human development and behavior,* 1. Proceedings of the First Meeting of the World Health Organization Study Group on the Psychological Development of the Child, Geneva, 1953. New York: Int. Univer. Press, 1953. (Portions reprinted in Kuhlen & Thompson, 1963, 28–48.)

Inhelder, Bärbel. Some aspects of Piaget's genetic approach to cognition. In J. Cohen (Ed.), *Readings in psychology.* London: Allen & Unwin, 1964, pp. 85–103.

King, W. H. The development of scientific concepts in children. *Brit. J. educ. Psychol.*, 1961, **31**, 1–20. (In Gordon, 1965, 265–276.)

Lovell, K. *The growth of basic mathematical and scientific concepts in children.* New York: Philosophical Library, 1962. Ch. 5: The concept of substance, 59–66; and Ch. 6: The concept of weight, 67–74. (In Mussen, Conger, & Kagan, 1965, 290–303.)

Luria, A. R. The directive function of speech in development and dissolution: Part I. Development of the directive function of speech in early childhood. *Word*, 1959, **15**, 341–352. (In Anderson & Ausubel, 1965, 350–363.)

Miller, G. A. Some psychological studies of grammar. *Amer. Psychologist,* 1962, **17**, 748–762. (In Anderson & Ausubel, 1965, 321–349.)

Piaget, J. The genetic approach to the psychology of thought. *J. educ. Psychol.,* 1961, **52**, 275–281. (In Gordon, 1965, 57–61.)

Wohlwill, J. F., & R. C. Lowe. Experimental analysis of the development of the conservation of number. *Child. Develpm.,* 1962, **33**, 153–167. (In Gordon, 1965, 193–201.)

REFERENCES

1. Ames, Louise B. The development of the sense of time in the young child. *J. genet. Psychol.,* 1946, **68**, 97–125.

2. Archer, E. J. Concept identification as a function of obviousness of relevant and irrelevant information. *J. exp. Psychol.,* 1962, **63**, 616–620.

3. Archer, E. J. On verbalization and concepts. In A. W. Melton (Ed.), *Categories of human learning.* New York: Academic, 1964, pp. 237–241.

4. Ausubel, D. P. A transfer of the training approach to improving the functional retention of medical knowledge. *J. med. Educ.,* 1962, **37**, 647–655.

5. Ausubel, D. P. *The psychology of meaningful verbal learning.* New York: Grune & Stratton, 1963.

6. Ausubel, D. P., & D. Fitzgerald. The role of discriminability in meaningful verbal learning and retention. *J. educ. Psychol.,* 1961, **52**, 266–274.

7. Ausubel, D. P., & D. Fitzgerald. Organizer, general background, and antecedent learning variables in sequential verbal learning. *J. educ. Psychol.,* 1962, **53**, 243–249.

8. Beberman, M. An emerging program of secondary school mathematics. In R. W. Heath (Ed.), *New curricula.* New York: Harper & Row, 1964, pp. 19–34.

9. Berrey, L. V. (Ed.) *Roget's international thesaurus.* (3rd ed.) New York: Crowell, 1962.

10. Braun, Jean S. Relation between concept formation ability and reading achievement at three developmental levels. *Child Develpm.,* 1963, **34**, 675–682.

11. Bruner, J. S. The course of cognitive growth. *Amer. Psychologist,* 1964, **19**, 1–15.

12. Cahill, H., & C. I. Hovland. The role of memory in the acquisition of concepts. *J. exp. Psychol.,* 1960, **59**, 137–144.

13. Campbell, J. A. CHEM study— an approach to chemistry based on experiments. In R. W. Heath (Ed.), *New curricula.* New York: Harper & Row, 1964, pp. 82–93.

14. Coleman, E. G. Verbal concept learning as a function of instructions and dominance level. *J. exp. Psychol.,* 1964, **68**, 213–214.

15. Craig, R. C. Directed versus independent discovery of established relations. *J. educ. Psychol.,* 1956, **47**, 223–234.

16. Danziger, C., & N. Sharp. The development of children's explanations of growth and movement. *Aust. J. Psychol.,* 1958, **10**, 196–207.

17. Elkind, D. Children's conceptions of right and left: Piaget replication study IV. *J. genet. Psychol.,* 1961, **99**, 269–276.

18. Elkind, D. Children's discovery of the conservation of mass, weight, and volume: Piaget replication study II. *J. genet. Psychol.,* 1961, **98**, 219–227.

19. Elkind, D. The development of quantitative thinking: A systematic replication of Piaget's studies. *J. genet. Psychol.,* 1961, **98**, 37–46.

20. Elkind, D. Quantity conceptions

in junior and senior high school students. *Child Develpm.*, 1961, **32**, 551–560.

21. Elkind, D. Children's conceptions of brother and sister: Piaget replication study V. *J. genet. Psychol.*, 1962, **100**, 129–136.

22. Elkind, D. Quantity conceptions in college students. *J. soc. Psychol.*, 1962, **57**, 459–465.

23. Elkind, D. Discrimination, seriation, and numeration of size and dimensional differences in young children: Piaget replication study VI. *J. genet. Psychol.*, 1964, **104**, 275–296.

24. Flavell, J. H. *The developmental psychology of Jean Piaget.* New York: Van Nostrand, 1963.

25. Glaser, R. Toward a behavioral science base for instructional design. In R. Glaser (Ed.). *Teaching machines and programed learning, II.* Washington, D.C.: NEA, 1965, pp. 771–809.

26. Haygood, R. C., & L. E. Bourne. Forms of relevant stimulus redundancy in concept identification. *J. exp. Psychol.*, 1964, **67**, 392–397.

27. Huttenlocher, Janellen. Some effects of negative instances on the formation of simple concepts. *Psychol. Rep.*, 1962, **11**, 35–42.

28. Jensen, A. Spelling errors and the serial-position effect. *J. educ. Psychol.*, 1962, **53**, 105–109.

29. Judd, C. H. The relation of special training to general intelligence. *Educ. Rev.*, 1908, **36**, 28–42.

30. Kates, S. L., & L. Yudin. Concept attainment and memory. *J. educ. Psychol.*, 1964, **55**, 103–109.

31. Kersh, B. Y., & M. C. Wittrock. Learning by discovery: An interpretation of recent research. *J. teacher Educ.*, 1962, **13**, 461–469.

32. Kilpatrick, W. H. We learn what we live. *N. Y. State Educ.*, 1946, **33**, 535–537.

33. Kittell, J. E. An experimental study of the effect of external direction during learning on transfer and retention of principles. *J. educ. Psychol.*, 1957, **48**, 391–405.

34. Klausmeier, H. J., & Katharine Dresden. *Teaching in the elementary school.* (2nd ed.) New York: Harper & Row, 1962.

35. Klausmeier, H. J., C. W. Harris, & W. Wiersma. *Strategies of learning and efficiency of concept attainment by individuals and groups.* U.S. Office of Education Cooperative Research Project No. 1442. Madison: Univer. of Wisconsin, 1964.

36. Krueger, W. C. F. Rate of progress as related to difficulty of assignment. *J. educ. Psychol.*, 1946, **37**, 247–249.

37. Lovell, K. A follow-up study of Inhelder and Piaget's "The Growth of Logical Thinking." *Brit. J. Psychol.*, 1961, **52**, 143–154.

38. Lovell, K. *The growth of basic mathematical and scientific concepts in children.* London: Univer. of London Press, Ltd., 1961.

39. Smedslund, J. The acquisition of transitivity of weight in five-to-seven-year-old children. *J. genet. Psychol.*, 1963, **102**, 245–255.

40. Smith, Mary K. Measurement of the size of the general English vocabulary through the elementary grades and high school. *Genet. Psychol. Monogr.*, 1941, **24**, 311–345.

41. Suchman, J. R. The child and the inquiry process. In A. H. Passow (Ed.), *Intellectual development: Another look.* Washington, D.C.: Association for Supervision and Curriculum Development, 1964, pp. 59–77.

42. Travers, R. M. W., Mary C. McCormick, A. P. Van Mondfrans, & F. E. Williams. *Research and theory related to audiovisual information transmission.* U. S. Office of Education Cooperative Research Project No. 3–20–003. Salt Lake City: Bur. Educ. Res., Univer. of Utah, 1964.

43. Underwood, B. J. Ten years of massed practice on distributed practice. *Psychol. Rev.*, 1961, **68**, 229–247.

44. Wallace, J. Concept dominance, type of feedback, and intensity of feedback as related to concept attainment. *J. educ. Psychol.,* 1964, **55,** 159–166.

45. Wittrock, M. C. The learning by discovery hypothesis. Paper read at The Conf. on Learning by Discovery, New York City, January, 1965.

46. Woodruff, A. D. *Basic concepts of teaching.* San Francisco: Chandler, 1962.

47. Wooton, W. The history and status of the school mathematics study group. In R. W. Heath (Ed.), *New curricula.* New York: Harper & Row, 1964, pp. 35–53.

CHAPTER 8

Problem Solving
and Creativity

Every human being needs to develop the abilities to think critically and to solve problems, often requiring creative solutions. These abilities, like others, are not merely present or absent in an individual. Instead each ability is distributed in a normal fashion among human beings of the same age. Although abilities range from low to high, the custodian in a four-room school, the pupil with an IQ below 70, the pupil with an IQ above 130, the teacher, the principal, and the superintendent all encounter many problems daily.

Many diversions keep children and adults from thinking for themselves and from identifying and solving significant problems. In many cases, rather than working toward expressing our best ideas and feelings in vocal and written form, in music, in drama, in art, or in physical movements, we are mesmerized by sterile television programs. We talk about trivialities or engage in other nonproductive activities. All of us can recall our drab conversations about the weather. Also some persons absorb information without processing or mediating it. No reflective or independent thought is given to interpreting the information. The development of high-level problem-solving abilities and creative thinking is indeed an objective of merit for our schools.

The importance of cognitive abilities in connection with factual information and concepts was shown in Chapter 7. They are given more attention now in connection with (1) the nature of thinking and problem solving, (2) the nature of creativity, (3) a model for improving problem-solving abilities, and (4) a model for encouraging creativity. As in Chapter 7, the discussion is intended to provide information not only for working with pupils but also for one's own improvement.

THE NATURE OF THINKING AND PROBLEM SOLVING

Problem solving is the most complex form of human behavior. One must think in order to solve problems. Everyone, except perhaps mentally deficient persons and extremely young children, can think and solve problems, but there are wide differences in these abilities among individuals at all age levels. When considering, however, what a teacher or parent can do to help children think more clearly or solve problems more efficiently, we encounter many questions, some of which are not fully answered. We may familiarize ourselves with the complexity of the situation by first considering ideas about thinking that have been generated over a period of many years.

Ideas about Thinking

Thinking has been of interest to mankind for a long time, in part because he can engage in the process but cannot define it. In this regard thinking is like learning. In fact, thinking may be considered as mental activity that is essential to learning most outcomes. Despite this apparent simplicity, thinking is as complex as learning itself. Though many attempts have been made to describe thinking, our knowledge about the improvement of thinking is incomplete. As you study the different ideas about thinking, try to discriminate among them and to identify some common elements. Try to decide whether adjectives such as reflective, productive, divergent, and critical make a difference.

REFLECTIVE THINKING
Dewey identified five phases or aspects of reflective thinking:

(1) suggestions, in which the mind leaps forward to possible solution; (2) an intellectualization of the difficulty or perplexity that has been *felt* (di-

rectly experienced) into a problem to be solved, a question for which the answer must be sought; (3) the use of one suggestion after another as a leading idea, or hypothesis, to initiate and guide observation and other operations in the collection of factual materials; (4) the mental elaboration of the idea or supposition . . . ; and (5) testing the hypothesis by overt or imaginative action (4, 107).

Dewey stressed particularly that thinking involves a state of doubt, perplexity, or felt mental difficulty in which the thinking originates, and, in addition, an act of searching, hunting, or inquiring to find material to resolve the doubt, and to settle and dispose of the perplexity. Dewey's concept of thinking serves as a basis for problem solving and is widely accepted as such. For example, the thought processes in problem solving have been summarized thus:

While the course of thinking out the solution of a problem varies somewhat for different cases, in general, examination reveals the following characteristic stages in the process: First, a difficulty is felt; second, the problem is clarified and defined; third, a search for clues is made; fourth, various suggestions appear and are evaluated or tried out; fifth, a suggested solution is accepted or the thinker gives up in defeat; and sixth, the solution is tested (28, 421–422).

PRODUCTIVE THINKING

Wertheimer summarized his ideas about productive thinking:

. . . in the desire to get at real understanding, requestioning and investigation start. A certain region in the field becomes crucial, is focused; but does not become isolated.

A new, deeper structural view of the situation develops, involving changes in the functional meaning, the grouping, etc. of the items.

Directed by what is required by the structure of a situation for a crucial region, one is led to a reasonable prediction, which—like the other parts of the structure—calls for verification, direct or indirect (61, 167).

If you were now to accept as an important question "What is thinking?" you would attempt to organize your present and past experiences into some sort of focus. This is your perceptual field as proposed by Wertheimer. In turn, if you are satisfied with your present meanings and organization, no productive thinking will occur. However, if you are dissatisfied you will attempt to seek closure, that is, to fill in the parts of the whole and in turn bring them into a fuller total organization which is satisfactory for you. In this process of acquiring a complete perceptual pattern with sufficient meaning to be satisfying, the emphasis is upon structuring and restructuring of one's perceptual field—a somewhat broader concept than Dewey's problem-solving approach.

CONVERGENT AND DIVERGENT THINKING

Guilford introduced fruitful ideas about thinking, as was indicated in Chapter 2 (13). Whereas Dewey and Wertheimer treated thinking as a process per se, Guilford differentiates between both the outcomes and the processes of thinking. He proposed five intellectual processes, including convergent and divergent thinking.

Cognition means discovery or rediscovery or recognition. Memory means retention of what is cognized. Two kinds of productive-thinking operations generate new information from known information and remembered information. In divergent-thinking operations we think in different directions sometimes searching, sometimes seeking variety. In convergent thinking the information leads to one right answer or to a recognized best or conventional answer. In evaluation we reach decision as to goodness, correctness, suitability or adequacy of what we know, what we remember, and what we produce in productive thinking. . . .

The unique feature of divergent production is that a *variety* of responses is produced. The product is not completely determined by the given information. This is not to say that divergent thinking does not come into play in the total process of reaching a unique conclusion, for it comes into play wherever there is trial-and-error thinking (13, 470, 473).

Here Guilford equates cognition and convergent thinking with what others call reasoning. On the other hand, the outcomes of divergent thinking are different from reasoning and can be most directly associated with creativity as will be shown subsequently in this chapter. Note that both convergent and divergent thinking are forms of productive thinking.

Convergent thinking and reasoning are similar processes. Our knowledge of reasoning is substantial. For example, four tests were arranged to measure reasoning: false premises, essential operations, syllogisms, and problem solving (40). Students who scored in the top 15 percent on the tests were classed as good reasoners and those in the bottom 15 percent as poor reasoners. The good reasoners were superior to the poor reasoners in accuracy of both deduction and induction processes and in speed of induction. The good reasoners were superior in eliminating sources of errors, in locating a crucial aspect of the problem, and in controlling various elements of the situation.

Just as there are differences in the abilities of good and poor reasoners, there also are differences between the sexes in reasoning (33). Three hundred high school boys were superior to an equal number of girls in drawing conclusions deductively. The boys' superiority over the girls was not related to intelligence, previous knowledge about the material, reading comprehension, reading preferences, practice effects, or knowledge of pertinent principles.

CRITICAL THINKING

Critical thinking corresponds closely to convergent thinking and evaluation (7). Decide which of the 12 following criteria of critical thinking involve Guilford's definition of evaluation or convergent thinking, previously discussed:

1. Grasping the meaning of a statement
2. Judging whether there is ambiguity in a line of reasoning
3. Judging whether certain statements contradict each other
4. Judging whether a conclusion follows necessarily
5. Judging whether a statement is specific enough
6. Judging whether a statement is actually the application of a certain principle
7. Judging whether an observation statement is reliable
8. Judging whether an inductive conclusion is warranted
9. Judging whether the problem has been identified
10. Judging whether something is an assumption
11. Judging whether a definition is adequate
12. Judging whether a statement made by an alleged authority is acceptable (7, 84)

Ennis proposed a three-dimensional model of critical thinking; namely logical, critical, and pragmatic dimensions. The logical dimension concerns judging alleged logical relationships between meanings of words and statements, while the critical dimension includes a knowledge of the criteria for judging statements (excluding the logical criteria inherent in the first dimension). The pragmatic dimension involves the impression of the background purpose of the judgment, including a decision whether the statement is good enough for the purpose. This dimension considers background factors preceding the judgment and highlights the fact that the criteria cannot be automatically and routinely applied in every situation. Intelligent judgment is needed in addition to applying criteria and knowing the meaning. Although not done in Ennis' article, it would seem that the criteria of critical thinking could be couched in behavioral terms and thereby be extended to application and evaluation in the classroom.

COMMON IDEAS ABOUT THINKING

What are the common elements ascribed to theories of thinking? First, thinking involves mental activity which originates with a feeling of perplexity, doubt, or dissatisfaction as the individual perceives something in his environment that is not completely satisfying or meaningful. Second, for the thinking to be productive, rather than aimless reverie or daydreaming, there is a focusing upon a problem or perceived elements of the environment. This situation or problem is intellectualized, formulated, or stated in such a way that it is relatively clear to the thinker. In mathematics, in painting a picture, in composing a song, in writing a short story, the individual must have a reasonably clear idea of what the problem is in order for him to focus upon it and to thing productively towards reaching some type of solution. Third, once the problem is intellectualized, thinking is directed toward the solution. In some problem situations the solution comes quickly; in others the individual may continue his efforts intermittently for months and years. Fourth, after a solution is tentatively accepted it is tested out or evaluated. The present information and methods one has, his hypotheses about the solution, and the particular social or other context of his efforts are all related to the testing or evaluating aspect of thinking. There also are at least two directions of thinking. One is toward acquiring a solution or closure to a problem for which there is a known or a generally accepted answer. *Logical thinking*, *critical thinking*, and *reasoning* are terms used quite generally to describe this direction. Another is that of seeking a new (at least to the thinker) or not generally accepted solution. This direction of thinking, called "divergent" by Guilford, has been termed by others "creative thinking," "imaginative thinking," and "original thinking."

Having now read about thinking, attempt to clarify what it means to help children to think clearly or productively. What does it mean for first-graders? fifth-grade children? high school students? college students? What directions of thinking are demanded? Those which lead to already known answers which we teachers can quite readily identify as right or wrong? Do we also want the direction of thinking which might lead to solutions of which we teachers are not aware? Consider, for example, the following question: "Are our school buildings and classrooms suitable for the efficient development of human abilities?" With the question so posed, we might limit our thinking and investigations to the school buildings and classrooms now in use and bring forth an affirmative or negative judgment. Now consider a different question: "What sort of spaces, equipment, and materials are needed to develop human abilities most efficiently?" The latter question might lead some persons to formulate ideas which up to the present time have been considered by few, if any, people.

Problem Solving

In the previous section it was shown that thinking is necessary for solving problems and that convergent and divergent thinking originate as the individual identifies and attempts to solve problems. From this we properly infer that if thinking is to be improved, problems must be identified and solved. We now consider in more detail the nature of problem solving, other concomitants of problem solving—insight, trial, and confirmation, success and failure, set, and problem solving by groups.

THE NATURE OF PROBLEM SOLVING

A problem exists for the individual when he encounters a situation where he must respond but does not have immediately available the methods, information, or both to arrive at a solution without further thinking. For example, a child encounters a situation where he must use long division to arrive at a solution but he does not have the needed method. Problem-solving activity in line with a sequence outlined in Table 8.1 is needed.

Note the parallel terminology in Table 8.1. For example, in the early part of the sequence we have these parallel terms: *setting a goal, appraising the situation; locating and defining the problem, mental elaboration of ideas; preparation, analysis; understanding the problem, working out connections between the known and unknown.* Other terminology is likewise parallel even though the number of processes is not identical in the five sequences. Johnson arrived at three processes after doing controlled experimentation in a laboratory (**25**). Merrifield, *et al.* arrived at their estimates about the number of processes through factor analytic studies (**44**). The other sequences are based on analysis and synthesis of research. Throughout, the terminology follows the preference of the particular writers. Other words might have been used to indicate the processes. Just as it is not necessary to have the same number of processes in the sequence because of the different degrees of inclusiveness of the terms, we do not need to think that problem solving always follows the sequence from top to bottom. It is important, however, to be aware that people from different disciplines and backgrounds do not use problem solving in exactly the same way.

Even though there is some difference concerning the exact meaning of *problem solving*, we seem to agree that problem solving is at the apex of human learning. On what is problem solving based? What must precede it? Figure 8.1 indicates that problem solving comes after certain other responses are learned. Going from the simplest type of learning by the infant, we find that first responses are learned, then chains of responses, associations of names with objects and events which we referred to as factual information in Chapter 7, concepts, and then principles that we called complex concepts in Chapter 7. We do not pose this basis of problem solving as the only correct one; however, it illustrates hierarchical patterning that is generally considered to be a requisite of problem solving. Also, this system of indicating content from simple to complex corresponds closely to a taxonomy proposed by Melton (43). In Fig. 8.1, no mention is given to creativity specifi-

Type	Paradigm[a]	Description	Example
Response learning	S-R	Establishment of a response-connection to a stimulus specified along physical dimensions.	Contact with fire (S) elicits startle movement (R).
Chaining	S-R~ S-R	Establishment of chains of response-connections.	Above paradigm is chained to presentation of heat (S) which elicits withdrawal (R).
Verbal learning (paired-associates)	S-r~~[s-R]	Establishment of labeling responses to stimuli varying physically within limits of primary stimulus generalization. Previous "response learning" assumed (as indicated by brackets).	Contact with fire (S) is associated with feeling of heat (r) and word **hot** (R) (association of heat sensation as s with word **hot** as R assumed).
Concept learning	S-r ~~ s / S-r ~~ s → Concept / S-r ~~ s	Establishment of mediating response to stimuli which differ from each other physically ("classifying").	Association of fire (S), steam (S), and hot metal (S) with feeling of heat (r) leads to association of heat with concept **hotness.**
Principle learning	— Concept \ / Rule / — Concept	Establishment of a process which functions like a rule "If A, then B," where A and B are concepts.	Concepts **hotness** and **sharpness** (similar paradigms assumed) lead to rule: "If hot or sharp, then painful."
Problem solving	—Rule \ Higher-order rule / —Rule	Establishment of a process which "combines" two or more previously learned rules in a "higher-order rule."	Solving "if water boils at 212°F, at what C does it boil, given F=9/5 C + 32."

[a] The paradigms shown have been designed to depict what is learned, and not the learning situation which leads to this result. In addition, it may be noted that beginning with concept learning, only the central portions of the inferred chains are shown.

Fig. 8.1. A suggested ordering of the types of human learning. (Adapted from R. M. Gagné. Problem solving. In A. W. Melton (Ed.), *Categories of human learning.* New York: Academic Press, 1964, p. 312.)

TABLE 8.1.

Parallel Relationships of Problem-Solving Processes as Specified in Five Sources

Klausmeier and Goodwin	Dewey (1933)	D. M. Johnson (1962)	Merrifield et al. (1960)	Polya (1945)
	Felt difficulty			
Setting a goal	Locating and defining problem	Preparation	Preparation	Understanding the problem
Appraising the situation	Mental elaboration of ideas		Analysis	Working out connections between the known and unknown, and deriving a plan of solution
Trying to attain goal: productive thinking and physical activity	Suggesting possible hypotheses	Production	Production	Carrying out the plan
Confirming or rejecting	Testing hypotheses	Judgment	Verification	Examining the solution
Reaching goal	Accepting one as correct		Reapplication	

cally. However, it is assumed that creativity is a form of problem solving.

In Fig. 8.1 we have seen a hierarchical arrangement of cognitive abilities which indicates one type of relationship. How does the ability to solve problems relate to other high-level cognitive abilities? Table 8.2 gives the correlations among various high-level abilities and problem solving (18). The high positive correlations are with reading, judgment, IQ, and problem recognition. Positive but lower correlations are shown between problem solving and word fluency, closure, and ideational fluency.

TABLE 8.2.

Correlations between Problem Solving and Other Variables

Variable	Problem Recognition	Word Fluency	Ideational Fluency	Closure	Judgment	IQ	Reading
1. Problem Solving	.62	.42	.29	.40	.71	.68	.73
2. Problem Recognition		.40	.56	.30	.55	.52	.60
3. Word Fluency			.46	.33	.37	.40	.49
4. Ideational Fluency				.17	.28	.32	.36
5. Closure					.27	.36	.35
6. Judgment						.54	.64
7. IQ							.56
8. Reading							

SOURCE: B. Harootunian, & M. W. Tate. The relationship of certain selected variables to problem solving ability. *J. educ. Psychol.,* 1960, **51**, 331.

Although high positive correlations are noted between problem solving and other high-level cognitive abilities, we should not infer that problem solving can be performed only by older persons who can read. Simple problems are solved by children at a relatively young age. Three- and 4-year-olds were required to manipulate strings leading to subgoals in a simple succession that would allow reaching the major goal; the nursery children were capable of inference (**26**). A similar conclusion was reached in a nonexperimental setting (**19**). Young children, when asked to solve a problem too difficult for them, merely drop it down to a simpler level and then respond. Their responses, although seemingly inappropriate to an adult observer, are plausible from their point of view. Some additional remarks are needed to relate problem solving to other outcomes of learning. Content is always involved in a problem and is not always purely semantic or symbolic. Many important problems cannot be solved simply by thought; very often the individual must actively seek information. If the solution of the problem involves production of anything—a poem, a short story, a musical composition, a design for a bridge or house—some psychomotor abilities also are required. Because many of the most critical problems facing mankind today are interpersonal, how the problem solver feels toward others and how they feel toward him affect his efficiency. Thus, the affective component also is present in problem solving.

INSIGHT, TRIAL, AND CONFIRMATION

Two different points of view have been expressed regarding the means of solving problems. One states that the solution to a problem is arrived at suddenly after some initial effort. Another point of view is that a problem gets solved through gradually eliminating errors and putting together correct responses. Although considerable argument has occurred concerning which is the correct interpretation, we accept the point of view that certain problems lend themselves to solution with fewer trials than others. Let us consider some examples.

Here is a problem that may be solved suddenly, without many previous trials. "With six matches of equal length, make four and only four equilateral triangles." Graduate students, given this problem verbally and told to manipulate the six matches, frequently are baffled and cannot reach a solution independently. They attempt to make the six equilateral triangles with the matches in a horizontal plane. However, after working with the matches they sometimes accidentally put one or two up from the horizontal plane into a pyramid form. Once the pyramid form is perceived, (and this perception appears suddenly), the individual does achieve the solution and thereafter can quickly reproduce the solution. This sudden perception and understanding of means-ends or method-solution relationships is characteristic of some problems. However, solution of many other problems involves trial and confirmation or, in the usual terminology of problem solving, the formulation and testing of successive hypotheses. Consider now an example of the latter type.

Imagine a committee of juniors and seniors in high school who must decide appropriate apparel for the Junior Prom. They know that about half of the students will not attend if formal dress is required. The committee members would like everyone to attend. In a problem situation such as this, the solution does not suddenly emerge as with the matches and equilateral triangles. Rather, many proposals or hypotheses are made. Each of these is discussed and tested as various persons give their reactions. Though someone in the group may quite suddenly perceive a solution, it is unlikely that sudden solutions will evolve.

More trial and confirmation and less insight is typical when a given class of problems is first encountered (17). Subjects of low mental ability were presented a series of simple discrimination problems, such as selecting the largest of two stimuli despite whether presented on the right or left. They displayed trial-and-error behavior, taking many trials to go through a series perfectly. After several hundred problems of the same class, the subjects would make the correct discrimination when the problem was first presented. This latter performance appears like insight learning, that is, suddenly getting the problem correct. However, the subjects had in previous trials learned how to learn the class of problems. They acquired what Harlow called a learning set. In more common terms, they acquired a method of learning which transferred positively to other problems of the same type. What is important here is that Harlow feels he has shown an orderly progression from trial and error to seemingly insightful learning and states the idea thus: "Generalizing broadly to human behavior, we hold that original learning within an area is difficult and frustrating, but after mastery, learning within the same area becomes simple and effortless" (17, 511).

To recapitulate, most likely insight is possible only after prior experience with the class of problems. In line with our previous discussion, some problems lend themselves to seeing means-end relationships more readily than others. Also, other things being equal, an older and more intelligent person solves a problem with less fumbling and fewer errors than a younger and less intelligent child. Further, teachers can arrange learning situations to facilitate achieving the correct solutions with fewer errors.

SUCCESS AND FAILURE

The effects of success and failure in problem solving are similar to the effects with other outcomes of learning. Repeated failures result in giving up, substituting a different goal, or showing other forms of unproductive behavior. The problem-solving processes of students after failure are significantly inferior to those following successful experiences (48). Success and failure produce differential effects at different points during problem solving. Students who withdraw from the prob-

267

lem-solving situation prior to achieving a solution set higher goals originally, use fewer alternative solutions in attempting to solve the problem, and perform less effectively after failure than do those who achieve solutions (**50**). Let us examine the differences between children of high and low intelligence who solve problems with different degrees of success.

Figure 8.2 shows differences in behavior involving problem solving among children of high, average, and low IQ. There were 40 children of the same age in each IQ grouping. On all the behavior, the children of low IQ were less effective than were those of high IQ. More important, the difference in behavior gives clues as to why failure was experienced more frequently by the children of low IQ. For example, more children of high than low IQ noted and corrected mistakes, verified solutions, and used a logical approach. More children of low than high IQ offered incorrect solutions, made random approaches to the problem, and did not persist in attempts at solving the problem. An actual description of the performance of a boy with a high IQ and of one with a low IQ may help to visualize some of these differences.

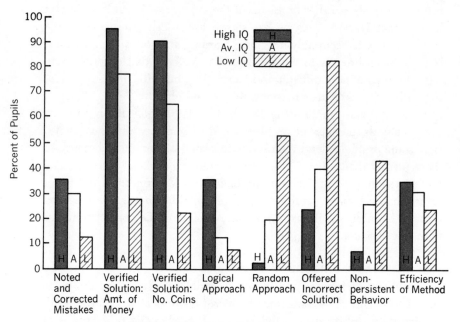

Fig. 8.2. Percent of pupils displaying problem-solving behaviors by type of behavior and IQ. (Adapted from H. J. Klausmeier & L. J. Loughlin. Behaviors during problem-solving among children of low, average, and high intelligence. *J. educ. Psychol.*, 1961, **52**, 149.)

Richard had a WISC IQ of 138 and used 585 seconds to solve the problem: "Make $9.77, using 12 bills and coins." He studied the situation and during the first 3 minutes made a first attempt at solution, getting the amount correct but using 13 instead of 12 bills and coins—9 one dollar bills, 1 half-dollar, 1 quarter, and 2 pennies. He checked the amount and number of coins and started over. During the next 3 minutes he made his second and third tries, each time starting with a five dollar bill. On the second he had 12 bills and coins but an incorrect amount; on the third try, neither was correct. Each time he checked amount and number of coins. During the third 3 minutes he made his fourth try, but made a mistake in adding the amount. Checking through his solution at the beginning of the fourth 3-minute period, he found the error and after 45 seconds offered as a correct solution 1 five dollar bill, 4 one dollar bills, 1 half dollar, 1 dime, 3 nickels, and 2 pennies. Richard made 25 separate moves, but only 6 were needed, as shown in the final solution. Therefore, his efficiency ratio was 6/25, or .24.

Michael, one of the more able low IQ boys, had a WISC IQ of 73 and used 805 seconds, to "Make 46¢, using 4 coins." Ten coins of each denomination—penny, nickel, dime, and quarter—had been placed on the table before him. (In a pretest it had been established that he had the requisite skill in adding and knowledge of coins to solve the problem.) Michael, as Richard, restated the problem correctly prior to attempting a solution. During the first 3 minutes, Michael took 3 dimes and 10 pennies from the supply, then returned to the supply 3 pennies, one at a time, and offered the remainder as a correct solution. Upon being told that it was incorrect and with all coins returned to the supply, he studied the coins and offered 1 quarter and 2 dimes as a second solution during the second 3 minute period. During the third 3 minutes, he withdrew from the supply 1 quarter, 1 dime, 1 nickel, and 1 penny and offered this as correct. When told it was incorrect and the coins had been returned, he again studied the coins, and during the fourth 3 minutes withdrew 1 quarter, 1 penny, 1 dime, then put the quarter back. During the fifth 3 minutes he again withdrew the quarter and another dime from the supply, thus having 1 quarter, 2 dimes, and 1 penny. This he offered as correct without observably checking accuracy of amount or number of coins. He made a total of 16 coin movements when only 3 were needed; his efficiency ratio was .188. At no point was it necessary to encourage Michael to continue or to keep at the task; however, like the majority of low IQ children, he offered incorrect solutions and did not verify amount of money nor the number of coins (31, 150–151).

As noted in the preceding descriptions, Richard was markedly superior to Michael in verification and reapplication, eventually arriving at the correct solution. Other children of low IQ, different from Michael, did not persist when informed that their solutions were wrong. After two or three such experiences, they manipulated the coins without producing a close approximation of the final correct solution. In this experiment we did not attempt to teach the child how to overcome his errors. In similar situations, however, we have taught individuals to use a particular strategy and this has improved learning efficiency. We are confident that more time should be spent in teaching children of all IQ levels methods for solving problems rather than giving them solutions or letting them fail repeatedly.

SET AND PROBLEM SOLVING

Set is usually defined as a predisposition to react to a situation in a certain way. Instructions are frequently used to establish a set. For example, four functions of instructions in problem solving are (1) to identify the terminal performance required, (2) to identify parts of the problem situation, (3) to recall relevant abilities, and (4) to guide thinking (10). When instructions achieve these purposes, the student receiving them behaves differently in the problem situation from the way he would without the instructions. In other words, each type of instruction establishes a set or predisposition concerning how to proceed or how to interpret the situation. It may be pointed out that instructions also may be used to increase motivation, arouse curiosity, induce stress, and the like.

That set influences problem solving has been demonstrated in a number of situations. Instructions to use a certain strategy resulted in improved performance on problems of the same class (30). Also, when individuals were taught to solve a series of related problems by one method, they persisted in using that method in solving other problems, even when the method repeatedly did not work (36, 51). Persons taught by a single method and having experienced success repeatedly in solving a series of related problems cling to the method even when repeated trials with it are found not to work in solving new problems of another class. In other words, the method leads to positive transfer with problems of the same class but to negative transfer to problems of another class.

The best example of negative transfer resulting from set is found in connection with using tools in solving problems (2). Preutilization with an electric relay and an electrical switch influenced behavior in a subsequent task. Those who had used the relay solely to complete an electrical circuit never utilized the relay as a pendulum weight in the solution of the new problem; the ones trained with the switch preponderantly used only the relay in the new problem, but the control group, which had not had any previous experience, used the relay and switch about equally. The prior use of the relay or the switch resulted in functional fixedness; the lack of prior experience permitted equal use of either tool by the control group.

We do not know why some intelligent individuals identify significant problems and achieve equally significant solutions, whereas others equally intelligent do not identify significant problems or, if so, they do not develop the methods or acquire the information needed to solve them. Some individuals rigidly persist with an already established method or a specific interpretation of information to solve one type of problem, whereas in other problems they may be quite flexible. We can, for example, be good problem solvers in the science laboratory but not apply problem-solving techniques to social problems in the community. In the laboratory we demand controlled experimental data; in the community we seek types of evidence to back up our already established biases.

Flexibility and rigidity are not generalized personality traits (24). Within individuals there is considerable variability in approaching problems with flexibility or rigidity, depending upon the inherent nature and content of the problem. For example, rigidity and flexibility are fairly consistent characteristics of individuals in meeting a series of similar tasks (12). However, when individuals are presented varying types of problem-solving tasks, they are rigid on one type but quite flexible on another.

PROBLEM SOLVING BY GROUPS

Teachers generally work with groups as well as individuals. How do groups perform on problem solving in comparison with individuals? Here we shall consider initial learning first and transfer later. Most researchers since 1950 find the average performance of small groups to be superior to that of individuals (9, 16, 21, 35, 59). However, a minority report that individuals do better than groups (6, 37, 45). In particular, Duncan stresses that the best individuals exceed the averages of groups (6). It is possible that group members would perform better after more experience in working together and after instruction. After six months of instruction and practice in group problem solving, the groups did out perform individuals (9).

Although individuals do not perform as well as small groups in most initial learning situations, how do they fare in transfer situations? In three different situations, groups of four did better initially than did individuals (23, 30, 60). In two of the three experiments, those who had learned initially as members of quads performed less well in a transfer situation when working alone. In the third experiment there was no difference (23).

Why is the average performance of small groups superior to that of individuals in most initial learning situations? During initial learning the small groups collectively arrive at an understanding of the problem more quickly than individuals, secure information more rapidly, cognize information more effectively, remember the relevant information better, bring a larger variety of methods to bear upon the solution, pose more solutions, and verify the solutions more reliably (30). However, when subsequently working as individuals on new transfer problems, those who initially were group members do all the things listed above less well on the average, apparently because they are not required to participate so actively initially. A person when working alone initially actively searches and arrives at a solution; some members of groups do not, or if they do, cannot transfer their knowledge effectively.

THE NATURE OF CREATIVITY

While visiting classrooms in elementary schools, high schools, and colleges, one looks at the students and wonders which of these will eventually be the outstanding musical composer, the great artist, the engineer, the scientist, the novelist, the statesman. What is happening in these classrooms that will encourage all of the students to develop their creative abilities, abilities which exist to some degree in each one? And what can be done, starting in kindergarten, to nurture the creative abilities of all children? As you have experienced education, thus far, how much of your instruction has been directed toward acquiring the knowledge and methods that mankind already possesses? How often were you encouraged to produce, to express yourself, to question present knowledge or methods, to try something different?

Visit the many high school classrooms now organized for academically talented students. Observe the content and method of instruction. You may experience the uncomfortable feeling that perhaps the creative individual of tomorrow will not come from these classroom groups. There is a possibility that a large number of the creative individuals are somehow lost by the criteria used in selecting the academically talented and that creativity in those identified is being submerged through instruction which focuses almost solely on the acquisition of larger and larger masses of already known facts and tested methods. Let us consider creative abilities, productivity, cognitive variables in creativity, and the school emphasis on creativity.

Creative Abilities

Although creativity is a widely used term, it is not defined clearly. Over a decade ago, 25 definitions of creativity had already appeared, most of them stressing the role of originality (**46**). We accept the following global definitions but point out that the factors which follow are useful also in delimiting creativity:

> . . . true creativeness fulfills at least three conditions. It involves a response or an idea that is novel or at the very least statistically infrequent. But novelty or originality of thought and action, while a necessary aspect of creativity is not sufficient . . . it must to some extent be adaptive to, or of, reality. It must serve to solve a problem, fit a situation, or accomplish some recognizable goal. And, thirdly, true creativeness involves a sustaining of the original insight, an evaluation and elaboration of it, a developing of it to the full (**38**, 485).

A distinction between productivity, creativity, and ingenuity has been advanced and is worth noting:

> *Productivity* is shown by bringing forth many ideas and solutions. It emphasizes both quantity and contribution . . . *Creativity* is shown by bringing something new into being. The emphasis here is on the newness and lack of previous existence of the idea or product. *Ingenuity* is shown by inventing or discovering a solution to a problem. The emphasis in this case is on the existence of a problem and the demonstration of a quality of genius in solving it in an unusually neat, clever, or surprising way (**8**, 92).

Ingenuity is closely related to adaptiveness in the previous quotation. A test of ingenuity and other tests will be discussed briefly in Chapter 16.

In Table 8.3 are given the names of creative abilities, the intellectual processes and the product, and the type of task used to measure the ability (**15**). Although only semantic content is given in Table 8.3, there are parallel abilities for figural and for symbolic content. You may recall from the discussion in Chapter 2 that figural abilities are thought to be more closely associated with performance in the visual arts and in the musical and architectural areas, while semantic content is more closely associated with performance in literature, science, mathematics, and related fields.

As indicated in Table 8.3 divergent-production abilities and other abilities involving transformations underlie creative performances. Note, however, that cognition and convergent production as well as divergent production are involved. Further, one must remember in order to use any prior experience in a current creative performance. We shall not elaborate on the types of tasks given in Table 8.3 except

TABLE 8.3.

Creative Ability Involving Semantic Content

Ability	Intellectual Process	Product	Type of Task Used To Measure Ability
Conceptual foresight	Cognition	Implications	List as many as six different ways to accomplish a certain task.
Ideational fluency	Divergent production	Units	Write names of things fitting broad classes; e.g., things that are white and edible.
Semantic spontaneous flexibility	Divergent production	Classes	List uses for a wooden lead pencil.
Associational fluency	Divergent production	Relations	Write synonyms for each of several words; e.g., for the word *hard*.
Expressional fluency	Divergent production	Systems	Construct a variety of four-word sentences, given four initial letters, no word to be used more than once; e.g., "W_____ f_____ r_____ d_____." Possible answer: "Who found Rover dead?"
Originality	Divergent production	Transformations	(Clever) Write titles for a short story. (Remote) Give remote (distant in time or in space or in sequence of events) consequences for a specified event.
Semantic elaboration	Divergent production	Implications	Add detailed operations needed to make a briefly outlined plan succeed.
Semantic redefinition	Convergent production	Transformations	Name an object that could readily be made by combining two given objects.

SOURCE: Based on J. P. Guilford, & R. Hoepfner. Current summary of structure-of-intellect factors and suggested tests. *Rep. psychol. Lab.*, No 30. Los Angeles: Univer. of Southern California, 1963.

to note that all of them require the person to produce something, rather than to recognize something as being a correct or appropriate response. Further, the scoring is not the usual scoring for right or wrong. Rather, the scores or ratings are usually in terms of the number of responses for the fluency abilities, in terms of cleverness for originality, and in terms of applicability for flexibility. You will find it interesting to respond to the tasks and to compare your responses with those of others.

We have now observed some of the intellectual or cognitive factors in creativity. Nearly everyone working in the field of creativity accepts fluency, flexibility, and originality as being associated with creativity.

Besides the cognitive abilities there are also personality traits associated with creativity. Persons high in ideational fluency also tend to be impulsive, self-confident, ascendant, more appreciative of originality, and somewhat less inclined toward neuroticism. Those who score high on originality tend to be more interested in aesthetic expression and meditative thinking, to be more tolerant of ambiguity, and to feel less need for discipline and orderliness. However, they do not have a strong need for adventure or variety, and they apparently recognize the need for cultural conformity (14).

Traits in living artists and writers with good reputations in their fields are noteworthy. The total group studied included 31 general writers, 64 artists, and 58 science-fiction writers. The creative artists and writers differed from the normal adult population in being more intelligent, emotionally mature, dominant, adventurous, emotionally sensitive, unconventional, radical, self-sufficient, and of high ergic-tension level. Artists in this group were found to be somewhat more unconventional and less intelligent than writers. The science-fiction writers appeared to be somewhat more radical than other writers or artists. The science-fiction writers also tended to be less emotionally sensitive than the artist or other writers (5). Here, too, the affective concomitants of creativity were much the same as noted in the previous study.

Productivity

Persons may have daydreams and do a great deal of thinking of the divergent sort. However, unless there is closure and the thoughts are incorporated into a product, the creative ideas do not become evident. This is true at all school levels, kindergarten through graduate school, and with all adults, including teachers.

An excellent source of information about productivity is Terman (**54**). After identifying children with IQs of 140 and higher in the early 1920s, Terman made several followup studies. When the males in the group were 25 years or older, the 150 rated highest in success as measured by productivity (not income) and the 150 lowest were compared on a number of items that had been gathered from their childhood. During the elementary school years the high and low success groups had been much alike, having about the same grades and test achievements. Early in high school the groups began to draw apart, with the success group getting higher grades. A far greater percent of the successful adult group had finished college. The most spectacular differences, however, showed up between the two groups in 1940, when they were 25 years old or older. The productive group, far more than the less productive, was superior in these personality characteristics: persistence in the accomplishment of ends, integration toward goals as contrasted to drifting, self-confidence, and freedom from inferiority feelings. The successful group appeared to have a much stronger drive to achieve good all-around mental and social adjustment and was relatively free from severe emotional tensions that bordered on the abnormal.

Other Cognitive Variables in Creativity

We have indicated in previous chapters that the concept of general intellectual ability (IQ) is not in harmony with the concept of many specific intellectual abilities. Although this is the case, tests of general intellectual ability do sample a composite of abilities that underlie broad classes of performance. Therefore, we might expect a positive correlation between general intellectual ability and creative performances, but the correlation would be far from perfect. When children representing the entire range of IQs from very low to very high are included in a sample, moderate positive correlations are secured between IQ and measures of specific divergent thinking abilities (**49**). Further, children of low IQ are consistently lower than children of average and high IQ in divergent thinking; however, they are lower in convergent than divergent thinking abilities (**32**).

Although we and others have discovered moderate positive correlations between divergent thinking and IQ, the correlations are not sufficiently high to justify intelligence tests being used to identify students who are high in creativity (**38**, **42**, **55**). Students of high IQ vary markedly in creativity and vice versa (11). This point of view is clearly stated: ". . . it is commonly observed that many children who are very high in intelligence as measured by IQ are not concomitantly high in such other intellectual functions as creativity, and many children who are very high in creativity are not concomitantly high in intelligence as measured by IQ" (11, 3). Here is a similar point of view: "The best conclusion at present is that intelligence, as measured, accounts for only a minor portion of the variation in creative performance and, by itself, is by no means an adequate measure of creativity" (52, 93–94).

Just as intelligence test scores and creativity do not correlate highly, neither do creativity and the grades assigned to students (53) nor ratings of creativity by teachers and scores of creativity (20, 29, 62). One explanation of the teacher's inability to rate creativity in students is related to the role of the school thus: "Since teachers are generally not expected to evaluate their children on the basis of creative performance, teacher ratings may be less accurate predictors of creative abilities than paper and pencil tests" (42, 31). Another possible interpretation is that the tests of creativity do not indicate real creativity any better than teachers' ratings.

The implication from the work thus far in relating creativity to other cognitive abilities is reasonably clear. We should not expect children of low and average IQ to be as creative as children of high IQ. At the same time we must not confuse IQ and creativity. There is wide variation among the children of the same IQ level in creativity. The same implications hold for grades made in the various school subjects and creativity.

Emphasis on Creativity in School

From reading popular magazines during recent years, one realizes that much is being written about the desirability of encouraging creativity in children and youth. Many professional journals and books emphasize the same point of view. Even though creativity is encouraged verbally, considerable sentiment also is expressed that teachers should concentrate upon securing high subject-matter achievements rather than creativity. Getzels and Jackson call for more emphasis on creativity and indicate that there is discrimination by teachers against creative students in the schools generally (11). Social-studies teachers generally are thought to avoid the elicitation and encouragement of most types of creative thought in their classes (**58**). Less emphatically, the statement is made that creative students will not always be to the liking of teachers (**38**).

Science teachers usually do not penalize creativity in their students (**3**). Similarly, in our studies of creativity over the years, the majority of teachers at all school levels did their best to encourage creativity. They were eager to discuss practical suggestions as well as general principles and theory regarding creativity. A small minority expressed negative points of view: the primary aim of the school is to encourage mental discipline; students cannot be creative until they have mastered a vast amount of the subject matter; therefore, any attempt to encourage creativity before Ph.D. study is ineffective. Our point of view is that creative abilities should be nurtured from the beginning of school life. We accept this objective completely and devote a later section to principles for encouraging creativity.

MODEL FOR DEVELOPING PROBLEM-SOLVING ABILITIES

Six generalizations and related principles are now set forth for nurturing problem-solving abilities:

GENERALIZATION	PRINCIPLE
1. Productive thinking originates with dissatisfaction about a problem.	1. Activate solvable problems.
2. Preparation for problem solving requires the recognition of and focusing upon the problem.	2. Assist students in stating and delimiting problems.
3. Background information and methods are necessary in order to avoid random trial, error, and subsequent failure.	3. Assist students in finding information.
4. Problem solving requires the application, analysis, and synthesis of information.	4. Help students process information.
5. The formulation of hypotheses and their subsequent conditional rejection or acceptance is essential.	5. Encourage the stating and testing of hypotheses.
6. Continuous improvement in problem solving is engendered through independently discovered methods and solutions.	6. Encourage independent discovery and evaluation.

To clarify each of these six principles, applications will be drawn from two sources in this manner: Each principle will be followed with a description of its implementation in a class in educational psychology and at the end of the section a lesson in ninth-grade biology will be presented. The class in educational psychology consisted of 25 university seniors. During the first five weeks of the semester, prospective teachers took an educational psychology class, methods classes, and one class in their major field. These classes met five days a week for 50 minutes daily. After five weeks the students went from the university campus into public high schools and did their student teaching for seven weeks. They were in the school throughout the school day, five days a week. After seven weeks of student teaching, the students returned to the campus for the last four weeks of the semester, their classes meeting daily as before their student teaching.

Activate Solvable Problems

On the first day of the class, the instructor passed out a mimeographed outline divided into three parts: an introductory statement, a list of problems which student teachers and teachers in service frequently experience, and a short reference list. The list of problems was written after a study of what research showed to be the main problems experienced by student teachers and teachers in service. In turn, the instructor decided which of the many problems were most appropriate for this particular course. The short introductory statement presented to the class follows:

Every attempt will be made by the instructor to conduct this course in line with what he thinks to be desirable conditions for promoting maximum efficiency of learning. In this connection, he assumes that

a. every student in this class wants to learn about human abilities and the nature of learning in order to become a successful student teacher;
b. the student will identify significant problems in order to learn efficiently;
c. the student will actively engage in finding solutions to his problems;
d. the resources among the students, the instructor, and the university are sufficient to enable each student to learn efficiently;
e. the student can learn through reading, discussing, thinking, and doing;
f. every student who is willing to accept the related responsibility should be given a wide degree of freedom in assuming direction of his own learning problems;
g. every student who is willing to accept the related responsibility should be treated as a mature individual and a beginning member of the teaching profession.

These ideas were discussed briefly on the first day of the class, and attention was directed toward the list of problems which was presented in the second part of the outline. After some discussion of the problems provided in the outline, the students proposed a few others.

As presented and first discussed, the problems were simply words for some of the students. Whole-class and small-group discussions clarified what they meant or might mean when the student was actually engaged in student teaching. The instructor and most of the students during the first week concluded that here were significant problems that could be partially, if not completely, solved during the semester.

Assist Students in Stating and Delimiting Problems

The students and instructor spent most of the first week in discussing possible delimitations of the problems in terms of the situation. From the total list of 18 problems, each student chose one which was of immediate concern to him and on which he would like to work before going into student teaching. The class was then organized into six groups, according to the first problem choice of each student. These six problems as finally stated by students were:

1. What are the attributes of a successful teacher?
2. How can I attain an orderly work situation in the classroom, free from disruptive incidents?
3. How can I provide for differences among pupils in rate of learning?
4. How can I encourage all pupils to want to learn?
5. What is the general course of purposeful learning?
6. What can or should I do to help pupils acquire well-integrated personalities and character?

During the first four weeks when the students were not actually working on the problems, the instructor presented his analysis of two other problems: (1) What principles would help me in teaching students psychomotor abilities in typewriting, sewing, swimming, and the like? (2) What principles would help me in teaching students knowledge and related cognitive abilities, such as comprehending, analyzing, evaluating, creating?

In attempting to solve the problem before going out for student teaching, the class agreed that three things would be done. First, each group would secure information about its problem, mainly through reading. An annotated bibliography was to be developed by each group and eventually distributed to the entire class with recommendations. Second, after each individual had acquired some information through reading and class discussions, a list of principles was to be developed by each group as the tentative solution to the problem. These principles also were to be distributed to the remainder of the class before the students left for student teaching. Third, the students and the instructor agreed that during regular class periods in the fourth and fifth weeks of the semester each group would demonstrate and subsequently discuss one or more of its principles. This, of course, took six class periods. The instructor encouraged the students to use this opportunity to get first-hand experience in teaching, and made it clear that he and the rest of the class also would try to make it a successful experience for the demonstrating group.

In this situation, then, there was delimitation of the problem in several steps. The first was to find out what the statement or problem really meant in practice and to state it in such way that there was reasonable opportunity for securing or making progress toward a solution during the semester. The second step was to decide the form in which the solution to the problem might appear. Three forms were agreed upon: first, a statement of generalizations; second, a demonstration of one or more of the generalizations in class; and third, a testing and evaluating of these generalizations during the student teaching.

During the first three weeks, at least half of the class periods were used in stating and delimiting the problem, in discussing information-gathering procedures, in analyzing information, and in organizing the generalizations. Also, individuals met with the instructor outside of class, and each of the groups met with him at least twice to consider various aspects of the problem-solving situation. It can be seen that delimitation of the problem did not occur suddenly but started in the first week and continued well into the third week. A considerable amount of the delimiting, of course, started after the students began securing information about the problems.

Assist Students in Finding Information

Once individuals selected a problem and subsequently organized themselves into groups, they needed information. Methods for getting information were devised by the groups, and procedures for bringing together and analyzing information were worked out. The instructor gave only a minimum reference list composed of one basic textbook, a supplementary textbook, and five books of readings. However, this list included a number of selections pertaining to each of the problems.

To this extent the instructor provided help, but he did not refer the students to any specific selection or group of selections that might be related to a particular problem. Students were helped in identifying various guides for use of the library, including the location of the current periodicals room and various reserve rooms. Only when individuals or groups asked for further specific help as to sources of information did the instructor give such help. From the start the students were encouraged to draw upon and contribute information in the smaller group from their previous experiences and knowledge about the problem.

In most groups it was a relatively simple matter to apportion responsibilities for examining the list of references in the course outline. Subsequently, each group developed procedures for going beyond the reference list. With occasional help they developed the means for recording their findings and for developing a fairly uniform system for writing the annotated bibliography. These bibliographies contained from 18 to 35 different entries. In checking these entries, the instructor found that about 60 percent of the entries were the same as those he had used in a previous topical outline of the course before attempting this problem-solving approach to instruction. The other 40 percent were new entries, most of which were excellent and of which the instructor had not been aware. For the most part, the new entries were drawn from the professional journals and from methods books in the major fields.

Help Students Process Information

When the students brought in information and started to write the generalizations in the small groups, considerable help was needed. Several class periods and meetings outside class with the instructor were needed to develop the first draft. As many as three out-of-class meetings were needed with some groups before a fairly well-organized statement of generalizations appeared.

One of the larger problems faced in interpreting and analyzing information was that, when the groups of three to six students started comparing what they had gathered, parts of it did not agree or, at least, needed to be analyzed in terms of the larger problem. The critical point came when the diverse information was to be incorporated in a fairly economical list of principles. The first list of principles tended to be exceedingly long, with 35 to 40 entries. Once a typewritten copy of these was available to all members of the group, careful analysis started. Overlappings and discrepancies were found. At this point the instructor volunteered help and was called upon frequently. Had there been more time available, most of the groups would probably have analyzed and organized the information reasonably well themselves.

Now follows the list of principles which a group of four students developed:

How Can I Attain an Orderly Work Situation
in the Classroom, Free from Disruptive Incidents?

1. Take it for granted that the class is well intentioned and expect good behavior from them.
2. Do whatever is necessary and appropriate to get a reasonable amount of order, especially in the first meeting with the class.
3. Let the pupils know what is expected of them and make sure the expectations are reasonable and appropriate, for example, with respect to (a) standards of conduct, (b) class assignments and activities, (c) homework and other out-of-class activities.
4. Teach and illustrate, giving due consideration to the students' interests and backgrounds such as learning ability, age, home background.
5. Maintain an active class with a variety of projects—not a monotonous routine.
6. Be consistent and impartial.
7. Be courteous to students—avoid the use of sarcasm and ridicule.
8. Promise only what can be carried out.
9. Arrange the situation so that crises are avoided.
10. Investigate the causes of misconduct carefully and take appropriate action, since the purpose of discipline is correction, not punishment.

This economical list of principles was based on information from 35 different sources and represents only a small portion of the many facts and concepts acquired by the students in their searching for a solution.

A second group of students had as their problem to provide for differences among pupils in rate of learning in skill subjects. Though the instructor had originally stated the problem in broad terms of providing for differences among pupils, these students delimited the problem to their specific interest. Their introductory statement and principles are now shown:

How Can I Provide for Differences Among Pupils in Rate
of Learning in Skill Subjects?

Up to the present time, extensive pretesting has not been used to determine different rates of learning ability in skill subjects. Therefore, we will make two assumptions:

1. Skill classes are heterogeneous.

2. The teacher will have to deal with individual differences within the classes.

The aim of the teacher in handling individual differences is not to mold every student to the same pattern, but to assay the assets and liabilities of each student and to work, with the individuals and groups so that members of the class, both individually and collectively, show a net profit at the end of the school year.

A. Dealing with individual differences within the classroom:
  1. Ask questions which in general vary from easy to more difficult, so that all will have an opportunity to respond successfully.
  2. Motivate the learners through praise and encouragement each day.
  3. Enliven your class by having each student keep his own daily personal progress chart.
  4. Give directions slowly, clearly, and simply.
  5. Organize groups within the class into ability levels and work with these individually with the help of audio aids.
  6. Let the fast learner occasionally help the slow learner. An example of this in a shorthand class would be to let the accelerated student dictate to the slower students and demonstrate shorthand outlines at the board.
  7. Use audiovisual aids, such as tape recorders, movies, and records, for supplementary demonstrations.
  8. Encourage the pupil to set his own goals, try for them, and decide for himself how good the results are.
  9. Manage practice so that the learners as individuals or in small groups can proceed at appropriate rates.

B. Dealing with individual differences outside of the classroom:
  1. Assign homework with different levels of difficulty that will be in line with the different interests and purposes of the major groups in the class.
  2. Have a classroom library with materials of several levels of difficulty relating to the skill subjects.
  3. Provide opportunities and facilities for students to improve their skills through purposeful practice in their spare time.
  4. Have out-of-class sessions to determine the root of trouble for any student encountering difficulty.

Recognize that these statements of principles were drawn up within a four-week period, that the students gathered information on other problems, that the instructor used about one-fourth of all class periods to present information on other problems, and that six days were used for demonstrating one or more of the principles by each group. The two groups of principles represent the students' best generalized conclusions about reasonable solutions to the problem prior to student teaching.

Encourage the Stating and Testing of Hypotheses

As soon as the student first identified a problem and started thinking about it individually and discussing it in his group, hypotheses were already being formulated. Thus, there were approximately three stages in hypothesis formulation and testing: first, securing the information and drawing up the list of principles; second, demonstrating one or more of the principles; third, actual student teaching. A considerable number of hypotheses were accepted and others were rejected—including, perhaps, some good ones. However, each list of principles was in fact a list of hypotheses which the students first tried out in discussions and subsequently in the demonstration before the class. The demonstration provided the first main test of one or more of the principles. Until students began planning for the demonstration, the principles did not carry the meaning which a principle should. However, when the students began deciding which one or more of the principles could be demonstrated in the classroom, the testing of the principle or hypothesis took form.

In the case of providing for differences in skill subjects, a very skillful demonstration was arranged in a business-education laboratory. One student acted as a teacher and dictated shorthand at a moderate speed to a second student while two other students took dictation from tape recorders, one at a low speed and the other at a high speed. The demonstration clearly showed that with sufficient equipment, shorthand dictation could be given at speeds suitable to the rate of at least three different groups of learners within a classroom.

Encourage Independent Discovery and Evaluation

This situation in educational psychology was excellent for encouraging independent discovery and evaluation. Only those students ready for student teaching during the semester were permitted to enroll, and during the five weeks preceding and the four weeks after student teaching, a relatively small number of other classes was taken. The arrangement enabled each student to plan his study and work schedule more efficiently than did the usual arrangement of taking five or six classes; in turn, the student had more time outside class meetings to gather information independently, to meet with other members of his group, and the like. Further, the students perceived themselves as full-time student teachers. Their motivation for identifying and solving problems was high.

The instructor generally withheld direct evaluation of the students' statements of principles and their demonstrations. He did not tell the students that anything was definitely right or wrong, that anything was complete or incomplete. Instead he raised questions. The raising of questions, along with discussions, served to help the students arrive at conclusions independently. Further, the instructor had as one main instructional goal the encouragement of independent discovery and evaluation by students so that, when they are subsequently on their own in teaching positions, they will not fall into a monotonous teaching method or way of life. The goal, if achieved, will lead toward their seeking to find better ways of improving problem-solving abilities of their pupils. They will not be satisfied with someone else telling them what, when, and how to teach.

On the basis of the instructor's day-to-day evaluation of this classroom situation, the independent discovery and evaluation by the students yielded excellent results. Under a previous instructional arrangement in which students took the class without doing student teaching, they had memorized principles and tried to associate as much meaning as possible with them. However, in the present situation the student did not have to memorize the principles he and his group developed, for they were already incorporated quite well into his total pattern of meaningful learning. Further, the principles drawn up by the other groups were demonstrated, discussed, and appeared to be as useful for guiding practices during student teaching as did those proposed by the instructor for the two problems he discussed. A small minority of students indicated that they would have preferred the instructor's handling all of the problems by presenting information and demonstrations and leading whole-class and small-group discussions. Over 80 percent of the students indicated that this was the first time they had been expected to accept the responsibility for their own learning efficiency. In addition some of them for the first time used the various library tools which had been available and were waiting for their use throughout the first three and one-half years of their university life. They felt that their skill in identifying and using sources of information was an important one which could be applied in their subsequent teaching careers.

Implementation in a Biology Class

Consider how some of the principles were implemented by a beginning science teacher:

I taught in a junior high school. The lesson I am about to describe was for my ninth-grade biology class which was composed of 13 high ability students. The specific topic being considered was the salivary digestion of starch. These instructional materials were used: 14 test tubes, 14 medicine droppers, starch suspension, dilute iodine solution, and Benedict's solution. All of these materials were available at the school.

When the class was asked, 'What effect has saliva on starch?' the ready answer was, 'It changes starch to sugar.' When asked how this could be verified, the students were less responsive. They were then instructed to carry out the test for the verification of the presence of starch. This test amounted to putting 5 milliliters of starch suspension in a test tube and then adding one drop of the iodine solution. If starch was really present, a dark blue color should result from the addition of the iodine. The test was positive.

The opening question was repeated and then I asked how to verify the answer given that saliva changes starch to sugar. One student proposed that some saliva be added to each test tube. All the students accepted and executed the proposal. Instructions were given to shake the tubes and to warm them in the fist for two minutes. During the hiatus, the reasons for the shaking and the warmth were discussed.

Observations disclosed that the blue-colored contents of the tubes had become colorless or nearly so. This quickly led to possible theories to explain the change. One student proposed that the iodine had been used up. He suggested that we add more iodine solution in order to test his theory. Each student did so, but no color change occurred. As expected, someone said that the starch had been changed to sugar. (Sugar suspension does not form a dark blue color with iodine solution.) At this point I explained that this might be so, but that the explanation should be regarded as a tentative one, subject to verification. Someone then suggested that we test for sugar with Benedict's solution, so this test was carried out and it was positive—sugar was present.

Henceforth the class seemed complacently satisfied until I asked, 'How can we explain the presence of the sugar?' Of course the forthcoming answer was, 'The starch changed into sugar; saliva caused it.' A classmate objected, 'Maybe there was sugar in the starch suspension.' It took but a moment to test the stock bottle of starch suspension for sugar. The test was negative, whereupon the following questions were raised. 'Is it possible that there was sugar in our saliva? Perhaps there was sugar in the iodine solution.' Tests were carried out; the results were all negative.

Since no other objections were presented, the findings were reviewed and listed on the blackboard as follows:

1. The bottle labeled starch suspension contained starch. It did not contain sugar.
2. There was no sugar in the iodine solution.
3. There was no sugar in the saliva.
4. After two minutes, the warmed mixture of starch and saliva gave a positive test for sugar.

Conclusions were called for and evaluated by the answers to the question,

'If we had not tested each substance for the presence of sugar, how would our conclusion have been affected?'

Examine the preceding discussion carefully. Which of the six principles were implemented? violated?

MODEL FOR ENCOURAGING CREATIVITY

All of the principles related to problem solving are applicable to creativity. In addition, a few principles are inferred from research on creativity as outlined in the first part of this chapter. These principles for encouraging creativity are not as firmly fixed in research findings as are those related to the learning of facts and concepts in Chapter 7 and those for problem solving in the preceding section. We do not know enough about the nature of creativity to identify reliably children now in school who may be the highly creative individuals of tomorrow. However, we do know that creativity is found to some extent in all individuals, except perhaps the mentally deficient.

MacLeish had this to say about the differences between the usual college course and the one set up to encourage creative writing:

> The truth is that the whole situation in a writing course is a reversal of the usual academic pattern. Not only is there no subject, there is no content either. Or, more precisely, the content is the work produced by students in the course. And the relation of the teacher to his students is thus the opposite of the relation one would expect to find. Ordinarily it is the teacher who knows, the student who learns. Here it is the student who knows, or should, and the teacher who learns or tries to. The student writes. The teacher reads. And the object of the teacher's reading is to learn if he can how closely the knowing of the words approximates the knowing of their writer. It may be less. It may be far, far more, for such is the nature of the struggle between a writer and the obdurate material of words in which he works. But whether less or more, the only question the man who undertakes to teach can ask, is the question of the adequacy of the writing to its own intent. As a writer himself he may call it "good" or "bad." As a man he may have this human opinion of the mind which conceived it. But as a teacher of writing it is not his task to tell his students what they should try to write or to judge their work by the standards he would apply to his own or his "betters" (39, 160).

The generalizations and principles which follow are intended to be applicable at all school levels.

GENERALIZATIONS	PRINCIPLES
1. Creativity is expressed in figural, symbolic, and semantic content and re-	1. Encourage creativity in many media.

quires mental and psychomotor activity.

2. Fluency, originality, flexibility, and other divergent-production abilities underlie creative performance.

2. Foster divergent-production.

3. Creative individuals tend to be emotionally sensitive, unconventional, independent, and self-confident.

3. Foster a creative personality.

4. Creative abilities require a nurturing environment over a period of time.

4. Encourage continuing creative expression.

5. Creativity is manifested in objects, ideas, compositions, and methods that are novel to the individual.

5. Encourage productivity.

Encourage Creativity in Many Media

If original expression in many media—written language, oral language, rhythms, music, and art—is to emerge, there must be opportunity in the school day for instruction directed toward this end (Fig. 8.3). The typical school curriculum, filled primarily with assignments and other activities through which the students are to learn and reproduce what mankind already knows, does not in itself encourage original expression. Further, creative expression is often stifled in order for students to devote more time to learning material that is not new even to the learner. Teachers can alleviate this situation in several ways, and one of the primary ones is by rewarding creative behavior (56). Merely letting the student present original ideas and earnestly attempting to understand his reasoning will often be reward enough. Recalling the tendency of youngsters to imitate, a teacher by displaying creative behavior can do much towards encouraging original expressions by her pupils. Some teachers have even become patrons for their students with creative promise; these teachers contribute their encouragement, guidance, and time.

The ideas above seem applicable to pupils of all age levels. Considerable success has been reported in fostering creative thinking in first-, second-, and third-graders (57). Children are taught how to use paper bags with which to trap ideas and are asked how to improve familiar toys. Indeed, not feeling constraints on responses as acutely, young children are likely to produce numerous thought-provoking ideas in many media.

Fig. 8.3. Inventiveness can be encouraged in many media.

Foster Divergent Production

Fluency, originality, and flexibility do not mean lawlessness or lack of values. Rather, they imply a readiness to make changes in behavior to meet circumstances that have not previously been met satisfactorily, or an ability to cope with completely new circumstances. Scientific knowledge and knowledge of the physical world generally are increasing so rapidly that we are constantly meeting situations for which we have no known means of responding productively. One factor that might inhibit divergent production is to teach only one strategy of learning or method of proceeding as the correct one.

This belief in correct method has done much to block divergent production. In athletics it is known that many records stood for years simply because coaches generally agreed that there was only one proper or correct form for such things as putting the shot, shooting a basketball, running the mile, running the 100-yard dash, and the like. Over long periods of time, fairly static top limits were expected. Then, a coach permitted a young man to follow his own method in putting the shot, and very soon the record went up markedly. A coach permitted basketball players to start shooting one handed, and soon a much higher percent of accuracy emerged. The forward pass greatly changed the character of football. To give examples from another area of learning, over many years a given content and methodology of oil painting was followed. Finally some nonconforming individual broke away from this method, and soon we had different forms and content in art expression. American composers required many years to depart from the style and general content of the Western European composers of music. Once the break was made, and aided by new means of communication such as radio and television, new forms of uniquely American composition emerged.

Divergent-production abilities improve with instruction. This is true for primary school (**57**) through college (**41**). Several persons recommend that pupils be given more leeway to express themselves creatively (**1, 22, 34**). Also, motivation is needed in the instructional program in connection with the nurturance of divergent-production abilities (**27**) as it is with convergent-production abilities.

Foster a Creative Personality

In the preceding discussion, we have emphasized cognitive abilities. These abilities do not develop, however, unrelated to the personality of the individuals. Inasmuch as Chapter 11 is devoted entirely to personality integration, we shall indicate here only a point of view regarding personality traits to be nurtured rather than discouraged.

Adjectives such as conforming, conventional, and dependent do not appear in the research as traits of creative individuals. Impulsive, sensitive, self-confident, independent, and unconventional do. Teachers and parents need to examine their own attitudes toward the behavior of children to decide which of these characteristics in children are associated with warm and accepting behavior on the part of the adult. It is clear, too, that creative individuals are not law breakers, seeking to destroy values and mores that have been decades and centuries in building. They are, however, more questioning of traditions, less inclined to consider all the possible outcomes before acting, and less concerned about how others regard them. In order for this kind of student to feel relatively comfortable in the school, we probably must encourage a wider range of approved behavior patterns than we do at the present time.

Encourage Continuing Creative Expression

The intellectual activities of poets and artists during four quarters of a creative enterprise are shown in Fig. 8.4. Notice that poets and

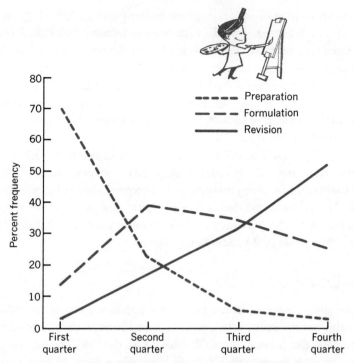

Fig. 8.4. Intellectual activities of poets and artists during four quarters of a creative enterprise. (Adapted from D. M. Johnson. *The psychology of thought and judgment.* New York: Harper & Row, 1955, p. 30.)

artists spend a great deal of time in early preparation. Then there is a considerable increase in the time given to formulation of the idea, whatever it is. As the preparation falls off from the third to the fourth quarter, revision increases markedly. There are, of course, wide differences in the total length of time required to bring forth the poem or the painting. Some poets and artists spend years on a large product. Smaller products are produced in a short time. Some novelists, too, start and complete a work in less than a year. Others spend as much as five or more years from the time they have the ideas about a novel until it is finished.

In a later revision the sequence was shown to be threefold: preparation, production, and judgment (**25**). In a test of ideational fluency where one is asked to give clever titles to a story, three phases are clearly evident: Preparation occurs as the plot is read, production as various titles are written for the plot, and judgment as the best of the titles is selected. Thus, even in a short time interval, the production of a creative response requires time, rather than emerging suddenly.

The above discussion suggests that a teacher cannot simply tell students that in a given length of time they are to produce something. He cannot stand before a class and say, "Now write a poem," or, "Get out your art materials and, before the period ends in 30 minutes, give me something to display on the bulletin board." From the idea to the finished product, time and effort are essential. Kindergarten children will, of course, do a finger painting in 3 to 5 minutes, wash their hands, and go to some other activity. If given a blank sheet of paper and crayon, primary school children in a relatively short time fill the page with something and are ready for another activity.

Such spontaneous expressions are to be highly encouraged. The teacher well knows that enthusiasm for and reinforcement of the child's early expressions, subsequent opportunities for continuing the expressions, and building essential skills will lead to creative projects satisfying to the individual. Some of these early projects may have lasting and permanent value not only to the individual but to the general school population, or even the larger population.

Many larger high schools now sponsor annual art exhibits of students' work, arrange programs which include musical compositions by the students, produce small volumes of their poetry and other literary work, print students' short poems, short stories, and essays in the newspaper, and stage students' plays. These are a few of the useful means for encouraging student creativity and for opening up opportunities for them to continue to produce after they finish school. These practices are in harmony with the ideas of encouraging creativity on a continuing basis throughout the school year.

Encourage Productivity

It is wise for the art teacher to display before the class an art product of each child. Girls in the modern dance class can profit from discussing and practicing before they bring a performance to a larger group. Students write several essays, stories, or biographies before one is selected for publication in the school newspaper or annual. For each pupil to have a reasonably good opportunity for having a better product displayed, he must produce several.

Most of the poets who are remembered for a few outstanding poems produced a large number, many of which were not published or at least were not well received. In school situations, also, we should encourage learners to transform some of their ideas rather consistently into a product, be it in written symbols, oral expression, art, music, or bodily expression such as in dance or dramatics. But productivity must be emphasized. Examination of the lives of men and women who have given something of permanent value to society leads to the inevitable conclusion that one must be productive.

When reading the following description of the attempts of an English teacher with creativity, decide which principles were implemented:

When I first told my classes [high school English] about April 23, the four-hundredth anniversary of William Shakespeare's birth, I gave them a list of approximately 14 projects from which they could choose. They were to select the one which interested them most and have it ready for April 23, which would be set aside for our celebration. The following is a list of some of these suggestions which could be done individually or in small groups:

1. Dramatizing a scene from *Macbeth*
2. Making a bulletin board display
3. Writing a poem in commemoration of Shakespeare
4. Drawing a character or scene from *Macbeth*
5. Designing a costume for one of the characters
6. Constructing or drawing a model of the Globe Theatre
7. Writing a report on some aspect of Shakespeare
8. Giving an oral report
9. Making a diorama of a scene from *Macbeth*
10. Memorizing a speech and presenting it before the class
11. Presenting a panel discussion

From the above list alone, students were given a variety from which to choose. The selections ranged from designing costumes which called for much creative imagination to writing reports which could be merely factual expositions. I did, however, tell them that they need not feel restricted to that list. I was certain that they would be able to think of other projects, and I wanted them to feel perfectly free to carry out their own ideas.

Flexibility, however, was more important in the actual carrying out of the projects. Students questioned me as to specific directions which they were to follow. For instance, students giving written or oral reports wished to know if they had to be a specific length. Those memorizing passages wondered if they could choose any speech, or if I required a certain number of lines. The four groups that worked on bulletin board displays asked if there were certain requirements which they had to meet. I set no specifications of this kind. In the case of reports, I merely said that they should be well developed. I had learned that if you require a student's written work to be 500 words long, for example, he spends most of his time counting the words. Because he does not have enough to say to equal 500 words, much of the work is superfluous.

Three of the students wrote poems in commemoration of Shakespeare. I had, of course, told the classes that I would give them all of the help that I could, and these three students sought help often. One of them brought four poems in after school and wanted my advice as to which was the best and should be read on April 23. By means of my questioning him, he decided which one was the best. He told me that he enjoyed writing poetry very much but just never had much occasion to do so. I suggested that he submit his poem to *Patterns In Print,* a publication of student work, which he did. It was accepted and will appear in this year's edition. The critical point is that he was interested enough to continue to produce until he was completely satisfied.

Another student enjoyed the projects so much that she worked on three of them, a bulletin board display, a written report, and a costume for Lady Macbeth.

Two days before the deadline, one of the students brought in a model of the Globe Theatre which she had made out of sugar cubes. A tremendous amount of time and talent was involved in its construction. The most rewarding aspect of this incident was that this girl was extremely withdrawn and previously had not volunteered. If I called on her, she would keep her eyes on her book and never offer an answer.

I had another student who also never took part in the discussion. However, he did not even listen to me or to his classmates. I had tried every imaginable means to get him interested in the class, but I was not successful. His project was three drawings of Macbeth which showed much artistic ability. I felt that he had perhaps learned something and enjoyed doing it.

One of the students designed and made a costume for Lady Macbeth which was itself an expression of creativity, but the colors she chose for it were even more so. The majority of the costume was black as she felt that Lady Macbeth played the part of an evil character. She used white trim, however, as she believed Lady Macbeth really had a pure heart.

SUMMARY

Thinking, problem solving, and creating always occur in a situation or context, not as abstract processes. Thinking is about something, problem solving is directed toward solution of a problem, and creativity involves expressing something in some form. Cognitive processes directed toward finding an already accepted or logical conclusion are usually designated by such terms as *reasoning, convergent thinking,* or *critical thinking.* Divergent, creative, and imaginative thinking are directed toward finding new or novel conclusions, methods, or forms of expression. Some convergent thinking is involved in divergent thinking, and vice versa.

Problem solving requires purposeful activity. The solution to some problems occurs suddenly with insight; in other problems, there is a continuing process of posing possible solutions, rejecting, and finally confirming one as most appropriate or correct. Problem-solving abilities of children and youth are improved through (1) activating solvable problems, (2) assisting the learner to state and delimit the problem, (3) assisting the learner in finding needed information and methods, (4) aiding the learner in processing information, (5) providing opportunities for stating and testing hypotheses, and (6) encouraging independent discovery and evaluation.

Developing new and better methods for solving problems and inventing new and better forms for expressing human experiences require divergent thinking. The school and society generally must identify more reliably and nurture more successfully the creative abilities of children and youth. Because little has been done in this area, particularly in social affairs, principles for improving creative abilities are necessarily tentative: (1) encourage creativity in many media, (2) foster divergent production, (3) foster a creative personality, (4) encourage continuing creative expression, and (5) encourage productivity.

QUESTIONS AND ACTIVITIES

1. a. In what respects is divergent thinking different from and similar to other thinking?
   b. In what respects are the outcomes of divergent thinking and convergent thinking the same or different?
   c. Discuss the thinking you engaged in to answer a or b.
2. a. How are problem solving and thinking alike and different?
   b. Compare and contrast two sequences in problem solving.
3. a. What do you consider to be the three main problems in college education today?
   b. Discuss the extent to which answering the above required convergent and divergent production.
4. a. Discuss insight, and trial and confirmation in problem solving.
   b. How do prior success and failure affect problem solving?
   c. What is the effect of set on problem solving?

5. Recall your school experiences at the college, high school, and elementary level. Estimate the percent of time given to instruction designed to encourage creative effort. Discuss briefly with examples.
6. a. How is productivity related to creativity?
   b. Discuss the conclusions of Terman regarding productivity.
7. Discuss the relationship between IQ and creativity.
8. Describe a classroom or other situation and give a concrete, specific description of how each principle for improving problem-solving abilities might be implemented.
9. a. Indicate briefly the subject field and school level in which you are most interested.
   b. Indicate which principle for encouraging creativity would be most difficult to implement in this situation and discuss why it would be more difficult than each of the other four.

SUGGESTIONS FOR FURTHER READING

Broudy, H. S. Dewey's analysis of the act of thought. *Bull. Sch. Educ., Ind. Univer.*, 1960, **36**, 15–26. (In Fullagar, *et al.*, 1964, 81–91.)

Cohen, J. *Humanistic psychology*. London: Allen & Unwin, 1958. Ch. 7: Contact of minds, 139–155. (Portions reprinted under the title "Contact between minds" in Cohen, 1964, 249–267.)

Duncan, C. P. Recent research on human problem solving. *Psychol. Bull.*, 1959, **56**, 397–429. (Abridged in De Cecco, 1963, 212–254.)

Ennis, R. H. A concept of critical thinking. *Harv. educ. Rev.*, 1962, **32**, 81–111. (Portions reprinted under the title "A definition of critical thinking" in Ripple, 1964, 286–304.)

Gagné, R. M., & E. C. Smith, Jr. A study of the effects of verbalization on problem solving. *J. exp. Psychol.*, 1962, **63**, 12–18. (In Anderson & Ausubel, 1965, 380–391.)

Guilford, J. P. The nature of creativity. In *Proceedings of the 1960 summer conference*, **13**. Bellingham: Western Washington State College Press, 1960, pp. 17–28. (In Russell, 1964, 125–131.)

Guilford, J. P. Factors that aid and hinder creativity. *Teachers Coll. Rec.*, 1962, **63**, 380–392. (In French, 1964, 429–447; Grinder, 1963, 484–500; and Seidman, 1965, 196–206.)

Klausmeier, H. J., & L. J. Loughlin. Behaviors during problem solving among children of low, average, and high intelligence. *J. educ. Psychol.*, 1961, **52**, 148–152. (In Ripple, 1964, 279–285.)

MacKinnon, D. W. The nature and nurture of creative talent. *Amer. Psychologist*, 1962, **17**, 484–495. (In Ripple, 1964, 305–323.)

Maltzman, I. On the training of originality. *Psychol. Rev.*, 1960, **67**, 229–242. (In Anderson & Ausubel, 1965, 657–678; and Staats, 1964, 259–273.)

Palmer, R. R. Straight and crooked thinking. *Clearing House*, 1958, **32**, 542–546. (In Crow & Crow, 1963, 394–400.)

Ripple, R. E., & F. B. May. Caution in comparing creativity and IQ. *Psychol. Rep.*, 1962, **10**, 229–230. (In Ripple, 1964, 324–326.)

Saugstad, P., & K. Raaheim. Problem-solving, past experience and availability of functions. *Brit. J. Psychol.*, 1960, **51**, 97–104. (In Gordon, 1965, 435–441.)

Torrance, E. P. Creativity. *What research says to the teacher*, No. 28. Washington, D.C.: National Education Association, 1963. (Portions reprinted under the title "Creativity: What can teachers do?" in Seidman, 1965, 161–164.)

REFERENCES

1. Barron, F. The psychology of imagination. *Scient. Amer.*, 1958, **199**, 150–170.

2. Birch, H. G., & H. S. Rabinowitz. The negative effect of previous experience on productive thinking. *J. exp. Psychol.*, 1951, **41**, 121–125.

3. Cline, V. B., J. M. Richards, Jr., & W. E. Needham. Creativity tests and achievement in high school science. *J. appl. Psychol.*, 1963, **47**, 184–189.

4. Dewey, J. *How we think*. New York: Heath, 1933.

5. Drevdahl, J. E., & R. B. Cattell. Personality and creativity in artists and writers. *J. clin. Psychol.*, 1958, **14**, 107–111.

6. Duncan, C. P. Recent research on human problem solving. *Psychol. Bull.*, 1959, **56**, 397–429.

7. Ennis, R. H. A concept of critical thinking. *Harv. educ. Rev.*, 1962, **32**, 81–111.

297

8. Flanagan, J. C. The definition and measurement of ingenuity. In C. W. Taylor, & F. Barron (Eds.), *Scientific creativity: Its recognition and development.* New York: Wiley, 1963, pp. 89–98.

9. Fox, D. J., & I. Lorge. The relative quality of decisions written by individuals and by groups as the available time for problem solving is increased. *J. soc. Psychol.,* 1962, **57**, 227–242.

10. Gagné, R. M. Problem solving. In A. W. Melton (Ed.), *Categories of human learning.* New York: Academic, 1964, pp. 293–317.

11. Getzels, J. W., & P. W. Jackson. *Creativity and intelligence: Explorations with gifted students.* New York: Wiley, 1962.

12. Goldner, R. H. Individual differences in whole-part approach and flexibility-rigidity in problem solving. *Psychol. Monogr.,* 1957, **71**, No. 21 (Whole No. 450).

13. Guilford, J. P. Three faces of intellect. *Amer. Psychologist,* 1959, **14**, 469–479.

14. Guilford, J. P., P. R. Christensen, J. W. Frick, & P. R. Merrifield. The relations of creative-thinking aptitudes to non-aptitude personality traits. *Rep. psychol. Lab.,* No. 20. Los Angeles: Univer. of Southern Calif., 1957.

15. Guilford, J. P., & R. Hoepfner. Current summary of structure-of-intellect factors and suggested tests. *Rep. psychol. Lab.,* No. 30. Los Angeles: Univer. of Southern Calif., 1963.

16. Hall, E. J., Jane S. Mouton, & R. R. Blake. Group problem solving effectiveness under conditions of pooling vs. interaction. *J. soc. Psychol.,* 1963, **59**, 147–157.

17. Harlow, H. F. Learning set and error factor theory. In S. Koch (Ed.), *Psychology: A study of a science.* Vol. 2. New York: McGraw-Hill, 1959, pp. 492–537.

18. Harootunian, B., & M. W. Tate. The relationship of certain selected variables to problem solving ability. *J. educ. Psychol.,* 1960, **51**, 326–333.

19. Hildreth, Gertrude. The difficulty reduction tendency in perception and problem solving. *J. educ. Psychol.,* 1941, **32**, 305–313.

20. Holland, J. L. Some limitations of teacher ratings as predictors of creativity. *J. educ. Psychol.,* 1959, **50**, 219–223.

21. Hoppe, R. A. Memorizing by individuals and groups. *J. abnorm. soc. Psychol.,* 1962, **65**, 64–67.

22. Horney, Karen. *Neurosis and human growth.* New York: Norton, 1950.

23. Hudgins, B. B. Effects of group experience on individual problem solving. *J. educ. Psychol.,* 1960, **51**, 37–42.

24. Johnson, D. M. *The psychology of thought and judgment.* New York: Harper & Row, 1955.

25. Johnson, D. M. Problem-solving processes. Paper read at Amer. Psychol. Ass., St. Louis, September, 1962.

26. Kendler, H. H., & Tracy S. Kendler. Inferential behavior in preschool children. *J. exp. Psychol.,* 1956, **51**, 311–314.

27. Kern, H. Motivating the pupil's creativity in the classroom. *Calif. J. secondary Educ.,* 1959, **34**, 263–268.

28. Kingsley, H. L., & R. Garry. *The nature and conditions of learning.* Englewood Cliffs, N.J.: Prentice-Hall, 1957.

29. Klausmeier, H. J., C. W. Harris, & Z. Ethnathios. Relationships between divergent thinking abilities and teacher ratings of high school students. *J. educ. Psychol.,* 1962, **53**, 72–75.

30. Klausmeier, H. J., C. W. Harris, & W. Wiersma. *Strategies of learning and efficiency of concept attainment by individuals and groups.* U.S. Office of Education Cooper-

ative Research Project No. 1442. Madison: Univer. of Wisconsin, 1964.

31. Klausmeier, H. J., & L. J. Loughlin. Behaviors during problem solving among children of low, average, and high intelligence. *J. educ. Psychol.*, 1961, **52**, 148–152.

32. Klausmeier, H. J., & W. Wiersma. The effects of IQ level and sex on divergent thinking of seventh grade pupils of low, average, and high IQ. *J. educ. Res.*, 1965, **58**, 300–302.

33. Kostick, M. M. A study of transfer: Sex differences in the reasoning process. *J. educ. Psychol.*, 1954, **45**, 449–458.

34. Levy, N. J. Notes on the creative process and the creative person. *Psychiat. Quart.*, 1961, **35**, 66–77.

35. Lorge, I., & H. Solomon. Group and individual performance in problem solving related to previous exposure to problem, level of aspiration, and group size. *Behav. Sci.*, 1960, **5**, 28–38.

36. Luchins, A. S. Mechanization in problem solving: The effect of Einstellung. *Psychol. Monogr.*, 1942, **54**, No. 6 (Whole No. 248).

37. McCurdy, H. G., & W. E. Lambert. The efficiency of small human groups in the solution of problems requiring genuine cooperation. *J. Pers.*, 1952, **20**, 478–494.

38. MacKinnon, D. W. The nature and nurture of creative talent. *Amer. Psychologist*, 1962, **17**, 484–495.

39. MacLeish, A. On the teaching of writing. *Harper's Magazine*, 1959, **219**, 158–161.

40. McNemar, Olga W. An attempt to differentiate between individuals with high and low reasoning ability. *Amer. J. Psychol.*, 1955, **68**, 20–36.

41. Maltzman, I. On the training of originality. *Psychol. Rev.*, 1960, **67**, 229–242.

42. May, F. B. Creative thinking: A factorial study of seventh-grade children. Unpublished doctoral dissertation, Univer. of Wisconsin, 1961.

43. Melton, A. W. The taxonomy of human learning: Overview. In A. W. Melton (Ed.), *Categories of human learning*. New York: Academic, 1964, pp. 325–339.

44. Merrifield, P. R., J. P. Guilford, P. R. Christensen, & J. W. Frick. A factor-analytic study of problem-solving abilities. *Rep. psychol. Lab.*, No. 22. Los Angeles: Univer. of Southern Calif., 1960.

45. Moore, O. K., & S. B. Anderson. Search behavior in individual and group problem solving. *Amer. sociol. Rev.*, 1954, **19**, 702–714.

46. Morgan, D. N. Creativity today. *J. Aesthet. Art Crit.*, 1953, **12**, 1–24.

47. Polya, G. *How to solve it.* Princeton: Princeton Univer., 1945.

48. Rhine, R. J. The effect on problem solving of success or failure as a function of cue specificity. *J. exp. Psychol.*, 1957, **53**, 121–125.

49. Ripple, R. E., & F. B. May. Caution in comparing creativity and IQ. *Psychol. Rep.*, 1962, **10**, 229–230.

50. Schroder, H. M., & D. E. Hunt. Failure-avoidance in situational interpretation and problem solving. *Psychol. Monogr.*, 1957, **71**, No. 3 (Whole No. 432).

51. Schroder, H. M., & J. B. Rotter. Rigidity as learned behavior. *J. exp. Psychol.*, 1953, **44**, 141–150.

52. Taylor, C. W., & J. L. Holland. Development and application of tests of creativity. *Rev. educ. Res.*, 1962, **32**, 91–102.

53. Taylor, C. W., W. R. Smith, & B. Ghiselin. The creative and other contributions of one sample of research scientists. In C. W. Taylor, & F. Barron (Eds.), *Scientific creativity: Its recognition and development*. New York: Wiley, 1963, pp. 53–76.

54. Terman, L. M. The discovery and encouragement of exceptional talent. *Amer. Psychologist,* 1954, **9,** 221–230.

55. Torrance, E. P. Explorations in creative thinking. *Education,* 1960, **81,** 216–220.

56. Torrance, E. P. *Role of evaluation in creative thinking.* U. S. Office of Education Cooperative Research Project No. 725. Minneapolis: Bur. of Educ. Res., Univer. of Minnesota, 1960.

57. Torrance, E. P. Priming creative thinking in the primary grades. *Elem. Sch. J.,* 1961, **62,** 34–41.

58. Torrance, E. P. *Education and the creative potential.* Minneapolis: Univer. of Minnesota, 1963.

59. Tuckman, J., & I. Lorge. Individual ability as a determinant of group superiority. *Hum. Relat.,* 1962, **15,** 45–51.

60. Wegner, Norma, & D. Zeaman. Team and individual performances on a motor learning task. *J. gen. Psychol.,* 1956, **55,** 127–142.

61. Wertheimer, M. *Productive thinking.* New York: Harper & Row, 1945.

62. Yamamoto, K. Relationships between creative thinking abilities of teachers and achievement and adjustment of pupils. *J. exp. Educ.,* 1963, **32,** 3–25.

CHAPTER 9

Psychomotor Abilities
and Skills

IT IS EASY to underestimate the importance of psychomotor abilities and skills in one's daily life. Many people depend upon the level of their psychomotor skills for a livelihood. This is true of typists and others in clerical positions, persons in the crafts, unskilled and semiskilled workers in many jobs, farmers, surgeons, artists, and musicians. As our society changes and fewer jobs require motor activity, there is a tendency for people to take up more physical activities for their avocations—skiing, camping, boating, golfing, and so on. In addition to the importance of physical skills in vocational and avocational pursuits, all of us require physical activity to maintain good health so that we are more productive mentally.

When we talk about psychomotor abilities and skills, we are not concerned primarily with interscholastic athletic activities. Physical education in the schools should be much more concerned about developing psychomotor abilities that will be used by the manual worker, the clerical worker, the surgeon, the musician, and the farmer than by athletes. The physical fitness of all children and youth is of far more importance than is any athletic program in which only a few excel. Further, psychomotor skills are relevant to every student in every subject field. Handwriting, drawing, typing—these and other skills can be developed in connection with any subject, and the higher level of skill one has in each, the more effective one is. Of course, music, visual arts, home economics, industrial arts, agriculture, and physical education require more use of motor skills than do mathematics, foreign language, and social studies. But the physical fitness of boys and girls is just as important to their excellent performance in the latter subjects as in the prior ones.

A clear differentiation between abilities and skills will make the study of this chapter more meaningful. A psychomotor ability is a process or factor combined with a part or parts of the body. For example, finger dexterity, trunk flexibility, and limb strength are psychomotor abilities. These abilities are partly a product of learning and partly a product of the innate structure of the individual. Abilities develop at different rates in growing human beings; also, the nature of abilities changes with maturation and learning. A skill refers to a combination of actions by which a task is performed. A psychomotor skill is one in which the motor or physical component is heavily involved, for example, hitting a baseball, writing cursively, typing, and playing the piano are psychomotor skills. Theoretically, how well an individual performs these skills is a function of the abilities he possesses. The same ability, such as motor coordination, may be important in all five skills.

In this chapter we are concerned with the nature of psychomotor abilities as well as the developmental trends in psychomotor abilities and skills. Of concern also are the changes that occur with increasing skill. The last section deals with a model for learning skills.

THE NATURE OF PSYCHOMOTOR ABILITIES

Some significant breakthroughs in identifying psychomotor abilities have occurred since the beginning of World War II. Two approaches are being pursued with enthusiasm and vigor. The first is to identify more positively the motor abilities which lay the basis for efficient motor acts. The second is to devise psychomotor tests, intended to identify the individuals who most likely would be successful in acquiring complex skills such as those required of pilots and navigators of aircraft. Furthermore there is continuing study of the abilities essential for students to develop proficiency in such fields as typewriting, playing musical instruments, and performing a variety of occupational tasks—clerical work and various skilled and semiskilled jobs.

A theoretical framework of psychomotor abilities is shown in Table 9.1 (18). Notice that strength, impulsion, speed, static precision, dy-

TABLE 9.1.

Matrix of Psychomotor Abilities

Part of Body Involved	Type of Factor						
	Strength	Impulsion	Speed	Static Precision	Dynamic Precision	Coordination	Flexibility
Gross	General strength	General reaction time		Static balance	Dynamic balance	Gross bodily coordination	
Trunk	Trunk strength						Trunk flexibility
Limbs	Limb strength	Limb thrust	Arm speed	Arm steadiness	Arm aiming		Leg flexibility
Hand		Tapping			Hand aiming	Hand dexterity	
Finger			Finger speed			Finger dexterity	

SOURCE: J. P. Guilford. A system of the psychomotor abilities. *Amer. J. Psychol.*, 1958, **71**, 165.

namic precision, coordination, and flexibility are called psychomotor factors. The psychomotor abilities are use or manipulation of some part of the body with relation to the psychomotor factors. For example, there is a general (gross) strength ability, trunk strength ability, and limb strength ability. Similarly, in the third column the abilities of general reaction time, limb thrust, and (hand) tapping are related to the psychomotor factor, impulsion. There are many blank spaces in Table 9.1. The theoretical framework is not, therefore, complete; and Guilford expressed the hope that further research would indicate what the missing abilities might be, so that the blank spaces would eventually be filled in. The technical difference between factors and abilities also is shown, but in common usage the factors also are treated as abilities. The tests used to secure measures of performance from which the factors and abilities were derived are mainly of three types:

tests of physical fitness, apparatus tests, and printed tests of one kind or another. The factors, of course, are inferred from performances on the tests, and it is through a statistical procedure that the so-called "factors" are derived.

A large amount of work needs to be done to relate the abilities shown in Table 9.1 to the many psychomotor skills which are learned and used in school and in our daily activities. For example, which abilities are required in playing a musical instrument? To what extent are limb strength, general reaction time, arm and finger speed, arm steadiness, dynamic balance, gross bodily coordination, hand dexterity, and finger dexterity involved in learning to play the violin or piano? These same questions, of course, can be asked about such curriculum areas as typewriting, art, industrial arts, swimming, and volleyball.

More recently the psychomotor abilities of boys and girls, derived from tests of physical fitness, were identified (13). A sample of 20,000 boys and girls from school systems throughout the United States participated in the study. Prior to this, extensive tests had been conducted for many years with Naval trainees (11). In Table 9.2 are given the abilities found in school-age children and young Naval trainees. A total of 25 abilities is given. This number should not be considered as final because the search for the abilities is still proceeding.

TABLE 9.2.

Psychomotor Abilities in High School Youth and Other Groups[a]

Ability	Characterization
High School Youth	
Explosive strength: General Leg emphasis Arm-shoulder emphasis	Ability to mobilize energy for a burst of effort rather than continuously or repeatedly, for example, when running and when throwing a softball.
Static strength: Trunk emphasis Arm-hand-shoulder emphasis	Ability to exert maximum force against objects, even for a brief period.
Dynamic strength: Arms—flexor emphasis Arms—extensor emphasis	Ability to exert muscular force repeatedly or continuously over a period of time; emphasizes resistance of the muscles to fatigue in doing pull-ups, for example.
Trunk strength	Ability to exert muscular force with trunk, particularly abdominal muscles.
Extent flexibility	Ability to stretch the trunk and back muscles forward, laterally, and backward as far as possible, not quickly.

T A B L E   9.2. *(Continued)*

Ability	Characterization
	High School Youth
Dynamic flexibility	Ability to make repeated, rapid, flexible movements recovering from strain effectively.
Gross body equilibrium	Ability to maintain equilibrium when depending on nonvisual cues; e.g., vestibular and kinesthetic cues.
Gross body coordination	Ability to coordinate the simultaneous actions of different parts of the body while making gross bodily movements.
Stamina-cardiovascular endurance	Ability to continue maximum effort requiring prolonged exertion; for example, in walking.
	Other Groups[a]
Balance—visual cues	Ability to maintain balance with the eyes open and the feet in various positions.
Speed of limb movement Arm Leg	Ability to move the arm or leg quickly where accuracy is not required.
Multilimb coordination	Ability to coordinate the movements of the limbs simultaneously—two hands, two feet, or feet and hands.
Control precision	Ability to make fine, highly controlled muscular adjustments, primarily where larger muscle groups are involved, with hands or feet.
Response orientation	Ability to make the correct movement in relation to the correct stimulus, especially under speeded conditions.
Reaction time	Ability to respond quickly to a stimulus.
Rate control	Ability to make continuous anticipatory motor adjustments relative to changes in speed and direction of a continuously moving target.
Manual dexterity	Ability to make skillful, well-directed arm-hand movements when manipulating fairly large objects under speed conditions.
Finger dexterity	Ability to make skillful, controlled manipulations of tiny objects involving use of the fingers.
Arm—hand steadiness	Ability to make precise arm-hand positioning movements where strength and speed are minimized; the critical feature is steadiness of the movements.
Wrist—finger speed	Ability to tap rapidly; pendular as well as rotary wrist-movements are involved.
Aiming	Ability to control hand and other movements when placing dots in small circles, for example. Some have previously referred to this as eye-hand coordination.

[a] Mainly U.S. Navy Trainees.
SOURCE: Based on E. A. Fleishman. *The structure and measurement of physical fitness.* Englewood Cliffs, N.J.: Prentice-Hall, 1964.

A comparison of the listing of abilities by Guilford and by Fleishman shows a larger number by Fleishman. Further, Fleishman tends to classify less by parts of the body and more by types of ability, regardless of part of the body. For example, he lists three kinds of strength —explosive, static, and dynamic—and then has trunk strength, which apparently fits none of the previous three types. Some of the difference in the terminology rests with preferences of the two men. Fleishman, however, has done the greater amount of study and also the more recent.

A large amount of work needs to be done to relate the abilities given in the two previous tables to the many skills learned in school. It seems unfortunate, for example, that someone has not worked as industriously as Fleishman to identify the abilities underlying performance in playing the piano, typing, and many other activities.

Interesting from the standpoint of learning more about psychomotor abilities, but somewhat discouraging from the standpoint of identifying precisely what these abilities may be, is another study of a complex psychomotor task. Systematic changes occurred in the pattern of abilities contributing to proficiency on the complex task from the beginning of the practice to the end. Some abilities increased in importance with practice, others decreased, and still others remained at a fairly stable level throughout the entire length of practice. In other words, certain abilities important in early performance of the task were not as important during final practice and vice versa. The relative importance of various abilities also changed with practice on a variety of other tasks (12, 15).

Abilities also change with practice on verbal skills, such as adding numbers, substituting digits for letters, reproducing patterns, and solving anagrams (38). No one general improvement factor underlies all of these skills. In addition, the amount of original ability, as measured before extended practice, has no bearing upon the change with practice; for example, the possession of high ability at the start does not assure a greater than average or smaller than average gain with practice.

In applying these conclusions to psychomotor learning in school situations, we would properly infer that reliable prediction of a student's performance at the end of a semester or year of instruction cannot be made from performances during the first month. Also, if one measured the performances of beginning piano players and identified the factors which comprised the beginners' abilities, one would have to make followup studies to ascertain the extent to which these abilities change with practice and improved performances. Unfortunately, we do not have, at the present, the needed information to relate all psychomotor abilities to the many instructional areas in school.

In summary, marked progress has been made in recent years to identify psychomotor abilities. Much still remains to be done in school settings to determine which abilities may subsequently be open to direct observation by the teacher or to indirect observation by testing. We must learn more about psychomotor abilities at various age levels before we can make reasonable estimates of the improvement in these abilities or the maximum limits of performance. At present, we can ascertain large differences in the motor performances among children of the same age, but often we cannot tell reliably what is associated with the varying levels of performance. We need to start with the best information available and move forward in this area just as was proposed in the previous chapter with respect to problem-solving abilities and creativity. In the meantime, we should do our best to provide optimum conditions for children and youth to develop whatever psychomotor abilities they may have.

DEVELOPMENTAL TRENDS

Within the same week or month try to observe the psychomotor abilities of four widely separated age groups. Go to a nursery room in a large hospital and notice the newborn infants and their behaviors. Observe children of ages 6 to 9 in the gymnasium or on the playground of an elementary school. Visit a comprehensive high school to observe an advanced typewriting class, an instrumental or vocal music class, an art or industrial arts class, an athletic team in practice, and a science class while experiments are being set up by the students. Finally, observe at work a surgeon, dancer, musician, or athlete. Though you would see only a small sample of each age group, the vast changes in psychomotor performances with age from infancy to maturity would be more immediately apparent than they can ever be through reading about them. Only a few descriptions of changes in abilities and skills with age are presented here.

Strength of Grip

Strength of grip of the hand is a measure of static strength. In Chapter 4, this was shown to be more highly correlated with intelligence and achievement in the cognitive domain than were four other physical measures—height, weight, number of permanent teeth, and bone development of the hand and wrist. Strength of grip also is correlated to some extent with vitality. Children of the same age who have the stronger grip seem to be able to mobilize their strength more effectively than do those with the weaker grip. This seems to carry over to mental tasks; mentally retarded children do not seem to be able to mobilize their energies for either physical or mental tasks as well as do bright children (**22**). Strength of grip correlates higher with other measures of strength than does any other single measure; in addition, it is easily secured with a hand dynamometer. For these reasons, it holds more promise of providing useful information to the teacher than do measures of height and weight.

Figure 9.1 shows growth curves for boys and girls ages 6 to 18 (**20**). The dynamometer readings are in kilograms, as noted in the left margin of Fig. 9.1. A rather steady increase in strength occurs with age and the rate is about the same for boys and girls until age 13. At this time the curve rises quite sharply for boys and continues to rise slowly but at a decelerating rate for girls. The influence of cultural factors on this difference between the sexes is not known. Boys, however, are encour-

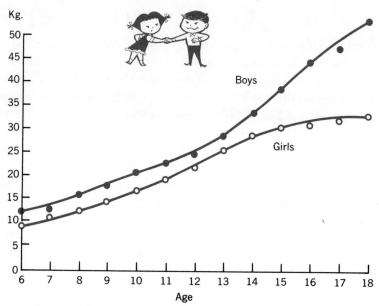

Fig. 9.1. Growth curve for strength of grip. (Adapted from H. E. Jones. The development of physical abilities. In N. B. Henry (Ed.), *Adolescence.* Yearb. Nat. Soc. Stud. Educ., 1944, **43**, Part I, 103.)

aged to participate in more strenuous physical activities than are girls. Furthermore, strength is usually considered a prestige gainer for boys, whereas many girls during adolescence want to give the impression of being dainty and feminine rather than strong and masculine.

Reaction Time

Reaction time is important in many activities. Emergency situations —braking an automobile, piloting an airplane under certain conditions, responding to a starter's signal in an athletic contest—require a quick motor response. Other tasks demanding rapid reactions to successive stimuli include playing a musical instrument, typing, dancing, and the like.

Figure 9.2 shows different measures of reaction time according to age (**28**). All reaction measures of the subjects were elicited by an auditory stimulus. The measures are pursuit reaction using the hands,

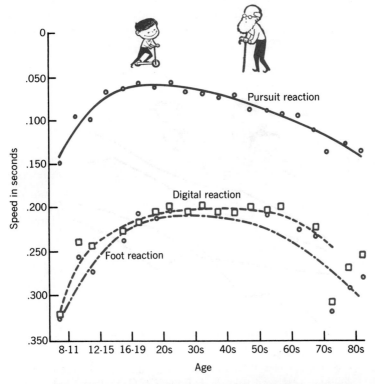

Fig. 9.2. Changes in reaction time with age. (Adapted from W. R. Miles. Measures of certain human abilities throughout the life span. *Proc. Nat. Acad. Sci.*, 1931, **17**, 631.)

digital reaction using the forefinger, and foot reaction. The speed of pursuit movements increases regularly until about age 18 and holds a fairly steady level until about age 30; then decline starts, becoming quite rapid at about age 70. Although the curves are somewhat different, the general pattern of digital and foot reaction is a rise until the 20s, and then a tendency to level off or decelerate until about age 60, when the deceleration becomes quite rapid. Figure 9.2 shows that during the school years reaction time increases noticeably. How much of this rapid increase is related to instruction and how much simply to maturation is unknown. Athletic coaches, and others, apparently believe that reaction time can be improved, for they spend much practice time toward achieving that end.

Speed

Speed of running is important in many physical activities. Arm and finger speed also are essential to the performance of many factory jobs, taking shorthand, playing a cello, etc. Usually, however, arm and fingers are tied in with responses to definite perceptual cues to a larger degree than is running. Various simple tests have been devised to assess arm and finger speed; however, the relationship between these

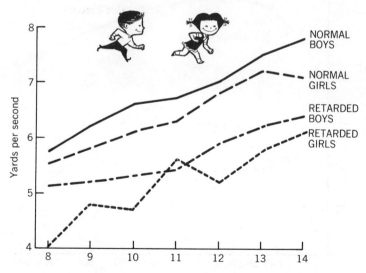

Fig. 9.3. Speed of running in normal and mentally retarded children. (Adapted from R. J. Francis & G. L. Rarick. Motor characteristics of the mentally retarded. *Amer. J. ment. Defic.*, 1959, **63**, 806.)

speed tests and performance in typing, for example, is not as clearly established as is that between speed of running and playing baseball, basketball, and football.

In Chapter 4, speed in running the 50-yard dash was given for boys and girls at ages 10, 13 and 16. Figure 9.3 shows speed in running the 35-yard dash for normally developed and mentally retarded children, ages 8 to 14 (**16**). The curve for normal boys shows a rather continuous increase from age 8 to 14 and beyond. With normal girls speed starts to fall off at about age 13. Notice that the mentally retarded boys were slower than the normal girls at all ages; however, the curve shows an increase with age for the mentally retarded boys, and at age 14 they are closing the gap between themselves and the normal girls. The irregular curve for retarded girls results partly from the small sample used in the study. Whether the relatively better performances for the retarded girls at ages 13 to 14 might continue is not known.

Balance

We know that young children have difficulty maintaining balance when learning to walk. What happens as they grow older? Table 9.3

TABLE 9.3.

Balance Scores by Sex and Age

Age Groups	Boys' Scores 0	1	2	3	4	5	6	Average	Girls' Scores 0	1	2	3	4	5	6	Average	N	Totals Average
13–15	3	2	2	8	11	2	7	3.7	1	7	4	5	2	0	0	2.0	54	3.1
12–13	2	1	7	4	12	6	4	3.6	2	6	2	7	3	0	1	2.3	57	3.1
11–12	0	3	4	8	7	6	6	3.8	2	3	3	5	3	2	0	2.5	52	3.3
10–11	3	9	6	5	7	8	3	3.0	2	5	4	6	0	4	0	2.4	62	2.8
9–10	2	8	7	7	5	4	3	2.8	5	4	7	7	4	1	0	2.1	64	2.5
8– 9	7	11	8	9	11	2	2	2.5	7	6	6	5	4	2	0	2.0	80	2.3
7– 8	12	10	9	7	0	4	0	1.6	5	3	3	3	3	2	0	2.1	61	1.8
6– 7	17	11	7	1	0	1	0	0.9	3	2	3	2	1	0	0	1.6	48	1.1
4– 6	10	1	0	0	0	0	0	0.1	9	1	2	0	0	0	0	0.5	23	0.3

SOURCE: G. W. Cron, & N. H. Pronko. Development of the sense of balance in school children. *J. educ. Res.*, 1957, **51**, 35.

shows a consistent rise in the mean or average balance scores for both boys and girls from age 4 to 6 until age 11 to 12. The gradual falling off from that age onward is somewhat more apparent for the girls than the boys. However, girls at age 13 and above appear more self-conscious than do younger girls or boys while performing the task. Therefore, the results for the older girls are questionable. It is interesting, too, that up through age 8 the girls had higher balance scores than the boys; thereafter, the boys scored consistently higher than the girls.

Flexibility

Extent flexibility is the ability to extend or stretch the whole body or parts of it as far as possible in various directions. Dynamic flexibility also involves the ability to extend and stretch; however, the criterion is not the extent or distance of maximum movement but the rapidity of repeated movements. Tests which measure the amount of abdominal and back stretching are used as indicators of extent flexibility, and more rapid bending and twisting activities are used to arrive at "cycle" scores of dynamic flexibility. Figure 9.4 shows growth curves for boys and girls for the two abilities (13).

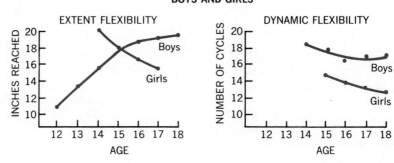

Fig. 9.4. Developmental curves for extent flexibility and dynamic flexibility in boys and girls. (Adapted from E. A. Fleishman. *The structure and measurement of physical fitness.* Englewood Cliffs: Prentice-Hall, 1964, pp. 122, 124.)

These curves are interesting. Extent flexibility in boys increases at a rapid rate from 12 to 15 and then at a decelerating rate from 15 to 18. An opposite pattern holds for girls, who show a decrease from age 14 to 17. Dynamic flexibility shows a decrease for both boys and girls from age 14 or 15 to 18. Of some 25 different abilities, dynamic flexibility is the only one that shows this pattern of decrease for boys prior to age 18. However, the performance of girls during the senior high school years deteriorates in a number of psychomotor abilities.

Writing Skill

Writing is one of the few activities highly dependent upon motor abilities in which most children receive formal instruction. It therefore should have much more careful investigation than it has received up to the present time. Ames and Ilg reported the developmental trends in writing behavior of younger children (1). Some of them are as follows:

SIX YEARS

Circle is now drawn counterclockwise, starting at the top.
Letters are printed, usually large and somewhat irregular.
Words are printed by some children at this age. Some reversals of single letters or order of letters in words may appear.
Name is printed in large letters.
Numbers from 1 to 20 or higher are written; some reversals of 3, 7, 9.

SEVEN YEARS

Words: The majority can now write, although an appreciable number prefer to print. The printing is now smaller and more regular.
Name: The majority can now write their given names and surnames; most still print.
Numbers: The majority write 1 to 20, with the figures now written smaller and in rows.

EIGHT YEARS

Words: The majority write single words, printing seldom being used. Important individual differences in writing skill are discernible. Reversals seldom appear.
Name: Nearly all write both their names, well spaced and small letters other than the initial letter of each word. Important variations in style of writing appear.
Numbers: Figures are much smaller and better spaced; few errors are made.

NINE YEARS

Words: Writing is smaller, neater, lighter, more even and slanted, though some still write straight up and down and about one-third still have very irregular letters. Letters are now much better proportioned.
Name: Beginning of individual styles, with sex differences being observed. Letters are more evenly made and more correctly proportioned.
Numbers: Numbers are now small and well formed (1, 32–34).

The above gradients in writing, like the curves that show the development of various psychomotor abilities throughout this section, conceal individual differences among the children at various age levels and do not present the wide overlapping between best and poorest performers at various ages. We have shown previously in Chapter 4 and also in Table 9.3 the wide range among boys of the same age. Referring back to Table 9.3, you will see that scores of 0 to 6 were made by boys from 8 through 15 years of age, except that none in the 11 to 12 group scored 0.

Factors that Affect the Growth of Abilities

The effects of instruction, including guided activity or practice, upon the development of psychomotor abilities and skills are not completely determined. We know, however, that people remain illiterate —they do not read or write—in an environment in which these skills are not taught to the children. Similarly, children do not learn the skills essential to winter sports when they live in a mild climate. Although the effect of excellent instruction in developing psychomotor abilities is not known, the effects of deprivation on physical characteristics, such as height, have been estimated (5). Figure 9.5 shows growth in height of boys under three different environmental conditions. The Tuddenham and Snyder data are based on children of above-average socioeconomic status growing up in Oakland, California (35). Measures of the Oakland children were taken in the late 1920s, the 1930s, and early 1940s. The Dreizen *et al.* children grew up in Alabama, and the measures for both the experimental (nutritive failure group) and the control group were secured, starting in 1941 (9). The two sets of Alabama children had identical ethnical backgrounds and came from the same geographical area. The conclusion is inescapable that inadequate nutrition has a permanent stunting effect. Similar adverse effects of orphanage life upon growth in height were established by Keys, *et al.* (21). The adverse effects of an impoverished environment are probably greatest in the period when growth is more rapid (5).

CHANGES THAT ACCOMPANY
SKILL LEARNING

The highly skilled performance, in comparison with the less skilled, is accomplished in less time, with less energy, greater accuracy, higher consistency, and more flexibility. In some skills all five are essential. We anticipate that fifth-graders, having developed better handwriting skill than third-graders, will write the same amount of material in less time, with less energy expenditure, with greater accuracy, with higher consistency from one word to the next, and with greater flexibility in

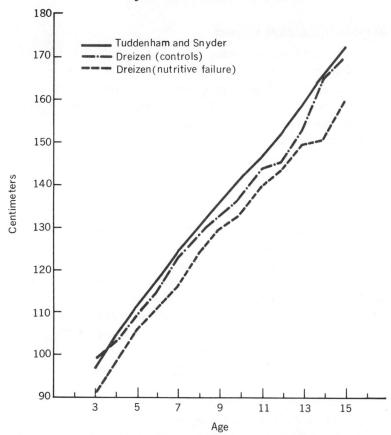

Fig. 9.5. Height growth for males under different environmental conditions. (Adapted from B. S. Bloom. *Stability and change in human characteristics.* New York: Wiley, 1964, p. 39.)

responding to a variety of writing tasks. Similarly, the person skilled in using a dictionary finds words in less time and with less energy, makes fewer errors or unproductive tries, consistently finds the words he seeks, and responds with more flexibility to a larger variety of words.

In the previous discussion of developmental trends, we pointed out that changes occur in abilities with increased practice. Other changes also occur, and these changes are gradual and continuous, rather than all or none. That is, the individual does not change suddenly from not being able to play golf or to type, for example, to being highly expert. As long as his motivation to improve continues, his performance will probably increase over many years. A number of changes occur with the improvement of a skill.

Voluntary to Involuntary Control

Miller *et al.* provide an interesting account of the transition of a skill in terms of cognitive controls (29). In the early phase, the movements are slow and unsure, each one controlled by a voluntary plan of the individual. In the later phase, the actions are rapid and precise, a series of movements controlled by an involuntary, hierarchical plan. The plan resides within the individual and may be compared to a program which controls the sequence by which events are carried out. For example, a phonograph has a program built into it for changing and playing records automatically. When the needle arm gets near enough to the spindle, the arm rises and gets out of the way, a record is released and drops into place, and the arm returns the needle to the outer position of the new record to start playing again. Engineers built the program into the phonograph. The program for executing a skill, such as typing or locating entries in an encyclopedia, cannot be built into the human organism by an outsider. The outsider can, however, give him a plan in the form of verbal instructions or a real-life model to copy and also may try to condition him to perform certain responses. Let us examine the characteristics of the plan in more detail before going to a further consideration of how the change from voluntary to involuntary occurs.

As indicated before in Chapter 3, in connection with processes of learning, the individual is capable of cognizing; that is, he senses events in his environment and associates meaning with them. These meanings are thought about productively. The transformed thoughts excite and energize the effector system in the case of psychomotor skills. In the system of Miller *et al.*, there is a complete cycle: receiving sensory impressions, acting upon the impressions mentally, energizing and carrying out a physical action, acting mentally upon the results of physical action to determine its appropriateness, and modifying the previous action, repeating it, or discontinuing it. The plan or program controls the entire sequence. Furthermore, plans are of a hierarchical nature. Thus, one might have an overall plan to control his actions when playing 18 holes of golf, less extensive plans or strategies for each of the 18 holes, and specific plans or tactics for executing each shot. There are even more specific plans in connection with each shot, such as lining it up, gripping the club, assuming a proper stance, and swinging.

Returning to the change in the plans for executing skills, we state that when an individual first starts to engage in the skill, his plans are voluntary, that is, he thinks about what he is doing. The beginning golfer, when putting for example, is very much concerned with the club grip, including the placement of each finger and the thumbs. He probably verbalizes to himself such things as "grasp the club firmly in the right hand, have both thumbs pointing down the shaft, and put the left index finger over the small right finger." When skilled, he takes the putter from the bag and grasps it without internal verbalization or thought about how to do so. Extensive practice has brought him to the point where his grip actions are automatic, or involuntary.

Miller *et al.* make an interesting comparison between the teacher and the learner in connection with skills. Typically, the teacher tries to communicate a global plan first and then comes to the more detailed plans. The learner, however, starts with the smaller units. In typing, for example, the teacher provides a model of an expert typist so that the learner may perceive the nature of the terminal performance that is desired. However, the learner starts by getting control over finger movements in response to individual letters. He may do this by writing words or phrases, rather than practicing the separate letters as discrete units. As he continues to practice, the smaller plans get integrated into larger and more complex ones. Eventually, he develops a set of hierarchical plans that control all his behavior, and these plans are run off automatically.

In this conception of skill learning practice is important to develop and integrate plans, but there is another reason. One may have a clear verbal description of how to putt, to play a piano, or to swim, but practice is needed in order to execute the plans. This does not mean that plans must be verbalized. A child can ride a bicycle very well without being able to describe his plan clearly. As Miller *et al.* point out, even physicists and manufacturers have not developed a clear statement of the principle underlying the cyclist's ability to keep his balance. Despite this, supplying the beginner with verbal descriptions and real-life models helps him to develop plans that work for him.

Differentiation of Cues

With motivated practice, one's skill improves through more effective utilization of cues. Imagine that you are walking from one place to another and are sure of your destination. The cues which guide your walking are within the environment and within yourself and may be seen, heard, and felt. As you walk, you see such things as the sidewalk or a brick wall, a stone, etc. Besides seeing things ahead and to the side, you hear sounds, particularly those behind you. These are external visual and auditory cues. They guide your walking without your being constantly aware of them. Although we are not generally conscious of it, there also are continuous internal kinesthetic stimuli and responses as we move. These tell us we are moving and in what direction.

More efficient use of cues is illustrated in finding the pronunciation of words in the dictionary. Suppose that the word is *panache*. The inexperienced individual uses more cues; that is, he looks at more of the letters in the thumb index of the dictionary before finding the *P*. After locating *P*, the inexperienced person uses more guide words at the top of the pages before finding the page on which *panache* appears. Once the word is found, the syllabication given in the phonetic pronunciation, the diacritical marks, and the accent marks must be used correctly. The beginner generally must pay closer attention to these three cues than does the more skillful person.

Another experience common to most of us is driving an automobile. Recall the many cues to which you responded in your first attempts at starting, stopping, or backing the car into a parallel parking space. Compare them with your present use of cues in performing the same activities. With increasing skill the individual uses fewer cues to guide his responses, and many of those he does use are the less obvious ones of which he was unaware as a beginner.

Feedback and Correction

Recall that a plan or program for executing a skill calls for mental operations preceding and following the movements. In the early phase, each action is evaluated in terms of comparing the present outcome to the desired outcome. Later, many previously separate movements are combined into what appear to be integrated single movements. They are so highly integrated that the results of performing one movement appear unrelated to the subsequent one. Again referring to the use of the dictionary in locating a particular word, we see that there is not one simple, rapid response unguided by cues from what comes next and what has just happened. Rather, when the individual locates the page on which the word is, he quickly scans the word entries; while doing so, he is making a very rapid series of trials and corrections before finding and confirming the word desired. Similarly, backing a car into a parallel parking space is not one action; rather, from the time one starts backing until the car is parked, there are rapid trials and corrections with continuous feedback from the previous responses.

The use of feedback from prior actions is not described readily. For a concrete example of this process, the reader might take a pencil and mirror to use in connection with tracing the outside of the star, given as Fig. 9.6. Place the mirror slightly above the star. Looking only at the mirror, not the outline, follow the original outline with a pencil. Note how you stop, look where you are, and correct for errors or difficulties.

Fig. 9.6.   Five-pointed star with mirror image.

Rapid and Accurate Movements

The change from a low level of skill to highly skilled action is accompanied with a change from slow and inaccurate movements to those that are rapid and accurate. If you could observe highly and moderately skilled typists as they reproduced this page, you would readily observe differences in the speed of hand and finger movements. The typist reproducing at 40 words per minute moves about half as rapidly as the one reproducing at 80 words per minute. There might be the same number of errors in the copy of both individuals. However, we would anticipate that the one with lower speed would either make more errors or else would take more time to strike the correct keys.

Coordination of Movement and Responses

Quick and accurate movements and other responses occur at precisely the right time in a skilled performance. In such an apparently simple task as writing a sentence legibly, there are many muscular movements and mental responses. The skilled writer does not hesitate about whether or not to capitalize words, how to punctuate, how to join letters within a word, or how to start and end words. As he writes, making rapid changes from vertical to horizontal to circular movements, there is a continuous series of correct movements and other responses coming at precisely the right time. The skilled person writes the word *women,* for example, in such a manner that the observer notices only a series of continuous smooth movements with no jerks or stops.

The skilled typist not only has integrated a series of movements and responses to reproduce individual words quickly, but also perceives a relatively long series of words in one visual fixation on the page. One fixation on five or six words provides all the cues needed to reproduce the words. Further, little or no conscious thought is given to such motor acts as striking the space bar, shift key, or the letters. Completing one word provides the cues for both the spacing and the starting of the next word. Similarly, as the expert typist takes material from a tape recorder, the auditory cues available through listening, and the production of successive words and other symbols, provide the continuous, steady cues essential to rapid production of evenly typed copy with few or no errors.

MODEL FOR IMPROVING SKILLS

Skills that are learned in school vary in the amount of motor and perceptual involvement, as shown in Fig. 9.7. Skills with high motor and low perceptual involvement include walking, running, swimming, bicycling, and gymnastics. The cues for the guidance of these skills are mostly internal and kinesthetic, rather than visual and auditory. Skills with a considerable perceptual and motor involvement include typing, playing a musical instrument, and others where the individual sees or hears the physical stimuli that, in turn, guide his motor responses. A third group of skills has low motor and high perceptual involvement. In silent reading, the motor component is low but includes focusing the eyes from left to right across the page, moving from top to bottom as successive lines are read, grouping the words to achieve a fast rate, and the like. However, the main component of reading silently is perceptual and cognitive, that is, recognizing words and associating meanings with them.

The amount of motor and perceptual learning in any of the skills

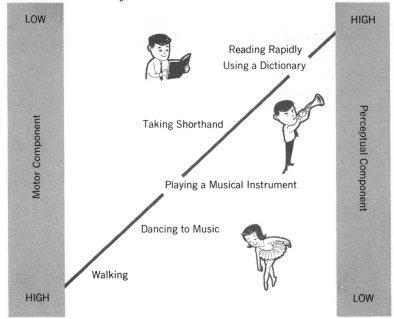

Fig. 9.7. Relative use of motor and perceptual components for different skills.

enumerated varies with the stage or level of skill development. Walking requires more attention to perceptual cues for the beginner than for the adult, just as attention to the motor component is less for the skilled than the beginning typist. Thus, when we discuss skill learning, we are concerned with skills of varying amounts of motor and perceptual involvement.

As in other chapters dealing with outcomes of learning, we shall set forth some generalizations and related principles of teaching, based on research and theory. Also, we shall view the partial implementation of each principle by a beginning speech correctionist. We shall not be directly concerned with motivation, retention, transfer, and individual differences because these are considered in detail in later chapters. The generalizations and principles regarding skill learning are these:

GENERALIZATION	PRINCIPLE
1. Learners vary in the abilities that are necessary for a skilled performance.	1. Analyze the skill in terms of the learner's abilities.
2. Many novel responses are acquired initially through observing and imitating a model.	2. Demonstrate the correct responses.

3. Plans within the individual control the order in which a sequence of operations is to be performed; plans for developing skills can be formulated into communicable instructions.

3. Guide initial responses verbally and physically.

4. Practice under desirable conditions facilitates the learning of skills through eliminating errors and strengthening and refining correct responses and form.

4. Arrange for appropriate practice.

5. Feedback facilitates skill learning through providing immediate knowledge of results.

5. Provide knowledge of results and correct inadequate responses.

6. Independent recognition and correction of errors, and independent identification and improvement of responses and form are essential for the continued improvement of skills.

6. Encourage independent evaluation.

Analyze the Skill in Terms of the Learner's Abilities

Implementation of this principle places three heavy demands upon the teacher—to understand the requirements of the skill, to understand the abilities of the learner, and to relate the two sets of knowledge. Teaching skills, like teaching other outcomes, involves knowledge of the subject matter, of the learners, and of principles of teaching; but it also requires expert judgment, guided by continuous feedback and correction while teaching. We cannot expect teachers to be thoroughly acquainted with knowledge of the requirements of a skill or of the abilities of the learners because no one has this complete knowledge. After nearly two decades of research, we have only a partial description of intellectual abilities (19) and of psychomotor abilities (13). Even though this is the case, there is sufficient knowledge that many of the gross violations of this principle can be eliminated, as illustrated in the ensuing discussion of handwriting for left- and right-handed children, vocal music for boys when the voice is changing, and accuracy and speed in beginning typing instruction.

Handwriting. How is handwriting different for left-handed and right-handed children? In most situations seats or desks are arranged so that the light comes from the left—proper for right handers, but not for left handers. Since one is taught to write from left to right on a page, the left-handed child is continuously covering what he has just written, whereas the right hander can see immediately what he has written. Most models of handwriting are for right-handed persons. The downward slant of letters is to the left; this is appropriate for the right handers, but without instruction, left-handed children normally slant the letters straight down or toward the right. Suppose, then, that a teacher has two or three left-handed children in a class. What sort of an analysis of the skill for the left-handed child should be made before instruction begins? Without careful analysis, it is possible that the teacher might insist that the left-handed children use precisely the same slant and spacing of letters as the right-handed, and do nothing to make other needed arrangements for seating and lighting.

Vocal Music for Adolescent Boys. A recent survey of high school boys and girls participating in chorus groups showed the ratio to be approximately four girls to one boy (34). A primary reason for this imbalance is that music teachers, particularly females, do not recognize the true nature of the singing task for boys going through the period of voice change. Music teachers in the junior high school generally pitch the music too high, select melodies which have far too broad a range for adolescent boys, and give instruction on songs which have little or no interest for boys of this age. Swanson found that a rating of pubic hair was useful for identifying the stage of voice change in adolescent boys. After rating the boys by this criterion, he regrouped junior high school classes for instruction in vocal music. When he arranged proper vocal exercises for the boys, selected interesting songs, rearranged many melodies, and proceeded to instruct them in groups brought together according to stage of voice change, they enjoyed the music activities as much as did the girls. When given the opportunity to volunteer to enroll in a vocal music class in the next grade, they did so.

We do not know how much direct damage to the singing voice and how much lack of interest in vocal music result because teachers do not understand the nature of the singing task for boys from about grade 5 to 9. Obviously, the female vocal-music teacher who has not experienced voice change and who insists that boys handle the same songs as girls is proceeding without accurate knowledge or is not using the knowledge she has.

Typing Instruction. The desired outcome of typing instruction is high speed, accuracy, and smooth, even copy. The question can properly be raised whether speed or accuracy should be emphasized in beginning typing instruction. Early in this century, accuracy was emphasized. Since 1950 considerable experimentation has been done to appraise the effects of emphasizing speed or emphasizing accuracy in the early phases of instruction in a variety of tasks. Now both speed and accuracy are emphasized in early typing instruction (**17, 33, 37**). However, in skills where speed is the predominant factor in later successful performances, speed rather than accuracy should be emphasized in early instruction; in skills where accuracy is the predominant factor required in later successful performances, attention should be given to accuracy early in the instruction. Thus, the teacher of any skill must understand the skill in order to ascertain whether speed, accuracy, or a combination of speed and accuracy is equally critical in later skilled performances.

Implementation in Speech Correction. Through the remainder of this chapter, implementation of the principles is described by a beginning speech therapist, working with a girl whom we shall call Sarah. In the last section of the discussion of each principle, we shall give the account in the first person by the speech therapist with only minor modifications to conserve space.

Before I met Sarah I had read about the correct means of producing the (s) sound, and I had identified the various auditory, visual, tactual, and kinesthetic aspects of the correct production of the sound. The objectives of my first meeting with Sarah were:

1. to discover how she produced the (s) sound;
2. to determine how her production of the sound differed from the correct production of the sound;
3. to determine the ways in which her means of production of the sound should be changed; and
4. to determine her abilities to correctly evaluate her production of the sound, to discriminate between correct and incorrect sounds and to identify the differences between them.

To accomplish the first objective in my first session with her, I watched her, listened to her, asked her to describe the tactual and kinesthetic elements of the sounds she produced, and tried to duplicate her production of the sound. I then analyzed my duplication in an effort to discover how she made the sound.

To accomplish the second and third objectives, I reviewed in my mind the correct means of producing the sound and compared her means of production to this mental model. I tried to determine which elements of her production were incorrect and the ways in which these elements were wrong. At this point I formed tentative judgments about how these incorrect elements should be changed.

To accomplish the fourth objective I presented her with a variety of tasks. To begin with, I had to produce the sound and then tell whether or not she thought her production was correct. I then presented her with a series of discrimination tasks. These required her to discriminate between correct and incorrect sounds when I made them, to point out differences between correct and incorrect sounds, to compare her production of the sound to my productions, and to try to point out differences between the productions made by her and by me. Among the various ways in which she performed these tasks were the following: with her unaided hearing alone, with an auditory training unit, with a tape recorder, with a mirror, with face to face contact, and with various combinations of these methods.

My evaluation showed that she was substituting (θ), the voiceless "th" sound, for the (s) sound. Her tongue was protruding between her teeth. In order to produce the sound correctly she would have to learn to place her tongue in the proper position behind her teeth. Regarding her feelings toward her production of the sound and her ability to discriminate between correct and incorrect sounds, I discovered that she knew her production was incorrect and had already learned to recognize the auditory and visual differences between correct and incorrect sounds.

She knew that she was not supposed to protrude her tongue, but she did not know the proper placement for it. When she tried to produce the sound with her tongue behind her teeth, she failed to groove it properly and she blocked the air stream from coming out of the center of her mouth.

As a result of my evaluation I formed the following plan of action:

1. to teach her to analyze more fully the various aspects of my correct and incorrect productions of the (s) sound;
2. to teach her to analyze more fully the various aspects of her production of the sound;
3. to teach her to compare the various aspects of her productions with those of my correct productions; and
4. to try to teach her to modify the incorrect aspects of her productions so she could learn to say the sound correctly.

Subsequent discussions of implementation of principles deal only with the fourth part of this plan of action.

Demonstrate the Correct Response

Novel responses may be learned through observation and imitation of a model; large segments of behavior rather than isolated units may be acquired (3). Further, the more competent the model, the greater is the acquisition of the imitative response (32). In some cases we cannot describe skilled actions in words (29), and in some instances the words we use cannot be understood or transformed into appropriate actions by the students. A good demonstration provides an overview of the skill to be acquired and a model to be imitated. The music teacher provides both when singing the melody through before having the children sing. In professional and collegiate football, the coaching team is comprised of a number of coaches—backfield, line, defense, offense —as many as seven or eight specialists. In part, the team of coaches is needed to demonstrate the particular skills involved in playing particular positions.

This principle, therefore, suggests that the correct response is to be demonstrated. This assumes that the teacher knows the one correct response or the several possible correct responses and can demonstrate them well. It does not mean, however, that the learner should or can always follow the demonstration precisely; as shown in the previous section, the left-handed child cannot follow the right-handed teacher exactly. In many demonstrations of physical movements, the teacher assumes that no individual will exactly duplicate the demonstration; instead, the learner will be encouraged to try to follow the demonstration and, at the same time, make the needed adaptations in terms of his own characteristics. The teacher knows that, though outstanding performers have some common characteristic movements and form, each is unique.

In certain situations it is appropriate not to demonstrate. If one wishes the learners to come up with new forms or unique expressions, demonstrating a particular form to be imitated does not yield desired results. The teacher of creative dance and the teacher of creative writing can demonstrate what creativity means to them. This demonstration should be simply to illustrate what creativity or appropriate expression is for the demonstrator. In art instruction a number of technical skills should probably be demonstrated and the learners should be helped to acquire them. However, when the individual is to develop his own art product, it is impossible for the teacher to demonstrate the learner's final product. The art teacher will perhaps suggest some possible themes and will help the student with the technical skills as necessary, but he will leave the main use of ideas, composition, and color to the learner.

Implementation in Speech Correction. It was relatively easy for the beginning speech correctionist to provide exemplary models and thus demonstrate correct responses. Notice how this was done.

After Sarah was able to analyze and compare the various aspects of her production of the "s" sound with my productions, it was time for her to learn to produce the sound correctly. As a first step in this process, I demonstrated the correct production for her.

As preparation for the demonstration I verbally reviewed the various aspects of the sound and asked her to watch and listen for them as I said the sound. After I had made the sound three times I helped her to give a verbal review of what she had seen and heard. I then produced the sound three more times.

Although the formal demonstration was thus concluded, it was to be repeated many times, both partially and completely, before she finally learned to produce the sound. In addition, demonstrations also were given of various methods and techniques throughout the corrective process. These demonstrations served more than one function. They provided a model for imitation, they showed how the various aspects of the sound were combined to form the whole, and they were a means of frequent review of the correct production of the sound.

Guide Initial Responses Verbally and Physically

Verbal instructions may be useful for describing the nature of the final performance desired, for indicating the abilities necessary to perform the task, for outlining a strategy or method of attack for developing the skill, and for clarifying previous achievements related to the task. In skill learning, the attempt is often made to incorporate a strategy for learning the skill into a set of instructions (29). Up to the present time, the precise purpose of instructions usually has not been given in written reports. Instead, it is mentioned that instructions are given and sometimes a condensed or complete version of the instructions is included. Thus, while we can establish whether or not the instructions are effective we cannot explain very clearly why they were or were not.

Giving students information about the general abilities that contribute to performance of the task and giving them information about the relation of specific components to the overall task proficiency contributed to improved performance in flying an aircraft (30). In an archery class, verbal instructions proved helpful (7). An experimental group was taught an accepted technique of shooting a bow and arrow and was referred to as the tuition group. The experimenter gave the tuition group the verbal instructions that she thought necessary for them to understand the nature of the skill and to become proficient in it. The women in the control group were given only the necessary equipment, minimum safety instructions, and thereafter proceeded on their own. Both groups met for 18 class sessions during a three-month period. At the end of the semester the tuition group performed better than the control group. Differences favoring the tuition group were apparent early in the semester and became greater as practice progressed. The control group tended to acquire an inefficient method and to stay with that method during successive class periods even though its progress was poor.

Davies (7) concluded that in at least three ways the teacher aids the learner to vary and improve his learning behavior: by directing the learner's attention to more adequate techniques than those he has acquired and has been employing; by promoting the growth of intellectual insight on the part of the learner into the factors related to his success; and by giving him a feeling of security and confidence in relinquishing a familiar mode of behavior and seeking one that is better. These three conclusions indicate the purpose of providing guidance of the learner's activities while he is developing a skill.

Verbal instructions for mental practice of a skill also are effective (36). Under the old system of teaching women students bowling, the usual verbal and manual instructions were given. In this experiment, however, three types of instruction were given with successive groups of students to encourage mental practice on the task. The first method was to have the mental practice in connection only with the arm swing in bowling. Before each attempt the student was instructed to think about such things as, "Let the arm go with the weight of the ball; resist the weight of the ball during the backswing by leaning forward from the ankle joint; follow through with the arm in the desired direction of the ball." This mental practice did not lead to the desired smooth, continuous pattern of movements.

With a second group, the instructions were expanded by preceding the suggestions above with, "Imagine or concentrate on a continuous movement pattern." With the third group and method the same instructions for mental practice were given. However, the bowling pins were placed at the end of the alley during the second week of instruction; this had not been done under the first two methods. Placing the pins in the proper position appeared to have the important psychological effect of giving further purpose to the practice. Although no more time was spent in practice by the second and third methods, efficiency in bowling increased by about one-third over the original method of instruction without mental practice.

Implementation in Speech Correction. We now continue with the beginning speech therapist and Sarah, the child. Before proceeding you may think of how you would verbally guide the responses of a beginner in some skill. Notice, too, the physical guidance provided to Sarah.

After the demonstration of the "s" sound was completed, I instructed Sarah to review verbally how to produce the sound and what she was to remember to do to change her present means of production. I then said the sound three times before she tried to say it. When she was yet unable to produce the sound correctly, this entire process was repeated several times. Throughout the repetitions I gave verbal suggestions before, during, and after her attempts at production.

When it became evident that verbal guidance was not sufficient, other methods were utilized. Among these were the following:

1. Sarah was instructed to move her tongue about randomly in an effort to come closer to the correct production. Evaluations of progress were made with and without mechanical aids.
2. She was instructed to move her tongue in directed ways. Evaluations were again made with and without mechanical aids.
3. She was instructed to put a toothpick on a certain place on her tongue while she made the sound. This served to hold her tongue in place and to help to groove the tongue properly.
4. She was instructed to hold a straw at a certain place in front of her teeth as she made the sound. This helped to establish the correct position of the tongue, the proper grooving of the tongue, and the proper emission of the air stream.

It was with the help of the straw that Sarah learned to produce the "s" sound correctly. The removal of the straw was gradual, beginning with removing it while she was in the process of production. Finally she was able to produce the sound without the help of the straw and with only occasional verbal reminders of things she was doing wrong. Throughout this corrective process I also gave many demonstrations of various types.

Arrange for Appropriate Practice

No one doubts that practice is essential to the improvement of skills. However, questions are constantly raised by the conscientious teacher concerning desirable conditions of practice. The questions are raised when children with instruction do not improve their skills. As indicated by the previous generalizations and principles, analyzing the skill, demonstrating it, and giving instructions about the procedure and other components only provides the basis for productive activity or practice. Practice itself is needed. Whole-part arrangements, the context in which the skills are practiced, variety in responses, and the length and spacing of practice sessions are the more important conditions, other than motivation, associated with effective practice.

WHOLE-PART ARRANGEMENTS

There is no abstract whole or part skill independent of the learner and the nature of the specific skill. What might be a whole skill for a beginner is a part for a more skilled performer, or vice versa. The within-tasks in many games and sports, for example, also pose questions. Is playing baseball a complex skill, or are there separate whole skills, such as pitching, catching, running, and batting? Is batting a whole skill or should it be broken up into smaller wholes? One useful way of looking at skills is from the standpoint of the organization of the skill itself. Some skills are closely knit; others are loosely organized. Diving is a closely knit skill, whereas football and baseball are aggregations of skills, each of which must receive concentrated practice. Any activity that requires an unbroken series of movements, such as diving, is a whole skill. Should complex skills consisting of aggregate skills and closely knit skills be taught as an entire unit during each practice session?

In juggling three balls, best results were obtained when the practice was done on the whole act, that is, juggling all three balls rather than one, then two, and finally three (24). Practice on the whole activity saved about 20 percent in time to reach a criterion of 100 successive catches. In rifle firing, going through an entire sequence of seven sub-tasks produced better results than practice first on one component, then combining the first and second; the first, second, third; and so on in a progressive-part method (26). The whole method produced considerably better results with a large number of people. For trainees with IQs 100 and above, the whole method was far superior to the part method; practice of the total act in each practice period provided for distributed practice on the parts. For trainees with IQs of 99 and below, only a small difference was found between the two methods.

The results of experiments completed from 1890 to 1952 in connection with learning to receive International Morse Code are most encouraging (39). In World War II there was much opportunity to try out efficient methods of teaching Morse Code. Among several features that were finally incorporated into the military teaching procedures, four are appropriate to the present discussion of skill learning: prompt reinforcement of the correct response, the whole method of teaching, a standard-speed presentation of signals, and distributed practice. In the whole method all 36 symbols of the code—26 letters and 10 digits—were introduced to the learners in the first practice session. This method contrasted sharply with previous ones wherein early instruction was devoted to lengthy practice on separate symbols (similar to the progressive-part method in rifle firing just mentioned). The application of our best information about skill learning led, in this case, to the following dramatic results:

Students spent 8 weeks at code school. Normally, they practiced code for 7 hours a day for the first 5 weeks, and devoted the last 3 weeks to other topics. Keller thought such massed practice might be wasteful, so he tried spreading out the code instruction over the whole 8 weeks, devoting 4 hours daily to code, and the rest to other topics. It turned out that the 4-hour group was as good as the usual 7-hour group at the end of 5 weeks, despite the shorter hours of practice. Of course they still had 3 more weeks to practice code, for they had been taking up their other topics along with the code; they ended up markedly superior to the massed group (39, 812).

THE CONTEXT FOR PRACTICE TASKS

It is not uncommon to find that some students who perform well in typing or shorthand are less proficient in these same skills in a regular office job after graduation. The classrooms in which the skills are developed are very different from the offices in which the skills are performed after graduation. Practice is not usually arranged in the context in which the skills will be used after graduation.

Many schools have overcome this difficulty by two methods. First, an office-practice class is offered. In it students carry out, in connection with the school's correspondence, duties similar to those they will perform after graduation. The room for the office practice class resembles general offices, with the usual filing cabinets, desks, typewriters, and other office equipment. In a second procedure the high school student goes into office work in a local business or other establishment for part of his instruction. In this manner he gets experience in the situational context in which the skills actually are used. Generally, these two procedures result in better performances after high school graduation, especially in the first weeks on the job.

Consider now other illustrations of the proper context for practice. The value of internship has been clearly demonstrated in medical education. Also, student teaching, in which the student teacher leaves the college or university for several weeks to a year to perform the duties of the regular teacher, is a form of internship different from and better than verbal classroom instruction about student teaching. Internship in the teaching profession is probably as useful as internship in the medical profession. In any event, the more closely the practice of complex skills is similar to the situations in which the skills are actually to be used, the more efficient the results. The medical intern, the teaching intern, and the student secretary "practice" more realistically than do most students in a regular classroom setting.

VARIETY OF RESPONSES

Blind adherence to a particular method or to a specific use of material—functional rigidity—was previously shown to interfere with efficient problem solving. It also interferes with skill learning. Even though the teacher thinks he knows the best approaches, he should reexamine them if his students do not make progress after repeated and consistent efforts. Students should be encouraged to try some other method, even though the teacher might not be aware of what it may be.

After working individually with a child from 15 to 20 minutes daily over a period of several weeks, only to find that the child is no better than when he started, the teacher should rightfully conclude that something is wrong with his method or that the child does not possess the essential abilities to profit from practice. Distributed practice, using a variety of methods, will usually produce the best results.

LENGTH AND SPACING OF PRACTICE SESSIONS

The dramatic results in learning Morse Code, achieved in part through distributing practice, were discussed in the previous section. Equally significant results have been obtained with other skills. For example, learning to juggle is more efficient when 5 minutes per day are used in practice, in comparison with using 15 minutes on alternate days (23). In fact, the distributed practice was almost twice as effective. Similar results have been attained with high-speed perceptual motor tasks (27) and with simple skills (2, 10). Figure 9.8 shows the effects of three different rest intervals—0, 30, and 60 seconds —in an initial set of 20 trials and also after a rest of 10 minutes (31). A main conclusion is that distributed practice yields better results both before and after a longer rest period.

Other things about Fig. 9.8 are noteworthy. Performance improved for all groups through the nineteenth trial, but it was least for the massed-practice group. With succeeding trials, fatigue and other conditions built up which could not be dissipated in the 0 interval of rest between trials, but could be in the 30- and 60-second intervals. After 10 minutes of rest, the massed-practice group showed marked improvement on the first trial. The 10 minutes of rest was sufficient to overcome some of the undesirable effects of the preceding massed practice. After the 10-minute rest interval, however, the distributed practice groups continued to perform better than the massed-practice group.

Many other studies could be cited to show that superior performance

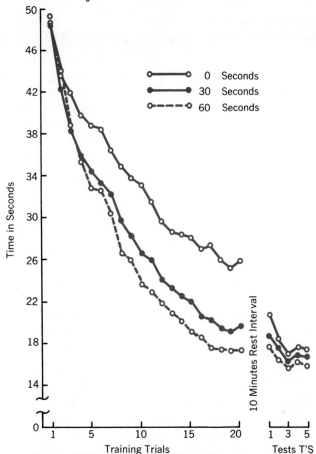

Fig. 9.8. Overall prerest and postrest performance under three degrees of distribution of practice. (A. S. Patel & D. A. Grant. Decrement and recovery effects in a perceptual-motor learning task as a function of effort, distribution of practice, and sex of subject. *J. gen. Psychol.*, 1964, **71**, 220.)

results from proper distribution of practice. However, the conclusion is clear that shorter practice sessions with an interval of time between sessions produce excellent results in any skill provided two conditions are met—the practice sessions must be sufficiently long to bring about improvement and the space between sessions must not be so long that forgetting occurs. The most important factor in being able to retain a skill from one session to the next, after a reasonable length of time, is the level of proficiency achieved during prior trials (**14**). Of course, if an objective of practice is to build endurance, then one would use longer practice periods. For example, in coaching athletes to run five miles, one has them run at least five miles in practice.

Teachers in junior and senior high schools usually have no control over the length of class periods. They work in schools where class periods in all subject fields are of the same length, usually from 45 to 75 minutes. In any subject where skills are part of the desired outcome the teacher should raise questions such as these: Within a class period of this length what is the best arrangement of active practice and rest? for a beginning class? for an advanced class? Will the students acquire skill more rapidly through active practice each day of the week or through active practice on alternate days?

In the elementary school, teachers have more opportunities to manipulate time arrangements since these schools are not as completely departmentalized as are junior and senior high schools. The elementary teacher has better opportunity to experiment with a variety of practice-rest arrangements. In the fourth grade, for example, experimenting could be done to ascertain whether children learn to spell as efficiently with 15 minutes of active practice on alternate days as with 15 minutes daily. When cursive handwriting is introduced, a test could be made to find whether 20 minutes of practice in four spaced 5-minute sessions during the school day would achieve the same or better results than 20 minutes at one time during the school day. Most teachers simply accept the arrangement that someone has previously set up without any evidence that it is the best.

Implementation in Speech Correction. The beginning therapist designed practice tasks with Sarah in making the "s" sound that were appropriate on several counts. Primary among these was the child's present ability level. The nature of the tasks changed as her abilities progressed:

The first practice tasks were of a type that did not require her to actually produce the sound. The tasks then progressed to having her produce the sound in isolation, to having her produce the sound in the various positions of syllables and words, and finally to having her produce the sound in words and sentences. When she reached the stage of syllables, it was necessary to first give her tasks which allowed her to say the "s" sound separated from the other sounds of the unit. After she mastered this, tasks were devised to give her practice at unifying the sound combinations.

The tasks were varied at each level and were performed with and without mechanical aids. At each level she was required to master tasks ranging in difficulty from simple to complex before she was allowed to progress to the next stage. Among the most difficult tasks at each level were those that required her to perform well at her present ability level in some situation other than the actual speech class.

Practice was distributed during the week rather than massed, since Sarah was seen each Monday, Wednesday, and Friday from 9:10 until 9:30 in the morning. When Sarah was learning to say the "s" sound, a typical session would begin with a quick review of the correct production of the sound. In this review I would make a series of correct and incorrect productions and she would tell me which were correct and incorrect and why. Then she would verbalize the things she had to remember in trying to make the sound and would try to produce the sound. She would usually produce the sound quite poorly on her first few attempts. With successive repetitions her productions would usually improve up to a point and then remain on a plateau. When this plateau was reached, or when it could be seen that she was not going to make any progress, a different method was used. If, for example, we had been working with only a mirror, some mechanical aid such as a toothpick would be introduced. If we were working with a toothpick a different aid such as a straw would be used. When it appeared that no further progress would be made immediately, even with a change in methods, practice on the production of the sound was discontinued and discrimination practice was given. After she had had a few minutes to rest from her attempts at production, these attempts were resumed.

After she was able to produce the sound correctly, distribution was accomplished primarily through the varying of activities. Throughout the corrective process it was noted that most progress was made when the session moved at a fairly rapid tempo and when the types of activities were varied often. In addition to these means of distributing the practice, Sarah was given various out-of-class assignments. These included such tasks as listening to herself and/or others, practicing with a straw, and doing exercises in her speech book.

Provide Knowledge of Results and Correct Inadequate Responses

Knowledge of results, or feedback, is one of the most powerful variables in skill learning; there is no improvement without knowledge of results, progressive improvement with it, and deterioration after its withdrawal (4). In many skills where the student can observe the results immediately, he guides his next tries on the basis of feedback from the previous ones. The student cannot always interpret his previous performances to determine their adequacy or inadequacy, correctness or incorrectness. The teacher, however, should provide arrangements so that knowledge of results is readily available. This principle has been thoroughly established for a long time (8, 39). Recently, knowledge of results have been shown to be less effective when followed by immediate motor movements rather than by a slight pause and then movement (25).

Progress in many skills is quite easily measured and a variety of means is available to the teacher to provide the learner with knowledge of his progress. Information can be given verbally in such simple statements as "correct" or "incorrect"; a verbal analysis can be given of any object which the student has produced; and the results of performance tests of all sorts can be incorporated in charts or given to the student directly. Verbal presentations, however, have some limitations. In some skills the actions cannot be explained verbally, nor can the accuracy or speed always be measured. In this case the teacher may demonstrate and the student, by observing, can compare his performance with that of the teacher. As was suggested previously in several studies, the learner also can be encouraged to engage in mental practice of the task both before and after he has completed it. This mental practicing is sometimes useful in helping the learner to intellectualize knowledge of results both with respect to ascertaining what he has done well and, possibly, where he has made an error.

Incorrect responses or poor movements should be corrected immediately. A primary determiner of the efficiency with which pupils acquire any skill is the quality of the help given at the time incorrect movements or responses are made. As was shown in Chapter 7, when the learner unknowingly misspells a word he tends to repeat the incorrect spelling. Similarly, if the individual performs a bodily movement incorrectly, he tends to repeat it. In some cases individuals overcome their deficiencies independently. In many cases, however, learning progresses only when the inadequacy is identified and appropriate methods are used to overcome it.

Implementation in Speech Correction. How often should knowledge of results be made available to a child who cannot evaluate the adequacy of his own responses? When should errors be corrected? In a few concise statements, the beginning therapist answers these questions.

This principle was implemented at all stages of the correction with Sarah in such a way as to also lay the basis for the next principle. In the early stages of therapy, I verbally evaluated each of her responses. Instead of merely labeling a response as correct or incorrect, I told her why it was right or wrong, gave her suggestions for the correction of inadequate responses, and informed her of progress toward or regression from the correct response. With the help of such mechanical aids as a mirror, an auditory training unit, and a tape recorder, I tried to help her to fully undersand the basis of my evaluations.

Encourage Independent Evaluation

This principle applied to skill learning carries the same meaning that it does to other learning outcomes that have been treated in Chapters 8 and 9. Under the direction of the teacher, the learner has the opportunity to profit from the guidance provided. Most skills, however, eventually are performed independently, and skills are taught in school so that learners can use them independently and in many activities. Besides the guiding and monitoring of active practice in school, there also should be discussion and analysis in which the learner acquires skill in evaluating and improving his performances independently. It is entirely possible that no person will acquire a high degree of skill as long as he remains completely dependent upon someone else for the guidance and monitoring of his activities.

Implementation in Speech Correction. When we work with 25 to 50 or more students in a class it is difficult to aid all students in evaluating their performances. In a one-to-one situation, as is the case in some speech therapy, it is easier to aid the child in self-evaluation. The beginning speech therapist, however, now presents some ingenious procedures with Sarah.

> Throughout corrective therapy I tried to teach Sarah to evaluate her own responses. Although I assumed the initial responsibility for the evaluations, I did so in such a way as to prepare her for making her own evaluations.
>
> I helped her to analyze the various aspects of the correct production of the "s" sound and helped her to learn to compare her productions to this model. I introduced the use of the tape recorder to help her to hear her errors. When she was able to do well at discrimination tasks, I helped her to evaluate her responses by asking questions in such a way that she would be able to arrive at the correct evaluations. When I felt that she was capable of evaluating her own responses, I let her try to do so. If she made errors in these evaluations, I helped her to correct those errors by again asking appropriate questions.
>
> Sarah eventually reached the point where she was able to correctly evaluate her own responses and to modify her incorrect productions of the sound without my help. She was then able to do much practicing of the sound outside of the actual speech class.

SUMMARY

Psychomotor abilities such as strength, speed, precision, coordination, and flexibility underlie skilled performances in typing, playing a musical instrument, drawing, and many others. The change from a lower to a higher level of skill is accompanied with voluntary to involuntary control of movements, better differentiation of cues, better feedback and correction, more rapid and accurate movements, and better coordination of movements and responses. Skills vary in the amount of involvement of motor and perceptual components. Walking, for example, is high in the motor and low in the perceptual component, whereas reading is high in the perceptual and low in the motor.

Psychological knowledge and theory permit the stating of principles that are applicable to all skill learning: (1) analyze the skill in terms of learner's abilities, (2) demonstrate the correct responses, (3) guide initial responses verbally and physically, (4) arrange for appropriate practice, (5) correct inadequate responses, and (6) encourage independent evaluation. The development of high-level skills in all children is necessary in attaining adequate vocational opportunities, avocational opportunities, and physical fitness and health.

QUESTIONS AND ACTIVITIES

1. a. Discuss the importance of psychomotor abilities in daily living.
   b. List a few things which you do that require a high level and others that require a low level of psychomotor ability. Which are most essential to your maintenance of life? Your enjoyment of life?
2. Compare the system of abilities of Guilford and Fleishman as shown in the two tables.
3. a. What are the main conclusions regarding the change in abilities with practice on a task?
   b. What are the implications of these conclusions for predicting success in skills?
4. a. State two or three conclusions about developmental trends in each of the following: strength of grip, reaction time, speed, balance, and handwriting.
   b. Which ability do you think is most, and which least, dependent upon instruction for its improvement? Give the basis of your opinion.

5. a. List and discuss the characteristics of a skilled performance.
   b. Identify a skill which you perform frequently but have not improved in recently; for example, handwriting or playing a musical instrument, and indicate why there has been no improvement.
   c. Demonstrate a skilled performance to someone and describe it in terms of the characteristics in (a).
6. Why is it important to analyze a skill before attempting to teach it to someone?
7. When should the teacher not demonstrate a skill to a beginner?
8. Discuss the effects of verbal guidance, physical guidance, mental practice, and overt practice in the learning of a psychomotor activity such as bowling.
9. For a skill in which you are most proficient or for one you may teach others, discuss practice tasks from the standpoint of:
   a. whole-part arrangements;
   b. context;
   c. variety of responses.

10. a. With what types of skills does distributed practice yield better results than massed practice? Give examples.
    b. When is a practice session too short?
    c. When is a practice session too long?
    d. To what extent is desirable length of practice sessions dependent upon the characteristics of the learner and the nature of the task? Give examples.
11. Under what conditions does knowledge of results facilitate skill learning?
12. List three of your skills that you could improve without instruction from another person. In one of these, describe how you would go about it.
13. Compare the principles for learning skills with those for learning concepts from the standpoint of their foundations in research.
14. Evaluate the implementation of each principle of skill learning by the speech correctionist.

SUGGESTIONS FOR FURTHER READING

Bayley, Nancy. Comparisons of mental and motor test scores for ages 1–15 months by sex, birth order, race, geographical location, and education of parents. *Child Develpm.*, 1965, **36**, 379–411.

Broadbent, D. E. Response to stress in military and other situations. In J. Cohen (Ed.), *Readings in psychology*. London: Allen & Unwin, 1964, pp. 325–340.

Espenschade, Anna S. Physical education in the elementary schools. *What research says to the teacher*, No. 27. Washington, D.C.: National Education Association, 1963.

Guilford, J. P. A system of the psychomotor abilities. *Amer. J. Psychol.*, 1958, 71, 164–174.

Hunsicker, P. Physical fitness. *What research says to the teacher*, No. 26. Washington, D.C.: National Education Association, 1963.

Priebe, R. E., & W. H. Burton. The slow-motion picture as a coaching device. *Sch. Rev.*, 1939, **47**, 192–198. (In Page, 1964, 198–203.)

Rosenbaum, M. E., & I. F. Tucker. The competence of the model and the learning of imitation and nonimitation. *J. exp. Psychol.*, 1962, **63**, 183–190.

REFERENCES

1. Ames, Louise B., & Frances L. Ilg. Developmental trends in writing behavior. *J. genet. Psychol.*, 1951, **79**, 29–46.
2. Ammons, R. B. Acquisition of a motor skill: III. Effects of initially distributed practice on rotary pursuit performance. *J. exp. Psychol.*, 1950, **40**, 777–787.
3. Bandura, A., & R. H. Walters. *Social learning and personality development*. New York: Holt, Rinehart, & Winston, 1963.
4. Bilodeau, E. A., & Ina M. Bilodeau. Motor-skills learning. In *Annual review of psychology*. Stanford: Stanford Univer. Press, 1961, pp. 243–280.
5. Bloom, B. S. *Stability and change in human characteristics*. New York: Wiley, 1964.
6. Cron, G. W., & N. H. Pronko. Development of the sense of balance in school children. *J. educ. Res.*, 1957, **51**, 33–37.
7. Davies, Dorothy R. The effect of

tuition upon the process of learning a complex motor skill. *J. educ. Psychol.*, 1945, **36**, 352–365.

8. Deese, J. *The psychology of learning.* New York: McGraw-Hill, 1958.

9. Dreizen, S., *et al.* The effects of nutritive failure on the growth patterns of white children in Alabama. *Child Develpm.*, 1953, **24**, 189–202.

10. Duncan, C. P. The effect of unequal amounts of practice on motor learning before and after rest. *J. exp. Psychol.*, 1951, **42**, 257–264.

11. Fleishman, E. A. A comparative study of aptitude patterns in unskilled and skilled psychomotor performances. *J. appl. Psychol.*, 1957, **41**, 263–272.

12. Fleishman, E. A. Abilities at different stages of practice in rotary pursuit performance. *J. exp. Psychol.*, 1960, **60**, 162–171.

13. Fleishman, E. A. *The structure and measurement of physical fitness.* Englewood Cliffs, N.J.: Prentice-Hall, 1964.

14. Fleishman, E. A., & J. F. Parker, Jr. Factors in the retention and relearning of perceptual-motor skill. *J. exp. Psychol.*, 1962, **64**, 215–226.

15. Fleishman, E. A., & S. Rich. Role of kinesthetic and spatial-visual abilities in perceptual-motor learning. *J. exp. Psychol.*, 1963, **66**, 6–11.

16. Francis, R. J., & G. L. Rarick. Motor characteristics of the mentally retarded. *Amer. J. ment. Defic.*, 1959, **63**, 792–811.

17. Green, L. A study of typewriting achievement in three high schools. *J. educ. Res.*, 1940, **34**, 209–217.

18. Guilford, J. P. A system of the psychomotor abilities. *Amer. J. Psychol.*, 1958, **71**, 164–174.

19. Guilford, J. P. Three faces of intellect. *Amer. Psychologist*, 1959, **14**, 469–479.

20. Jones, H. E. The development of

physical abilities. In N. B. Henry (Ed.), *Adolescence.* Yearb. nat. Soc. Stud. Educ., 1944, **43**, Part I, pp. 100–122.

21. Keys, A., A. Henschel, *et al. The biology of human starvation.* Minneapolis: Univer. of Minnesota, 1950. 2 vols.

22. Klausmeier, H. J., J. Feldhusen, & J. Check. *An analysis of learning efficiency in arithmetic of mentally retarded children in comparison with children of average and high intelligence.* U.S. Office of Education Cooperative Research Project No. 153. Madison: Univer. of Wisconsin, 1959.

23. Knapp, C. G., & W. R. Dixon. Learning to juggle: I. A study to determine the effect of two different distributions of practice on learning efficiency. *Res. Quart. Amer. Ass. Hlth Phys. Educ. Recr.*, 1950, **21**, 331–336.

24. Knapp, C. G., & W. R. Dixon. Learning to juggle: II. A study of whole and part methods. *Res. Quart. Amer. Ass. Hlth. Phys. Educ. Recr.*, 1952, **23**, 398–401.

25. McGuigan, F. J., Carolyn Hutchens, Nancy Eason, & T. Reynolds. The retroactive interference of motor activity with knowledge of results. *J. gen. Psychol.*, 1964, **70**, 279–281.

26. McGuigan, F. J., & E. F. MacCaslin. Whole and part methods in learning a perceptual motor skill. *Amer. J. Psychol.*, 1955, **68**, 658–661.

27. Mackworth, Jane. Performance decrement in vigilance, threshold, and high-speed perceptual motor tasks. *Canad. J. Psychol.*, 1964, **18**, 209–223.

28. Miles, W. R. Measures of certain human abilities throughout the life span. *Proc. Nat. Acad. Sci.*, 1931, **17**, 627–633.

29. Miller, G. A., E. Galanter, & K. H. Pribram. *Plans and the structure of behavior.* New York: Holt, Rinehart, & Winston, 1960.

30. Parker, J. F., Jr., & E. A. Fleishman. Use of analytical information concerning task requirements to increase the effectiveness of skill training. *J. appl. Psychol.*, 1961, **45**, 295–302.

31. Patel, A. S., & D. A. Grant. Decrement and recovery effects in a perceptual-motor learning task as a function of effort, distribution of practice, and sex of subject. *J. gen. Psychol.*, 1964, **71**, 217–231.

32. Rosenbaum, M. E., & I. F. Tucker. The competence of the model and the learning of imitation and non-imitation. *J. exp. Psychol.*, 1962, **63**, 183–190.

33. Solley, W. H. The effects of verbal instruction of speed and accuracy upon the learning of a motor skill. *Res. Quart. Amer. Ass. Hlth Phys. Educ. Recr.*, 1952, **23**, 231–240.

34. Swanson, F. J. Voice mutation in the adolescent male: An experiment in guiding the voice development of adolescent boys in general music classes. Unpublished doctoral dissertation, Univer. of Wisconsin, 1959.

35. Tuddenham, R. D., & M. M. Snyder. Physical growth of California boys and girls from birth to 18 years. *Child Develpm.*, 1954, **1**, 183–364.

36. Waterland, J. C. The effect of mental practice combined with kinesthetic perception when the practice precedes each overt performance of a motor skill. Unpublished master's thesis, Univer. of Wisconsin, 1956.

37. West, L. J. Verbally induced sets toward speed and accuracy in elementary typewriting. *Nat. Bus. Educ. Quart.*, 1953, **21** (3), 46–55.

38. Woodrow, H. The relation between abilities and improvement with practice. *J. educ. Psychol.*, 1938, **29**, 215–230.

39. Woodworth, R. S., & H. Schlosberg. *Experimental psychology.* New York: Holt, Rinehart & Winston, 1954.

CHAPTER 10

Attitudes and Values

Wwhat attitudes and values should children learn in school? The answer to this question is less clear than are answers to similar questions dealing with psychomotor and cognitive outcomes. Agencies such as the home and church supposedly are more responsible than the school for attitude learning. Also, people in most communities differ as to which attitudes and values should be acquired by children and youth; therefore, the school has difficulty in deciding which set of conflicting attitudes and values to incorporate in the school curriculum. In addition, the learning of attitudes is not as well understood as the learning of cognitive and psychomotor outcomes. Teachers must proceed in the teaching of attitudes with lesser assurance than in the teaching of skills.

The authors believe that the learning of attitudes and values is an important objective of the school, and that careful attention should be given to (1) tastes, attitudes, and values; (2) developmental trends; (3) a model for facilitating attitude learning; and (4) the problem of extreme attitudes.

TASTES, ATTITUDES, AND VALUES

An attitude is a learned, emotionally toned predisposition to react in a consistent way, favorable or unfavorable, toward a person, object, or idea. An attitude of an individual is inferred from his behavior and cannot be measured as directly as skills, facts, and concepts. The main difference between a concept, as defined in Chapter 8, and an attitude is that an attitude influences the individual's acceptance or rejection of persons, things, and ideas, hereafter referred to as attitude objects. An attitude does have meaning for the individual, as does a concept.

As shown in Fig. 10.1, there is no sharp dividing line or distinction between tastes or preferences, attitudes, and values. From the stand-

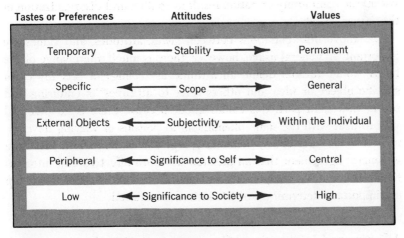

Fig. 10.1. Schematic organization of tastes, attitudes, and values.

point of stability, tastes are most temporary and values are most stable, with attitudes somewhere between. Tastes may shift readily from day to day or week to week, attitudes change less frequently, and values are quite resistant to change. Tastes refer to something specific, such as the like or dislike of a particular animal, color, or flavor; values are more general and encompass large areas of experience. For example, we might think of a *taste* as applying to a specific arrangement of a musical composition, an *attitude* as acceptance or rejection of certain categories of music such as sacred, classical, or jazz, and a *value* as the entire scope of music in the life of the individual.

In connection with the subjectivity dimension shown in Fig. 10.1, tastes are usually thought of as the individual's perception of the attractiveness or unattractiveness of an external object; attitudes are involved in the relationship between a person and the object; and values more intimately inhere within the individual. As applied to significance to the self, an individual's tastes may change without much modification in his total personality or self-organization. Attitudes also can change, but with many changes of attitude there also is an accompanying change in the self; and with large and significant changes in the value system, there is also basic change in personality. On the last dimension—significance to society—tastes are not considered of high importance, being unique to individuals within the larger social group. Values, however, are of high importance to organized segments of society, such as the community, state, and nation. Large differences in values or in the means of achieving the same values by subgroups within the community or nation result in conflict and disorganization of the larger society.

The above differentiations between tastes, attitudes, and values are important. In general usage, however, there is much interchange of the terms. Some authors define an attitude as feelings or sets toward a specific object or idea and others refer to attitudes as enduring and stable values. In part, this comes about because there is no practical way to deal with the same phenomena in persons of varying developmental levels—preschool, elementary, high school, and adult. Yet, there is general agreement that an attitude has both affective and informational or cognitive components and that the individual and the group are important determiners of the attitudes acquired.

Affective and Informational Components of Attitudes

Occasionally attitudes are acquired through one traumatic emotional experience, but with little information about the attitude object; more often they are acquired through a series of lesser emotional experiences and with more information; some are acquired with considerable information about the attitude object and little accompanying feeling or emotion. Figure 10.2 shows theoretical weightings of the feeling and informational components in attitude acquisition. The weighting may vary from very high to very low for both the feeling and the informational components. It is possible for the attitudes toward three subjects (A, B, C) to be held by the same individual. Attitude A might be favorable or unfavorable and is based largely on emotional experiences and little on informational experiences with de-

HIGH

LOW

G
N
I
L
E
E
F

N
O
I
T
A
M
R
O
F
N
I

LOW

HIGH

A Attitude toward denominational religions.

B Attitude toward group work.

C Attitude toward research into the causes
and cures of diseases.

Fig. 10.2. Theoretical weighting of the feeling and informational components of attitudes.

nominational religions. Attitude B is based about equally on informational and emotional experiences with group work. Attitude C is heavily based on informational experiences with a relatively low degree of emotional experience.

In general, commercial advertising uses the "A" approach, whereas schools use the "C" approach. The advertiser, of course, wishes individuals to acquire a favorable attitude toward a product, so he presents it in a most pleasant emotional setting with a minimum amount of information which is all favorable. When the teacher wishes individuals to acquire an attitude without attempting to influence the accepting-rejecting dimension, he gives all information—favorable, unfavorable, and neutral. No matter how an attitude is acquired—through emotional or informational experiences—it guides behavior in a consistent way. For example, if the individual has a strong negative attitude toward religion, he probably will not attend church regularly or will go but not for the same purposes as most church members. If he has a strong positive attitude toward research into the causes and cures of disease, he will probably contribute to various fund-raising campaigns to extend medical research. It is possible, of course, to have attitudes that at times are contradictory. Someone may have a strong antimedical attitude toward the treatment of illness and a strong positive attitude toward the curative powers of faith; however, when his appendix ruptures, this person may be forced to make a decision.

Individual and Group Bases of Attitudes

Just as an individual acquires his own facts and concepts, so he acquires his own attitudes. However, membership in groups, particularly primary groups, exercises an important influence on the acquisition of attitudes, more so than on concepts and psychomotor skills. Primary groups such as the family, the neighborhood play group, the high school crowd, and cliques, usually have a core of common attitudes which holds the members together. New members coming into these already formed primary groups tend to accept the established attitudes of the group. This does not mean that diverse attitudes are never acquired by members of the same group. Though a core of common attitudes serves to consolidate a small neighborhood group, the various members also may have markedly different attitudes which affect areas of life outside the neighborhood group. Such factors as the purposes or functions of the group, the feelings among the members, the amount and closeness of associations among the members, and the type of leadership affect the extent to which common or diverse attitudes emerge.

Applying these group characteristics to large college classes, we frequently find groups in which the students hold a vague but common purpose of learning certain subject matter. There is not a strong like or dislike among members of the class, there are few close associations made during regular class periods, and the leadership is vested in one person—the teacher. In such a classroom we do not expect to find a core of common attitudes. Instead, each individual has unique attitudes affecting most areas of life except for a small segment within the particular classroom. But such groups can be organized and led so that attitudes are influenced. In an experiment with college students (1) the attitudes of individuals shifted with their perceived estimates of how most of the members of their group reacted to the particular attitude object; (2) classes taught by a group-centered technique created more amiability among members than did leader-centered classes; (3) a group-decision method was more effective than a lecture in reaching a conclusion about an attitude object; and (4) individuals within groups and the groups themselves did not change all attitudes in the same manner—certain attitudes apparently were more resistant to modification than others (16). The importance of the group and of group management in the acquisition and modification of attitudes will be given more consideration in a later discussion.

Imitation and Conditioning in Attitude Learning

Earlier in Chapter 3, we noted that much social learning occurs through imitation of models (1). A brief recapitulation of the main concepts of imitation with specific application to the learning of attitudes will lay the basis for some of the generalizations and principles that will be discussed later in this chapter.

Imitation works in three ways to increase the number, range, and intensity of the observer's matching response. First, the observer acquires new behavior that he has not previously manifested. For example, a child observes a model and subsequently manifests large units of behavior. Second, observing a model may strengthen or weaken inhibitory responses of the observer. Here the observer already has the behavior in his repertoire, but it has been inhibited. Inhibited behavior seen in a model that is punished is inhibited further or weakened; that seen in a model that is rewarded is disinhibited or strengthened. Third, observing a model may have the effect of eliciting previously learned behavior that has not been manifested recently. The difference between the disinhibiting effects of imitation and the eliciting effects can be determined only by knowing the history of the observer. The extent of imitation depends mainly on two factors: punishment and reward. The observer will tend not to imitate if the model is punished for his behavior; however, if a certain behavior brings reward, the observer is more likely to imitate. Individual characteristics and circumstances also are influential. Imitation is strengthened if the person lacks self-esteem, lacks competence, or believes he is very similar to a model. One is also more likely to imitate if in the past he has been rewarded for conforming or for copying someone else's behavior.

As you remember, a response made for the first time is strengthened through reinforcement. Except in the laboratory, the schedule of reinforcement is not well controlled and is intermittent, rather than systematic. Nonetheless, even if reinforcement by an authority figure such as a parent or teacher is intermittent, it has a strengthening effect. On the other hand, responses already in the learner's repertoire are inhibited by punishment and nonreward. When a child's responses are considered to be a threat to himself or to society, positive reinforcers are

347

removed (a privilege taken away) or an aversive stimulus such as punishment is used. While these active techniques lead to inhibition of undesired responses, they may not result in permanent extinction. They may be only temporary. As noted in Chapter 3, classical conditioning procedures may be more effective than punishment and nonreward because they eliminate an undesirable response by establishing a desired one that is incompatible.

The main types of behavior that respond to principles of imitation and reinforcement and that have been studied experimentally are aggression, dependency, and sexual behavior. From these types of behavior we can infer attitudes. As an example let us consider aggressive behavior as a favorable means of coping with certain situations. If in a number of situations we observe a child handling a book carefully and reading attentively, we infer that he has developed a favorable attitude toward reading or toward books. We thus assume that the same principles which explain the learning of the behavior also are useful in explaining the learning of attitudes associated with behavior.

Considerable evidence for the learning of attitudes through imitation and through reinforcement of desired responses and punishment of undesired responses is found in studies of the attitudes and prejudices of young children. For example, 250 children of kindergarten, first, and second grades were found to demonstrate stereotyping and rejecting of other groups of human beings, such as the Negro, white, Jew, Catholic, and Protestant (21). We observe also that young children may acquire the religious beliefs of their parents through imitation, reinforcement, and punishment. This does not mean that attitudes are learned only through imitation, followed by reinforcement or punishment. As noted in the previous discussion in this chapter, the development of attitudes is influenced by cognizing information about attitude objects as well as by interacting in primary groups.

DEVELOPMENTAL TRENDS

Much remains to be learned about the acquisition and change in attitudes from infancy into adult life. Some attitudes appear to be acquired in early childhood and remain fairly stable thereafter; others are not acquired until considerably later in adolescence and are readily subject to modification. A general sequence in the learning of attitudes involves being aware of and receiving stimuli, responding to stimuli from mere acquiescence through obtaining satisfaction in the response, forming values from first acceptance through commitment, conceptualization of values, and finally characterization in a philosophy of life (Fig. 2.5). In line with the previous outline of a developmental sequence in concept learning in Chapter 7, we would not expect conceptualization of favorable or unfavorable feelings to occur, except at a most elementary level, prior to the school years. However, emotionalized reactions—pleasant and unpleasant—are present as early as the second year of life and parents report that their children express favorable attitudes toward school before starting the first grade (25). Thus, being aware of and responding affectively to stimuli occur early in life in preschool years while valuing, conceptualization, and characterization come later. As we consider some highpoints of the learning of attitudes during the school years, inferences about learning processes and a developmental sequence may be drawn.

Elementary School Years

Children's social perceptions, including attitudes toward a number of pervasive and significant attitude objects, are stable in some regards and change in others from first to sixth grade (5). In both grades children had more favorable attitudes toward rural situations than urban. Most children regarded the country as a place where they could go sight seeing, ride ponies, roam about the fields, and have opportunities to play. In contrast, the city was seen as a place of excitement where one could take bus rides and go shopping. However, most children did not associate going downtown or going to the city in general with recreational pursuits, and for some, shopping was regarded as something that had to be done—a chore interfering with play activities. The first-graders were found to have more negative attitudes toward urban situations than did the sixth-graders, and, to a lesser extent, more negative attitudes toward rural situations than did the sixth-graders. The Estvans, who conducted this study, interpreted the more general negative or mixed feelings on the part of the first-graders as associated with lack of understanding or knowledge of the situation.

Negative attitudes toward lower-status living were acquired before the children reached first grade and remained relatively unchanged through the sixth grade. The children acquired favorable attitudes for upper-status living during the first six years of school. The sixth-graders showed many more positive and many fewer negative attitudes toward upper-status living than did the first-graders. Although boys and girls had similar attitudes and feelings about lower-status situations,

349

the girls were more attracted to upper-status situations than were the boys. The Estvans interpreted this to mean that the girls were more socially responsive and had internalized attitudes at a younger age than boys.

Positive attitudes toward the school were expressed by 49 percent of the children, negative attitudes by 20 percent, mixed attitudes by 22 percent, and no expression of attitude by 9 percent. Although there were negative and mixed attitudes toward the school, the children expressed only favorable attitudes toward learning as one aspect of schooling. The first-graders were more favorable toward the school than the sixth-graders. The Estvans interpreted the more unfavorable attitudes toward the school by the sixth-graders as follows:

Vacillating between child and adult roles, there is both a resistance to symbols of authority as represented in the school, and a negation of childish things associated with "grade" schools. Furthermore, their quest for new experiences and expanding interests may come in direct competition with school concerns which have lost much of their novelty by this time. This lessening of enthusiasm for school may also be an outcome of the kinds of experiences the child has had in school some of which, apparently, have not kept the original flame burning as brightly as before (5, 231).

The above conclusions suggest that some attitudes—for example, those toward social status and rural–urban living—are acquired quite early in life and become more fixed with further learning. Other attitudes—for instance, those toward school—appear less stable and change direction. The precise circumstances associated with the strengthening or the weakening of particular attitudes were not discussed by the Estvans.

High School Years

Some attitudes become more stable and others change from age 10 to 16 (6). Let us consider growth gradients as applied to cheating and stealing:

10 YEARS

Cheating. Ten has a strict code, and feels that "cheating is awful." Most Tens say specifically that they would not cheat, though a few report one or two children at school who do.

Stealing. No children admit to stealing. Many comment that stealing is very bad. Some might be tempted, but many know they would feel "awful" if they did; others know the consequences would be too bad. Several say they know children who do steal, and remark on the badness of this. . . .

11 YEARS

Cheating. Though stating that they themselves would not cheat, many Elevens show much concern (as did Six) about others who do. Most report that some of the children at school cheat, girls frequently saying that most boys cheat on exams.

Some say they used to cheat when younger, though they no longer do.

Stealing. Most say that they never do, but that they know people (even own twin) who steal either from stores or from their mother's pocketbook. Many are troubled about this, and most comment that it is a bad idea or wrong. One or two admit they used to, but say, "No longer."

From reports other than their own, it appears that more girls than boys are likely to be involved in an episode of pilfering at eleven. . . .

12 YEARS

Cheating. Compared with Ten, Twelve shows a very casual attitude toward cheating. Many say they would not cheat, but others say they might if they had to, and quite a few say that they do ("All the kids do—we help each other out").

Stealing. A similar change appears. Most say that they themselves do not steal. But a few—boys more than girls—admit to occasional stealing, several mentioning the "fun" of it. A great many say they "know kids" who steal, mostly from ten-cent stores, and many add, "They charge too much anyway."

Some seem mildly admiring of others who steal. . . .

13 YEARS

Cheating. Thirteen reports that a few classmates cheat, but most do not. Most 13-year-olds disapprove of others' cheating, and do not admit to doing so themselves—unless there is some good reason.

Stealing. Pilfering from stores is less frequently reported—even in Thirteen's mention of "the other kids." The thrill element is somewhat discounted: "What's the use of going and lifting little whistles?" . . .

14 YEARS

Cheating. Boys and girls have more to say about cheating now than they did earlier. Most feel that there is not too much cheating at school: "I think most kids are pretty honest. A few will cheat if they have the advantage." But the situation clearly differs from school to school, and even from class to class. Some report that "75 to 80 per cent of the kids" cheat; others that school is run on the honor system, and almost no one cheats.

In their own practices, a slightly qualified honesty seems to prevail—some are honest *except* ("except in Latin") and others are honest *if* (if they respect the teacher). Some say it is confusing because some teachers allow you to check your work with other pupils more than others do.

Stealing. As usual, they do not admit to stealing themselves. When discussing others' stealing, Fourteen no longer appears shocked (as at ten) or slightly admiring (as at twelve), but rather understanding: "I think it's something she'll grow out of." . . .

15 YEARS

Cheating. Fifteen seems to feel more strongly about cheating. Most say that they themselves do not cheat, and some say they would rather flunk than cheat. Nearly all state that a few in their class do, but all seem to think this wrong. "I will not help a person who wants an answer."

Stealing. Most of our subjects say not only that they do not steal, but that they do not know anyone who does. Increasingly cited is the concept that it really doesn't pay, because if you steal people don't trust you. . . .

16 YEARS

Cheating. All our Sixteens say they would not cheat in any situation, except perhaps examinations. Here they differ widely. Some say, "Oh, we all cheat in exams," others say they don't know anybody who cheats. Still others say there is no point in cheating except getting better marks, so it's not worth it since "cheating isn't you."

Stealing. As at fifteen, no stealing is reported by our subjects, either by themselves or by acquaintances . . . (**6**, 480–483).

Attitudes toward cheating and stealing undergo change from age 10 to 16, but the change is not consistent. At age 10 there is a strong attitude against cheating and stealing but, at age 12, both cheating and stealing are not strongly disapproved. By age 16, these youths of the middle class and above-average intelligence frown upon stealing; however, there is still some acceptance of cheating, especially in examination situations.

In a study of how high school youth believe children should be brought up, 3000 students were given a combination factual and opinion test based on the judgment of experts (**22**). Table 10.1 shows the responses to six of the attitudinal items. The students were in general agreement with the experts on most of the 90 items. But, of the six reported in Table 10.1, the majority of high school students differed with the experts on items 30 and 52. Fifty-seven percent of high school students agreed that a child should be made to attend church services and 65 percent would punish a child for swearing. The experts disagreed. On items 1, 47, 69, and 85 the majority of high school students responded as the experts did. Although results are not given in Table 10.1, there was little difference between the responses of ninth- and tenth-graders and those of the eleventh- and twelfth-graders.

It appears, then, that attitudes toward child rearing are quite similar for high school students and adult experts. Whether there might have been higher agreement between the students and their parents is unknown. One also might interpret the information in Table 10.1 as showing considerable difference in attitudes among high school students. For example, 57 percent agree and 27 percent disagree to item 30.

TABLE 10.1.

Responses of 3000 High School Students to Selected Items of Purdue Opinion Panel

Item	Total			Boys			Girls		
	% Agree	% Disagree	% ?	% Agree	% Disagree	% ?	% Agree	% Disagree	% ?
1. More important child be emotionally well adjusted than do superior work in school (A)[a]	75	8	17	72	9	19	79	6	15
30. Make child attend church services. (D)	57	27	16	55	27	18	58	26	16
47. Child needs to learn when, what, and how to fight. (A)	68	17	15	74	12	14	64	20	14
52. Should punish child for swearing. (D)	65	19	16	62	21	17	70	16	14
69. Provide special classes for dull and superior students. (A)	68	19	13	62	22	16	73	17	10
85. Give child regular allowance. (A)	80	10	10	74	14	12	83	8	9

[a] Letters in parenthesis at ends of each statement indicate judgment of experts.

SOURCE: Adapted from H. H. Remmers, & A. J. Drucker. How high school youth believe children should be brought up. In H. H. Remmers, *et al.* (Eds.), *Growth, teaching and learning: A book of readings.* New York: Harper & Row, 1957.

Having established that attitudes toward social class are already present by the first grade, we may reasonably inquire about ethnic attitudes during the high school years. Table 10.2 shows the mean level of attitudes for three age groups—13 to 14, 15 to 16, 17 to 18—attending a suburban school near Boston (27). A low score indicates a more favorable attitude, a high score a less favorable attitude. Attitudes toward Jews and Negroes improved slightly with increasing age while those toward Southerners deteriorated. However, with the exception of the latter the change was small. Apparently, events in the South in the early 1960s were associated with the last phenomenon. Although

TABLE 10.2.

Mean Level of Attitude by Age for Five Scales

	Age		
Scales	13–14 (N:317[a])	15–16 (N:150[a])	17–18 (N:150[a])
Opinion of Jews	31.4	31.7	29.9
Opinion of Negroes	32.7	32.5	31.7
Behavior toward Negroes	18.4	20.5	18.7
Negro Social Distance	22.4	26.2	25.3
Opinion of Southerners	31.7	33.4	33.7

[a] Ns for the "Opinion of Negroes" scale were 288, 194, and 193. This scale was based on a questionnaire administered on a different day from the one containing the other scales.
Source: Adapted from W. C. Wilson. Development of ethnic attitudes in adolescence. *Child Develpm.*, 1963, **34**, 251.

not shown, the attitudes among the boys did not vary as widely at the oldest age as at the youngest age. The mean scores made by all groups at all ages were neither highly favorable nor unfavorable toward the ethnic groups.

College Years

With increasing college enrollments, attitude development from the freshman through the senior year has become more important. Information has been collected in two ways: through interviews with the students while in college and through testing and observation of graduates (26). A test has been designed to measure such characteristics as freedom from compulsiveness, flexibility, tolerance for ambiguity, impunitive attitudes, critical attitudes toward authority (including parents or family, the state, religion, rules, etc.), mature interests, unconventionality or nonconformity, rejection of traditional feminine roles, freedom from cynicism about others, and realism. The general factor found to underlie most of these separate characteristics was called "rebellious independence." Here are some of the items in the test which measure this factor. The information in parentheses shows the percent of true responses of the Vassar women, first as freshmen and then as seniors:

I would rather be a steady and dependable worker than a brilliant but unstable one. (T: 69–45)
I have never done anything dangerous for the thrill of it. (T: 45–30)
I believe in a life hereafter. (T: 61–47)
A strong person will be able to make up his mind even on the most difficult questions. (T: 48–37)
I don't like to work on a problem unless there is the possibility of coming out with a clear-cut and unambiguous answer. (T: 40–22)
For most questions there is just one right answer, once a person is able to get all the facts. (T: 35–07)
I think I am stricter about right and wrong than most people. (T: 42–30)
Disobedience to the government is never justified. (T: 35–17)
Communism is the most hateful thing in the world today (T: 33–13) (**26**, 112–113).

Table 10.3 shows the mean scores of various groups of females and males on the 72-item test from which the above items were drawn

TABLE 10.3.

*Comparison of Various Groups on the Short Form
Developmental Scale*

Sex	Class	College	N	Mean Score
F	Freshmen	Vassar	321	23.157
F	Freshmen	Beirut	28	24.193
F	Freshmen	Paine	58	16.160
M	Freshmen	Paine	30	19.187
F	Sophomores	Paine	44	17.184
M	Sophomores	Paine	18	18.189
F	Juniors	Paine	28	21.157
M	Juniors	Paine	14	24.136
F	Seniors	Paine	26	19.100
M	Seniors	Paine	21	23.129
F	Seniors	Vassar	197	34.170
F	Seniors	Beirut	33	25.167

SOURCE: H. Webster. Changes in attitudes during college. *J. educ. Psychol.*, 1958, **49**, 114.

(26). Vassar is a women's college, Paine is a coeducational college for southern Negroes, and Beirut is for Arab girls. In the three colleges the mean scores go up—in the direction of greater rebellious independence—from the freshman to the senior year, with the Vassar group showing an increase from 23.57 to 34.70. Webster interpreted the data gathered in several studies as supporting these conclusions: There are substantial changes in attitudes during college; the attitudes of the students vary according to age, sex, and culture; and college students do not become more alike in their general attitudes while attending college.

Besides becoming more independent, students also might be expected to manifest less ethnocentric ideology (the tendency to exalt the superiority of the group to which one belongs). Furthermore, males change less than females during the four-year college period (19). Also, at the end of the first two years of college, the females are less ethnocentric than the males, and there is no difference between members of fraternities or sororities and nonmembers. Further, intelligence is not associated with change in ethnocentrism (20).

We can conclude that changes in attitudes do occur during college years. Part of this change results from maturation and part from education. It is not known how much might be associated with the change in environment from the home to the college community, with the students' new identifications with age-mates, instructors, and the institution, and with emotional experiences.

MODEL FOR FACILITATING ATTITUDE LEARNING

A model for facilitating attitude learning, comprised of seven generalizations and related principles, is presented in the same manner as in the preceding chapters. These principles are applicable not only to the class of affective outcomes that we have put on the continuum—*tastes* and *preferences, attitudes,* and *values*—but also to other outcomes that have a high affective component, namely *interests* and *motives.* We could substitute any of the above terms for attitudes in the model.

Although each principle is stated with the teacher as the assumed doer or subject of each verb, we do not imply that the teacher is to be highly directive and assume all responsibility for decision making about the learning of attitudes. Rather, the teacher is to serve as a guide and organizer. In many situations, starting as early as kindergarten and extending through college, the students should participate in implementing the principles. Careful scrutiny of the generalizations will show that the middle five follow a sequence of learning and instruction, from initial acquisition through use. The first principle is included because the schools have not done an adequate job of determining their role in the learning of attitudes. Even though a clear indication is given by the schools concerning mathematics, language arts, and other subject matter, most schools have not outlined a program of instruction concerning attitudes. The last principle is included to assist individuals in deliberately modifying their attitudes.

GENERALIZATION	PRINCIPLE
1. Attitudes, as other outcomes, are learned and can be taught.	1. Identify the attitudes to be taught.
2. A receptive, responding observer incorporates a model's behavior into his own repertoire through imitation.	2. Provide exemplary models.
3. Positive reinforcers strengthen attitudes through contiguity of response and reinforcement and through the linking of pleasantness with the reinforced response.	3. Provide pleasant emotional experiences with attitude objects.
4. Cognizing information and thinking productively modify attitudes differentially, according to the strength of the attitude.	4. Extend informative experiences.
5. Group interaction provides for testing of and commitment to behavior in harmony with group standards.	5. Use group techniques to facilitate commitment.
6. Practicing an attitude in relevant situations provides for stable organization.	6. Arrange for appropriate practice.
7. Purposeful learning may be initiated by an individual in order to acquire or modify attitudes.	7. Encourage independent attitude cultivation.

Identify Attitudes to be Taught

If ours were a completely static society and world, this principle would perhaps be unnecessary. Our society and world are, however, rapidly changing, and much confusion arises as to which attitudes should be taught. A rapid change in attitudes by large segments of the adult population is clearly revealed in their reactions toward Germany and Japan during World War II and shortly thereafter. With such shifts in attitudes, not only toward these nations, but also toward others, what might be a core of attitudes to teach children in school? The list which follows is incomplete but could be used by teachers to ascertain which items should be taught in school. Though the list is organized under two headings—values and attitudes—recall that the distinction between attitudes and values is not clear-cut and that application of the terminology to children of varying school levels must be different.

Values

1. Good physical and mental health
2. Pleasant home (school) life
3. Comfortable living (school) conditions
4. Many good friends
5. Stimulating intellectual activity
6. Service to society
7. Ability to identify, recognize, and work toward the solution of significant problems
8. Wealth
9. Opportunity for relaxation and recreation
10. Respect from others as a worthwhile person
11. Acceptance of responsibility for the result of one's own actions
12. Use of intelligence rather than force in the solution of problems
13. Respect for the individuality of others
14. Satisfying religious experiences

Attitudes Directly Connected with School

(The attitudes are inferred from the behavioral statements; the student is the assumed subject of each verb.)

15. Likes the subject matter
16. Likes the teacher or teachers
17. Likes classmates
18. Likes the school generally

19. Starts work promptly
20. Works with enthusiasm and vigor
21. Uses spare time advantageously
22. Follows directions
23. Takes good care of own property
24. Takes good care of others' and public property
25. Works well with others
26. Observes safety rules
27. Practices good health habits
28. Shows courtesy to others

Although the values listed are generally considered more appropriate for adolescents and adults than for younger children, it is possible that, starting in kindergarten, the school can contribute toward the pupils' acquisition of these values if they are agreed upon as desirable. If a group of teachers and parents were to discuss them, questions of definition would immediately arise. What are the precise meanings of such terms as *comfortable school conditions, pleasant school life, wealth,* and *satisfying religious experiences.* After the meanings were clarified there would undoubtedly be considerable disagreement about applying the values to daily situations. For example, though people verbally subscribe to the use of intelligence rather than force in the solution of problems, in application by parents and teachers this belief is often restated as a question: "When can intelligence rather than force be used with children in the solving of immediate daily behavior problems?"

How much agreement might be reached among a group of elementary, high school, or college teachers about the attitudes implied in items 15 through 28? There appears to be considerable disagreement on items 15, 16, 17, and 18; some teachers do not care whether or not pupils like the subject matter, the teacher, their classmates, and the school. Some teachers, because of their own attitudes or personalities, may not be able to accept items 15 through 18 as desirable. If, however, agreement could be reached that the implied attitudes should be acquired by the pupils, implementing the next six principles should prove effective in achieving them.

Provide Exemplary Models

One way to examine the effects of models is to control the behavior of the model and analyze the behaviors of observers before and after observing the model. This may lead to stating functional relationships between the model's behavior and the behavior of the observer; however, it makes no attempt to explain why the observer imitates the model (1). The same procedure may be followed with the attempt to explain just why an observer imitates a model.

A common interpretation is that the observer identifies with the model (11). When one identifies with a model, he behaves, feels, and thinks as if the attributes and behavior of the model belong to him. One may do this without actually being aware that he is identifying with or imitating the model. In other words, a child does not deliberately set out to behave like a model in the same manner that he tries to read or to write. A young child identifies with his parent early in life. Two conditions are necessary for this identification to occur. One, the child wants to possess some of the parent's characteristics; two, he has some basis for feeling that he and his parent are similar. Associated with wanting to possess some of the characteristics of the parent is the warm, nurturant relationship between the child and his parent. If a parent is cold and rejecting rather than warm and accepting, the child will not readily identify. A parent controls goals that the child desires, including power over the child and other people, mastery over the environment, and love. Identification with the parent is fostered through the desire to possess what the goals imply (18).

Behaving and feeling like the model also imply that the observer is similar to the model. The feeling emerges in two ways. As stated above, a child adopts his parent's attributes and behavior. Second, others may tell a child that he is similar to his parent. As the child perceives similarity of behavior with the model and is told that in mastery over the environment, power over other people, etc., he is like the model, identification with the model is strengthened. A brief sketch of the changes in identifying figures with age gives an indication of the role of the school in providing exemplary models.

Before he is 5, a boy accepts his father as the person after whom to model his behavior; the same is true of a girl and her mother. A boy imitates his father, and a girl, her mother in such matters as using the toilet, dressing, talking, eating, playing, and working. On starting school a girl often identifies with a woman teacher, but many boys continue to identify with their fathers, for generally there are no male teachers in the primary grades. In the second and third grade and as the children learn to read, they often identify with characters they read about—girls with women characters and boys with men. A boy at this level who receives physical education instruction from a man teacher whom he admires is likely to identify with him. A boy's most popular elementary teacher is often his physical education teacher, in many cases his only male teacher.

As a child grows older his parents become relatively less important as models to imitate. His social groups widen and he may pattern his behavior after an age-mate or an older child of the same sex. States- men, athletes, cowboys, and adventurers often become models for boys in the upper elementary grades. These men may be in direct contact with a boy or they may exist only through his experience with reading, movies, radio, or television. Girls in the upper elementary grades often select as their ideal a famous woman of history, a nurse, or a teacher. With adolescence, girls often shift to glamorous women—the movie star, the ballet dancer, the poetess, or the religious worker—and boys tend toward correspondingly glamorous men. Both boys and girls be- come more realistic in later adolescence when the need to decide on a career forces them to modify their attitudes toward adult life.

Rejection, the opposite of identification, also can occur. A child can reject a parent or teacher if the person does not offer what the child needs: satisfaction, help in overcoming rough spots, and demonstration of love even though some behavior is disapproved. The adult who gives these to a child is not likely to be rejected. Instead he will likely receive affection and cooperation from the child, and he can assume that the child will accept many of his mannerisms, attitudes, and values with- out much questioning.

The importance of identifying figures is well illustrated in modern advertising, especially that done by television. A principal technique is to have the hero or heroine endorse the product. Other techniques are embodied in statements trying to associate prestige with the product: "Scientists have found . . .," "Four out of five doctors recommend . . .," "The thinking man. . . ." So personal is this advertising that by buying the product the user feels better, because he is like whoever does the endorsing or recommending.

In at least two respects the schools have not been successful in pro- viding exemplary models; teachers too frequently have not regarded themselves as possible identifying figures for pupils, and the reading materials presented to children and youth do not contain a sufficiently broad scope of possible exemplary models to appeal to the many pupils. In Chapter 6 it was shown that three main behavior patterns of teachers were associated with desirable classroom behavior: being friendly and understanding; being responsible, businesslike, and sys- tematic; and being stimulating and imaginative. Recall the teachers you admired most. To what extent did they display one or more of the patterns above? An adult who is friendly, understanding, and imaginative is generally admired by children and youth. Although difficult (or almost impossible for some teachers), the attempt should be made to be friendly and understanding even though the student may have personal characteristics, attitudes, and values that differ markedly from those held by the teacher. It is quite certain that the student who rejects the teacher emotionally also will reject the attitudes and values proposed by the teacher.

Instructional materials used in the school also need careful examination. The basic textbooks and library books, including fiction and biography, are often inadequate for many pupils because the central character is too unrealistic to serve as an exemplary model. In many books the hero is too magnificently successful and the circumstances are so different from usual life that many boys, especially from lower and upper social classes, will not imitate him. Female characters are usually of two types—highly ambitious and eminently successful or excessively kind, timid, and lacking in intelligence and ambition. Many girls do not imitate either type of heroine. Careful examination should be made of reading material to ascertain the attitudes and values engendered. For example, how many stories or biographies are available of men who have become famous through victory in war as compared with men who have worked industriously for peace? men who have shown leadership in labor organizations, teaching, and the ministry? men who have achieved eminence from wealthy as compared with poor economic backgrounds? women who have achieved prominence in the theater and music as compared to teaching, stenographic work, and homemaking? A disproportionate share of school literature depicts the lives and circumstances of only a small segment of the total population and is not representative of the family and home situations from which most children come or of the occupations and successes they will achieve as adults.

The preceding discussion emphasizes that imitation is more an affective than a cognitive process and that attitudes acquired through imitation are not given thoughtful consideration by the acquirer. For these reasons some psychologists disagree with the principle. The same psychologists agree, however, that rejection is also more emotional than intellectual, and that it is accompanied by nonacceptance of attitudes and behaviors. Because the learning of attitudes is a relevant educational objective, the principle is included in this section so that proper consideration is given to providing exemplary models for all students.

Provide Pleasant Emotional Experiences with Attitude Objects

Large units of behavior are incorporated into the observer's repertoire through imitation. This behavior is indicative of the attitudes
expressed in the behavior of the model. Informative experiences also
influence attitudes. For example, learning why there are school rules
and why they are to be obeyed affects attitudes toward both socially
approved and disapproved behavior. Imitation and incorporating informative experiences into the cognitive structure will have more permanent and lasting effects upon attitudes when the attitude behavior
is reinforced. Positive reinforcers strengthen attitudes through associating pleasantness with attitude. This is accomplished best when there is
close temporal contiguity of the reinforcer with the behavior indicative
of the attitude. Further, after an attitude becomes internalized, behavior not in accordance with it produces anxiety. In this manner
reinforcements eventually are not needed for the continuation of behavior that is in line with an internalized attitudinal system.

Although the withholding of a positive reinforcer and the administration of punishment tend to force compliance and to inhibit the punished
responses, positive reinforcers more reliably strengthen desired responses. The hedonistic principle carries strong weight in the learning
of attitudes. If a teacher wishes to have children develop favorable
attitudes toward school, he will make the classroom more attractive and
comfortable, present a good personal appearance and dress attractively,
show warmth and enthusiasm to the children, demonstrate interest in
the subject matter, and make it possible for each child to experience
success with some school learning tasks. If the opposite of these five
things is done, it is certain that some children will develop unfavorable
attitudes toward both the classroom and the school.

In those instances where unfavorable attitudes are already firmly
fixed, neither pleasant emotional experiences with the attitude object
nor objective information changes the attitude; students' self-perceptions and feelings toward themselves must change. For example, unfavorable, firmly fixed race attitudes are more effectively modified
through attempting to give insight into the self than through giving
insight into the objective nature of the problem. Individuals highest in
ego defensiveness were most resistant to accepting insight into self
(12). Also making persons aware that important values can be attained
by changing their attitudes tends to result in changed attitudes except
with persons who are extremely prejudiced (3). Thus, modification and
change are possible if the individual can accept a change as being more

pleasant or rewarding than holding fast to the already established attitude.

Extend Informative Experiences

Accurate information about the attitude object facilitates its initial acquisition. However, if the attitude is already firmly established and the individual has openly expressed himself on it, further information may do little to modify the attitude. The means of acquiring information are manifold and include direct experiences with persons, ideas, and objects, reading books and other material, listening to radio, watching television, seeing sound movie films, and the like. The effects of these different means of influencing attitudes are now considered.

Three information-giving procedures were used with students to ascertain which might be most effective in changing attitudes toward and acceptance of persons of different nationality backgrounds (7). First, members of the various majority and minority groups were grouped together on the basis of expressed interests in particular work and play activities. Second, factual information about various nationality groups was presented to the students in lectures, discussions, and reading assignments. Third, the students as classroom groups were provided a minimum amount of factual information but were given a variety of short stories, novels, and plays to read; some informal dramatizing also was done. The third method achieved the best results; in the two schools in which it was used there was a greater increase in acceptance between majority and minority groups than in the schools in which the first two approaches were used.

One possible difficulty in arranging direct experiences with the attitude objects is that unpleasant emotions may be experienced and unfavorable information gathered. Having children from residential or rural areas visit the section of a city where a minority group is concentrated may result in even less favorable and more prejudiced attitudes toward that group. Similarly, taking children from large cities into a barren rural area may not result in more favorable attitudes toward life in the country.

Under various exchange programs between the United States and other countries, high school and college students are studying in foreign countries on the assumption that these exchange programs will result in better understanding and more favorable attitudes (14, 15). An experimental group of Hollins College students studied in Europe for one year. Each student lived with a French family during the school year and spent the summer session traveling throughout Europe. The students left in the middle of their sophomore year and returned in the middle of their junior year. A control group of students from the same class at Hollins did not go to Europe. In most attitudes and personality chararacteristics there was little or no difference between the groups who studied abroad and those who remained at home. However, the effect of a year abroad, in comparison with the year at home, led to (1) a slight decrease in prejudice, (2) a tendency toward the development of less favorable feelings toward Americans and more favorable feelings toward Europeans, (3) more submissive social adjustment, (4) less independence, and (5) the development of higher social values.

Changes in attitude may accompany studying a particular course or unit. Taking any one of three science courses—biology, chemistry, or anatomy—resulted in more acceptant attitudes toward evolution at all high school grade levels (2). Ninth-grade students who took no science course did not change their attitudes, and the ninth-graders as a group at the start of the freshman year tended toward nonacceptance of evolution. In a college setting, a marked shift in the direction of more favorable attitudes resulted from a two-week workshop for teachers and other educational personnel (23).

Although changes in attitudes sometimes occur even after short instructional periods, new information in itself does not always direct opinions in the desired direction. When the distance is small between the individual's own attitude and that presented to him, he judges the information as fair and factual; however, with increasing distance between the individual's attitude and that presented in the information, the favorable judgment is sharply reduced, and the information is perceived as propagandistic and unfair. In addition, individuals whose attitudes or whose opinions are greatly different from those advocated in the information do not change their opinions or attitudes (8). The type of information presented also affects the modification of attitudes (9). Information which advocated the most extreme change had more effect in bringing about the change than did that which advocated moderate or a small amount of change. Further, the number of persons changing in the direction opposite to that advocated was about the same for the three degrees of advocated change.

Implementation of Extended Informative Experience. Let us examine how this principle was implemented. In a class in Problems of Democracy, one unit of study was the Cold War. A beginning teacher decided that two appropriate attitudes for the students to learn were that the problems of the Cold War could not be solved through atomic warfare and that the continued existence of civilization depended upon the settlement of the Cold War. Various means were used to extend informative experiences with the attitudes during a period of about two weeks:

1. A movie on the bombing of Nagasaki and Hiroshima was shown and was followed with a whole-class discussion of the effects that could be wrought with modern bombs and missiles.
2. Comments of Arnold Toynbee about atomic warfare and editorial comments in local newspapers related thereto were duplicated and discussed by small groups within the class. Subsequent reports were made to the whole class on the most important ideas.
3. Chapters in the basic text were assigned, discussed, and related to the current scene and topic.
4. Two filmstrips were shown and discussed by the whole class and in small groups. One dealt with the ideological conflict between Russia and China; the other covered the major Cold War conflicts and confrontations between the Communist countries and the Western countries for the period 1945 to 1963.
5. A minister, visiting the United States from West Germany, gave a vivid account of what life is like under Fascism and Communism. His father also had been a minister, imprisoned during the Nazi regime. The minister's original remarks were received with rapt attention and the question period following his presentation was lively.
6. An essay was assigned on the topic "How can I help to bring about a more peaceful world and better understanding among my fellow men?" This required the student to seek more information. Many responses were given other than joining the Peace Corps.

Use Group Techniques to Facilitate Commitment

We have now outlined a sequence by which behavior indicative of certain attitudes is acquired and strengthened. Earlier in the chapter the importance of primary groups in the formation of attitudes was indicated. Among school-age children, informal groups are highly important sources of information, reinforcement, and emotional release. As we expect and as it should be, parents and teachers become relatively less influential in the life of the child as he grows older and as he identifies with his generation. All of us are aware that wishing to be a member of an age group is a powerful motivating force. It is in the informal groups of childhood and adolescence that many attitudes are tested out, and eventually the individual commits himself to living up to standards implied by the attitude. Teachers have the opportunity to influence attitude development through working with children in groups within and outside regular classroom hours. Deserving special consideration in this regard are role playing, sound films and discussions, and group decision making (Fig. 10.3).

1. Role Playing

2. Sound films and discussion

3. Group decision making

Fig. 10.3. Group interaction encourages commitment to positive attitudes and values.

ROLE PLAYING

Role playing in various forms is unrehearsed dramatization dealing with a social or psychological problem. In most role-playing situations students use only the information they already have, but in some instances information is provided to the students. There is no rehearsing, no memorizing of lines, and no coaching as in ordinary dramatic presentations. Role playing in classroom settings is generally based on informal class discussions dealing with a wide variety of topics. The students informally dramatize such behavorial characteristics as shyness, aggressiveness, good manners, prejudice, courtesy, and dishonesty. Also, they can carry out roles drawn from novels, short stories, newspaper stories, and plays which the class has studied.

Role playing markedly affected ethnocentricism in college students (4). Each role player was instructed to advocate in the community an educational program completely in favor of integrating Negroes into the community in connection with defense work. A test was administered to the students about two weeks before and again seven to ten days after the role playing. The pretest and posttest scores indicated a decided shift in attitudes in the direction of the role playing; that is, the students who played the roles became more favorable toward having Negroes move into a white neighborhood and also became more favorably inclined toward Negroes in general. A control group of students who did not see the role playing did not change attitudes; students who observed but did not participate in the role playing did not shift their attitudes to the extent that the participants did. In this experiment, as in role playing generally, the participants expressed their feelings as they portrayed a role and presented information. Role playing thus combines informational and emotional experiences related to the underlying attitudes.

In another situation college students were first given a test to sample their opinions about international organizations, and on the basis of this test the students with extreme attitudes—favorable and unfavorable—were identified (24). After identifying these students and assigning them to one of the three groups—role playing, observer, and nonparticipant—role-playing situations were arranged so that each role player assumed a role which advocated attitudes directly opposite to his as expressed on the test. The role playing had no effect upon the attitudes as measured by a test two days after the role playing was completed. By the design of the experiment it was impossible to ascertain what might have resulted had the students been chosen to play roles in harmony with their originally expressed attitudes.

In another situation role players were presented a prepared outline of information (10). The control group received the same written information and listened to the role playing. The role players changed opinions in the direction of the role played more than did the control group. The role players whose attitudes changed markedly displayed considerable improvisation of the supplied information in their presentations and appeared well satisfied with their oral presentations. This suggests that changes resulting from role playing may come about because the role player is impressed by his own arguments, illustrations, and the convincing appeals that he uses to stimulate others; or the role player interprets his performance as a rewarding experience that gives him emotional satisfaction. The latter factor was felt to be important in the change because the students who indicated immediately after role playing that their performance had been satisfactory were subsequently found to have changed their opinions considerably.

The effect of role playing on children and youth of school age is not clearly established. It is hypothesized, however, that role playing would probably be more powerful in helping individuals to acquire new attitudes than in changing attitudes already firmly fixed, and that it might be more effective with school-age children than with adults. Some cautions in the use of role playing also are necessary. One should not put a student in a role-playing situation in which he would feel highly uncomfortable. For example, it would be most unfortunate to have a shy, withdrawing child try to play the role of a shy, withdrawing child or of a boisterous, aggressive child before his classmates. The favored procedure for a teacher who might not know the children well is to discuss with the whole class the role-playing situation, including the various characters or roles, and then to ask for volunteers.

SOUND FILMS AND GROUP DISCUSSION

The sound motion picture and television, properly used, influence attitudes in that information is presented, identifying figures are shown, and pleasant emotions are experienced by the observer. Discussion both before and after the film presentation is needed in order to profit most from it. Direct involvement of the pupils in the discussion also is needed.

An exciting experiment was carried out with high school students (17). Students who scored high, middle, and low in ethnocentrism were identified and were then assigned randomly to one of three groups. One group saw a film unfavorable to ethnocentrism but did not discuss it; another group saw and discussed the film; the control group neither saw nor discussed the film. Five important results were obtained. First, a significant reduction in ethnocentric attitudes occurred in the group who had seen the film and followed the viewing with discussion; however, those students who did not actively take part in the discussion after seeing the film did not change attitudes. Second, the stability of the attitude change after an elapsed time of one month was higher for the discussion groups than for the film-alone group; the film-alone group had regressed significantly toward their original attitudes. Third, the amount of information learned from the film and discussion was related to the degree of ethnocentrism held by the individual—the higher the degree of ethnocentrism, the less he learned. Fourth, active participants in the film-plus-discussion group learned more from the film than did students who were passive during the discussion. Fifth, no significant relationship was found between intelligence and attitude.

Discussion without films also is useful for presenting and clarifying information. In small-group or whole-class discussions, pupils have the opportunity to try out their ideas with one another and with the teacher. In this trying out certain expressions and behavior are confirmed, others are denied. Beyond this, classroom discussions serve the useful purpose of helping learners evaluate propaganda. Many agencies and groups are using television presentations, often filmed or recorded, to influence people's attitudes on controversial issues. By definition, there are at least two sides or points of view on a controversial issue. One can easily be misled by being acquainted with only one point of view. Whether the controversy is presented by an educational film, a commercial film, or television, students at the time of graduation from high school or earlier should be competent in checking whether facts representing both sides of the issue have been included.

GROUP DECISION MAKING

There is a vast difference between being presented information about appropriate and inappropriate conduct and arriving at group decision. When an individual shares in making a decision, he abides by that decision to a greater extent than when he does not take an active part. In group decision making the individual members are face to face and do not feel separated from others as they do when they listen to a lecture, read a book, or view a television production. Some of the effects of decision making in groups compared with other means merit special attention (13).

In an attempt to get housewives to use meats that they were not using—beef hearts, sweetbreads, and kidneys—researchers presented information in attractively arranged lectures to one group; another group, led by a trained leader, discussed the possibility of using these meats until a decision was reached. A subsequent check showed that only 3 percent of those who listened to the lecture were using the recommended meats, but 32 percent of those who shared in the group decision were. In another experiment some groups of housewives were presented lectures for the purpose of increasing their home consumption of milk. Other groups were led in discussion and arrived at a group decision. The same information about milk consumption was presented to both the lecture and decision making groups. In this experiment, about 45 percent of those who had shared in decision making and about 15 percent of those who heard the lectures were using more whole milk two and four weeks later. In a third experiment completely individualized instruction about the importance of cod liver oil and orange juice in the baby's diet was given to a group of mothers preparing to leave the hospital. Other mothers participated in group discussions, leading to decisions about using the juice and oil. The individualized instruction was managed well; however, after two and four weeks the mothers who participated in the group decision were carrying out the practices recommended by the hospital nutritionist to a greater extent than those who received individualized instruction.

The groups in the preceding experiments were small, usually from 6 to 17 persons. This small number of members permitted relatively free discussion. It is possible that attitudes and behavior were changed by the give and take in the discussions, the reinforcing and negating of expressions by the members, and the informational content and emotional commitment involved in the decision making. In the school, situations could be arranged whereby a large majority of the student body, organized into small groups, would agree to keep the corridors relatively clean and quiet, to get to class on time, to start work promptly when getting to class, to respect the ideas and property of others, and to display many other behaviors implied in the attitudes listed earlier in this chapter. The result would be less need for the policing and rule pronouncing now required in many schools. Commitment to socially approved attitudes is sorely needed.

Arrange for Appropriate Practice

This principle carries the same meaning as in previous chapters. Attitudes are not acquired through memorizing and talking about verbal statements. Rather, from many specific experiences the individual integrates the meaning and feeling components into increasingly larger and more stable behavior patterns. The school that proposes to influence pupil attitudes must provide appropriate practice contexts within the classroom, the school building, and the school-community environs. If having pupils like one another is desired, what kind of practice opportunities might be arranged? First of all, the teacher, recognizing the possibility of being an exemplary model, makes certain that he manifests lively, favorable interest in the pupils. Second, as the pupils show their liking for one another, the teacher confirms or reinforces these responses with verbal statements, positive remarks about the behavior of good friends, an approving nod, a smile, or other gestures. Third, the teacher does not reject any child or condone rejection. To accomplish the latter, many adjustments are needed. The child who comes to school dirty is sent to the washroom to clean up when he first arrives at school; a suitable task is found for the slow-learning child; the highly aggressive child is given opportunity to express his aggressive feelings against indestructible objects or in other ways; the withdrawing child is helped to develop some skill or interest gradually and then is incorporated into smaller groups of two or three and finally into the total classroom group.

Kindergarten and primary school teachers are generally successful in helping most children make at least one or two good friends in the classroom group; so are a smaller proportion of intermediate and upper-grade teachers. High school and college teachers frequently do not accept this as a worthwhile objective and are unconcerned or are unaware that one or two children may be completely rejected by the rest of the class. Some boys and girls sit through five or six high school classes daily, knowing that among all members of the various classes there is not a single other adolescent whom they can call a friend.

Consider for further clarification one of the values listed previously in the chapter—to make a unique contribution to society. The child's society is the classroom or other school group. Each pupil is helped to identify something unique he can accomplish for the group. In the primary grades the "conversation" or "sharing" periods serve this purpose. During these periods the children report out-of-school incidents or bring objects to school, and each has opportunity to bring something of high interest to the classroom group. In the intermediate grades making a mural, decorating the room, and finding and bringing together various collections provide practice opportunities. In high school and college classes the tendency is not to engage in these sharing activities in regular class settings. Students make their unique contributions to a group in extraclass or cocurricular activities such as the school play, the annual, the athletic events, and the many clubs.

We now combine three attitudes for discussion—respect for others, respect for property, and honesty. What does practice of these attitudes mean? High school students are given opportunity and responsibility through the student council or student government to practice these attitudes. One applies the three attitudes named above by leaving lockers unlocked, the idea being that if students accept the attitudes they will not steal property from the lockers of their schoolmates. After all, if students cannot practice these attitudes in school, how can they be expected not to steal from strangers in the larger community outside the school?

Encourage Independent Attitude Cultivation

At some point the individual might decide that he would get along better with himself and others if he could acquire a friendly attitude toward his associates. How can this be done? The process of acquiring a new attitude is much the same as acquiring any new habitual way of behaving, for example, brushing one's teeth after eating, or writing more legibly, or spelling more correctly. One begins with intent and practices. Carefully considering the importance of the attitude in one's life, deciding to carry out the behavior implied by the attitude, allowing no exception in the behavior, and taking every opportunity to act upon the new attitude lead to stability and eventual incorporation of the attitude without conscious effort.

It is easier to read the above words than to carry out what they imply. A deeply ingrained habit, such as cigarette smoking or writing rapidly and illegibly, is not easily broken. A firmly established attitude, such as a prejudice in the area of religion, race, or politics, is perhaps equally difficult to change deliberately. Thus, the above suggestions are more applicable to the acquisition and establishment of a new attitude than to extinction of one already firmly established. This has serious implications for teachers and teaching. If for any reason a prospective teacher cannot acquire a liking for the subject matter, for teaching duties generally, or for living in a classroom with pupils and cannot deliberately change his own attitudes, he should consider another career.

THE PROBLEM OF EXTREME ATTITUDES

For no apparent reason a child may have an aversion to some object in the room; for example, chalk or paste. Another child may have deeply engrained prejudices against those of a different race, religion, or nationality background, including the teacher. Many youth attending high school have been apprehended for delinquent behavior and regularly report to a parole officer or social worker. Some groups in the United States hold extremely destructive attitudes toward other groups. Conformity or agreement upon all attitudes and values is, of course, not the goal. However, people must have a sufficiently large core of common attitudes and values in order to live together reasonably well. A balance somehow must be found between encouraging uniqueness in individuals and requiring compliance to reasonable group standards and to the codified laws of the land.

In working with children who demonstrate extreme attitudes, the teacher first does all that is possible within the classroom setting. He is an understanding teacher, a person who shows interest in the student as a human being as well as a learner of certain subject matter. He maintains an open relationship with the student, makes a special effort to serve as an exemplary model, uses films and reading materials that present exemplary models, reinforces any expression of desirable attitudes, arranges group activities in which the student may arrive at a better understanding of himself and of socially accepted attitudes, and tries to get desired responses substituted for the undesirable. If these best efforts fail, help is sought from school psychologists, counselors, social workers, and others. The history of racial and religious prejudice throughout the world suggests that all the resources of a community must be mobilized to develop the attitudes necessary for the survival of civilization.

SUMMARY

Attitudes and values are among the most important outcomes learned in school for they are important determiners of how the individual reacts to situations and also to what he seeks in life. Thus, attitudes and values serve both as responses and as motivational forces. The main difference between an attitude and a concept is that the former directly influences the individual's acceptance or rejection of attitude objects —ideas, persons, things, situations. Attitudes, to a greater extent than concepts and psychomotor abilities, are acquired through conditioning and identification. Membership in primary groups, such as the family and informal neighborhood and school groups, markedly influences attitude development.

Some attitudes are learned early and become more firmly established with increasing experience; others undergo change. Attitude learning and modification have been demonstrated at all school levels, but more so in children than in adolescents and adults. Pleasant feelings, success, and rewards produce favorable and lasting attitudes; unpleasant feeling, failure, and punishments lead to unfavorable attitudes and also, in some cases, to the extinction of previously favorable attitudes.

When agreement is reached concerning which attitudes children and youth should learn in school, a program of instruction can be organized that will result in efficient learning of attitudes. The learning of attitudes is facilitated through (1) providing exemplary models, (2) providing pleasant emotional experiences, (3) extending informative experiences, (4) using group techniques, (5) arranging for appropriate practice, and (6) encouraging independent attitude cultivation. These principles, as the discussions throughout the chapter imply, are applicable to all outcomes in the affective domain—*tastes, attitudes, preferences, values, interests,* and *motives.*

QUESTIONS AND ACTIVITIES

1. a. Discuss the differences among tastes or preferences, attitudes, and values.
   b. Give three examples of each applied to yourself at present.
2. Discuss the affective, informational, and group bases of attitudes, applying the discussion to attitudes or values which you hold.
3. Based on your personal experiences, discuss the extent to which attitudes are learned through imitation and conditioning.
4. a. Identify and discuss two or three conclusions about attitude formation and modification during elementary school years
   b. during high school years
   c. during college years
   d. Why are attitudes less stable than concepts or psychomotor skills?
5. a. Study and define the 14 statements of values on page 358 and clarify their meanings.

Then arrange them in order, from highest to lowest, on the basis of their importance in your life.
   b. Arrange them from highest to lowest on the basis of their importance to adults generally.
6. Classify statements 15–28, on pages 358–359, as A, B, or C: A to mean the school should encourage the behavior in all students, B to mean the school should encourage the behavior in the majority of students, and C to mean the school should encourage the behavior in a minority of the students.
7. Discuss the extent to which education should clarify meanings of and provide informative experiences about attitudes rather than indoctrinate.
8. Discuss the means and extent to which identification is important in acquiring attitudes, relating the discussion to:
   a. your own attitudes

375

b. learning of attitudes in school
9. Why are pleasant emotional experiences especially important in the modification of attitudes?
10. Compare the effects on students of listening to and discussing statements of attitudes with discussing the statements and practicing what they imply for behavior.
11. a. Indicate possible uses of each of the following in school situations:
    role playing

sound films and group discussion
group decision making
b. Under what conditions might each of the above produce attitudes opposite to those which the teacher desires the students to acquire?
12. Discuss the possibilities of deliberate cultivation of an attitude. Attempt to identify and deliberately cultivate an attitude.

SUGGESTIONS FOR FURTHER READING

Allport, G. W. Values and our youth. *Teachers Coll. Rec.*, 1961, **63**, 211–219. (In Grinder, 1963, 17–27; Fullagar, et al., 1964, 289–299; and Seidman, 1965, 257–264.)

Bandura, A. Social learning through imitation. *Nebraska symposium on motivation.* Lincoln: Univer. of Nebraska Press, 1962, pp. 211–274. (Excerpt in Page, 1964, 274–288.)

Bostrom, R. N., J. W. Vlandis, & M. E. Rosenbaum. Grades as reinforcing contingencies and attitude change. *J. educ. Psychol.*, 1961, **52**, 112–115. (Revised under the title "Grades as reinforcers in the production of attitude change" in DeCecco, 1963, 129–135.)

Bowers, Patricia, & P. London. Developmental correlates of role-playing ability. *Child Develpm.*, 1965, **36**, 499–508.

deCharms, R., & G. H. Moeller. Values expressed in American children's readers: 1800–1950. *J. abnorm. soc.*

Psychol., 1962, **64**, 136–142. (In Kuhlen & Thompson, 1963, 264–273.)

Janis, I. L., & B. T. King. The influence of role playing on opinion change. *J. abnorm. soc. Psychol.*, 1954, **49**, 211–218. (In Page, 1964, 262–273.)

McKeachie, W. J. Individual conformity to attitudes of classroom groups. *J. abnorm. soc. Psychol.*, 1954, **49**, 282–289.

Pettigrew, T. F. Regional differences in anti-Negro prejudice. *J. abnorm. soc. Psychol.*, 1959, **59**, 28–36. (In Rosenblith & Allinsmith, 1962, 180–188.)

Rogers, C. R. The significance of the self–regarding attitudes and perceptions. In M. L. Reymert (Ed.), *Feelings and emotions.* New York: McGraw-Hill, 1950, pp. 374–382.

Staats, A. W., & Carolyn K. Staats. Attitudes established by classical conditioning. *J. abnorm. soc. Psychol.*, 1958, **57**, 37–40. (In Staats, 1964, 322–328.)

REFERENCES

1. Bandura, A., & R. Walters. *Social learning and personality development.* New York: Holt, Rinehart, & Winston, 1963.
2. Barkley, K. L. Influence of college science courses on the development of attitudes toward evaluation. *J. appl. Psychol.*, 1948, **32**, 200–208.
3. Carlson, E. R. Attitude change through modification of attitude structure. *J. abnorm. soc. Psychol.*, 1956, **52**, 256–261.
4. Culbertson, Frances M. Modification of an emotionally held attitude through role playing. *J. abnorm. soc. Psychol.*, 1957, **54**, 230–233.

5. Estvan, F. J., & Elizabeth W. Estvan. *The child's world: His social perception.* New York: Putnam, 1959.

6. Gesell, A., Frances L. Ilg, & Louise B. Ames. *Youth: The years from ten to sixteen.* New York: Harper & Row, 1956.

7. Hayes, Margaret L., & Mary E. Conklin. Intergroup attitudes and experimental change. *J. exp. Educ.,* 1953, **22,** 19–36.

8. Hovland, C. I., O. J. Harvey, & M. Sherif. Assimilation and contrast effects in reactions to communication and attitude change. *J. abnorm. soc. Psychol.,* 1957, **55,** 244–252.

9. Hovland, C. I., & H. A. Pritzker. Extent of opinion change as a function of amount of change advocated. *J. abnorm. soc. Psychol.,* 1957, **54,** 257–261.

10. Janis, I. L., & B. T. King. The influence of role playing on opinion change. *J. abnorm. soc. Psychol.,* 1954, **49,** 211–218.

11. Kagan, J. The concept of identification. *Psychol. Rev.,* 1958, **65,** 296–305.

12. Katz, D., I. Sarnoff, & C. McClintock. Ego-defense and attitude change. *Hum. Relat.,* 1956, **9,** 27–45.

13. Lewin, K. Group decision and social change. In E. Maccoby, T. M. Newcomb, & E. L. Hartley (Eds.), *Readings in social psychology.* (3rd ed.) New York: Holt, Rinehart and Winston, 1958, pp. 197–211.

14. McGuigan, F. J. Psychological changes related to intercultural experiences. *Psychol. Rep.,* 1958, **4,** 55–60.

15. McGuigan, F. J. Further study of psychological changes related to intercultural experiences. *Psychol. Rep.,* 1959, **5,** 244–248.

16. McKeachie, W. J. Individual conformity to attitudes of classroom groups. *J. abnorm. soc. Psychol.,* 1954, **49,** 282–289.

17. Mitnick, L. L., & E. McGinnies. Influencing ethnocentrism in small discussion groups through a film communication. *J. abnorm. soc. Psychol.,* 1958, **56,** 82–90.

18. Mussen, P. H., J. J. Conger, & J. Kagan. *Child development and personality.* New York: Harper & Row, 1963.

19. Plant, W. T. Changes in ethnocentrism associated with a four-year college education. *J. educ. Psychol.,* 1958, **49,** 162–165.

20. Plant, W. T. Sex, intelligence, and sorority or fraternity membership and changes in ethnocentrism over a two-year period. *J. genet. Psychol.,* 1958, **93,** 53–57.

21. Radke, M. J., H. G. Trager, & H. Davis. Social perceptions and attitudes of children. *Genet. Psychol. Monogr.,* 1949, **40,** 327–447.

22. Remmers, H. H., & A. J. Drucker. How high school youth believe children should be brought up. In H. H. Remmers, H. N. Tivlin, D. G. Ryans, & E. R. Ryden (Eds.), *Growth, teaching and learning: A book of readings.* New York: Harper & Row, 1957, pp. 32–53.

23. Shaw, J., H. J. Klausmeier, A. Luker, & H. Reid. Changes occurring in teacher-pupil attitudes during a two-weeks guidance workshop. *J. appl. Psychol.,* 1952, **36,** 304–306.

24. Stanley, J. C., & H. J. Klausmeier. Opinion constancy after formal role playing. *J. soc. Psychol.,* 1957, **46,** 11–18.

25. Stendler, Celia B. Social class differences in parental attitudes toward school at grade I level. *Child Develpm.,* 1951, **22,** 36–46.

26. Webster, H. Changes in attitudes during college. *J. educ. Psychol.,* 1958, **49,** 109–117.

27. Wilson, W. C. Development of ethnic attitudes in adolescence. *Child Develpm.,* 1963, **34,** 247–256.

CHAPTER 11

Personality Integration
and Character

ONE'S TASTES and preferences for specific objects and events merge into more inclusive attitudes as shown earlier in Chapter 2. The attitudes toward a broader class of objects and events merge into a value system of greater permanency, generality, and significance to the self and society. Eventually a network of values is conceptualized and organized into a complex system. With organization the more specific sets typical of attitudes and values are transformed into generalized sets. Generalized sets emerge from a hierarchically organized system of value complexes and lay the basis of characterization. So pervasive is the behavior associated with a stable value system that it characterizes the individual almost completely (20).

Personality integration and character are the product of the individual's value system and environment and are inferred from his behavior. The role of education in personality integration and character development may be clarified from careful study of (1) the nature of personality integration, (2) the bases of personality integration, (3) developmental trends, and (4) a model for encouraging personality integration.

As you already know, the study of personality is fascinating whether approached from introspection or from understanding and guiding children and youth. A discussion of personality, to be moderately complete, is necessarily comprehensive. Therefore, relax with this chapter. Try not to rush through it; take the pressures off yourself. Many mature, and personally secure, individuals have found this the most rewarding chapter in the book and return to it after completing the course.

NATURE OF PERSONALITY INTEGRATION

What is personality? It is a construct, or concept, that indicates the uniqueness and totality of an individual as a social being. "Personality is the dynamic organization within the individual of those psychophysical systems that determine his unique adjustment to his environment" (2, 48). Dynamic implies adaptation to changing circumstances, and organization indicates stability. Personality also may be considered as "the distinct and unique organization of traits in an individual as reflected in how he reacts to himself and others and in how they react to him, and also in how he meets frustrations and conflicts—that is, in how he adjusts to his environment" (17, 444). Close scrutiny of these two definitions leads to the conclusion that personality has more than one attribute. The principal attribute of personality is the organization of the psychophysical systems within the individual. These systems include the knowledge and skills of the individual, his values, and his motives. Other corollary attributes include the individual's reactions to others, others' reactions to him, and his methods of adjusting to his environment. As implied in the chapter title, the goal of education in both the home and school is to facilitate the development of an individual whose knowledge, skills, value system, and motives comprise an integrated whole.

A model of integrative adjustment may be summarized:

This model of integrative adjustment as characterized by self-control, personal responsibility, social responsibility, democratic social interest, and ideals must be regarded only in the most tentative fashion. Nevertheless, it does seem to take into account some realistic considerations. It avoids the impossible conception of the normal person as one who is always happy, free from conflict, and without problems. Rather, it suggests that he may often fall short of his ideals; and because of ignorance, the limitations under which an individual lives in a complex world, or the strength of immediate pressures, he may sometimes behave in ways that prove to be shortsighted or self-defeating. Consequently, he knows something of the experience of guilt at times, and because he tries to be fully aware of the risks he takes, he can hardly be entirely free from fear and worry. On the other hand, a person who is congruent to the model is likely to be one who enjoys a relatively consistent and high degree of self-respect and who elicits a predominantly positive and warm reaction from others. Moreover, it is such a person who seems to learn wisdom rather than hostile bitterness or pathologically frightened withdrawal from whatever disappointments or suffering may be his lot. . . . (**31**, 188–189).

Notice that in evaluating adjustment one must make judgments about self-control, personal responsibility, social responsibility, democratic social interest, and ideals. This means that one would not conclude that the thief, the murderer, and the delinquent are well adjusted personalities, however well they may satisfy their own needs or however rational their behavior may appear to themselves. Ethical values, including what is generally considered character, cannot be reasonably treated as separate from personality integration or integrative adjustment.

Character development usually refers to the internalization of ethical values. Separating character development from personality integration is impractical in education at home or in school. Teaching ethics unrelated to the emergent personality of the student is similar to being concerned with the student's actions but not his motives and goals. Encouraging student acceptance of ethical values is an entirely justifiable objective of education. However, this is part of the broader objective of influencing his personality.

THE BASES OF PERSONALITY INTEGRATION

The educational objective in connection with personality integration is to get a larger number of individuals who can live fairly comfortably with themselves, and who also accept a reasonable amount of responsibility for the welfare of others. On the preventive side this would reduce unhappiness and delinquency in children and youth and mental illness and criminality in adults. Pep pills and tranquilizers would disappear from the college campus. On the positive side, this objective would result in buoyant, productive individuals with much zest for life and learning. Conditions within the individual and the environment are now discussed as the bases of personality integration (Fig. 11.1).

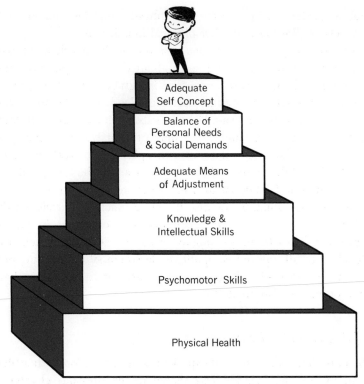

Fig. 11.1.   The building blocks of personality integration.

Health and Psychomotor Skills

We have already pointed out in Chapter 9 the nature of psycho-motor abilities and skills. Here we briefly relate these and health to personality integration.

Chronic poor health or a physical handicap may color unfavorably the individual's entire perceptions of himself and the world about him and may prevent him from acquiring adequate means of adjustment. It may interfere with, or at least limit, his acquisition or use of motor and intellectual abilities. Not everyone with a chronic illness is mal-adjusted, of course. Some people with severe handicaps such as being blind or deaf, being crippled, or being shut in for long periods of time have made excellent adjustments. These people have themselves found adequate means of adjusting, despite their handicap or illness. In gen-eral, however, the school and the home justifiably attempt to promote good physical health in children and give considerable attention to such matters as adequate nutrition, adequate facilities for rest and relaxation, protection from disease and physical injuries, and correction of a variety of illnesses and other physical impairments.

Being extremely deficient in one or more of the psychomotor skills that are common to other children of about the same age may constitute a serious block toward personality integration. Not being able to perform prestige-giving physical skills may lead the child to perceive himself in an unfavorable way. He may subsequently show withdrawal or aggressive behavior. Similarly, it may prevent his experiencing the usual give-and-take social relationships in play and recreational activities that other children normally enjoy. Just as the handicapped child with an amputated finger or arm can learn to adjust to a variety of home and school situations, so also the child much less proficient than others in such tasks as writing, singing, and engaging in physical activities can learn to adjust, but to do so he needs much help from the teacher. In all types of competitive classroom situations, low proficiency in any skill—handwriting, music, art—often results in being ignored or unfavorably treated.

Satisfying Emotional Experiences

The importance of emotional experiences in connection with attitude acquisition and modification was shown in the previous chapter. In the broader society, too, it is apparent that much behavior is governed by emotions. World leaders deliberating about peace and war in the United Nations or a family discussing a television program bring emotion as well as information to their debate. The importance of emotions to the individual and society is stated thus:

It is evident that for full-functioning, adult living, the capacity for emotional response is essential. We cannot destroy or completely suppress normal functional processes without stunting and distorting the personality and creating individuals who, because they lack capacity for emotions or are so very rigidly and unchangingly fixated, may be as menacing and destructive as the individuals who are completely impulsive and unable to regulate their emotional reactions. . . .

Emotional integrity, as a goal for adult living, requires flexible, nonrigid personalities capable of reacting emotionally, of experiencing anxiety, guilt, and hostility, when these are appropriate and legitimate responses to life experiences. An adult cannot live as a whole person, as an integrated organism-personality, capable of meeting life tasks and maintaining productive interpersonal relations unless he can react emotionally and have feelings when these are normal, wholesome reactions. But emotional integrity has to be achieved through progressive but gradual maturation of the personality from infancy onward. . . .

If we ask how we can foster emotional maturity and guard the emotional integrity of the developing child and adolescent, we cannot offer any very clear and sure answers. There are, however, some promising leads we should recognize and a few beginnings of improved procedures. Basically, the problem is to provide the child with materials, situations, practices, and relationships in which he can react emotionally when provoked, but release or express those reactions in ways that are not self-defeating (bottling up, repressing, etc.) nor socially destructive (complete permissiveness). This means providing at each stage of his development what will be adequate equivalents for earlier expressions or releases. They may be symbolic surrogates or substitutes through which an emotional reaction may be released, channeled, transformed. . . .

In our educational processes in the family, in schools, increasingly in nursery schools and kindergartens, in our high schools of varied kinds, in our colleges, in our many agencies for children and youth, in organizations for recreation and leisure time, in summer camps and work camps—everywhere there are possibilities for helping to develop wholesome personalities who from early infancy have courage, confidence in themselves, trust in people, and faith in our enduring goal values. Giving the emerging personalities of children and adolescents much-needed help to mature emotionally and to maintain their emotional integrity as organism-personalities offers the most promising and rewarding ways of developing a better social order and orienting our children as future members of a world community. . . .[1]

This point of view about the critical role of emotions in daily living may be elucidated. Emotions are felt by children as well as by adults and may be pleasant or unpleasant. As early as age 2, children have already experienced excitement, delight, elation, affection, and joy. They also have known distress, anger, disgust, and fear (5). Emotions, even the unpleasant ones, are not necessarily disorganizing, contrary to what many writers have expressed. Pleasant emotions and nonintense unpleasant emotions of short duration, such as anger and fear, mobilize the individual's physical energy (21). The extremely angry or fearful person does not think clearly but he can mobilize his physical energy effectively, to strike harder or to run faster, for example. Long-lasting unpleasant emotions do have a disorganizing effect on both physical and mental behavior, and intense unpleasant emotions of short duration disrupt intellectual processes even though they mobilize physical energy.

Knowledge and Intellectual Skills

As health and psychomotor skills affect personality integration, so do intelligence and cognitive abilities. Children and youth of low in-

[1] Reprinted by permission L. K. Frank. *Feelings and emotions: Doubleday papers in psychology.* New York: Random House, 1954, pp. 28, 32, 34, 38.

telligence and academic achievement are often less well accepted in the classroom than are those of low psychomotor abilities. Parents also seem to accept small stature, physical handicaps, and low motor performances in children more readily than lower intellectual abilities. Because of unfavorable reactions from others and less ability to deal with symbolic learning, the child of low ability may experience relatively severe adjustment problems. He has difficulty in accepting himself, especially if he feels that his teacher and classmates do not accept him. It is not surprising, therefore, that anxiety and emotional disturbance are higher in children of low and average abilities than in children of high abilities (11).

Adequate Means of Adjustment

In a broad sense, all learning is adjusting. Through learning one acquires knowledge, skills, and attitudes to meet various situations with increased efficiency and satisfaction. Learning adequate means of psychological adjustment refers more specifically to intrapersonal and interpersonal relationships, especially in frustrating situations. The appropriateness of the means of adjustment used by students can be ascertained by answering these questions:

1. Do they lead to good health and avoidance of injury?
2. Do they lead to satisfying relationships for the individual and the members of the group to which he belongs?
3. Do they lead to later successful adjustment?
4. Do they comply with codified laws?
5. Do they conform to unwritten but generally accepted ethical principles as embodied in the value system of the school and the teachers?

These questions imply that psychological adjustment is not simply accepting the status quo or conforming to present conditions and group demands with no attempt to improve oneself or to change circumstances, including the social groups in which one lives.

Individuals inevitably experience frustrating situations and their adjustment does not involve all five preceding criteria. Often, a person must choose between two desired goals or between two unpleasant tasks—a frustrating circumstance. But more often frustration is experienced when a desired goal cannot be achieved immediately. Some condition within himself, his physical environment, or his social environment prevents the individual from reaching the goal. When the block cannot be overcome with persistent effort, tension increases, especially if the goal is highly desired. A high school boy, for example, may strongly desire approval from his classmates; but his classmates do not accept him, much less give him recognition and approval. This boy, then, becomes frustrated. Different adjustments to frustrating situations of this type might be made: (1) goal-oriented effort, (2) reinterpretation of self and situation, (3) pursuit of a substitute goal, (4) withdrawal, (5) aggression and related reactions, (6) suppression and related reactions, and (7) anxiety and related reactions. These are not equally effective means of adjustment. Goal-oriented effort, reinterpretation of self and situation, and pursuit of an appropriate substitute goal generally lead to better future adjustments than do withdrawal, aggression, suppression, and anxiety. However, in some situations the last four are the only means that the individual perceives as being appropriate to maintain his physical existence or his self-esteem. Let us consider all of these means of psychological adjustment in more detail.

GOAL-DIRECTED EFFORT

A student who lacks skill in reading, swimming, public speaking, playing a musical instrument, or other skills common to his age-mates may experience frustration in his early attempts in these activities, or he may feel left out if he does not try to participate. Usually the level of skill or knowledge itself is not as critical as the way in which the individual perceives it. In situations where the person must perform but feels that he cannot do as well as he desires or as well as others expect of him, he becomes frustrated. When frustrated, he may simply continue making the same responses even though they do not achieve the desired end. In most situations an altered response is required rather than repeating the same response. To alter and improve a response requires additional information or further practice of some skill. At this point the problem-solving approach to social and emotional problems can be as productive as it is when applied to more purely intellectual problems such as those encountered in science, mathematics, English, and other subject-matter fields. Once the new information or the higher-level skills are acquired, a situation which was frustrating can, when encountered again, be a source of satisfaction. Resolute trying is to be encouraged. Goal-oriented effort toward achievable goals is socially approved and, if developed in younger children, should prove useful throughout life.

REINTERPRETING SELF AND SITUATION

One difficulty in applying problem-solving techniques to frustrating interpersonal problems is that self-esteem cannot easily be maintained while the individual is securing information or developing the higher-level skill. The adolescent who is fearful of having to be the announcer of an assembly program hesitates to ask for help from his teacher or classmates, feeling that this would lower his status in the eyes of those who selected him. Starting in the elementary grades, many children will not attempt a new activity in a group situation for fear of presenting an unfavorable performance or appearance in the presence of others.

In many situations where the individual feels inadequate, one means of adjustment is through a better understanding of oneself and the situation. If the classroom is a nurturing environment, as it properly should be, the student recognizes that the teacher and classmates are helpful people. They want to help him learn and are not negatively critical. The teacher can do much to create this type of environment and to facilitate better understanding. Obviously, if the teacher often disapproves or encourages class members to be highly critical of one another, better understanding of self and the situation by a frustrated student will achieve negative rather than positive results.

PURSUIT OF A SUBSTITUTE GOAL

Sometimes effort to reach an unattainable goal is stopped, and an attainable goal is substituted. Some who try out for the athletic team, the play, the music festival, the art exhibit are not accepted. Frustration can be quite intense for those who highly desire to be accepted but are rejected. In some cases, continued trying may lead to acceptance; in other cases, the teacher's best judgment may be that the individual does not and probably will not have the needed knowledge, skills, and other characteristics to be accepted. These latter individuals need help in identifying and accepting substitute goals that are attainable.

In helping students find appropriate substitute goals, one has at least three concerns: to make certain that a student does not give up his original goal, if he has reasonable possibility of success; to try to find a substitute goal, if a substitute seems advisable, which will help the student satisfy the same needs as his original goal; to be particularly careful about suggesting a substitute that involves little or no opportunity for achieving an equally desirable end. For example, the tenth-grader who wants to be a scientist but who is having difficulty in chemistry should not be encouraged to accept a substitute goal if there is reason to believe that he may do better in this and other science courses with improved or more persistent efforts. If this student has, with great effort, performed at a mediocre level in previous science and mathematics courses, a substitute goal for course work in high school and an eventual career must be considered. Perhaps the student's interest in science could be related to mechanical drawing, advertising, or the like. Instead of the more difficult science and mathematics courses, general courses could be substituted. It would be unwise, however, to deny the student any goal in connection with science by not permitting him to take any science courses in his last three years of high school.

WITHDRAWAL

To avoid bodily injury and maintain physical health we must avoid many harmful situations. We do not dive into deep water unless we can swim, nor do we plan a long trip in an automobile when the roads are icy. Sometimes we also must avoid situations which might be detrimental to our emotional well-being. Many adults deliberately excuse themselves from a discussion if they know that someone in the group is likely to become emotionally upset or abusive. If a person already has experienced unpleasant emotions in a first situation, he reasonably avoids the same situation until he can acquire knowledge or skills to meet it more adequately. But the individual, facing many potentially harmful situations daily, cannot avoid or withdraw from all of them and be reasonably well adjusted. Escape from meeting important life situations by chronic and repeated withdrawal eventually leads to severe maladjustment.

Permitting or even encouraging occasional withdrawal achieves better results than continuous forcing. The high school girl who comes to class in an ill-fitting dress or who feels that her appearance for any reason will be pitied or disapproved by classmates should not be forced to rise when speaking or reciting. Many elementary, high school, and college girls come from economic backgrounds that do not permit large expenditure on clothing, hairdressers, and other niceties that some of their classmates may enjoy. Too, some children do not go on vacation trips or engage in other prestigious activities during the summer recess; older ones may work at many jobs for little money or idle away time because they cannot find work. For this reason, if there is class discussion of the interesting things done during the summer, participation in the discussion should be voluntary, not forced. Potentially frustrating and personality-damaging situations should be handled in the same way as physically dangerous situations. Children should be taught the information and skills needed to cope with these difficult situations.

AGGRESSION AND RELATED REACTIONS

Aggression, as used here, designates hostility directed against the perceived source of frustration—usually another person, but at times an object or oneself. Aggressive reactions are hostile attacks with the purpose of removing or injuring the source of the frustration. Aggression with physical reactions is often observed in smaller children; one child takes a toy from another and hitting, biting, scratching, gouging, or hair-pulling ensues. In older children and adults, aggression generally takes the form of verbal attacks.

Figure 11.2 shows a sequence of aggression and counter-aggression between two individuals. Bill, frustrated by Henry (A), attacks him (B). Henry strikes back (C); Bill retaliates more strongly (D); but Henry overpowers him (E). Bill, in turn, may withdraw or acquiesce

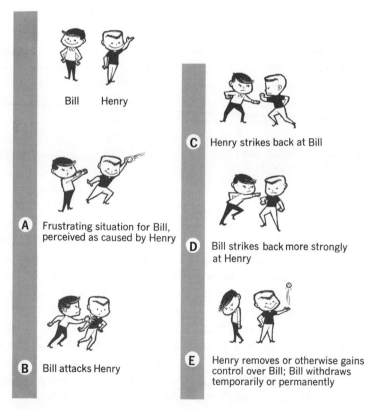

Bill   Henry

C Henry strikes back at Bill

A Frustrating situation for Bill, perceived as caused by Henry

D Bill strikes back more strongly at Henry

B Bill attacks Henry

E Henry removes or otherwise gains control over Bill; Bill withdraws temporarily or permanently

Fig. 11.2.   Sequence of frustration, aggression, and counteraggression.

outwardly, or both boys may reinterpret their attitudes toward themselves and the situation and return to the status preceding the frustrating situation. In verbal situations, aggression does not stop after its first expression. On the contrary, when the individual does not perceive his initial verbal attacks as eliminating the perceived source of frustration, aggression increases (10).

Aggressive reactions in American culture are widespread and, at least in younger children, are approved by many adults. Quite early in life, children recognize their own physical strength and verbal abilities, and some learn to achieve their ends primarily through aggressive acts. Solutions attained by superior force are accompanied by submission or lack of resistance in others. In many situations, the weaker individual cannot strike back against the frustrating person in the position of authority. This often leads to displaced aggression. The child, frustrated by the teacher but unable to withdraw from the situation, does not strike back at the teacher physically or verbally. Instead, he tears up his book, breaks his pencil, slams a door, and the like. Or, on arriving home, he may kick his dog—not because the dog has hurt him but because he must show his superiority in a fashion similar to the teacher's power over him. Also, the individual who cannot strike back against a more powerful figure may turn his aggressive feeling inward, blame himself, or otherwise punish himself as a means of relieving his tension.

Response to aggression varies with the situation and the personality of the individual. In an experimentally arranged situation, aggressive behavior increased from the first four to the last four trials with a corresponding decrease in submissive–complaisant behavior in all children (22). Young children with high power-dominance needs showed more aggressive reactions than did children with high affection needs. The children with high affection needs showed less increase in aggressive behavior and more submissive–complaisant behavior. The boys as a group demonstrated more aggressive and less submissive–complaisant behavior than girls. Also, children who had attended a permissive experimental preschool for a longer period of time exhibited higher aggression and lower submissive behavior during frustration than did children who had very recently come to the school.

Personally secure and insecure college students also varied in their aggressive reactions to an experimentally induced frustration (3). The insecure group was more extrapunative—that is, they showed greater hostility or greater aggression against persons or things than did the more secure group. There was no difference between the two groups in the extent to which they blamed or punished themselves. One concludes from both experiments that children of preschool age with a high affection need and secure college students less frequently resort to aggressive reactions in frustrating circumstances than do children with high-dominance needs and personally insecure college students.

SUPPRESSION AND RELATED REACTIONS

Suppression implies a form of self-control by which emotional reactions or tendencies to action are kept from overt expression. *Repression* implies the same process except at a less conscious level. *Daydreaming* and *fantasy* permit the individual to escape from reality and to carry out his desires imaginatively. *Rationalization* implies concocting ideas and justifying them on individually approved rather than generally approved bases. These means of adjustment enable a person to meet a frustrating situation without taking goal-directed, aggressive, or any new overt actions to meet situations. All of us at one time or another have used them without always being aware that we are doing so.

These, like other adjustment techniques, are neither desirable nor undesirable in themselves. Yet, if they are used in meeting a large number of situations for long periods of time, the effect is highly undesirable. Suppressing and repressing such emotional feelings as jealousy, anger, fear, affection, and elation repeatedly leads to physical illness as well as to severe psychological disturbance. Fantasy can be used to avoid so many important life situations that eventually the individual creates a world out of his fantasies and loses touch with reality. Chronic rationalization also can lead to much unethical behavior which the individual interprets as reasonable and appropriate. Observant teachers can detect the appearance of many of these mechanisms in students, but what to do about them is not well understood. As will be suggested in later discussion of principles of personality integration, attempting to create and maintain a secure emotional environment in the classroom is a positive approach to the problem.

ANXIETY AND RELATED REACTIONS

Anxiety, different from most other means of adjustment, is not as much a response to frustration as it is a fusion of low fear with the anticipation of possible failure or punishment. Sometimes the source of the anxiety is not clear to the individual. However, anxiety is a powerful factor in individual behavior as we shall observe when noting two types of anxiety, some effects of anxiety generally, and other variables associated with anxiety.

Manifest anxiety is a generalized state, applicable to broad classes of behavior. Manifest anxiety is nonspecific, and the highly-anxious person reacts to many different situations in the same manner. Test anxiety is more specific and applies primarily to testing situations as we usually think of them. In a pioneer study, students high in test anxiety scored low on a college-entrance examination and made low grade-point averages; however, a positive relationship was found between general anxiety scores and grade-point average (28). Thus, test anxiety and general anxiety did not produce the same effects.

How is general anxiety related to motivation? Mild anxiety with a low degree of tension, particularly in problem-solving situations, is not harmful to learning; it may be a positive motivation influence (35). However, the teacher should not deliberately create frustrations or arouse anxiety because most learning situations are anxiety producing in themselves. The better approach is to reduce rather than to increase anxiety.

What is the relationship of anxiety, test and general, to performance? Here we cannot determine whether anxiety affects motivation only, performance only, or both. However, shown in Fig. 11.3 are data for two groups having the highest and the lowest scores on a test of manifest, general anxiety. The low-anxiety group of fourth-graders made consistently fewer errors than the high-anxiety group, suggesting that high anxiety reduced efficient performance (24). More anxious college students also scored lower in reading speed, reading comprehension, and recall (8).

Stress generally produces anxiety although the two cannot be clearly shown to be correlated. Stress affects performance in the same manner as anxiety and also is associated with personality disorganization. Four degrees of stress, ranging from a relaxed environment with little or no stress to high stress, produced dramatic results. Inability to perceive new relationships in problem-solving situations (rigidity) was greater under stress than under nonstress; however, the degree of rigidity did not increase significantly as the experimentally induced stress was increased. Under stress, the group showing higher insecurity to general life situations was subject to more rigidity than was the more secure group. Some students became disorganized under high stress. As stress increased, they tended toward diffused and disorganized responses; and subsequently, as a defensive reaction, they exhibited greater rigidity in solving the problems (1).

Other variables are associated with anxiety. Test anxiety is more closely related to intellectual performance of boys than girls (30). The

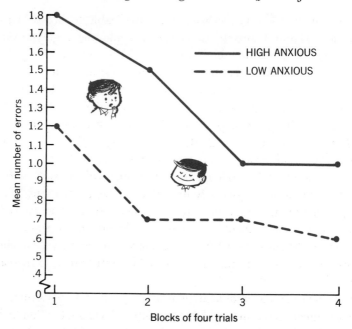

Fig. 11.3. Error curves for anxious and nonanxious subjects plotted in blocks of four trials. (Adapted from D. S.
Palermo, A. Castaneda, & B. R. McCandless. The relationship of anxiety in children to performance in a complex
learning task. *Child Develpm.*, 1956, **27**, 335. By permission of the authors and The Society for Research in Child
Development, Inc. Copyright 1956 by the Society for Research in Child Development, Inc.)

effects of test anxiety also are related to the amount of stress. High-
anxiety students under stress did not perform as well as the low- and
the middle-anxiety students; whereas under no stress, the high-anxiety
students did better than the others (**29**). The effects of general anxiety
upon performance vary with the intelligence level of the students, the
type of task to be performed, and the nature of the instructions (**27**).

More specific conclusions are possible regarding anxiety, achievement in different curriculum areas, and intelligence (**11**). Children
with low IQs, who were enrolled in special classes for the educable
mentally retarded, were more anxious than those with average IQs,
and children with average IQs were more anxious than those with high
IQs. In reading, arithmetic, and language, the more anxious children
did not perform as well as those of lower anxiety. The highly-anxious
children with low IQs performed less well in arithmetic; whereas the
highly-anxious children with average IQs performed less well in lan-

guage and reading. Apparently reading and language are more important for children with average IQs enrolled in regular school classes, but arithmetic is more important for children with low IQs enrolled in special classes.

Why is it that children of lower mental ability generally demonstrate higher anxiety? High mental ability may make it possible for the child to assess the environment more realistically—the real and present dangers in any current threatening object, situation, or person. His fears thus may be specific and identifiable. Children of lower IQs may show greater anxiety, that is, generalized fear of a nonspecific nature, because of their limited ability to evaluate the threat in objects, situations, or people that interact with them. The high-anxious child of lower IQ is less free to respond to the teacher, the learning material, and the learning situation. The anxious child of any IQ level may expend much of his energy in dealing with the general fear responses to the school environment. In this way high general anxiety, rather than enhancing motivation, is debilitating and interferes with the learning process. It is possible, too, that a vicious cycle is engendered through high anxiety and low achievement. Lack of achievement in reading, arithmetic and language heightens anxiety and, in turn, heightened anxiety further depresses achievement.

Current knowledge about anxiety implies that it is unwise to increase anxiety deliberately, except for research purposes, because performances tend to deteriorate under stress. Also, because high-anxious individuals do not perform generally as well as those individuals with low anxiety, it is appropriate to try to reduce anxiety in order to improve learning efficiency.

Integration of Personal Needs and Social Demands

Living represents a continuous series of adjustments between satisfaction of individual needs and satisfaction of the demands of the group to which one belongs. Various degrees of integration of personal needs with social demands are found in children and adults. One important dimension in this integration is conformity *vs.* rebellious independence. Early in life, especially during school years when age-mates become important, some persons develop a high degree of conformity to group standards and values. Conforming is entirely acceptable if the individual has independently arrived at the judgment that the particular code or value is good. There is, however, another type of conformity that is irrational.

A series of experiments with college students and other adults was arranged to investigate irrational conformity to group norms (9). Each individual in the experimental group was deliberately deceived by being told privately that other members of his group had agreed unanimously upon certain responses to situational items. Each individual then responded to the items. For example, an expression of agreement or disagreement was called for on this statement: "Free speech being a privilege rather than a right, it is proper for a society to suspend free speech whenever it feels itself threatened." Whereas only 19 percent of the control subjects expressed agreement with the statement, 58 percent of the experimental subjects (each of whom had been told that the group agreed to it) did so.

Another item on the same list was as follows: "Which one of the following do you feel is the most important problem facing our country today? (1) Economic recession; (2) educational facilities; (3) subversive activities; (4) mental health; (5) crime and corruption." Before answering, each member of the experimental group was told privately that "subversive activities" was unanimously agreed upon by their group as the most important; the control group was not given any information. Forty-eight percent of the experimental and 12 percent of the control subjects chose "subversive activities" as their answer to the item. The difference between the control and the experimental group on both items suggests that group pressure is important in securing conformity and that some individuals conform to be like the group rather than assuming initiative and responsibility for forming and expressing their own opinions.

The minority of one conforms not only to the valid judgments of the group but also to the invalid judgments (12). Here the judgments involved the length of lines, not a social or political problem; and the result was for the minority of one to conform to the group judgment. This conclusion holds generally for groups of individuals. However, children having high need for social approval, in comparison with those who are more independent, comply more readily to the judgments of others and to the perceived expectations of the group (33).

The integration of personal needs and societal demands, as may be seen, loses meaning when the person denies his individuality by conforming to group pressures. On the other hand, satisfying one's personal needs without considering the demands of society leads to anarchy, to deterioration of civilized life. Civilization is based on the assumption that the strong help the weak, rather than destroy them. Further possible evidence of lack of sufficient conforming to societal demands is represented in discipline problems in the school and delinquency and criminality in the larger society. We shall be concerned with discipline and delinquency after considering the self-concept as a basis of personality integration.

Adequate Self-Concept

The self-concept is what the individual refers to as "I" or "me" and is the totality of meanings, attitudes, and feelings which the individual has of himself—the most complete description one could give of his present self. It is his private conception of his own personality. The self-concept develops over a period of time and is learned, albeit incidentally and in part through conditioning, identification, and imitation, as well as with awareness. The infant is not aware of himself as a person, but as he grows and learns, he acquires an awareness of self. This awareness subsequently broadens to include more complete interpretations. With increasing age the self-concept becomes stable; the individual does not markedly change his attitudes, feelings, or ideas about himself. To illustrate, a prospective teacher may think that she is quite attractive, has acceptable social attitudes and goals, and is congenial but has enough independence to maintain her self-esteem and individuality in thought and action. She sees herself as a wholesome person and has interrelated many important facets of her own life. She has an adequate and well-organized self-concept.

The self-ideal is the desired self—what the person wishes most to be like and to do. A large discrepancy between the self-concept and self-ideal indicates maladjustment. The person who is strongly dissatisfied with his present self but has accepted a high self-ideal may be overly anxious and make poor adjustments in present situations. Persons dissatisfied with their present traits and living conditions may internalize a self-ideal which cannot be achieved but which serves as a basis for continuing self-criticism. Regardless of age, having a reasonably well-integrated personality calls for acceptance of the present self, comfortable feelings in a variety of present situations, and sufficiently stable self-perceptions whereby most situations encountered do not threaten one's feelings toward self as a worthwhile individual.

Acceptance of self is positively associated with acceptance of others. Positive correlations ranging from .36 to .70 were found between scores of self-acceptance and acceptance of others (4). Different combinations of self-acceptance and acceptance of others are related to personality integration (13):

1. Students high in self-acceptance, but low in acceptance of others, overestimated their personal acceptability to others while ascribing degraded motives to others about them.
2. Those high in self-acceptance and in acceptance of others were healthiest in their positive confidence in self and others, and asserted considerable self-determination and acceptance of personal responsibility for conduct and actions.
3. Those low in acceptance of self and high in acceptance of others shunned leadership almost completely.
4. Those low in acceptance of self and in acceptance of others exhibited high anxiety, impulsivity, low morale, overdependence, and a marked tendency to accommodate others.

These same clear-cut conclusions regarding acceptance of self and of others have been drawn in another experiment (38). Even more comprehensively, acceptance of self, acceptance of others, acceptance by others in a larger group, and acceptance by best friends are positively correlated (26). It is clear that an adequate self-concept, acceptance of others, and acceptance by others are positively related. This is not to say that one is cause and the other effect. Apparently acceptance of and by others and having an adequate self-concept are part of the mutually interrelated attributes of personality integration. It is thus possible that if an adult helps the student with one of the attributes, there will be positive transfer to the other.

Means of improving the self-concept have been tried in several settings. Instruction during grades 6 to 8 that was designed to help children acquire a more understanding and analytical approach to their own and others' behavior, resulted in higher self-acceptance and lower feelings of anxiety and insecurity in the children (6). College students became more positive toward themselves and the experimenter when favorably evaluated by the experimenter. Authoritarian and more rigid individuals responded less well toward self and to the favorable evaluations than did those who were less authoritarian. Negative evaluations by the experimenter did not affect the students' self-evaluations as much as positive evaluations (16). Boys experiencing behavior problems in school met in small groups for ten 50-minute counseling interviews with their regular high school counselors. In early meetings held in a fairly permissive environment, the boys spent a considerable amount of the time relating lurid stories of their real and fancied misdeeds. Once the boys were satisfied that the counselor could be trusted, they released many violent and aggressive feelings, some against the school, some against teachers, and some against parents. In the later sessions, they discussed freely with the counselor their in-school behavior, rules and regulations set up by the school, and other requirements that had been placed upon them. The boys' concepts of themselves as worthwhile individuals improved from the beginning to the end of the group counseling. Desirable change in behavior and attitudes toward self occurred first, followed by an attitude change toward others (7).

DEVELOPMENTAL TRENDS

We have already indicated a general trend in personality development in Fig. 10.1 of the previous chapter. This broad sweep in development becomes more precise in the consideration of developmental changes of a more specific nature.

As we mature, we go through various stages in developing our self-concept. Sixth-graders differentiate the external environment from self more clearly than do third-graders. The self-perceptions of sixth-graders are more realistic and less influenced by egocentrism, than are those of third-graders (25). Differences between high school students and college students in mature self-concepts also are marked (37). College men are different from high school boys, the former being more inner controlling and self-actualizing. However, the difference between girls in high school and college is not marked, probably because high school girls are relatively more mature than high school boys. High school girls are already more nearly like college women. Both inner controlling and self-actualizing behavior is considered to represent the highest levels of maturity of the self-concept.

Figure 11.4 shows correlations between ratings of a number of personality variables at various points in the lives of individuals as children and young adults (18, 267). Although the behavior of the children was rated as early as during the first three years of life, it is at the ages given in the figure that there is considerable stability with similar behavior in young adulthood. Indication of what the terms imply may be helpful in interpreting the results.

Passivity refers to acquiescing or withdrawing in the face of attack or frustrating situations. *Affectional dependence* involves seeking affection, acceptance, and emotional reassurance from adults. *Behavior disorganization* implies uncontrolled behavior such as violent crying and tantrums during the early years and uncontrolled destructive ac-

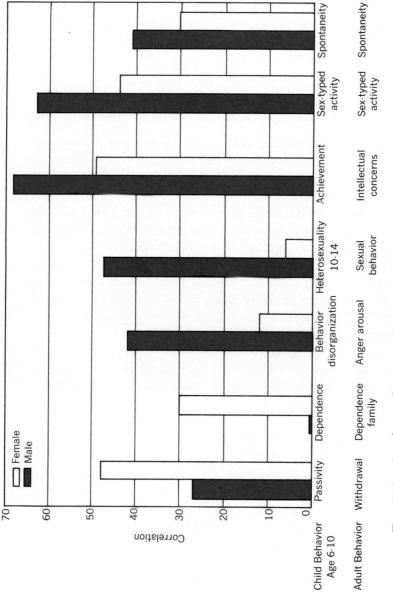

Fig. 11.4. Correlations between selected child behaviors (6 to 10 years of age) and phenotypically similar adult behaviors. (J. Kagan & H. A. Moss. *Birth to maturity: A study in psychological development.* New York: Wiley, 1962, p. 267.)

tivity, rages, and tantrums during the schools years. *Heterosexuality* during ages 10 to 14 involves the interactions with members of the opposite sex, with special attention given to dating behavior. *Intellectual achievement* designates mastery over school tasks, including involvement in knowledge acquisition, amount of time spent in reading, and interest in scientific projects. *Sex-typed activity* is activity during childhood in line with the role of the particular sex. *Spontaneity* is the opposite of inhibition and apprehension with peers; one who is spontaneous interacts freely with his peers, without tension and discomfort in social situations.

A brief examination of Fig. 11.4 shows that there are sharp sex differences on many variables, especially dependence, behavior disorganization, and heterosexuality. One should, therefore, not generalize to both sexes. For example, on the basis of heterosexual activity at age 10 to 14 one could predict sexual behavior in adult males with a fair degree of reliability; however, with females the prediction would not be better than chance. On the other hand, achievement and spontaneity show about the same correlations for both sexes from age childhood to young adulthood.

Inasmuch as the correlations between younger ages and young adulthood are even lower than those given in Fig. 11.4, one cannot predict later behavior from knowing the child during the preschool years. Nevertheless, the reader is invited to read the extensive first-hand information (18). The richness and variety of personality development is well documented.

The previous study went only to young adulthood. Attitudes toward education have been found to be fairly stable from 18 to 33 years (36). Values remain fairly stable from age 25 to 55 (19) and vocational interests from 19 to 38 (34). Other personality variables, including attitudes toward church, toward God as reality and toward war, are subject to fairly rapid shifts, even in later adolescence and early adulthood. The safest conclusion that one can draw from all the information is that it is unwise to attempt long-term predictions about the personality of maturing children and youth, infancy through high school. Pervasive traits, such as achievement, sex-typed activity, and physical characteristics, such as height, are more readily predictable from age 6 to 10 to young adulthood. These traits are less influenced by environmental factors and more by biological factors than are passivity, dependence, behavior disorganization, spontaneity, vocational interests, and values.

An example of the discontinuity in aggressive behavior between early childhood and young adulthood is shown in the following excerpts drawn from longitudinal information from the Fels Institute (**18**). You will note that this girl was aggressive and destructive as a child, but as adolescence approached, she began to suppress this behavior. As an adult, she did not display her hostile feelings and was not aggressive because this would have violated her standards that she had set for herself as a young woman.

At 2 years of age S's nursery-school behavior was often punctuated with aggressive outbursts.

"S seldom talks or shows any outward sign of emotion. She is by far the most physically bold child, doing much jumping and climbing. She often reacts to other children destructively, pushing them down, pulling out hair, and absconding with toys. . . ."

Two years later, at 4 years of age, S's nursery-school behavior was clearly competitive and aggressive.

"S was habitually aggressive, but she was not a successful leader. She was very competitive and seized every opportunity to equal or excel the feats of the other children. She liked to tease, and she had great sport with Mary and Peter, both of whom would yell or whine when she plagued them. Occasionally she played cooperatively with others, but more often she put herself in the role of a rival. S complied with adult requests at times, but at other times resisted with all her might. She needed to be reminded to take turns and to respect property rights. It was not because she did not know about these nursery-school principles, but rather because she could get such a rise out of other children by pushing in front of them or by snatching at their toys."

When S visited day camp at 6½, the predisposition toward unprovoked aggression was still clearly present.

"S was somewhat shy and wary in social situations and made few social advances. She was almost eager in her response when others made advances to her. She seemed to expect that she might not be accepted and was surprised and pleased when other children were nice to her. S was very easy to have around when she was busy. Sometimes in free moments she went a little wild. The other children complained that she pushed them, knocked their sand constructions down, or poked her finger in their clay work. These outbursts were over in a flash. She needed no provocation other than idleness to start her off. She never made excuses for her behavior or even admitted anything about it. S was out for her own advancement and was sort of a lone wolf. She seemed to feel no deep identification with the group or with any of its members."

During the early school years S was independent, and verbally rebellious and attacking. She was competitive with peers and began to gain some peer respect because of her daring, verbal skills and athletic prowess. By age 10 a dramatic shift occurred in her behavior. She became interested in her attractiveness to boys, and this new motive was accompanied by a sharp decrease in overt aggression. At age 10 the day-camp observer wrote:

"There has been a good deal of change in S's appearance: straightened posture, hair washed clean with French braids, and frilly, nice clothes. The big thing seems to be the big shift in S herself. She no longer needs to express her hostility and alienation toward the world. She has the possibilities of becoming a very attractive little girl. Socially S has loosened up a great deal. Though no one in this group was congenial with her, she was much more out-going than in previous years. At the races she got to the tomboy state, loudly boasting and jeering at one girl for being so awkward. *Most of the time she had a quiet, almost demure, air about her, listening to what others had to say and smiling in a friendly fashion. . . ."*

By 12½ years this girl had adopted more completely the traditional feminine-role behaviors. The home visitor wrote:

"S has passed conspicuously into adolescence. Since the last time I saw her, her breasts have developed noticeably, and she has a very pretty figure and is becoming quite attractive. The mother told me privately that S had bought a new bathing suit, a one-piece affair, and when she tried it on for the family, her older brother gave a long, low whistle, which embarrassed her terribly. Mother shows considerable interest in S's appearance and in helping her to become attractive. She mentioned today that before school starts, she plans to take S to a hair stylist for a special cut. She also remarked that S says she wants to grow up and marry and have children, 'so that's what we're get-ting ready for.' "

S did very well academically in high school and college and decided to go to graduate school. On first impression S appeared quiet, reserved, and neither competitive nor aggressive. She became conflicted over an intellectual career because the required competition in graduate school threatened the self-image she was trying so hard to retain. She was sufficiently insecure about her conception of herself as a woman that intense involvement in an intellectually aggressive atmosphere made her uncomfortable. During the adult interview she tried to explain why she withdrew from graduate school (**18**, 112–115).

In this case, a marked change in aggressive behavior is seen from early childhood to adolescence. However, from adolescence into young adulthood, the pattern is quite stable. In connection with achievement, which shows a higher correlation between childhood and adulthood than does aggression, there is often discontinuity from early life into adulthood as shown in excerpts which follow about a boy.

S was a highly motivated and excellent student in elementary and high school. He received a scholarship to college, graduated valedictorian of his college class, and won a competitive fellowship to graduate school. When interviewed as an adult, he expressed a strong motivation for achievement and recognition, and he looked forward with confidence to an intellectually creative career.

However, at age 2½ S was distractible and gave no clue to his future achievements.

"S spent an unhappy first week at nursery school. He cried a great deal and looked ready to cry even when he was not actually doing it. He drew away when other children approached him as if he were afraid of them. He required much adult attention to get him to do anything. He stood around, did nothing, and looked rather lost. After the first week, he became happier and played primitively in the sand out-of-doors. He did some climbing on ladders and slid alone. *In the room, his activity was not constructive. He did a lot of wandering from room to room, and he liked to throw things: balls, colored cubes, or tin dishes.* He watched the other children a great deal, identifying himself with the play of others by laughing when they did. Despite S's lively coloring he was not a lively, dramatic child. In fact, the teachers remarked that when they were tallying up the children to see who was there, they were always most likely to forget S's presence."

Let us contrast this summary at 2½ with a nursery-school report three years later, at 5½ years of age.

"S was one of the most adult-centered children in the group. The particular quality of his relationship is hard to describe. It was on a very verbal level. He came to tell you things, show you things, act things out, and explain things. S has a very active play life. There was a constant stream of verbal descriptions, and an observer would know every minute of the time what S was doing, what technique he was using, and why he was doing it. S *seemed to have a very strong calvinist sense of needing to get things done and not wasting time.* He would say, 'In a few minutes I will be through with this.' Although he was still ineffectual in holding on to things, he had really become more skilled."

"By choosing the less coveted objects and getting into an obscure corner in which to work, he had a chance of carrying his projects through. S *seemed really happy just to be making things.* There was a great emphasis on the detail without an over-all pattern. The Christmas tree gave him a very good goal to work toward, and he did more than his share of hanging materials. At the end of the session S was one of the most jubilant in wrapping up his booty to take home."

"In his scrutiny of the books and the retelling of the stories there was an emphasis on every tiny detail; every part coming in its sequence. S often asked questions to find out where parts fit in; how this different world of nursery school was supposed to run; what peoples' ideas about things were. Once told, he would store the knowledge away for the future. S was a great storyteller; long lectures on how things worked and on events at home. S's exceedingly high standards and an inability to relate to the world are his most salient features."

At 16½ years of age he was interviewed at the Institute.

E: "Would you tell me some of the things you are interested in?"

S: "Oh—my grade standards, various forms of amateur scientific research—I like to play around with. Like down at school, every once in a while I read about something interesting that someone has done, and if facilities permit, I like to try it out."

E: "Anything else you are interested in?"

S: "Well—I read a good bit—my main format of reading is in the science

402

fiction class. I kind of enjoy learning. Of course, I may be rather con-
ceited, but I don't think, except in a few classes, I actually learn anything.
However, it excites my interest toward discovering things for myself."
E: "Are your grades important to you?"
S: "Oh, I like to have them—I figure I should get along with a B just as well
as an A, but then I don't have to work much harder to get an A, so I
might as well have it" (18, 126–127).

Obviously, one cannot make predictions from two cases. One does,
however, get the clear impression that marked changes occur as late
as adolescence in important personality variables. From other information, we also know that some personality change occurs in adults. The
teacher thus operates on the assumption that changes in desirable directions are possible.

MODEL FOR ENCOURAGING
PERSONALITY INTEGRATION

The principles previously discussed in Chapter 10 in connection with
attitudes and values are relevant also to personality integration. Providing exemplary models to students, extending informative experience
about attitudes and values, providing for pleasant emotional experience, using group techniques to facilitate commitment to socially approved attitudes and values, arranging appropriate practice opportunities to implement more stable organization of the value system, and
encouraging deliberate cultivation of attitudes and values apply to
personality integration. Four other generalizations and related principles are now considered.

GENERALIZATION	PRINCIPLE
1. Stable personality organiza- tion develops in a secure emo- tional environment; high stress and chronic anxiety produce inefficient learning and even- tual personality disorganiza- tion.	1. Develop an emotionally se- cure environment.
2. An adequate self-concept, ac- ceptance by others, and ac- ceptance of others are inter- dependent and are requisite for personality integration.	2. Encourage self-understanding and self-acceptance.

3. Independence and a sense of achievement, attained through successful experiences, are essential to personality integration.

3. Help student to attain realistic goals.

4. Methods of adjusting to frustrating circumstances are learned; rational methods may replace undue aggressiveness, anxiety, and withdrawal.

4. Provide practice in meeting conflict.

These principles should be considered as useful hypotheses to guide behavior in teaching and other situations, rather than as established laws. Another person with a different concept of personality, analyzing the same large body of research and expert opinion, might use different terminology.

Develop an Emotionally Secure Environment

The classroom environment, more than the organized subject matter, serves to facilitate personality integration. In the emotionally secure classroom, standards of conduct are understood and accepted, feelings of acceptance and belonging are encouraged, pleasant emotions are freely expressed, help is given with unpleasant emotions, frustration and anxiety are reduced, friendly interactions are promoted, and a zest for learning is nurtured.

Standards of Conduct. Children and youth feel quite secure emotionally if the demands on them are made known and are consistent. Insecurity develops in a highly permissive group situation where inexperienced or immature members must originate their own standards, or in a situation wherein the demands vary from day to day or are inconsistently enforced by the leader. Most pupils do not resent reasonable rules and regulations; on the contrary, they prefer to know the kind of behavior that the leader consistently will approve or disapprove. They often test the new teacher to ascertain what the limits are. Particularly in the upper elementary grades and high school, an effective means of getting behavioral standards clarified and accepted by the pupils is to have them participate in the formulation. This technique has proved useful in a variety of usual school situations, as well as in high school classes composed of students already apprehended by the law but attending school while on probation. In many instances, older students come up with reasonable proposals to guide their conduct and try to live up to them.

Feelings of Acceptance. A feeling of acceptance and belonging is important in achieving an emotionally secure classroom. This does not mean that the teacher must spend a great deal of time making it obvious that he accepts each student in the class. Rather, as the learning activities start and progress, the teacher shows in facial expressions and words that he is pleased to have each student in his class. Misbehavior is corrected and occasionally an individual may be privately reprimanded or punished. Though it is relatively impossible for the younger child to disassociate himself from his conduct, the teacher can make it clear that it is the misbehavior which is disapproved, not the child.

Emotional Expression. Pleasant emotions are too infrequently expressed in many classroom situations by both the teacher and the pupils, and there is probably too much suppression of feelings generally. In the kindergarten and primary grades the tendency is for the teacher to express her own pleasant feelings quite freely and to encourage pleasant emotional expressions in pupils. However, as the demand to learn more organized subject matter increases, both the teacher and pupils sometimes feel that not nearly enough is being accomplished, with the result that there are few happy experiences and pleasant emotional expressions in the classroom. As was shown in Chapters 4 and 10, interest and liking for school decreases from first to sixth grade, and schooling becomes less pleasant for a variety of reasons. The emotional atmosphere might be improved if the instructional program elicited more pleasant reactions and if time were spent helping youngsters deal more effectively with their unpleasant emotions.

Friendly Interactions. Having one or two good friends in class and being able to discuss interests and problems that have arisen are important for personality integration. A most constructive goal of the teacher is to make sure that each child in the room has one or more good friends. Further, elementary and high school students desire membership in groups. Occasional class discussions and appropriate reading material can provide the informational bases for making friends and affiliating with groups. The cliques and crowds with ethical standards contradictory to those generally accepted usually cannot be broken up by rules and regulations because the cliques satisfy the members' needs for affection and friendship. Rather than attempting to separate friends or to sever friendships, the better procedure generally is to help these students as groups to reappraise their attitudes, values, and behaviors.

Enthusiasm for Learning. Most observers of young children marvel

405

at their exploratory behavior. Young children raise all sorts of questions about themselves and their environment. They are curious and want to learn. For many children this zest for learning is somehow blunted during elementary and secondary school years by restrictions arising in the home, the neighborhood, and the school. Beginning in the first grade, the urge for activity which leads to new discovery is thwarted by the pressure to conform to a confining situation, the classroom. Answers which the child needs to solve an important problem are deferred because a problem which an adult wants solved takes precedence. Teachers often feel, too, that it is their job to give answers rather than to help pupils find the answers. Mastering specified learning tasks suited mainly to the middle group of students becomes more important than does encouraging them to raise questions and seek solutions. Eventually the student no longer finds a challenge in the classroom learning situation; his previous eager searching for solutions becomes passive tolerance or even open resistance. When this happens undesirable means of adjusting, such as suppression, daydreaming, repression, and aggression, become prevalent. It is impossible to have an emotionally secure classroom environment when even a minority feel that there is nothing worthwhile to be obtained.

Encourage Self-Understanding and Self-Acceptance

By the time the student finishes high school, he should have a fairly realistic appraisal of himself, his motor skills, his knowledge and intellectual abilities, his interests, and his emotional make-up. One of the weaknesses of our total educational program, including the college level, is that we do not give sufficient help to students in understanding their strengths and weaknesses. Often a counselor makes a fairly adequate appraisal of the student's assets and limitations and uses this for placing him in various curricula and classes. However, the information on which the appraisal is based is not interpreted to the student so that he himself can understand the strengths which he may capitalize on, weaknesses which he may overcome through persistent effort, and possible limitations which he cannot overcome but must accept.

Besides some inadequacies in encouraging self-understanding, there is even less deliberate attempt to encourage self-acceptance. Rather than helping students accept and appreciate their special individual selves, we encourage unrealistic striving: "Anyone can become President of the United States." "Everyone should make a perfect score on this test." "Everyone should finish in ten minutes." Similarly, the grading system of "A-F" or "H-S-U" tends to encourage lack of self-acceptance except in those who receive high marks. Though giving students low or failing marks may encourage self-understanding and realism, it does not lead to self-acceptance, especially if the idea also is expressed that one should not be satisfied with low marks even though he has done his best.

Although desire to improve coupled with some dissatisfaction with present performance is necessary for progress, extreme self-rejection or unrealistic striving leads to poor personality integration and, at times, to deliberate violation of ethical principles. The person who continually strives for higher success than that attained does not get reasonable satisfaction from his achievements. Many American children and adults are not satisfied with achievements which are adequate for themselves; they are dissatisfied unless they are the wealthiest in their group, the highest in the class, the best athletic performer, and the like. And much of the deliberate cheating and rationalizing of unethical behavior in human affairs generally results from this compulsive desire to appear better than one really is.

Self-acceptance is the primary requisite for an adequate self-concept. Further, acceptance by others and acceptance of others is positively related to acceptance of self. One cannot determine which is cause and effect. Inasmuch as this is the case, it is well to work on all of them simultaneously. The teacher's rejecting a child or condoning classmates' rejection of him will not encourage self-acceptance. Similarly, permitting a child to gain a better perception of self through bullying others and treating them as inferior will not encourage a healthy self-concept. We do not imply that blind conformity to group opinion is desirable; it is undesirable. Nevertheless, accepting some other children and being accepted by them appears to be essential for normal social and emotional development, for normal personality integration.

This point of view about the members of a family applies equally well to the school:

We might set down here three insights that have become so well established that we can call them psychological axioms. One is that no human being can be his best self if he is always trying to be someone else instead of himself. The second is that he cannot be his best self unless he enjoys a reasonable self-respect and sense of worth. The third is that—particularly in childhood, but in some measure throughout life—his estimate of himself reflects the treatment he receives from the key figures in his environment; it is not something he makes out of nothing, but something he makes of other people's responses to him. As others see him, so he gradually tends to see himself (**23**, 91).

Help Student to Attain Realistic Goals

Some adults still believe that the pupil ought to experience failure in school as preparation to meet failure in adult life. However, the evidence is clear that highly productive, happy adults have a backlog of previous successes starting in childhood, and that repeated successes do not necessarily lead to an inflated opinion of self nor to undue self-centeredness. Our psychiatric wards and penal institutions are occupied primarily by persons who have repeatedly experienced failure.

As discussed in the preceding section, it is important that pupils not only learn to understand themselves but also that they have experience in setting and reaching goals. Many pupils set their sights too high in learning tasks such as spelling, arithmetic, science, or other fields. With the recent emphasis on science and mathematics as preparation for careers in engineering or science, high school students of relatively low ability are taking more of the advanced classes in science and mathematics. Large numbers of them, however, are experiencing failure rather than success. And many high school graduates of lower abstract abilities who enter college are disappointed and at times become seriously disturbed upon being dropped for academic failure. As will be discussed further in Chapter 12, some goals are set too low. This, too, does not facilitate personality integration.

Provide Practice in Meeting Conflict

Conflict situations inevitably arise in the classroom. The first response to such situations is often emotional. We expect younger children to respond with rather free expression of emotions in conflict situations. Although this free emotional expression tends to relieve tension, it does not resolve the conflict. If we are to make progress in human affairs, more conflict situations such as those between minority–majority groups, labor and management, nation and nation, will have to be solved in a manner more rational and less emotional. Youth in school today need practice in rational or intelligent methods for meeting the various conflict situations they encounter.

Conflict situations in school may provide the basis for fruitful learning experiences which promote personality integration. As was suggested in the previous chapter, role playing, group discussions, and group decision-making promote better understanding of social and ethical values and acceptance of such values. Disagreements among pupils about such matters as responsibility for performing various tasks, appropriate conduct, and the cause of conflict can initiate a role-playing situation or a group discussion in which the emphasis is on rational means of solution rather than on fighting, arguing, blaming, and punishing.

A further word is in order concerning frustration. In our increasingly complex society, everyone experiences many unavoidable frustrations and accompanying anxieties. The role of the school and the teacher is to reduce frustration rather than deliberately to arrange frustrating situations. It is clear from the experiments reported that high stress can be induced in people by one who has sufficient control over their lives and activities. High frustration with accompanying lack of need satisfaction results in undesirable responses such as aggression, disorganization, regression, rigidity, and anxiety. Nosebleeding, severe headache, frequent need to go to the bathroom, muscular tics—all possible symptoms of severe emotional strain—are sometimes induced by placing too heavy demands on children. And it is difficult to arrange purposefully work activities and assignments so that some pupils do not become highly frustrated because they misinterpret or perceive differently the demands of the teacher. A fine balance, often hard to achieve, must be maintained between encouraging persistent trying and accidentally creating too much tension, with resulting inefficiency and personal disorganization.

PERSONALITY INTEGRATION AND DISCIPLINE

In the discussion in this and the preceding chapter, we have outlined a positive approach for encouraging an excellent work situation and self-discipline. This approach implies that the teacher's behavior should be directed toward producing self-disciplined individuals and that a good learning situation should be maintained for all students. In Chapters 5 and 6 we have dealt with characteristics of teachers and teacher–pupil interaction that should be helpful in maintaining a good work situation. In most school situations, discipline depends primarily upon the leadership characteristics of the teacher, the types of interaction between the teacher and the students, and the teacher's organization and direction of the learning activities. There are, however, two other very important variables—the students and the forces outside a classroom. Some students do not come to school to learn and consequently they have negative attitudes toward the entire situation. Outside forces, including the neighborhood and the school administration, are not conducive to high morale in some schools. If this is the case, more positive leadership is required from the teacher.

Let us make two assumptions in this discussion of discipline. First, a beginning teacher may not know how to establish his leadership role. Second, correction and sometimes punishment are required.

Establishing a Leadership Role

At first a beginning teacher might have difficulty in establishing his role as a leader. On the basis of our experiences as teachers at all school levels—elementary through college—we offer the following suggestions in connection with first meetings with a class.

1. Plan carefully and in detail what will be done before meeting the class. Make sure that the subject matter is known well so that reference to books is not necessary.
2. Know the plan so well that reference to it is not needed during the class period. When a teacher has to rely on written notes to ascertain what will come next, students lose confidence in his competence.
3. In making the opening presentation stand still and establish direct eye contact. Walking about the room with eyes diverted from the students invites whispering and inattention.
4. Consciously speak slowly for under stress there is a tendency to talk more rapidly than usual.
5. Use only a few minutes, not more than five, for an initial verbal presentation; students tire very quickly of sitting and listening. Also, refrain from doing what so many beginning teachers tend to do—overestimate the interest value of their material and the vocabulary level of the students.
6. Demonstrate high enthusiasm for the subject matter and the particular class. Point out the social values, as well as the knowledge, that may be attained through study and mastery of the subject.
7. Make a clear, definite assignment to the students early in the class period so that they begin constructive activity.
8. Change activities during a class period often rather than continuing the same activity throughout the period.
9. Exercise tight control in early class meetings with incisive but courteous requests to students to accomplish what you desire.

When your role as the leader is established, disruptive incidents will still arise. However, you may decrease them.

1. Know each student by name so that you can call on anyone who may be starting a problem, thus diverting his attention from the problem to you. In smaller classes the teacher knows each individual after the first day of classes. In other situations, a seating chart permits the teacher to call on students by name. Besides drawing attention, calling a student by name assures him that he will be treated as an individual.
2. Identify the students who appear immature in self-control and self-direction. Give particular attention to the learning problems of these students and have individual conferences with them.
3. Identify the student leaders and secure their cooperation. Sociometric tests and information from teachers already in the system may be helpful in this. Classes of 30 to 40 students have from 3 to 5 highly popular students who are also the leaders. When the popular students cooperate with the teacher, the other students are likely to follow.

Correction and Punishment

The effects of punishment are not well understood. It is possible, however, that punishment is a very powerful influence in bringing about change in behavior and that punishment, properly administered, does not result in permanent emotional disturbance (**32**). Punishment to divert attention from antisocial conduct and to prevent one individual from interfering with the progress of the group may be the most constructive procedure a teacher can use in special cases. There are situations in which punishing an individual is necessary to maintain high morale within the group.

Problems involving the use of punishment are (1) criteria for deciding whether to punish, (2) time of punishment, (3) form of punishment, and (4) severity of punishment.

CRITERIA FOR PUNISHMENT

One may decide whether to punish by answering first, "Will punishing help the individual grow in self-discipline and self-control?" and second, "Will punishing contribute to a more effective working situation for the group?" Frequently, both of these questions cannot be answered positively, and one decides to punish an individual for the good of the group. If time were available to investigate the causes of the misconduct, punishment might not be necessary. Serious misconduct often appears suddenly and action has to be taken at that time to prevent the situation from getting out of control or to prevent disruption of the group's activities.

Punishment may be used as an effective means for diverting attention or activity from an undesirable end. The student who is chasing another in a crowded corridor may be brought up sharply with a teacher command to stop and an order for both students to go into the classroom. An individual in the woodwork shop may maliciously use a saw on metal to produce a grating sound which hinders other students' work. In the crafts class, a student may go from one person to another interfering with their work and accomplishing nothing constructive himself. The teacher's asking these students to desist and giving them some work to perform, such as cleaning up the room, may serve to divert their attention.

The following criteria may be useful in deciding whether to punish. First, how serious is the misconduct? Generally, cursing, using vulgar language, destroying property, and fighting need to be curbed as they appear. Punishing the individual immediately may be the most constructive solution at a given time. Second, for what length of time has less serious misconduct persisted? If an individual persists in less serious but disruptive conduct and fails to respond to group stimulation and teacher interest, punishment may be necessary until a solution is effected. Third, how seriously does the individual's conduct disturb progress in learning activities? When the individual's actions do not greatly interfere with conduct and activity of the group, it is better not to punish immediately but to investigate causes and try to work out a solution.

TIME OF PUNISHMENT

According to one theory, punishment should come at the time the misbehavior occurs. According to a second theory, the misbehavior should be stopped but the punishment itself should come at some later time. These are quite contradictory; therefore their application will be illustrated in one situation.

John, an eighth-grader, comes into the classroom and in a clear voice uses profane language. Should he be punished then or later? According to the first theory, the punishment should come immediately so that its unpleasantness is closely associated in time with the misconduct. This theory assumes that punishment conditions John not to curse again because he associates the unpleasant punishment with using profane language. According to the second theory, John should be informed that he has committed a serious offense and will be punished later. The teacher makes provision to see him at some later time and punishment is then decided.

Immediate punishment is better than delay in connection with corporal punishment or sharp disapproval with smaller children in the home. Delaying punishment for long periods of time, for example, unfavorable comments on report cards, is quite ineffective. One must decide whether to punish immediately or later by analyzing the seriousness of the offense and the probable effects on the individual and the group. In analyzing time for punishment, one also should consider the form of the punishment and the procedures for changing the attitude of the individual.

FORM OF PUNISHMENT

The form of punishment should be related to the nature of the misbehavior in specific situations. The offender who mars school property or personal effects of classmates should be required to make restitution. Thus, if one student maliciously breaks another's glasses, he should make restitution. Any malicious destruction of property may be handled in this way provided it does not cause extreme hardship on the offender and thus lead to more serious misconduct.

Loss of privilege is frequently used as punishment for using profane language, cheating, or creating a classroom disturbance—offenses which have no closely related punishment. Extra work also fits into this category. Here we face one of the difficult problems in use of punishment. When the individual is punished in some form not closely related to the misconduct, it is possible that the punisher and not the punishment will be associated with unpleasantness. Thus, when the punisher is not present, the individual continues the misconduct.

Forced apology to the teacher or to classmates is sometimes employed, as is expulsion from the room or school. These forms of punishment are probably more severe than moderate corporal punishment, privately administered. Unless the individual seriously interferes with progress of the group, these forms of punishment should not be used. Some persons recommend never using them.

Mass punishment is extremely dangerous, particularly when the whole class or several in a group are punished for the offense one individual has committed. It is unwise to try to force students to reveal the identity of an offender by punishing all of them. Whole-school strikes and class strikes against a teacher are frequently incited in this way.

For minor offenses in which punishment is employed, it is best not to call the attention of the class to the offense or to the punishment. The teacher should handle the situation firmly, quickly, and with little class-room disturbance. In most cases, some classmates will identify them-selves with the student being punished; therefore, advertising it causes widespread resentment against the teacher. Also, the student loses pres-tige with his classmates and may become antagonistic toward the teacher. In all forms of punishment except for serious offenses, the ef-fective procedure is to get the punishment over quickly, to make sure that resentment is not continued between student and teacher, and to get productive work started immediately.

SEVERITY OF PUNISHMENT

When punishment is so severe that the individual does not want to return to the classroom, to improve his conduct, or to work with a teacher who administered the punishment, the student cannot be helped by the teacher. Opportunity for helping the student grow in self-discipline is lost and the punishment intensifies the individual's maladjustment. Except for the most serious offenses which greatly im-pede progress of the group, punishment should not be so severe as to produce these results.

One cannot predict accurately how severe a punishment is for an individual except through knowing him and his home situation. A sar-castic verbal attack may be more severe for the timid, shy girl than a hard whipping for the boy who receives whippings frequently at home. To decide severity of punishment for an individual, one must take into account the individual's feeling about it.

SUBSTITUTION OF DESIRABLE BEHAVIOR

Punishing should be followed with correction. One of the best pro-cedures for eliminating antisocial behavior, as noted in Chapter 3, is to substitute and reinforce other behavior which leads to the same de-sirable goal. For example, if a child seeks attention and gains it through disruptive acts such as throwing paper or screaming, punishment may lead to suppression of these instrumental behaviors. However, securing attention may be a reasonable goal of the student. If doing well in a learning task, helping with a class project, or keeping a library shelf in order can be interpreted by the teacher to the rest of the class in such way that the student gets attention, the acts should be reinforced. Substitution of socially approved behavior for misbehavior is perhaps the most constructive means of correcting behavior.

We also must assume that the student, whatever his misbehavior, is doing what he thinks is best for him at the time. He may have inadequate knowledge or skills as to how to gain his objectives through socially approved behavior. Simply teaching the student new knowledge and skills may be most helpful in correcting his misbehavior.

Teachers may have unusual conceptions of what constitutes misbehavior and also about the causes of misbehavior. Most of the nine classes of misbehavior mentioned most frequently by teachers and for which the students were punished do not seem to be serious (**15**). The percents indicate the frequency with which the misbehavior was mentioned by a group of teachers:

Talking	21.4	Inattention	6.4
Disobedience	16.8	Tardiness	5.8
Carelessness	9.8	Cheating	4.6
Defiance of authority	8.7	Throwing objects	3.5
Cutting class	8.1		

The extent to which misbehavior of this type might be prevented by the teacher cannot be determined immediately. It is reasonable to expect that more teachers should try to provide sufficiently interesting learning activities so that talking, carelessness, and inattention are reduced.

SUMMARY

Becoming a person is at the apex of learning. What the person is, how he reacts to others, how others react to him, his motives, his adjustment to self and others, all of these and more are included in the concept of personality. Personality is not something unrelated to learning. It is based on health and psychomotor skills, emotional experiences, knowledge and related intellectual skills, adequate means of psychological adjustment, integration of personal needs and social demands, and the self-concept. Although the school may not explicitly try to shape the personality through an organized program of instruction, children and youth when in school learn knowledge, abilities, skills, attitudes, values, motives, and interests which are at the very heart of personality. Therefore, the school has the responsibility for exercising a strong positive force in building healthy, zestful personalities.

Caution and confidence are essential when dealing with the developing personality of the child. Caution is required in predicting what the child will be like as an adolescent and adult on the basis of what he is today. Marked changes occur in personality traits from childhood into adulthood. Even from adolescence into adulthood there are considerable changes. Here is where confidence is needed. Although a child may already demonstrate unfavorable attitudes toward himself or others or may already manifest undue aggression or dependence, we can be confident that changes in desirable directions are possible. This is not to say that experiences in early life are not important; however, we do emphasize that change is possible, even in adults.

Inasmuch as attitudes and values are integral components of personality, the principles for facilitating the learning of attitudes and values given in Chapter 10 are applicable for personality. Four additional principles require thoughtful examination in connection with the teacher's role in personality development: (1) Develop an emotionally secure environment, (2) encourage self-understanding and self-acceptance, (3) help student to aid each learner to attain realistic goals, and (4) provide practice in meeting conflict.

Discipline and personality integration are related. The goal of discipline is self-direction and self-control, rather than external direction and control. Although this is the case, we still live in an imperfect world and punishment and correction are sometimes necessary. The use of punishment requires careful consideration in terms of establishing a leadership role in the classroom, criteria for punishment, time of punishment, form of punishment, severity of punishment, and the substitution of desirable for undesirable behavior.

QUESTIONS AND ACTIVITIES

1. a. Define personality.
   b. Evaluate Shoben's description of integrative adjustment, referring to the original article if necessary.
2. a. Rate yourself on the six bases of personality integration, using an A to mean you are particularly strong in relation to it, B to indicate moderately strong, C to indicate moderately weak, and D to indicate particularly weak.
   b. Discuss the role of the teacher and the school in connection with each of the six, as applied to students at any school level.
3. a. Give an example of each of the seven means of adjustment.
   b. In your opinion, which of the seven are less appropriate for a teacher than a student? Why?

4. a. Indicate two or three generalizations about the stability of personality.
   b. What are the implications for education?
5. Related to your interest in level of schooling and subject field, give an example of implementing each of the four principles of personality integration.
6. Drawing from your own school experiences, discuss the extent to which each of the four principles have been implemented. Devote two or three paragraphs to each and include illustrations.
7. Evaluate the suggestions for establishing a leadership role. Add, delete, and rewrite suggestions as appropriate.
8. a. Under what circumstances do you think a teacher should punish a child?
   b. Do you think you are more prone to punish than were most teachers you had? Explain.
   c. Do you think children of today need more correction than did the children with whom you went to school? Explain.

SUGGESTIONS FOR FURTHER READING

Bandura, A., & R. H. Walters. *Social learning and personality development.* New York: Holt, Rinehart, & Winston, 1963. Ch. 4: Reinforcement patterns and disciplinary techniques, pp. 188–200.

Beilin, H. The prediction of adjustment over a four year interval. *J. clin. Psychol.,* 1957, **13,** 270–274.

Bronfenbrenner, U. Soviet methods of character education: Some implications for research. In *Review of recent research bearing on religious and character formation.* New York: Religious Education Association, 1962, pp. 45–61. (In Page, 1964, 382–390.)

Grimes, J. W., & W. Allinsmith. Compulsivity, anxiety, and school achievement. *Merrill-Palmer Quart.,* 1961, **7,** 247–271. (In Rosenblith & Allinsmith, 1962, 420–433.)

Horwitz, M. Hostility and its management in classroom groups. In W. W. Charters, Jr., & N. L. Gage (Eds.), *Readings in the social psychology of education.* Boston: Allyn & Bacon, 1963, pp. 196–212.

Ingersoll, Hazel L. The transmission of authority patterns in the family. *Genet. Psychol. Monogr.,* 1948, **38,** 225–302.

Jones, V. Character development in children: An objective approach. In L. E. Carmichael (Ed.), *Manual of child psychology.* (2nd ed.) New York: Wiley, 1954, pp. 781–832.

Kagan, J., & H. A. Moss. The stability of passive and dependent behavior from childhood through adulthood. *Child Develpm.,* 1960, **31,** 577–591. (In Mussen, Conger, & Kagan, 1965, 327–344.)

Kounin, J. S., & P. V. Gump. The comparative influence of punitive and nonpunitive teachers upon children's concepts of school misconduct. *J. educ. Psychol.,* 1961, **52,** 44–49. (In Gordon, 1965, 231–236; and Ripple, 1964, 190–198.)

Lighthall, F. F. Anxiety as related to thinking and forgetting. *What research says to the teacher,* No. 30. Washington, D.C.: National Education Association, 1964.

McKeachie, W. J., D. Pollie, & J. Speisman. Relieving anxiety in classroom examinations. *J. abnorm. soc. Psychol.,* 1955, **50,** 93–98. (In Charters & Gage, 1963, 212–219; and Page, 1964, 370–380.)

Maslow, A. H. Cognition of being in the peak experiences. *J. genet. Psychol.,* 1959, **94,** 43–66. (In Fullagar, *et al.,* 1964, 359–379.)

Peck, R. F., & J. V. Mitchell, Jr. Mental health. *What research says to the teacher,* No. 24. Washington, D.C.: National Education Association, 1962. (Portions reprinted under the title "The mental health of the teacher" in Seidman, 1965, 77–79.)

Sheviakov, G. V., & F. Redl. *Discipline for today's children and youth.* Wash-ington, D.C.: National Education Association, 1956.

Symonds, P. M. Classroom discipline. *Teachers Coll. Rec.,* 1949, **51,** 147–158. (In Page, 1964, 290–300; and Seidman, 1965, 69–76.)

REFERENCES

1. Ainsworth, L. H. Rigidity, inse-curity, and stress. *J. abnorm. soc. Psychol.,* 1958, **56,** 67–74.

2. Allport, G. W. *Personality: A psy-chological interpretation.* New York: Holt, Rinehart and Winston, 1937.

3. Bennett, C. M., & T. E. Jordan. Security-insecurity and the direc-tion of aggressive responses to frustration. *J. clin. Psychol.,* 1958, **14,** 166–167.

4. Berger, E. Relation between ex-pressed acceptance of self and ex-pressed acceptance of others. *J. abnorm. soc. Psychol.,* 1952, **47,** 778–782.

5. Bridges, K. M. B. Emotional de-velopment in early infancy. *Child Develpm.,* 1932, **3,** 324–341.

6. Bruce, P. Relationship of self-ac-ceptance to other variables with sixth grade children oriented in self-understanding. *J. educ. Psy-chol.,* 1958, **49,** 229–238.

7. Caplan, S. W. The effect of group counseling on junior high school boys' concepts of themselves in school. *J. counsel. Psychol.,* 1957, **4,** 124–128.

8. Chansky, N. M. Threat, anxiety, and reading behavior. *J. educ. Res.,* 1958, **51,** 333–340.

9. Crutchfield, R. S. Conformity and character. *Amer. Psychologist,* 1955, **10,** 191–198.

10. deCharms, R., & E. J. Wilkins. Some effects of verbal expression of hostility. *J. abnorm. soc. Psy-chol.,* 1963, **66,** 462–470.

11. Feldhusen, J. K., & H. J. Klaus-meier. Anxiety, intelligence, and achievement in children of low, average, and high intelligence. *Child Develpm.,* 1962, **33,** 403–409.

12. Feldman, M. J., & M. R. Gold-fried. Validity of group judgment as a factor affecting independent and conformity behavior. *J. soc. Psychol.,* 1962, **58,** 289–294.

13. Fey, W. F. Correlates of certain subjective attitudes toward self and others. *J. clin. Psychol.,* 1957, **13,** 44–49.

14. Frank, L. K. *Feelings and emo-tions: Doubleday papers in psy-chology.* New York: Random House, 1954.

15. Greene, J. E., Sr. Alleged "mis-behaviors" among senior high school students. *J. soc. Psychol.,* 1962, **58,** 371–382.

16. Harvey, O. J. Reactions to nega-tive information about the self as a function of the unfavorableness of the information, source of the evalutions and personality char-acteristics of the recipient. *Tech-nical Report No. 8.* Washington, D.C.: Office of Naval Research, 1958.

17. Johnson, R. C., & G. R. Medin-nus. *Child psychology: Behavior and development.* New York: Wiley, 1965.

18. Kagan, J., & H. A. Moss. *Birth to maturity: A study in pyscho-logical development.* New York: Wiley, 1962.

19. Kelly, G. A. *The psychology of personal constructs.* New York: Norton, 1955. 2 vols.

20. Krathwohl, D. R., B. S. Bloom,

& B. B. Masia. *Taxonomy of objectives: The classification of educational goals. Handbook II: Affective domain.* New York: McKay, 1964.

21. Leeper, R. W. A motivational theory of emotion to replace "emotion as disorganized response." *Psychol. Rev.,* 1948, **55,** 5–21.

22. Otis, Nancy B., & B. McCandless. Responses to repeated frustrations of young children differentiated according to need area. *J. abnorm. soc. Psychol.,* 1955, **50,** 349–353.

23. Overstreet, B. W. The role of the home in mental health. In N. B. Henry (Ed.), *Mental health in modern education.* Yearb. nat. Soc. Stud. Educ., 1955, **54,** Part II, pp. 82–98.

24. Palermo, D. S., A. Castaneda, & B. R. McCandless. The relationship of anxiety in children to performance in a complex learning task. *Child Develpm.,* 1956, **27,** 333–337.

25. Phillips, B. N. Age changes in accuracy of self-perceptions. *Child Develpm.,* 1963, **34,** 1041–1046.

26. Reese, H. W. Relationships between self-acceptance and sociometric choices. *J. abnorm. soc. Psychol.,* 1961, **62,** 472–474.

27. Ruebush, B. K. Interfering and facilitating effects of test anxiety. *J. abnorm. soc. Psychol.,* 1960, **60,** 205–212.

28. Sarason, I. G. Test anxiety, general anxiety, and intellectual performance. *J. counsel. Psychol.,* 1957, **21,** 485–490.

29. Sarason, I. G. The effects of anxiety and threat on the solution of a different task. *J. abnorm. soc. Psychol.,* 1961, **62,** 165–168.

30. Sarason, I. G. Critique and notes: Test anxiety and intellectual performance. *J. abnorm. soc. Psychol.,* 1963, **66,** 73–75.

31. Shoben, E. J., Jr. Toward a concept of the normal personality. *Amer. Psychologist,* 1957, **12,** 183–189.

32. Solomon, R. L. Punishment. *Amer. Psychologist,* 1964, **19,** 239–253.

33. Strickland, Bonnie R., & D. P. Crowne. Conformity under conditions of simulated group pressure as a function of the need for social approval. *J. soc. Psychol.,* 1962, **58,** 171–181.

34. Strong, E. K., Jr. Nineteen year follow-up of engineer interests. *J. appl. Psychol.,* 1952, **36,** 65–74.

35. Symonds, P. M. *What education has to learn from psychology.* New York: Bureau of Publications, Teachers College, Columbia Univer., 1958.

36. Tuddenham, R. D. Constancy of personal morale over a fifteen-year interval. *Child Develpm.,* 1962, **33,** 663–673.

37. Washburn, W. C. Patterns of self-conceptualization in high school and college students. *J. educ. Psychol.,* 1961, **52,** 123–131.

38. Williams, J. E. Acceptance by others and its relationship to acceptance of self and others: A repeat of Fey's study. *J. abnorm. soc. Psychol.,* 1962, **65,** 438–442.

PART III

Desirable Conditions for Learning

*M*ODELS of instruction have been presented for seven outcomes: factual information (Chapter 7), concepts (Chapter 7), problem solving (Chapter 8), creativity (Chapter 8), psychomotor abilities and skills (Chapter 9), attitudes and values (Chapter 10), and personality integration (Chapter 11). Take time now to give an example of each outcome and two or three of the related teaching principles. If you have studied the previous chapters and cannot do this readily, consider reviewing until you can. The above information must be clearly in mind so that it does not become entangled with the ensuing conditions for efficient learning. As you study the key questions related to conditions of learning, you will see how closely the models for achieving outcomes and the conditions for efficient learning are related.

How is student motivation increased?	Chapter 12. Motivation
How are retention and transfer improved?	Chapter 13. Retention and Transfer
What must be done to provide well for each child?	Chapter 14. Providing for Individual Differences
How are the new materials, media, and organizations of instruction used effectively?	Chapter 15. Instructional Media and Organization

You have had many experiences with the concepts implied in each of these questions. As you read, try to recall these experiences. For example, when studying motivation, recall the attempts of your teachers to get students to accomplish various tasks. Why did some procedures work with some students? Why did all fail with some? Relating your experiences to the following material will help to make it clear, and will help you to learn, to remember, and to apply it.

CHAPTER 12

Motivation

THE MAJORITY of the readers of
this material are, or soon will be, directly and vitally concerned with
motivating students to learn. This important task should serve as an
incentive to consider carefully the contents of this chapter. However,
the authors are reminded when writing a chapter on motivation that
they have the responsibility of motivating the reader initially to such
an extent that he eagerly delves into the material presented. It is
hardly expected that this chapter will hold one's interest to the degree
that it would be classified in the "I-couldn't-put-it-down" category. But,
as a motivator, consider the interesting study discussed below.

The Minnesota Starvation Studies involved 36 normal young men
who were put on a six-month, semistarvation diet of the European
famine type (20). The men lost approximately one-fourth of their previous weight and developed the classic signs of semistarvation. No
other abnormal physical stresses were applied: The men were comfortably housed and clothed, exercised frequently, and provided with
a pleasant social environment. The men were conscientious objectors
who volunteered to make sacrifices for the common good.

The men's behavior was characterized by increasing inertia and
apathy. Men began to conserve energy in all possible ways. A few of

the men displayed serious behavioral disorders; many of them increasingly daydreamed, especially about fanciful ideas related to food.

Bizarre behavior in connection with food was almost universal and often took the form of compulsive action or of ritual. Some of this behavior was obviously motivated by desire to increase food satisfaction—plate licking, "souping" everything with water, eating extremely slowly and arranging the food in fantastic ways. Other peculiar behavior and ideas were likewise indicative of obsessions about food—resentment of fat people, compulsions to look in garbage cans, refusal to talk at meals, and the like. All of these attitudes about food may be considered relatively reasonable under the circumstances, though the casual onlooker would be mystified, for example, by the expression of anger provoked by a simple joke about food (20, 523).

The implications of the starvation studies are many, but the crucial one is that extreme "drive" conditions such as those described would not be optimal for human learning. The question then arises as to the appropriateness of conclusions reached in deprivation studies, prevalent in experimentation with animals, for human learning. The authors are uncertain that the internal physiological state of the motivated child, trying earnestly to learn to read new words and enjoying the activity, is identical with or even similar to that of an animal that has been deprived of food or water for hours. In any event, the child's outward behavior appears very different.

If all students wanted to learn what the school and teacher desired, and if all had the ability to perform the desired tasks efficiently, this chapter would be short. But some students are forced to go to school rather than desiring to do so; some do not want to learn what the schools want them to, at least not when and as the teacher desires; and some cannot perform the learning tasks well for a variety of reasons. Further, in some classrooms, motivation for learning is exceedingly low among most pupils, while in other classes of the same school, it is high. In this chapter, the point of view is that the goal of the school and of the teacher is to organize and manipulate the physical and social environment so that most students want to learn, are confident that they can learn what the teacher desires, and believe that what they learn is worthwhile for them.

We are properly concerned with what the teacher can do to increase the motivation of students. First, discussions may be held with the class, printed and other material may be used, and activities in addition to discussion may be engaged in so that students determine what is to be learned. Second, the situation may be organized so that the students' biological and social needs are satisfied. In turn, satisfaction of higher-level needs, such as the needs to know and understand and to achieve mastery over things, including subject matter, takes precedence. Third, rewards and punishments, cooperation and competition, and other incentives may be manipulated. Fourth, the learning activities may be made more meaningful to the students, as was shown in Chapters 3 and 7 in the discussions of meaningful learning. Also, the teacher may, through class, group, and individual discussions with students, help them set and attain realistic goals. Fifth, as discussed in Chapters 6, 10, and 11, interaction with students may be businesslike, enthusiastic, and warm. Further, prestigeful exemplary models may be provided for imitation. This brief overview of what is meant by organizing and manipulating the physical and social environment to enhance motivation will be clarified in the discussion of (1) human needs, (2) human interests, (3) goals and goal setting, (4) cooperation and competition, and (5) a model for motivating students.

HUMAN NEEDS

Unsatisfied human needs, with their resulting tension inside the organism, serve as motives to arouse and direct behavior toward goals which the individual perceives as satisfying the need and thereby reducing the tension. There are many classifications of needs; however, we will consider only the following: Maslow's economical list, important school-related needs, and Murray's system of needs.

A Hierarchy of Needs—Motives

Maslow set forth a theory of human motivation which brought together many ideas proposed up to that time, and his theory still merits careful study by anyone who accepts the idea of human needs as being important in energizing and directing behavior (25). The needs in order of importance to the individual are: (1) physiological needs, (2) safety needs, (3) love and belonging needs, (4) esteem needs, (5) self-actualization needs, (6) the desires to know and understand.

Maslow lists physiological needs—those necessary to maintain life —as the needs for food, oxygen, and rest, and suggests that one could make an exceedingly long list, depending upon the degree of specificity of description desired. The specific minerals and vitamins alone could comprise a very long list. He makes two other important points related to the satisfaction of the physiological needs. First, an almost certain way of getting a lopsided view of human capacities and human nature is to make the organism extremely and chronically hungry or thirsty. Extreme hunger or thirst dominates the entire organism's behavior and gives a very untrue picture of most of his higher motivations, including the social. Second, gratification is more important than deprivation in motivational theory. Once the physiological needs are gratified, other more commonly observed human needs and related goal-directed behavior emerge.

Safety needs in infants and children are demonstrated by their preference for some kind of routine or rhythm rather than disorder, their avoidance of various forms of perceived danger situations, and their withdrawal from strange and unfamiliar situations that elicit danger and terror reactions. In general, the safety need in children and adults is observed as an active and dominant mobilizer of the organism's resources in emergencies—war, disease, injury, natural catastrophes, and the like.

The love need is described as a desire or a hunger for affectionate relations with people in general and for a place in the group. Strength of this need is observed in the person who feels keenly the absence of friends, wife or husband, children, or people more generally.

Esteem needs most clearly suggest receiving recognition as a worthwhile person. Satisfaction of the esteem needs is accompanied by feelings of confidence, worth, strength, and usefulness. The thwarting of these needs produces feelings of inferiority, weakness, or helplessness.

The need for self-actualization is the need to be or to become the person one can be; for example, the tendency for the individual to become in actuality what he is potentially. Satisfaction of this need is expressed in various ways. One person becomes a good mother, another an athlete, another a musician, another a teacher, and so on. The persons in whom these needs have been relatively well satisfied are the healthiest in our society.

Maslow was uncertain that the desires to know and to understand —cognitive needs—were as clearly established in all human beings as were the others. Although curiosity, exploration, and the desire to acquire further knowledge can be readily observed, they are more evident in persons of higher intelligence than in those of lower intelligence. Where the need is present and strong, it is accompanied by wanting to systematize, to organize, to analyze, and to look for relationships.

The order of the need categories is important for they must normally be satisfied in the order given; that is, the physiological needs must be satisfied before there can be satisfaction of the safety needs; similarly, the safety needs must be met before the needs for love and belonging come into play. A summary statement helps to clarify the idea:

These basic goals are related to each other, being arranged in a hierarchy of prepotency. This means that the most prepotent goal will monopolize consciousness and will tend of itself to organize the recruitment of the various capacities of the organism. The less prepotent needs are minimized, even forgotten or denied. But when a need is fairly well satisfied, the next prepotent ("higher") need emerges, in turn to dominate the conscious life and to serve as the center of organization of behavior, since gratified needs are not active motivators.

Thus man is a perpetually wanting animal. Ordinarily the satisfaction of these wants is not altogether mutually exclusive, but only tends to be. The average member of our society is most often partially satisfied and partially unsatisfied in all of his wants. The hierarchy principle is usually empirically observed in terms of increasing percentages of non-satisfaction as we go up the hierarchy. Reversals of the average order of the hierarchy are sometimes observed. Also it has been observed that an individual may permanently lose the higher wants in the hierarchy under special conditions. There are not only ordinarily multiple motivations for usual behavior, but in addition many determinants other than motives (**25**, 394–395).

Figure 12.1 visualizes the hierarchy of prepotency. The hierarchical aspect is shown by successive needs being built on the one below. The prepotency idea suggests that at any given time the esteem needs, for

Fig. 12.1. Hierarchy and prepotency of needs. (Based on A. H. Maslow. A theory of human motivation. *Psychol. Rev.*, 1943, **50**, 370–396.)

example, might take precedence over the love and belonging needs or the safety needs. Similarly, if the basic needs in the hierarchy are temporarily satisfied, the self-actualization need would determine the goals of the individual.

The above ideas have important implications for education. For example, the teacher wants the pupils to acquire certain knowledge, but it is possible that a particular child's needs for love or esteem are not satisfied. The child's goals to satisfy these needs take precedence in energizing and directing his behavior. A rejected child, for example, may have a much stronger need for love and belonging than desire to know and understand and, therefore, he directs his energy toward satisfaction of this need rather than toward the learning task.

In fact, strict adherence to Maslow's model would necessitate satisfaction of all five of the pupil's needs below it in the hierarchy before the desire to know and understand is activated (becomes prepotent). The acquisition of knowledge and understanding are also basic elements in Bloom's cognitive taxonomy, presented in Chapter 2. The many subsidiary functions performed by the school, often criticized as "frills" by many laymen and even some educators, can be seen as attempts to satisfy those needs in the hierarchy normally prepotent over the desire to know and understand. Thus, the school lunch program and physical education classes operate to allay physiological needs; teacher acceptance of the pupil as a worthy individual helps meet love and belonging needs; while guidance services, classes in fine arts, and vocational training serve to promote satisfaction of esteem and self-actualization needs. According to Maslow's theory, these "frills" are quite necessary if the child is to experience the cognitive needs to know and understand.

Other School-Related Needs

The human being has other needs that are, in some respects, related to the cognitive needs to know and understand. Chief among these are the need to explore (or to manipulate) and the need to achieve, sometimes called the achievement motive (abbreviated "n Ach").

THE NEED TO EXPLORE OR TO MANIPULATE

Behavior described by such terms as *exploration, manipulation,* and *curiosity* is very much alike and belongs to a general class of behavior called "attention" (10). Attention is aroused by presenting stimuli different from the organism's expectations and is satiated by repeatedly presenting these originally discrepant or novel stimuli.

Early in life children demonstrate exploratory behavior. When the child can walk, or on occasion even before, he leaves his room, his house, and his play area to explore the bright objects elsewhere, to find the source of the loud and different sounds, and to learn what is on the other side of the street. His hands are used to feel and manipulate new materials, and his mouth to experiment with new foods and to make new sounds.

Some interesting experiments conducted with monkeys are pertinent to this discussion of the exploratory motive. For example, monkeys open a clasp device over and over again for no apparent reason other than the satisfaction of manipulating it (16). In the presence of visual stimuli, and in the absence of any reinforcement, monkeys actively explore their environment (7). Rather than searching for food, the monkeys appear to engage in searching behavior from curiosity. Another manifestation of curiosity is shown by monkeys learning responses for the reward of being allowed to look briefly out of a window in their otherwise opaque cages. With increasing time away from the window, the monkeys increase the rate of responding (4, 5, 6). Evidence of this type contradicts the idea of motivation resulting primarily from the deprivation of food, water, and other materials and activities associated with biological needs. Monkeys do not learn best under extreme drive conditions (15). Indeed, the source of motivation seems external to the learner and seems to result from environmental cues.

The need to explore also is observable in young children. Children of age 5 through 9 were assigned to three treatment groups. All groups had to learn which button to press to make a signal light flash. The children in one group were promised a sack of candy after they had made the light go on a given number of times. The children in a manipulation group, on the other hand, got the same promise of a sack of candy but, enroute, were made to believe that each time the light went on, they reached into a large bag of candy and took a piece of candy to put into their own imaginary candy sack. The third treatment, control, received only a light flash after the correct response. The results showed that the manipulation group solved the problem in significantly fewer trials than either of the other two groups (44).

The distinction between curiosity and exploration can be applied to school situations. If the pupils' behavior is characterized by physical movements, *exploratory* or *manipulatory* is appropriate terminology and subsumes curiosity; if the individual focuses attention upon some object or phenomena without overt approach movements, *curiosity* is the appropriate term.

Curiosity is being given increasing attention with elementary school pupils. The importance of curiosity is threefold: Learning depends on curiosity, creativity requires curiosity, and sound mental health demands curiosity. Despite its apparent importance, curiosity is not rated or tested reliably. An individually administered test of curiosity is apparently needed (**26**).

The most important implication of the recent research on exploratory behavior and curiosity is that these can and should be capitalized upon in the school. Much needs to be done, even such a rudimentary thing as ascertaining those subjects and objects about which pupils are most curious. This task may not be as simple as it appears at first glance; consider the frustrated parent who spends many hours and several dollars buying his youngster a gigantic fascinating toy, only to find that the child quickly discards the toy and instead is obsessed by playing with the cardboard box in which it came.

THE NEED TO ACHIEVE

The persistent and varied attempts that children make to learn to ride bicycles, to skate, to read, and to write suggest that there is strong need to secure mastery over things and ideas. As long as the person feels uncomfortable with himself in relation to a learning task, he expends considerable effort in activities which lead to mastery such as studying, practicing, and getting new information. The need to achieve mastery over things and ideas is so prevalent in American society that it can be used effectively in classroom motivation. Achieving mastery over people is also sufficiently strong in some children to require substitution of other goals. On occasion it occurs that a person's need to achieve in a school situation overshadows his need for moral integrity. Recall from an earlier chapter that classroom association is the most important concomitant of deceit (**17**).

Teachers estimate the need to achieve by observing pupils' activities in the classroom. Instead of saying that a child has a high need to achieve, the teacher normally says that he is highly motivated. It is important to distinguish between a student's need to achieve and his actual achievement. A pupil may have a very strong need to achieve, but low aptitude; this combination would not result in high achievement. This idea can be clarified by the simple equation:

$$\text{Aptitude} + \text{Motivation} = \text{Achievement}$$
$$\text{(Need to achieve)}$$

Attempts to measure aptitude and achievement in given subject areas

430

have been moderately successful (more so for achievement than for aptitude) and thus, motivation can be inferred indirectly if the two other quantities are given.

Efforts to measure motivation (or need achievement) directly have not been completely successful. For example, one instrument, intended to measure the strength or intensity of the need to achieve as a general characteristic, involves the scoring of imaginative stories or responses given by subjects when presented with a series of pictures (24). By careful scoring in several categories, a trained administrator can establish an achievement-need score for the subject. The reliability of this motivation test is not high (3). Table 12.1 shows a positive correlation over a relatively short period of time between two successive sets of scores; but with longer passage of time, the correlation is quite low. Thus, based on this test, the achievement motive is situational in character; otherwise, it would not vary so much over relatively short periods of time.

TABLE 12.1.

Coefficients of Equivalence Stability for Need Achievement

	February, 1957 (N:40)	April, 1957 (N:26)	August, 1955 (N:46)
October, 1956 (N = 46)	+.29	+.56*	+.15
February, 1957		+.20	+.40*
April, 1957			+.03

NOTE: Asterisks denote p < .05.
SOURCE: R. C. Birney. The reliability of the achievement motive. *J. abnorm. soc. Psychol.,* 1959, **58**, 267.

Although the objective scores derived from achievement-motivation tests are not highly consistent over longer periods of time, those who scored high and low on an achievement-motivation test differed significantly on a problem-solving task (12). The mean motivation score of those who solved the problem was 9.28, whereas the nonsolvers had a mean score of 7.34. As shown in Fig. 12.2, among those with high achievement motivation scores, 25 solved the problem and 22 did not. On the other hand, there were 14 solvers and 31 nonsolvers in the low motivation group. This result is similar to other reports of differences

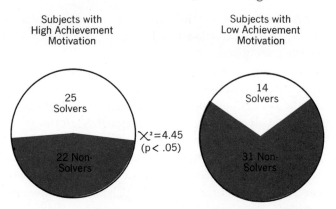

Fig. 12.2. Number of problem solvers in high and low achievement-motivation groups. (Adapted from Elizabeth G. French & F. H. Thomas. The relation of achievement motivation to problem solving effectiveness. *J. abnorm. soc. Psychol.*, 1958, **56**, 46.)

in achievement between students who score high or low on tests of achievement motivation.

Little has been done to measure achievement motivation directly in school-age children although some recent instruments are reported to be useful in judging the level of motivation. Because motivation scores seem unreliable, direct observation of pupil behavior in the classroom often serves better than tests in ascertaining the strength and direction of the achievement motive in individual pupils. However, the achievement motive, although elusive to measure, is quite clearly established as an important determiner of the direction and intensity of an individual's behavior. Furthermore, differences in strength of need to achieve are reflected in varying levels of achievement.

A Psychogenic Need System

A nonhierarchical classification of human needs has been developed (27). In addition to the viscerogenic needs such as eating, elimination, etc., a taxonomy of psychogenic needs originating in the mind is outlined. The needs are listed with brief definitions in Table 12.2. Our purpose in presenting them is to acquaint you with the terminology which is encountered later in this chapter, and in studies of human motivation. A widely used projective personality test—the Thematic Apperception Test (28)—several personality inventories, and a test of motivation are based on the framework of needs provided by Murray.

TABLE 12.2.

Psychogenic Need System

Need	Behaviors Associated With Need
Abasement	To surrender; to comply and accept punishment; to apologize, confess.
Achievement	To overcome obstacles, to exercise power.
Affiliation	To greet, join; to form friendships, associations; to love.
Aggression	To assault or injure; to belittle, harm, blame; to punish severely.
Autonomy	To resist coercion or influence; to defy authority; to seek independence.
Counteraction	To defend honor; to refuse admission of defeat by retaliating.
Deference	To cooperate; to serve gladly.
Defendance	To defend oneself against belittlement or blame; to justify one's actions.
Dominance	To influence or control others; to persuade or dictate; to lead and direct; to organize the behavior of a group.
Exhibition	To attract attention to one's person; to excite, shock others.
Harmavoidance	To avoid pain, physical injury, illness and death; to take precautionary measures.
Infavoidance	To avoid failure, shame, ridicule; to conceal disfigurement.
Nurturance	To nourish, aid, or protect others; to express sympathy.
Order	To organize, arrange; to be tidy and clean.
Play	To relax, seek diversion; to avoid serious tension.
Rejection	To snub, ignore; to remain indifferent and aloof.
Sentience	To seek and enjoy sensuous impressions.
Sex	To form and further an erotic relationship, sexual relationship.
Succorance	To seek sympathy, aid, protection; to plead for mercy; to be dependent.
Understanding	To analyze experience, to discriminate among concepts, to define relations, to synthesize ideas.

SOURCE: Adapted from *Explorations in Personality* by Henry A. Murray. Copyright 1938 by Oxford University Press, Inc. Reprinted by permission.

HUMAN INTERESTS

The usual means of ascertaining an individual's interests in activities is to observe his behavior or to ask him more directly to state his preference for a number of activities. Vocational interests in secondary students and adults have been studied rather extensively. Interests are believed to have five characteristics:

First, they are acquired in the sense that feeling becomes associated with the activity. We are not referring to the learning of an activity itself, such as writing one's name, which usually requires many repetitions. We are referring to the associating of feeling with an activity. . . .

Second, interests are persistent. Sometimes disliking is replaced by liking

433

and vice versa; many start out disliking olives and acquire a taste, a pleasant feeling for them. But, all in all, interests are surprisingly permanent.

A third characteristic of interests is intensity. One can not only immediately indicate whether he likes or dislikes an activity, but one can also immediately indicate his relative preferences for different activities.

The fourth and fifth characteristics are acceptance-rejection and readiness to act. . . . The associated value, or feeling quality, determines whether the activity will be accepted or rejected, whether the organism will go toward or away from, whether it will continue the status quo or discontinue it. It must also be noted that many activities develop in time so as to bring sufficient pleasure to be employed for their own sake. So we smoke, chew gum, play bridge, or golf for the fun of it (**43**, 452–453).

The persistence of interest noted above is based on tested preference for activities in persons in the age group 25 to 55. The recall of interests by adults also is revealing. Seventy-five male and 75 female teachers and 43 male factory workers were asked to recall their first interests in occupations (**29**). At the time of the interview, these people were between 28 and 40 years of age, with a mean age of 34. The development of interests in jobs was different in women than in men teachers and, also, the interests of men who became teachers differed markedly from those of men who became factory laborers. Fifty percent of the women recalled a vocational preference at about age 9, 50 percent of the men teachers did at about age 11, and 50 percent of the factory workers did at about 14. Interestingly, 100 percent of the teachers reported a definite vocational interest at age 21, while factory workers in considerable numbers reported no vocational interest at any point in their lives.

In an exciting study, first-grade children were found to have four main kinds of interests: active play outdoors, playing with toys indoors, written activities, and helping adults with work (**46, 47**). Marked sex differences were found in the interests of boys and girls. The sex differences became even more pronounced in fourth-grade children. The boys' interests were characterized as rejecting inappropriate activities, things associated with being a sissy and girls' work. Girls rejected physical activities, aggression, and all sorts of activities they considered inappropriate for girls. Tyler strongly believes that interest patterns result from the development of dislike of many activities by both boys and girls who originally had a liking toward the same activities. Further, it is the broad interest in sexually determined activities, in work, and in aggression rather than specific similarities between activities that seems to determine interest patterns in children of this age.

Table 12.3 shows the items of the total interest test on which the

TABLE 12.3.

Items Showing Greatest Individual Differences in Responses (Boys; N:96)[a]

	Item	Like	Indifferent	Dislike	Undecided
Part 1.	Reading				
	Love stories	23	15	48	8
	To read aloud	37	18	35	3
Part 2.	Movies				
	Love stories	22	17	45	7
	Movies about rich people	35	21	32	6
	Sad movies	30	20	38	5
Part 3.	Radio				
	Classical music	30	24	35	6
	To have the radio on while reading	34	21	36	3
Part 4.	Games and toys				
	Blocks	29	22	41	3
	Dancing	37	19	35	8
	Hopscotch	27	22	33	10
	Jacks	30	17	36	10
	Jumping rope	22	21	45	8
	Playing doctor or nurse	32	17	40	5
	Playing school	29	19	40	5
Part 9.	Occupations				
	Barber	29	20	38	7
	Bookkeeper	39	19	32	4
	Dentist	32	18	35	8
	Orchestra leader	29	24	30	7
Part 10A.	Activities				
	Be in a fight	30	17	43	1
	Clean house	33	19	38	2
	Sew	28	15	46	3
	Sing in choir or glee club	37	12	33	10
	Study	42	18	28	3
	Wash dishes	31	16	42	3
Part 10B.	School play				
	Make the costumes	34	17	38	3
	Write the play	46	8	34	4

[a] Sums of tabulations vary because of omissions and multiple responses.

SOURCE: Leona E. Tyler. The development of "vocational interests": I. The organization of likes and dislikes in ten-year-old children. *J. genet. Psychol.*, 1955, **86**, 36.

differences among fourth-grade boys was greatest. It is surprising to see the small difference in the number of boys who showed like and dislike for various activities such as reading aloud, seeing sad movies, the occupation of orchestra leader, being in a fight, studying, washing dishes, and writing the school play. Note that these are activities which show the disagreement among the fourth-grade boys. Nearly the same number liked as disliked them. On many other activities there was much higher agreement.

Although we know that vocational interests become relatively stable somewhere around age 20 and that differences among pupils in school activities are far ranging, we are less certain as to the process by which interests are originally acquired. Tyler's theory, that dislike of activities is learned, is crucial if fully supported in school situations, for it means that the child probably acquires disinterest or dislike for certain learning activities as shown in Table 12.3 after he starts school.

GOALS AND GOAL SETTING

The goal is the end result which the individual seeks. Goal setting implies conscious awareness of what is being sought. The close relationship between needs and goals will become more apparent when we discuss: (1) remote, intermediate, and immediate goals, (2) setting and attaining immediate goals, (3) factors affecting goal setting, and (4) overcoming the effects of failure.

Remote, Intermediate, and Immediate Goals

Remote, intermediate, and immediate goals are related to the developmental level of the individual. For a first-grade child, a remote goal might be something he wishes to achieve four weeks in the future, an intermediate goal would be achieved within a week, and an immediate goal, within a few minutes or an hour. The college freshman sets a remote goal of becoming a successful teacher four years hence, an intermediate goal of completing the required courses in the freshman year, and an immediate goal of reading and understanding a chapter in a book within a two-hour period of study. *Level of aspiration,* the term generally used to describe an immediate goal, will be discussed later.

Goals vary in complexity. Remote goals are usually multiple. The freshman who sets the goal of becoming a successful teacher perceives in this not only doing an excellent job in a classroom but also earning his livelihood and securing many other satisfactions from teaching. His needs for achievement, exploration, affection, esteem, and self-actualization are met if his remote goal is achieved. Immediate goals, on the other hand, are usually less involved and have fewer facets.

Setting and Attaining Immediate Goals

The level of aspiration is the level of performance in a familiar task which an individual tries for or thinks he can accomplish on the next performance. Table 12.4 shows the process of goal setting and some of

TABLE 12.4.

Level of Aspiration

	Last Perform- ance	Level of Aspiration or Goal	Goal Discrep- ancy	Actual Perform- ance	Attain- ment Discrep- ancy	Feelings of Success or Failure
Bill	20	40	+20	18	−22	Failure
Mary	30	33	+3	30	−3	Failure
George	35	33	−2	38	+5	Success
Susan	40	43	+3	45	+2	Success

the terminology connected with level of aspiration. Imagine that Bill, Mary, George, and Susan are in a typing class. Their last performances, point A, are shown as 20, 30, 35, and 40 words per minute on a five-minute test. The teacher asks them to indicate how many words per minute they expect to type in a five-minute test two days later. As shown, their levels of aspiration or immediate goals are set as follows: Bill—40, Mary—33, George—33, and Susan—43. The difference between the last performance and the level of aspiration now set, *goal discrepancy*, can be positive or negative. Notice that Bill shows a positive goal discrepancy of 20 and George a negative goal discrepancy of 2. These students continue their class work and two days later take another five-minute test. Bill now achieves a speed of 18, Mary —30, George—38, and Susan—45. The attainment discrepancy is again either negative or positive. Bill shows a negative attainment discrepancy of 22 and Mary of 3; George and Susan show positive attainment discrepancies of 5 and 2. If these students were all ego-involved —actually had set the goals and tried to attain them—Bill and Mary would have experienced failure feelings.

What is the effect of prior success and failure on goal setting? Fourth-, fifth-, and sixth-grade children were arranged in three experimental groups based on their previous school experience (36). Children in the success group had shown subjective and objective evidence of success in all academic school subjects, including reading and arithmetic; those in the failure group had the opposite experience; and the differential group had experienced success in reading and failure in arithmetic. These groups were given familiar reading and arithmetic tasks and, after the first goal-setting sequence, feelings of success and failure were experimentally induced in them by telling them that they either had not done well or had done well, regardless of how they had actually performed. The child's level of aspiration was ascertained by asking him how many seconds he thought would be needed for him to complete the reading or to solve the arithmetic problem.

Figure 12.3 presents a comparison of the academically successful, failure, and differential groups in terms of goal-discrepancy scores—the difference between actual performance on the first trial and the level of aspiration set for the next trial. Most children in the success group set levels of aspiration in the reading task slightly above their past performances; however, the failure group set them erratically—three set goals below previous achievement and seven set goals five or

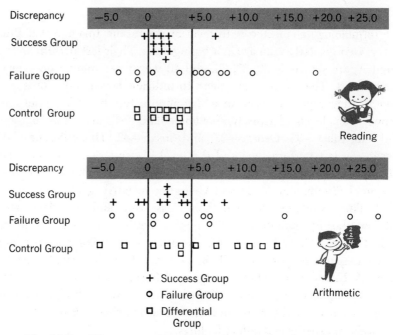

Fig. 12.3. Discrepancy scores of groups varying in past experience of success or failure. (Adapted from Pauline S. Sears. Levels of aspiration in academically successful and unsuccessful children. *J. abnorm. soc. Psychol.*, 1940, **35**, 511.)

more seconds above their previous achievement. The differential group was more like the success group in dispersion on the reading task. The pattern in arithmetic showed the success group less widely dispersed than the failure group and the differential group in between. The success group in both tasks set the most realistic goals.

After this initial work, failure and success feelings were induced experimentally in the three groups. Induced feelings of success in all three groups led to more realistic goal setting; that is, the level of aspiration was set more in line with the past performance; and induced feelings of failure produced greater variability in subsequent goal setting.

Part of the previous experiment was replicated in three eleventh-grade classes in United States history, but there was no attempt to induce feelings of success or failure experimentally (8). The students were divided into two groups. One had experienced previous academic success, and the other had experienced lack of success as indicated by grade-point average. These students then set six consecutive goals throughout the academic year. The students with a record of previous academic success achieved higher and set goals more realistically (usually above previous performance), whereas those with previous failures achieved lower and set goals less realistically—sometimes above previous performance and sometimes below. The actual experience of success and failure in attaining goals had similar effects on later goal setting, as did the induced feelings of failure and success reported earlier. However, more eleventh-grade students than younger children who had experienced success tended to set the next goal lower.

More informal evidence about level of aspiration was secured with college students in realistic situations (9). The main conclusions are summarized in five statements:

1. Success generally leads to raising the level of aspiration; failure, to lowering.
2. The stronger the success, the greater the probability of a rise in the level of aspiration; the stronger the failure, the greater the probability of a lowering.
3. Shifts in the level of aspiration are partly a function of changes in the subject's confidence in his ability to attain goals.
4. Failure is more likely than success to lead to withdrawal from goal setting.
5. Effects of failure on the level of aspiration are more varied than effects of success. In a similar study, other college students who

experienced more successes on training trials had significantly greater verbalized expectancies and confidence than did others who experienced fewer successes in training (40).

Both objectively measured success and subjective feelings of success are accompanied by realistic goal setting, higher achievement, and higher motivation for the learning task. Repeated failures produce undesirable emotional effects. This does not mean that immediate success is necessary. Even though a student experiences failure on his first try, he will continue to try if he has confidence that he can be successful.

College girls were given nine puzzles and each was asked to tell which puzzle she would most enjoy doing, which one she would enjoy second best, and so on (13). The puzzle that each girl ranked fifth was identified and then the entire group was divided into four subgroups. Each subgroup was then given a different experimental treatment in connection with the fifth-ranked task. One group experienced success and expected further success on the subsequent tasks, another group experienced failure but expected future success, a third group experienced success but expected future failure, and the fourth group experienced failure and expected failure on other tasks. After all the tasks were finished, the girls were again asked to rank the nine puzzles in order of preference for doing. The average ranking of the task that had previously been ranked fifth follows:

Success on first task, expecting further success	3.85
Failure on first task, expecting future success	4.75
Success on first task, expecting future failure	4.80
Failure on first task, expecting further failure	5.85

Feelings of success combined with expectation of further success led to higher preference for the particular puzzle, and failure with expectation of further failure led to lowest preference. Although present success and expectation of future success resulted in greater liking for continuing an activity, some girls who failed and expected further failure persisted in desiring to continue with the same task.

Factors Affecting Goal Setting

Present success and expectation of further success have a desirable effect on motivation, achievement, and subsequent goal setting; repeated failure has a definitely undesirable effect.

Other factors affecting goal setting include the nature of the task and various personality variables not directly associated with the task.

An analysis of 59 studies dealing with level of aspiration led to several conclusions of importance to education (18). First, a task can be so difficult that no student can realistically set a goal or hope to achieve success on it; also, a task can be so easy and accomplished with such little effort that no feeling of success is experienced. Second, children who are realistic and confident and have comfortable feelings toward themselves and school set goals more realistically, and they strive more persistently to achieve those goals than do students with the opposite traits. Third, low goal setting is often accompanied by high need to avoid failure; some individuals protect their self-esteem by setting goals low enough to be achieved easily. Fourth, insecure individuals experience a feeling of success by publicly setting high goals which they know they cannot attain; approval is generally given for "hitching to a star," even though one never rises from the smog. Fifth, the group influences goal setting of members. After the goals of the entire group are known, there is a tendency for those with higher goals to lower them somewhat and those with lower goals to raise them somewhat.

Overcoming the Effects of Failure

Repeated failures in grades or in subjective feelings indicate that the student is not learning efficiently and may be acquiring undesirable attitudes toward himself and school. This does not mean that an occasional pupil should not be failed by objective standards. If, however, a student fails for no reason of his own or for reasons that he cannot overcome, the situation has not been arranged to meet some of his important needs. Children can be helped to overcome the undesirable effects of failure.

Children of preschool age were placed in two experimental situations for 15 and 8 minutes to perform an attractive task, but one so difficult that they could not accomplish it readily, if at all, with persistent effort (19). The experiment was arranged to induce feelings of failure. The responses of the children in the two situations showed considerable variation and 15 of them demonstrated exceedingly immature behavior. In the second part of the experiment, 12 of those of immature behavior participated in a training program designed to ascertain the extent and the means by which the undesirable effects of failure could be overcome. In this experimental program, four similar but not identical attractive tasks were arranged according to level of difficulty, from quite easy to difficult but solvable with persistent effort. During the reeducation period the experimenter started with the easiest task, helped each child at times, encouraged him to continue at times, and arranged the situation so that the child could see his progress and was aware of his success with the first task. Figure 12.4 shows the responses of the group on a task similar to the original difficult tasks before and after the experimental training. Marked improvement occurred in three kinds of behavior: attempting to solve the problem alone, interest in the task, and amount of crying. The training did not have much effect on the children's asking for help; however, on all other behavior the small differences show that the training did produce more desirable responses.

Another study, an extension of the Keister-Updegraff study, was concerned primarily with age and sex differences in regard to training (**49**). Four-year-olds were found to use more facial expressions and rationalizing behavior, while 3-year-olds expressed significantly more behavior such as making no attempt, seeking help, and seeking infor-

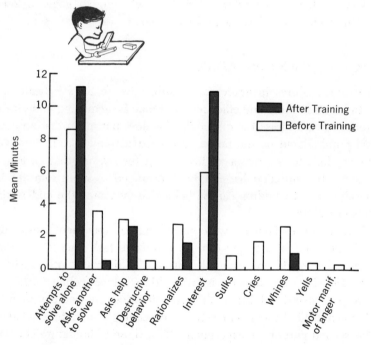

Fig. 12.4. Responses of trained group on puzzle-box test before and after training. (Mary E. Keister & Ruth Updegraff. A study of children's reactions to failure and an experimental attempt to modify them. *Child Devlpm.*, 1937, 8, 246. By permission of the authors and the Society for Research in Child Development, Inc. Copyright 1937 by the Society for Research in Child Development, Inc.)

mation. Boys displayed significantly more facial expressions and more destructive, emotional responses. They had a tendency to rationalize and to seek help. In contrast, girls made more attempts to solve the task alone, to seek contact, and to seek information.

Inasmuch as these were studies of preschool children, it is difficult to project the results to elementary and secondary grades. We cannot directly answer the question of whether or not giving individual help and easier tasks to failing students will be effective. We have, however, analyzed the level of aspiration. This analysis indicates that there are several ways a teacher may encourage the failing student to be persistent in his efforts. One way is to build the student's self-confidence so that he feels secure in striving toward a particular goal. Someone who is not afraid of being hurt by failure will be more willing to renew his efforts. A teacher should deliberately arrange pleasant learning situations in which the student feels successful. In addition to fostering self-confidence, this will help him set realistic goals. Also, the student should be told when he makes progress, even if the amount of improvement seems small and insignificant to the teacher.

COOPERATION AND COMPETITION

We are somewhat schizophrenic in that we encourage cooperation in the home, the school, and the neighborhood, yet simultaneously we encourage competition for rewards. The outcomes of training in cooperation and competition are not clear. They are dependent upon the age of the individuals, the forms of cooperation and competition, and the areas in which the competition and cooperation are carried out. We do know that the values from competition and cooperation are somewhat different. In competing with others one wishes to win or to do better for personal gain or prestige. In cooperative activities, one wishes to improve himself and to make a significant contribution to the group. If the competition is friendly and organized so that every student has an opportunity at some time to win, motivation, achievement, and interpersonal relations may be excellent; however, in poorly managed competition, hostility between members of the group develops, and, in younger children, outward aggression occurs. In cooperative activities, there is no reason for hostility or aggression to develop; on the contrary, the group members are encouraged to help one another. We turn now to some outcomes of cooperation and competition in people of varying ages and under varying arrangements.

Second-grade pupils were asked to paint two murals during noon hour. Before painting the first one, they were told that, if everyone painted well and if the mural was a good one, everyone would receive a prize—a package of colorful stickers. Before painting the second mural, they were told that only the best painters would receive prizes. The children were then observed during the painting sessions and in subsequent play activities; check lists and stenographic recordings were made during the observation. In these situations, there was no difference during the painting sessions between instances of positive and negative interaction among the children; the effects of cooperation and competition were the same (42).

Within two seventh-grade classes, students tried to better their own previous performances (individual competition) and in two other classes, the students competed against one another for three days (14). On Monday, and again on Friday, a self-scoring test was given to the students to determine whether or not the pupils changed answers—cheated—when given the opportunity to do so. The individual competition consisted of having each child keep a record of his progress on Tuesday, Wednesday, and Thursday. The group competition consisted of telling children how their scores compared with the scores of pupils in the other class. Wide variation in the number of children who cheated was found under both competitive arrangements, but no difference was observed in the amount of cheating between the two forms of competition—individual and group. Two-thirds of the children who cheated did so on only one of the days, Monday or Friday. Children of higher intelligence and higher achievement cheated less frequently than those of lower intelligence and lower achievement. Achievement was the same under the two forms of competition, although the fact that all pupils had knowledge of the results for each day may have been a stronger motivating force than either form of competition; also, the entire learning time was only a brief portion of the school day for one week.

Three forms of motivation—curiosity and creative drive, cooperative group activity, and competition—were applied to primary school children. Competition produced the lowest motivation and performance in reading; curiosity and creative drive, the highest (34).

Four groups of high cohesiveness and four groups of low cohesiveness were drawn from a number of fourth-grade classes (31). Two of the high-cohesive and two of the low-cohesive groups worked under cooperative conditions while the other four groups worked under competitive conditions. The task was a modification of the game

"Twenty Questions." In the cooperative arrangement, the members of the group shared equally in a reward, but in the competitive group they shared in accordance with their relative contributions. Under cooperative conditions, the groups which were already cohesive increased in their cohesiveness; under competition there was no change in cohesiveness. The children in the competitive arrangement shared about equally in the rewards. This led to a final conclusion that, if the results of competition lead to a fairly uniform distribution of rewards in the group, the effects of competition may be similar to that of cooperation; however, if only one or two members receive the rewards, competition will likely lead to a decrease in group cohesiveness.

An interesting task was arranged for college students in which there was no need to use an external incentive to keep the students working (39). The students worked under three experimental conditions: one in which the subject perceived himself to be in a cooperative situation, one in which he saw himself as competing with another, and the third in which he worked alone. Two relatively simple tasks that could be performed in a few minutes were used. On both of these tasks, the cooperative situation yielded most efficient learning, the individual situation next, and the competitive situation least. Other information showed that the students in the competitive situation rated their motivation highest, rated their enjoyment of the task highest, and thought they expended the most energy. For some unexplained reason, the higher motivation with possible threat to self-esteem in the competitive situation led to some disruption of response and therefore to less effective learning. The students in the cooperative situation appeared to be relaxed and stated they were; they felt that the other person would either perform well or share the blame for the poor performance.

In none of the preceding studies did competition yield more efficient learning than cooperation. Inasmuch as cooperative activities also reduce the threat of failure and frustration for pupils of lower ability, the school should seriously consider reducing competition among pupils in regular classroom learning situations. This is in line also with the previously discussed ideas about individual goal setting.

MODEL FOR MOTIVATING THE STUDENT

The significance of motivation for learning is usually assumed without question. On the one hand, the promise of reward or the threat of punishment provides means by which the teacher can keep the pupil at work; on the other hand, interest, curiosity, and self-selected goals keep the learner at work without pressure from the teacher. The teacher has a choice between using specific goads or enlisting self-activating motives, or perhaps employing some combination of these (38, 182).

This point of view is similar to ours except that we feel the teacher must be prepared to apply different principles with different children. As was stated earlier, some pupils come to school and want to learn everything the school and the teacher desire. With these pupils, the principal motivational task is to find sufficient and appropriate learning activities for them. Many pupils, however, either do not want to learn what the school and teacher offer, or they do not want to learn it the way it is being presented. All the principles which follow are applicable to the second group and, to a lesser extent, to the first group.

GENERALIZATION	PRINCIPLE
1. When certain objectives are to be achieved, the students' attention must be directed toward those objectives.	1. Focus student attention on desired objectives.
2. Curiosity, interest, and achievement are positive motives that may be manipulated readily to focus student behavior toward desired objectives.	2. Encourage the development of positive motives.
3. Meaningful learning sets and advance organizers enhance motivation for learning new material by relating previous abilities and knowledge to the present task.	3. Use learning sets and advance organizers.
4. Setting and attaining goals encourage consistent effort and permit knowledge of progress and feelings of success to operate effectively.	4. Help students to set and attain realistic goals.
5. A warm, businesslike environment promotes continued effort and favorable attitudes toward learning.	5. Create a warm, orderly atmosphere.
6. Rewards are effective with some children in initiating and directing behavior; punishment may suppress undesirable behavior.	6. Provide incentives and punish, if necessary.
7. Extended intense motivation, accompanied by anxiety, disorganizes behavior and impairs learning efficiency.	7. Avoid high stress and disorganization.

Focus Attention on Desired Goals

Many elements of the physical environment of the classroom may be manipulated to direct pupil attention toward the objectives. Here is how a fourth-grade teacher focused attention on the study of "Cold Lands" at the beginning of a unit in social studies. The pupils arrived at school the first day after the Christmas holidays on a cold morning. After two weeks of vacation, 32 children, anxious to get in from the cold, hurried to Room 120. The thermometer registered 55 degrees in the corner of the room with a north exposure. This was probably the first time the majority of these children realized quite fully the meaning of the word, *cold*.

With stormcoats and snowsuits on, the children examined the totem pole, the walrus tooth, actual photographs of Lapps with reindeer herds, laughing Eskimos in Baffin Island, Aleuts ice fishing, and numerous pictures displayed on bulletin boards. After spending a few minutes looking at these various things, some of the children started examining library books that had been placed conspicuously on tables. One or two others began to find the Cold Lands on globes and maps. The environment of the room, mingled with the cold feeling, may have prompted Barbara to remark that, "We are like Eskimos this morning, all bundled up to keep warm."

A teacher of an eighth-grade general science class began a unit on electrical current, the second unit on electricity, with these words and a demonstration:

I have a large coil which, as you can see, is insulated wire wound together. I am going to connect the two ends of the coil to this current-measuring instrument called a galvanometer. Here is a friend we have already studied, a bar magnet. Watch what happens to the needle of the galvanometer when I push the North pole of the magnet inside the coil of wire [needle moves to the left]. Now watch when I pull the magnet out this way [needle moves to the right]. Now I am going to go through the same operations once more. You ask me questions that will help you to decide why the galvanometer reacted the way it did.

In geography a beginning teacher described attempts to focus attention on a study of Japan:

The first day of the unit the students walked into an environment which was definitely Japanese. In the front of the room was a wall map of Japan and a travel poster. Bulletin boards were filled with pictures of Japan. But, the best materials were on the table in the front of the room, some of the many

447

products made in Japan. Few students were in their seats when the bell rang. Students were raising questions, but instead of answering, I asked more questions. Every student was trying to identify and name the products made in Japan.

These illustrations show that pupil attention can be focused through the use of materials and activities that involve a number of sensory perceptions. In the fourth-grade class, seeing, hearing, and feeling were all involved. In the science classroom, only seeing and hearing were involved. To focus class attention toward the desired outcomes, it is essential to appeal to more than one sense, because the usual class always has some pupils who respond better to visual material than they do to spoken words. The teacher takes a positive role in order to make certain that the necessary materials are arranged and available; in addition, he decides whether or not, once their attention has been generally directed toward a learning outcome, the pupils will begin studying from books directly or will engage with him in planning activities.

In some situations it is not necessary to do any more than let the pupils know, by oral or written suggestions, what is expected. In certain skill classes a self-activating routine may become quickly established whereby pupils come in even before the bell rings and start to work without the teacher's giving any specific instruction. Further, when projects or activities are started but not finished on one day, the tendency is for the pupils to come back and start immediately where they have left off.

Encourage the Development of Positive Motives

In the previous sections of this chapter, we have indicated that the needs to know and understand, to manipulate and explore, and to achieve are powerful motives because they direct activity toward some end. One does not have to deprive the individual of his biological, safety, love and belonging, or esteem needs in order for these other needs to take over in guiding and directing behavior. In fact, the biological needs must be satisfied before these higher level needs related to learning can operate. Representative of positive motives are curiosity and interest which we shall treat briefly.

As discussed earlier, human beings are curious about objects and phenomena in the environment. Curiosity is generally expressed toward new and novel objects, ideas, and events rather than toward familiar ones. The arousal of curiosity is not dependent on any form of reward or punishment nor is it attached to any specific drive situation, such as hunger or thirst. Also, after an object, idea, or material is no longer novel it loses its curiosity value. Novel ideas and material can be used purposefully to arouse curiosity. Any other activity or goal setting connected with the unit of work is then designed to capitalize upon aroused curiosity.

It is possible that some activities will arouse so much curiosity that the individual will persist in them and, in the process, will learn efficiently. Instructors in science, psychology, and other classes often introduce a puzzle or a game of some sort in order to clarify a major idea. Even college students become so absorbed in completing the puzzle that, if permitted, they spend the entire class period trying to work it out. Unless brought back by the instructor, they completely miss the idea that the puzzle supposedly illustrates. The need to explore is quite pervasive and can be capitalized upon daily. The objective here is to encourage students to seek the novel and the fascinating in their daily activities. If school learning activities do not entirely satisfy this need, gratifications outside the school may be sought. In addition, if the individual is thwarted or directly punished for showing curiosity, he may eventually acquire substitute goals or suppress his curiosity.

Interests are also positive motives because the individual purposefully seeks to do something. One way to find out about students' interests is to ask them which of several classroom activities they most prefer. Even though they might not be highly interested in any, giving them the choice itself may encourage interest. When students feel that subsequent instructional arrangements will be based upon their stated interests, they express themselves freely and reliably. In elementary, high school, and college classes, expressed interests are frequently used as a basis for dividing classes into smaller groups. When five or more different activities are to be undertaken, the entire class is invited to express interest in the activities, and then the subgroups are arranged accordingly. The idea underlying interest grouping is that motivation is higher because the students are working on activities which attract and hold their attention.

A boy should not be excused indefinitely from arithmetic class simply because he is interested in science, not mathematics. Instead, the teacher should utilize this interest in science by helping the boy see the relationship between arithmetic and his existing interest. Likewise, if a teacher wants to build a boy's interest in silent reading, she can capitalize on his fondness for dogs by giving him books and pamphlets about dogs and their care. Interest gathers momentum when the activities are satisfying and rewarding. Getting a student to see the satisfaction in an activity may lead to the formation of a very stable interest.

Let us examine some attempts of beginning teachers to utilize the curiosity and interests of students. In an English class studying mythology, one question proved especially fruitful in arousing curiosity: "Where do myths come from and why were they told in the first place?" Upon answering this question, the ninth-graders realized that myths were created by people, not greatly different from themselves.

As a means of discovering the students' interests in India, a teacher first held a class discussion in which the students indicated whatever came first to their minds when they thought of India. Then, each student wrote a "pretend" letter to a high school student in India, asking whatever questions he was most concerned with. The letters helped the teacher to discover any preconceptions (and possible misconceptions) the students had and to evaluate their existing interests.

A beginning history teacher found several techniques to arouse curiosity each day that the class was studying a unit on World War II. Two photographs were passed quickly around the room, and then the students were asked what the photographs meant to them. One was a monument erected in honor of persons exterminated during World War II at Buchenwald; the other showed the burning chambers in which bodies were cremated. Another item was an extra edition of the *Washington Daily News* with the huge headline, "Allies Invade France." The presentations of news stories, journal articles, pictures, and editorials, with a stimulating question, aroused much curiosity.

Use Learning Sets and Advance Organizers

Short instructions should be given to students before starting a task. These instructions may have different purposes, such as prompting the student to recall relevant knowledge, to think of the abilities or skills needed for the new task, to understand the final outcome desired, or to compare or contrast ideas in the task. Instructions of this type comprise a learning set, a predisposition to proceed in a certain manner rather than another. As we noted previously, advance organizers may be prepared and presented to the student for two main purposes: to provide an organizational framework for the new material so that it will be understood better, and to provide transitional material between what is already known and the new material. If knowing how to proceed and what will be learned produces a desire to learn, these techniques are motivating. The major effect of learning sets and of advance organizers is to produce more efficient learning. For example, one group of students were told to read a selection on Buddhism while remembering similarities between the Buddhist and Judeo-Christian religions; a second to remember the differences between them; a third to remember the similarities and differences; and a fourth merely to understand and to remember the passage. On two subsequent tests, the differences and the similarities-and-differences groups did better than the understand-and-remember group (48). The facilitating effects of advance organizers that compare and discriminate between prior and new material is well documented (2).

Help Students to Set and Attain Realistic Goals

Although this same principle has been discussed in connection with personality integration, and has been implied in the discussion of all learning outcomes mentioned in Chapters 7 through 10, it is treated here because it is probably the most important principle of this group. When a person sets a goal, he tries to attain it. Attaining goals is accompanied with feelings of success, as noted in the sequence of purposeful learning in Chapter 3. Nothing encourages continued effort and further realistic goal setting more effectively than a backlog of goals successfully attained. Why then do students so infrequently set individual goals in the classroom? There are three main reasons. First, even though individual students vary widely in readiness to learn, they are all given the same material. Second, teachers do not take the time or have the ability to help each student set and attain realistic goals. Third, instructional materials and activities are often not available to permit the kind of instruction which individual goal setting requires. Let us consider these and other matters associated with helping each student to set and attain realistic goals.

When a teacher has students representing a wide range of capability for learning new tasks, realistic goal setting by each student, rather than all by students dealing with the same assignment, requires much knowledge and skill. The teacher must:

1. have a fairly accurate estimate of each student's abilities
2. have a good estimate of the difficulty of the learning activities
3. encourage varying levels of performance by pupils
4. permit students of all abilities to experience many successes and occasional feelings of failure in reaching their goals

451

5. realize that the goal-setting process takes considerably more class time than does giving the same assignments to all students in the class

Realistic goal setting also requires that each pupil have a fairly reliable estimate of his own abilities in relation to the learning activity and a rough estimate of the difficulty of the learning activity. The pupil must also have an interest in the learning activity and some previous success in connection with school learning.

When the teacher has fairly reliable information about the students, class discussion is profitable for arriving at a better understanding of the proposed activities and for encouraging group decision or commitment to study and work with enthusiasm and persistence. In most situations, dividing a group of 20 to 35 pupils into three to five smaller groups in which everyone has better opportunity to discuss possible activities is appropriate. Finally, there must be individual teacher—pupil conferences with some pupils to help each to set a realistic goal.

How might individual goal setting proceed in a beginning typewriting class? All students start at the same point—not being able to type—and engage in the usual instruction and demonstration procedures, including distributed practice to increase speed and accuracy. Six or more weeks might be needed to reach this point. Once it is reached and the students know their speed and accuracy, each sets the goal he expects to attain one week hence in terms of number of words per minute and number of errors on a timed test. At the end of the week, the timed tests are used to ascertain the extent to which the goal is achieved. After this first experience, the goal set for one week later should be more realistic. After several experiences in goal setting at weekly intervals, more distant goals of two or more weeks in the future are appropriate. Along the way, the teacher continuously acquires better estimates of the students' abilities, and helps them raise or lower goals as the situation demands. At the end of the year, we properly anticipate that some students would set and achieve goals in terms of speed twice to three times as high as others.

Many teachers object to the above procedure because of the grading system. What grade should a student receive who has done his best and types at 25 words per minute? the one who has done his best and achieved a stable speed of 60 words per minute? Procedures to handle the vexing problem of grading have been discussed fully elsewhere (21, 22). Our point of view is that any grading system which prevents teachers from helping pupils learn as well as they might should be carefully examined and changed as necessary. The function of the school is to nurture and to improve human abilities and human beings, not to grade and categorize.

In the second week of a seminar for highly talented high school seniors, each student set goals for the semester; no one set the same goal. One girl set a goal of writing children's literature. With professional guidance from her teacher, she identified a vast amount of children's literature during the first weeks and started to read and study it and to try out some selections with neighborhood children. Upon becoming better acquainted with the literature, she had to readjust her goal in the early part of the semester to complete more of the reading. After spending much time in these activities, she then started her first writing. In this case, the teacher helped her both to readjust her goal and to make progress toward achieving it. In the same seminar, another student set the goal of getting a better understanding of "beatnik" literature. After reading several novels, she found difficulty in understanding and evaluating them. The teacher then helped her develop criteria and locate critical reviews of the entire "beatnik" movement and of specific novels.

These examples from the typing class and the seminar show that class activities and discussions led by the teacher, smaller-group discussion led by the teacher or by designated pupil chairmen, and individual conferences between the teacher and pupil are essential for implementing purposeful and efficient learning based upon goal-setting procedures. In Chapter 15, we shall discuss programed instruction, instructional teams, and other recent innovations designed to make individual goal setting by students more workable.

Create a Warm, Orderly Atmosphere

In Table 6.4 information was summarized which indicated that warm, businesslike, imaginative teacher behavior is associated with high and consistent pupil achievement and high emotional security. Sentimental and unplanned teacher behavior is associated with inconsistent student achievement and low achievement for insecure children. Aloof and routine teacher behavior is associated with low achievement in rebellious students and low emotional security in most children. The association of lower and higher achievement with certain kinds of teacher behavior involves motivation. A few examples will clarify this point.

Three pairs of punitive and nonpunitive teachers were selected. Children in various classes were asked about pupil misconduct. Those who had the punitive teachers were less concerned about learning and school values than were the children whose teachers were nonpunitive. Also, children under punitive teachers manifested more aggression in their misconduct and were more unsettled about misconduct (23). Personal warmth of the teacher and student interest in science also are highly related (33).

Creativity also is fostered better in a warm, nurturant environment without teacher domination, than in a nonsupportive environment with teacher domination. Formal group instruction in which shame was used as punishment had a negative relation with creativity (41). On the other hand, the teacher's manifesting interest in the child's ideas and listening to the child was positively correlated with creativity (37).

Provide Incentives and Punish if Necessary

In Chapter 11, we noted that punishment may be used to suppress undesired behavior. Further, the threat of punishment may be used in order to get the student to perform some task which he would prefer not to do. However, the effects of punishment and threat of punishment are much less predictable than are the effects of positive incentives. Further, the use of punishment tends to put the teacher in an unfavorable light with students and also may cause personal problems for the student. You may wish to review the previous discussion of punishment prior to continuing with the study of positive incentives.

Concrete and symbolic rewards are sought by adults as well as children and can serve the purpose of getting people to perform inherently unpleasant tasks. If the tasks were pleasant or undertaken to achieve important goals, no rewards would be necessary. Rewards used in the schools are of two main types: concrete and symbolic. Concrete rewards take the form of money, pencils, an excuse from class, and the like. Symbolic rewards include letter grades, favorable comments, nonmonetary awards, and others. Rewards may be given for individual effort, competitive effort, or cooperative effort. Let us consider briefly the effects of different types of rewards.

Five types of rewards were used with 9-year-old children: no reward, a verbal reward, a penny reward, a promise of 25 cents upon completing the task, and combinations of these four at various points in the task. The results were of practical significance. First, efficient learning was in the reverse order of the incentive conditions listed. The most effective incentive was the promise of 25 cents. Second, the verbal reward when repeated more than four times lost its effectiveness. Third, the concrete reward—giving a penny—was just as effective when administered during the last 15 trials as when administered during the entire series of 30 trials. Fourth, and most important, since the promise of 25 cents yielded the most efficient learning, it was the goal of receiving the 25 cents which stimulated the learning, not actually getting the money. The goal energized the individual, whereas actually receiving the penny or the verbal reward tended to bring about quiescence and lack of further consistent effort (1).

If the rewards are kept small and given early in the learning situation to get initial effort started on inherently meaningful learning tasks, it is possible that the learner will associate the pleasantness of receiving the reward with the task. Further, as progress on the task itself is made, the accompanying experience of success and knowledge of progress make continuing rewards unnecessary. As shown in the previous chapters dealing with factual and skill learning, reinforcement of correct responses promotes efficient learning. Students cannot always evaluate their own responses without help and need reinforcements in order to confirm correct or appropriate responses. For example, one group of students received its test papers back corrected and was given five minutes to go over the papers. The second group did not have its papers returned. One week later the test was again administered to the students. The results were clear cut and decisive. Students who were given the opportunity to inspect their papers scored considerably higher, one week later, than did those who did not inspect their papers (32).

In a similar study, 74 teachers administered whatever test would next occur in the usual course of instruction for their own pupils. Pupils were unaware that an experiment was in progress and were randomly assigned to one of three experimental treatments: one-third had their tests returned with no teacher comments, another third with free teacher comments (that is, natural and appropriate for the particular students concerned), and the final third of the pupils had their tests returned with specified, but generally encouraging, teacher comments. In their next objective exam, the free-comment group scored significantly high and the no-comment group significantly low. Thus, appropriate and natural teacher comments had a facilitating effect on student motivation (30).

A considerable number of students from families that have a high interest in education work industriously to achieve desired learning outcomes without any form of external incentive, including grades. Even these highly motivated pupils respond well to occasional praise from the teacher, not only for good achievement, but also for persistent effort. Approval from classmates and others within the school also works well with most students, though some need much less approval from their classmates and teachers than do others.

The teacher must be alert in using rewards, for pupils are indeed different. Differential effects of material and nonmaterial rewards are noted on children of lower and middle social class (**45**). Nonmaterial rewards were quite effective with pupils of middle social class, but ineffective with pupils of lower social class.

In addition, a teacher must be alert when "dispensing" rewards and praise, for students quickly ascertain the "worth" of teacher actions in this regard. Students distinguish between two types of disapproval by teachers: disapproval of inadequate performance and disapproval when the student has done his best (**35**). The former has a favorable effect on motivational aspirations while the latter has a detrimental effect. Further, indiscriminate bestowal of rewards by the teacher minimizes the teacher's influence, while rewards given only for adequate performances increases the teacher's influence.

In summary, the widespread use of concrete and symbolic rewards as motivational devices has many dangers. However, when a teacher cannot get pupils to perform worthwhile learning tasks by other means, it is better to use rewards than to use punishments or simply to allow students to sit day after day in the classroom without making any effort to learn.

Avoid High Stress and Disorganization

Trying to achieve a desired goal is always accompanied by some tension. As shown in Chapter 11, anxiety and stress may become so high that the student's responses become disorganized; he does not learn efficiently. This is not likely to occur if the situation permits him to lower his goal; however, persons typically set their goals too high and experience frustration in not attaining them when they feel that they will lose the approval of peers or other persons whom they admire. Frequently, students who set goals such as making all A's experience severe frustration when it becomes apparent that they will receive C's or even B's in one or two courses. The frustration comes not because they feel they are not learning enough or that the learning in itself is not valuable, but because some reward, such as a desired scholarship, will be denied or disapproval from parents or teachers will result.

SUMMARY

Motivation is a salient concept in American society today. As Fitts has pointed out, human motivation has largely been ignored by human engineers (11). For a century, jobs have tended to become intrinsically less interesting and motivating. Yet few studies in human engineering have had as their goal determining ways to make them more interesting. In the human's earlier life, motivation is an integral component of learning and a critical problem in educational settings.

Unsatisfied needs, with the accompanying tensions, arouse and direct activity toward goals which the individual perceives as satisfying those needs. A classification scheme which incorporates most human needs includes: physiological needs, safety needs, love and belonging needs, esteem needs, self-actualization needs, the need to explore, and the need to achieve.

Interests are probably acquired in the same way as attitudes. An interest may be persistent and intense, and may serve as a set toward acceptance or rejection of an activity. When given a choice, the individual engages in an activity which he perceives as interesting rather than one he dislikes or sees as uninteresting.

Goals may be remote, intermediate, or immediate. A variety of organismic and situational factors affect goal setting and goal attainment in learning situations as well as in life. Experiencing success and anticipating further success result in higher achievement and better personality integration than do experiencing failure and anticipating further failure. Cooperative activities offer opportunity for more students to experience success than do competitive activities where only a few receive the rewards.

High motivation can be attained in group situations by: (1) focusing attention on desired goals, (2) encouraging the development of positive motives, (3) using learning sets and advance organizers, (4) helping student to set and attain realistic goals, (5) creating a warm, orderly atmosphere, (6) providing suitable rewards and punishing if necessary, and (7) avoiding high stress and disorganization.

QUESTIONS AND ACTIVITIES

1. In what activities may the teacher engage to increase the motivation of students?

2. a. Critically evaluate the concept of a hierarchy of needs.

   b. How might this concept be

useful in appraising intensity of student motivation for classroom activities?

3. Describe your present needs to achieve and to explore. Are they intense? Already gratified? Connected with which facets of your daily life?

4. Referring to the research of Sears and others, discuss briefly the effects of setting and attaining immediate goals.

5. a. State two goals you intend to reach this week, two others one year hence, and two others ten years hence.
   b. What is the relationship between these goals and your needs as you perceive them? Your interests?

6. a. Classify the five factors affecting goal setting into two groups, organismic and situational.
   b. Put the five in the order from highest to lowest to indicate your judgment as to which a teacher can exercise most control over in a classroom setting.

7. Outline and discuss a plan for overcoming the effects of failure in students of the developmental level in which you are most interested.

8. a. Summarize the results of the research reported on cooperation and competition.
   b. Why does research not yield clear-cut and final conclusions about the effects of cooperation and competition in school situations?

9. a. Describe a classroom situation, including the number of students, sex, school level, range of general intellectual abilities, and range of achievement levels represented in the group.
   b. Indicate how you would implement each principle of motivation in this situation.

10. a. Drawing on your own experiences as a student, list the three principles you judge were least frequently applied by your teachers.
    b. Why were they least frequently applied?

<hr>

SUGGESTIONS FOR FURTHER READING

Coleman, J. S. The adolescent subculture and academic achievement. *Amer. J. Sociol.*, 1960, **65**, 337–347. (In Charters & Gage, 1963, 87–94; and Ripple, 1964, 135–147.)

Fowler, H. *Curiosity and exploratory behavior.* New York: Macmillan, 1965, pp. 3–77.

Harlow, H. F. Motivation in monkeys— and men. In F. L. Ruch (Ed.), *Psychology and life.* Chicago: Scott, Foresman, 1963, pp. 589–594. (In Russell, 1964, 67–72.)

Kennedy, W. A., & H. C. Willcutt. Praise and blame as incentives. *Psychol. Bull.*, 1964, **62**, 323–332.

Kersh, B. Y. The motivating effect of learning by directed discovery. *J. educ. Psychol.*, 1962, **53**, 65–71. (In DeCecco, 1963, 277–287; Gordon,

1965, 431–435; Ripple, 1964, 396–404; and Seidman, 1965, 104–109.)

Lachman, S. J. Level of aspiration: A classroom demonstration of phenomena and principles. *J. gen. Psychol.*, 1961, **65**, 357–363. (In Seidman, 1965, 114–118.)

McClelland, D. C., J. W. Atkinson, R. A. Clark, & E. L. Lowell. *The achievement motive.* New York: Appleton–Century–Crofts, 1953. (Portions reprinted under the title "Origins of achievement motivation" in Kuhlen & Thompson, 1963, 217–224.)

Page, E. B. Teacher comments and student performance: A seventy-four classroom experiment in school motivation. *J. educ. Psychol.*, 1958, **49**, 173–181. (In Charters & Gage, 1963, 219–225; and Page, 1964, 310–319.)

Prentice, W. C. H. Some cognitive aspects of motivation. *Amer. Psychologist,* 1961, **16**, 503–511. (In Crow & Crow, 1963, 356–370; and Harper, et al., 1964, 400–411.)

Rosenfeld, H., & A. Zander. The influence of teachers on aspirations of students. *J. educ. Psychol.,* 1961, **52**, 1–11.

Sears, Pauline S., & E. R. Hilgard. The teacher's role in the motivation of the learner. In E. R. Hilgard (Ed.), *Theories of learning and instruction.* Yearb. nat. Soc. Stud. Educ., 1964, **63**, Part I, pp. 182–209.

White, R. W. Motivation reconsidered: The concept of competence. *Psychol. Rev.,* 1959, **66**, 297–323. (In Gordon, 1965, 10–23.)

Zunich, M. Children's reactions to failure. *J. genet. Psychol.,* 1964, **104**, 19–24.

REFERENCES

1. Abel, L. B. The effects of shift in motivation upon the learning of a sensori-motor task. *Arch. Psychol.,* 1936, **29**, 205.

2. Ausubel, D. P. *The psychology of meaningful verbal learning.* New York: Grune & Stratton, 1963.

3. Birney, R. C. The reliability of the achievement motive. *J. abnorm. soc. Psychol.,* 1959, **58**, 266–267.

4. Butler, R. A. Discrimination learning by rhesus monkeys to visual-exploration motivation. *J. comp. physiol. Psychol.,* 1953, **46**, 95–98.

5. Butler, R. A. Incentive conditions which influence visual exploration. *J. exp. Psychol.,* 1954, **48**, 19–23.

6. Butler, R. A. The effect of deprivation of visual incentives on visual exploration motivation in monkeys. *J. comp. physiol. Psychol.,* 1957, **50**, 177–179.

7. Butler, R. A., & H. F. Harlow. Persistence of visual exploration in monkeys. *J. comp. physiol. Psychol.,* 1954, **47**, 258–263.

8. Byers, J. L. An investigation of the goal patterns of academically successful and unsuccessful children in a United States history class. Unpublished master's thesis, Univer. of Wisconsin, 1958.

9. Child, I. L., & J. Whiting. Determinants of level of aspiration: Evidence from everyday life. *J. abnorm. soc. Psychol.,* 1949, **44**, 303–314.

10. Dember, W. N., & R. W. Earl. Analysis of exploratory, manipulatory, and curiosity behaviors. *Psychol. Rev.,* 1957, **64**, 91–96.

11. Fitts, P. M. Engineering psychology. In S. Koch (Ed.), *Psychology: A study of a science.* Vol. 5. New York: McGraw-Hill, 1963, pp. 908–933.

12. French, Elizabeth G., & F. H. Thomas. The relation of achievement motivation to problem-solving effectiveness. *J. abnorm. soc. Psychol.,* 1958, **56**, 45–48.

13. Gebhard, Mildred E. The effect of success and failure upon the attractiveness of activities as a function of experience, expectation, and need. *J. exp. Psychol.,* 1948, **38**, 371–388.

14. Gross, M. M. The effect of certain types of motivation on the "honesty" of children. *J. educ. Res.,* 1946, **40**, 133–140.

15. Harlow, H. F. Mice, monkeys, men, and motives. *Psychol. Rev.,* 1953, **60**, 23–32.

16. Harlow, H. F., Margaret K. Harlow, & D. R. Meyer. Learning motivated by a manipulation drive. *J. exp. Psychol.,* 1950, **40**, 228–234.

17. Hartshorne, H., & M. A. May. *Studies in the nature of character: I. Studies in deceit.* New York: Macmillan, 1928.

18. Holmes, Charlotte C. An examination of goal-directed behavior in terms of level of aspiration. Unpublished master's thesis, Univer. of Wisconsin, 1959.

19. Keister, Mary E., & Ruth Upde-

graff. A study of children's reactions to failure and an experimental attempt to modify them. *Child. Develpm.*, 1937, **8**, 241–248.

20. Keys, A. Experimental induction of psychoneuroses by starvation. In *The biology of mental health and disease.* 27th ann. Conf. Milbank Memor. Fund. New York: Harper & Row, 1952, pp. 515–525.

21. Klausmeier, H. J. *Teaching in the secondary school.* (2nd ed.) New York: Harper & Row, 1958.

22. Klausmeier, H. J., & Katharine Dresden. *Teaching in the elementary school.* (2nd ed.) New York: Harper & Row, 1962.

23. Kounin, J. S., & P. V. Gump. The comparative influence of punitive and nonpunitive teachers upon children's concepts of school misconduct. *J. educ. Psychol.*, 1961, **52**, 44–49.

24. McClelland, D. C., J. W. Atkinson, R. A. Clark, & E. H. Lowell. *The achievement motive.* New York: Appleton-Century-Crofts, 1953.

25. Maslow, A. H. A theory of human motivation. *Psychol. Rev.*, 1943, **50**, 370–396.

26. Maw, W. H., & Ethel W. Maw. *An exploratory investigation into the measurement of curiosity in elementary school children.* U.S. Office of Education Cooperative Research Project No. 801. Washington, D.C.: Dept. Hlth, Educ., & Welfare, 1964.

27. Murray, H. A. *Explorations in personality.* New York: Oxford, 1938.

28. Murray, H. A. *Thematic Apperception Test.* Cambridge: Harvard, 1943.

29. Norton, J. L. Patterns of vocational interest development and actual job choice. *J. genet. Psychol.*, 1953, **82**, 235–262.

30. Page, E. B. Teacher comments and student performance: A seventy-four classroom experiment in school motivation. *J. educ. Psychol.*, 1958, **49**, 173–181.

31. Phillips, B. N., & L. A. D'Amico.

Effects of cooperation and competition on the cohesiveness of small face-to-face groups. *J. educ. Psychol.*, 1956, **47**, 65–70.

32. Plowman, L., & J. B. Stroud. Effect of informing pupils of the correctness of their responses to objective test questions. *J. educ. Res.*, 1942, **36**, 16–20.

33. Reed, H. B. Implications for science education of a teacher competence research. *Sci. Educ.*, 1962, **46**, 473–486.

34. Roberts, G. R. A study of motivation in remedial reading. *Brit. J. educ. Psychol.*, 1960, **30**, 176–179.

35. Rosenfeld, H., & A. Zander. The influence of teachers on aspirations of students. *J. educ. Psychol.*, 1961, **52**, 1–11.

36. Sears, Pauline S. Levels of aspiration in academically successful and unsuccessful children. *J. abnorm. soc. Psychol.*, 1940, **35**, 498–536.

37. Sears, Pauline S. *The effect of classroom conditions on strength of achievement motive and work output of elementary-school children.* U.S. Office of Education Cooperative Research Project No. 873. Stanford: Stanford, 1963.

38. Sears, Pauline S., & E. R. Hilgard. The teacher's role in the motivation of the learner. In E. R. Hilgard (Ed.), *Theories of learning and instruction.* Yearb. nat. Soc. Stud. Educ., 1964, **63**, Part I, 182–209.

39. Shaw, M. E. Some motivational factors in cooperation and competition. *J. Pers.*, 1958, **26**, 155–169.

40. Slovin, T., H. Schumer, & J. L. Myers. Effects of success and instructions on verbalized expectancies and amount bet in a two-choice situation. *Tech. Rep. No. 10.* Amherst: Dept. Psychol., Univer. of Massachusetts, 1963.

41. Spaulding, R. *Achievement, creativity, and self-concept correlates of teacher-pupil transactions in elementary schools.* U.S. Office of Education Cooperative Research

Project No. 1352. Urbana: Univer. of Illinois Press, 1963.

42. Stendler, Celia, D. Damrin, & A. Haines. Studies of cooperation and competition: I. The effects of working for group and individual rewards on the social climate of children's groups. *J. genet. Psychol.*, 1951, **79**, 173–197.

43. Strong, E. K., Jr. Satisfactions and interests. *Amer. Psychologist,* 1958, **13**, 449–456.

44. Terrell, G. Manipulatory motivation in children. *J. comp. physiol. Psychol.*, 1959, **52**, 705–709.

45. Terrell, G., Jr., Kathryn Durkin, & M. Wiesley. Social class and the nature of the incentive in dis-crimination learning. *J. abnorm. soc. Psychol.*, 1959, **59**, 270–272.

46. Tyler, Leona E. The relationship of interests to abilities and reputation among first-grade children. *Educ. psychol. Measmt,* 1951, **11**, 255–264.

47. Tyler, Leona E. The development of "vocational interests": I. The organization of likes and dislikes in ten-year-old children. *J. genet. Psychol.*, 1955, **86**, 33–44.

48. Wittrock, M. C. Effect of certain sets upon complex verbal learning. *J. educ. Psychol.*, 1963, **54**, 85–88.

49. Zunich, M. Children's reactions to failure. *J. genet. Psychol.*, 1964, **104**, 19–24.

CHAPTER 13

Retention
and Transfer

THE TEACHER is concerned about the extent to which material learned during a day, week, or month will be remembered at a subsequent time. He also is concerned about transfer of learning—whether what is learned and remembered will help in meeting new or different situations. A main reason for formal education in school is to facilitate learning in situations outside school. The conditions and relationships among original learning, remembering, and transfer of learning are treated in the subsequent discussion of: (1) outcomes that are remembered and transferred; (2) retention and forgetting; (3) viewpoints about transfer; (4) a model for encouraging retention and transfer.

OUTCOMES THAT ARE REMEMBERED AND TRANSFERRED

An outcome may be said to have been acquired when it is first incorporated into the learner's behavior pattern; for example, when the child correctly spells a word or solves a problem, we properly say that at that time he has *acquired* the particular outcome. If at a later time the same child correctly repeats the performance, we say that he has *remembered* or *retained* what he acquired. *Transfer* of learning occurs when whatever is learned in one situation is used in a new or different situation.

Transfer may be lateral or vertical (13). In *lateral* transfer the individual is able to perform a novel task of about the same level of complexity as that which he has learned. For example, a child has learned at school to recognize new words. He then recognizes in a newspaper article words of about the same difficulty as those read in school. Lateral transfer has taken place. Instruction in reading is based on the assumption that there will be lateral transfer; that is, formal instruction in reading will lead to better reading in other subject fields.

Through *vertical* transfer, the person is able to learn more advanced or more complex outcomes. For example, being able to add, subtract, and multiply lays the basis for performing long division. Any hierarchical organization of knowledge follows a similar pattern as that given in the mathematics example. Subordinate concepts lay the basis for the subsequent learning of superordinate concepts. Thus, possessing the concepts of subject and predicate is essential to learning the concept of sentence. Similarly, the ability to read at one level permits learning to read at the next higher level.

Whether transfer is lateral or vertical, there are three main requirements. The individual must possess favorable attitudes toward new learning, essential knowledge, and requisite abilities. Wanting to continue to learn is essential. Knowledge also is prerequisite for positive transfer. We cannot teach children to think, independent of subject matter. For example, if the young child does not yet have mathematical concepts, he cannot be taught to think using these concepts. In any subject the child can learn to think only as he has the prerequisite knowledge. At an advanced level, the more systematic knowledge the scientist possesses, the greater his chances for discovering new knowledge. Although the abilities of mankind are not yet fully catalogued, they, too, are essential for transfer. Methods of learning, also referred to as *strategies* of learning and *learning-to-learn* techniques, make it possible to apply knowledge to new situations. We may similarly think of methods of adjusting as being essential for transfer in social situations. In the following paragraphs, we will give brief attention to concepts, methods of learning, and methods of adjusting in order to emphasize learning outcomes that are especially amenable to retention and transfer.

Concepts, based on a relatively larger number of facts, are retained better than the facts themselves and also show greater possibility for transferring to a variety of new situations. This was shown when 172 students were given a pretest, the same test at the end of the semester, and the same test four months later (**30**). After four months they remembered the concepts better than the specific information on which the concepts were based. Thus, separate facts do not transfer so readily as concepts, in part because facts are forgotten more rapidly and in part because they are less applicable to a variety of situations.

Methods of learning are indicated by a variety of terms such as *work methods, study methods,* and *work-study skills.* All the terms refer to the process of learning how to learn. Whether the original learning is the running of mazes by lower animals or the solving of problems by human beings, the methods of learning are the highly pervasive outcomes that are retained and that transfer to many subsequent situations. Harlow demonstrated that learning to learn was an important characteristic of apes and younger children and concluded that learning to learn efficiently transforms the human organism from a creature that adapts to a changing environment by trial and error to one that adapts by seeming hypothesis and insight. He further postulated that learning to learn is a more important variable in most learning tasks than is making correct responses in the presence of certain stimuli (**17**).

From grades 4 through 8 there is a consistent increase in work-study skills, also referred to as *abilities,* such as reading a map; using references, an index, or a dictionary; and alphabetizing. In addition, a considerable difference exists in these abilities between children of low and high intelligence enrolled in the same class. Therefore, every school should have a good central library in which to give instruction in work-study skills. Work-study skills should be incorporated into the entire instructional program each day, for slow-learning groups as well as fast-learning groups profit from instruction in work-study skills. Planned instruction should begin not later than the fourth grade (**20**). These abilities have high prospect for transfer and facilitating new learning in a variety of in- and out-of-school situations.

Methods of adjusting include goal-oriented effort, reinterpretation of one's own behavior in a situation, and pursuit of substitute goals. Methods of adjustment are learned at a young age and subsequently have a very important impact on one's life. Though it is difficult to ascertain precisely how a particular method of adjustment is originally acquired, it is certain that it is applied later to new or somewhat different situations—that is, the individual responds to the new situation with a previously learned method of adjustment.

RETENTION AND FORGETTING

Try to recall everything that occurred during the third, sixth, or tenth year of your life. You cannot recall perfectly, but why have you forgotten? Various explanations are given of why some material and experiences are remembered and others are forgotten. We shall consider general explanations, the type of material that aids retention, and a unique feature of memory and forgetting, namely, *reminiscence*.

One explanation of retention is that, when something is learned and used, it is remembered but, when it is not used, it is forgotten. This explanation in terms of *disuse* suggests deterioration or decay of the connections in the brain as the basis for forgetting and some sort of strengthening of connections when the response is used.

Interference of present learning with what has been previously learned also leads to forgetting. For example, you read and studied the preceding chapter on motivation and remembered much of what you studied. Now you are into this chapter; it is possible that your reading here will interfere with your remembering the materials on motivation. This phenomenon is called *retroactive inhibition*. Another kind of interference works in the opposite direction. In what we call *proactive inhibition*, initial learning interferes with subsequent learning. Sequence is the main difference between proactive and retroactive inhibition. In proactive inhibition, the interfering material is encountered first, in retroactive it is encountered last. One can reduce the undesirable effects of retroactive inhibition through the use of advance organizers which tend to make new and old material more readily discriminable (4). Similarly, the negative effects of proactive inhibition can be eliminated by giving instructions to the students to notice and remember differences between sets of material (41).

Reorganization also is a basis of forgetting. In this process, someone learns certain material or a skill, but does not learn it well and does not use it for some time. He then has need to use it and, in the process of recall, reorganizes what he had previously acquired into some new patterns which make sense to him now. For example, a child learned to spell *believe* correctly as part of the organized program of spelling instruction, but did not write it again for several weeks. Now he needs the word in a story. His best present version is *beleve;* in the active reorganizing process to meet the present situation an incorrect spelling is accepted.

A slightly different viewpoint about forgetting is that embodied in *subsumption* theory as was discussed in Chapter 3 (3). For example, a person now has learned the concept of *red circle.* Although he remembers the attributes of red circle so that he will correctly label any such object encountered, he probably has forgotten the many individual objects which he encountered in forming the concepts of *red* and *circle.* The more individual experiences which were eventually subsumed under the concepts *red* and *circle* have lost their dissociability and have, therefore, been forgotten. They are no longer discriminable and hence are incapable of being remembered because they have been incorporated into the more general and inclusive concepts.

Another theory of forgetting is *motivated forgetting,* but it is less well established than are the theories of disuse, interference, and reorganization. Apparently, as we learn we constantly decide what we will try to remember and what is not worth remembering; part of this deciding not to remember could represent motivated forgetting. Further, most human beings try to forget unpleasant experiences but are not completely successful; others sometimes forget so completely as to experience amnesia—the inability, not associated with known damage to the brain or central nervous system, to recall past experiences. In some cases the individual can recall nothing of his previous experiences; in other cases there is recall of events only up to a certain period. Because most amnesia victims are helped by various therapeutic processes to recall the experiences they previously could not, it is assumed that they wanted to forget but now no longer do. Amnesia victims usually have experienced exceedingly unpleasant events before the onset of the condition.

In daily affairs, there also is some suggestion of motivated forgetting. Some adults forget appointments which they anticipate to be unpleasant. Also, the boy who is ordered to see the principal immediately after school may honestly forget that he was to do so, even though he remembers that his gang is to meet a week hence for a football game. Though the bases of motivated forgetting are not fully understood, the teacher or parents should not immediately conclude that a child is deliberately lying when he states that he forgot an appointment or forgot to carry out some activity he perceived as being rather unpleasant. We do not treat the adult amnesia victim as a deliberate liar and should not so treat the child.

466

Type of Material and Retention

The degree of meaningfulness of material is related to retention. Figure 13.1 shows that unrelated material committed to memory by rote procedures is forgotten very rapidly, with more than 70 percent loss at the end of one day and 80 percent loss at the end of the second day (37). This curve is typical of those in many experiments in which *nonsense material* is committed to memory by rote, and the learning stops when the subject reaches a criterion of one perfect recitation.

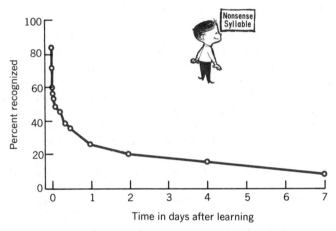

Fig. 13.1. Curve of retention as determined by recognition. (Adapted from E. K. Strong. The effect of time-interval upon recognition memory. *Psychol. Rev.*, 1913, **20**, 357.)

Table 13.1 shows the percent of correct answers to examination items made by students enrolled first in a general psychology course and later in a beginning course in educational psychology. Nearly 86 percent of the items answered correctly in June also were answered correctly in September; and 81 percent of the items answered correctly in February were answered correctly in September (31). This high degree of retention suggests that a curve of retention for material of low meaningfulness as shown in Fig. 13.1 does not apply to more meaningful material. The same conclusion was reached about retention of socially useful and meaningful arithmetic problems by children of low, average, and high intelligence (11, 25).

An extensive review of studies dealing with retention of subject matter by elementary, high school, and college students points to differential retention of various outcomes:

1. *Elementary-school subjects.* Studies in elementary-school subjects indicate that reading ability tends to increase during summer vacation. Studies of history show a difference in the rate of forgetting types of historical material: a gain in the second test in the case of easy material but a loss for more difficult material. Arithmetic studies tend to show that advanced material is more easily lost than fundamentals. The degree of difficulty of the material studied appears to affect the rate and amount of loss.

2. *Secondary-school subjects.* Studies conducted in mathematics in secondary schools showed a definite loss varying from ten per cent during the summer vacation to as much as thirty-three and one-third per cent during a year interval. In a standardized algebra test some items were retained by one hundred per cent of the class whereas other items showed a one hundred per cent loss. In some of these studies there would appear to be little relation between amount of initial acquisition and the amount retained. Studies in science show a definite loss varying with different types of material. Retention appears higher in the area of general information and application of facts and lower in ability to recall chemical terms and to write equations. In a study of high-school and college chemistry, high-school seniors showed a forty-two per cent loss of informational material after a period of three months. After a five-year period college students were able to recall approximately nineteen per cent of the informational material studied in high-school chemistry.

3. *College subjects.* Studies in college science courses show a definite loss over the time intervals measured. The amount of loss varies from fifty per cent over a four-month period to as high as ninety-four per cent loss of initial gain after one year. The greatest loss appears to be in technical information with little loss in ability to apply principles to new situations. Retention in general subject-matter areas after an interval of four years or more indicated

TABLE 13.1.

Percent of Correct Answers to Examination Items

	Pretest	End of General Psychology Course	Beginning of Educational Psychology Course Sept., 1954	% Retention
19 items common to June, 1954, and educational psychology tests	54.03	73.5	70.7	85.6
18 items common to Feb., 1954, and educational psychology tests	41.12	78.0	71.1	81.3

SOURCE: W. J. McKeachie, & D. Solomon. Retention of general psychology. *J. educ. Psychol.,* 1957, **48**, 111.

highest retention in United States history, ancient history, and geometry whereas the lowest retention was in physics, chemistry, and Latin. In a world history test given to college freshmen, retention scores appeared to be closely related to grades received in high-school courses. In an American history test based upon factual information, a group of college girls showed a loss of forty per cent of the initial acquisition after one year (**36**, 455–456).

The above summary shows that retention is related to varying types of learning outcomes and to their difficulty. In general, factual and technical information is forgotten rapidly; more general information, application of facts, and principles are retained better.

Reminiscence

A person juggles two balls for the first time in his life for 10 minutes. At the end of 10 minutes he makes 50 consecutive catches. He then rests for 5 minutes and, upon juggling again, makes 60 consecutive catches. Without practice and without further learning of any sort he has performed better than he did previously. In another situation, a student is given 40 words to spell. He studies these words for 20 minutes and spells 25 correctly. For the next 10 minutes he engages in a physical activity without further study of the words. Thereupon, he takes the same list of words and spells 30 correctly; it appears that he remembers more than he originally learned. These better performances after a change in activity or rest are referred to by the term *reminiscence*.

The better performance in juggling after rest is usually explained on two bases. With each successive try during the first learning there was some lessening of efficiency produced by fatigue or reactive inhibition; when the individual had completed 10 minutes of active practice some efficiency was already lost. The rest interval provided the needed time for the effect of fatigue, or reactive inhibition, to dissipate; when the juggling was started after rest, a better performance resulted. Another explanation is improvement with practice from the first to the second try. A level of skill was built during the first practice session and, after rest, further improvement occurred. Though both of these are reasonable explanations of reminiscence in connection with motor tasks, they are not as appropriate for such tasks as spelling and arithmetic, in which the amount of physical energy is negligible and in which individual items are missed—not learned. At the present there is no completely adequate explanation of improved performance in such cases—in the spelling example, for instance. Higher motivation might have been present in the second situation because the individual has already experienced some success in the first situation. Although these explanations are tentative, the important point is that in many school situations we expect to observe reminiscence, especially with psychomotor tasks.

VIEWPOINTS ABOUT TRANSFER

The teacher, as well as others who decide what to teach, explicitly or implictly accepts a theory or combination of theories of transfer in making his decisions. Understanding the theories will make the decisions more rational. Four theories in order of their historical origin are formal discipline, identical elements, generalization, and transposition. These four theories are discussed first; then agreements about theories and negative and positive transfer are treated.

Formal-Discipline Theory

The formal-discipline theory of transfer arose before the brain and central nervous system were adequately understood, and it was assumed that the mind was composed of many separate faculties such as memory, reason, attention, will, and imagination. According to the theory, these faculties should be strengthened through practice much as muscles are strengthened; systematic drill in certain subject fields was thought to have the same effect as physical exercise of the body. Inasmuch as the most difficult subjects in the late 1800s were supposedly Latin, Greek, and mathematics, they were thought to be the most desirable subjects and most useful for strengthening these faculties and for improving the mind generally. In accordance with the theory, memory drills (it made little difference what was memorized) were employed to develop the memory faculties. Long and difficult assignments were supposed to develop the faculties of will power and attention. Further, subjects such as Latin, Greek, and mathematics were thought to have inherent qualities which enabled the simultaneous development of many other faculties. In turn, as these faculties were well developed through education in the school, the results would automatically transfer to out-of-school situations, including the practical daily affairs of life.

Thorndike, after studying the effects of different subjects taken in high school upon increase in students' ability to reason, concluded that one subject was no better than another for improving reasoning ability (39). As the courses were then taught, physics, trigonometry, Greek, and Latin produced no better reasoners than did physical education and dramatic arts; however, students who were enrolled in the more difficult courses made higher scores initially than did those who were enrolled in the more practical courses. Humphreys also concluded that (1) taking a course in English literature does not automatically result in the students' showing higher appreciation of literature outside the course, (2) teaching moral or ethical values in Sunday School does not necessarily have any effect on moral behavior outside the class, (3) a foreign-language course does not sharpen the intellect of those who take the course, (4) a laboratory course in physical science does not necessarily result in carry-over of scientific method to social sciences or biological sciences, and (5) a traditional geometry course does not necessarily result in an increase in ability to solve problems, except in geometry (21). It is a mistake to assume that there is automatic transfer from any subject field to any other subject field or to situations outside the school.

Though the theory of formal discipline has been disproved, considerable teaching is yet based on it, though it is stated in such terms as *mental discipline* or *intellectual discipline*. Some teachers still justify the subject matter and their instructional procedures on such bases. In the previous discussion of outcomes of learning which may transfer it was shown that attitudes toward study, methods of study, and methods of adjustment which students acquire in some subjects may transfer to other subjects or situations. A generalized attitude toward doing one's best, an efficient method of acquiring facts and concepts, and adjusting to new situations by goal-oriented effort do transfer to a variety of situations. It is possible that some teachers who use such terms as *intellectual discipline* and *mental discipline* are referring to these generalized attitudes and methods.

The above discussion is not meant to imply that students should not work persistently to acquire learnings which challenge their best abilities. Nor does it deny that the teaching of moral and ethical beliefs, combined with punishment or creation of guilt feelings, can lead to firm acceptance of those beliefs. However, we may safely infer that the school which wishes children to develop speaking facility in French offers French instruction with emphasis on speaking, for a child does not learn to speak French fluently by studying Latin or Greek. The school which intends to prepare girls for secretarial positions after graduation offers some instruction in typing, shorthand, and bookkeeping. Equally important, the bright high school student intending to enter a profession, via higher education, concentrates most of his studies in English, mathematics, science, social studies, and foreign language—not to train his mind, but to acquire such outcomes and abilities as mentioned early in this chapter which will transfer to higher education and an eventual career.

Identical-Elements Theory

The identical-elements theory of transfer assumes that elements present in the original learning situation also must be present in the new learning. The identical elements may be facts, skills, or methods. Thus, after the student has mastered the addition facts, he can use them for other problems in which the same facts appear. After he has mastered skill in using an index in one book, the skill transfers to other indexes that are organized in a similar way. The theory set forth by Thorndike provides a more reliable basis for considering transfer than does the formal-discipline theory (38).

If one follows this theory in curriculum construction and teaching practice, he puts into the school instructional program the more specific facts and skills which are used outside the school situation. When an educational goal is to help boys get jobs in factories, courses in welding, machine operation, woodworking, auto mechanics, blueprinting, and the like are offered. In rural areas boys are given instruction in animal husbandry, soil conservation, and allied subjects in order to help them assume their role as farmers. The hundreds of different courses of a vocational nature now offered in large high schools, colleges, and universities suggest the importance of the identical-elements theory. Many universities offer graduate programs leading to the Ph.D. degree in agriculture, music, art, home economics, physical education, and the like. Though the requirements for these advanced degrees include some study in general education areas such as English, social studies, science, and language, a heavy portion of the graduate requirements are highly specialized courses in the particular field. On the other hand, a large number of persons with Ph.D.'s in English, social studies, and science, make their livelihood through teaching and related activities; their Ph.D. preparation is vocational to about the same extent as that of agriculturists, home economists, and the like.

In elementary education, the idea of identical elements led to identifying vocabulary and arithmetic facts used by children and adults. In turn these many specific facts were incorporated into the curriculum requirements or course of study. The large mass of specific facts or specific skills resulted in much drill with low meaning; further, situations may be very much alike and yet be perceived as quite different, so that the specific facts and skills are not applied. In multiplication, for example, placing a decimal point in the multiplier and multiplicand makes the problem different in some respects. Some pupils perceive the problem as so different that they do not attempt to transfer their facts and skills in adding, subtracting, and multiplying by which they could solve the problem (except for the proper placement of the decimal point in the answer).

Generalization Theory

In one experiment two groups of boys threw a small dart at a target placed under water (23). One group was given a full theoretical explanation of refraction before starting and the other group was given no explanation of the principle. Both groups began their practice with the target placed under 12 inches of water; the same amount of practice was required for both groups to reach the same results. At this point, knowledge of the principle appeared to be of no value; however, the task was now changed only to the extent of reducing the level of the water. The difference between the performance of the two groups was striking in that the boys with the understanding of the principle performed the task much more efficiently than did those without the understanding. It was not the identical elements in the two situations which transferred but the understanding of the principle of refraction.

The preceding experiment by Judd was replicated as nearly as possible with these results: (1) understanding the principle facilitated positive transfer, (2) understanding the principle also facilitated the original learning, and (3) the completeness of the theoretical information had a direct effect upon both initial learning and transfer—the more complete the information the better the results (18). The preceding examples deal with skill learning. Understanding a principle also facilitates the learning of outcomes in the cognitive domain (27, 42).

Transfer by generalization is an extension of transfer by identical elements. Unless the new situation has enough in common with the previous one for the learner to perceive applications, no transfer occurs. Generalization provides a more mature and a broader viewpoint toward effective curriculum and teaching practices. When the teacher is freed from attempting to teach a large number of specific facts and skills in many different subjects, other more interesting and meaningful activities can be organized and more efficient learning is achieved. More longterm projects and assignments, problem-solving activities, class discussions, and units of work which stress broad principles and generalizations can be used, rather than short, unrelated daily lessons which emphasize the acquisition of many specific facts, skills, and attitudes.

Transposition Theory

The gestalt psychologists of Germany, credited with the theory of transfer by transposition, transmitted their ideas to us upon their emigration to the United States with the rise of Hitler. The theory of transposition goes farther than that of generalization in that the entire pattern of means-ends relationships is proposed as the basis of transfer. For example, after an individual recognizes the "Star Spangled Banner" in the key of F, he readily recognizes it when it is transposed into the key of G, though no individual note is the same in the two keys. Applied to the dart-throwing experiment of Judd, the gestalt theory would suggest that it is not only the principle but the individual's entire perceptions of the relationships between the principle, the use of the dart, the depth of the water, and the placement of the target that transferred. Transposition applied to arithmetic means that the specific facts and skills of addition, even the principle underlying addition, are not the basis of transfer from in-school to out-of-school situations, instead, it is the understanding of the *relationships* among the facts, processes, and principles. The more extensive the knowledge of relationships gained during initial learning, the greater the transfer (22).

Some curriculum improvement programs specifically intend to have students better understand the organization of the subject matter, acquire the major concepts and the principles which express relationships among concepts, and develop abilities. For example, an experimental program for instruction in science was prepared in brief outline form for use in the early grades (10). One idea in this program is to teach general abilities which will be needed later to develop more specialized abilities and knowledge. The abilities given special attention are observing and classifying, describing, recognizing and using numbers and number relations, recognizing and using space and time relations, measuring, inferring, and predicting. The conceptual knowledge to be developed simultaneously is shown in the vocabulary of the first three proposed exercises: *liquid, solid state, dissolve, solution, gas, gaseous state, carbon dioxide, oxygen.* The relationships among concepts to be identified by the children are represented in desired outcomes such as classifying matter in any of three states—solid, liquid, and gas—and inferring that air makes water disappear. These abilities and concepts are to be learned through an instructional program in which the teacher provides experimental materials and questions while the children manipulate, raise questions, respond to the teacher's questions, observe, describe, etc. No evidence is presented as to whether this instructional program achieves the desired objectives; however, the attempt to secure transfer by emphasizing concepts and abilities is noteworthy.

Agreements About Transfer

The last three transfer theories are based on reliable evidence that transfer does occur, but are not in agreement concerning exactly what it is that transfers. In the identical-elements theory it is the more specific facts, skills, or attitudes; in generalization theory it is the principles and ability to apply the principles; and in the transposition theory it is the broader patterns of means-ends relationships and the related abilities required to perceive and apply the relationships. However, for a response made to one event or in one situation to transfer to other events or situations, the individual must perceive the other situations as similar to the initial one. Further, the conditions of the initial learning are related to the amount of transfer. Partially learned material shows less transfer than that which is well learned.

Positive and Negative Transfer

Although an outcome may be acquired and remembered well, transfer of learning is not automatic and may be negative or positive. Negative transfer was discussed in some detail in Chapter 8 in connection with problem solving.

When an individual learns to use some information, instrument, or method of approach in a particular way to solve a problem successfully, he tends to persist in the same way even though it does not lead to solution of a new problem (7). Positive transfer occurs when an outcome learned in one situation is remembered and is applied to a new situation. Neither negative nor positive transfer occurs when the learning in one situation is not perceived by the individual as related to a new situation.

Proponents of the idea of learning for its own sake, that is, the acquiring of knowledge or skills simply in order to understand or to perform better, are justified in suggesting that every student should engage in some of this type of activity; however, those who are concerned that the school should encourage outcomes which will transfer to situations outside the school are very much concerned with positive and negative transfer. For example, an individual who spends four or five years after high school graduation to become a teacher and one who spends eight or more years to become a psychologist or physician are wasting much time and energy in higher education if there is negative or no transfer to their subsequent careers.

MODEL FOR ENCOURAGING RETENTION AND TRANSFER

A discussion of retention and transfer follows logically from the preceding chapters dealing with outcomes of learning and motivation. As may be properly inferred from the discussion thus far, no learning outcome transfers to a new situation unless it is retained, and no retention occurs unless something is learned initially. Therefore, in the model for encouraging retention and transfer, we highlight motivation, initial acquisition, retention, and transfer successively.

GENERALIZATION	PRINCIPLE
1. Intention energizes and focuses behavior toward a goal.	1. Foster intent to learn and remember.
2. Meaningful material, that which manifests relatedness among parts and which the individual can incorporate into his cognitive structure, is readily learned and remembered.	2. Make the initial learning meaningful.
3. Positive reinforcers strengthen behaviors, thereby facilitating retention.	3. Provide for satisfying consequences of correct responses.
4. Practice increases the stability and clarity of the individual's knowledge and thus reduces forgetting.	4. Distribute practice and review.

5. Proactive and retroactive inhibition and lack of relatability of material result in poor initial acquisition and poor retention.

5. Avoid interference and faulty organization.

6. Generalized attitudes, knowledge, and abilities transfer readily to new situations.

6. Emphasize general concepts and abilities.

7. The inclusiveness and generality of one's attitudes, knowledge, and abilities are extended through use in a variety of situations.

7. Provide for application.

8. Attitudes, knowledge, and abilities acquire stable organization through productive learning experiences extending over a period of time.

8. Provide for sequential, cumulative learning.

Foster Intent to Learn and Remember

All acts have in common the character of being intended or willed. But one act is distinguishable from another by the content of it, the expected result of it, which is here spoken of as its intent. There is no obvious way in which we can say what act it is which is thought of or is done except by specifying this intent of it (28, 367).

What makes actions meaningful is the intent of the acting person. A motive consists of a value regarding something and an intent to carry out a sequence of operations to achieve a valued goal (32). Intentions to perform certain behavior not only energize and direct immediate actions in a goal direction but also continue to operate in this fashion even after intervening activities prevent their final execution, thus facilitating retention. As indicated in Chapter 12, aiding learners to set realistic goals is a powerful motivating device. Another way of stating this in the terminology of intentions is to foster intent to learn well and to remember. The principle derives from empirical evidence as well as theory.

Undergraduates in an educational psychology course were given a passage of about 1400 words on the history of dope addiction (6). One group (the control group) was instructed to read the passage at normal speed, to use the remainder of the period to study the facts and ideas in the selection, and to be prepared for a test that would immediately follow their reading and study. Fourteen days later they were given a second unannounced test of retention, using an equivalent form. The same procedure was used with an experimental group except that immediately after completing the first test this group was told that another test on similar material would be given in 14 days. The scores of the two groups were about the same on the first test. The experimental group, told at the end of the first test that it would be retested in 14 days, scored lower than did the control group on the retention test. These results led to the conclusion that intent to learn facilitated retention and that intent to remember when introduced after learning had little effect on retention. The implication for classroom teaching situations is that intent to learn and remember should be encouraged before the pupils start the learning task rather than after the teaching is completed.

Intent to remember is inherent in goal setting and attainment, as discussed in Chapter 12. The student who has set a realistic goal in connection with school learning tasks achieves higher than one who has set no goal or an unrealistic one. Further, if the goal is not immediately attained, there is high intent during each successive practice or study period to recall what has been learned previously in order to make progress toward the goal. Thus, with material as shown in the paragraph above, the teacher may use a test as an external incentive to promote intention to learn and remember, whereas in goal-setting situations the incentive is not necessary. But in both cases, intent to learn and remember facilitates retention.

Make the Initial Learning Meaningful

We have shown previously in Chapters 3 and 7 that meaningfulness has two aspects: the relatedness of the parts of the material and the ability of the individual to incorporate new material into his cognitive structure. Let us consider a brief illustration of each. Were we to scramble the words in the preceding sentence, you would probably come up with the same sentence in a short period of time because the syntactic and semantic meanings of the words are either known or readily identified. On the other hand, given a list of syllables, such as gnx, fzb, and mlt, you could not find relationships among them on a syntactic or semantic basis. This material is potentially not meaningful to us who have learned to speak and read the English language. Consider an example of psychological meaningfulness. In the preceding sentences *syntactic* conveys little meaning to the person who does not know (have in his cognitive structure) the concept of syntax. Therefore, the idea in the sentence is not meaningful because he cannot relate syntactic to any prior knowledge. (Syntax refers to the rules of grammar by which sentences are formed.)

Figure 13.2 shows curves of forgetting for material of different degrees of potential meaningfulness (**15**). The curves are for nonsense material, poetry, observational material, and loss in confidence. The nonsense material was forgotten very rapidly, about 70 percent after 24 hours, whereas the loss in poetry and observational material was much less rapid. The observational material was based on a picture of an office scene; the details of this scene were remembered well, over 80 percent, after 25 days. The subjects also were asked to indicate their confidence in the answers given, that is, if they would be "willing to swear" to the correctness of their answers. Confidence showed more rapid loss than did recall of facts.

Meaningful material is recalled better after sleep and also after regular daily activities than is meaningless material. Accepting the idea

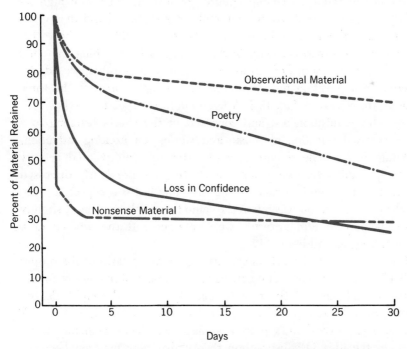

Fig. 13.2. Typical rates of forgetting for different kinds of material. (Adapted from A. R. Gilliland. The rate of forgetting. *J. educ. Psychol.*, 1948, **39**, 23.)

that forgetting is an active process influenced by various activities interpolated between the original learning and later testing, Newman selected stories to be learned so that the content could be readily divided into two classes—essential material needed to understand the stories and nonessential material (**34**). The essential material was reproduced with 87 percent accuracy after eight hours of sleep and with 84 and 87 percent accuracy, respectively, after eight hours of waking activities during the morning and afternoon. Only 47 percent of the nonessential material was reproduced accurately after eight hours of sleep and the amount of reproduction dropped to 25 and 19 percent after the eight-hour waking intervals. The nonessential material showed much the same rate of loss as did nonsense material (Fig. 13.2); however, the essential material showed little loss after interpolated activity between the acquisition and retention tests.

Given the same material to learn, the less intelligent pupils forget more than do the more intelligent, mainly because the less intelligent do not acquire it so well or do not understand it fully. But when the material is appropriate to each child's achievement level, there is no difference in retention among children of low, average, and high intelligence (**26**). In this study each child was pretested and then given a series of ten items in subtraction at the level of difficulty above that which he performed correctly in the pretest. After teaching the child each item in the series of ten as meaningfully as possible, we administered an acquisition test; the mean or average scores for the three groups are shown in Fig. 13.3. A five-minute interpolated activity followed the acquisition test and consisted of the child's listening to a tape-recorded selection of music and stories, an exciting, attention-holding device. The retention scores after this interpolated activity went up slightly for two groups, illustrating the previously discussed phenomenon of reminiscence. When the same test was repeated seven weeks later, retention was much the same for the three groups, slightly above 90 percent. Similar results were obtained with the same children in counting and addition (**12**).

Precisely how well teachers can arrange learning tasks of the proper difficulty level for each child in usual classroom situations is uncertain. The difficulty of the task is related to what the child already knows, as indicated in the preceding discussion of finding a new task appropriate to the child's present achievement level. Difficulty is related to the idea in subsumption theory that new material becomes meaningful, and more readily learned, when it is relatable to existing knowledge. Both theory and research are clear that material which

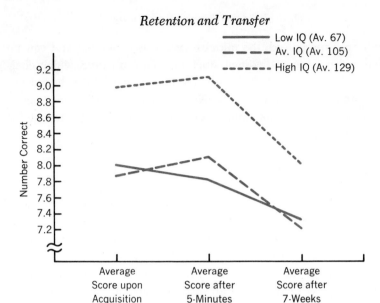

Fig. 13.3. Retention in subtraction problems by children of low, average, and high intelligence. (Based on H. J. Klausmeier, J. Feldhusen, & J. Check. *An analysis of learning efficiency in arithmetic of mentally retarded children in comparison with children of average and high intelligence.* U.S. Office of Education Cooperative Research Project No. 153. Madison: Univer. of Wisconsin, 1959, **12**, 69.)

is inherently meaningful and which can become meaningful to the learner is learned more rapidly initially and also' is retained well.

Provide Satisfying Consequences of Correct Responses

As was shown in previous chapters, the unpleasant effects of failure and punishment retard learning, whereas the pleasant effects of success and reward facilitate it. In about the same way feelings of success and pleasantness and of failure and dissatisfaction are related to recall. Experimentally induced threat to the individual results in poorer recall of material than does no threat, and subsequent alleviation of threat results in better recall (1). A more pleasant, cooperative atmosphere under a democratic leader facilitates the recall of factual information more than a competitive atmosphere under authoritarian leadership (45).

Consequently, deliberate attempts to produce unpleasant feelings in connection with learning activities should be avoided. Instead, when initial learning activities are managed so that satisfying consequences are experienced, the initial behavior is confirmed and can be recalled and used in subsequent situations. Difficult tasks which challenge the learner but which he can master are recalled well and are not inherently unpleasant. They may become so if the learner is punished or reproved for not doing well, rather than being praised for consistent trying.

Distribute Practice and Review

The desirability of distributing practice was shown in previous chapters dealing with factual information and skills. Some important factual material in most subject fields cannot be acquired with a high degree of meaning. Overlearning of spelling words, some arithmetic facts, and facts in social studies and science is accomplished through systematic review. That is, after 20 spelling words are acquired during one week, systematic review of these words is given during the remainder of a semester or year. This overlearning, repeating the correct spellings in each review session, facilitates permanent retention through increasing the stability and clarity of the individual's knowledge and abilities (3). To illustrate, a situation was arranged whereby testing and reviewing were accomplished simultaneously with prearranged groups of children at intervals of 1 day, 14 days, 28 days, and 63 days (40). Retention of many important outcomes improved significantly with systematic review. Best results were secured when the review tests were administered one day after initial instruction rather than later. Also, incorrect or erroneous concepts that were not corrected persisted; if the pupils made errors which were not corrected, they tended to accept and retain the errors as correct.

Many critics of programed instruction have claimed that repetition of the same items in one sitting makes the instructional situation monotonous. It may have this effect for it does not improve immediate or long-term retention (35). However, interspersing short reviews of the preceding material in subsequent short instructional sequences greatly improves retention. Thus in programed instruction, as in regular instruction, spaced review proves effective in encouraging retention.

The amount of review needed in various classroom situations cannot be prescribed; but we are certain that the less meaningful and less well-aquired material must be overlearned immediately, and must subsequently be reviewed more often than meaningful and well-acquired material. Also, if initial outcomes and abilities were acquired more completely, more meaningfully, and were used more frequently in subsequent ongoing learning activities, there would be less need for formal reviews. For example, if eleventh-grade students learned history more completely and used what they learned subsequently in the twelfth grade, less review of the same material would be needed in college courses.

Avoid Interference and Faulty Reorganization

Table 13.2 is an application of the effects of interference on remembering. Suppose that students take beginning conversational Spanish during the first period. This class period might be followed by Spanish

TABLE 13.2.

Effects of Interpolated Activities on Remembering

I. Learning Activity, First Class Period	II. Interpolated Learning Activity, Second Class Period	Effect of II on Remembering I
Beginning Spanish	Spanish history	Positive and small
Beginning Spanish	Mathematics	Small and possibly negative
Beginning Spanish	Beginning French	Negative and large

history, mathematics, or beginning conversational French. Spanish history immediately following conversational Spanish has a positive effect on remembering conversational Spanish, because the two are complementary and do not interfere with one another. A mathematics class has little effect on subsequent recall of conversational Spanish, because it neither complements nor interferes with it. French immediately following Spanish has a large and undesired negative effect on remembering the Spanish. French, though similar to Spanish, does not complement but interferes with the Spanish; the same stimuli, English words, call for different responses in Spanish and in French, and this is the source of interference and confusion. It is possible that the French might be taught in such manner as not to interfere with beginning Spanish. However, if the emphasis is on acquiring vocabulary and the same words in English are used in both beginning Spanish and French, two undesirable effects are possible: the French decidedly interferes with remembering the Spanish, and the initial Spanish instruction markedly interferes with acquiring beginning French. As previously stated, the terms ascribed to these phenomena are *retroactive inhibition* and *proactive inhibition*.

Meaningful material is not subject to interference to the same degree as nonsense material as shown in Table 13.3 (**16**). The control group received rest after the original learning; experimental group one received dissimilar material that supposedly would not produce interference; experimental group two received similar material that would supposedly produce interference. Immediately after these interpolated activities, there was practically no difference in recall of the original learning by the three groups; and after 45 minutes and after 21 days, the amount recalled was much the same for the three groups. Thus, interpolated activity similar to the original learning did not produce forgetting. It is of some interest, too, that after 45 minutes the experimental group which had received dissimilar material for the interpolated activity showed some reminiscence.

TABLE 13.3.

Number of Completion Items Correctly Recalled

Group	Kind of Interpolated Material	N	Immediate		After 45 min.			After 21 days		
			Mean	σ	Mean	σ	% Recalled	Mean	σ	% Recalled
Control	Rest	14	23.36	3.80	23.14	3.56	99.1	18.93	3.08	81.0
Exp. Gp. 1	Dissimilar material	15	23.20	3.27	23.53	3.34	101.4	19.33	3.93	83.3
Exp. Gp. 2	Similar material	16	23.31	2.14	22.94	3.84	98.4	18.81	4.59	80.7

SOURCE: J. F. Hall. Retroactive inhibition in meaningful material. *J. educ. Psychol.* 1955, **46**, 50.

Similar results were obtained when another group of students successively studied meaningful material dealing with Buddhism and Christianity (**5**). Here, too, retroactive inhibition was found to have a negligible effect on retention of newly learned meaningful material. However, the acquisition of a foreign language, the learning of shorthand symbols, and the learning of important facts in many subject-matter fields cannot be highly meaningful for all pupils the first time new material is studied. Therefore, the negative effects of interference should be avoided.

Faulty reorganization results not so much from retroactive inhibition as from lack of thorough learning in the first place. At this point try to recall the principles for improving retention discussed thus far. If you can recall them, neither interference nor faulty reorganization have occurred; however, it is possible that after reading and studying the first four principles and then following with study of the present principle, you may not be able to recall them because you did not master them fully in your first study. In any event, the statements which you recall as the principles are your reorganized version of them which you are likely to accept as correct unless you check back with the original statements.

Both interference and reorganization hinder initial learning and retention. The best possibility for improving retention is to make the original learning meaningful and thorough. Beyond this, students should not be scheduled for successive classes wherein similar but noncomplementary material may result in either proactive or retroactive inhibition.

Emphasize General Concepts and Abilities

When transfer is sought, it is important for the teacher to identify the outcomes and abilities to be learned well, retained, and transferred by the students. We cannot assume that students studying Latin will independently select Latin words on which many English words are based. Students in geometry cannot identify the many possible applications of geometric facts and principles to their daily activities or to subsequent careers in engineering or architecture. Besides identifying, the teacher also has responsibility for emphasizing those outcomes which have greatest possibility for transfer. The previous discussions have shown that general information, concepts, and principles, methods of learning, generalized attitudes, and methods of adjustment have greater possibility of transfer to many situations than do specific facts and attitudes and technical information. Also, outcomes acquired meaningfully transfer better than do those acquired by rote memory.

For example, children were taught subtraction either by a meaningful (rational) method or by a mechanical (rote) method (8). Those taught by the rational method were given a variety of suggestions in understanding the process of borrowing in subtraction. The other group was taught one mechanical method and then drilled, using exercises wherein borrowing was required. Those taught by the rote method made more rapid progress in the first few days because the meaningful method required more time to learn; however, at the end of 15 days they were already dropping behind those taught by the meaningful method. More important, when a transfer situation was arranged, those who had been taught understanding of subtraction performed far better than those who had not. An example clarifies the basis on which these and similar results are obtained. If a child understands that adding is counting upward and is taught, when first encountering 3 + 3, to count 3 somethings (dots) and 3 more somethings (dots) to get 6, as he subsequently meets a new fact such as 6 + 4, he can independently get the correct answer by making 6 dots and 4 dots to get 10. If the child is taught the addition facts by rote, that is, if he is presented the facts to memorize but does not understand that adding is counting upward, when he meets the transfer situation, 6 + 4, he does not know what to do. Some children, of course, arrive at the generalization of counting upward independently. However, in this study even bright children did not understand the process of borrowing when taught by rote methods and therefore were unable to transfer.

In another situation problem-solving tasks were presented to 60 students with one group being taught the solution by memorizing and the other by understanding (19). In this situation: (1) more time was required to teach the problem initially to the understanding group than to the memorizing group, (2) overnight retention was equal for the two groups, and (3) the understanding group did significantly better than the memorizing group on all three problems used in measuring transfer. Mentally retarded children, children of average intelligence, and children of high intelligence remembered equally well and also transferred their knowledge to a new situation equally well when the initial mathematics material was graded at their achievement levels and taught in a meaningful fashion (24).

Understanding of the material facilitates transfer. What effect does the method of learning have upon transfer? If we think of one method of learning as being on a continuum of discovery, we may examine how method affects transfer. Let us think of a "pure" discovery method as being characterized by the student discovering an answer rather than having it told to him, identifying a procedure rather than having it told to him, identifying a principle or generalization rather than having it told to him, and selecting the information which he acts upon rather than having it presented to him. Given all these criteria, there is indeed very little "pure" discovery. However, one or more of the conditions is met to some extent in the various descriptions of the discovery methods of learning.

In order to arrive at a solution in discovery learning, the learner must secure information, transform it in some way so as to arrive at a desired solution, find a missing relationship, or create a novel response. Young children learn many new concepts through discovery, especially when in the stage of concrete operations as described previously in Chapter 7. Further, some learning-to-learn procedures are acquired independently as are some problem-solving skills. This type of discovery, when successful, leads to somewhat better initial learning; retention and transfer are definitely improved (2).

Note that the critical point is whether the student learns independently. Our schools are bulging with students who do not learn well by themselves. It is true that most students profit from being given some information rather than no information about a strategy to use in attaining concepts (27). They also profit from being given some assistance in identifying a principle or generalization that, in turn, helps in securing the response. This is true for kindergarten children (43) and also for college students (42). But many of the new curricula emphasizing discovery as the method of learning very carefully sequence the printed material to make sure that the student "discovers" the solution which the writer intended. Further, helpful suggestions are given teachers concerning how to proceed, including questions to ask and materials to have available, in order to get the student to arrive at a solution, method, or generalization which is already known and is part of the structured discipline.

Independent discovery facilitates retention and improves motivation when the student arrives at an appropriate solution. Props, hints, and instructions help the student arrive at the solution without giving too much help and they facilitate initial learning, retention, and transfer for the large majority of the students. Further, knowledge that is hierarchically organized requires that certain abilities be acquired before others. These basic abilities and knowledge must be incorporated into the learner's cognitive structure, using meaningful reception learning and other procedures, if there is to be transfer (13). Thus, the previous knowledge and abilities of the student are very important factors in transfer.

Provide for Application

Students may study and enjoy Shakespearean plays for the inherent satisfaction derived. If, however, the purpose of such a study is to assist in better interpretation of English history or of the present scene in England or America, most students need help in applying the pertinent ideas from the plays to the modern scene. The applications might take the form of comparing Shakespeare's style of writing and modern writing, the characters in his plays and in modern plays or in life generally, the themes of his plays and themes that exist in modern living, and so on.

Suppose that a teacher intends to secure horizontal transfer from one problem to similar problems. Practice on a variety of problems like the initial one rather than on the same ones facilitates transfer (29, 33). Does the same conclusion hold when the attempt is made to secure transfer from one class to other classes of problems or knowledge? Here, also, practice on several classes of problems in the initial situation produces more transfer than does practice on problems of the same class (44). Teachers who know the subject matter well and its applications can be more effective in securing transfer than can those who know the subject matter but are weak on its application.

What is the effect on transfer of having the student verbalize the generalization, rule, description of the method, or statement of relationships among means-ends relationships? This question was answered regarding concept learning in Chapter 7. Naming pictures facilitates transfer by young children (9). Verbalizing the method one is using while solving a problem also facilitates transfer by high school students (14). Students, who verbalize during initial learning, discover principles and methods more readily and easily apply these principles to new problems. Although a teacher might not have students verbalize their methods in independent study, a class discussion of methods and principles used to solve problems would be very helpful. Also, students could be encouraged to think through their procedures silently while they conduct an experiment, read a book, and so on.

Provide for Sequential, Cumulative Learning

Most skills, concepts, attitudes, and abilities are not fully acquired in one day, week, or year but cumulatively through distributed practice and study over a period of time. The various disciplines require many years of study in order for one to become moderately literate. The people who outline a general sequence of instruction from kindergarten through grade 12 must give careful consideration to encouraging continuity in learning. At the same time the teacher is daily faced with the problem of deciding how large or comprehensive a unit of learning to attempt in order for the student to acquire something that can be carried through to the next day or week.

Obviously if nothing is learned today, it cannot be retained or used tomorrow. In spelling, for example, it is better to learn 3 words well each day of the week than to be given 15 words at one time and end up at the end of the week not knowing any of them. In foreign language instruction it also is better to emphasize a smaller dialogue than to assign a long one and, in the process, encourage so much interference and reorganization that nothing is recalled. Science instruction is much the same. To attempt to make physicists out of tenth- or eleventh-grade pupils is unrealistic. Instead, the study of physics in high school must be organized into appropriate segments by which the student learns well; his knowledge, skills, interests, and abilities in turn will enable him to continue further study of physics in college. Only then will he become a physicist.

SUMMARY

General information is remembered and transfers more readily to new situations than does specific information. Concepts and generalizations transfer more readily than other information. Strategies or methods of learning, methods of adjusting, generalized attitudes, and values — these are the pervasive outcomes that transfer from one class of events and situations to many others. Abilities that are developed in one situation also transfer to other situations of a like nature. The type and amount of transfer ranges from high positive to high negative.

Forgetting is explained by different theorists as resulting from disuse, interference, reorganization, obliterative subsumption, and motivated forgetting. The evidence is now clear that (1) meaningful material is retained better than meaningless, (2) material acquired with purpose is retained better than material learned incidentally, and (3) having knowledge enables one to retain new knowledge better.

Three generally accepted theories of transfer are identical elements, generalization, and transposition. All incorporate the idea of positive transfer but disagree on precisely what transfers. According to any theory, however, the individual must perceive the new situation as being similar to that in which the initial learning occurred.

Retention and transfer are closely related in that if something is not remembered it cannot be transferred subsequently when a new situation is encountered. Retention is related to initial learning in that something must be learned in order to be remembered. For facilitating retention and transfer then, the teacher (1) fosters intent to learn well and remember, (2) makes the initial learning meaningful, (3) arranges for satisfying consequences of correct responses, (4) distributes practice and review, (5) avoids interference between learning situations, (6) emphasizes general concepts and abilities, (7) provides for application, and (8) provides for sequential, cumulative learning. Instructional materials should be written according to the same principles.

QUESTIONS AND ACTIVITIES

1. a. Contrast lateral and vertical transfer, giving concrete illustrations.
   b. Discuss the three conditions in the learner that are essential for either type of transfer.
2. On the basis of your own experiences, which of the outcomes has the most possibility for retention and transfer?
3. a. Discuss each of the five explanations of forgetting.
   b. Which is least useful in explaining why forgetting occurs? Give reasons for your choice.
4. a. State three or four generalizations from the research cited about relation of the type of material to retention.
   b. Discuss one possible application of each to a classroom situation.
5. Discuss the nature and educational implications of reminiscence.
6. a. Describe briefly the four theories of transfer.
   b. Which theory is least satis-

factory for you? Most satisfactory? Give reasons for your choices.

7. Discuss the meaning of positive and negative transfer, giving at least two examples of each from your own experiences.
8. Discuss the relationship among initial learning, retention, and transfer.
9. a. Select and restate the eight principles of retention and transfer.
   b. Give an example of implementing each principle, related to your interest in subject matter and level of schooling.
10. Briefly summarize and discuss the research on which one principle is based. Refer as necessary to further sources of information.
11. It is now proposed that preschool education of culturally disadvantaged children will help them succeed in school. Discuss this proposition in connection with outcomes of learning that transfer and theories of transfer.

SUGGESTIONS FOR FURTHER READING

Briggs, Leslie J., & Nancy R. Hamilton. Meaningful learning and retention: Practice and feedback variables. *Rev. educ. Res.*, 1964, 34, 545–558.

Duncan, C. P. Transfer after training with single versus multiple tasks. *J. exp. Psychol.*, 1958, 55, 63–72. (In Anderson & Ausubel, 1965, 641–656.)

Ellis, H. *The transfer of learning.* New York: Macmillan, 1965, pp. 3–85.

Harlow, H. F. The formation of learning sets. *Psychol. Rev.,* 1949, **56,** 51–65. (Portions reprinted in Kuhlen & Thompson, 1963, 178–185.)

Klausmeier, H. J., & J. Check. Retention and transfer in children of low, average, and high intelligence. *J. educ. Res.,* 1962, **55,** 319–322 (In Ripple, 1964, 428–434.)

Klausmeier, H. J., W. Wiersma, & C. W. Harris. Efficiency of initial learning and transfer by individuals, pairs, and quads. *J. educ. Psychol.,* 1963, **54,** 160–164. (In Seidman, 1965, 185–189.)

Miller, G. A., E. Galanter, & K. H. Pribram. *Plans and the structure of behavior.* New York: Holt, Rinehart and Winston, 1960. Ch. 10: Plans for remembering, 125–138. (In Russell, 1964, 141–147.)

Newman, E. B. Forgetting of meaningful material during sleep and waking. *Amer. J. Psychol.,* 1939, **52,** 65–71. (In Anderson & Ausubel, 1965, 281–289.)

Reynolds J. H., & R. Glaser. Effects of repetition and spaced review upon retention of a complex learning task. *J. educ. Psychol.,* 1964, **55,** 297–308.

Staats, A. W. Comments on Professor Russell's paper. In C. N. Cofer, & Barbara S. Musgrave (Eds.), *Verbal behavior and learning.* New York: McGraw-Hill, 1963, pp. 271–290. (Reprinted under the title "Verbal mechanisms in purpose and set" in Staats, 1964, 214–230.)

Wittrock, M. C. Set applied to student teaching. In J. P. DeCecco (Ed.), *Human learning in the school.* New York: Holt, Rinehart and Winston, 1963, pp. 107–117.

Wittrock, M. C., & P. A. Twelker. Verbal cues and variety of classes of problems in transfer of training. *Psychol. Rep.,* 1964, **14,** 827–830.

REFERENCES

1. Aborn, M. The influence of experimentally induced failure on the retention of material acquired through set and incidental learning. *J. exp. Psychol.,* 1953, **45,** 225–231.

2. Ausubel, D. P. Learning by discovery: Rationale and mystique. *Bull. nat. Ass. sec. sch. Principals,* 1961, **45,** 18–58.

3. Ausubel, D. P. *The psychology of meaningful verbal learning.* New York: Grune & Stratton, 1963.

4. Ausubel, D. P., & D. Fitzgerald. The role of discriminability in meaningful verbal learning and retention. *J. educ. Psychol.,* 1961, **52,** 266–274.

5. Ausubel, D. P., Lillian C. Robbins, & E. Blake, Jr. Retroactive inhibition and facilitation in the learning of school materials. *J. educ. Psychol.,* 1957, **48,** 334–343.

6. Ausubel, D. P., S. H. Schpoont, & Lillian Cukier. The influence of intention on the retention of school materials. *J. educ. Psychol.,* 1957, **48,** 87–92.

7. Birch, H. G., & H. S. Rabinowitz. The negative effect of previous experience on productive learning. *J. exp. Psychol.,* 1951, **41,** 121–125.

8. Brownell, W. A., *et al.* Meaningful versus mechanical learning: A study in grade III subtraction. *Duke Univer. Studies Educ.,* No. 8. Durham, N.C.: Duke Univer. Press, 1949.

9. Cantor, G. N. Effects of three types of pretraining on discrimination learning in preschool children. *J. exp. Psychol.,* 1955, **49,** 339–342.

10. Commission on Science Education. *Science—a process approach; Part Four* (Experimental ed.) Washington, D.C.: Amer. Ass. for the Advancement of Sci., 1963.

491

11. Feldhusen, J., J. Check, & H. J. Klausmeier. Achievement in subtraction. *Elem. Sch. J.*, 1961, **61**, 322–327.

12. Feldhusen, J. F., & H. J. Klausmeier. Achievement in counting and addition. *Elem. Sch. J.*, 1959, **59**, 388–393.

13. Gagné, R. M. *The conditions of learning.* New York: Holt, Rinehart and Winston, 1965.

14. Gagné, R. M., & E. C. Smith. A study of the effects of verbalization on problem solving. *J. exp. Psychol.*, 1962, **63**, 12–18.

15. Gilliland, A. R. The rate of forgetting. *J. educ. Psychol.*, 1948, **39**, 19–26.

16. Hall, J. F. Retroactive inhibition in meaningful material. *J. educ. Psychol.*, 1955, **46**, 47–52.

17. Harlow, H. F. The formation of learning sets. *Psychol. Rev.*, 1949, **56**, 51–65.

18. Hendrickson, G., & W. H. Schroeder. Transfer of training in learning to hit a submerged target. *J. educ. Psychol.*, 1941, **32**, 205–213.

19. Hilgard, E. R., R. P. Irvine, & J. E. Whipple. Rote memorization, understanding, and transfer: An extension of Katona's card-trick experiments. *J. exp. Psychol.*, 1953, **46**, 288–292.

20. Howell, W. J. Work-study skills of children in grades IV–VIII. *Elem. Sch. J.*, 1950, **50**, 384–389.

21. Humphreys, L. G. Transfer of training in general education. *J. gen. Educ.*, 1951, **5**, 210–216.

22. Johnson, R. C., & R. C. Zara. Relational learning in young children. *J. comp. physiol. Psychol.*, 1960, **53**, 594–597.

23. Judd, C. H. The relation of special training to general intelligence. *Educ. Rev.*, 1908, **36**, 28–42.

24. Klausmeier, H. J., & J. Check. Retention and transfer in children of low, average, and high intelligence. *J. educ. Res.*, 1962, **55**, 319–322.

25. Klausmeier, H. J., & J. Feldhusen. Retention in arithmetic among children of low, average, and high intelligence at 117 months of age. *J. educ. Psychol.*, 1959, **50**, 88–92.

26. Klausmeier, H. J., J. Feldhusen, & J. Check. *An analysis of learning efficiency in arithmetic of mentally retarded children in comparison with children of average and high intelligence.* U.S. Office of Education Cooperative Research Project No. 153. Madison: Univer. of Wisconsin, 1959.

27. Klausmeier, H. J., C. W. Harris, & W. Wiersma. *Strategies of learning and efficiency of concept attainment by individuals and groups.* U.S. Office of Education Cooperative Research Project No. 1442. Madison: Univer. of Wisconsin, 1964.

28. Lewis, C. I. *An analysis of knowledge and valuation.* La Salle, Ill.: Open Court, 1946.

29. Lloyd, K. E. Supplementary report: Retention and transfer of responses to stimulus classes. *J. exp. Psychol.*, 1960, **59**, 206–207.

30. McDougall, W. P. Differential retention of course outcomes in educational psychology. *J. educ. Psychol.*, 1958, **49**, 53–60.

31. McKeachie, W. J., & D. Solomon. Retention of general psychology. *J. educ. Psychol.*, 1957, **48**, 110–112.

32. Miller, G. A., E. Galanter, & K. H. Pribram. *Plans and the structure of behavior.* New York: Holt, Rinehart and Winston, 1960.

33. Morrisett, L., & C. I. Hovland. A comparison of three varieties of training in human problem solving. *J. exp. Psychol.*, 1959, **58**, 52–55.

34. Newman, E. B. Forgetting of meaningful material during sleep and waking. *Amer. J. Psychol.*, 1939, **52**, 65–71.

35. Reynolds, J. H., & R. Glaser. Effects of repetition and spaced review upon retention of a complex learning task. *J. educ. Psychol.*, 1964, **55**, 297–308.

36. Sterrett, M. D., & R. A. Davis. The permanence of school learning: A review of studies. *Educ. Admin. Supervis.*, 1954, **40**, 449–460.

37. Strong, E. K. The effect of time-interval upon recognition memory. *Psychol. Rev.*, 1913, **20**, 339–372.

38. Thorndike, E. L. *The psychology of learning: Educational psychology*. Vol. 2. New York: Bureau of Publications, Teachers College, Columbia Univer. Press, 1913.

39. Thorndike, E. L. Mental discipline in high school studies. *J. educ. Psychol.*, 1924, **15**, 1–22, 83–98.

40. Tiederman, H. R. A study of retention in classroom learning. *J. educ. Res.*, 1948, **42**, 516–531.

41. Wittrock, M. C. Set to learn and proactive inhibition. *J. educ. Res.*, 1963, **57**, 72–75.

42. Wittrock, M. C. Verbal stimuli in concept formation: Learning by discovery. *J. educ. Psychol.*, 1963, **54**, 183–190.

43. Wittrock, M. C., E. R. Keislar, & Carolyn Stern. Verbal cues in concept identification. *J. educ. Psychol.*, 1964, **55**, 195–200.

44. Wittrock, M. C., & P. A. Twelker. Verbal cues and variety of classes of problems in transfer of training. *Psychol. Rep.*, 1964, **14**, 827–830.

45. Yuker, H. E. Group atmosphere and memory. *J. abnorm. soc. Psychol.*, 1955, **51**, 17–23.

CHAPTER 14

Providing for
Individual Differences

IN THE late 1950s, the race into outer space set off a national concern for identifying and providing for gifted students. The Civil Rights movement in the United States in the 1960s generated a national effort for better education of the culturally disadvantaged. The rising incidence of delinquency and technological unemployment has forced us to reexamine the role of the school in educating many students for useful citizenship through becoming an economically independent worker. Along with these newer concerns, we continue to try to make education more valuable for children and youth who are not in any way handicapped. We realize more clearly that the schools have an important function in the development of the individual and in the preservation and improvement of group living. Also, we know that this education cannot be identical mass education, the same prescription of 12 years of schooling for all using the identical instructional materials and activities. Instead, the plea for individualization that psychologists and educators have been making for the past half century is assuming greater significance.

In Part II of this book, we outlined principles of instruction. This was followed with a discussion of principles of motivation and retention and transfer in the next two chapters. These principles are intended

494

to be applicable to all groups of children as well as to individuals. However, the applications vary. In this chapter, we are concerned with applications to gifted and talented children, the mentally retarded and slow learners, the culturally deprived, and the antisocial delinquents. Before reading about these different groups, identify one principle from each of the preceding seven chapters that is most interesting to you and try to determine its application to each of the groups mentioned in the preceding sentence. Recognize, too, that if a school system has done nothing to identify the children who fit the above categories and if the teacher does nothing, no applications can be made. We shall briefly consider differences in abilities and some general provisions that are needed in the school system to provide adequately for students of varying abilities.

DIFFERENCE IN ABILITIES

Considering the diverse and often conflicting proposals made by adults about the proper education of children, it is important for school personnel to formulate their own conceptions clearly. The authors' point of view is now presented. You are invited to examine the following eight generalizations critically and add, delete, or modify as you deem appropriate in terms of your values and knowledge:

1. Recognize variations in abilities.
2. Nurture emergent abilities.
3. Identify all abilities.
4. Provide for educational continuity.
5. Provide adequate materials.
6. Secure competent staff.
7. Provide for individualizing and grouping.
8. Continue the common elementary school and the comprehensive high school.

Recognize Variations in Abilities

Suppose that in an elementary school the attempt is made to identify pupils who fit the following polar descriptions: intelligent-unintelligent, superior in reading-inferior in reading, skilled in handwriting-unskilled in handwriting. Before making the identification, a criterion of intelligence, a criterion of reading proficiency, and a criterion of writing proficiency would be necessary. After the criteria were agreed upon, what percent of the pupils would be classed intelligent and what percent unintelligent? superior in reading and inferior in reading? skilled in writing and unskilled in writing? Undoubtedly, only a small percent of the total child population would be placed in any one of these six classes. The top 10 percent might be classed as superior in reading and the bottom 5 percent as inferior, leaving 85 percent as neither superior nor inferior.

Though a larger group can be divided readily into two groups on such bases as male or female and above or below median chronological age, most individuals possess cognitive and psychomotor abilities ranging from very low to very high. One of the major problems in providing adequately for children is assessing their abilities accurately. The more reliable the assessment, the more likely are we to learn that there are many abilities, not just a few, and that these abilities vary not only among individuals but within the same individual. The extent of this multiple variation has been documented in Chapter 4 and other chapters. You may wish to refer back to Chapter 4 to observe the figures and tables which indicate these variations.

Nurture Emergent Abilities

Outstanding or poor performances in adulthood are not assured at the time the individual is conceived. Although heredity contributes to determining eventual adult performances, the environment—home, neighborhood, school—is also very important. The blighting effects of an impoverished home and neighborhood upon subsequent achievement are becoming increasingly obvious in our nation. Younger children particularly must have rich opportunities for self-expression and excellent guidance of their emerging abilities. Otherwise, we shall never know how they as adults may have achieved in an enriched environment. All children of the entire range of abilities and affective characterics require good education, and much of it, in order to develop whatever talents they may have.

Identify All Abilities

We may properly conclude that not all abilities of mankind have yet been identified and therefore cannot be provided for adequately. However, a substantial number of abilities have been identified, especially those associated with achievement in the various subject areas (See Chapters 4 and 16·). We have stated that these abilities emerge and are improved with nurture. Therefore, a systematic and continuous effort must be made by the schools to identify children's abilities. In order for this to be accomplished, there must be a widespread attitude that schooling is for the nurturance of the abilities of children and youth, not for teachers and other school people to make a livelihood. We must be governed by the fact that every child, except possibly the most deficient mentally and physically, possesses some abilities that can be nurtured in an excellent educational environment and that it is the job of the school to identify these abilities.

Later in this chapter, we shall indicate identification procedures used with gifted and talented children. These same procedures, involving the use of standardized tests and teacher judgment, simultaneously provide the means for identifying other exceptional children such as the slow learning, the mentally retarded, the antisocial, and the emotionally disturbed. School systems and teachers must plan to identify the abilities and deficiencies of all children, rather than a single group, or too much time is lost. Refer now to the rating scale used in Racine, Wisconsin, shown in the next chapter, to see how a rating scale may be used to identify children of the entire range of achievements and characteristics.

Provide for Educational Continuity

Young children lack knowledge, experience and judgment. Compared with adults they are physically and socially immature. With an enriched environment in the home and neighborhood, and excellent teaching in the school, they develop physically, mentally, and affectively. Before finishing high school, they may be superior to their parents and teachers in many cognitive and psychomotor abilities. Without guidance and help they do not move suddenly from being first-grade children to being outstanding poets, artists, or even useful citizens. Slow-learning children and the large middle group also require continuity in education so that previously acquired skills and knowledge are extended.

Here are some examples of lack of continuity. In one school, bright pupils were grouped together for instruction in the sixth grade and mastered most of the curriculum requirements of the eighth grade in language arts, mathematics, social studies, and science. Upon completing the sixth grade, they went to a junior high school but were put in regular seventh-grade classes and treated as "average" seventh-graders even though they already knew most of the subject matter of the seventh grade. Slow-learning children were given special attention

throughout their elementary school years and made reasonable progress. However, upon completing the sixth grade they also went to regular seventh-grade classes and were treated as "average" achievers.
But they could not read the textbooks of the seventh grade, were only
at fourth-grade level in arithmetic, and could not understand the technical vocabulary of science. In another school, instruction in French
for all children was started in the fourth grade and continued through
the sixth. No further instruction in French was available until the ninth
grade for any of the children who went to junior high schools in the
community.

At present, the greatest difficulties in providing adequately for children of the entire range of abilities are encountered in the transition
from home to school in early childhood, from elementary school to
junior high school, from junior high school to senior high school, and
from senior high school to college or to adult life without further education. We still do not provide continuity of instruction from one school
level to the next and from school to adult life so that severe problems
for many children and youth are avoided. About 30 percent do not
graduate from high school, and many of these do not secure gainful
employment.

Provide Adequate Materials

Since World War II, marked progress has been made in getting new
buildings, classrooms, and teachers for a rapidly increasing child population. This in itself is a highly significant accomplishment. However,
in the planning of new buildings and in the securing of school facilities and equipment, the tendency has been to make only minor changes
from the arrangements of the past, on the assumption that the same
equipment and instructional materials could serve equally well for the
nurturance of all forms of abilities in all children. This practice may
meet the needs of the larger percent in the middle but is inadequate
for the smaller percent who learn exceedingly well or with much
difficulty.

Whether in heterogeneous age-graded classes with other children or
in special sections, bright children need some instructional materials
more advanced than those for the other children. The slow learners
also require reading material different from the rest of the group. Children in the underprivileged areas need compensatory educational materials. Just as swimming pools are needed for swimming instruction,
science laboratories for science instruction, and typewriters for typing

instruction, so also space and the proper materials are needed to nurture the creative abilities of pupils in English, mathematics, art, and other areas. The sensory handicapped, the antisocial, and the emotionally disturbed children also require special materials, equipment, and space that are usually not available in regular classrooms.

Secure Competent Staff

The shortage of competent teachers, school psychologists, guidance counselors, curriculum supervisors, and administrators continues. Even with the best facilities, the education of children cannot be better than the school personnel doing the work. The abilities of many children will continue to go unidentified—much less well provided for—until society recognizes the importance of well-educated and competent school staff and gives the necessary financial support to schools.

School personnel, when considering this challenge, are much the same as the general population, clinging to outmoded and inefficient practices and procedures. We still have many small high schools with enrollments of less than 100 students. A considerable number of one-room elementary schools are found with fewer than 30 pupils in all eight grades. Until recently, educational opportunities grew worse in the slums of our large cities as well as in many rural areas. A large number of young persons still start to teach in the elementary school with less than the baccalaureate. Many persons unfamiliar with job requirements or counseling procedures attempt to counsel students about critical educational and vocational matters. In part, these undesirable conditions persist because present school personnel are opposed to any proposals for improving the profession and related learning opportunities for children.

Provide for Individualizing and Grouping

The principal means of providing for pupils of varying abilities and levels of achievement is through individualization and various forms of grouping. Opportunities for individualization are much better now than in the past and will be discussed more fully in the next chapter. Programed instructional materials in printed form make it possible for each child to study material best suited to his rate of learning. These materials used with electronic equipment enable a child to speak a second language, to learn shorthand dictation, and to study other subject matter at a rate suitable for him. Instructional teams and modern space facilities also lend opportunities for individual attention. New school buildings are being constructed in which individual study booths replace the old auditorium. Modern schools are being equipped with libraries that make available not only books, but also recordings and television. Most important, individualization is now being considered as essential to quality education and is receiving more attention since the logistics of providing a quantity of classrooms and teachers for the expanding population are being met more adequately.

For years people have believed that children should be grouped into classes of about 30 to 45 students with one teacher giving the same instructional assignments to all. Slowly, against the force of tradition, this idea is giving way to the concept of arranging groups according to the purpose of instruction. If this purpose is to present the same new information via words, demonstrations, pictures, and other means, one teacher can now reach large numbers of students simultaneously with television. However, only a limited number of objectives can be achieved by this means. Social skills and abilities, such as the application, synthesis, and evaluation of newly acquired ideas, can be learned more readily in small discussion groups of about five to ten. Groups of this size can be arranged at all school levels, and one teacher may work with several groups. Let us examine the bases of forming small groups for achieving these objectives.

Friendship grouping is useful for getting students already friendly with one another started quickly on tasks. The advantage here is that time is not spent becoming acquainted with one another. *Interest grouping* is an effective means of putting students with like interests to work on problems of mutual concern. Arranging a large group into smaller work groups on the basis of mutual interests is highly effective when performance at the same level is not critical. *Achievement-level grouping* is useful in getting students together who can handle work of the same level of difficulty. For example, when children are to read the same material or do the same arithmetic exercises grouping those on the same achievement level works very well. *Differential-ability grouping* is useful when a teacher wants different abilities represented in the same group. For example, in an American history class the teacher might want a number of small groups, each having a student who can lead discussion well, another who reads and writes well, another who can visualize information well. When working with a large heterogeneous group that will subsequently be divided into smaller working groups, the teacher needs to use the differential abilities of the students intelligently in order to nurture the abilities of all students.

Continue the Common Elementary School and the Comprehensive High School

If instruction in art or foreign language is required of a portion of the children in an elementary school, should it also be available and required of all children? This question is concerned with the function of the common public school in America. Our tradition has been to make the subject-matter areas the same for all children, but to provide for differences in learning abilities within the various subject fields. Most schools still follow this practice through the sixth grade, with electives starting in junior high school. Some schools, however, are offering foreign language, music, or art only to those children who achieve higher than most. It is possible that these schools are inadvertently and perhaps unintentionally drifting into the European pattern of education, attempting to identify the university-bound children at age 9 or 10 and then providing a different education for them. The authors' judgment is that the elementary school, of all schools in the United States, has most clearly demonstrated its superiority over the European system of expensive education for the elite, and inexpensive, little, or no education for the masses. And European schools are increasingly patterning their system after that of the United States.

The comprehensive high school can meet the needs of students representing the entire range of abilities and interests if it is adequately supported financially and has adequate staff and instructional materials. But it cannot work well when one English teacher is expected to provide effectively for 150 or more students representing the entire range of abilities, or when business education, home economics, industrial arts, and fine arts are treated as odious appendages rather than as essential components of the total instructional program. If the comprehensive high school is to survive, it must accept all students as they come and provide instruction and guidance in which each pupil is placed in classes profitable for him. It is possible that more combined work-study arrangements are needed for many students, and other special provisions may be required for delinquents and culturally disadvantaged youth.

GIFTED AND TALENTED CHILDREN

In Chapter 2, we showed that abilities are readily identified in four areas: figural, semantic, social, and psychomotor. A person might be superior in one or all of these. Most academic subject matter is concerned with semantic content. The child who is consistently superior in most academic subjects, or who promises to be, is called a "gifted student." One who is superior in only one field such as music, art, foreign language, or mathematics is called "talented." These designations have emerged historically and the terminology is not critical. One may prefer to call an individual "gifted" who is superior only in social relations. As long as we clearly indicate the behavioral characteristics of those we refer to by name, we can communicate adequately. Here we shall use the terms *gifted* and *talented* as we have defined them in this paragraph and shall subsequently describe procedures for identifying each type. Children and youth superior in any area of human endeavor are included in the following discussion of objectives, identification procedures, and provisions.

Objectives

What do we want gifted children to be and do as a result of education? Should their self-realization or their usefulness to society be given prior consideration, if this choice must be made? Should they become more alike or more different from one another with increasing education? more alike or more different from other children? The answers to these questions involve objectives based on value systems related to the individual and his contributions to society. Parents, and the children as they mature, should share these decisions with school personnel. The decisions in part determine who is selected as gifted and what educational provisions are made. It is unwise for a school system to embark on special programs until the objectives have been clearly formulated.

A statement of objectives to be achieved at various school levels—primary through high school—has been agreed upon in a number of Wisconsin schools in which the senior author conducted experiments. The following eight objectives guided the evaluation of experimental arrangements for gifted and talented children. In comparison with others, children of superior ability are:

1. To acquire the subject matter more efficiently; their more efficient acquisition of subject matter is to result in fuller knowledge and understanding of the physical and social world.
2. To develop better work-study skills, including learning-to-learn procedures; in turn, this should lead to a higher degree of independence in learning efficiency in and out of school.

3. To develop higher-level problem-solving abilities, sometimes stated as *effective thinking, critical thinking,* or *reasoning.*
4. To develop higher-level expressive abilities in such areas as oral and written expression, art, music, dramatics, and physical activities.
5. To acquire appreciations of beauty in more fields.
6. To develop equally effective citizenship behavior.
7. To develop equally good personal-emotional adjustment as other children.
8. To develop similar high-level ethical conduct and character.

Whether reaching these educational objectives will lead to desirable outcomes for the individuals in adulthood cannot be determined except through longitudinal study. For clarification of what gifted persons themselves value at mid-life we turn to Terman's work. The values expressed at mid-life by persons who were originally identified in the early 1920s as gifted children are noteworthy (32). Their responses to the question "From your point of view, what constitutes success in life?" were as follows:

a. Realization of goals, vocational satisfaction, a sense of achievement
b. A happy marriage and home life, bringing up a family satisfactorily
c. Adequate income for comfortable living (but this was mentioned by only 20 percent of women)
d. Contributing to knowledge or welfare of mankind; helping others, leaving the world a better place
e. Peace of mind, well-adjusted personality, adaptability, emotional maturity (32, 152)

The above categories of responses were given by about 40 to 50 percent of the entire group of males and females, except for (c) as noted. If these are acceptable goals to be achieved by the age of 35 to 50, then the more immediate objectives stated previously should contribute to their eventual realization.

Gifted high school pupils also indicate that they receive specific values from schooling. At the end of the first year in an honors class in American history, the exceptionally able high school juniors enrolled in it said that they valued most from the course:

1. Learning how to study
2. Learning how to secure reliable information and to write research reports
3. Having long-range assignments rather than daily, short ones
4. Participating in panel discussions, whole-class discussions, and debates

5. Reading documentary and current material
6. Forming of better reading habits
7. Learning to budget time
8. Gaining feelings of confidence when presenting information orally
9. Having freedom from routine assignments, including the learning of large amounts of factual information in chronological sequence

These bright students, like Terman's adults, want considerable independence and respect as individuals; they want to feel secure with themselves and others; and they hope to contribute to the group. Undoubtedly, if asked why they valued the above, the students would reveal that their choices bore some relationship to their plans for later life—marriage and vocational success, for example.

Identification

Gifted and talented children are identified through use of standardized intelligence tests, standardized achievement tests, teacher observation, and other means of appraisal. Further, whether mental age, IQ, or scholastic-aptitude scores are obtained from the tests, the tendency is to use some form of percentile score or other deviation score so that, regardless of the test used, the lower limit is the same; for example, ninety-ninth, nintieth, or seventy-fifth percentile. Many schools are now setting the lower limit of IQ at the eighty-fifth and of achievement at the seventy-fifth percentile, intending to identify the top 10 percent or thereabouts. In some large city systems, the criteria are purposefully varied among schools within the city. In schools which draw pupils almost totally from lower socioeconomic status, it is assumed that an impoverished environment will depress intelligence and achievement scores in relation to those of other children in favored environments; therefore, the criteria are at times lowered in these schools.

Examine this specific procedure used to identify bright, older second-graders for subsequent attendance in a five-week summer school followed by enrollment in the fourth grade at the start of the next school year (23). First, all children in the second grade were administered a group intelligence test. Second, those who scored 115 or higher and who were above the median chronological age of all second-graders were identified. Third, the teachers were asked to rate the children on achievement and other characteristics and to recommend any other older second-graders who might profit from acceleration. Fourth, these children, recommended by the teacher or identified by the intelligence testing, were administered a group educational achievement battery.

Those who made a total score equivalent to the eightieth percentile or higher were identified. All children who met the four criteria thus far were recommended for summer session attendance and subsequent enrollment in the fourth grade. The four criteria were age above the median of second-graders, IQ of 115 or higher, achievement at the eightieth percentile or higher, and teacher recommendation. A child who did not meet the standardized criteria or teacher recommendation was given an individual intelligence test and overall assessment by the school psychologist. The psychologist then recommended for or against acceleration. Next, the parents were called in for a conference to provide information about the child and the home and to participate in the final decision regarding acceleration. On the basis of all the information, certain children went to summer school and some were subsequently accelerated. The final decision against a child going into the fourth grade was made by the teacher during the five-week summer session.

In order to identify abilities and deficiencies of all pupils, the following procedures are recommended. First, a group intelligence test and a battery of educational achievement tests should be administered to all students every two years, starting in the second grade. Second, teacher observation and rating of each child's achievement, personal characteristics, and special abilities or deficiencies should be secured each year. Third, additional group testing should be done as necessary to provide for children who transfer into the school system. Fourth, a school psychologist should make an individual assessment of every child recommended for any special program. Fifth, conferences with parents should be held. In certain cases, the school nurse, the social worker, and other specialists may also provide useful information. This type of comprehensive program is used to identify any special talents or any specific deficiency a child may possess. More specialized testing and other diagnositic procedures are often needed to identify disabilities.

Physical, social, and emotional maturity should be considered in identifying gifted children. As shown in Chapter 4, the difference between elementary school children of low (average IQ 67) and high intelligence (average IQ 127) in such physical measures as height, weight, number of permanent teeth, and bone development is of no practical significance for any educational purpose. Similarly, emotional adjustment was found to be about the same for the children of low and high intelligence. If a special educational provision is to be made for gifted and talented children, no child should be eliminated simply because he is below the average of all children in physical development or because he is less well adjusted socially or emotionally than most children (19). It is possible that poorer social and emotional adjustment in a bright child might result because the instruction is not suited to his needs; if special provision were made, his adjustment might improve markedly.

Educational Provisions

We have already indicated that individualization and grouping are the two possible organizational arrangements. Within these arrangements, provisions intended to be helpful to gifted and talented students are usually classified as enrichment, acceleration, sectioning and special classes, instructional teams, and nongraded classes. Special schools are applicable only to our largest school systems and will not be discussed further. Instructional teams and nongraded classes are very promising, but will not be discussed in this chapter inasmuch as they are given considerable attention in the next chapter.

All of these provisions are merely means for bringing instructional content in line with the abilities of the student. They are organizational patterns that do nothing unless the instructional program for the gifted student is changed. For example, special sections or classes for bright children do nothing in themselves to improve instruction. However, in special sections we can bring higher-level content to bright children and we can more readily use discovery methods of teaching. We can emphasize creative activities. One teacher working with a group of bright individuals can do these things better than ten different teachers, each individualizing instruction for three bright children out of a heterogeneous class of 30 to 45. All the special provisions which we discuss are based on the assumption that instructional materials and activities should and can be different for gifted and talented children than for those not gifted.

ENRICHMENT IN HETEROGENEOUS CLASSES

Enrichment is possible in all types of organization; however, it is the principal means of providing for the gifted in heterogeneous classes. The small school that has only one first-grade class of 25 pupils can enrich instruction for the brighter ones, as can the larger school with 90 first-graders. Descriptions of enrichment procedures are manifold (6, 26, 28). In Milwaukee the main categories of enrichment applied generally to all school levels and subject fields are: research activities, creative projects, experimentation and demonstration, leadership opportunities, club work, service to school and community, and special talent activities—music, dramatics, dance, and athletics.

In addition to the fact that enrichment can be done in the smallest to the largest schools, judgments favoring enrichment for gifted pupils in regular classes rather than grouping or accelerating include:

1. Enrichment can provide for each child to develop his abilities to the fullest.
2. Children of varying abilities and levels of abilities have opportunity to work and play together and benefit from these contacts with one another.
3. The less able pupils are encouraged by the presence of the more able.
4. This type of school situation more closely parallels that outside of school.
5. It is desirable for the more able pupils at times not only to live with but to help those of lower abilities.

There are drawbacks to enrichment in the upper elementary grades and thereafter:

1. It is difficult to provide competent teachers who have sufficient knowledge in several subject fields to do a good job of enrichment.
2. There is insufficient time to work well with the gifted students, particularly in the junior and senior high school where the teacher has as many as 150 students daily.
3. It is exceedingly difficult, if not impossible, to do a good job of enriching instruction without drawing subject-matter content from the next higher grade level.

This last drawback is critical in connection with enrichment in heterogeneous classes, for most schools have not found adequate means whereby the bright fifth-grade pupils, for example, use regular sixth-grade textbooks, while the more average and slower students use fifth- and fourth-grade texts, respectively.

ACCELERATION

In this discussion acceleration means that the students will finish 12 grades in less than 12 school years or, after finishing high school in 12 years, will receive college credit which permits completing the requirements for the baccalaureate in less than 4 years. The principal means of acceleration are early admission to kindergarten or first grade, double promotion, concentrating instruction in shorter time periods, lengthening the school year to permit graduation in less than 12 school years, early admission to college, and admission to college with advanced standing. Acceleration, like enrichment, can be applied from the very smallest one- or two-room rural school to the largest city school system.

One of the strongest cases for *early admission to kindergarten,* and subsequently to first grade, on the basis of mental age rather than chronological age is made by Worcester (34). He studied the performances of children in later elementary grades whose average admission age was eight months younger than that of pupils admitted regularly. The pupils who had been admitted early were found not to differ in physical development from those regularly admitted. In academic work, the younger pupils did as well or better than their older classmates. As judged by their classmates or by teachers' ratings, they were as well or better adjusted socially and emotionally than the other pupils. They had as good or better psychomotor coordination, were well accepted by their peers, liked school, and did as well or better than those of the same age who were a year later in getting started to school. No negative effect of the early admission was noted, although some individual pupils were found not to have made good progress. Observe that the children admitted early were only eight months younger than those normally admitted and were thus primarily drawn from the group which was born from a day to a few months too late to enter normally. However, had they not been admitted early, they would have lost a whole year, except in schools which admit at the beginning of the second semester.

Double promotion, having a child skip a grade, for example, from second to fourth or from sixth to eighth, presents many difficulties and should probably not be practiced except in small rural or other poor schools which cannot provide more adequate means of acceleration. The disadvantage of double promotion is that the pupil often skips some important learning which is difficult to accomplish in the next grade or which is never accomplished. Nevertheless, if a school has no better means of providing for exceptionally gifted pupils than through double promotion, skipping may be desirable.

Concentrating instruction into shorter time periods is more efficient than double promotion or skipping and offers opportunities not provided by early entrance into kindergarten or first grade. In the ungraded primary school, the bright child can complete the normal first three grades in two years if the school is operating on a yearly plan, and in four or five semesters if it is operating on a semester plan. No skipping of instruction need occur. Similarly, bright students can finish three years of junior high school in two, four years of high school in three, or four years of college in three when arrangements are made to concentrate instruction into shorter periods of time, for example, six semesters of algebra and geometry in four. Condensing three years of junior high school mathematics into two years was found completely satisfactory for boys and for most girls; however, some girls experienced difficulty with geometry in the ninth grade. Condensing three years of science was completely satisfactory for both sexes; the bright children achieved just as high when taking biology in the ninth grade as did equally bright tenth-graders who had not experienced the condensed program (25). In this connection, we point out that condensing instruction works best in large junior high schools by putting students together in the same section for the condensed instruction.

The lengthened school year and the assignment of additional work during the regular school year enable gifted and talented students to complete 12 years of schooling in less than 12 years without skipping content. As noted earlier, bright, older second-graders are identified toward the end of the second grade. They then attend a five-week summer session and enroll in the fourth grade in September. During the summer session they complete the essential content of the third grade which has not been included in the second grade. Cursive handwriting, language arts, arithmetic, and expressive abilities—verbal, artistic, musical, and physical—receive main attention. The accelerates meet with their teacher in the summer session for five weeks in a self-contained classroom from 8:00 to 12 A.M., Monday through Friday. By the end of the fifth grade, the accelerates who first participated in this program had caught up with equally bright children, who were one year older, in 30 of 33 measures (21). They were not significantly lower than the older bright children in any of the usual subject-matter fields, except word knowledge, or in any of ten tests of creative thinking. They were lower in only one of six psychomotor abilities—handwriting legibility, but not handwriting speed. They were not lower in ethical values, attitudes toward school, or in teacher ratings of their social and emotional adjustment.

During World War II, a considerable number of students finished four years of college in three years by going regularly to summer school, receiving credit for courses by examination, and taking more courses than most students during each semester or quarter. Pressey and Flesher studied a group of such accelerated female students while they were in college and again ten years after they graduated (29).

Ten years after graduation a lower percent of the accelerated students had married and had children; however, they were a year younger than the control group. About the same number of accelerates and nonaccelerates were active in community affairs ten years after graduation; however, twice as many of the accelerates had earned a further academic degree and almost twice as many of the married accelerates were continuing in a career other than that of a housewife. Although the accelerates probably had higher motivation and ambition originally, the general conclusion was that completing the four years of college in three had many desirable and no undesirable effects. Only women were included in the experimental and control group; it was hypothesized that the accelerated program might have been even more beneficial for males.

Early admission to college can be accomplished in several ways. One is to accelerate pupils by some means as indicated previously without their skipping any essential subject matter. Another is simply to take them out of high school in the junior or senior year and put them into college. Tenth- and eleventh-grade students were selected and admitted early to 12 participating colleges under an arrangement sponsored by the Fund for the Advancement of Education (8). As college seniors, the majority of those who had entered early were favorable to the program and indicated that early admission was very profitable for them. A control group did not favor the program.

This program of early admission through skipping the last part of high school received unfavorable evaluation from the high school principals from the outset. With the many other means available for getting students into college by age 17 without skipping essential content or other experiences, it would appear unwise to use this type of early admission program. Only in poorly managed schools that do not have systematic provisions for the gifted would it appear wise to get exceptionally bright students out of the school for the senior year and into college.

Admission to college with advanced standing is being accomplished through high school seniors' taking advanced placement tests in various college subjects. Unlike the student who enters college without having completed all high school work, the advanced-placement student is graduated with other students at the end of the senior year but receives credit for course work in college. Also, some school systems are working out arrangements directly with colleges in which certain courses in high school are automatically accepted as equivalent to the same course in the freshman or sophomore year of college. A program of advanced placement that started at the University of Buffalo in the 1930s has proven very effective (2).

The most difficult remaining problem in connection with early admission and advanced placement is that of cooperation between the high schools and colleges (27). The Bronx High School of Science in New York City (a special school for students talented in science) and several others entered into a project in which such courses as English literature and composition, biology, chemistry, physics, and mathematics were taught in high school as they supposedly are in colleges during the freshman and sophomore year. In 11 different subjects

TABLE 14.1.

Methods for Accelerating Pupils Without Skipping Subject Content

Method	Level	Investigator
Early admittance to kindergarten or first grade	Preschool	Hobson, Birch, Worcester.[a]
Condensation of 6 semesters of non-graded primary school into 4 or 5 semesters	Primary	Klausmeier.[b]
Summer-session attendance for entry into higher grade in the fall	Elementary	Klausmeier & Ripple, Klausmeier.[c]
Condensation of content into less time; e.g., 3 years of English in 2 years	Junior high	Justman, Klausmeier, Klausmeier, & Wiersma.[d]
Taking advanced college placement courses in the senior year of high school	Senior high	Meister, Barnette.[e]
Taking additional courses; summer session attendance	College	Pressey & Flesher.[f]

[a] J. R. Hobson. Mental age as a workable criterion for school admission. *Elem. Sch. J.*, 1948, **48**. Birch, J. W. Early school admission for mentally advanced children. *Except. Child.*, 1954, **21**. Worcester, D. A. *The education of children of above average mentality.* Lincoln: Univer. of Nebraska Press, 1956.

[b] H. J. Klausmeier. *Summary report of research completed, 1958–1961, on educational provisions for children and youth of superior learning abilities, Milwaukee Public Schools.* Milwaukee: Board of School Directors, 1962.

[c] H. J. Klausmeier, & R. E. Ripple. Effects of accelerating bright older pupils from second to fourth grade. *J. educ. Psychol.*, 1962., **53**. Klausmeier, H. J. Effects of accelerating bright older elementary pupils: A follow-up. *J. educ. Psychol.*, 1963, **54**.

[d] J. Justman. Academic achievement of intellectually gifted accelerants and non-accelerants in junior high school. *Sch. Rev.*, 1954, **62**. Justman, J. Academic achievement of intellectually gifted accelerants and non-accelerants in senior high school. *Sch. Rev.*, 1954, **62**. Klausmeier, H. J. (see [b] above). Klausmeier, H. J., & W. Wiersma. Effects of condensing content in mathematics and science in the junior and senior high school. *Sch. Sci. Math.*, 1964, **64**.

[e] M. Meister. Cooperation of secondary schools and colleges in acceleration of gifted students. *J. educ. Sociol.*, 1956, **29**. Barnette, W. L. Advanced credit for the superior high school student. *J. higher Educ.*, 1957, **28**.

[f] S. L. Pressey, & Marie A. Flesher. Wartime accelerates ten years after. *J. educ. Psychol.*, 1955, **46**.

offered this way, the same tests were administered to large numbers of high school seniors and college freshmen. The achievements of the seniors compared favorably with those of college freshmen. However, some colleges will not credit these high school courses toward college graduation.

Table 14.1 presents a summary of the methods of acceleration which do not involve skipping of content, the school level at which experimentation has been done, and the reference in which the results are reported. Completely favorable results in terms of the educational achievements and the social, emotional, and physical adjustment of the accelerates were observed by all the researchers. Our own research has clearly shown that acceleration does not result in lower educational achievements or in social or emotional adjustment. Besides the researchers listed in Table 14.1, Terman (31) and Shannon (30) reported the same conclusions. With this type and amount of evidence mounting over the years, and with the present shortage of teachers and other educated talent, an appropriate national goal might be to have all bright students awarded the baccalaureate by their twenty-first birthday and the most able and rapidly maturing by age 20. Human resources are wasted by forcing bright students to spend 12 years completing their education through high school and 16 years in completing all requirements for the baccalaureate.

SECTIONING AND SPECIAL CLASSES

Any school that has enough pupils for two sections can arrange them into a higher and a lower group. The school with as many as 150 or more students at each grade level can also section readily. If the high section contains only students of superior learning ability, it may be designated a special class for the gifted. The lowest section may be designated a class for slow-learning students. It is unfair to children, of course, to place them in these sections if they do not meet commonly accepted criteria of giftedness or slow learning. Unfortunately, some schools attempt to keep all sections equal in number, and this often determines the criteria used in placement in sections.

When sectioning is done in the larger elementary schools, the pupils receive instruction in most if not all subject-matter fields as sectioned groups. Some special groupings from among sections, for example, in music, art, or arithmetic, might produce more homogeneity. In the junior and senior high schools, the better procedure is to section students according to achievement level in particular subject fields, giving due consideration to pupils of high intellectual abilities and other criteria of identification.

Special classes for gifted children, called the "major work program for gifted children," have been in operation for many years in the public schools of Cleveland, Ohio. The program starts in the primary school although some pupils are added during the intermediate grades. The pupils have most of their work in special classes, but take physical education, music, and crafts with the rest of their age group and participate in other regular school activities. As part of the enrichment program a foreign language is taught, although it is not offered to other children enrolled in the same school. Further, the enrollments, about 20 pupils per class, are considerably smaller than regular classes, thus permitting more individualization of instruction. A questionnaire was administered to all the high school graduates of the program between the years 1938 and 1952 (1). About 84 percent of these students expressed favorable attitudes about the special classes and more than 50 percent of both the men and women had no suggestions for improving the program.

The best-liked aspects of the program included foreign language, opportunity to express individuality, curriculum differences from regular classes, and freedom from regimentation. The least-liked features of the program were the somewhat unfavorable attitudes of other students and teachers toward the program and the lack of social contact with other pupils. The most frequent suggestion for improvement was that there should be more associating with other pupils. Other school systems report similarly desirable results for their special classes. As shown previously, equally desirable results also are reported for acceleration and enrichment in heterogeneous age-graded classes, particularly at the elementary school level.

Until recently special classes for the gifted in the elementary school have been operated primarily in large cities like Cleveland. However, sectioning and special classes are common in junior and senior high schools which have enrollments of 150 or more pupils per grade. If special classes and sectioning are to work well in any school, differentiation of instructional materials and activities must be made in the various sections. Table 14.2 shows some features of the sectioning arrangements in the required English and history classes of Waukesha Senior High School. The total enrollment in English is 644 and in history, 666. The higher number in history results from more students failing the first time and repeating as seniors.

TABLE 14.2.

Features of Sections in Eleventh-Grade English and History
(Waukesha High School, Wis.)

| | Number of Students Enrolled | | Criteria of Selection in Both Subjects | |
Section Designation	English	History	Scholastic aptitude, local norms (Percentile Rank)	Achievement test, national norms (Percentile Rank)
Honors	24	25	90—higher	90—higher
One	262	264	60—99	75—99
Regular	264	279	18—59	25—74
Low Regular	74	78	1—17	1—24
				Previous history of difficulty in the subject
Special	20	20	Individual appraisal	Individual appraisal
Total	644	666		

The juniors are invited to enroll in the honors sections, provided their scholastic-aptitude test score is at the ninetieth percentile or higher on local norms and their tested achievement in the particular subject is at the ninetieth percentile score or higher on national norms. Only four honors sections are available, one each in English, history, mathematics, and science. Though some students are eligible for all four, most enroll in only the two in which they are most interested and enroll in one sections for the other subjects.

Students are given no choice in enrolling in the other sections for which they are eligible by the criteria. All students with scholastic aptitude at the sixtieth percentile or higher and with achievement in the particular subject at the seventy-fifth percentile or higher must enroll in the one sections. Teachers' grades and recommendations are given some consideration in admission to the honors sections and to the low regular sections. The special classes are for students identified as educable mentally retarded while still in the elementary grades. Class size is lowest in the special classes (20), about equal in the honors and low regular sections (about 25), and highest in the regular and one sections (about 30).

Other interesting features of the program concern reading materials and instructional activities. The required textbook is different for every sectional level. In the honors section in history, for example, a book normally used at the college level and supplementary readings of documentary materials are used. The low regular sections use a junior high school history book with a low level of reading difficulty; the same type of reading material is used in the low regular sections in English. However, in the honors section in English, a regular high school text is used. The amount of writing activity goes up successively in all sections, regardless of subject, from low regular through honors. The amount of assigned reading goes up successively from low regular through one; in the honors sections the assigned reading drops off but is replaced with a heavier volume of voluntary reading. Objective tests are generally used from low regular through the one sections; in the honors sections, almost no objective tests are used.

The most heterogeneous sections are the regular, and the most difficult for which to find appropriate activities are the low regular. Publishers are just beginning to provide instructional materials for high school students whose reading achievements are at the junior high school level. Also, supplementary and general library books which have interesting content for students at about age 17 have quite advanced vocabulary. The teachers at Waukesha are earnestly attempting to provide differentiated instruction in line with the level of abilities and achievements of the students in the various sections.

When sectioning and related instruction are managed well, teachers and students of all ability levels in small (S), medium-sized (M), and large (L) high schools are favorable to the arrangements, as shown in Table 14.3. We also found that the students of all ability levels formed their friendships primarily on the basis of being in the same after-

TABLE 14.3.

Reactions of Students and Teachers to Continuing Sectioning Arrangements
(Three High Schools)

	Students' Responses						Teachers' Responses		
	High Ability		Middle Ability		Low Ability				No Response
School	Yes	No	Yes	No	Yes	No	Yes	No	
S	18	0	17	1	17	1	18	1	3
M	15	2	11	6	14	3	30	3	7
L[a]	17	2	17	2	13	4[b]	25	2	2
Total	50	4	45	9	44	8	73	6	12

[a] Only teachers of eleventh-grade classes were invited to respond.
[b] Two students did not respond.
Source: H. J. Klausmeier, J. Mulhern, & H. Wakefield. High school students evaluate sectioning. *Educ. Leadership*, 1960, **17**, 222.

school activities rather than being in the same elective or required classes; thus the sectioning was not considered to have promoted undesirable social relationships among students in the three ability groups. The information in Table 14.3 should not be interpreted to mean that high school students and teachers in other schools might not be equally favorable to some other arrangements, such as heterogeneous classes with enrichment and no sectioning.

MULTIPLE PROVISIONS

Many provisions are necessary to meet the needs of the gifted and talented in medium-sized and large cities. After five years of intensive research, the following provisions were incorporated into the operating procedures of the Milwaukee Public Schools:

1. In the primary school, special attention is given to early identification and acceleration of children of superior ability. About four per cent of the children of above median CA and about one per cent of the younger children who demonstrate exceptionally high abilities are accelerated one or two semesters at some point between kindergarten entrance and completion of fourth grade.

2. In the fourth grade, children of superior ability are placed in regular heterogeneous classes and appropriate enrichment opportunities are provided for them. Fourth-grade teachers are informed of identified children of superior ability in their classes. The fourth-grade program is intended to help the pupils acquire additional growth in independence, aid them in adjusting to the expanded curriculum of the intermediate grades before placement in special classes in the fifth grade, and help those accelerated in the primary school adjust to the higher grade before placing them in special classes.

3. In the fifth and sixth grades, children of superior ability are placed in special self-contained classes in certain elementary schools, or, in locations where special self-contained classes are not feasible, in a comparable alternative arrangement such as special classes which meet periodically with an itinerant teacher. In these special classes, there is some condensation of content in subject areas to permit progress in a designated subject at an accelerated rate, and there is enrichment of the entire curriculum to achieve higher level competency than may be attained in the regular classroom.

Some pupils of superior ability are accelerated placement-wise during Grades 4, 5, and 6, especially those who are in the older age group for their actual grade placement.

4. In the junior and senior high school, provisions for youth of superior abilities include courses in the regular program sequence for students talented in any one subject field or in several subject fields. In addition, specific opportunities for enrichment, acceleration, and condensed instruction are available. . . .

The superior ability student at the junior and senior high school level typically pursues one or more courses one year in advance of the regular sequential program; e.g., ninth-grade algebra, general science, and English may be taken in the eighth grade. High school credit toward graduation is given to eighth-grade pupils who satisfactorily complete these high school courses. . . .

Students of superior ability in the senior high school, having completed seven units by the end of grade 9, choose among three options: graduation one or two semesters early upon completing the 17 recommended units, remaining through Grade 12 with some released time for enrollment at a college or university, or remaining through Grade 12 with some released time for employment (**24**, 4–5).[1]

SLOW-LEARNING AND MENTALLY RETARDED CHILDREN

Slow-learning and mentally retarded children comprise about 15 percent of the total child population of school age, according to criteria of IQ based on the Revised Stanford-Binet Scale. Slow-learning children have IQs or scholastic aptitude ranging from the third to fifteenth percentile and have equally low achievements in the usual school subjects. Some children with IQs as low as 70 learn reasonably well and are properly classified as slow learners rather than mentally retarded, and some with IQs as high as 75 who do not learn well are properly classified as mentally retarded. Dunn and Capobianco summarized some general agreements about terminology and definitions of mental retardation:

Within the last six years, educators arrived at functional, though tentative, subdivisions of mentally retarded children. These categories are: (a) the "Educable mentally retarded," with IQ's of approximately 50 to 75, who appear to have sufficient potential to acquire skills in the basic school subjects; (b) the "trainable mentally retarded," with IQ's of approximately 30 to 50, who seem to have the capacity to communicate orally, to care for themselves physically, and to become economically productive in sheltered environments, yet who cannot be expected to become literate; and (c) the "custodial mentally retarded," with IQ's below approximately 30, who are unable to acquire skills even in self-help and thus require permanent care (**7**, 453).

We now turn briefly to considerations of provisions for slow-learning, educable mentally retarded, and trainable mentally retarded children. The custodial mentally retarded are usually placed in residential institutions and remain there for life.

[1] Reprinted from *Education* magazine. Copyright, 1964, by the Bobbs-Merrill Company, Inc., Indianapolis, Indiana.

Slow-Learning Children

The provisions for slow-learning children vary according to the size of the school and the abilities of the staff. The general objective is to identify whatever abilities the slow-learning child possesses and to develop those abilities to the fullest. In the elementary grades, slow learners are usually kept in the same heterogeneous classes with other pupils; special sections are arranged for them, however, in some larger elementary schools. In the larger junior and senior high schools which have special provisions for gifted children, there are usually comparable classes for the slow learners also.

Nonpromotion of slow learners is more widely practiced than is acceleration of gifted students, with far more boys than girls being held back. What are the criteria for acceleration and nonpromotion? Reading vocabulary and spelling achievement are the most important determiners of whether or not a child is promoted to the next grade (15). Equally important skills, such as in reading comprehension, arithmetic fundamentals, and arithmetic reasoning, are not related to promotion. Boys as a group do not achieve as high in reading vocabulary and spelling as do girls; however, they do as well or better in arithmetic fundamentals and in arithmetic reasoning.

Holding back slow learners usually does not improve their achievement or help their adjustment to school. The effects of a change in promotional policy on pupils' achievement in reading were studied in one district of the Phoenix schools (12). The traditional basis for promotion was academic achievement, a policy which resulted in the nonpromotion of a large number of bilingual and underprivileged children. A change was made to continuous promotion, on the assumption that all the pupils would make continuous progress more readily by being promoted each year than by being kept back. Under the new policy, some nonpromotion continued; however, the number of pupils not promoted was markedly reduced. On the basis of achievement tests administered for ten consecutive years, the new program of continuous promotion did not result in lower reading achievement; on the contrary, slight improvement resulted for the entire group, including those who would have been kept back under the traditional policy.

Teachers in junior and senior high school frequently experience ethical conflicts within themselves when they must make decisions as to whether to maintain a minimum standard of achievement and fail the slow learner who has done his best or to pass him along even though he has not achieved a minimum standard. There is no point in having slow-learning children attend high school classes if they do not learn as well as they might or if they continuously experience failure in many subjects. The better approach, psychologically and ethically, in providing for slow-learning students in high school is to arrange special sections for them, make certain that they learn as well as they can, and to set up standards of achievement in terms of their abilities, not in terms of the entire high school population.

Education must help most slow learners become relatively independent economically and stable emotionally and socially. Though an exceedingly wealthy country, the United States cannot look forward to supporting slower learners throughout life through tax monies or charities. Depriving them of further education at around age 16 or not having them learn well in usual classes almost assures that a considerable number will never become economically self-sufficient. As will now be shown, a considerable number of educable mentally retarded children with special education eventually become independent of others, find employment, and make useful contributions to community life as adults in labor and service occupations.

Educable Mentally Retarded Children

In the more backward states and communities, educable mentally retarded children are institutionalized at a young age and remain wards of the state for the remainder of their lives. In some smaller, more isolated schools, mentally retarded children are kept in regular classes until they are hopelessly incompetent to perform the class work, at high school age if not earlier, whereupon they quit school and remain with the family or are institutionalized. In the more progressive communities and states, the educable mentally retarded are identified at some time between kindergarten and fourth grade and are placed in special classes in a regular elementary school. As they are able to participate in the regular program of music, art, physical education, and other school activities, they do so; but their instruction in the usual school subjects is in a separate class. At about age 16, they are placed in special classes until they reach ages 18 to 21, and receive vocational education; or they go to vocational high schools; or they are placed in other specialized vocational arrangements. By age 21, some assume rather complete independence and responsibility for their own adult lives. Some marry and have a successful home life; some subsequently have normal children, particularly the more attractive females and the occupationally successful males who marry mates of average abilities.

Many others, however, although able to perform adequately a variety of skilled, semiskilled, and unskilled tasks, need a protected environment throughout adult life to help them with their social and economic affairs. Still others do not make a successful life and, by delinquency, criminality, emotional disturbance, or general incompetence, become permanent wards of the state.

The objective of education for educable mentally retarded children is to develop to the fullest what abilities they do have. However, to expect the majority of them to achieve well in an algebra class, to read at the ninth-grade level, or to understand abstract ideas, is unrealistic. The related problem of family life and marriage is also complex. Sex generally becomes a critical problem at adolescence, especially with girls. Although sterilization of some mentally retarded people is permitted in some states, it is frowned upon by some religious and ethnic groups. So, too, is the encouragement of effective birth control. It is common to find mentally retarded children now enrolled in special classes whose parents also were enrolled in them as children.

Trainable Mentally Retarded Children

Trainable mentally retarded children are usually cared for by institutions, but recently a new program has been set up. In this arrangement, the child lives at home and attends a special class. Because the program is so recent, the outcomes are highly tentative. The senior author conducted research in different classrooms for educable mentally retarded children and in four classrooms for the trainable. The enrollment is typically kept at 18 or lower for the educable retarded and at 12 or lower for the trainable.

The difference between the performances of these two groups at the same age is very sharp. Although a trainable child occasionally performs as well as one in the retarded group, at age 10 most of the trainables cannot count ten pennies correctly. They have difficulty with outer garments such as overshoes and buttons and are difficult to communicate with. Simple quantitative terms, such as *faster* and *slower*, *more* and *less*, cannot be communicated to them at this age. If even a small percent of them can become relatively self-sufficient and can make their own way economically as adults, the efforts of the teachers and the public in supporting the special classes are worthwhile. A considerable portion of them will need continuing help throughout life. Perhaps when their homes are broken by death or other causes, they will become wards of the state.

CULTURALLY DEPRIVED CHILDREN

In the United States, completion of high school is a prerequisite for subsequent gainful employment and participation in the economic, political, and social affairs of the community. About one-third of our youth, however, do not complete high school (33). This proportion is considerably higher in cities where slum living and segregation are prevalent. This is the group generally referred to as culturally disadvantaged or culturally deprived. Illiterate parents, poverty, large family size, broken homes, and impoverished neighborhood conditions contribute to the deprivation. However, cultural deprivation is not limited to the large cities or to any ethnic or racial group. Rural areas also have young people who do not profit from schooling and will not become economically independent adults. Inasmuch as the home and other agencies are not meeting the problems of cultural deprivation, the schools must take a more active role (4).

What should the schools do about cultural deprivation? Consider an abbreviated summary of the original recommendations developed in a conference on education and cultural deprivation (4).

1. Breakfast and lunch, medical and dental care, and necessary clothing should be provided by the school or community.

2. Nursery schools and kindergarten should be organized for culturally deprived children. A national commission composed of teachers and other specialists should develop and coordinate this program. The teachers should be specially trained for this type of teaching. Parents must be sufficiently involved and committed to this type of schooling that they insure continuity in the child's experience. The main objectives of the preschool education are to improve the child's perceptual ability, language development, mastery over various aspects of the environment, enthusiasm for learning, thinking and reasoning abilities, and attention span for purposive-learning activities.

3. Special attention should be given to education of the culturally disadvantaged children during elementary school years. His perceptual development, language development, motivation, and ability to attend should be appraised at the beginning of the first grade. Appropriate instruction for each child should be arranged. The emphasis during the first three years should be on the development of each child's knowledge, abilities, and attitudes. A national commission of teachers and other specialists should develop and coordinate the instructional program. A variety of different educational approaches should be tried

out and their effectiveness evaluated. The teaching staff must be carefully selected and educated in order to help each child master the fundamental skills in language, reading, and arithmetic and a general skill in learning itself. Home-school relations must be cooperative. Every available resource should be utilized with culturally deprived children who have not had preschool educational opportunity.

4. With special regard to Negro students, all children must learn under the most positive set of human interactions under teachers who are warm and supportive to all children. Children of all races should engage in common activities. With the rapid changes resulting from the civil rights movement, Negro children will need more educational and vocational guidance than other children. Beginning with secondary school, Negro students should have periodic interviews with capable guidance workers.

5. A major effort should be made at the beginning of secondary education to identify culturally deprived students who will begin higher education upon completion of high school. Special instructional programs, tutorial help, counseling, and help with the basic skills must be provided. Modifications for those who are having difficulty with regular school subjects are needed whereby they specialize in an area of interest and continue to develop the basic skills in language and reading. Work-study plans are necessary, requiring effective cooperation between schools, industry, and public agencies. Especially for the culturally disadvantaged youth, there should be peer societies which have continuity over the age period 14 to 19. These societies should provide opportunities for social relations, service to others, and the development of meaningful value patterns.

If a program such as this is put into effect, will it accomplish the primary objective of raising the level of educational achievement and changing the values of culturally disadvantaged children and youth? This question cannot be answered definitively at this time; however, some evidence from projects underway in large cities suggests the feasibility of making the effort. Let us consider the preschool program.

Several misconceptions about the high importance of heredity and the relative unimportance of environment are now giving way to more reasonable interpretations (16). The concept of fixed general intelligence is being replaced with a concept of more specialized abilities that are dependent upon environmental nurturance, including instruction. The notion of predetermined development is yielding to a concept of development influenced by environmental considerations. The early years of life, once regarded as unimportant in intellectual development, are now regarded as highly important. The idea of motivation as a result of unpleasant drive states is being superseded by concepts of achievement motivation and the desires to know and understand. All of these viewpoints have been encountered in previous chapters and are therefore mentioned only briefly.

Cognitive stimulation in the preschool years may be highly effective in accelerating intellectual functions. In these years, the child is highly receptive to learning. Furthermore, less has to be compensated for at the preschool age than later. The development in preschool years of language and verbal behaviors, auditory and visual discrimination, general environmental orientation, adequate self-concepts and motivation, and concept formation is essential for later school learning. A child with an intact brain who is not severely disturbed can learn all the basic scholastic skills. Failure of these children to learn comes about when the school fails to develop adequate curricula, including methods and materials (5).

From this it is apparent that the culturally disadvantaged child will be reasonably well educated only if school personnel commit themselves to the task. At the high school level, this means securing a vast number of teachers who will work as cheerfully with the culturally disadvantaged as with other children more nearly like themselves. Large financial outlays for education are required. Along with more interested and well prepared teachers and more monies, continuous experimentation is required so that education is kept up to date. Education now serves the culturally disadvantaged poorly because outmoded concepts are still practiced.

DELINQUENCY

A delinquent is a child or youth between the age of 7 and 17 who repeatedly commits acts which, when carried out beyond the statutory juvenile age of 16, are punishable as crimes (11). Like any other behavior, delinquent behavior results from the interaction of the individual with his environment. Delinquent boys differ in their interaction from nondelinquent boys through an interplay of somatic, temperamental, psychological, and social influences that may be summarized thus:

. . . (1) *physically*, in being essentially mesomorphic in constitution (solid, closely knit, muscular); (2) *temperamentally*, in being restlessly energetic, impulsive, extroverted, aggressive, destructive (often sadistic) . . .; (3) *in attitude,* by being hostile, defiant, resentful, suspicious, stubborn, socially assertive, adventurous, unconventional, nonsubmissive to authority; (4) *psychologically,* in tending to direct and concrete, rather than symbolic, intellectual expression, and in being less methodical in their approach to problems; (5) *socioculturally,* in having been reared to a far greater extent than the control group in homes of little understanding, affection, stability, or moral fibre by parents usually unfit to be effective guides and protectors or . . . desirable sources for emulation and the construction of a consistent, well-balanced, and socially normal superego during the early stages of character development. While in individual cases the stresses contributed by any one of the above pressure-areas of dissocial-behavior tendency may adequately account for persistence in delinquency, in general the high probability is dependent upon the interplay of the conditions and forces from all these areas.

In the exciting, stimulating, but little-controlled and culturally inconsistent environment of the underprivileged area, such boys readily give expression to their untamed impulses and their self-centered desires by means of various forms of delinquent behavior. Their tendencies toward uninhibited energy-expression are deeply anchored in soma and psyche and in the malformations of character during the first few years of life (9, 281–282).

DELINQUENCY IN A MIDWESTERN CITY

We should not infer from the preceding quotation that having a mesomorphic body build or being reared in a family and neighborhood in an underprivileged area always result in delinquent behavior. Instead, it is the interplay of *all* these factors. From studies of delinquents and nondelinquents extending over many years, a prediction scale has been developed (9) and subsequently validated (10). This scale was used in a longitudinal study of boys growing up in a small city in the Midwest (13). Table 14.4 shows the boys' scores which were based on home visits. Certain information is given in the note accompanying Table 14.4 that is helpful in understanding it. Other essential information regarding each column is now presented.

Social class B, C, and D refer to lower-middle, upper-lower, and lower-lower respectively. Social class A refers to upper and upper-middle; however, none of the boys and girls in this category became delinquent in this particular study. Aggressive maladjustment indicates behaviors such as fighting, bullying, stealing, breaking rules, and being truant from school. This was rated by the teacher and also secured from sociometric tests; it is not a prediction factor of the Gluecks. A high score on discipline of the boy by the father indicates overstrict or erratic discipline in comparison with firm but kindly discipline. Supervision of the boy by the mother is also a composite of a number of ratings, and a high score indicates unsuitable supervision. A high score in affection of the father and mother for the boy indicates hostility in

TABLE 14.4.

Delinquency and Family Relations[a]

Social Class of Boy	Aggressive Maladjustment T-Score[b]	Discipline by Father	Family Relations Category				Prediction Score	Actual Level of Delinquency
			Supervision by Mother	Affec'n fr. Father	Affec'n fr. Moth.	Cohesiveness of Family		
D	76	60	83	73	86	97	399	II
D	75	60	83	73	86	97	399	II
C	67	60	83	73	86	61	375	I
D	73	72	83	73	43	97	368	I
D	74	72	58	73	43	61	307	II
B	70	60	58	73	43	61	295	II
D	75	60	10	73	86	61	290	III
D	—	9	58	73	86	61	287	II
C	70	9	58	73	86	61	287	III
D	69	60	58	73	43	21	255	III
D	70	60	10	73	43	61	247	III
C	76	9	10	73	86	61	239	I
D	66	72	10	34	43	61	220	No
C	63	60	10	73	43	21	207	No
C	72	60	10	34	43	21	168	No
C	66	9	58	34	43	21	165	No
B	65	9	10	34	43	21	117	III
D	51	9	10	34	43	21	117	No
B	47	9	10	34	43	21	117	No
C	38	9	10	34	43	21	117	No
C	60	9	10	34	43	21	117	No
B	66	9	10	34	43	21	117	No

[a] Prediction and delinquency based on home visits, scored in relation to record of actual delinquency.

[b] The score for Aggressive Maladjustment is a *T*-score, with the mean at 50. The 90th percentile is about 63 on this scale, and the 95th percentile is 67.

Prediction Score	Chances of Becoming Delinquent
less than 200	8 in 100
200–249	37 in 100
250–299	64 in 100
300 and over	89 in 100

SOURCE: R. J. Havighurst, *et al. Growing up in River City*. New York: Wiley, 1962.

comparison with warmth. A high score in cohesiveness of family indicates an unintegrated family in comparison with a cohesive one. These five ratings of the home in the Glueck system are based on visits to the home and interviews with the child and one or both parents. The prediction score is the total of the five scores; the key for interpreting it is given in the note at the bottom of Table 14.4.

The actual level of delinquency was obtained in this manner (13).

Police records were consulted, and a rating was made for each contact the student had with the police. Contacts were rated from 1 to 4 for seriousness of the offense, and from 1 to 4 for the disposition of the case: Whether the individual was let off with a warning, brought to court, declared delinquent, fined, put in prison, sent to the reformatory, and so on. The total delinquency scores ranged from 2 to 35. These, in turn, were put into four levels or categories.

Category IV was least serious with a score below five; Category III had scores of five to eight, characterized by two contacts with the police for relatively slight offenses. Categories II and I indicate more serious behaviors and Category I implied real danger of a criminal career. Two instances of Category I clarify this rating.

Rex. Rex was a boy of low mentality (IQ 77) who hated school and was frequently truant. His father was a steady worker but would frequently get angry with the boy and beat him. At the age of thirteen the boy was picked up by the police and admitted stealing $20 from the pocketbook of a lady in a store. His mother repaid the money and no charges were pressed. At fourteen he was arrested for an attempted breakin at a filling station. He was later declared delinquent by the county court, placed in a detention home, and later transferred to a foster home for a short period. He was given a medical examination but no pathology was found. At eighteen he was picked up several times for drunkenness, fined several times, and finally jailed. He is fast becoming an habitual drunkard. This is a case of emotional maladjustment abetted by a delinquent subculture.

Sue. Sue was first picked up at the age of fifteen for hanging around downtown with a group of girls. A month later she was reported to the police by her father for being truant, not coming home nights, and being unmanageable. She was married at sixteen but was reported to the police shortly afterward by her neighbors who complained of the filthiness of the apartment and the neglect of her small baby. The police found her at that time in a tavern. Two months later she was brought in for soliciting men in a tavern. She continues to live with her parents and to practice prostitution (13, 70).

Referring back to Table 14.4 you note the relationship between the prediction scores and the actual delinquency observed. That is, 12 delinquents had the 12 highest scores and only 1 lowest scorer became a delinquent. The relationship is not perfect; however, it is sufficiently close that those concerned with the prevention of delinquency should carry out the visits in the home in order to identify possible predelinquents. Use of both the Glueck Prediction Scale and the rating of aggressive maladjustment as outlined by Havighurst *et al.*, with boys and girls in grades 5 through 8 would prove useful in identifying future delinquents.

Our purpose is not to clarify procedures for identifying predelinquents but to indicate some of the psychological, sociological, and educational factors related to delinquency. The prevention of delinquency is a complex task, one of the most important problems faced by the United States, because the incidence of delinquency has risen in recent decades. The solution to the problem requires the active cooperation of many people and agencies.

The most effective preventive measures against juvenile delinquency seem to be (1) finding ways of improving the family life of socially and economically underprivileged boys and girls and (2) finding ways of making school a more successful and satisfying part of their lives, or (3) creating an alternative pathway to adulthood for boys through work experience and helping them to follow this pathway (13, 88).

SUMMARY

Many social, economic, and political forces exert continuing pressure on the schools to provide education of high quality for all children. All the abilities of all children must be nurtured adequately in order that each child may achieve self-realization and contribute to the general welfare as a human being, a citizen, and a worker. At present about 30 percent of our youth of all ability levels do not complete high school. Some children who learn with difficulty do not profit much from attending school. Some bright and talented students do not learn well. In fact, efficiency of learning in all domains—cognitive, psychomotor, and affective—is low when all children are considered.

Certain groups of children merit special consideration—the gifted and talented, the slow learning and mentally retarded, the culturally disadvantaged, and potential delinquents. Provisions for these children and others must be varied, taking into account the characteristics of the community, the school system, the home, and the children themselves. However, this variation in provisions does not mean that little or nothing will be done by the schools. Until recently the plight of the culturally disadvantaged has deteriorated in our large cities and rural areas.

We must open the gates of innovation, not insist on only old methods that have proved ineffective for decades. Acceleration of some students, enrichment for all students, grouping on such bases as achievements and interests, special classes for groups of any size that will profit from them, special schools for children who cannot be accommodated in our present structures—these and other arrangements need to be perfected.

Not discussed in this chapter but outlined in the next one are better means of individualization—autoinstruction of many types, nongraded schools, and instructional teams. Already these arrangements have been defined, but they are only a beginning. Needed are creative teachers, teachers who will appraise the situation and come up with novel solutions that cannot be described in this book because they are still unknown.

QUESTIONS AND ACTIVITIES

1. a. In your judgment, which of the eight generalizations about differences in abilities and general provisions are accepted least by the population generally?
    b. Which generalizations do you think are least accepted by teachers and other persons in educational positions?
2. a. Give an example of each of the bases of grouping, applied to elementary school, junior high school, or senior school.
    b. Provide an example of each applied to a classroom setting.
3. Give your opinions of the ideas presented about the common elementary school and the comprehensive high school.
4. a. Discuss the adequacy of the objectives of education for children of superior ability in Wisconsin.
    b. Do you think these objectives will lead toward the values of Terman's subjects at mid-life? Explain.
5. Discuss the extent to which general intellectual ability, achievement, physical characteristics, and emotional adjustment are useful in identifying gifted children, talented children.
6. Discuss the pros and cons of enrichment as a primary means of providing for differences among students.
7. Describe the conditions under which each of the six means of acceleration might be better or more appropriate than the other five in providing for a gifted child. Refer to the Suggestions for Further Readings as necessary to secure further information.
8. Would you place students of high intellectual ability in the same sections or special classes for all high school subjects or would you section in each subject according to achievement level? Why?
9. Give your opinions of the Waukesha plan in high school English and social studies.
10. Evaluate the multiple provisions for gifted students in Milwaukee.
11. a. If you had a child of your own who was a slow learner, what educational provisions would you want for him? If educable mentally retarded?
    b. At what age or developmental level would you wish publicly supported education to cease for the child?
    c. How often would you want the school to evaluate your child's abilities and progress?
12. a. Which provisions are recommended for the culturally disadvantaged that were not

operative in the schools you attended?

b. Which of the different provisions do you accept as desirable?

c. What other provisions do you think the schools should make for the culturally disadvantaged?

13. a. What is the legal definition of a delinquent?

b. What are the characteristics of delinquents?

14. Three broad provisions are stated for dealing with delinquency. Discuss the specific implications of these provisions for teachers or any other group of educational workers.

SUGGESTIONS FOR FURTHER READING

Burt, C. Francis Galton and his contributions to psychology. *Brit. J. statist. Psychol.,* 1962, **15**, 1–41. (Portions reprinted in Cohen, 1964, 49–65.)

Carriker, W. R. (Ed.) Role of the school in prevention of juvenile delinquency. *Coop. Res. Monogr.,* No. 10. Washington, D.C.: U.S. Office of Education, 1963.

Conger, J. J., W. C. Miller, & C. R. Walsmith. Antecedents of delinquency: Personality, social class, and intelligence. In P. H. Mussen, J. J. Conger, & J. Kagan (Eds.), *Readings in child development and personality.* New York: Harper & Row, 1965, pp. 442–468.

Davis, D. A. An experimental study of potential dropouts. *Personnel Guid. J.,* 1962, **40**, 799–802. (In Seidman, 1965, 322–325.)

Deutsch, Cynthia P. Education for disadvantaged groups. *Rev. educ. Res.,* 1965, **35**, 140–146.

Eckland, B. K. College dropouts who came back. *Harv. educ. Rev.,* 1964, **34**, 402–420.

Goldstein, H. The educable mentally retarded child in the elementary school. *What research says to the teacher,* No. 25. Washington, D.C.: National Education Association, 1962.

Havighurst, R. J. Conditions productive of superior children. *Teachers Coll. Rec.,* 1961, **62**, 524–531. (In French, 1964, 137–147; Fullagar, *et al.,* 1964, 209–217; and Grinder, 1963, 501–510.)

Hock, Louise E. Classroom grouping for effective learning. *Educ. Leadership,* 1961, **18**, 420–424. (In Seidman, 1965, 136–140.)

Hunt, J. T., *et al.* Education of exceptional children. *Rev. educ. Res.,* 1963, **33**, 1–138.

Jensen, A. Learning ability in retarded, average, and gifted children. *Merrill-Palmer Quart.,* 1963, **9**, 124–140. (In DeCecco, 1964, 356–376.)

Kirk, S. A. *Early education of the mentally retarded.* Urbana: Univer. of Illinois Press, 1958. (Excerpts in Rosenblith & Allinsmith, 1962, 317–323.)

Klausmeier, H. J., & R. E. Ripple. Effects of accelerating bright older pupils from second to fourth grade. *J. educ. Psychol.,* 1962, **53**, 93–100. (In Ripple, 1964, 118–127.)

Passow, A. H. The maze of the research on ability grouping. *Educ. Forum.,* 1962, **26**, 281–288. (In French, 1964, 238–248.)

Pressey, S. L. Educational acceleration: Occasional procedure or major issue? *Personnel Guid. J.,* 1962, **41**, 12–17. (In French, 1964, 310–318.)

Schreiber, D. The dropout and the delinquent: Promising practices gleaned from a year of study. *Phi Delta Kappan,* 1963, **44**, 215–221. (In Seidman, 1965, 168–176.)

Shaw, M. C., & J. T. McCuen. The onset of academic underachievement in bright children. *J. educ. Psychol.,* 1960, **51**, 103–108. (In Kuhlen & Thompson, 1963, 519–524.)

Terman, L. M. The discovery and encouragement of exceptional talent. *Amer. Psychologist,* 1954, **9**, 221–230. (In French, 1964, 35–47; and Rosenblith & Allinsmith, 1962, 303–312.)

Vernon, P. E. Education and the psychology of individual differences. *Harv. educ. Rev.,* 1958, **28**, 91–104. (In DeCecco, 1963, 482–501; and Ripple, 1964, 103–117.)

REFERENCES

1. Barbe, W. B. Evaluation of special classes for gifted children. *Except. Child.,* 1955, **22**, 60–62.
2. Barnette, W. L. Advanced credit for the superior high school student. *J. higher Educ.,* 1957, **28**, 15–20.
3. Birch, J. W. Early school admission for mentally advanced children. *Except. Child.,* 1954, **21**, 84–87.
4. Bloom, B. S., A. Davis, & R. Hess. *Compensatory education for cultural deprivation.* New York: Holt, Rinehart and Winston, 1965.
5. Deutsch, M. Facilitating development in the pre-school child: Social and psychological perspectives. *Merrill-Palmer Quart.,* 1964, **10**, 249–264.
6. Dunlap, J. M. Gifted children in an enriched program. *Except. Child.,* 1955, **21**, 135–137.
7. Dunn, L. M., & R. J. Capobianco. Mental retardation. *Rev. educ. Res.,* 1959, **29**, 451–470.
8. Fund for the Advancement of Education. *They went to college early.* New York: Author, 1957.
9. Glueck, S., & Eleanor T. Glueck. *Unraveling juvenile delinquency.* New York: The Commonwealth Fund, 1950.
10. Glueck, S., & Eleanor T. Glueck. *Predicting delinquency and crime.* Cambridge: Harvard, 1959.
11. Glueck, S., & Eleanor T. Glueck. *Family environment and delinquency.* Boston: Houghton Mifflin, 1962.
12. Hall, W. F., & Ruth Demarest. Effect on achievement scores of a change in promotional policy. *Elem. Sch. J.,* 1958, **58**, 204–207.
13. Havighurst, R. J., *et al. Growing up in River City.* New York: Wiley, 1962.
14. Hobson, J. R. Mental age as a workable criterion for school admission. *Elem. Sch. J.,* 1948, **48**, 312–321.
15. Holmes, J. A., & Cecile J. Finley. Under- and over-age grade-placements and school achievement. *J. educ. Psychol.,* 1957, **48**, 447–456.
16. Hunt, J. M. The psychological basis for using pre-school enrichment as an antidote for cultural deprivation. *Merrill-Palmer Quart.,* 1964, **10**, 209–248.
17. Justman, J. Academic achievement of intellectually gifted accelerants and non-accelerants in junior high school. *Sch. Rev.,* 1954, **62**, 142–150.
18. Justman, J. Academic achievement of intellectually gifted accelerants and non-accelerants in senior high school. *Sch. Rev.,* 1954, **62**, 469–473.
19. Klausmeier, H. J. Identifying children through measurements. *Education,* 1959, **80**, 167–171.
20. Klausmeier, H. J. *Summary report of research completed, 1958–1961, on educational provisions for children and youth of superior learning abilities, Milwaukee Public Schools.* Milwaukee: Board of School Directors, 1962.
21. Klausmeier, H. J. Effects of accelerating bright older elementary pupils: A follow-up. *J. educ. Psychol.,* 1963, **54**, 165–171.
22. Klausmeier, H. J., J. Mulhern, & H. Wakefield. High school students evaluate sectioning. *Educ. Leadership,* 1960, **17**, 221–225.

23. Klausmeier, H. J., & R. E. Ripple. Effects of accelerating bright older pupils from second to fourth grade. *J. educ. Psychol.*, 1962, **53**, 93–100.

24. Klausmeier, H. J., & D. Teel. A research-based program for gifted children. *Education*, 1964, **85**, 1–6.

25. Klausmeier, H. J., & W. Wiersma. Effects of condensing content in mathematics and science in the junior and senior high school. *Sch. Sci. Math.*, 1964, **64**, 4–11.

26. McWilliams, E. M. Enrichment practices for gifted junior high school pupils. *Bull. nat. Ass. sec. sch. Principals*, 1956, **40**, 72–81.

27. Meister, M. Cooperation of secondary schools and colleges in acceleration of gifted students. *J. educ. Sociol.*, 1956, **29**, 220–227.

28. Pregler, H. The Colfax plan. *Except. Child.*, 1954, **20**, 198–201.

29. Pressey, S. L., & Marie A. Flesher. Wartime accelerates ten years after. *J. educ. Psychol.*, 1955, **46**, 228–238.

30. Shannon, D.C. What research says about acceleration. *Phi Delta Kappan*, 1957, **39**, 70–72.

31. Terman, L. M. The discovery and encouragement of exceptional talent. *Amer. Psychologist*, 1954, **9**, 221–230.

32. Terman, L. M., & Melita H. Oden. *The gifted group at midlife: Thirty-five year's follow-up of the superior child.* Stanford: Stanford, 1959.

33. U.S. Office of Education. *Status of education in the U.S.* Bull No. 1. Washington, D.C.: Government Printing Office, 1959.

34. Worcester, D. A. *The education of children of above average mentality.* Lincoln: Univer. of Nebraska Press, 1956.

CHAPTER 15

Instructional Media and Organization

Tᴇᴄʜɴᴏʟᴏɢʏ is having a profound effect upon education. A vision of an automatic classroom, made possible through advancing technology, is described:

> The fourth development that can be anticipated is the most spectacular. Essentially it is based on a systems concept. It is theoretically possible now to design an automatic classroom under the control of the teacher. Such a classroom would have total light and air control, automatic projection and television systems, technical provision for the possible discussion environments, display situations, etc., which could be changed at will. By planned programming, the classroom could be made to function for major presentations, small group discussions, individual work at teaching machines, creative periods and the like. As we said, all of this *could be* under the control of the teacher. The classroom then would become the teaching machine. . . . An acquaintance of mine refers to this concept as the "mad scientist" classroom (11, 376).

As we indicated in Chapters 5 and 6, the teacher will continue to be the key figure in the instructional process. Nevertheless, new media of instruction and new organizations for instruction are having a pronounced effect upon learning and teaching. The effects of recent technology are showing up in the schools, especially in connection with instructional television and other electronic equipment, autoinstruction that is taking various forms, and new organizations for instruction. These and other material innovations are accompanied by new concepts concerning the responsibility of instructional personnel.

We are entering an era when it is possible to individualize instruction much better than before, to humanize and personalize education, to improve the quality of education, and to provide more education for more students, especially for that 30 percent who do not now graduate from high school. The new media and organization for instruction will contribute toward this end.

Let us examine how some of the early optimists of the late 1950s viewed TV and electronic laboratories. The goal of educational television as mass education is presented by an ardent enthusiast:

A determination to serve "all the people" from preschool to octogenarians, the glorious new generation of oldsters modern times now gives us, is the ideal of every single educational station. Good programs need not be expensive to produce; they are just hard to conceive and develop. Simplicity is a cardinal virtue in education, at all times, and necessity forces it on educational television. So the subjects of home life, travel, recreation, child care, reading, listening, resting, playing, the art of conversation, the arts of acquired skills in music, photography, design, and dance, play acting, participating in all forms of a "gainful occupation" as a person, become bridges that open up the gateways of the arts, the sciences, literature, philosophy, psychology, anthropology, and all the other subjects residing in the liberal education of today, produced by our educational institutions.

Educational television is making them "come alive" for increased millions of viewers, who in the ease and comfort of their modern homes now may find an interesting new highway to the promise of an abundant life (**7**, 617).

Another enthusiast describes the individualization possible with electronic equipment and related methods in foreign-language teaching: "With automated teaching all the students can speak at the same time. With automated teaching all the students can speak all the time. . . . Every student has a private tutor. The rapid learner is not hampered by the slow learner" (**23**, 6–7).

We still question whether TV or teaching machines should be used in foreign language, shorthand, and music instruction in a large school system. One teacher, providing a daily program on television which thousands of students view simultaneously, or the electronic equipment and a teacher in each of the 100 or more elementary school buildings? At present, some school systems are proceeding with TV; others are using the electronic equipment. The decisions are often made on such practical considerations as availability of teachers and cost. If a school system already is equipped for TV instruction, the cost is much less

533

when instruction is handled through television. The language laboratory is less expensive if the school is not equipped for TV and if only a few school buildings are involved.

There seems to be little doubt that the age of technology will have a profound effect upon education. The various types of electronic equipment now available vastly increase the flexibility of school systems. For example, the Victor Electro-Writer in combination with the Bell System's Tele-Lecture offers promise in the areas of facilitating extension educational services and of enriching programs in schools otherwise isolated. The Tele-Lecture system allows a lecturer, using regular telephone lines, to speak to large groups in scattered areas across the country (wherever telephone service is available). The speaker's voice is amplified at the receiving stations. The electro-writer equipment allows the lecturer to send live blackboard notes electronically to the same remote stations. The lecturer can be seated at his desk in his home or office, speaking on the phone and jotting notes on the electro-writer equipment before him. At the receiving stations students hear the lecturer's voice, see his notes projected on a screen in front of them, and are able to ask questions of the lecturer. This equipment provides everything that television does except the visual image, and the cost is substantially smaller than television.

The important point in this discussion is that the emphasis should continue to be on the educational opportunities afforded to children. The electronic equipment presently available is merely one of many currently available means toward this overall objective. Although the practical factors presently determine important educational decisions, psychologists and educators, concerned with the long-term effects and widespread usage of various educational media and instruments, are concerned with research problems such as:

1. Which human abilities and characteristics can be nurtured most effectively through which media and by which procedures? For example, can the ability to communicate effectively in a foreign language be nurtured as well in hundreds or thousands of students simultaneously viewing and responding to TV instruction as by use of electronic equipment, managed by a teacher, within each school building?

2. Is one or another medium or technique more effective in achieving certain learning outcomes than others? Is TV equally appropriate for developing independence in problem-solving techniques and for presenting factual material? Is autoinstruction equally effective in developing good citizenship behavior and in conditioning persons to respond correctly to certain stimuli?

534

3. Is educational TV equally appropriate for all age groups in all types of behavioral settings? For example, is televising most of the instructional program equally appropriate for first-graders in regular classroom settings and for high school seniors or university students under the direction of one teacher?

4. How long will students of any age in any setting respond with sufficient motivation to the device to learn well? If a college should decide to offer an entire instructional program through the baccalaureate via TV, how many students would remain in the program? What would be the effects of one TV course per semester? two per semester? Similarly, if the entire instructional program in a twelfth grade is offered by machines, will the students continue to learn, or even continue to use the machines, throughout the year?

Other questions might be raised. However, we are learning more about both TV and autoinstruction, as will be shown in the remainder of this chapter, devoted to selected examples of (1) TV instruction, (2) electronic foreign-language instruction, (3) autoinstruction, and (4) new organizations for instruction, including team teaching and nongraded approaches (Fig. 15.1). The primary purpose is to present an overview of instructional media and organization to which psychologists, educators, and teachers must give increasing attention.

TELEVISION INSTRUCTION

There are many open-circuit educational TV stations and also commercial stations that carry TV instruction. The amount of instruction by open-circuit TV increases each year. The use of closed-circuit TV in schools and colleges also is increasing very rapidly. Closed-circuit TV within a school does not require the usual broadcasting facility. The cost of closed-circuit TV is decreasing markedly, principally because of better equipment at lower cost. Colleges are now equipping dormitories with TV viewing rooms so that students may take courses outside the usual class hours and classrooms. Undoubtedly the number of TV courses taken by students of all ages will continue to increase rapidly. The program to be described in the following paragraphs, however, utilizes a more conventional setting for TV instruction.

Closed-Circuit TV in One University

A comprehensive study of various instructional procedures, including closed-circuit TV, was conducted at Miami University (22). It is

Fig. 15.1.

Four aids in modern teaching

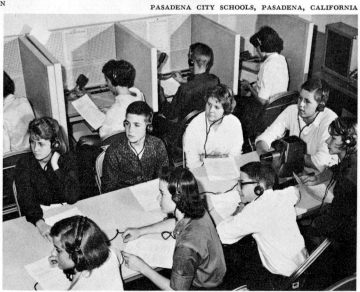

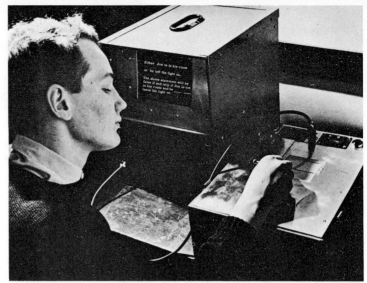

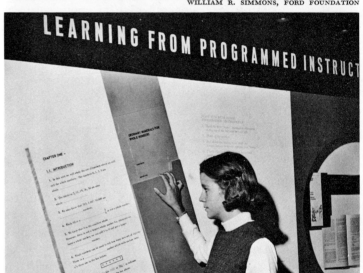

one of the best longitudinal investigations thus far completed. This entire section is devoted to it; the conclusions and other information are drawn directly from the study and include no interpretive comments by the present authors.

PURPOSES AND SCOPE

The major purpose was to determine the relative effectiveness of large- and small-group instruction at the college level. Closely related purposes were (1) to improve large-group teaching procedures so that the claimed advantages of small-group instruction could be realized in large-group teaching to the greatest extent possible; (2) to study and improve facilities, including TV, utilized in large-group instruction; and (3) to develop and encourage the use of a more adequate instructional aids center for the improvement of college teaching. Inasmuch as the intent was to gain accurate information on the effectiveness of both large- and small-group instruction and of different teaching procedures and course organizations, rather than to substantiate any preconceived notions about methods of instruction or forms of class organization, evaluation was done from beginning to end of the study.

DESIGN

The courses were taught under experimental conditions and under control conditions. The experimental conditions generally involved some variant of large-group instruction, with sections arranged in various ways to permit a single instructor to extend his influence as a teacher to a greater number of students than in the teaching of small classes. The control condition consisted of course sections which were conventional or typical in size for Miami University. A section was considered large if the instructor was responsible for at least twice the number of students ordinarily taught by him in a conventional section. Since the typical enrollment in a conventional course section at Miami University does not exceed 25 to 35 students, sections which enrolled in excess of 50 students were usually designated as large. As a rule, however, sections classed as "large" had enrollments in excess of 80 students.

Four different types of large-group procedures and experimental sections were investigated:

1. Sections were taught by closed-circuit television, designated simply as TV courses.
2. Large sections (designated LC) in which the instructor was physi-

cally present in the room were tried. These include courses taught by means of some variant of the lecture or interrupted-lecture method and courses taught by the case or problem procedure.

3. Independent study (IS) sections were instituted, wherein the number of scheduled formal class meetings was reduced below the usual requirement of one meeting per week for each hour of credit.

4. Sections were taught by graduate student assistants (GS).

The control sections for the TV, LC, and IS courses were conventional classes consisting of 25 to 35 students. These sections were taught by the same instructors responsible for the experimental sections of a particular course. Thus, the basic type of comparison of student achievement and attitude was a comparison between criterion scores obtained under experimental and conventional conditions. Because much of the analysis required comparisons between data obtained from experimental and control sections, students were matched in all courses on the basis of various standardized tests. Also, a brief pretest of factual knowledge was administered in a number of courses, and the experimental and control sections of virtually all courses purportedly were equated with respect to proportional distributions by sex and class standing.

Evaluative instruments were developed in the areas of student achievement, student attitudes and opinions, and faculty attitudes and opinions. The measures of student achievement were course examinations; tests of synthesis, problem solving and critical thinking; and tests of stereotypes and misconceptions. The student attitudes measured were those toward large-group instruction and toward the course and the instructor.

Various questionnaires concerning the relative strengths and weaknesses of the experimental procedures were submitted to the participating instructors. In addition, an open-ended type of questionnaire concerning large-group instruction was distributed to the entire faculty.

RESULTS

The principal results as applied to TV classes are now given in abbreviated form. Differences significant at or beyond the .05 level are reported. This level of significance means that there are 95 chances in 100 that the obtained difference is a true, not chance, difference.

1. With few exceptions, in large-group instruction (including TV) subject-matter achievement as measured by course examinations was as high as in small-group (conventional) instruction. Of 28 comparisons between TV and conventional classes, only four differences were

significant at or beyond the .05 level and three favored conventional classes. Of 45 comparisons between large (not TV) and conventional classes, three of four differences significant at or beyond the .05 level favored conventional classes.

2. The experimental procedures did not lead to reduced proficiency in achievement defined as the ability to solve problems and to synthesize information. Of 22 comparisons between large classes, including TV, and conventional classes, only five were significant at or beyond the .05 level; all five favored conventional classes.

3. Subject-matter retention after periods ranging from one to two years, measured by using the same type of objective final examinations as at the end of the course, was unaffected by increased class size or by instructional procedure.

4. Students in the TV and in the large nontelevised sections rated the course content somewhat less favorably than did students in the control sections of these same courses.

5. Student motivation and interest in the specific subject matter were not adversely affected by assignment to experimental rather than to control sections.

6. The students, with few exceptions, judged the experimental procedures to reduce the instructor's effectiveness somewhat. This perceived reduction in teaching effectiveness was not paralleled by a corresponding decrement in actual achievement of students in the experimental sections as shown in the previous statements, 1 to 3.

7. Students in most courses preferred small classes to both large classes and TV classes. In total preference, not simply of the content or the instructional procedures reported in (4) and (6), the students in all 27 comparisons favored conventional over TV courses. And in all 29 comparisons they also favored conventional to large classes.

8. The instructor himself is a major determinant of student attitudes about TV and large-class instruction. There was a pronounced tendency for students to react either favorably or unfavorably to both their instructor and large-class procedures. The majority of students consistently indicated that they would enroll in a TV class or a large class (even though they preferred small classes) if they would be assured thereby of being taught by an excellent teacher.

9. Practically all instructors who tried TV teaching liked it better than they thought they would. Although most would still prefer to teach conventional classes, there was considerable feeling that TV classes are superior to other large-group teaching procedures. The major defects inherent in TV, as far as the instructors were concerned,

are related to the physical barrier between student and teacher and the lengthy preparation time required for each TV presentation.

The reactions to TV of faculty members who did not try TV teaching are probably best described as "moderately favorable." About one-third of this group believed that televised instruction has a definite place on the campus for course work. Another third felt that TV should be used primarily for off-campus instruction and for supplemental work on the campus. The remaining third were approximately equally divided in their feelings: Either they felt that television should be abandoned or they were uncertain about its place in the university setting.

Some concluding comments about TV teaching are significant:

Television is an effective means of communication for instructional purposes. The costs for purchase and maintenance of equipment and for course production are high; consequently TV teaching is not economical except as a mass medium. In general the cost factor makes televised teaching feasible only for courses of fairly large enrollment. Costs are quite variable, depending upon such factors as the kind and type of studio equipment purchased, open- or closed-circuit instruction, and the salaries and load credit for professional and technical personnel involved in course production. The "break even" point for this university is between 250 and 300 students enrolled in a given course at a given time. The ultimate use of video tape will, of course, materially affect the problem of optimal enrollments. It will increase the original cost of a lesson production considerably, but will make repeat performances possible at greatly decreased costs. The use of tape will add a very desirable degree of flexibility in scheduling courses and, consequently, add greatly to the utility of television as a medium of instruction.

Possibly the greatest handicap to large group teaching other than the lecture method is, on most campuses, the lack of rooms planned to facilitate those procedures which are dependent upon class discussion. The lack of rooms designed for TV reception is of equal concern. The conventional class room with its bank of windows along one side, its overhead direct lights, and generally poor acoustical properties makes a very inadequate TV receiving room. Poor seating arrangement for TV viewing, the difficulty of eliminating receiving set glare, poor acoustics, and generally poor ventilation when shades must be used, puts TV teaching at a great disadvantage over the small group instruction for which the rooms were designed.

The conventional rectangular room, even though of sufficient size to accommodate 60 to 80 students, normally discourages anything but a lecture, or at the best, an "interrupted lecture" as the basic teaching procedure. Auditoriums, while often excellent in acoustical properties and in ventilation, are not at all conducive to the development of class discussion. . . .

Another serious handicap to televised teaching is the lack of receiving sets of adequate screen size and of picture quality needed for class viewing. This is a technical problem which is being increasingly recognized by manufacturers of receiving sets, and as the demand increases, it is expected that special classroom receivers can and will be designed especially for this market. The average commercial receiver, designed as it is for the home receiver market, is inadequate for instructional use, even when provided with special control and safety gadgets. Research is needed to better identify classroom needs so that TV receivers may be developed especially to meet these needs (22, 5).

The Effectiveness of Instructional TV

The relative effectiveness of TV instruction at Miami University was shown to be modest. However, it has become remarkably widespread at all school levels in a relatively short period of time. An early impetus to educational TV was the Midwest Program on Airborne Television Instruction (MPATI). Beginning actual operation in 1961, MPATI involved transmitting programs (via aircraft flying over north-central Indiana) to over 2,000,000 pupils in six states. Video tapes have been made in virtually all subject areas by teachers specially trained to teach via television. Special texts, study guides, and other materials have been prepared for use with the television courses. Schools participating in MPATI equip their schools with conventional UHF receiving sets and make other necessary arrangements to insure good reception of the programs.

An evaluation of the effectiveness of instructional television is a monumental task, but fortunately has been efficiently done by Schramm (29). Table 15.1 consolidates the results of 393 studies reviewed by Schramm. As can be seen in the table, the preponderant finding was that there was no significant difference between TV and other instructional procedures. Note also from the table that, although subject matter seems to make little difference in the results, school level does. At successively higher school levels, TV is relatively less effective. A thorough and recent estimate of educational TV is stated thus:

It must be acknowledged, however, that ETV has never quite fulfilled the dream that some of its founders had for it—that it would become the school and the university of people who had little opportunity for education. Its audiences are highly skewed toward the people who *have* had opportunity for education. . . .

Educational television as it functions today is very little competition for commercial television in furnishing an entertainment service, in swift handling of news, or in extensive coverage of public events. Its special place, so far, is in the area of providing cultural programs, intellectual challenge and stimulation, information other than spot news, and educational opportunities. . . .

542

TABLE 15.1.

The Effectiveness of Instructional TV

Grade Level	Direction of Findings[a]	Math	Science	Social Studies	Humanities	Language Skills	Health Safety	Total[a]
3rd–6th	+TV	14	8	12	0	14	2	50 +TV
	n.s.d.	21	14	11	0	36	4	86 n.s.d.
	–TV	3	1	1	0	10	1	16 –TV
7th–9th	+TV	4	9	0	2	0	3	18 +TV
	n.s.d.	11	8	1	7	0	1	28 n.s.d.
	–TV	2	3	0	0	0	0	5 –TV
10th–12th	+TV	0	3	3	4	1	1	12 +TV
	n.s.d.	10	7	17	17	6	0	57 n.s.d.
	–TV	5	3	0	9	4	0	21 –TV
College	+TV	0	1	1	0	0	1	3 +TV
	n.s.d.	4	26	24	11	12	7	84 n.s.d.
	–TV	0	1	4	3	1	4	13 –TV
Total	+TV	18	21	16	6	15	7	83 +TV
	n.s.d.	46	55	53	35	54	12	255 n.s.d.
	–TV	10	8	5	12	15	5	55 –TV
							Total	393

[a] + TV: difference found favoring instructional TV (p. < .05).
n.s.d.: no significant difference found.
– TV: difference found favoring conventional instructional[1] techniques.

SOURCE: W. L. Schramm. Learning from instructional television. *Rev. educ. Res.*, 1962, **32**, p. 157.

The import of this study is that, in nine years, educational television has won a beachhead. It has 75 stations, a central program service which operates like a network by mail, a small but loyal and important audience, and enough good programing to whet the appetites of the viewers. This is a significant accomplishment. Now, does it rest with this, or does it go ahead? If it rests, the chances are that it will become increasingly a channel for school broadcasts rather than for community broadcasts. If it goes ahead, then it must have more and better programing, and to have more and better programing it must have more adequate financing. . . .

But just as financing will make it easier to find and develop talent for distinguished programs, so will an infusion of talent, skill, and imagination make it easier to obtain financing. This is the destiny that beckons to educational television if it can muster the strength to go beyond its beachhead (**31**, 166–174).

Thus, instructional TV is substantially entrenched, but still falls short of attaining what many expected of it. In general, teacher-education institutions have not dealt intelligently with TV instruction. Prospective teachers and experienced teachers returning for education are not being instructed concerning TV instruction on a widespread basis. They should be learning to evaluate TV instruction and some should be developing skills as TV teachers.

FOREIGN-LANGUAGE LABORATORIES

A native language is acquired in stages. First comes the listening period; speaking is the second. The third and fourth stages of language development manifest themselves through education. The child learns to read and write. Through orthography, the child learns to record human speech. Not everyone passes into the third and fourth phases of language learning, but individuals of every culture engage in the listening and speaking phases of language. It is for the student who is studying a foreign language with intentions of developing aural-oral skills that the electronic laboratory is arranged.

Problems in Foreign-Language Teaching

The development of aural-oral skills in an efficient manner demands close observation and direction from the first day of instruction. In the native environment, a child has at least one full-time language teacher, his mother or another older person. His pronunciation, sentence structure, etc., are closely supervised. His progress in developing linguistic habits depends in part upon his individual abilities and skills and in part upon the persons imitated.

One teacher cannot listen to and correct individual oral utterances of 30 students simultaneously. But the individual student cannot be left unsupervised; he is in the most critical period of language learning. He must form correct speech habits. If he does not learn to pronounce words and utter phrases correctly, he will not be understood.

Each language has its own distinctive sound patterns. The language student must be educated to form these new sounds physically and to recognize these new sounds acoustically. The electronic language laboratory provides for individual supervision by the teacher in the development and perfection of aural-oral skills at rates appropriate to the individual student.

Components of a Foreign-Language Laboratory

In order to describe a proposed program of instruction, it is necessary to indicate the main components of a language laboratory. These are given in Table 15.2 (**16**). Three laboratory arrangements are possible.

TABLE 15.2.

Major Laboratory Components

Component	Listen Only	Listen-Speak	Listen-Speak-Record
Console:			
Master Magnetic Player(s)	Yes	Yes	Yes
Phonograph	Yes	Yes	Yes
Monitor & Intercom	No	Yes	Yes
Student Position:			
Headphones	Yes	Yes	Yes
Microphones	No	Yes	Yes
Activated Amplifier	No	Yes	Yes
Magnetic Recorder	No	No	Yes
Booths	No	Yes	Yes
Installation:			
Electronic Wiring	No	Yes	Yes
Other Items:			
Portable Master Recorder	Yes	Yes	Yes
Accessories	Yes	Yes	Yes

SOURCE: J. S. Holton, *et al. Sound language teaching, the state of the art today.* New York: University Publishers, 1961, p. 9.

In one the students listen only, in another they listen and speak, and in the third they listen, speak, and record. The major components of the listen-speak-record laboratory require further description.

The master magnetic player and the phonograph provide two means of playing a program for the students to listen to and also for recording the students' responses. The important function of these components, however, is to present instructional programs. Some consoles have four or more magnetic players which enable four different programs to be heard simultaneously. The monitor and intercom enable the teacher to listen to students and speak to them. The critical problem in foreign-language laboratories is not with this equipment. Instead it is with the programs which contain the instruction.

At each student position in the language laboratory there are headphones for listening, a microphone for speaking, an activated amplifier to boost the level of sound, a magnetic recorder on which the student can make a permanent record of his speaking, and a sound-conditioned booth. The earphones permit sound to be heard only by the student The booth should be relatively soundproof so that when the student records he neither disturbs others nor has his concentration interrupted. A portable master recorder permits greater flexibility in presenting programs and in student recording.

Master Instructional Programs

Electronic equipment is useful only to the extent that master instructional programs are available for use. A typical master program is organized as shown in Fig. 15.2. On the master tape a problem,

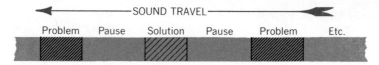

Fig. 15.2. Typical master program. (J. S. Holton, P. E. King, G. Mathieu, & K. S. Pond. *Sound language teaching, the state of the art today.* New York: University Publishers, 1961, p. 11.)

question, or bit of material is presented. Then there is a pause during which the student responds. Next a solution, usually called a "master solution" is presented. When attempting to develop speech, the problem incorporates the word, phrase, or sentence; the student speaks the same word, phrase, or sentence; then the word, phrase, or sentence is again presented.

A principal problem in foreign-language instruction with laboratories is the master program and the relationship of the laboratory to the total instructional program in the language. A notable attempt to co-ordinate a complete program in high school French is incorporated in *Learning French the Modern Way* (9). Level I of this program consists of a book, 8 filmstrips, 4 motion pictures, 24 tape recordings for use in the language laboratory, 3 reels of taped tests, and printed test booklets. The second level for the high school has similar material. The entire program is designed to develop listening and speaking skills in French and abilities of reading and writing French with facility, and to gain appreciation of the French culture. The taped record-ings and programs are designed especially to facilitate listening and speaking.

The Daily Program

In a class period of 50 minutes, how is the total time spent, once the unit or semester has started? One plan is to give 25 minutes to labora-tory activities and the other 25 minutes to other activities. The 25 minutes for laboratory activities are further divided as shown in Table 15.3. Study this arrangement to note the amount of activity by the student.

Effectiveness of Language Laboratories

The number of language laboratories in the United States is increas-ing partly because of the provisions of the National Defense Educa-tion Act of 1958; the increase was from 304 in 1958 to 6700 in 1962 (14). Based on a criterion of widespread use, language laboratories are successful. However, it is too early to pass final judgment on their effectiveness (15). For example, children in New York taught in con-ventional classes achieved higher than those taught primarily in lan-guage laboratories (19). Here, too, the language laboratory was ef-fective in developing speech production, principally during the first year of study. Although problems are still encountered in teaching foreign languages in language laboratories, it is certain that the tra-ditional approach has failed to teach the majority of our students a second language. We expect that as more teachers learn to speak a second language well and to use electronic equipment effectively, boys and girls also will learn foreign languages efficiently. There is no doubt whatsoever that most children can learn to speak a second language. Those who move to a second country do so readily.

TABLE 15.3.

Laboratory Activities of Students and Teachers in Foreign Language[a]

Section	Master Tape Min	Master Tape Contents	Student Activity	Teacher Activity
A	1	Start instructions	Listens and does as instructed	Conducts visual lookout for needed student help
B	4	"Listen"-Lesson (no pauses)	Listens	—
C	½	Instructions	Does as instructed	—
D	8	"Listen-Speak" Lesson (spaced pauses)	Listens and speaks into his microphone (audio-active participation)	Supervises remotely or personally
E	½	Instructions	Does as instructed	—
F	4	"Listen-Speak-Record" Lesson	Listens and speaks into his microphone, and both "Master" and "Student" are recorded (on Magnetic Disc or Tape)	Supervises remotely or personally
G	½	Instructions	Does as instructed	—
H	4	(Tape continues to run "blank" without sound)	Plays back recording—"compares" (self-evaluates)	Supervises remotely or personally
J	2	Summation of completed lesson	Listens or does as instructed	—
K	½	Final instructions	Does as instructed	—

[a] 25 Minutes Total Automated Lesson
SOURCE: J. S. Holton, *et al. Sound language teaching, the state of the art today.* New York: University Publishers, 1961, p. 37.

In passing, it should be noted that electronic equipment, including tape recorders, is being used in other subject fields besides language. For example, the study of shorthand can be divided into three major phases: recognizing symbols and reading shorthand; taking dictation at increasing rates and transcribing it into longhand; and taking office-type dictation and accurately typing transcripts from the shorthand notes. The second phase is the one during which electronic devices are used most advantageously. Dictation, recorded at four different speeds, is made available to students in the same room via earphones. This procedure makes it possible for each student, without interruption, to select a speed appropriate for him, simply by turning a knob. The teacher is free to observe the class. All dictation can be stopped with a master switch, and whole-class discussion, practice, or any other classroom activity may be undertaken. This type of instruction that provides effectively for individual differences is making rapid headway.

AUTOINSTRUCTION

"Autoinstruction is probably the most publicized, most exploited, possibly most errant, and potentially most valuable of all contributions of American psychology to education" (**26**, 354). Here Pressey is referring to programed instruction, teaching machines including foreign-language laboratories, programed textbooks, and other devices which present material to which the student responds. In this section, we are concerned primarily with what is commonly referred to as programed instruction. Brief mention is also made of computer-based teaching.

The entry of programed instruction into education has been moderately rapid, but there are pockets of resistance (**10**, **40**). In addition to criticism from outside the movement, there has been considerable disagreement among the proponents as to how to construct programs. The basic split has been over the relative merits of linear and branching programing, championed by Skinner (**35**) and Crowder (**6**), respectively. Another approach is Pressey's adjunct programing (**27**). We shall first consider the approaches of these three men and then will indicate some problems existing in the field.

Skinner's Linear Programing

Skinner is generally credited for the recent revival of interest in teaching machines and programed instruction (**34**). His basic propositions are fivefold, mainly drawn from animal experimentation and from cursory experiences in educational settings. They may be summarized briefly.

First, a satisfying consequence or reinforcement immediately following a response facilitates permanent acquisition of the response. Many other psychologists also have high confidence in the efficacy of reinforcement, but Skinner has made the application directly to classroom learning situations. The teacher with even 25 students cannot possibly provide the necessary reinforcements to each pupil's responses. Thus, many pupils do not learn efficiently because their correct responses are not reinforced. In fact, many make errors, and it is not until long after the errors have been made that the teacher informs them of their errors. Well-designed machines, readily available to each pupil, can overcome this deficiency.

Second, not only should a response be reinforced immediately, but reinforcements must be made long after the individual has first acquired the response. In school situations, periodic review of material is made by students under teacher guidance. Here also the teacher cannot reinforce the desired responses of each individual in a group situation. But material can be programed for machine use whereby the proper number and spacing of reinforcements for previously acquired responses can be ascertained and subsequently accomplished. Instead of the ineffective and sometimes haphazard procedures frequently seen in classroom situations, Skinner would make a science of this phase of the instructional program.

Third, there is uncertainty as to the proper number and spacing of reinforcements in early acquisition of behavior. The well-designed machine and program enables us to ascertain more precisely what this number and spacing should be with each learner and with learners of varying characteristics acquiring varying types of simple responses and more complex behavior patterns. Skinner has found, however, that pigeons, rats, dogs, monkeys, and children show surprisingly little difference in acquiring behavior patterns.

Fourth, there has been a tendency to use threat of punishment as a means of getting students to learn. This is undesirable because of the possible anxiety produced in the students. The teaching machine not only eliminates this threat, but is designed to help the learner move through a carefully graded, progressive program whereby he continuously experiences success along with learning more efficiently. Mechanical and electrical devices can provide the progressive sequences and reinforcements far more efficiently and successfully than a teacher. Skinner reports that a human being cannot arrange the reinforcements and related human variables between experimenter and subject; machines must be used.

Finally, the technical problems and cost of machine instruction are not large in terms of the possible increase in learning efficiency. The necessary techniques are known; the equipment can readily be provided. In relation to the costs of the many labor-saving devices in the home, the costs of teaching machines in the school are minor.

To meet the objectives implied by these propositions, Skinner has advocated the use of linear programing. In linear programing, each student goes through an identical sequence of small steps; he responds to each step and is immediately reinforced by knowledge of results, that is, a correct answer is presented. The steps are made small enough that the student's performance is essentially errorless. Skinner is convinced that learning should be as nearly errorless as possible, thus necessitating fairly routine questions (**35**). Skinner also feels that the student should construct his response rather than select it from a choice of alternatives, for example, he wants recall, not recognition. In brief, he sees a proper program functioning in small steps to lead the student by successive approximations to the desired understanding; in multiple-choice items the wrong alternatives must be somewhat plausible and therefore, Skinner feels that they hurt the delicate process of "shaping" appropriate behavior. He even goes so far as to label them a great evil in education, inasmuch as having once seen the wrong alternative, the student may some day call forth the wrong answer instead of the right one.

Figure 15.3 is the first page of a linear programed textbook dealing with ratios and proportions (**37**). Notice that the exercises appear in the left column and the answers are in the right column. An ingenious method is incorporated in the book so that the answers are covered until the student is ready to check his answer against the one given.

Crowder's Branching Programing

Branching, or intrinsic, programing is different from linear and assumes that misunderstanding inevitably occurs during learning, and that the program has the responsibility of resolving any learner's particular misunderstanding before he moves on through the program (**6**). The pupil is presented with a multiple-choice question; the correct response allows him to move on through the program, while an incorrect response causes him to be directed to appropriate material to clear up his misunderstanding. The student who makes an incorrect response follows a branch of the main program, returning to the same question he initially missed after the additional material has been covered. Thus, Crowder has no addiction to errorless learning; the questions in a branching program have a diagnostic function. Crowder has developed the scrambled text to implement his view; the student, depending upon the response he selects to a question, is directed to different pages in the text.

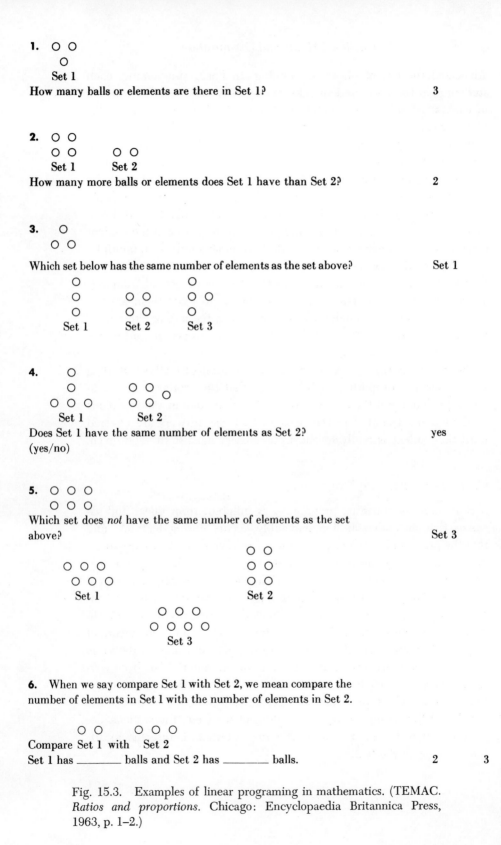

1. ○ ○
　　○
Set 1

How many balls or elements are there in Set 1?　　　　　　　　　　3

2. ○ ○
　　○ ○　　　○ ○
Set 1　　　Set 2

How many more balls or elements does Set 1 have than Set 2?　　　　2

3. ○
　　○ ○

Which set below has the same number of elements as the set above?　　Set 1

　　　○　　　　　　　○
　　　○　　○ ○　　○ ○
　　　○　　○ ○　　○
　Set 1　Set 2　　Set 3

4. ○
　　○
○ ○ ○　　　○ ○
Set 1　　　○ ○ ○
　　　Set 2

Does Set 1 have the same number of elements as Set 2?　　　　　　yes
(yes/no)

5. ○ ○ ○
　　○ ○ ○

Which set does *not* have the same number of elements as the set
above?　　　　　　　　　　　　　　　　　　　　　　　　　　Set 3

　　　　　　　　　　　　○ ○
　　○ ○ ○　　　　　　○ ○
　　○ ○ ○　　　　　　○ ○
　　Set 1　　　　　　Set 2

　　　　○ ○ ○
　　○ ○ ○ ○
　　　Set 3

6. When we say compare Set 1 with Set 2, we mean compare the
number of elements in Set 1 with the number of elements in Set 2.

　　　○ ○　　　○ ○ ○
Compare Set 1 with　Set 2
Set 1 has _____ balls and Set 2 has _____ balls.　　　　2　　　3

Fig. 15.3.　Examples of linear programing in mathematics. (TEMAC.
Ratios and proportions. Chicago: Encyclopaedia Britannica Press,
1963, p. 1–2.)

7.   O   O O
         O O   O O

Compare Set 1 with Set 2

Set 1 has _____ balls and Set 2 has _____ balls.   3   4

8. The symbol ÷ means "divided by."

Copy the symbol which means "divided by."   ÷

    ;

    ÷

    Ɂ

    =

9. The symbol ÷ means _____.   divided by
    multiply by
    divided by
    added to
    subtracted from

10. Set 1 can be compared with Set 2 by *subtraction* or by *division*.
Copy the symbols which express the two ways numbers can be compared.   ÷   —
    +
    ÷
    —
    ×

11. Subtraction or division may be used to compare the number
of elements in two _____.   sets
    bets
    sets
    for
    plus

12. Make the symbol that means "divided by."   ÷

13. O O O   O O
    Set 1   Set 2

Set 1 has 1 more ball than Set 2; that is, $3 - 2 = 1$.

Set 1 has been compared with Set 2 by _____.   subtraction
    subtraction
    addition

Fig. 15.3.   *(Continued)*.

A good explanation of *branching* is contained in a programed text designed to teach the principles of linear and intrinsic programing (**5**). Figure 15.4 shows two pages from this text dealing with intrinsic programing. Read the content carefully for it gives the purposes of intrinsic programing and also its characteristics. Notice that much information is presented without asking for a response. Also, one can go to several different pages after reading the two pages given as Fig. 15.4.

Even though intrinsic programing differs markedly from linear, both have some common points (**36**). Teaching must be more effectively individualized; each student should be actively engaged in the learning process; and knowledge of the appropriateness of a given response should be forthcoming without delay. In actuality, linear programs are much more in evidence than the branching variety, possibly because they are easier to construct.

Pressey's Adjunct Programing

Pressey is often credited with devising the first teaching machine in the 1920s. Years ago, he described the use of a simple machine to test the pupil and to inform him of the correct answers (**24**), the use of an apparatus for automatically teaching drill material (**25**), and the elements of a machine for scoring tests and tabulating by item. At that time he predicted that an "industrial revolution" might occur in education using mechanical devices to free the teacher from routine tasks.

It is interesting that recently Pressey has serious misgivings about the direction that the autoinstructional movement has taken. He believes the basic difficulty has been engendered by an unjustified application of an animal-based learning theory to meaningful human learning (**27**). He has advocated the use of programs in an adjunct or facilitating role rather than in a primary role. He would use material much as it is presented in a well-written textbook and then present multiple-choice items, with answers, based on the material.

An adjunct program might serve as a device for relearning material, reviewing it, or evaluating one's knowledge of it. A principal advantage of an adjunct program over linear programing is that the structure of the knowledge can be presented to the student. In an adjunct program one can present an advance organizer, a topical outline, or some other classification scheme so that the student more readily perceives relationships among parts.

554

Problems to be Overcome

It would be misleading to infer from the foregoing that the road ahead for programed learning and teaching machines is paved with roses. Besides cultural inertia other problems must be considered. The main one, also alluded to above, is that the learning is no better than the program involved. The questions quite naturally arise, even within a given subject field, as to what material should be programed and where the emphasis should be placed. There is nothing beneficial about a more efficient means of learning if the wrong material is selected to be learned.

Stake outlines other shortcomings in programs as they are currently used (36). First, the programs deal almost solely with subject-matter objectives; little or no effort is made by programers toward accomplishing other educational objectives such as awakening creativity and nourishing evaluative abilities. As a second limitation, Stake sees the program as an extremely poor reference source. To overcome this situation, he suggests emphasizing the use of appropriate reference materials.[1] The final questionable assumption detailed by Stake is that the same material is suitable for all learners; obviously this criticism is much more pertinent to linear programs than it is to branching programs. As a practical solution, he suggests an assortment of programs for a given curricular objective, each program designed for students with specified capabilities and educational background.

Another potential problem is pupil boredom that may result from programed instruction. Initial enthusiasm for a programed book by freshmen and graduate students soon was replaced by restlessness and resentment because of the program's "unceasing, impersonal, robot-like progression of minutiae" (28). Other sources, however, report more learner satisfaction with the teaching machine than with the programed text (17) and wide variability in student attitudes toward programed instruction (8).

Added to the problems above is an overriding critical requirement for any innovation in education: that it be established as effective by research. A considerable amount of research has already been done (21, 30, 33). It is difficult to resolve unambiguously all the research findings in the area, but it is apparent that programed instruction has been suitable for some purposes and not for others. Possibly its great-

[1] For example, see Wendt and Rust's library-usage instructional program, now employed at Southern Illinois University (38).

Branching, in an elementary form, can be used as a way of explaining why wrong answers are wrong. After each explanation the student can be sent back to the last page to try again:

Branching can be used remedially to catch the student who does not understand what has been covered:

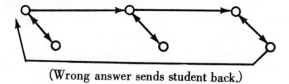

(Wrong answer sends student back.)

Branching can be used to enable the student with a good background to get through faster than the student who needs additional work:

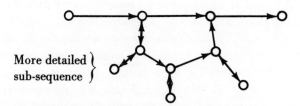

More detailed } sub-sequence

Branching can be used to give the student a choice — he can judge how deeply he wants to go, as you did on page 36.

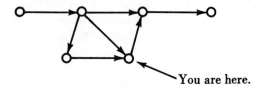

You are here.

Now turn to page 39.

Fig. 15.4. Mechanics of intrinsic programing. (D. Cram. *Explaining "teaching machines" and programing.* San Francisco: Fearon, 1961, pp. 38–39.)

Why branching? Well, as we said earlier, "The alternatives lead somewhere."

Wrong answers, while not encouraged, are not avoided in a branching program as they are in a linear program, since they may be corrected before the learner moves on.

The assumption in branching programming is that a wrong response does not necessarily hinder the learning of a correct response. The *response is useful mainly in guiding the student through the program.* Each response is used to test the success of the latest communication to the student, and in that sense, it "lets the program know" where to take the student next.

The differences in approaches to programming, then, lie in what is considered to be the function of the overt or motor response. The advocates of branching programs believe that:

Page 41   The overt response is not fundamental to the learning process but is useful as a means of supplying feedback to the program.

Page 44   The overt response is fundamental to the learning process.

Page 47   No answer is ever completely wrong.

Fig. 15.4.   *(Continued).*

est service to date has been the freeing of the teacher from spending time imparting routine factual information to her pupils. The preponderance of evidence indicates that the use of programed instruction has become an accepted educational practice. That it can be effective has been amply demonstrated. The task remaining is to determine its best possible uses. Also, more teachers should be instructed in programing. Student teachers given instruction and practice in program writing perform better than those who do not (39).

Computer-Based Teaching Machines

This very short section is included only to acquaint the reader with some long-range projections of autoinstruction in the form of computer-based teaching. The Computer-Based Laboratory for Automated School Systems (CLASS) has as its nucleus a digital computer (32). Contained in the individual mode classroom, controlled by the computer, are display units (physically resembling portable TV sets) and response devices for the pupils, plus monitoring equipment for the teacher. Note the description of the operation of the classroom presented below:

Each student in the class has a display unit and a response device. The student typically reads an item on his film viewer and then enters a multiple choice answer on his response device. Answers are recorded and evaluated in the computer, and feedback is supplied by small lights on the response device. The computer then determines which the student should see next. The number of the next item is displayed on the student's response device. The student then turns to the indicated item on his film viewer and repeats the cycle. In this fashion each of twenty students in the class receives simultaneously individualized instruction from the computer.

The teacher has special monitoring equipment to keep track of what is going on in the classroom. When a student is having trouble an alarm light on the teacher's monitor console is activated. The teacher may defer action if he is busy or he may press a button on his console corresponding to that student's position and take a number of actions. For example, one action button will cause his response unit to be connected in parallel with that student's response device. He may then observe that student's responses to each item. Another action button will call up further information, on a cathode ray tube, about this student's performance. This information will assist the teacher in locating the source of the student's difficulty. A brief discussion with the student may help clear up his problem, and the incident will be recorded for future reference when the program is being revised (32, 349–350).

A discussion of the CLASS facility in the group mode also is provided in the article. It might be noted that CLASS uses a branching technique.

558

The PLATO II project put into effect a computer-based system using only two students (1). Each pupil had a number of "logic" keys on his keyboard to use as the computer presented a program sequence. Six of the more important keys and their functions are listed in Table 15.4. Based upon the insights achieved using PLATO II, a new system

TABLE 15.4.

PLATO II; Logic Keys and Functions

Key	Function
Continue	Display following slide.
Reverse	Display preceding slide.
Judge	Judge answer just entered as correct or incorrect.
Erase	Erase last answer (only incorrect answers may be erased).
Help	Display first slide of appropriate help sequence.
Aha!	Help sequence no longer desired, return to main sequence.

SOURCE: Adapted from P. G. Braunfeld. Problems and prospects of teaching with a computer. *J. educ. Psychol.*, 1964, **55**, 204.

is being developed. Logically dubbed PLATO III, the improved system, using a larger computer, will greatly increase the student stations to at least 500 and will feature error-detecting routines as well as complex-judging functions.

Although exciting in their potential, computer-based teaching machine systems essentially are still experimental.

NEW ORGANIZATIONS FOR INSTRUCTION

Education in the United States is in a process of rapid change, almost a revolution, relative to prior decades. Under both the Kennedy and Johnson administrations, the federal government entered into education on a broad scale. On the local scene, no less than the national, an increased willingness to try new organizational structures has been evident. The central concept linking most of the new instructional organizations is flexibility. This section will consider instructional teams, including the use of noncertified personnel, and nongraded approaches.

Instructional Teams

A variety of new approaches, defining the functions and responsibilities of the classroom teacher, are being tried. Most of these are

559

based upon one or all of the four following ideas. First, the traditional arrangement of having one teacher instruct a classroom group of 25 to 40 pupils is not resulting in the most desirable teaching-learning situations in many cases. Second, because so few persons make classroom teaching a life career, arrangements must be found whereby those who assume this professional responsibility are rewarded accordingly. Third, a better way to attract the most able young people into a life career of teaching is to make certain that a portion of all teachers, perhaps one-fourth to one-half, perform and are rewarded at a professional level. Fourth, some duties currently performed by experienced teachers can be performed equally well (or better) by other persons, for example, secretaries.

Team teaching is a relatively new concept; the first reference to team teaching did not appear in *The Education Index* until Volume 11 (1957–1959). Instructional teams redeploy teachers in such manner that the particular strengths of each teacher may fully be utilized. The volume of knowledge in nearly all subject areas has mushroomed to the extent that it is impossible for a teacher to be well prepared in all subject areas. In a multisubject team, for example, one teaching English, social studies, mathematics, etc., a teacher normally teaches only in his stronger areas; in a single-subject team, on the other hand, a teacher can concentrate on areas within the subject field in which he is particularly interested and prepared. The specialties of different teachers complement one another. Most important, the pupil is provided with instruction from well-prepared teachers in all subject areas. The diverse structural models that may be emulated include single-subject teams or all combinations of subjects within a single grade or across several grades (3).

Additional benefits can accrue to the teacher in the teaching team. The inexperienced beginning teacher can draw upon the expertise surrounding him on a teaching team, selectively choosing and imitating the most effective techniques used by the various teachers. Experienced teachers have close, daily professional contacts with knowledgeable critics, rather than seeing their peers only occasionally over coffee or in the office before or after school. Continuity of instruction is assured, even when substitute teachers are used. When a hierarchical team is established, it is possible to pay the team leaders additional increments above their regular salary, increments that serve as one inducement to make teaching a life career. At the same time, cooperating or regular teachers, those paid the base salary, have an incentive to increase their subject-matter proficiency and improve their teaching techniques.

Quite obviously the students assigned to a team can be grouped in many diverse ways. In the usual self-contained classroom, the teacher does some grouping. But if she has only two very advanced readers she cannot arrange a special group for them. In the team groups, the entire pool of 70 to 80 youngsters is available. From this pool six or seven advanced readers may be grouped together. Many of the disadvantages usually mentioned in the ancient argument on homogeneous *vs.* heterogeneous grouping are avoided. With the pool of youngsters, grouping homogenously is done for some purposes and grouping heterogeneously for others.

Aside from achievement-level groupings, the size of pupil groups also can be varied. Contrary to a common conception, team teaching is not normally characterized by all large-group instruction. Rather there is usually provision for small-group instruction or seminar-type discussion, as well as independent study by the pupils.

Controlled evaluation of instructional teams has been limited to date. In general, articles on the subject usually describe favorable attitudes on the part of participating teachers, pupils, and their parents. In controlled investigations, there has been no preponderance of evidence supporting the belief that personal and social adjustment of pupils would be impaired by the team approach. Indeed, for most pupils, there seems to be the advantage of having several teacher models to imitate selectively. The usual findings in controlled studies in regard to pupil achievement under team and self-contained organization have been of no significant differences or of small differences favoring the team (20). A team comprised of university professors, principals, supervising teachers, and student teachers achieved good results (4). Because there is not consistently greater achievement under the team approach, some persons favor abandoning it.

Yet there is an inherent appeal to the logic in the assumptions underlying the team approach: making better use of teachers' strengths, flexible grouping of pupils, greater incentives for professional teacher performance, etc. There are possible explanations why the team approach typically has not led to greater achievement results. Possibly standardized achievement tests do not measure much of the information imparted by teams. In addition, evaluation in the past typically may have taken place before the team had established stable, working relationships. Thus, in many cases, the effects of unstable team organizations on pupil achievements were compared to the effects of teachers with from 2 to 30 years' experience in self-contained classroom methods and techniques. The position of the authors is that team teaching is a technique of considerable promise.

For example, if 80 percent of the teaching is by instructional team in the junior high school, about 20 percent of the total staff would be team leaders. With a graduate degree and three to ten years of experience, the team leader should be paid $9,000 to $14,000 per year, even when this gives the leader a salary equal to the school principal. The interns should earn about $2500 and the other teachers from $4800 to $8000, whether they work in the team or individually. Most of the other teachers will be beginning teachers, married women who are experienced teachers, and others who enjoy teaching but who do not wish to assume the responsibilities of leadership or put in the 50 or more hours of work per week which is required of the team leader.

Team teaching is now popular; many school systems are trying out different types of teams. If educators could capitalize upon its real merit of giving high responsibility and reasonably adequate pay to teachers who want, need, and earn both, the instructional-team concept might result in greatly improved pupil learning and adjustment over a longer period of time. Probably no administrative arrangement or instructional device will have much effect upon improving the quality of education unless many more young men of high caliber can be attracted to classroom teaching as a lifetime career. The team-leader concept as outlined could accomplish this.

Noncertified Personnel in Teams

The use of instructional secretaries was tried in two high schools and four elementary schools of Davidson County, Tennessee. In the first year the question was raised: Can teachers extend their talents and improve their effectiveness if relieved of time-consuming clerical duties through the use of secretarial help? Six part-time instructional secretaries were employed at a salary of $25 for a 20-hour week. They were married women with excellent training and extensive secretarial experience.

Each secretary was assigned to several rooms, usually six. The principals and teachers outlined the assignments, all secretarial or clerical. The secretaries were not assistant teachers and did not work directly with the children. Among other things, they kept teachers' registers and checked rolls, posted data on school forms, typed letters to parents, cut stencils for tests and prepared other instructional materials, scored and recorded objective tests, operated audiovisual equipment, and wrote letters to make appointments for parent-teacher conferences. During one typical, 20-day period, these secretaries completed work on 1,028 job assignments which included the handling of some 37,000 pieces of material. One-third of their time was devoted to duplication of teacher-prepared materials.

The 32 teachers participating during the first year were high in their praise of the arrangement, and they reported 297 changes in their teaching practices. Most affected practices were related to individualization of instruction, home-school relations, increased use of audiovisual aids, and testing and evaluation.

Participating teachers were asked to choose between working with a secretary or without one. Four-fifths of the teachers indicated that a better learning situation could prevail if as many as 4 pupils were added to any of the four basic class sizes—25, 30, 35, and 40 pupils—and if three hours of secretarial help per week were provided. All teachers agreed that they could teach 39 pupils more effectively than 35 with the three hours of secretarial service. This result was significant, particularly because most experimentation of this nature has been looked upon by teachers as increasing their work load. These results, however, do not indicate the desirability of any particular class size, with or without secretarial help.

During the second year of the experiment, the service was continued in the same six schools. By the addition of three secretaries, the service was extended to all teachers in two elementary schools; however, in the other two schools, it was withdrawn from six teachers who had received it the first year. During this second year, the service was provided for 61 teachers. Generally, appraisals were more favorable and utilization of the secretaries was more effective in the second year. A definite pattern developed toward greater use of the secretaries for direct improvement of the teaching–learning situation as opposed to the more indirect approach of securing relief from clerical and routine tasks.

The reactions of the six teachers who lost the secretarial help are noteworthy. As compensation for the loss, each teacher's class size was reduced by 5 to 13 pupils. These six teachers listed a total of 144 separate pieces of duplicated material, 13 educational pamphlets ordered by the secretary the previous year, and one set of bulletin board captions still in use during the second year. Of 59 changes in practice listed by them the first year, 9 were no longer employed,

33 were used less frequently, and 17 were still fully in existence. Of the service missed most, four teachers mentioned help in preparing materials of instruction, four listed help in checking and recording, and one missed the help in preparing bulletin board materials. All teachers indicated that their out-of-school activities were more restricted. Only one teacher felt her instruction had not been impaired by the withdrawal of the service.

After two years, the results are fourfold: (1) the school people have learned to use secretarial help effectively, (2) the plan to use secretarial help in the manner described is financially feasible, (3) the use of secretarial help leads to improved teaching, and (4) there is an adequate supply of secretarial help available for the schools.

Interns in Teams

Among the most successful arrangements of instructional teams is one at the University of Wisconsin in which an intern works with an experienced teacher as part of a two-member team, or as a member of a larger team that includes only certified personnel, or as one member of a larger team that includes certified and noncertified personnel (12). Four teacher-education programs include internships in teams.

There is a fifth-year program designed to attract qualified liberal-arts graduates into teaching careers. During the fifth year, the candidate serves a full semester as a salaried intern in one of many instructional teams affiliated with the Wisconsin Improvement Program and the School of Education. Another semester and summer session are devoted to academic work.

Another arrangement involves five years, and an internship as in the preceding, but the student plans this program prior to graduation. This plan permits a greater amount of general education and specialization in a major than does a four-year program.

A third plan involves one semester of internship after completing the baccalaureate. Here, the candidate plans his program well in advance of graduation. A final plan incorporates the internship in the last semester of the senior year. This requires at least an additional summer session of work. In general, elementary education candidates pursue the last plan most frequently and secondary education candidates the first two.

A brief account of one team (at the time of writing 600 interns were participating in the program annually) will clarify some of the team operations (12).

PERSONNEL

Two experienced teachers, one University of Wisconsin intern each semester, and one secretary for two and a half hours a day. (The intern is a liberal-arts graduate and usually a United States history major without teaching experience or training except for some postgraduate training in education done through the Wisconsin Improvement Program at the University.)

PLANS

The preceding personnel teach four classes of about 75 students each, handling the whole junior class in U.S. history and a few seniors for a total of about 300 students. Therefore, each experienced teacher is responsible for 150 students. The experienced teachers also help to train the intern for a teaching career. Instead of hiring a part-time teacher for the extra two periods a day, the intern and secretary are used.

From the teachers' standpoint, the team arrangement enhanced the teachers' abilities and opportunities to:

1. Stimulate students by developing her strengths.
2. Avoid duplication of effort by giving presentations in the large group.
3. Check regularly on the progress of students.
4. Counsel with individual students when necessary and at least twice a year with each student.
5. Plan together with a colleague, pooling resources and ideas to come up with the best approach.
6. Use new approaches to teaching and evaluate them.
7. Be secure in the knowledge that classwork will continue even if she is absent.
8. Guide a newcomer to the profession, the intern, in learning to teach
9. Accumulate resource material and bibliographies for all levels within the group.
10. Meet the needs of the various levels of student ability.

Some difficulties were experienced in this situation. The room lacked adequate lighting, ventilation, electrical outlets, maps, microphone facilities, central screen, and flag. There was also a shortage of filmstrips, records, books, and motion picture films. (University advisors feel that the school should have a film library of its own.) And the amount of time required during this first year of team teaching was unbelievable; virtually no day's work was done in as little as eight hours.

565

NONGRADED SCHOOLS

Why is there increasing dissatisfaction with graded classes and favor of nongraded classes? Graded classes have tended to promote a lockstep system of education. Each student, regardless of his intellectual abilities and achievements, is required to take 12 years to complete 12 grades of school. Nongraded schools intend to overcome this:

> The nongraded school is designed to implement a theory of continuous pupil progress: since the differences among children are great and since these differences cannot be substantially modified, school structure must facilitate the continuous progress of each pupil. Some pupils, therefore, will require a longer period of time than others for achieving certain learnings and attaining certain developmental levels. This theory of continuous progress differs markedly from two other prevailing theories of pupil progress: the theory of grade standards and the theory of "social" promotion. The authors reject both of these conflicting theories (13, 44).

Two widely publicized, nongraded high schools—both in Florida— are described for illustrative purposes. The principal at the first of these, Melbourne High School, readily disposes of the graded concept:

> The durable attractiveness of the grade lies in its administrative convenience. It serves as a comfortable holding pool in which school administrators can and do throw youngsters for custodial purposes and forget them for a year. By comparison, non-grading is an administrative prickly pear constantly needling for attention to the learning needs of youngsters (2, 206).

Instead of grades, Melbourne uses *ad hoc* learning arrangements called "phases." Students are assigned to these phases on the basis of their scores on standardized achievement tests, rather than on IQ or age. Note the descriptions of the phases provided:

Phase 1: Subjects are centered around remedial work.
Phase 2: Subjects are concerned with basic skills.
Phase 3: Subjects are designed for students seeking an average education.
Phase 4: Subjects are available for students desiring education in considerable depth.
Phase 5: Subjects are open to students who are willing to assume responsibility for their own learning and plan to go far beyond the boundaries of a single course.
Phase Q: Students whose creative talents are well developed in special areas should give consideration to this "Quest" phase of the curriculum. This is an important dimension of the phased organization designed to give thrust in the direction of individual fulfillment. In this phase a student may research an area in which he is deeply

curious, either to develop creative powers or in the quest of knowledge. A student may spend from one to three hours a day in Quest.

Phase X: Non-academic subjects which do not accommodate student mobility; e.g., typing, physical education. These subjects are ungraded but unphased (2, 207).

Thus, a student may be enrolled at different phases in each subject he takes.

Other characteristics of Melbourne High School also are unusual. There are no study halls or standard texts and typing classes average 125 students with a single teacher.

Another attempt to break away from "the graded-lockstep" and, indeed, from a multiplicity of traditional educational practices is seen at Nova High School. The director of the school spent three years visiting outstanding schools throughout the country to incorporate into the plans for the Nova High School all the best modern educational methods for improving instruction. The advocates of the school believe that all the equipment, teaching aids, and instructional methods have been tested and proved in other school systems. The curriculum of the school is described in the following paragraph:

Nova is a space age school. Its philosophy is based on a concept best described as scientific learning for a scientific age. Interestingly, to achieve the goals of such a philosophy, there has been a return to a "hard-core" curriculum. Each Nova student pursues a schedule of studies which includes mathematics, foreign language, English, science, social studies, technical science, special studies, and physical education. A student may choose a foreign language from among Latin, Spanish, French, Russian, and German. His choice of a technical science or special studies course comes from electronics, mechanical and scale drawing, music, home economics, art, personal typing, mechanical technology, safety and driver education, physiology, and home nursing (18, 9).

Recall that, with the nongraded approach, this rather rigid-sounding curriculum loosens up considerably. Thus, seventh-year students may be studying mathematics on what is traditionally thought of as a tenth-grade level. Of course, Nova does not have grades; in their place, the school uses numerous short achievement levels called "units" in each subject area. Capable students finish a unit in about a month; below-average pupils take up to six weeks. To pass from one unit to the next, the student must pass a final unit test. The trimester plan is used with a single month's vacation; only near the end of the trimester preceding the vacation is there any pressure on students to complete all units in progress.

The techniques and media used at Nova include team teaching, closed-circuit television, overhead projection in every room, a reading laboratory, science and language laboratories, and varying sizes of group instruction. Unusual facilities include wall-to-wall carpeting, resource centers, teaching machines, microfilm readers, and complete air-conditioning. Supposedly, these innovations were made possible by excluding a large auditorium and a cafeteria kitchen from the building plans. Personally, these authors can go along with the purpose and innovations at Nova, but without wanting to sound facetious, we wonder about the advantages of wall-to-wall carpeting over a well-planned hot-lunch program.

SUMMARY

Television, language laboratories, and programed instruction, in their infancy only a few years ago, have become accepted in the schools throughout the United States. The graded organization of the school with a single teacher for 25 to 40 students is giving way to nongraded schools and instructional teams. Computer-based instructional systems are leaving the planning boards and are being incorporated into experimental equipment and facilities. We are entering an era when it is possible to individualize instruction better than ever before, to improve the quality of education for all children and youth, to humanize education, and to provide more and better education to larger numbers for a longer period of time, especially to that 30 percent of youth who do not graduate from high school at the present time.

Not one of the above media or organizations will revolutionize education. However, these with better preparation of teachers, better quality of other instructional materials and media, better facilities, more specially educated personnel to perform other duties, and heightened concern for improved education at all governmental levels are resulting in greatly improved educational opportunities for all children and youth. We may not have dramatic improvements in achievements whereby we suddenly have students achieving at 14 what they do now at 16. By increasing achievements through more efficient learning by only a modest percent each year for the next decade, we shall have high school seniors at the level of many of our current college graduates. The level of educational attainments will increase markedly in the future.

For these goals to be realized, experimentation must continue in the laboratories, and programs and materials must be tested in the field, in the classrooms with teachers and students in usual situations. Subject matter must be selected wisely. Appropriate subject matter in learnable programs must be incorporated in TV and autoinstruction of all types. The teacher continues to be the key person in the educative process. The more children and youth who learn independently, the more time will the teacher have to humanize education, to help each child achieve a full measure of self-realization.

QUESTIONS AND ACTIVITIES

1. Describe how TV, language laboratories, and autoinstruction might improve education.

2. Give your opinions of how the four research questions dealing with media and materials will be answered eventually.

3. a. If you were an undergraduate student at Miami University, would you prefer instruction by TV, large lecture classes, or a combination of these? Why?

    b. In TV classes, conventional classes, or a combination? Why?

    c. If you were responsible for the instructional program and had plentiful funds, which arrangements would you make available? Why? (Base your remarks on the information presented in the description of the experiment, not on your personal experiences or opinions.)

4. a. Discuss the possibilities for improving human abilities through in- and out-of-class use of electronic equipment and related instructional procedures in foreign language or other instruction.

    b. Which principles given in Chapters 8 and 12 might be implemented more readily with the equipment and related procedures than without them?

5. a. In what respects are linear, branching, and adjunct programing alike and different?

    b. Which seems to be most appropriate for outcomes related to your interest in subject field and level of schooling? Explain.

6. Indicate the main outcomes you wish students to learn and write a two-page sample of each type of programing for it. Consult books and articles on how to write programs or the books from which the samples are taken. (See Suggestions for Further Reading.)

7. a. Keeping in mind your major interest, discuss your present competence as a program writer.

    b. Should the classroom teacher be competent in writing programs? Why or why not?

8. Which one of the following principles of instruction seems best suited and which seems least suited for implementation by autoinstruction? Explain.
    a. Sequence instruction properly.
    b. Assist the learner to delimit problems.
    c. Encourage original expression in many media.

9. a. List all the possible advantages of team teaching for the

students and for the teacher as given in the book.

b. Add to this list from your own analysis and experience.

c. List all the conditions that you think are essential to make instructional teams successful.

10. Given all the necessary physical arrangements, materials and supplies, and personnel, would you prefer to teach individually or as a member of a team? Explain fully.

11. a. How are nongraded classes different from graded classes?

b. Based on your analysis, what

conditions for placing students in classes and for materials and facilities are essential for successful nongraded classes?

12. a. Given complete freedom to arrange nongraded instructional groups at the school level in which you are most interested, what criteria would you use for placing students in groups? Explain why you would use these criteria.

b. What educational improvements would you anticipate from the grouping that you propose?

SUGGESTIONS FOR FURTHER READING

Brown, B. F. The non-graded high school. *Phi Delta Kappan,* 1963, 44, 206–209. (In Seidman, 1965, 125–129.)

Crowder, N. A. On the differences between linear and intrinsic programming. *Phi Delta Kappan,* 1963, 44, 250–254. (In DeCecco, 1964, 142–151.)

Finn, J. D. Technology in the instructional process. *Audiovis. Commun. Rev.,* 1960, 8(1), 5–26. (Reprinted under the title "A new theory for instructional technology" in Russell, 1964, 59–66.)

Fitzgerald, H. T. Teaching machines: A demurrer. *Sch. Rev.,* 1962, 70, 247–256. (In Fullagar, *et al.,* 1964, 630–636.)

Keislar, E. R., & J. D. McNeil. Teaching scientific theory to first grade pupils by auto-instructional device. *Harv. educ. Rev.,* 1961, 31, 73–83. (In Seidman, 1965, 178–184.)

Lumsdaine, A. A. Instruments and media of instruction. In N. L. Gage (Ed.), *Handbook of research on teaching.* Chicago: Rand McNally, 1963, pp. 583–682.

Pressey, S. L. Teaching machine (and learning theory) crisis. *J. appl. Psychol.,* 1963, 47, 1–6. (Portions reprinted in DeCecco, 1964, 446–457; and reprinted in Fullagar, *et al.,* 1964, 618–625.)

Quackenbush, J. How effective are the new auto-instructional materials and devices? *IRE transactions on education,* 1961, pp. 144–150. (In Fullagar, *et al.,* 1964, 585–600.)

Schramm, W., J. Lyle, & E. B. Parker. Children's learning from television. In E. C. Uliassi (Ed.), *Studies in public communication.* No. 3. Chicago: Univer. of Chicago, 1961, pp. 86–98. (In Gordon, 1965, 315–323.)

Shaplin, J. T., & H. F. Olds (Eds.), *Team teaching.* New York: Harper & Row, 1964.

Sherburne, E. G., Jr. ETV research in the decade ahead. *Audiovis. Commun. Rev.,* 1960, 8(4), 192–201. (Portions reprinted in DeCecco, 1963, 394–403.)

Skinner, B. F. Why we need teaching machines. *Harv. educ. Rev.,* 1961, 31, 377–398. (Portions reprinted in DeCecco, 1964, 92–112; reprinted in Fullagar, *et al.,* 1964, 600–618.)

Stolurow, L. M. Teaching by machine. *Coop. Res. Monogr.,* No. 6. Washington, D.C.: U.S. Office of Education, 1961.

Thelen, H. A. Programmed materials today: Critique and proposal. *Elem. Sch. J.,* 1963, 63, 180–196. (In Page, 1964, 253–259.)

Trump, J. L. Flexible scheduling: Fad or fundamental? *Phi Delta Kappan,* 1963, 44, 367–371. (In Seidman, 1965, 119–125.)

570

REFERENCES

1. Braunfeld, P. G. Problems and prospects of teaching with a computer. *J. educ. Psychol.*, 1964, **55**, 201–211.
2. Brown, B. F. The non-graded high school. *Phi Delta Kappan*, 1963, **44**, 206–209.
3. Brownell, J. A., & H. A. Taylor. Theoretical perspectives for teaching teams. *Phi Delta Kappan*, 1962, **43**, 150–157.
4. Chorny, M., & A. G. Storey. A team approach to student teaching. *Canad. Educ. Res. Dig.*, 1965, **5**, 60–65.
5. Cram, D. *Explaining "teaching machines" and programming.* San Francisco: Fearon, 1961.
6. Crowder, N. A. On the differences between linear and intrinsic programming. *Phi Delta Kappan*, 1963, **44**, 250–254.
7. Dunham, F. A new road to the abundant life: A survey of educational television. *Amer. Psychologist*, 1955, **10**, 615–617.
8. Eigen, L. D. High-school student reactions to programmed instruction. *Phi Delta Kappan*, 1963, **44**, 282–285.
9. Evans, J. A., & Marie Baldwin. *Learning French the modern way. Book I.* New York: McGraw-Hill, 1961.
10. Feldhusen, J. F. Taps for teaching machines. *Phi Delta Kappan*, 1963, **44**, 265–267.
11. Finn, J. D. Technology and the instructional process. *Phi Delta Kappan*, 1960, **41**, 371–378.
12. Fowlkes, J. G. (Ed.) *Experiences in team teaching.* Madison: Wisconsin Improvement Program, School of Education, Univer. of Wisconsin, 1963.
13. Goodlad, J. I., & R. H. Anderson. *The nongraded elementary school.* New York: Harcourt, Brace, & World, 1959.
14. Gray, Genevieve. Educational technology and the individual student. *Phi Delta Kappan*, 1964, **46**, 6–8.
15. Grittner, F. M. The language lab —gadget or godsend. *Wisconsin J. Educ.*, 1963, **95**, 15–16.
16. Holton, J. S., P. E. King, G. Mathieu, & K. S. Pond. *Sound language teaching, the state of the art today.* New York: University Publishers, 1961.
17. Hough, J. B., & B. Revsin. Programmed instruction at the college level: A study of several factors influencing learning. *Phi Delta Kappan*, 1963, **44**, 286–291.
18. Kaufman, B., & P. Bethune. Nova High space age school. *Phi Delta Kappan*, 1964, **46**, 9–11.
19. Keating, R. F. *A study of the effectiveness of language laboratories.* New York: Institute of Administrative Research, Teachers College, Columbia, 1963.
20. Klausmeier, H. J., & W. Wiersma. The effects of IQ level and sex on divergent thinking of seventh grade pupils of low, average, and high IQ. *J. educ. Res.*, 1965, **58**, 300–302.
21. Lumsdaine, A. A. Educational technology, programed learning, and instructional science. In E. R. Hilgard (Ed.), *Theories of learning and instruction.* Yearb. nat. Soc. Stud. Educ., 1964, **63**, Part I, pp. 371–401.
22. Macomber, F. G., & L. Siegel. *Final report on the experimental study in instructional procedures.* Oxford, Ohio: Miami Univer., 1960.
23. Mathieu, G. Automated language instruction: A new deal for student and teacher. *Automated Teaching Bull.*, 1959, **1**, 5–9.
24. Pressey, S. L. A simple apparatus which gives tests and scores—and teaches. *Sch. & Soc.*, 1926, **23**, 373–376.

25. Pressey, S. L. A machine for automatic teaching of drill material. *Sch. & Soc.*, 1927, **25**, 549–552.

26. Pressey, S. L. Autoinstruction: Perspectives, problems, potentials. In E. R. Hilgard (Ed.), *Theories of learning and instruction.* Yearb. nat. Soc. Stud. Educ., 1964, 63, Part I, pp. 354–370.

27. Pressey, S. L. A puncture of the huge "programing" boom? *Teachers Coll. Rec.*, 1964, **65**, 413–418.

28. Roth, R. H. Student reactions to programed learning. *Phi Delta Kappan*, 1963, **44**, 278–281.

29. Schramm, W. L. Learning from instructional television. *Rev. educ. Res.*, 1962, **32**, 156–167.

30. Schramm, W. L. *Programed instruction, today and tomorrow.* New York: The Fund for the Advancement of Education, 1962.

31. Schramm, W. L., J. Lyle, & I. deSola Pool. *The people look at educational television.* Stanford: Stanford, 1963.

32. Silberman, H. F. The digital computer in education. *Phi Delta Kappan*, 1962, **43**, 345–350.

33. Silberman, H. F. Self-teaching devices and programmed materials. *Rev. educ. Res.*, 1962, **32**, 179–193.

34. Skinner, B. F. The science of learning and the art of teaching. *Harv. educ. Rev.*, 1954, **24**, 86–97.

35. Skinner, B. F. Teaching machines. *Science*, 1958, **128**, 969–977.

36. Stake, R. E. The teaching machine: Tool of the future or passing fancy? *Phi Delta Kappan,* 1963, **44**, 247–249.

37. TEMAC. *Ratios and proportions.* Chicago: Encyclopedia Britannica Inc., 1963.

38. Wendt, P. R., & G. C. Rust. Programed instruction for transfer to the real life situation. *Phi Delta Kappan*, 1963, **44**, 273–277.

39. Wisenthal, M. Programmed instruction and teacher education. *Canad. Educ. Res. Dig.*, 1965, **5**, 66–76.

40. Wohlwill, J. F. The teaching machine: Psychology's new hobbyhorse. *Teachers Coll. Rec.*, 1962, **64**, 139–146.

PART IV

Evaluation and Measurement

*E*NGENDERING adequate motivation in students (Chapter 12), encouraging retention and transfer (Chapter 13), providing for individual differences (Chapter 14), and using new instructional materials and organizations (Chapter 15) are essential to efficient learning. In order to determine the effectiveness of learning, evaluation and measurement of achievements and abilities in the cognitive and psychomotor domains, and outcomes in the affective domain, are required. Statistical techniques are helpful in summarizing and interpreting measurements. Consider two key questions related to each chapter in Part IV:

We get the wrong impression about measurement, evaluation, and statistics when we consider them to be completely unfamiliar. College students have been measuring height, weight, miles traveled, etc. for many years and they have been summarizing these measurements. Presumably they also have sufficient knowledge of arithmetic to do the simple computations required in most statistics. Relating prior knowledge to the present material and utilizing skills already developed will aid the study of these chapters.

CHAPTER 16

Standardized Tests

Evaluation requires making judgments about the relative desirability of something in terms of a standard. Thus, we evaluate how well a student is performing in any subject field, his conduct on the playground, his motives, and the like. Evaluation is a comprehensive term. Measurement is more restricted. Measurement is concerned with the administration and scoring of tests of all types. We can measure through administering and scoring an achievement test. Also, we could count the errors in capitalization, spelling, punctuation, and sentence structure in a theme. Likewise, the number of exercises correct on an arithmetic assignment may be counted. These measurements are useful in subsequent evaluation. For example, we administer and score an achievement test at the beginning and end of the unit. This measurement helps us in evaluating the progress made by the student. Evaluation and measurement by school personnel are concerned with the students' abilities and characteristics and with student progress toward achieving outcomes of learning as set forth in Chapters 7 through 11.

The nature of evaluation and measurement is clarified in the discussions of (1) the purposes of evaluation and measurement, (2) characteristics of a good evaluation procedure, (3) characteristics of standardized tests, and (4) widely used standardized tests. The purposes of evaluation and the characteristics of a good evaluation procedure considered in this chapter refer not only to published tests, but also to informal evaluation procedures treated in Chapter 17.

THE PURPOSES OF EVALUATION AND MEASUREMENT

Whether in a ten-cent store, supermarket, or large department store, we see many instances of the customers and the sales people evaluating and measuring. One objective of education is to assist learners in developing knowledge and skills of evaluation and measurement in their many daily activities. The more specific purposes of teachers and other educational personnel in evaluating and measuring are to:

1. Facilitate student progress.
2. Assess student progress.
3. Understand the individual student.
4. Facilitate self-understanding by the student.
5. Evaluate instructional programs.
6. Assist in administrative judgments.
7. Contribute to knowledge of abilities and instruction.

Facilitate Student Progress

The student needs to know whether he is spelling a word correctly, punctuating properly, or using an appropriate method to solve a problem. He cannot make progress without this information and must either get the information himself or receive help. A most important task of the teacher is to know what is correct or acceptable and to help the student learn this.

To overcome incorrect responses or inappropriate methods, causes of a student's lack of progress must be appraised. A variety of informal procedures and published tests, inventories, and check lists are available for this purpose. The most important purpose of evaluation is to help the student make progress in achieving learning outcomes considered by society, the teacher, and himself to be of value.

Assess Student Progress

In the process of helping the student make progress in daily, weekly, and longer-term learning tasks, the teacher can also ascertain how well the student is learning; however, in many situations the emphasis is simply to ascertain what the student knows and, on this basis, to award him a grade or rating. In more desirable situations, the attempt is made to ascertain what the student knows at the start of a day, semester, or year, and also what he has learned at points along the way. For example, one form of a standardized test in reading may be given at the beginning of the school year and an equivalent form of the same test toward the end of the school year. To the extent that this standardized test measures the objectives of the instructional program in reading, the test results may be used to determine how well the students have learned during the school year.

Recognizing the importance still attached to grades at the high school and college level, we must make accurate judgments about what the student knows, how well he performs a variety of tasks, and how well he has learned. If we continue to use grades, the best evaluative devices should be used to help us make these judgments accurately. The more important purpose, however, is to get reliable information on how well the student is learning; and if it is found that the student is not making reasonable progress, to do whatever is necessary to improve the situation.

Understand the Individual Student

Higher education is elective and not required. The college instructor frequently is not interested in the abilities and other characteristics of the students. If they achieve sufficiently well to meet his standards, they are passed in the course; otherwise, they fail. But students are required by law to attend elementary and secondary schools; their parents and they cannot avoid this. The elementary and secondary teacher cannot proceed like the college instructor. To decide whether a child, required to attend school, is making the progress of which he is capable, and whether he is learning as well as can reasonably be expected of him, the teacher needs information about each child's cognitive abilities, psychomotor abilities, and other characteristics.

A variety of informal observational procedures can be used to appraise the abilities and characteristics of students. However, it is in this area particularly that published tests are used. Measures of intellectual ability, sometimes called scholastic or academic aptitude tests, educational achievement tests, interest inventories, and the like, are available to facilitate the appraisal of abilities.

Consider a city in which there are four large high schools. English is required of all students in the ninth grade. In each high school, there are a number of beginning, as well as experienced, English teachers. Each teacher is able to observe only the students in the classes taught. How well can each teacher know the intellectual abilities of all of the students during the first week or even during the first month? How well can the pupil's ability to read the required textbook be appraised? Tests of intellectual ability and reading achievement, though far from perfect, may provide useful information for appraising pupil abilities and other characteristics.

One of the important and often neglected components of an overall evaluation program in the school is the understanding of abilities and characteristics of students. Teachers at all school levels, including college, are meeting their students for the first day, week, or even months without attempting to ascertain the kind of abilities essential for achieving the objectives of instruction. Better results would be possible if the level of abilities and affective characteristics of the student were understood in relation to demands of the learning tasks.

Facilitate Self-Understanding

Students are staying in school longer now than ever before, yet the time is relatively short compared to one's total life span and is crucial in its impact on one's later life. One purpose of formal education is to help students understand themselves as individuals and as members of groups. By the time they finish high school, if not earlier, they are expected to set realistic goals and to evaluate their progress toward these goals. Further, they are to make decisions about what is important in life and what they can attain with regard to the kinds of abilities and characteristics they possess.

It is the teacher's responsibility to determine the extent to which students share in gathering, interpreting, and using information that might help them understand their abilities. The teacher might obtain information from problem check lists and interest blanks and from intelligence tests, achievement tests, sociometric tests, and so on. All this needs to be interpreted to the students if they are to achieve self-understanding. The greater part of this information should not be presented to students as a classroom group but in individual conferences or in smaller groups. Further, information that might have a pronounced detrimental effect upon a student should be withheld from him. But, in those areas directly related to progress in learning and ability to learn, students should share in all phases of information gathering and interpreting. In this way, they can identify their strengths and weaknesses and use the information for self-understanding and improvement. Many references on interpreting test scores are available (**26**).

Evaluate Instructional Programs

Assume that a teacher has set the objective of all students' learning to recognize participial phrases. The first part of the class period is spent in teaching; toward the end a short test is given. This test not only tells the extent to which the students have learned to recognize participial phrases, but also suggests whether the teaching method was effective and whether the teacher's objective was realistic. If most students had half of the test items wrong, many alternative explanations could be made; either the objective was not realistic, the method of teaching was ineffective, the test was too hard, or the characteristics of the students led to the poor performance. Careful analysis of the situation may help in deciding the causes of the poor learning situation.

Take another example related to guidance. Tenth-grade students are randomly put into two groups, one to receive six counseling interviews during the year, the other to receive none. One purpose of the counseling interviews is to help the students understand their own abilities. At the end of the year a skilled person evaluates the effects of the counseling. If a difference is found in self-understanding favoring those counseled, the conclusion may be safely drawn that the counseling procedures achieved the desired objective.

Assist in Administrative Judgments

Which children shall be retained in a grade? promoted? accelerated? If classes are arranged for educable mentally retarded children and for those of superior learning ability, which students shall be selected for these classes? Among the high school seniors, which shall be recommended for matriculating in a college or university and which shall not? What kinds of reading materials are most appropriate for students in the seventh (or any other) grade? These are types of curriculum and administrative decisions that are continually being made. It is only through a comprehensive program of evaluation and measurement that these decisions can be made intelligently.

Contribute to Knowledge of Abilities and Instruction

Measurement in the physical sciences is highly precise and accurate; in the biological sciences, measurement is less exact, apparently because the things measured are more complex than those in the physical sciences. In the behavioral sciences, where study is focused on human beings, the most complex of all biological organisms, measurements are less exact than in either the physical or biological sciences. In most educational settings, there are many human beings who continually interact. The problem of making value judgments about human abilities and teaching–learning processes is much more complex than making similar judgments about the properties and interactions of various chemicals or of lower forms of animals.

As we have mentioned many times in the previous chapters, our knowledge about human abilities, including the realm of teaching–learning processes, is not perfect. The great advances in recent years in identifying abilities have occurred in military settings. We are just beginning to carry out the kind of research with children of school age that is so vital for the improvement of teaching–learning processes. We still proceed on a trial-and-confirmation basis in many areas of learning; that is, the students are enrolled in the school, they engage in various learning activities, and, on the basis of our daily judgments of their performances, we estimate how they should perform.

CHARACTERISTICS OF A GOOD
EVALUATION PROCEDURE

Any evaluation procedure, whether it be a standardized educational achievement test or an informal method of observing and evaluating the students' performance, should be *valid, reliable,* and *useable.* These terms have special significance for published tests and, to a lesser extent, for the daily and informal evaluation procedures used by teachers.

Validity

In using a commercially printed or a self-devised test, a teacher should be concerned with how valid the test is for achieving specific purposes. The different types of validity and related purposes which follow require careful study.

Four types of validity have been distinguished, namely, content validity, concurrent validity, predictive validity, and construct validity.

Content validity is concerned with the sampling of a specified universe of content.

Concurrent validity is concerned with the relation of test scores to an accepted contemporary criterion of performance on the variable which the test is intended to measure.

Predictive validity is concerned with the relation of test scores to measures on a criterion based on performance at some later time.

Construct validity. More indirect validating procedures, which we refer to under the name *construct validation,* are invoked when the preceding three methods are insufficient to indicate the degree to which the test measures what it is intended to measure.

We can illustrate these concepts by examining various ways in which a test of interpretive reading in science might be employed. A science teacher may wish to determine the proficiency of his students with respect to this teaching objective. Interpreting the test for this purpose requires information on *content validity:* Does the test present the types of situations to which the teacher is trying to teach students to respond?

The teacher would examine the evidence furnished by the producer of the test specifying the universe from which reading selections were sampled, and he would examine the types of questions included in the test. The teacher might be interested in knowing either whether the paragraphs and questions asked are representative of the reading materials his students have been studying, or whether they are representative of the science reading materials encountered in adult activities.

The teacher may also be interested in using the objective test to replace the much more time consuming and difficult method he now employs to evaluate the achievements of the students in a particular course. A decision as to whether this test is a satisfactory substitute requires evidence of *concurrent validity.* If the teacher, for instance, is satisfied that the students' ability to make critical interpretations and applications in free response to a paragraph is a good measure of the objective, he may inquire whether ability to select the best of several interpretations offered in a multiple choice test measures the same ability.

The guidance counselor may have occasion to consult the same test scores for the purpose of advising students concerning election of a science course in college. Such use of test scores involves prediction of later performance and, hence, depends on *predictive validity.* The counselor would need to know how accurately scores on this test predict achievement in college science courses. He would consult the evidence concerning the correlation of the test scores with measures of achievement in college science courses accepted as criteria for the purpose.

It may be noted that concurrent validity refers to the relation between test scores and criterion scores which can be obtained at the same time, while predictive validity refers to the relation between test scores and criterion scores which cannot be secured until some time later. The former answers the question, "With what degree of accuracy can the test scores replace the scores on an existing criterion?" The latter answers the question, "With what degree of accuracy can the test scores estimate the scores on the criterion that the test subjects would achieve some time later?"

For any of the three purposes described above, the specified types of evidence of validity may not be available, either because the universe of content cannot adequately be specified or because an acceptable criterion is not available. In such cases the test user must judge the validity of the test for his purpose on the basis of such evidence as the test producer presents. The use of logical inferences from experimental evidence or other information relevant to any aspect of test validity has been termed *construct validity.*

Construct validity is highly important in achievement testing. In the first place, universes of content, while relatively easy to specify in the traditional school subjects, nevertheless are very difficult to specify in many important areas such as study skills, attitudes, interests, understandings, and appreciations. Second, although in some cases criteria for concurrent validity can be obtained, as in the example above, this is not generally the case. In fact, for the purposes of most educational achievement tests, no suitable concurrent criterion of performance has usually been available to determine validity in terms of a correlation coefficient or other quantitative objective measure. Such criterion data as teachers' ratings, course grades, or teacher-constructed examination grades are generally inadequate for this purpose and frequently inferior to the tests for which they are to be used. The same considerations apply to predictive validity in many situations.

The most typical example of construct validity applied to an achievement test in a traditional subject in which the universe of content is accepted, but a suitable (concurrent) criterion is not available, is the procedure by means of which the discrimination of the test scores is measured between successive grades in a sequence of courses. The information obtained by this means permits the logical inference that those grade groups in the sequence which have received more instruction attain a higher level of achievement. The same or experimentally similar approaches may be followed to adduce information bearing on construct validity for any use of a test. Content, concurrent, and predictive validity may be thought of as specialized aspects of construct validity. . . .

It may be advisable to point out that for instructional uses of achievement tests (diagnosis and analysis of achievement, planning of remedial work, and determination of supervisory needs of the teacher) content validity is important. For administrative uses of test scores (classification of pupils, promotion, and school records of achievement) it is only the concurrent and construct validity that are important. It is the measure of the accuracy of the inferences which determine administrative decisions. In such cases content validity is important primarily as it lends logical support to concurrent or construct validity (2, 16–19).

These examples refer to achievement tests. Present achievement tests meet the various criteria of validity to a higher degree than do many other types of published tests. It is important that the test user makes certain that any test he uses is valid for his purposes. The test manual which accompanies any published test should clearly indicate the types of validity described above, as well as other characteristics of the test, including reliability.

Reliability

Reliability refers to the degree to which the measurements yielded by a test are consistent or stable. There are several types of reliability and related methods for ascertaining the degree of reliability.

One procedure is to ascertain how consistently the test measures at two points in time. For example, a group of students takes the same test on two occasions; the two sets of scores are correlated, and the result obtained is the *coefficient of stability*. If a spelling test of 50 words were given on two consecutive days to the same students, and each student obtained the same score both times (or scores changed an identical amount in the same direction), the coefficient of stability would be positive and perfect, + 1.00. If, however, the scores changed in different directions or in varying amounts, the coefficient would be lower. The greater the inconsistency between tests, the less reliable the test. Note that the coefficient of stability would vary depending upon the time interval between the two testings.

A second procedure is to construct two forms of the same test and to administer them in close succession, usually on the same day, to the same students. This considerably reduces any day-to-day variation that would lower the comparability of the results of the two forms. A correlation, called a *coefficient of equivalence*, is computed. This is an indication of the degree of equivalence between the results yielded by the two forms. Test makers often produce several forms of the same type of test. The equivalent forms are needed to prevent practice or learning effects from influencing scores when the same test is given repeatedly to some students but not to others. Equivalent forms of an achievement test at the beginning and end of a unit, semester, or year are useful to ascertain generally what a group of students has achieved.

A logical extension of the two forms of reliability just discussed is the *coefficient of equivalence and stability* which is the correlation between the results produced by two forms of the same test given at points separated in time.

When only one form of a test is available, the split-half method is used to ascertain reliability, usually referred to as the *coefficient of internal consistency;* in effect it is the coefficient of equivalence between the two halves of the test. Each half of the test is considered an equivalent and independent form of the same test. Various means are used to make certain that the items in each half of the test are independent and that the students have sufficient time for answering all items in the entire test when it is administered. A correlation between the two sets of scores is then obtained as a measure of equivalence. This method can be applicable to teacher-made tests and to many experiments in which only a single test is utilized. Obviously temporary factors influencing the testing should be equal. The various coefficients discussed are summarized in Table 16.1.

TABLE 16.1.

Types of Test Reliability

Coefficient	Correlation Between:		Time Interval Between Administrations?
Coefficient of Stability	Test A	Test A	Yes; of arbitrary but meaningful length.
Coefficient of Equivalence	Form 1 of Test A	Form 2 of Test A	No.
Coefficient of Equivalence and Stability	Form 1 of Test A	Form 2 of Test A	Yes, of arbitrary but meaningful length.
Coefficient of Internal Consistency	Random Half 1 of Test A	Random Half 2 of Test A	No (single administration).

Other means of determining internal consistency can be applied to single tests in which each correct response is scored one and each incorrect response zero. Reference to a procedure most applicable to teacher-made tests is given in Chapter 17.

Why are accurate, consistent measures needed? Why is the test maker so concerned about reliability? The test maker wants to produce accurate measuring instruments for the same reasons that manufacturers want precise tools for linear measurement, liquid measurement, and the like. If a measuring instrument has low reliability, it also has low concurrent and predictive validity. For example, an unreliable achievement test in reading, administered early in the first grade, is of no value in ascertaining children's present reading achievements or in predicting future achievements. Neither is an unreliable spring scale useful in determining a child's present or subsequent weight.

What conditions may result in the low reliability of a test? The most important five are as follows. First, a test may be unreliable because of poorly constructed items that do not discriminate between students who possess the knowledge, skill, or other attributes being tested and those who do not. More attention will be given in Chapter 17 to constructing tests to avoid this.

Second, even well-constructed items may be unreliable. This happens when they are so easy that most students get all of them correct or so difficult that most students cannot answer them. Items too easy or too difficult do not spread the scores of the students. Thus, a test may be reliable for 9-year-olds but quite unreliable for 7- and 11-year-olds; it may be reliable for 9-year-olds in the average achievement range but unreliable for those of exceptionally high or low achievement. Also, a test that has high reliability after a year of instruction may show low reliability if administered at the beginning of the year.

The length of the test also can be responsible for low reliability. A single spelling word or science concept is a poor and inadequate sample of a student's performance. If only ten items are given, one student may guess three or four correctly. Thus, chance would be an important determiner of the scores obtained. In a longer test of perhaps 50 items we get more dependable scores as there is a better possibility that variations accounted for by guessing cancel out. A test can, however, be made so long that students become tired or bored and respond unreliably.

Inadequate scoring methods, too, may produce low reliability. This is one of the principal weaknesses of essay tests, as we shall see in Chapter 17. Besides essay tests, other tests in which unequal weights are given to items also are subject to low reliability, particularly if the students are unaware of the unequal weights. For example, if four items of a 44-item test are scored ten points each and the other 40 are scored one point each, missing one or two of the former greatly lowers the score. It is good practice to inform students of the weights assigned to each item so that they may use the available time accordingly.

Finally, inadequate time to complete a test lowers reliability in any test where time is not a criterion of performance. This is a difficult problem to overcome, for the rate at which students respond to a test varies markedly. If time is called when the first half of the group is finished, one cannot be certain how the other half would have scored had time been allotted for them to finish.

Useability

In addition to the more theoretical considerations of validity and reliability a number of practical considerations must be taken into account. These are designated by the term *useability,* the extent to which the test can be used. The teacher must consider the amount of time required to administer the test; the amount of preparation or education required to administer, score, and interpret the test; the amount of time required to score the test; the ease of interpreting the test results after the scores are obtained; the cost; and the mechanical make-up of the test. Because these considerations are important, published tests usually provide such information in the test manual.

The best source book for finding this information is the *Mental Measurements Yearbook* series (Buros: 1938, 1940, 1949, 1953, and 1959). Often used in conjunction with *Tests in Print* (6), the yearbooks include not only descriptive information concerning many published tests, but also critical reviews of the various tests and a bibliography of articles and books which have appeared about each test.

Buros's work presents extensive coverage of standardized tests, however, we shall mention only a few most widely used.[1]

CHARACTERISTICS OF STANDARDIZED TESTS

A standardized (standard) test has four distinguishing characteristics:

1. The items have been carefully selected, and if the technical recommendations concerning requirements of an evaluative instrument (as outlined previously) are followed, systematic study has been made of the test to determine its reliability, validity, and useability. The type of validity and reliability is reported in the test manual. The items in the test constitute a systematic sample of the universe of performances or abilities which the test purports to measure.

2. A second characteristic of a standardized test is the standardized administration of the test. These instructions are in the manual for guidance of the test administrator and, as necessary, on the test copy

---

[1] Interested readers will be able to learn much about a particular test by following the procedures set forth in *Tests in Print* (pp. xxi–xxvi) and the particular yearbook of interest (in the *Fifth Mental Measurements Yearbook,* 1959, see pp. xxiv–xxvi). Most of the evaluative comments which appear about the well-known tests described in the subsequent section of this chapter are based on the authors' study of the test, the manual, and the critical review in Buros.

for the person being tested. The exact words to use in administering the test, the amount of time to allow for completion, and the type and amount of help and encouragement to give are clearly specified. For example, the *Teacher's Manual, Iowa Tests of Basic Skills* gives a brief overview of the test, and then instructions for preparing to administer the test, including advance arrangements about seating, pencils, and scratch paper; administering the entire battery of tests within a time schedule; distributing and collecting test materials; timing the tests; marking the tests properly; and preparing the pupils for taking the tests (22). (These are also important in preparing to administer a test that the teacher has constructed.)

Specific instructions for opening the first test period are given next. After these appear the instructions for pupils' putting their names on the answer sheets and for marking the answer sheets properly. The directions for administering the vocabulary test start as follows, with the first paragraph for the teacher's information and the next paragraph to be read to the pupils:

This test requires 17 minutes of actual working time. It should be administered immediately after giving instructions to pupils for marking the answer sheets, as directed in the preceding section.

(1) Begin by saying:

"We are now ready to begin work on the first test. This is a vocabulary test like the practice test we just studied. Find the section labeled Test V, Vocabulary, on your answer sheet near the top on the front side. (Pause.) Now place your answer sheet beside page 3 of your test booklet. (Pause.) We will read the directions at the top of page 3 to remind you of what you are to do. Read them silently while I read them aloud. They say:

"In each exercise, you are to decide which one of the four words has most nearly the same meaning as the word in heavy black type above them. Then, on the answer sheet, find the row of circles numbered the same as the exercise you are working on. You are to fill in the circle on the answer sheet that has the same number as the answer you picked. The sample exercise in the box at the right has already been marked correctly on the answer sheet" (22, 9).

This is followed with instructions for the test administrator to make certain that the procedures are clearly understood by the pupils and to get them started with the first test item.

3. A third feature of a standardized test, but not of all published tests, is the standardized scoring. Whether the student enters his response on the test copy or answer sheet, a scoring key is provided. For tests in which the items cannot be scored as right or wrong the instructions needed for making judgments are given. The *Handbook for Essay Tests, Level 1, College Sequential Tests of Educational Progress*

suggests that students' essays be rated from one to seven, seven being the highest rating (28). In the original scoring on which the subsequent norms were based, the readers scored on the basis of three factors: quality of thought—50 percent, style—30 percent, and conventions—20 percent.

Quality of thought was defined as "the selection and the adequacy of ideas and supplementary details, and the manner of their organization (i.e., the way in which their connections are derived from the arrangement of parts)."

Style was defined as "clearness, effectiveness, and appropriateness, including matters of structure and diction, emphasis, the *means* of transition between ideas, and the finer points of simplicity, economy, variety, and exactness of expression."

Conventions was defined as "the properties of mechanical form, including grammar and usage, capitalization, punctuation, and the mechanical aspects of the structure of sentences." A number of essays are then presented in the handbook with ratings and comments to guide the rater in making his judgments.

4. A final characteristic of standardized tests is the presence of established norms with which test scores can be interpreted in terms of grade equivalent, percentile, or other forms of derived scores. You should realize that a norm is not a standard to be reached, but a range of values or scores, constituting the performances or scores made by the group on which the test was standardized. It is well to remember that by design and definition, half the pupils in the nation will be below average. The user has the responsibility to use the norm appropriate for his students; in many cases, the development of local norms is desirable.

In the *Manual for Administrators, Supervisors, and Counselors, Iowa Tests of Basic Skills*, we find that a total of 74,174 pupils from 213 school systems in 46 states was included in the normative sample (21). This total was distributed about equally among the grades in which the tests are intended for use, namely, grades 3 through 8. The manual also gives the percent of the normative sample from the various geographical regions of the United States. Based upon this sample, tables were developed whereby the actual scores made by the pupils can be interpreted in grade equivalents or in percentile ranks under three time conditions: tests administered at the beginning of the school year, at the middle, and at the end. These grade equivalents are available for a total battery score as well as for five main tests—vocabulary, reading, language skills, work-study skills, and arithmetic skills. Figure

16.1 shows the grade equivalents in profile form of Frank Smith as a fourth-grader (broken line) and as a fifth-grader (solid line) on achievements as measured by this test.

WIDELY USED STANDARDIZED TESTS

The principal published tests administered by teachers are educational achievement tests, intellectual ability tests, often referred to as scholastic or academic aptitude tests, interest inventories, and personality inventories. Other tests and inventories are used by school psychologists and counselors and are frequently administered to the student individually; also quite a number of instruments are used for research purposes.

TABLE 16.2.

Kinds of Tests Used by Schools Using Each Kind

| | Schools | |
Tests	N	%
Achievement	492	96.9
Academic aptitude	497	97.8
Nonacademic aptitude	271	53.3
Interest inventories	433	85.2
Personality inventories	244	44.1

SOURCE: C. A. Larson, & W. H. McCreary. Testing programs and practices in California public secondary schools. *Calif. J. secondary Educ.*, 1956, **31**, 391.

Table 16.2 shows the extent of the use of tests in California junior and senior high schools that enroll students in grades 7 through 12 (20). Academic aptitude tests are most widely used, in 97.8 percent of the schools, followed closely by achievement tests, 96.9 percent. The heaviest concentration of testing was done in grades 9 and 12. This use of tests is not considered desirable or undesirable but merely indicates incidence of various types of tests used.

Individual Intelligence Tests

The three individual intelligence tests most widely used today are the Revised Stanford-Binet Intelligence Scales (32), the Wechsler

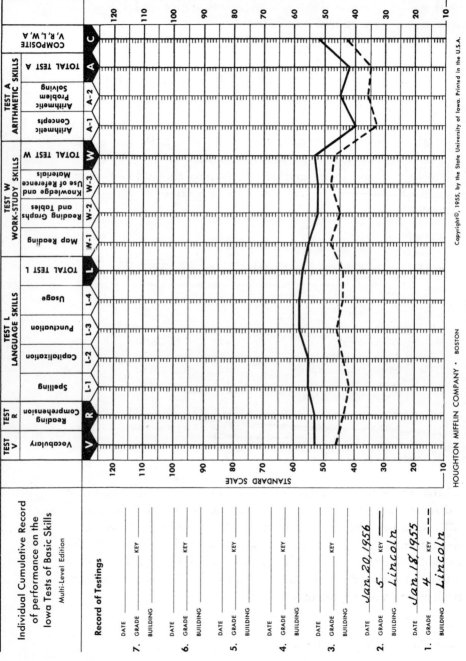

Fig. 16.1. Pupil profile chart. (E. F. Lindquist, & A. N. Hieronymus. *Teacher's Manual. Iowa Test of Basic Skills.* Boston: Houghton Mifflin, 1956, p. 19.)

Intelligence Scale for Children (**39**), and the Wechsler Adult Intelligence Scale (**40**). These tests are administered to an individual by a skilled examiner and are more reliable and valid measures of general intellectual ability than are printed tests administered to groups. However, as has been pointed out previously, general intellectual ability changes to some extent with age and is subject to environmental influences. Also, we accept the idea of group abilities and of specific intellectual abilities, as well as general intellectual ability although tests of specific abilities have not been used widely except in research. Thus, when describing the first two of these individual intelligence tests, we are not implying that intelligence is a unitary, fixed, or unchangeable characteristic. The limitations of the concept of general intellectual ability that we spoke of in earlier chapters apply to these individual tests and to the group tests of intelligence to be mentioned later in this chapter.

REVISED STANFORD-BINET INTELLIGENCE SCALE

The new 1960 Form L-M tests levels of mental development from age 2 to superior adult III, much as did the 1937 Forms L and M. However, Form L-M consists of the best items from the two previous forms. From ages 2 to 5, there are six tests at each half year of chronological age. For each chronological age thereafter to age 14, there are six tests for each year. After age 14 the levels are average adult and superior adult I, II, and III, as shown in Fig. 16.2.

The examiner administers the scale, starting at the age level at which the subject passes all six subtests, and continues upward until reaching the level at which no test is passed. For example, if an 8-year-old passes all tests for age 8, he receives 96 months mental age; for each of the six subtests at each age level passed thereafter, he receives an additional 2 months. From this, his total mental age is computed (this is his raw score); the obtained M. A. is divided by his actual chronological age (C. A.) and multiplied by 100; the resulting score is his IQ. The 8-year-old with an M. A. of 120 months has an IQ of 125 (120/96 × 100).

The older forms were based on the assumption that mental growth started slowing down at age 13 and reached its maximum at age 16. The new Form L-M is not based upon this assumption and, although the idea of mental age is not abandoned, the IQ may now be converted into a deviation IQ. (For a more complete consideration of how scores are changed into deviation scores, see Chapter 18.) The principal advantage of the deviation IQ over the older ratio IQs, M. A./C. A. ×

RECORD BOOKLET—Form L-M

Stanford-Binet Intelligence Scale

		Year	Month	Day
Name... Sex............... Date of test ....
Address... Birthdate ....
School............................... Grade......... Examiner............... Age ....
Parent.................................... [From............... Agency...............]

Birthplace........................ of father........................ of mother........................
Occupation of father........................ of mother........................

CA ....
MA ....
IQ ....

TEST SUMMARY

	Yrs.	Mos.
II		
II-6		
III		
III-6		
IV		
IV-6		
V		
VI		
VII		
VIII		
IX		
X		
XI		
XII		
XIII		
XIV		
AA		
SA I		
SA II		
SA III		
Total		
MA Score...............		
Testing time...............		

FACTORS AFFECTING TEST PERFORMANCE
OVERALL RATING OF CONDITIONS

	Optimal	Good	Average	Detrimental	Seriously detrimental

Attention
a) Absorbed by task..Easily distracted

Reactions During Test Performance
a) Normal activity level..Hyperactive or depressed
b) Initiates activity...Waits to be told
c) Quick to respond..Urging needed

Emotional Independence
a) Socially confident..Shy, reserved, reticent
b) Realistically self-confident..............Distrusts own ability or overconfident
c) Comfortable in adult company..Ill-at-ease
d) Assured...Anxious about success

Problem Solving Behavior
a) Persistent..Gives up easily or can't give up
b) Reacts to failure realistically............Withdrawing, hostile, or denying
c) Eager to continue...Seeks to terminate
d) Challenged by hard tasks.......................................Prefers only easy tasks

Independence of Examiner Support
a) Needs minimum of commendation....................Needs constant praise and encouragement

Was it hard to establish a positive relationship with this person? ....

Houghton Mifflin Company, Boston
FGHIJ-R-73210/6987654

Fig. 16.2. Record Booklet—Form L-M, Stanford-Binet Intelligence Scale (L.M. Terman & Maud A. Merrill. Revised Stanford-Binet Intelligence Scales. Boston: Houghton Mifflin, 1960.)

100, is that with the earlier forms, changes in ratio IQ occurred in the same children with age, simply because the test was inadequately scored. In older forms, a child at age 16 years 6 months received an IQ of 138 by having passed certain tests; in the new form his deviation IQ is 132 for passing the same tests. Besides getting a reliable estimate of IQ the examiner observes and rates characteristics of the child affecting test performance: attention, reactions during test performance, emotional independence, problem-solving behavior, and independence of examiner support, as shown in the excerpt from the record notebook in Fig. 16.2.

Form L-M, like the 1937 forms, is based on the assumption that intelligence is an overall or general intellectual ability which is reflected in almost any activity undertaken. The items in the test, therefore, sample a wide variety of cognitive processes and, to a more limited extent, motor abilities. Memory, verbal reasoning, mathematical reasoning, vocabulary, drawing, and motor manipulation are required to pass certain items. The earlier forms showed quite high predictive validity, and it is possible that Form L-M will yield even higher correlations with achievements in mathematics, science, language arts, and social studies.

No test is perfect. The Stanford-Binet is heavily weighted with items calling for verbal abilities; and the correlations in the older forms between the IQs of children at age 4 and of the same children at later ages have been significant and positive but of modest size, indicating that, whatever the general ability is as measured in preschool children, it is not exactly the same as during school years.

WECHSLER INTELLIGENCE SCALE FOR CHILDREN (WISC)

This individual test, like the Wechsler Adult Intelligence Scale, is not based on the idea of mental age as an acceptable measure of intelligence (39). It was the first individual intelligence test to employ deviation IQ scores. Wechsler proposed a concept of global intelligence rather than one of general intelligence. According to Wechsler:

Intelligence is the aggregate or global capacity of the individual to act purposefully, to think rationally and to deal effectively with his environment. It is global because it characterizes the individual's behavior as a whole; it is an aggregate because it is composed of elements or abilities which, though not entirely independent, are qualitatively differentiable. By measurement of these abilities, we ultimately evaluate intelligence. But intelligence is not identical with the mere sum of these abilities, however inclusive. There are three important reasons for this: (1) The ultimate products of intelligent behavior are not only a function of the number of abilities or their quality but also of the way in which they are combined, that is, upon their configuration. (2) Factors other than intellectual ability, for example, those of drive and incentive, enter into intelligent behavior. (3) Finally, while different orders of intelligent behavior may require varying degrees of intellectual ability, an excess of any given ability may add relatively little to the effectivenesses of the behavior as a whole. It would seem that, so far as general intelligence is concerned, intellectual ability, as such, merely enters as a necessary minimum. Thus, to act intelligently, one must be able to recall numerous items, i.e., have a retentive memory. But beyond a certain point this ability will not help much in coping with life situations successfully. This is true of even more important capacities, such as the ability to reason, particularly when specialized. The unusual reasoning abilities of the mathematician are more highly correlated with the thing that we ultimately measure as intelligence than sheer memory is, but possession of this ability is no surety that behavior as a whole will be very intelligent in the sense above defined. Every reader will be able to recall persons of high intellectual ability in some particular field, whom they would unhesitatingly characterize as below average in general intelligence (**37**, 3–4).

The WISC consists of 12 main tests which are divided into two subgroups, called "Verbal" and "Performance." The six Verbal tests are information, comprehension, arithmetic, similarities, vocabulary, and digit span; the six Performance tests are picture completion, picture arrangement, block design, object assembly, coding, and mazes. The digit span and maze tests are supplementary and are not used with normal subjects. According to Wechsler:

Most of the verbal tests correlate better with each other than with tests of the performance group, and vice versa. But, while the tests identified as verbal and performance differ as the labels indicate, they each tap other factors, among them non-intellective ones, which cut across the groups to produce other classifications or categories that are equally important to consider in evaluating the individual's performance (**38**, 5).

The skilled examiner administers the test to the individual child according to standardized instructions and scores according to standardized procedures. The raw scores in each subtest are changed to scaled scores, using appropriate tables for children of various chronological ages, starting at 5 years and proceeding in three-month steps to 15 years 11 months. The Verbal score is secured by adding the five scaled scores of the verbal tests; the Performance score is the sum of the five performance tests; and the full-scale score is the sum of the Verbal score and the Performance score. The examiner then uses appropriate tables to ascertain the Verbal IQ, Performance IQ, and full-scale IQ. Fig. 16.3 is the WISC Record Form for entering results of the test.

The WISC is easier to administer than the Stanford-Binet, but its

WISC RECORD FORM

NAME_____AGE____SEX___

ADDRESS_____

PARENT'S NAME_____

SCHOOL_____GRADE_____

REFERRED BY_____

	Raw Score	Scaled Score
VERBAL TESTS		
Information	____	____
Comprehension	____	____
Arithmetic	____	____
Similarities	____	____
Vocabulary	____	____
(Digit Span)	____	____
Sum of Verbal Tests		____
PERFORMANCE TESTS		
Picture Completion	____	____
Picture Arrangement	____	____
Block Design	____	____
Object Assembly	____	____
Coding	____	____
(Mazes)	____	____
Sum of Performance Tests		____

	Year Month Day		Scaled Score	IQ
Date Tested	____ ____ ____	Verbal Scale	____*	____
Date of Birth	____ ____ ____	Performance Scale	____*	____
Age	____ ____ ____	Full Scale	____	____
		*Prorated if necessary		

NOTES

_____
Examiner

Printed in U. S. A.   0130

57-200 AS

Fig. 16.3. WISC record form. (D. Wechsler. Wechsler Intelligence Scale for Children. New York: Psychological Corporation, 1949. Reproduced by permission. Copyright © 1949, The Psychological Corporation, New York, N.Y. All rights reserved.

scoring requires more sensitive judgments. The WISC yields considerably lower IQs, especially at 115 and above, than did the older forms of the Stanford-Binet. The Verbal IQ correlates higher with school achievements than does the Performance IQ; and considerable research is still needed to interpret the large differences found occasionally between Verbal IQ and Performance IQ in some subjects. It has been suggested that a pupil with a language problem will score markedly

597

higher on the Performance IQ while the occurrence of the reverse situation (Verbal IQ considerably higher than Performance IQ) might be indicative of emotional blocking (8).

One can plot a profile of the ten subtest scores. Some clinicians find the profile useful in diagnosis of brain injury, personality disorders, and the like; for this reason the WISC is used widely in clinical settings. The WISC represents an important contribution in the field of individual testing and appraisal, meriting equal consideration with the Stanford-Binet.

Group Tests of General Intellectual Ability

Group tests of general intellectual ability, sometimes called "scholastic aptitude" and "mental ability," are used far more extensively in schools after grade 1 than are individual tests. The group tests do not require specially trained testers. Many group tests have predictive validity for certain school objectives equally as high as the Stanford-Binet and Wechsler tests.

The administration of any group test requires that each student taking it understands the directions, wants to do his best, and is physically and emotionally in good condition. In small classroom groups, the tester, usually the teacher, can observe each student fairly well to see that these conditions are met. When these tests are administered to large groups, it is more difficult to make certain that the three conditions are met. When a purpose of testing is to secure a more thorough understanding of a student, an individual intelligence test is far superior to group tests. Also, it is obvious that group verbal tests are not as useful as individual tests with younger children who cannot read, children with any sort of severe handicap, and any person who had not had the opportunity to learn to use the English language.

Group tests of intellectual ability for use in school situations have been developed primarily to help make two types of decisions—what the student is ready to learn now and how well he will achieve in the future, in school or in an occupation. In many cases, educational achievement tests give more direct answers to these questions, so that group intellectual ability tests are valuable supplements to achievement testing and provide good information in the absence of achievement testing. The achievement battery requires much more administration time than the intellectual ability test.

To what extent are IQs from different group tests comparable? Some tests yield higher IQs than others for all students, for the higher-IQ group only, or for the lower-IQ group only. Reports of differences among several commonly used group tests for small samples of subjects are available and may be consulted by school administrators. However, a better way for a large school system to determine the best testing program is to set up carefully designed studies to ascertain testing needs. Further, the increasing (and desirable) tendency of test makers and publishers is to include in the test manual the necessary data by which raw scores or IQs can be changed to percentile scores or other meaningful deviation scores. Table 16.3, part of a larger table from the *Examiner's Manual, California Short-Form Test of Mental Maturity, Level 2, 1963, S-Form,* shows the percentile equivalents for the four main subtests, the language and nonlanguage parts of the test, and total. For example, raw scores of 22 to 24 in language and of 27 to 29 in nonlanguage are equivalent to the fiftieth percentile for children of 114 to 119 months. Other tables and descriptions in the same manual show how to use raw scores to arrive at standard scores, stanines, mental age, IQ, grade equivalent, and how to change IQ to percentile scores. The important point is that, on the other group tests also, the percentile scores are more comparable from one test to another than are the IQs.

Items used in group tests of intellectual ability vary widely. Some are purely measures of educational outcomes which supposedly all pupils have had equal opportunity to learn; other items are intended to be novel, met for the first time in the test. The five sample items in Fig. 16.4 taken from the Lorge-Thorndike Intelligence Test, Form 1, Levels A-H, are indicative of the type of item used in verbal group tests of intelligence for elementary school pupils.

There are several other notable group tests of general intellectual ability. Among them are the College Qualifications Test (CQT), the Cooperative School and College Ability Tests (SCAT), the Henmon-Nelson Tests of Mental Ability, the Kuhlmann-Anderson Intelligence Tests, the Miller Analogies Test, and the SRA Tests of Educational Ability. Although certain tests yield separate subtest scores, any test which combines all the subtest scores by any method is put in this category, for the total is a summary measure of general intellectual ability.

Aptitude Tests

Test makers and others have been concerned for years with devising tests that will be better than the general intellectual ability tests in pre-

TABLE 16.3.

Percentile Norms—California Short-Form Test of Mental Maturity; Level 2, 1963 S-Form (Age: 9 yrs. 6 mos.–9 yrs. 11 mos.)[a]

Per-centile	Factor				Section		
	Logical Reasoning	Numerical Reasoning	Verbal Concepts	Memory	Language	Non-Language	Total
99	42+	22+	25	25	53+	51+	99+
98	40–41	21	24	24	50–52	49–50	95–98
95	36–39	17–20	20–23	20–23	43–49	43–48	83–94
90	33–35	15–16	17–19	18–19	38–42	39–42	74–82
80	30–32	12–14	15–16	15–17	32–37	35–38	65–73
70	28–29	11	13–14	13–14	28–31	32–34	59–64
60	26–27	9–10	12	12	25–27	30–31	54–58
50	24–25	7–8	10–11	10–11	22–24	27–29	48–53
40	22–23	6	8–9	8–9	19–21	24–26	43–47
30	20–21	4–5	7	6–7	15–18	22–23	37–42
20	16–19	2–3	4–6	4–5	10–14	17–21	28–36
10	13–15	1	1–3	1–3	4–9	13–16	19–27
5	9–12	—	—	—	1–3	7–12	7–18
2	8	—	—	—	—	6	3–6
1	7–	—	—	—	—	5–	2–

[a] Values in all columns (except percentile) are in raw score units.

SOURCE: Adapted from *Examiner's Manual, California Short-Form Test of Mental Maturity, Level 2, 1963 S-Form*, Monterey, California: California Test Bureau.

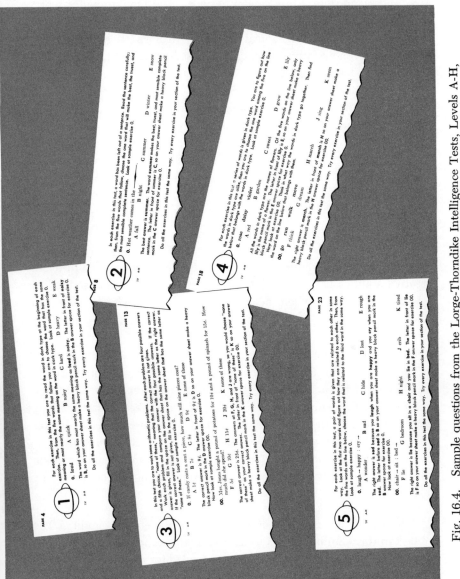

Fig. 16.4. Sample questions from the Lorge-Thorndike Intelligence Tests, Levels A–H, Form 1. (I. Lorge, R. L. Thorndike, & Elizabeth Hagen. The Lorge-Thorndike Intelligence Tests. Boston: Houghton Mifflin, 1964, pp. 4, 8, 13, 18, and 23. Copyright © 1964 by Houghton Mifflin Company. All rights reserved. Reprinted by permission of the publisher.)

dicting success in the separate subjects, vocations, and the fine arts.

Most notable in this area are the Differential Aptitude Tests (DAT) and the General Aptitude Test Battery (GATB), the latter used by the U.S., and many state, Employment Services. The DAT provides scores for eight factors: verbal reasoning, numerical ability, abstract reasoning, space relations, mechanical speed, clerical speed and accuracy, and two vocabulary scores (spelling and sentences) (3). The GATB, on the other hand, provides measurements for nine abilities: general reasoning ability, vocabulary, numerical aptitude, spatial aptitude, form perception, clerical perception, motor coordination, finger dexterity, and manual dexterity (12). Other tests in this category are the Meier Art Judgment Test, the Employer Aptitude Survey, the Flanagan Aptitude Classification Tests, the Holzinger-Crowder Unifactor Tests, the Multiple Aptitude Tests, and the SRA Primary Mental Abilities Test.

Experimental Tests of Creativity

In recent years, a large number of tests which purport to measure creative abilities have been devised. A few of these are described in this section and the whole field of testing for creativity is evaluated briefly.

THE KIT OF REFERENCE TESTS FOR COGNITIVE FACTORS

The complete Kit of Reference Tests for Cognitive Factors purports to measure 24 factors; however, the tests are all in experimental form, not intended for general use (18). Many of the 24 factors have already been identified in the structure of intellect (13), discussed in Chapter 8. Four tests from the kit have been used extensively in studies of creativity and are now described briefly. More complete information concerning each is given in a manual accompanying the copies of the tests (11).

1. Alternate Uses is a test of semantic spontaneous flexibility. The task in this Guilford test is to list different uses for common objects, such as a chair and shoe. The test is intended for grades 6 through 16.
2. Associations IV is a test of associational fluency. The task in this Guilford test is to produce a word that is associated with both the two stimulus words but which is related to the two stimulus words in different ways. For example,

jewelry. . . . . bell.

The keyed response is *ring*. The test is listed as suitable for grades 10 through 16.

3. Plot Titles is a test of originality. The task is to write relevant and clever titles for a given story plot. Responses—titles—are categorized as high descriptive, low descriptive, high commentary, and low commentary. Only the "highs" are considered to indicate originality. The test is listed as suitable for grades 10 through 16.

4. Consequences is also a test of originality. The task is to list the consequences of certain hypothetical occurrences or situations. The test is suitable for grades 10 through 16.

THE TORRANCE COMPENDIUM

In these creativity tests, a number of tasks appear in more than one test (33, 34, 35). Therefore, some of the tasks are described rather than the tests:

1. Picture Construction. Here the respondent uses a shaped piece of colored paper as the nucleus for a drawing. He has ten minutes to draw a picture or object "that no one else will think of" incorporating the piece of colored paper and to title his drawing.

2. Circles. This task requires the respondent to draw pictures using circles as the main part of the picture. Originality is stressed. A similar task uses squares instead of circles. Ten minutes are allowed.

3. Product Improvement. This task presents a picture of a stuffed animal and allows the pupil ten minutes to list "the cleverest, most interesting and unusual ways" he can think of for changing the product to make it more fun to play with as a toy, regardless of cost.

4. Unusual Uses. The respondent is given ten minutes to list "interesting and unusual uses" for a common object, such as a tin can or a cardboard box.

5. Just Suppose. Here the respondent is asked to guess what would happen if a certain situation occurred; for example, "Just suppose clouds had strings attached to them which hang down to earth. What would happen?" Five minutes are allowed for the test.

6. Creative Writing. The respondent chooses one of ten topics that are given; for example, "The duck that doesn't quack" or "The flying monkey." He is "to write the most interesting and exciting story" he can compose on the topic. Twenty minutes are given.

Responses to these tasks are scored according to the specified instructions and the tasks, singly or in combination, yield four factors of divergent thinking—fluency, flexibility, originality, and elaboration.

FLANAGAN INGENUITY TEST

This test is part of the FACT (Flanagan Aptitude Clasification Test) Battery (9). Recall from Chapter 8 that Flanagan defines *ingenuity* as involving the invention or discovery of a solution to a problem. The manual for the test states:

> The items in this test require the examinee to find "ingenious" solutions that are: (1) practical and useful solutions to a real problem; (2) clever, unusually fitting, and clearly better than solutions which might be expected from typical persons working on these problems; and (3) novel in the sense of providing a surprisingly good solution to the special problem involved (versus one which could be obtained by logical, routine, or mechanical process) (**10**, 3).

The test consists of 24 items; the time limit is 24 minutes. Each item consists of a situation with the last sentence left uncompleted. The respondent completes the last sentence by "ingeniously solving the problem" and selecting the correct response. The responses are normally just one word, with the first and last letters furnished. A sample item is given below for the reader's information:

> A hostess for a children's party wanted to serve ice cream in an interesting manner, and she decided to make a clown for each child. She placed a ball of ice cream to represent the clown's head on a round cookie which served for a collar, and on top of this she inverted a

a. t __ __ e
b. u __ __ i
c. r __ __ s
d. c __ __ e
e. t __ __ r

The keyed response is d ("cone"). The score on the test is the total number of correct responses.

REMOTE ASSOCIATES TEST

This test (abbreviated RAT) was developed by Mednick and was possibly so named to win the favor of experimental psychologists. The discussion of this test is based on two articles—Houston, and Mednick (16) and Mednick (25). A good description of the test is stated thus:

> Several words from mutually distant associative clusters must be presented to the subject; his task must be to provide mediating links between them. Further, (a factor of extreme importance), the mediating link must be strictly associative rather than being of a sort that follows elaborate rules of logic, concept formation, or problem solving. In their final (or at least present) form, the test items consist of sets of three words drawn from mutually remote associative clusters (**25**, 227).

Two forms exist for the college level, each consisting of 30 items. The time limit is 40 minutes. Two examples of items are given below:

> Example a: Surprise   line   birthday
> Example b: Wheel   electric   high

The keyed answers are "party" and "chair" (**25**, 227).

ADEQUACY OF TESTS OF CREATIVITY

The preceding tests of creativity have four weaknesses in general. Reliability is usually low. They have not been carefully validated against external criteria of validity; thus, it is uncertain how well the test scores correlate with actual creativity. The tests are timed; in general, timed tests do not enable all respondents to manifest all their abilities. Finally, the number of responses on some tests is the score; this emphasizes quantity, perhaps at the expense of quality. Although creativity tests in general have these weaknesses, most of them also are clearly indicated by the publisher as experimental, not for general use in the schools.

Should they even be used in experiments on creativity? MacKinnon's conception of creativity forced him ". . . to reject as indicators or criteria of creativeness the performance of individuals on so called tests of creativity" because ". . . they fail to reveal the extent to which the subject faced with real life problems is likely to come up with solutions that are novel and adaptive and which he will be motivated to apply in all of their ramifications" (**24**, 485).

We do not feel that modern tests of creativity should be discarded; however, they must be improved. In some respects, the test movement in creativity today is comparable to that in intelligence testing a half century ago. An attempt is being made now as then to measure something that is not clearly defined. The early years of creative testing are characterized by conflicting and confusing results similar to the early years of intelligence testing. Especially critical are matters of reliability and validity. Until test scores indicate more reliable and more valid estimates of actual creativity, they cannot be interpreted reliably.

Tests of Educational Achievement

Educational achievement tests are designed to measure the extent to which pupils have acquired various outcomes of instruction. As suggested in Chapters 7 through 11, a large number of these outcomes in any subject field at any school level can be stated as facts, concepts, problem-solving abilities, and psychomotor and other skills. Further, attitudes, values, interests, motives, and methods of adjustment also are learned in school. The present discussion is devoted primarily to tests which measure outcomes in the cognitive domain; however, the teacher or any other person selecting tests of educational achievement should make certain of the relationship between the objectives of instruction and what is measured by the achievement test. If, for example, one wishes to ascertain the more specific concepts and processes in arithmetic related to a child's experiencing difficulty in reading or arithmetic, he will use a specially designed diagnostic test, not a general achievement test in reading or arithmetic. Similarly, if one wishes to ascertain the extent to which problem-solving abilities and concepts are being acquired in mathematics, one does not use a test which includes only computational exercises.

The early educational achievement tests measured knowledge and routine skills closely related to specific subject fields; they gave little attention to such outcomes as problem-solving abilities, understanding of principles, application of principles or knowledge, or evaluation of facts. More recent tests are attempting to measure the latter type of outcomes. However, the best tests currently available in any subject field or fields (and there are many excellent ones) should not be treated as providing complete evidence about the quality or effectiveness of the educational program of a school, of a teacher's work in the school, or as an adequate basis for deciding what the objectives of instruction should be. Instead, they provide some evidence which fits into a balanced continuous evaluation program in which the objectives of education are stated clearly and a variety of teacher judgments and informal evaluation procedures also is used. In general, standardized achievement tests have been used too little to provide understanding of a pupil's present achievements and too much to categorize pupils and for grading.

Of all types of available group tests, achievement tests are the most valuable for use in a variety of school situations. They provide more direct information about each child's performances and abilities in relation to the school's central objectives than do any other currently available type of test, including those discussed in the previous sections. Further, one of the better sources of information to which a teacher can turn for finding models of well-constructed achievement test items is printed tests. Consider for example, the items in Fig. 16.5 taken from Word Meaning, Arithmetic Applications, Social Studies (Part B: Study Skills), and Science tests of the Stanford Achievement

TEST 1: Word Meaning

DIRECTIONS: Read the beginning part of each sentence and the words under it. Decide which of the answers given is *best*. Look at the answer spaces at the right or on your answer sheet (if you have one). Fill in the space which has the same number as the word you have chosen.

SAMPLES

A The name of a color is —

1 farm   3 red
2 milk   4 pet   A ○ ○ ● ○ (1 2 3 4)

B The day that comes after Monday is —

5 Sunday   7 Wednesday
6 Tuesday   8 Saturday   B ○ ○ ○ ○ (5 6 7 8)

11 The giving up of something which is wanted or needed is —

1 a sacrifice   3 a benefit
2 a relief   4 an assistance   11 ○ ○ ○ ○ (1 2 3 4)

12 A business transaction in which one gains by selling is said to be —

5 miserable   7 bankruptcy
6 penurious   8 profitable   12 ○ ○ ○ ○ (5 6 7 8)

13 A group of people gathered for religious worship is called a —

1 colony   3 congregation
2 convention   4 committee   13 ○ ○ ○ ○ (1 2 3 4)

TEST 7: Arithmetic Applications

DIRECTIONS: Work each problem. Then look at the possible answers under the problem and see if your answer is given. If it is, fill in the answer space at the right or on your answer sheet (if you have one) which has the same letter as the answer you have chosen. If your answer is not given, fill in the space which has the same letter as the letter beside NG (which means "not given"). If NG is not listed for an example, one of the given answers is the correct answer. There is no sales tax in any problem on the test unless you are told otherwise. Use a separate sheet of paper for all figuring.

1 One hundred fifty children come to school on three buses. What is the average number of children on a bus?

a 30   b 50   c 100   d 450   e NG   1 ○ ○ ○ ○ ○ (a b c d e)

2 Candy bars are 6 for 25¢. How many could you buy for $1.00?

f 12   g 30   h 24   i 60   j NG   2 ○ ○ ○ ○ ○ (f g h i j)

3 Adults' tickets are 90¢ and children's are 35¢. How much will 3 children's and 2 adults' tickets cost?

a $2.85   b $1.25   c $1.80   d $1.05   e NG   3 ○ ○ ○ ○ ○ (a b c d e)

TEST 8: Social Studies (Continued)   Part B: Study Skills

DIRECTIONS: Look at each graph or map and read the questions that go with it. Decide which of the answers given is *best*. Then fill in the answer space which has the same number as the answer you have chosen.

Use the table below in answering questions 46–50

The Great Lakes

Name of Lake	Area in Square Miles	Length in Miles	Maximum Depth in Feet	Elevation in Feet
Erie	9,940	241	210	572
Huron	23,010	206	750	581
Michigan	22,400	321	923	581
Ontario	7,540	193	778	246
Superior	31,820	383	1,302	622

46 The deepest lake is —

1 Huron   3 Ontario
2 Michigan   4 Superior   46 ○ ○ ○ ○ (1 2 3 4)

47 What is the length in miles of Lake Ontario?

5 7540   6 193   7 778   8 246   47 ○ ○ ○ ○ (5 6 7 8)

48 The lake with the greatest elevation is also —

1 smaller than Lake Erie
2 more shallow than Lake Michigan
3 shorter than Lake Huron
4 the largest, the longest, and the deepest   48 ○ ○ ○ ○ (1 2 3 4)

49 How many lakes have a greater elevation than Lake Huron?

5 none   6 one   7 two   8 three   49 ○ ○ ○ ○ (5 6 7 8)

50 How many lakes are both deeper and larger in area than Lake Michigan?

1 none   2 one   3 two   4 three   50 ○ ○ ○ ○ (1 2 3 4)

TEST 9: Science

DIRECTIONS: Read each question. Decide which of the answers given below is *best*. Look at the answer spaces at the right or on your answer sheet (if you have one). Fill in the space which has the same number as the answer you have chosen.

SAMPLE

A As water boils, it changes to —

1 ice   3 steam
2 dew   4 snow   A ○ ○ ● ○ (1 2 3 4)

1

SALT WATER   FRESH WATER

A girl wants to see if her boats float higher in salt water than in fresh water. To be sure of the answer, the boats must be —

1 in the same kind of water
2 turned the other way
3 the same color
4 the same size   1 ○ ○ ○ ○ (1 2 3 4)

6 The metal cover of a jelly jar is too tight to twist off. What would be *best* to do next?

5 break the jar carefully at the bottom
6 use a can opener to open the top
7 let hot water run on the cover and try again
8 put the jar in a cold place for a while and try again   6 ○ ○ ○ ○ (5 6 7 8)

7 Scientists most often learn new facts by —

1 working alone
2 debating with their friends
3 making observations and doing experiments
4 writing down everything they do   7 ○ ○ ○ ○ (1 2 3 4)

8 Which group of foods would give the widest range of necessary food values?

5 meat, vegetables, fruit
6 meat, eggs, beans
7 milk, ice cream, vegetables
8 rice, potatoes, fruit   8 ○ ○ ○ ○ (5 6 7 8)

Fig. 16.5. Sample questions from the Stanford Achievement Test, Form W Intermediate I. (T. L. Kelley, R. Madden, E. F. Gardner, & H. Rudman. Stanford Achievement Test, Intermediate II Complete Battery: Form W. Copyright 1964 by Harcourt, Brace and World, Inc., New York. Copyright in Great Britain. All rights reserved. Reproduced by permission.)

Test. Other widely used achievement batteries are the California Achievement Tests, the Iowa Tests of Educational Development, the Metropolitan Achievement Tests, the SRA Achievement Series, and the Sequential Tests of Educational Progress (STEP). The subtests in most achievement batteries also are available as separate tests or can be administered separately from a complete booklet. A large number and wide variety of tests are published as separates in the usual junior and senior high school subjects.

Interest Inventories

Interests tend to become stable during later adolescence. Also, expressed interest in an immediate activity in the classroom provides a favorable motivational set toward the activity. Though a teacher can readily ascertain the interests of students in immediate classroom activities, deciding which of many possible courses of study and occupations will be of interest over a period of time is a more difficult task. Interest inventories have been developed mainly to facilitate this type of educational and vocational decision making.

In an interest inventory of many items, the respondent in a short time period checks his preferences for a large number of activities. In this manner, the preferences of the respondent to many activities can be compared with those of other individuals in the standardization populations. The administration of interest inventories is fully as standardized as administration of educational achievement tests. However, interpretation of interest inventories is not standardized, especially for junior and senior high school students who are not yet in adult occupations and whose interests are still in the formative stage. This will become more apparent in the subsequent discussion of two notable inventories—the Strong Vocational Interest Blanks and the Kuder Preference Record.

The Strong Vocational Interest Blank for Men, Revised (29) is intended for use with males, age 17 and over. There are 57 scoring scales (47 occupations, 6 occupational group scales, and 4 nonvocational scales). The clusters for the 47 occupations and 6 occupational groups are as follows:

Group I: artist, psychologist, architect, physician, psychiatrist, osteopath, dentist, veterinarian (group scale)
Group II: physicist, chemist, mathematician, engineer (group scale)
Group III: production manager

Group IV: farmer, carpenter, printer, mathematics–physical science teacher, policeman, forest service man, army officer, aviator

Group V: Y.M.C.A. physical director, personnel manager, public administrator, vocational counselor, Y.M.C.A. secretary, social science high school teacher, city school superintendent, minister, social worker (group scale)

Group VI: music performer, music teacher

Group VII: certified public accountant

Group VIII: senior C.P.A., accountant, office worker, purchasing agent, banker, mortician, pharmacist (group scale)

Group IX: sales manager, real estate salesman, life insurance salesman (group scale)

Group X: advertising man, lawyer, author-journalist (group scale)

Group XI: president of manufacturing concern

The four nonvocational scales are occupational level, masculinity–femininity, specialization level, and interest maturity.

In the Blank for Men the respondent encircles L to indicate a like for, I to indicate indifferent to, and D to indicate dislike for 400 activities incorporated in as many items, four of which are:

1. Actor (not movie)	L	I	D
9. Author of novel	L	I	D
10. Author of technical book	L	I	D
11. Auto salesman	L	I	D
	(29, 2)		

The responses, usually on IBM Answer Sheets, are subsequently scored at various centers, where they can be processed electronically. In turn, the obtained scores are keyed according to the various occupational and other categories previously reported.

The Strong Vocational Interest Blank for Women, Revised (30) is for age 17 and over and has 28 occupational scales and 1 nonvocational scale as follows: artist, author, librarian, English teacher, social worker, psychologist, social science teacher, Y.W.C.A. secretary, lawyer, life insurance saleswoman, buyer, business education teacher, office worker, stenographer–secretary, housewife, elementary teacher, music performer, music teacher, home economics teacher, dietitian, college physical education teacher, high school physical education teacher, occupational therapist, nurse, mathematics–science teacher, dentist, laboratory technician, physician, and masculinity–femininity.

These Strong Vocational Interest Blanks have been widely used and the scoring keys, during the many years of continuous use and revision, were developed on the basis of correlations between the inventory scores and criteria. The criteria were drawn from responses of successful adults in the various occupations. This selection of items by trial-and-confirmation procedures enabled Strong to relate expressed preferences of respondents to the preferences of successful adults in specific occupations and in broad groups of occupations listed above.

Note that one blank is for males and another for females. Certain fields of teaching are listed for both males and females; some, only for males; others, only for females. Though sex differences in interests are pronounced, males and females in the same teaching field, for example, mathematics, have more similar occupational interests than do males in architecture and males in Y.M.C.A. positions. Beyond this also, younger females, particularly, have a broad global interest in marriage and family that is quite different from interests of males; this has been a persistent and troublesome problem in devising and validating interest inventories for use with females (36).

The Kuder Preference Record–Vocational, Form CH (19), is intended for use in Grades 9–16 and with adults. Form CH yields scores related to 10 clusters of occupational interests: outdoor, mechanical, computational, scientific, persuasive, artistic, literary, musical, social service, and clerical. The eleventh scale is masculinity–femininity. Not to be confused with this vocational inventory are Form A, a personality scale, and Forms D and DD, intended to yield scores related to more specific vocations.

Kuder developed his inventory by a procedure almost opposite to that of Strong. As stated earlier, Strong keyed his inventory by relating it to interests of successful persons in various occupations. He was not concerned whether a group of items were interrelated but with how successful persons responded to items. Kuder began with factor analysis of items to identify clusters of interests, and then organized these related items into the ten descriptive scales noted above. Thus, the early scales were not validated against the interests of adults in the occupational fields. Many subsequent studies of these relationships have been completed and the inventory scores can be related to more specific vocations.

The items are so arranged that the respondent indicates which activity in a group of three he likes most and which he dislikes most (Fig. 16.6).

The best use of the Kuder scores and profiles is to treat them as one source of information for helping the student to understand himself

KUDER PREFERENCE RECORD
VOCATIONAL
FORM CH

Prepared by **G. Frederic Kuder**, Editor, *Educational and Psychological Measurement*

Professor of Psychology, Duke University

This blank is used for obtaining a record of your preferences. It is not a test. There are no right or wrong answers. An answer is right if it is true of you.

A number of activities are listed in groups of three. Read over the three activities in each group. Decide which of the three activities you like **most**. There are two circles on the same line as this activity. Punch a hole with the pin through the left-hand circle following this activity. Then decide which activity you like **least** and punch a hole through the right-hand circle of the two circles following this activity.

In the examples below, the person answering has indicated for the first group of three activities, that he would usually like to **visit a museum most**, and **browse in a library least**. In the second group of three activities he has indicated he would ordinarily like to **collect autographs most** and **collect butterflies least**.

EXAMPLES

Put your answers to these questions in column O.

P.   Visit an art gallery . . . .

Q.   Browse in a library . . . .   ←LEAST

R.   Visit a museum . . . .   MOST→

S.   Collect autographs . . . .   MOST→

T.   Collect coins . . . .

U.   Collect butterflies . . . .   ←LEAST

Some of the activities involve preparation and training. In such cases, please suppose that you could first have the necessary training. Do not choose an activity merely because it is new or unusual. Choose what you would like to do if you were equally familiar with all of the activities.

In some cases you may like all three activities in a group. In other cases you may find all three activities unpleasant. Please show what your first and last choices would be, however, if you *had* to choose.

Some activities may seem trivial or foolish. Please indicate your choices, anyway, for all of the groups. Otherwise we cannot give you a complete report. Your answers will be kept strictly confidential.

Please do not spend a lot of time on one group. Put down your first reaction and go on. Do not discuss the activities with anyone. An answer is worthless unless it is your own judgment.

If you want to change an answer, punch two more holes close to the answer you wish to change; then punch the new answer in the usual way. Hold the pin straight up and down when you punch your answers.

Now go ahead with the activities on the next page.

Published by SCIENCE RESEARCH ASSOCIATES, 259 East Erie Street, Chicago 11, Illinois
Copyright under International Copyright Union. All rights reserved under Fourth International
American Convention (1910). Copyright 1948, by G. Frederic Kuder. Copyright 1948 in Canada.
Registered under Patent Nos. 1,500,777 and 2,052,369. Printed in the U.S.A.
To Reorder Use Code Number 7-291

Fig. 16.6.   The Kuder vocational interest form. Note the range of activities covered as illustrated in the practice examples. (G. F. Kuder. Kuder Preference Record—Vocational, Form CH. Chicago: Science Research Associates, 1948.)

better in planning a high school and perhaps a post-high-school program of study or work. At present, school people properly give much more weight to results from achievement and intellectual ability tests than to results from interest inventories in planning high school courses with the students.

Other interest inventories published in the United States which require more caution in interpretation than the previous two are the Brainard Occupational Preference Inventory, the Inventory of Occupational Interests, and the Occupational Interest Inventory (Lee-Thorpe).

Personality Inventories and Check Lists

Some theorists classify interest and intelligence as personality traits. In Chapter 10, such outcomes of learning as interests, motives, attitudes, values, and personality integration were put in the affective domain rather than in the intellectual or psychomotor. Also, it was pointed out that outcomes in the affective domain are related to efficiency of learning in the cognitive and psychomotor domains, and vice versa.

Problems in personality testing are presented by Cronbach, including such matters as the respondent's faking the answers, the concealing of the purpose of the test from the respondent, and ethical issues in personality testing. This last is of highest importance. Cronbach concludes:

> There remains the question of using personality tests when the tester has authority over the person tested. The psychologist diagnosing mental patients, the military psychologist, or the school teacher can enforce tests on his charges. The standards with regard to such practice probably should vary from institution to institution. In general, it seems that subtle tests may properly be used if they are valid and relevant in making decisions which would otherwise rest on less valid information. The tester should avoid misrepresentation in giving the tests. For example, it is quite improper to study an individual's beliefs under the guise of an opinion poll. Test records made for employee counseling should never be made available to the employee's superior (8, 462).

As we have become increasingly aware of and concerned with personality integration, many published tests have appeared to appraise personality traits, personality organization, personal and social problems, personal and social adjustment, and other affective characteristics. Some of the more notable published instruments are described to present the sweep of this movement at all age levels. Considerable attention is given to instruments used in research in teacher education, particularly those mentioned earlier in Chapters 5 and 6.

The publishers of personality tests intend them to be used primarily in understanding and guiding the child more effectively. In this respect, it should be noted that the meaning of these test results is not as clear as results from intelligence and achievement tests; we have not yet defined personality as clearly as we have intellectual abilities and educational achievements. The school system which uses personality inventories would do well to carry out longitudinal research to ascertain the meaning of the scores and profiles.

The Minnesota Multiphasic Personality Inventory or MMPI (14) has status among personal inventories similar to that of the Strong Vocational Interest Blanks in the field of interest testing and the Stanford-Binet Intelligence Scale in the field of general intellectual ability. Even so, the MMPI is not generally considered sufficiently valid in itself to provide a completely accurate diagnosis of an individual's personality or to predict adjustment of individuals over a period of time. At present, research with college students is in progress in the attempt to find patterns of scores which may serve such purposes as discriminating groups of freshmen who will graduate, who will be subsequently successful in a career, and who need immediate counseling or other therapy.

The MMPI is intended for use with individuals of age 16 and over; forms are available for administration to individuals and to groups. The original psychiatric scales incorporated in the Inventory and still used are hypochondriasis, depression, hysteria, psychopathic deviate, masculinity and femininity, paranoia, psychasthenia, schizophrenia, and hypomania. Besides these nine scales, there are four correction or control scores: a ? score indicates the total number of items omitted by the respondent; the L score indicates the total number of improbable answers given; the F score acts as a check on the validity of the whole record; and the K score is a correction key applied to certain of the psychiatric scale scores.

The instructions suggest that each statement be read and marked as being "true as applied to you" or "false as applied to you." Every statement is to be responded to; however, "If a statement does not apply to you or if it is something that you don't know about, make no mark on the answer sheet." Four items show the style but do not sample the content of the 561 items included in the 1943 form:

1. I like mechanics magazines.
100. I have met problems so full of possibilities that I have been unable to make up my mind about them.
200. There are persons who are trying to steal my thoughts and ideas.
300. There never was a time in my life when I liked to play with dolls.

Another personality instrument, referred to in Chapter 5, is the Minnesota Teacher Attitude Inventory which is now described. The MTAI, consists of 150 statements designed to sample opinions of prospective teachers and other school personnel about teacher–pupil relations (7). About 30 minutes are required for administration, and scoring is simple. To each statement, the person responds with: strongly agree, agree, undecided or uncertain, disagree, or strongly disagree. Four items are:

1. Most children are obedient.
2. Pupils who "act smart" probably have too high an opinion of themselves.
5. Teaching never gets monotonous.
14. Young people are difficult to understand these days.

This inventory is one of the few instruments designed to measure attitudes in relation to vocational success. The scoring is standardized and, on the basis of the scores obtained, one uses tables to convert raw scores to percentile ranks for such populations as beginning education majors, graduating education seniors, experienced elementary teachers, and experienced secondary teachers. The concurrent validity as well as the scoring procedures are based upon responses of experienced teachers who were judged to show varying degrees of excellence in the management of teacher–pupil relations. Though this is the case, there are many disagreements about desirable attitudes toward various teacher–pupil relations. The school administrator or other person who might use the test for selecting teachers should first take it himself, learn how he scores, and then decide whether or not he wishes his candidates for teaching positions to respond as he does.

A simple check list of personal problems is often useful in facilitating counseling interviews, in making group surveys leading to plans for individualized action with a student, as a basis for guidance programs of the homeroom and orientation type, as a means of increasing teacher understanding of students in regular classroom situations, and in conducting research on the problems of youth. When students know that their responses will be kept confidential and that they will be given assistance with the problems that they have checked as troublesome, they tend to respond freely and frankly. Not intended as a refined measure of any aspect of personality, the check list can be used by teaching staff and counselors to good advantage, provided they know how to use it and are able to help the student with the problems he reveals. The Mooney Problem Check List, the SRA Junior Inventory, and the SRA Youth Inventory are a few of the better-known check lists available.

Two other inventories in this category are most often used for college students: the Study of Values (1) and the Survey of Study Habits and Attitudes (4). The Study of Values aims to measure the relative prominence of six basic interests or motives in personality: theoretical, economic, aesthetic, social, political, and religious. The test scoring procedure is ipsative; that is, a high score on one scale can be obtained only at the expense of other scales. A profile can be constructed on the basis of the responses made. Figure 16.7 shows the profile of values for average males and average females and indicates the region of average, high, and low scores. The Study of Values is widely used in psychological and educational research and in counseling and interview sessions with individuals. The purpose of the Survey of Study Habits and Attitudes is to promote self-understanding in the student taking it and to provide information which can be used in counseling the student.

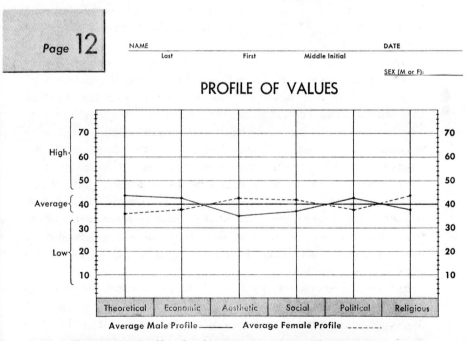

Fig. 16.7. Profile of values (From G. W. Allport, P. E. Vernon, & G. Lindzey. Study of Values. Boston: Houghton Mifflin Company, 1960, p. 12.)

Projective Tests of Personality

A projective test is a relatively unstructured, yet standard situation to which a person is asked to respond, but with as few restrictions as possible upon the mode or content of response. The purpose of projective testing is to ascertain the respondent's characteristic mode of behavior, including attitudes, motivations, and dynamic personality traits, by observing his behavior in response to some standard stimulus. Although teachers and others at times use simple projective devices to elicit pupil responses, the three principal projective tests—the Thematic Apperception Test, the Children's Apperception Test, and the Rorschach Technique—are administered only by psychologists or psychiatrists. Interpretation of the responses is highly dependent upon the experience of the examiner. Though these projective tests are used widely in clinical situations, their status is more dubious at present than it was some 15 to 20 years ago.

The Rorschach Technique is a projective test for use with individuals, age 3 and over (27). There are many adaptations and revisions; the original test consists of 10 ink blots of varying colors and irregular forms. The subject is shown the ink blot and asked to tell what he sees in the blot. The trained clinician questions and encourages the subject to respond.

Upon securing the responses, the clinician follows one or another fairly objective procedure for deriving scores from the obtained responses. Generally, the scores fall into three major categories: location, determinants, and content. The location of the response refers to whether the whole blot, subdivisions, or unusual details of it were responded to. Determinants take into account the shape, color, and shading of the blot to which the subject responded. Content refers to whether the subject saw in the blot a person or persons, parts of persons, clothing, an inanimate object, and the like. On the basis of these responses, the clinician infers the total personality organization of the individual and some of the possible perceptions of the individual to self and to others which may be related to one or more facets of his personality organization.

In a hospital or other diagnostic and treatment center, the psychologist, psychiatrist, social worker, and others use all the information each has collected, confer about the individual, and arrive at decisions as to the present status of the individual's psychological health, the need for further diagnosis, possible forms and duration of treatment, possible release date, and the like. Many institutions rely quite heavily upon

Rorschach data in diagnosis of personality disorders, even though attempts to score and interpret the Rorschach responses objectively have not proven completely successful.

Hertz summarized interpretation of the Rorschach thus:

. . . it should be noted that the final analysis in the procedure of the interpretation in terms of other clinical and test data defies standardization, as Rorschach originally contended. The information gleaned from the Rorschach material is projected against family background, education, training, health history, past life, qualitative judgments of the examiner and of other people, and other clinical and test data. This is then interpreted in terms of the examiner's experiential knowledge of the dynamics of human behavior. Final conclusions are made by inference and analogy depending upon the experience, ingenuity, the fertility of insight, and, not to be forgotten, the common sense of the examiner. Prolonged and extensive experience is necessary, not only with human personality but with all kinds of clinical problems. This last step by definition, therefore, is personal to the examiner and subjective in him. It permits of no norm, and it eludes all standardization (**15**, 538).

Four recent reviewers of the Rorschach indicate skepticism about continued heavy reliance on this test by clinicians and suggest the need for more refined measures of personality organization and dynamics. One of the reviewers, L. F. Shaffer, indicates, however, why it may receive continued use:

In view of the relatively unfavorable evidence, why is the Rorschach held in such high esteem? Without attempting to be comprehensive, three reasons may be suggested. First, we have an intense need for a subtle and comprehensive instrument to assess personality. As recent research in social psychology shows, motivation and belief are highly related. When one has a strong need, evidence of little objective merit may be perceived as conclusive. Second, the Rorschach is projective for the examiner as well as for the examinee. One readily "reads into" the vague verbalizations of the Rorschach protocol all that one already knows and believes about the examinee. For each individual examiner, therefore, the Rorschach seems to confirm his other knowledge and he has an intuitive and personal sense of the validity of the instrument. Third, the Rorschach is not wholly without validity—it is sometimes "right" (**5**, 288).

SUMMARY

The main purposes of evaluating and measuring are to (1) help the student progress in learning tasks, (2) ascertain how well the student is learning, (3) understand abilities and other characteristics of students, (4) facilitate the student's self-evaluation and self-understanding, (5) judge the effectiveness of instructional and related programs, (6) assist in making curriculum and administrative judgments, and (7) extend knowledge about human abilities and teaching–learning processes. A suitable evaluation instrument must be valid, reliable, and useable.

Standardized tests are widely used to evaluate outcomes of instruction and to assess abilities and other student characteristics. Good standardized tests likewise must meet the criteria of validity, reliability, and useability. Standardized tests have the following characteristics: (1) the administration of the test is standardized, (2) the scoring of the test is standardized, and (3) the comparison of the tested group with other groups is possible because norms are available.

Commonly used published tests include both individual and group tests of general intellectual ability, single and multiaptitude tests, experimental tests of creativity, single tests and batteries of educational achievement, interest inventories, personality inventories and checklists, and projective tests of personality. Group tests of general intellectual ability, of aptitude, and of educational achievement are usually intended to be administered, scored, and interpreted by teachers. On the other hand, other tests and inventories generally require more education by the administrator, scorer, and interpreter; some personality tests require a large amount of specialized education.

QUESTIONS AND ACTIVITIES

1. a. List and discuss briefly the two purposes of evaluating and measuring which have been achieved best in your college classes.
   b. State and discuss the two which have been achieved least well in your college classes.

2. a. Discuss the test results which have been most helpful to you in self-evaluation thus far.
   b. Discuss other evaluation procedures which have been helpful to you in self-evaluation.

3. a. Discuss the main types of test validity.
   b. Discuss the main types of test reliability.

4. a. What are the main characteristics of standardized tests?
   b. Which of the same characteristics would be most difficult to incorporate in a test you might construct?

5. Referring to the appropriate references as necessary, compare the ideas about intelligence underlying Terman's and Wechsler's tests.

6. What are the advantages and disadvantages of the individual intelligence test in comparison with the group test of general intellectual ability?

7. Secure test manuals and test copies for at least two group tests of general intellectual ability and com-

pare them on the characteristics set forth previously for standardized tests.

8. Compare items intended to measure creative abilities with items of a group test of general intellectual ability. In what respect are the items different?

9. Would you use a group test of general intellectual ability or an educational achievement test to predict subsequent achievements of eighth-graders in high school English, social studies, science, and mathematics? Why?

10. What are the limitations of educational achievement tests?

11. a. What values may accrue from the use of interest inventories?

b. In what respects are the Strong Vocational Interest Blank for Men and the Kuder Preference Record—Vocational alike? Different?

12. Why must school personnel exercise more caution in the use of personality tests than educational achievement tests?

13. Why should the teacher understand the purpose and the use of the Rorschach Technique?

14. Suppose that no published tests were available. What effect would this have on attaining each of the eight purposes of evaluation indicated in the first part of the chapter?

SUGGESTIONS FOR FURTHER READING

Antastasi, Anne. *Psychological testing.* (2nd ed.) New York: Macmillan, 1961. Ch. 2: Principal characteristics of psychological tests, pp. 21–43; and Ch. 3: Use of psychological tests, pp. 44–75.

Binet, A., & T. Simon. The development of the Binet–Simon Scale. In Judy F. Rosenblith & W. Allinsmith (Eds.), *The causes of behavior: Readings in child development and educational psychology.* Boston: Allyn & Bacon, 1962, pp. 286–290.

Bloom, B. S. Testing cognitive ability and achievement. In N. L. Gage (Ed.), *Handbook of research on teaching.* Chicago: Rand McNally, 1963, pp. 379–397.

Brim, O. G., Jr. American attitudes toward intelligence tests. *Amer. Psychologist*, 1965, **20**, 125–130.

Dyer, H. L. On the assessment of academic achievement. *Teachers Coll. Rec.*, 1960, **62**, 164–172. (In Crow & Crow, 1963, 466–478; and Ripple, 1964, 536–548.)

Dyer, H. L. Is testing a menace to education? *N.Y. State Educ.*, 1961, **49** (1), 16–19. (In Fullagar, *et al.*, 1964, 573–578.)

Fishman, J. A., & P. I. Clifford. What can mass-testing programs do for-and-to the pursuit of excellence in American education. *Harv. educ. Rev.*, 1964, **34**, 63–79.

Gulliksen, H. Measurement of learning and mental abilities. *Psychometrika*, 1961, **26**, 93–107. (In Crow & Crow, 1963, 288–303.)

Hagen, Elizabeth. Analyzing test results. *Nat. elem. Principal*, 1961, **41**, 11–17. (In Fullagar *et al.*, 1964, 562–572.)

Mayo, S. T., *et al.* Educational and psychological testing. *Rev. educ. Res.*, 1965, **35**, 1–99.

Seashore, H. G., & J. H. Ricks, Jr. *Test Service Bulletin*, No. 39. New York: The Psychological Corporation, 1950, pp. 16–19. (Reprinted under the title "Norms must be relevant" in Crow & Crow, 1963, 479–485.)

Thorndike, R. L. The measurement of creativity. *Teachers Coll. Rec.*, 1963, **64**, 422–424. (In Seidman, 1965, 206–208.)

619

REFERENCES

1. Allport, G. W., P. E. Vernon, & G. Lindzey. Study of Values. Boston: Houghton Mifflin, 1960.
2. American Educational Research Association & National Council on Measurements Used in Education. *Technical recommendations for achievement tests.* Washington, D.C.: National Education Association, 1955.
3. Bennett, G. K., H. G. Seashore, & A. G. Wesman. Differential Aptitude Tests. New York: Psychological Corporation, 1959.
4. Brown, W. F., & W. H. Holtzman. Survey of Study Habits and Attitudes. New York: Psychological Corporation, 1953.
5. Buros, O. K. *The fifth mental measurement yearbook.* Highland Park, N.J.: Gryphon Press, 1959.
6. Buros, O. K. (Ed.) *Tests in print.* Highland Park, N.J.: Gryphon Press, 1961.
7. Cook, W. W., C. H. Leeds, & R. Callis. Minnesota Teacher Attitude Inventory. New York: Psychological Corporation, 1951.
8. Cronbach, L. J. *Essentials of psychological testing.* (2nd ed.) New York: Harper & Row, 1960.
9. Flanagan, J. C. Flanagan Aptitude Classification Test, Ingenuity. Chicago: Science Research Associates, 1957.
10. Flanagan, J. C. *Manual for Flanagan Aptitude Classification Tests, Ingenuity.* Chicago: Science Research Associates, 1960.
11. French, J. W., Ruth B. Ekstrom, & L. A. Price. *Manual for kit of reference tests for cognitive factors.* Princeton: Educational Testing Service, 1963.
12. General Aptitude Test Battery. Washington: U.S. Employment Services, 1959.
13. Guilford, J. P. Intellectual resources and their values as seen by scientists. In C. W. Taylor &

F. Barron (Eds.), *Scientific creativity: Its recognition and development.* New York: Wiley, 1963, pp. 101–118.
14. Hathaway, S. R., & J. C. McKinley. Minnesota Multiphasic Personality Inventory. New York: Psychological Corporation, 1951.
15. Hertz, Marguerite R. Rorschach: Twenty years after. *Psychol. Bull.,* 1942, 39, 529–572.
16. Houston, J. P., & S. A. Mednick. Creativity and the need for novelty. *J. abnorm. soc. Psychol.,* 1963, 66, 137–141.
17. Kelley, T. L., R. Madden, E. F. Gardner, & H. C. Rudman. Stanford Achievement Test, Intermediate II Battery, Form W. New York: Harcourt, Brace, & World, 1964.
18. *Kit of reference tests for cognitive factors.* Princeton: Educational Testing Service, 1963.
19. Kuder, G. F. Kuder Preference Record–Vocational, Form CH. Chicago: Science Research Associates, 1948.
20. Larson, C. A., & W. H. McCreary. Testing programs and practices in California public secondary schools. *Calif. J. secondary Educ.,* 1956, 31, 389–401.
21. Lindquist, E. F., & A. N. Hieronymus. *Manual for administrators, supervisors, and counselors, Iowa Tests of Basic Skills.* Boston: Houghton Mifflin, 1956.
22. Lindquist, E. F., & A. N. Hieronymus. *Teacher's manual, Iowa Tests of Basic Skills,* Boston: Houghton Mifflin, 1956.
23. Lorge, I., R. L. Thorndike, & Elizabeth Hagen. Lorge-Thorndike Intelligence Test, Form 1, Levels A–H. Boston: Houghton Mifflin, 1964.
24. MacKinnon, D. W. The nature and nurture of creative talent. *Amer. Psychologist,* 1962, 17, 484–495.
25. Mednick, S. A. The associative

basis of the creative process. *Psychol. Rev.*, 1962, **69**, 220–232.

26. Ohlsen, M. M. Interpretation of test scores. In W. G. Findley (Ed.), *The impact and improvement of school testing programs.* Yearb. nat. Soc. Stud. Educ., 1963, **62**, Part II, pp. 254–294.

27. Rorschach, H. Rorschach Technique. New York: Grune & Stratton, 1960.

28. *Sequential Tests of Educational Progress, Handbook for essay tests, Level I, College.* Princeton: Educational Testing Service, 1957.

29. Strong, E. K., Jr. Strong Vocational Interest Blank for Men, Revised. New York: Psychological Corporation, 1959.

30. Strong, E. K., Jr. Strong Vocational Interest Blank for Women, Revised. New York: Psychological Corporation, 1959.

31. Sullivan, Elizabeth T., W. W. Clark, & E. W. Tiegs. *Examiner's manual, California Short-Form Test of Mental Maturity, Level 2, S-Form,* Monterey: California Test Bureau, 1963.

32. Terman, L. M., & Maud A. Merrill. Revised Stanford-Binet Intelligence Scales. Boston: Houghton Mifflin, 1937, 1960.

33. Torrance, E. P. Non-verbal Minnesota Tests of Creative Thinking, Forms A, B, and NVA. Minneapolis: Bur. of Educ. Res., Univer. Minnesota, 1960 (Form NVA), 1962 (Form A), and 1963 (Form B).

34. Torrance, E. P. *Administration and scoring manual for Abbreviated Form VII, Minnesota Tests of Creative Thinking.* Minneapolis: Bur. of Educ. Res., Univer. Minnesota, 1962.

35. Torrance, E. P., & D. E. Templeton. *Manual for Verbal Form A, Minnesota Tests of Creative Thinking.* Minneapolis: Bur. of Educ. Res., Univer. Minnesota, 1963.

36. Tyler, Leona E. *The psychology of human differences.* New York: Appleton-Century-Crofts, 1956.

37. Wechsler, D. *The measurement of adult intelligence.* Baltimore: Williams & Wilkins, 1944.

38. Wechsler, D. *Manual, Wechsler Intelligence Scale for Children.* New York: Psychological Corporation, 1949.

39. Wechsler, D. Wechsler Intelligence Scale for Children. New York: Psychological Corporation, 1949.

40. Wechsler, D. Wechsler Adult Intelligence Scale. New York: Psychological Corporation, 1955.

CHAPTER 17

Teacher Evaluation Procedures

Evaluation is a continuous process of securing and interpreting information to ascertain the quality and amount of student progress toward educational objectives. A comprehensive evaluation program requires the use of various instruments such as the standardized and other published tests discussed in Chapter 16, teacher-made tests, and informal procedures. You may review briefly the purposes of evaluation and the characteristics of a good evaluation procedure reported in the first sections of Chapter 16 before considering: (1) observation and rating of performance; (2) teacher-made tests; and (3) self-reporting devices.

OBSERVATION AND RATING OF PERFORMANCE

By observing the pupils as they engage in various learning activities, the teacher gains important information about such things as future plans of the pupils; the quality of performance in art, swimming, typing, and many other areas; the conduct of the pupils; level of motivation and interest in school activities; and attitudes toward classmates, teachers, and self. It is exceedingly difficult, if not impossible, to obtain published tests or to devise written tests to secure this type of information as reliably as it can be secured through systematic observation of daily performances.

Types of Informal Observation and Rating

Teachers are not interested only in observing pupil performances; in many school systems, they are required to rate and to report their ratings to the students, parents, and school officials. Frequently the school system incorporates its objectives in the report form submitted to the student and parents. Though the main purpose of teacher observation and subsequent rating of performances is not to provide information to the students or parents, two excellent report forms are now presented and discussed to illustrate the variety of evaluative information the teacher is expected to provide.

Figure 17.1 is the front side of the comprehensive report form of the Monona Grove High School, Madison, Wisconsin. The parents receive a quarterly report for each subject in which the student is enrolled in school. A letter grade of *A* to *F* is given in each of the three main areas: "individual performance," "school citizenship," and "knowledge and skills in subject." These three areas are given equal weight in assigning the letter grade for "total growth and performance." The various marks —plus, minus, and no—are entered as appropriate for the 13 subareas: "Works up to ability," "Has a positive attitude," "Shows self-direction," etc. Space is provided on the back of the report form for parent and teacher comments, and the parent is asked to telephone the school if a conference is desired.

Notice that each teacher who has the student in his class must observe and rate behavior in connection with the three main objectives of the high school: to encourage desirable individual growth in each pupil, to encourage desirable citizenship behavior, and to encourage optimum development of knowledge and skills in the subject.

At the Monona Grove High School, individual performance is appraised as a valuable indication of the present and future success of the student in any type of work or play; the ability to plan, organize, and follow through on the plan; the skills developed in supervised study, in solving problems, in group research, in group discussion, and in individual research. All such habits and skills are part of the total growth of the students. Evaluation in this area is in relation to the student's *own* ability.

623

REPORT TO STUDENTS AND PARENTS

MONONA GROVE HIGH SCHOOL — MADISON, WIS.

Fr. ☐ Jr. ☐

Name _____ So. ☐ Sr. ☐

Mr.

Subject _____ Teacher Mrs. _____
Miss

Home Room Teacher

Term beginning September 8, 1964 — ending June 15, 1965

GRADING SYSTEM

A=4.4 - 3.6   D=1.4 - 0.6   **+ Mark** indicates superior achievement
B=3.4 - 2.6   F=0.4 - 0.0   **No Mark** indicates average achievement
C=2.4 - 1.6   Inc=Incomplete   **— Mark** indicates need for improvement

	First Quarter	Second Quarter	Third Quarter	Fourth Quarter		FINAL EVALUATION	KNOWLEDGE AND SKILLS AVERAGE
INDIVIDUAL PERFORMANCE							
Works up to ability							
Has a positive attitude							
Shows self-direction							
Plans work wisely							
SCHOOL CITIZENSHIP							
Is courteous and considerate of others							
Is responsible							
Contributes his share							
Is a good leader or follower							
Takes care of school, personal property							
KNOWLEDGE & SKILLS IN SUBJECT							
Develops skills							
Indicates knowledge by assignments							
Recites effectively							
Scores satisfactorily on examinations							
TOTAL GROWTH & PERFORMANCE ACCUMULATED GRADE POINT							
Days Absent							
Times Tardy						(over)	

Fig. 17.1. Report to students and parents. (Courtesy Monona Grove High School, Madison, Wisconsin.)

School citizenship represents the observed performance and growth toward the qualities of a competent, cooperative, participating school citizen. Such factors as care of personal and school property, the ability either to lead in worthwhile activities or to take an active part in carrying them out, and effective cooperation in group projects are important. Citizenship includes contributing something to the good of the school. A student who causes no trouble in school is not necessarily a

ACCUMULATED GRADE POINT INTERPRETATION

QUARTER			FINAL GRADE	
FIRST	.7 to 0 = A+ to F		4.4 - 3.6	A
SECOND	.9 to 0 = A+ to F		3.5 - 2.6	B
THIRD	1.1 to 0 = A+ to F		2.5 - 1.6	C
FOURTH	1.3 to 0 = A+ to F		1.5 - .6	D
			.5 - .0	F

TO PARENTS—

We share with you a mutual interest in helping your son or daughter become an academically and socially competent person. We encourage your understanding and ask for your cooperation.

THE FACULTY
Monona Grove High School

DATE	PARENT OR TEACHER COMMENTS

SIGNATURE OF PARENT OR GUARDIAN

FIRST QUARTER --- ☐

SECOND QUARTER --- ☐

THIRD QUARTER --- ☐

If a conference with the teacher is desired,
please check space above or telephone 222-1291

Fig. 17.1. *(Continued).*

good citizen; good citizenship involves contribution to the welfare of others.

Knowledge and skills in the subject include the appraisal of strictly academic achievement through tests, reports, notebooks, projects, discussions, demonstrations, and the like. Subject knowledge and skills are more than memorization of facts and acquisition of skills, but less than total growth and performance related to all the educational objectives.

Figure 17.2 shows the wide range of objectives of instruction for an elementary school. In Fig. 17.2, observe the number of pupil perform-

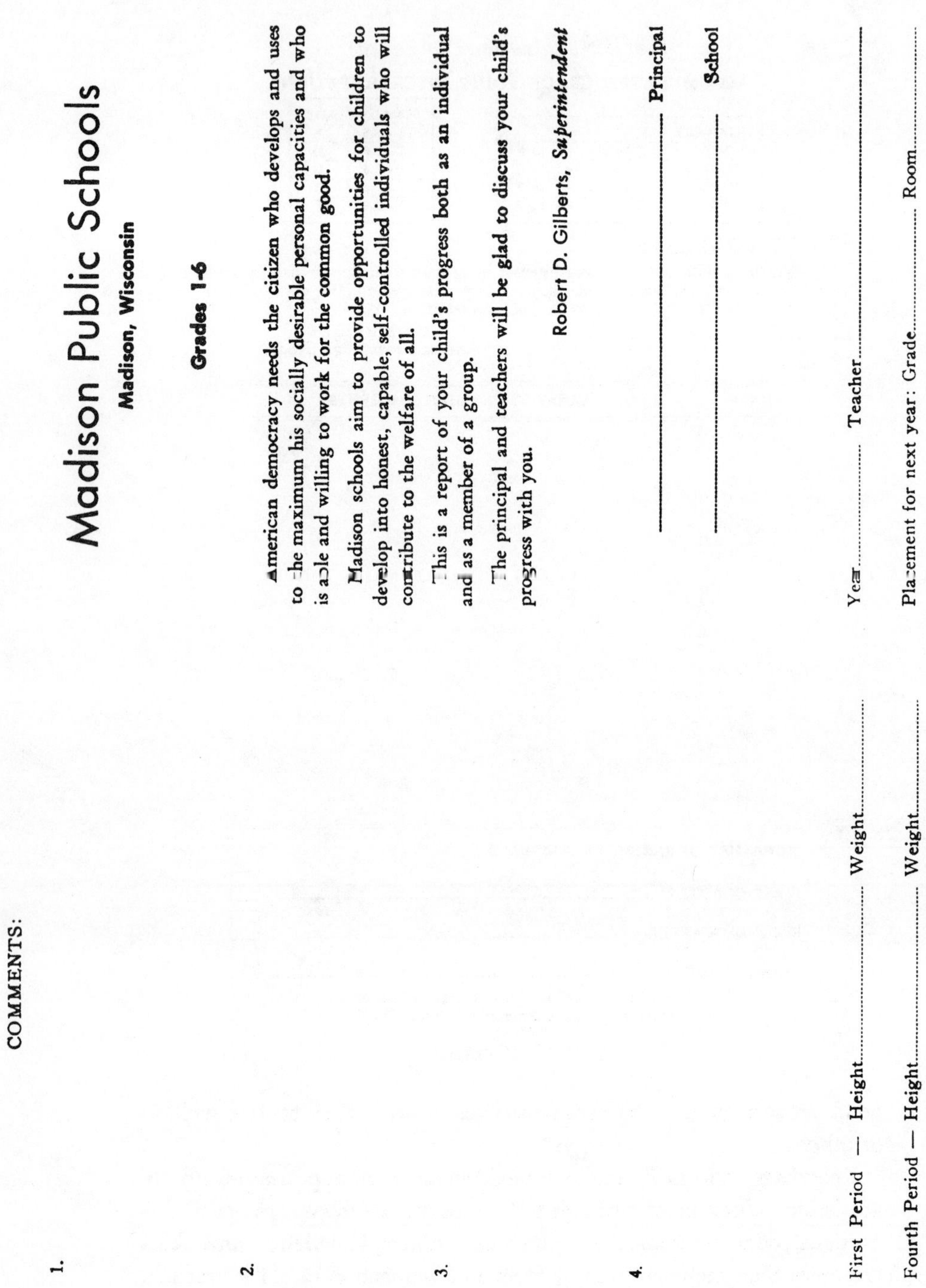

Madison Public Schools

Madison, Wisconsin

Grades 1-6

American democracy needs the citizen who develops and uses to the maximum his socially desirable personal capacities and who is able and willing to work for the common good.

Madison schools aim to provide opportunities for children to develop into honest, capable, self-controlled individuals who will contribute to the welfare of all.

This is a report of your child's progress both as an individual and as a member of a group.

The principal and teachers will be glad to discuss your child's progress with you.

Robert D. Gilberts, *Superintendent*

Principal

School

Year............ Teacher............

Placement for next year: Grade............ Room............

COMMENTS:

1.

2.

3.

4.

First Period — Height............ Weight............

Fourth Period — Height............ Weight............

Fig. 17.2. Report card used by the Madison Public Schools is accompanied by an explanation sheet to help parents understand the fine points behind the grading system of the schools. (Courtesy Madison Public Schools, Madison, Wisconsin.)

Report of .... Grade ....

Good citizenship and good work habits are necessary for satisfactory school progress.

The items checked suggest ways in which your child can and should improve:

CITIZENSHIP

	Report Periods			
	1	2	3	4
Being self reliant				
Working well with others				
Playing well with others				
Observing rules of safety				
Practicing good health habits				
Showing regard for property				
Respecting rightful authority				
Showing courtesy to others				

WORK HABITS

	Report Periods			
	1	2	3	4
Working carefully and accurately				
Getting to work promptly				
Completing work promptly				
Using spare time to advantage				
Listening to and following directions				
Sharing in group planning				

A conference with parent is desired
(Call school for an appointment)

SCHOOL SUBJECTS

√—Indicates how your child compares with other children of this grade level.   X—Losing position (little or no progress)

Effort: S—Satisfactory; U—Unsatisfactory; I—Improving

	1st Report Period					2nd Report Period					3rd Report Period					4th Report Period				
	Above Grade Level	At Grade Level	Below Grade Level	Effort S I I U		Above Grade Level	At Grade Level	Below Grade Level	Effort S I I U		Above Grade Level	At Grade Level	Below Grade Level	Effort S I I U		Above Grade Level	At Grade Level	Below Grade Level	Effort S I I U	
Reading																				
Language																				
Spelling																				
Writing																				
Social Studies																				
Science																				
Arithmetic																				
Music																				
Art																				
Physical Education																				

Attendance	Days Present	Days Absent	Times Tardy	Days Present	Days Absent	Times Tardy	Days Present	Days Absent	Times Tardy	Days Present	Days Absent	Times Tardy

TOTALS FOR THE YEAR

Parent's Signature

Fig. 17.2.   *(Continued)*.

627

EXPLANATION OF REPORT CARD

1. **Grade Level:**

   A check in the "At Grade Level" column indicates achievement about equal to the average for that grade. "Above Grade Level" indicates achievement above the average for that grade; while a check in the "Below Grade Level" column indicates achievement below the average for that grade. An "X" indicates grade level and also that the child is not progressing as well as we think he should in that particular subject. Note that grade level is not a stationary position. A child who is checked "At grade level" each report period is making normal growth for the year.

2. **Effort:**

   Some of the children who find school subjects difficult are among the best of workers, and deserve credit for their efforts. On the other hand, some children with much ability do not apply themselves and never reach their best potential. Such a pupil might be checked "Above Grade Level" but "Unsatisfactory" for effort. This would mean that he is capable of doing much better and should be urged to do so.

3. **A Confidential Report:**

   Children often compare marks and, unfortunately, parents sometimes do also. This is very unfair for the children. It often inflates the ego of some and causes resentment and discouragement among others.
   You should receive the card in a sealed envelope. It should be discussed privately with your child, signed, and sealed in the enclosed envelope before returning.

4. **Citizenship:**

   One of the most important phases of a child's growth. (See reverse side for items included in citizenship.)

5. **Work Habits:**

   Good work habits are a necessity for good progress.

6. **A Conference With Parent is Desired:**

   If you find a check here, arrange a conference with the teacher as soon as possible. Many problems are prevented or corrected by close parent-teacher cooperation.

If you have questions about the report card, please feel free to call the teacher or principal.

Fig. 17.2. *(Continued).*

CITIZENSHIP

This outline is included with your child's report to better enable you to interpret citizenship marks on the report card. Please keep it for future reference.

1. **BEING SELF RELIANT**—refers to the pupil's habit of depending on himself rather than on others.
   a. Has confidence in himself.
   b. Works independently.
   c. Assumes responsibility for doing things without being reminded.
   d. Can be trusted to do special tasks alone or with a group without constant supervision.
   e. Does not ask for unnecessary assistance.
   f. Can go ahead without constant prodding or praise from the teacher.

2. **WORKING WELL WITH OTHERS**—refers to the pupil's ability and willingness to cooperate with others, to act in desirable ways in work situations involving himself and others.
   a. Contributes something to the group.
   b. Can accept leadership.
   c. Can follow well.
   d. Has a "give and take" attitude.
   e. Does not interfere with the work of others.
   f. Accepts criticism and suggestions from the group graciously.

3. **PLAYING WELL WITH OTHERS**—refers to the pupil's ability and willingness to cooperate with others, to act in desirable ways in play situations involving himself and others.
   a. Works for his team rather than for himself.
   b. Follows the rules of the game.
   c. Gives others their turn.
   d. Does not isolate himself from the group.
   e. Is willing to share with others.
   f. Can control his temper.
   g. Is good natured.

4. **OBSERVING RULES OF SAFETY**—refers to the behavior of the pupil in relation to such basic safety practices as obedience to safety rules; also, in being mindful of the consequences of his acts which might possibly be injurious to others.
   a. Obeys traffic laws, including city bicycle ordinance.
   b. Uses care in handling tools and materials.
   c. Conducts himself properly during fire drill.
   d. Is careful at drinking fountains, on stairs, in halls, etc.
   e. Cooperates with boy patrols and traffic officers.
   f. Keeps away from railroad tracks and other dangerous places in going to and from school.
   g. Does not play with sticks, guns or dangerous toys.

5. **PRACTICING GOOD HEALTH HABITS**—refers to the behavior of the pupil in relation to those basic health practices designed to promote his own well-being and to protect the health of others.
   a. Is clean in dress, habits, and person.
   b. Stays home when there is evidence of a cold.
   c. Puts on wraps according to the weather.
   d. Sits and stands correctly.

6. **SHOWING REGARD FOR PROPERTY**—refers to the pupil's attitude toward the best possible care of all property whether it belongs to him or not.
   a. Handles school materials carefully and economically.
   b. Does not deface desks, walls, or materials.
   c. Does not trespass on lawns or disturb the peace or property of others.
   d. Is careful of and responsible for playground equipment.
   e. Takes good care of personal belongings, such as clothing, books, and supplies.

7. **RESPECTING RIGHTFUL AUTHORITY**—For every freedom that we have in our democracy we have a corresponding obligation. Freedom of speech, press, etc., is acceptable only as far as it is good for all. Recognition and acceptance of social discipline and lawful authority is of prime importance in good citizenship.
   a. Cooperates with boy or girl patrols and crossing guards.
   b. Responds promptly and cheerfully to teachers' directions.
   c. Accepts and gives constructive criticism.
   d. Shows growth in the use of the democratic process as it applies to the organization of room, clubs, committees, etc.

8. **SHOWING COURTESY TO OTHERS**—refers to the pupil's attitude and his willingness to act with consideration, tolerance, and respect in situations involving others.
   a. Helps others when there is need.
   b. Is considerate of a newcomer in the group.
   c. Does not tease others in embarrassing situations.
   d. Refrains from making unkind remarks.
   e. Shows racial and social tolerance.
   f. Is thoughtful of giving pleasure or comfort to others.
   g. Listens to what others have to say.
   h. Does not interrupt.

Fig. 17.2. *(Continued)*.

ances and other behavior which the teacher would most likely observe and rate rather than using any form of published or teacher-made tests. In the primary school as well as in the intermediate grades, other performances and behavior also might be rated through observation rather than with tests. But in both the high school and elementary school report form, the teacher is required to make certain ratings on the basis of the pupil's ability. Standardized tests like those discussed in Chapter 16 and written tests constructed by the teacher are often used in estimating the abilities of individual pupils.

What does the teacher observe in order to help pupils acquire the objectives stated above and learn efficiently? Two examples, one in arithmetic and the other in science, clarify the observational procedures.

Performance in Arithmetic. Computational skill in arithmetic may be readily appraised by means of written tests once the child can read and write the symbols used in the test. But how well does the child understand the arithmetic concepts and processes underlying the skill? Can he use these skills in written problems and in problems which come up in his everyday life? How does he attack problems?

Does the child understand the process? This will be discussed in terms of a procedure for appraising and understanding the process of multiplication; the procedure may be applied to other arithmetic concepts and processes.

After the children have learned to add objects in groups of two, their knowledge of these addition facts is incorporated in a multiplication table in three steps:

One 2	$= 2$	$2 + 0 = 2$	$1 \times 2 = 2$
Two 2's	$= 4$	$2 + 2 = 4$	$2 \times 2 = 4$
Three 2's	$= 6$	$2 + 2 + 2 = 6$	$3 \times 2 = 6$
Four 2's	$= 8$	$2 + 2 + 2 + 2 = 8$	$4 \times 2 = 8$
Five 2's	$= 10$	$2 + 2 + 2 + 2 + 2 = 10$	$5 \times 2 = 10$
Six 2's	$= 12$	$2 + 2 + 2 + 2 + 2 + 2 = 12$	$6 \times 2 = 12$

When and how should the child's understanding that multiplication is a process of addition be appraised? The most appropriate time is when the concept is being taught, for unless appraisal is made at this time, the teacher cannot determine whether more work is needed. Direct observation of the children when they are engaged in the activity is the best appraisal method.

Can the child use his computational skills and understanding of processes in solving problems? The teacher says to the class: "We have $5.00 to spend for our birthday party. Mary's committee has spent 39¢

for decorations. Bob's committee says that 2 gallons of ice cream will cost $3.00, and 5 dozen cones will cost $1.25. Susan's committee wants to buy 5 dozen fancy napkins. They cost 5¢ a dozen. Have we enough money for all this? Each of you work on this to see if there is enough money, how much will be left over, or how much more we need." Children attempt solution of the problem, working in pairs with the teacher observing their work. One child then writes the correct solution on the chalk board and explains how he arrived at the solution. Here, too, the teacher observes the explanation. Observation and related guidance in many situations like these aid children in applying computational skills to real problems and provide the means whereby the teacher can observe the extent to which the children are learning application of those skills.

To determine how the child attacks problems, the teacher observes him in situations like that above. How he goes about getting a solution also is checked carefully in his written work. In the above example, one child may first multiply 5×5¢ to get 25¢, the cost of the napkins, and then add 39¢, $3.00, $1.25, and 25¢, for a total of $4.89. Subtracting this from $5.00 gives the remainder of 11¢. There are numerous possibilities of making errors in computation and in method of attack in this problem. The method used may be appraised by careful observation.

The teacher can help the children improve their attack on both oral and written problems by asking such questions as: What is the problem? What do we want to find out in this problem? What should we do first? What is our next step? How can we check whether our answer is correct? In addition to discussing such questions orally the teacher can observe as the answers are applied in a variety of situations. In the process the correct or appropriate method is approved or reinforced and possible errors are identified and corrected.

Performance in Science. Assume that two objectives of science instruction are to build problem-solving techniques and to develop a scientific attitude toward the solution of problems. How do informal observation and related guidance assist pupils in acquiring problem-solving techniques and scientific attitudes? The following example will help to answer this question.

Early in the year, fourth-grade children and their teacher identify the problem: How can soil be conserved? This leads to a discussion of the social implications of erosion. The teacher proposes that the class first study soil formation so that they will understand better what causes erosion.

The children engage in such activities as making dirt by sandpapering rock, stirring coarse sand and pebbles together in a large jar of water, putting a water-soaked porous rock into a plastic bag and freezing it in the refrigerator, and taking a field trip to see how tree roots break the pavement.

When the children understand how to sandpaper the rocks, the teacher asks: "What are we looking for?" and this leads to a statement of the problem. The teacher helps the children develop skill in stating it and also sets the stage for more careful observation as the experiment proceeds. The rocks may be weighed before they are sandpapered, and later the rocks and dirt may be weighed, if the children are ready for this more technical instruction and if sufficiently accurate scales are available.

When the coarse sand and pebbles are stirred in the water, the children notice that only the sand moves when the water is stirred slowly, but that both sand and pebbles move when it is stirred rapidly, and that the heavier particles remain toward the bottom. "How does this form soil?" asks the teacher. Observant Harry says that stirring the water did the same thing as sandpapering the rock. Everyone agrees that this is a good observation, and the ensuing discussion leads to the writing of preliminary guides for observation.

"The water dissolved some sand, didn't it?" This question from Pamela is pursued further to determine whether the coarse grains of sand and pebbles really dissolved or whether they broke into finer particles by striking against each other. Pamela has identified a more complex problem which the teacher points out and discusses with the class.

Chester suddenly wants to know what makes deltas. "Does the water make the soil or just carry it?" The children are now exhibiting a scientific attitude; they want to find correct answers. The teacher observes the attitudes each child expresses. She makes a point of encouraging the children to discover the answers for themselves. "I am not sure exactly what the answers to these questions are. We need more information. We know that when rocks are carried by water and strike against each other they chip and break. How can we find out if water really makes the large particles dissolve? How can we find out how deltas are formed?"

The discussion which now begins leads to further research. It is decided that one group of children will repeat the water-stirring experiment using only washed sand and pebbles, and another group will have water trickle slowly down a small mound of dirt, coarse sand,

and pebbles. The children who want to find out more about deltas are referred to appropriate reading materials.

Before any of this work is begun, each child is asked to write out what the problem is and how he intends to get further information and record his results. This is handed in for the teacher's appraisal and then returned to the child, with appropriate suggestions. Throughout all these activities, the teacher gives individual help and group guidance in observing carefully and recording accurately, working with the children continuously. When results of the experiments and reading are reported to the class, facts on which there is agreement and those on which there is disagreement are noted and discussed further. Thus, a child whose information is inaccurate learns not only that it is inaccurate, but what he can do to correct it.

By means of careful observation the teacher appraises and may rate the pupil's growth or present status in problem-solving techniques and a scientific attitude. This appraisal is not postponed until the end of a unit, semester, or year; instead it begins as soon as the development of problem-solving techniques and a scientific attitude are identified as objectives of science instruction. It receives special emphasis when a problem is identified and it remains an essential component of an effective, progressive teaching-learning situation.

These descriptions of observing and rating in arithmetic and science imply that the characteristics or criteria of a good performance are known to the teacher and serve to guide the observation and rating. This is, of course, true for evaluating all performances: the making of a garment or preparation of food in home economics, diving or hitting a baseball in physical education, writing a story or giving a talk in the language arts, learning to speak a foreign language, or making a map or display in social studies. The teacher's observation and guidance are helpful to the extent that the teacher knows the characteristics of effective performance by students of the particular age or grade level.

Rating Scales

A rating scale provides a means for putting the results of observation in numerical form. The simplest rating scales indicate two degrees, for example, "excellent" and "poor." More discriminating scales use more ratings—as many as the rater can reliably differentiate.

The main factors which determine the objectivity and accuracy of ratings are the exactness with which a performance being rated is defined, the discrimination with which the various ratings are made, and the competence of the person performing the rating. A scale may be devised for rating any performance—a theme, a painting, the playing of a musical instrument; and for rating conduct—behavior toward the opposite and own sex, domination and withdrawal, and the like. A comprehensive rating scale used in a controlled experiment and another rating scale of creativity will illustrate the form and use of rating scales.

In the Racine, Wisconsin, Public Schools, a controlled experiment was designed to ascertain the effects of acceleration on pupils presently enrolled in the second grade. Let us review briefly the procedure to indicate how the rating scale was used. First, the entire child population of the second grade was given a group intelligence test and the scores were changed to percentile scores. Next, the second-graders above the median age of all the pupils enrolled in the second grade, whose scores were at or above the eighty-second percentile, were identified, and those who were at the ninety-ninth percentile and above in the younger age group were identified. This was the first screening to find those who might profit most from acceleration. Each child so identified was then rated by his teacher, using the scale shown in Fig. 17.3. Each teacher was invited to nominate other children who might profit by acceleration and rate them, using the same form. Subsequently, all children identified by the intelligence testing and by teacher nomination were given a standardized educational achievement battery.

On the basis of the three types of information—IQ, teacher rating, and achievement tests—a sample of 60 children was identified. This group was then divided randomly, half to receive five weeks of instruction during the summer and be promoted subsequently to the fourth grade, with the other half proceeding as usual into the third grade. As noted previously in Chapter 14, the results of the acceleration program were completely favorable. Toward the end of the fourth grade, the accelerated children had not caught up with equally bright, nonaccelerated fourth-graders who were a year older (**6**). Toward the end of the fifth-grade, the older nonaccelerated bright children were ahead of the accelerates on only 3 of 33 tests of convergent and divergent thinking, school achievement, and ratings in the social and emotional areas (**5**). The program was judged so successful at the end of the fourth grade that most of the original control group not accelerated at the end of the third grade were accelerated at the end of the fourth grade. It should be noted that no accelerated child will finish high school before the age of 17 years and 1 month. Had acceleration

Racine Public Schools
Teacher Rating Scale of Second Grade Children

Child's Name _____
  Teacher _____
School _____
  Date _____

Directions: This form is to be used to secure your appraisals of second-grade
children who might qualify for acceleration. The child whose name is listed
above has already met certain age and IQ criteria and will subsequently be
given an achievement test. Place a check ✓ in the space to the left of the
subitem which most adequately describes the child. Use only one check for each
item. Not all items carry equal weight. As a guide for rating in some of the
areas, you may wish to refer to Explanatory Sub-Statements for Knowledge and
Skills of Reporting Pupil Progress, Teachers Handbook, Second and Third Grades,
Racine Public Schools (pp. 10-19)

1. Artistic Ability (Shows growth in expressing ideas creatively. Uses art
   materials with care and understanding.)

_____ Outstanding
_____ Above average
_____ Average
_____ Below average

2. Musical Ability (Responds to and enjoys music. Shows growth in musical
   activities.)

_____ Outstanding
_____ Above average
_____ Average
_____ Below average

3. Dramatic Ability (Is expressive and enjoys dramatic play.)

_____ Outstanding
_____ Above average
_____ Average
_____ Below average

4. Vocabulary Development (Uses a reasonably large and appropriate vocabulary.)

_____ Outstanding
_____ Above average
_____ Average
_____ Below average

5. Language Arts (Expresses written ideas effectively. Expresses oral ideas
   effectively.)

_____ Outstanding
_____ Above average
_____ Average
_____ Below average

Fig. 17.3. Teacher rating scale of second-grade children.
(Racine Public Schools, Racine, Wisconsin.)

635

6. Handwriting (Writes rapidly, neatly, legibly.)

_____Outstanding
_____Above average
_____Average
_____Below average

7. Reading (Reads with understanding. Applies phonetic understandings. Uses skills in word structure. Reads well orally. Likes to read.)

_____Outstanding
_____Above average
_____Average
_____Below average

8. Spelling (Spells correctly in all written work.)

_____Outstanding
_____Above average
_____Average
_____Below average

9. Arithmetic (Understands meanings of numbers taught. Understands processes in arithmetic work. Works accurately. Applies arithmetic to everyday problems.)

_____Outstanding
_____Above average
_____Average
_____Below average

10. Intellectual Curiosity (Asks many questions. Has wide range of interests. Discusses new ideas eagerly. Observes unusual things.)

_____Outstanding
_____Above average
_____Average
_____Below average

11. Pride in Accomplishments (Is satisfied with only high-quality work. Enjoys doing well in most school work.)

_____Outstanding
_____Above average
_____Average
_____Below average

12. Persistence (Plans and carries through work consistently. Continues with difficult tasks.)

_____Outstanding
_____Above average
_____Average
_____Below average

Fig. 17.3. *(Continued).*

13. Emotional Development

_____ Normal
_____ Unusual

If checked unusual, describe: _____
_____
_____
_____

14. Social Development

_____ Normal
_____ Unusual

If checked unusual, describe: _____
_____
_____
_____

15. Physical Coordination

_____ Normal
_____ Unusual

If checked unusual, describe: _____
_____
_____
_____

16. This Child Is Accomplishing the Regular Second-Grade Work

_____ With ease
_____ With considerable individual help from the teacher
_____ With difficulty

17. This Child Could Now Do Regular Beginning Third-Grade Work

_____ With ease
_____ With a little further study and work
_____ With considerable individual help from a third-grade teacher
_____ With difficulty

18. This Child Could Now Do Regular Beginning Fourth-Grade Work

_____ With ease
_____ With a little further study and work
_____ With considerable individual help from a fourth-grade teacher
_____ With difficulty

Fig. 17.3. *(Continued).*

637

not occurred the youngest would be 18 years and 1 month when they graduated.

The purpose of the rating scale was to get information from teachers, based upon their observation of the pupils during the first seven months of the second grade. For this reason it is comprehensive and does not define each area being rated in great detail. For the particular purpose, however, the administrative, curriculum, psychological, and teaching staffs of the school, as well as the experimenters, felt that it would provide useful information on which to base decisions.

Also in Wisconsin, a longitudinal research project concerning creativity was conducted in the Milwaukee Public Schools. Creativity is an objective of education for all children, but particularly for those of above-average learning abilities. Some experimental tests of creativity were devised and administered to tenth- and eleventh-grade students of superior learning abilities. Did the tests measure creativity? To obtain a partial answer the experimenters turned to teacher observations and ratings.

A problem was arranged to elicit student responses during one class period. For example, in social studies the students wrote an essay on the topic, "One state, one nation, one world." With no previous practice or coaching, the students appeared at a regular class meeting and received the following instruction in order to elicit the essays:

As part of a study in creative thinking, I (the teacher) am working with the University of Wisconsin. We have agreed to provide the University with samples of creative work, so we have arranged the following exercise for you today instead of your regular assignment. This is an exercise in creative thinking. It will not count for your grade, and there are no right or wrong answers. How clearly you write, how you organize your ideas, and how neatly you write are not important. Write as many ideas as you can about the topic now presented. Remember, give as many original, sound, and clever ideas as you can think of. I cannot answer any questions you might have during the rest of the period.

The chart in Fig. 17.4 gives the rating scale of creative expression

Rating Scale of Creative Expression

	5	4	3	2	1
Number of ideas					
Originality of ideas					
Quality of ideas					

Fig. 17.4. Rating scale of creative expression.

used for evaluating what each student produced. The number of ideas each student expressed was counted. After a distribution was made of this count, the students in the upper 20 percent were assigned a rating of five, the next 20 percent a rating of four, and so on, with the bottom 20 percent assigned a rating of one. Originality was defined as new, different, and clever ideas not normally expressed by other students of this age, with a five being considered high and one low. Quality of ideas was rated in terms of what the rater considered to be quality in the particular subject field. Each of the three characteristics rated was given equal weight in arriving at a total score; for example, if a paper was rated five in number of ideas, two in originality, and four in quality of ideas, the total rating was 11.

The classroom teacher, the curriculum coordinator in the particular subject field, and a member of the university staff rated each paper. The average of the three ratings was used as the score of creative expression. This procedure whereby three competent persons rate the same performance improves the accuracy of the ratings. There is no better way for a teacher to check the reliability of his ratings of pupils' performances than to have another equally competent teacher rate the same performance and then compare the two sets of ratings.

These general guides may be useful in constructing rating scales:

1. Select qualities and performances for rating in relation to objectives. Generally, it is unwise to rate students on a quality or performance which you do not attempt to develop in class.
2. Use rating scales for important objectives which cannot be appraised by other means. It is better to rate performance related to one or two objectives, and to do it well, than to organize many scales which result in snap judgments.
3. Carefully describe each rating in terms of your ability to discriminate performance and behavior related to it. It is better to use only three ratings—excellent, average, poor—which you can discriminate than to further subdivide into five, eight, or ten ratings which you have difficulty in discriminating.
4. Compare your ratings of an individual's performance with the ratings of another teacher who understands the scale and performs the rating at the same time.
5. Make your scales understandable to students so that they aspire to achieve higher performance and so that they may rate themselves. Along with the usual areas of achievement and conduct, self-rating scales facilitate learning and self-evaluation by the students.

Check List

The check list used in the "count down" before firing a manned space ship is one of the most complex check lists ever devised by man. It serves the purpose of checking things off according to a fixed schedule which must be followed if the firing is to be successful. In the assembly of complex machinery such as an electronic computer, a detailed check list also is used. The teacher does not devise such elaborate instruments; however, whether the student is making a formal dress or conducting an experiment, the teacher often has developed a check list, either mentally or explicitly in written form. While observing the students' performances, he checks the sequence and accuracy of the students' activities. This check list, of course, may become a rating scale if each step is rated on two or more bases such as right-wrong or appropriate-inappropriate.

Figure 17.5 presents a check list for observing work methods of students. It is generalized rather than highly specific, but has been found useful by many teachers to guide their observation of students' work methods. Notice that the only checks are "Yes" and "No." The checking in itself does not help the student or the teacher. A check of "No" should be interpreted to mean that the student has not yet acquired the behavior and needs help to improve his performance.

Anecdotal Records

Behavior varies to some extent with the situation. The child who shows a great deal of interest and gets to work immediately with enthusiasm in the classroom may show no interest and accomplish little on the playground. Objective records of behavior in different situations give important clues to understanding the child and identifying the characteristics which make him unique. The following procedures are helpful in making anecdotal records of behavior: (1) Briefly, but in enough detail to reveal important aspects, describe the situation in which the behavior occurs. (2) Record the pupil's behavior exactly as it occurs; include specific details. (3) Check what has been recorded to make sure that it contains no subjective elements—adjectives such as "good" or "bad," "bright" or "dull," "lazy" or "industrious." (4) Interpret the behavior if there is enough information to reveal a pattern. Indicate clearly that it is your interpretation, and keep it separate from the objective portion of the record.

Studying a child in different situations enables one to learn much

Does the child attend to the task?		Yes No
Does he have all the supplies ready that he needs for the work?		Yes No
Does he start work immediately?		Yes No
Does he concentrate on the task?		Yes No
Does he finish most of the things he starts?		Yes No
Does he know how to attack the particular task?		Yes No

Fig. 17.5.   Check list for observing work methods.

about behavior in general and to gain insight into the various methods for best coping with certain behavior. Anecdotal records for one child, contributed by several teachers who have the child in class, are especially valuable for gaining better understanding of a child whom teachers do not understand well or who is not making good progress.

TEACHER-MADE OBJECTIVE ACHIEVEMENT TESTS

In the intermediate grades, high school, and college, the majority of tests used are of the written type, comprised of objective items. In many instances the teacher-made test has higher content validity for the classes of that particular teacher than does the standardized educational achievement test. The teacher designs the test to measure the objectives of a particular class, whereas the standardized educational achievement test is intended to measure outcomes in a large number of school situations.

The Objective Test

Less than a half century ago, the objective test was rarely used in American education. McCall played a leading role in establishing the true–false test for everyday use in the schools of the United States. He

641

urged teachers to use objective tests more frequently than once a year (for example, the standardized achievement test); he offered the true-false test as a supplement to, not a replacement for, the "traditional" test (for example, the "Compare," "Discuss" essay variety).

McCall's article on the true–false test appeared in the first volume of the *Journal of Educational Research*. The presentation is delightful and thorough. Especially enjoyable were the reasons he gave for using the test, two of which are quoted below:

> The traditional examination endangers a pleasant relationship because pupils more or less justly suspect that the score they make depends almost as much upon their conduct as upon their product. . . .
> The true-false examination is more enjoyable for the pupils. "Children cry for it" may be a bit exaggerated, but at any rate they hate it less. . . . It is agonizing for a pupil to describe at length a knowledge which he does not have in the hope that his command of English will camouflage his lack of information (7, 42, 43).

To facilitate understanding of and to improve skill in writing various types of items, consider the more complete discussion of: (1) types of objective test items; (2) abilities measured by written tests, (3) tests of work samples; (4) guides for constructing objective tests.

TYPES OF OBJECTIVE TEST ITEMS

The principal types of objective test items are alternate-choice, multiple-choice and multiple-response, matching, and completion. There are many variations of each type.

Alternate-Choice. An alternate-choice item requires the student to choose one of two answers as being more nearly correct.

Two Option:

The revised Stanford-Binet Scale is administered (1) individually, (2) to groups.

The Kuder Preference Record measures (1) interest, (2) aptitude.

True–False:

Evaluation is more comprehensive than is measurement.

Discovering the relative position of students in the class is a primary purpose of evaluation.

Yes–No:

Are all tests reported in *The Fifth Mental Measurements Yearbook* standardized?

Do both the Revised Stanford-Binet Scale and the Wechsler Intelligence Scale for Children yield a total IQ?

Right–Wrong:

A primary purpose of evaluation is to help students progress on learning tasks.

The Strong Interest Blank for Men is a self-report inventory.

Agree–Disagree:

The Rorschach Technique is widely used by teachers.

The Iowa Test of Basic Skills is a standardized educational achievement test.

Same–Different:

Ratio IQ–Deviation IQ

General Intellectual Ability–Scholastic Aptitude

Examine these true–false items to discover poor construction:

Standardized tests scarcely ever have reliability coefficients of 1.00.

Essay tests should not be used infrequently in any course.

Aptitude and *ability* are synonymous.

The title of Chapter 9 of this book is: "Psychomotor Skills and Abilities."

You probably agree that "scarcely ever" is vague; "not infrequently" makes the second item difficult, if not impossible, to answer; "aptitude" and "ability" usually have different meanings but may not always, depending on the context in which they are used; and the last item demands recall of specific words from the text—also, it could readily be a "trick" question because it is correct except that "Skills" and "Abilities" are reversed.

Some strengths of alternate-choice tests are that they may be adapted to testing in many classes, a great deal of material may be tested in a short time, and they are easily scored. In testing achievement, the weakness of alternate-choice tests is apparent: guessing is encouraged, the learner is presented with a wrong as well as a right response, and it is extremely difficult to construct alternate-choice items in which either choice is always correct or always incorrect. When part of the items in the test are usually true and others are always true, the student is faced with the problem of deciding whether a usually true item should be marked "true" or "false."

Multiple-Choice and Multiple-Response. The sample items from a standardized educational achievement battery presented in Chapter 16 (p. 607) are multiple-choice items in which the student selects one of three, four, or five choices as correct or better than the others. The multiple-choice item is used widely in standardized educational achievement tests because it is adaptable to measuring such outcomes as facts, understanding of concepts, the ability to apply information,

643

and the ability to evaluate, as will be shown in a later discussion of outcomes measured by written tests.

Multiple-response items require the student to choose all the correct choices in a series. The following are examples of multiple-choice and multiple-response items:

Multiple-choice:

To ascertain the effects on students' attitudes of a unit on food selection, the best evaluation procedure is to

A. use a teacher-made objective test over the unit.
B. use an essay test over the unit.
C. have the students plan menus for a hypothetical family for the week.
D. observe the students' food choices at lunch in the school cafeteria.

Multiple-response:

Which of the following are educational achievement batteries?

A. Iowa Test of Basic Skills.
B. Differential Aptitude Tests.
C. California Test of Mental Maturity.
D. Sequential Tests of Educational Progress.
E. WISC.

Multiple-choice items are more difficult to construct than are alternate-choice. Here are some general suggestions that may be used as a check list in making multiple-choice tests:

1. Select for each test item a concept or generalization of significance.
2. State the introductory statement and the choices clearly and concisely.
3. Avoid use of identical words in the introductory statement and the correct choice.
4. Include at least four choices to minimize guessing.
5. Make the choices parallel in English construction, for example, start all choices with a verb, a noun, or a preposition, etc.
6. Make only one choice correct; in part this is accomplished through careful wording of the introductory statement.
7. Make all choices plausible. Choices readily recognized as incorrect are useless for testing purposes.
8. Make the choices of equal length. When the correct choice is longer or shorter than the incorrect choices, the student may select it for that reason.
9. Distribute the correct choices randomly in the total test; that is, by

a random procedure, determine whether A, B, C, or D will be the slot used for the correct responses.

10. Set up clear instructions for the students to follow and arrange for quick and accurate scoring of the test.

11. In an untimed test have easy items first with items going in the direction of increasing difficulty. In a timed test, include difficult items early in smaller groups of easy-to-hard items.

Matching. Sets of matching items call for pairing an item in the first column with a word or phrase in the second column. There are many kinds of learnings which involve association of two things. Generally, matching items measure only whether the association has been made and whether the student recognizes it; matching items do not usually measure the extent to which meaning has been established. Matching items may have no distracters or several; now follow a set of matching items with no distracter and a set with one distracter.

Matching items with no distracter:
Match each item with the proper entry, A–D.

1. Denying the existence of some troublesome drive.

A. Rationalization.

2. Taking pride in the success of someone else.

B. Identification.

3. Accusing others of sins which tempt us.

C. Repression.

4. Finding excuses for our behavior which we know is improper.

D. Projection.

Matching items with a distracter:
Match each item with the proper entry,
A–E. (Based on 1937 Revision of Stanford-Binet Scale.)

1. Includes about 45 percent of the population.

A. IQ 70 and lower.

2. Includes about 2 percent of the population.

B. IQ 115–130.

3. Includes about 14 percent of the population.

C. IQ 90–110.

4. Can learn to read at a low level.

D. IQ 45–65.

E. IQ 25–45.

In constructing matching items it is well to use related materials within groups of items to be matched. For example, if you wish to test association of synonyms and association of men and events, use two sets of items—the first dealing with synonyms and the second with men and events. Also, do not provide clues to the answers. Notice in the example with no distracter that each item begins with a participle and the things to be matched are all nouns.

Including a distracter eliminates some possibility of guessing. For example, in the example with no distracter if the student knows two of the answers, he then has a 50–50 chance of guessing the other two correctly. Further, he may give the same answer for both unknowns, thus assuring himself that one is correct.

Sets of matching items should take into account the developmental level of the learners and the difficulty of the items. Long sets of items with several distracters are difficult; more important, when many errors are made by the students the test has little diagnostic value.

Completion. Completion tests are those in which words or phrases have been omitted in sentences; the student is to fill in the omitted word or phrases. This kind of test may measure ability to recall or to perceive relationships. Here is a sample of each:

Standardized tests that are consistent, that is, give similar results over time, are said to be_____ .

An aptitude test that predicts accurately college achievement has high predictive_____ .

The following are examples of poorly constructed completion items:

A_____test score is meaningless until converted into a derived score.

The_____Test measures intelligence.

_____tests may be grouped into categories: _____ .

You will probably agree that in the first poorly constructed item, the use of the article "A" gives a clue to the answer; the second is vague and indefinite and any one of several answers is correct; and the third has so many missing words that it is impossible to tell what is wanted.

To facilitate scoring of completion tests, consecutive numbers may be placed in the blanks, with instructions that the answers corresponding to the numbers be placed in the left margin.

ABILITIES MEASURED BY WRITTEN TESTS

Progress is being made in devising written tests which measure more than understanding of facts and concepts. The student's ability to apply factual information, to analyze it, to come up with the proper conclusion, and to evaluate may be appraised with skillfully constructed tests.

Whether a test simply measures memory of factual information or measures application of facts depends in part upon what the student

646

already knows. For example, in the previous matching items based on Stanford-Binet IQ's, if a person knows that the mean IQ is 100 with a standard deviation of 16 and knows the area under various portions of the normal probability curve, he can get all the items right by applying this information. In this case the matching items measure application. However, if the student does not know the above information but must rely upon his recall of a table or chart, the items measure recall of factual information.

With this in mind we turn now to sample items intended to measure the ability to apply information, the ability to analyze information, and the ability to evaluate information. These examples and the related discussion are drawn from Bloom, who in turn selected the items from the *Yearbook* of the National Society for the Study of Education (3):

APPLICATION:

The italicized statement at the end of the problem is assumed to be a correct answer. You are to explain the italicized conclusion by selecting statements from the list following the problem. (The student checks the explanations.)

If a person is planning to bathe in the sun, at what time of day is he most likely to receive a severe sunburn? *He is most likely to receive a severe sunburn in the middle of the day (11 A.M. to 1 P.M.) because:*

————We are slightly closer to the sun at noon than in the morning or afternoon.

————The noon sun will produce more "burn" than the morning or afternoon sun.

————When the sun's rays fall directly (straight down) on a surface, more energy is received by that surface than when the rays fall obliquely on the surface.

————When the sun's rays fall directly (straight down) on a surface, less sunshine is reflected from the surface than when the sun's rays fall obliquely on that surface.

————When the sun is directly overhead the sun's rays pass through less absorbing atmosphere than when the sun is lower in the sky.

————Just as a bullet shot straight into a block of wood penetrates farther into the wood, so will the direct rays at noon penetrate more deeply into the skin.

————The air is usually warmer at noon than at other times of the day.

————The ultraviolet of the sunlight is mainly responsible for sunburn.

It is assumed that this is a new problem for the student and that the task is one of selecting the correct explanatory principle. Some of the alternatives offered are factually correct while others are incorrect. Some are relevant, others are irrelevant. Some merely repeat the conclusion, while others state the generalizations or principles which have explanatory value. Selecting the appropriate explanatory generalizations requires that the student be able to relate the appropriate generalizations to the situation (2, 52–53).

647

ANALYSIS:

Statement of facts. The following table represents the relationship between the yearly income of certain families and the medical attention they receive.

Family Income	Percent of Family Members Who Received No Medical Attention During the Year
Under $1200	47
$1200 to $3000	40
$3000 to $5000	33
$5000 to $10,000	24
Over $10,000	14

Conclusion: Members of families with small incomes are healthier than members of families with large incomes.

Assumption (Select one):

1. Wealthy families had more money to spend for medical care.
2. All members of families who needed medical attention received it.
3. Many members of families with low incomes were not able to pay their doctor bills.
4. Members of families with low incomes did not receive medical attention [3, 127].

If it is assumed that the data and the problem are essentially new to the student, it requires that the student be able to identify the assumption which must be made to support the conclusion in relation to the data.

Evaluation: A 6A class was studying the geography of Europe and the land of the Dutch people. Someone in the class said that the homes of the Dutch people who live in America are always neat and clean. The teacher asked this question, "What reasons can you give for thinking that they are always neat and clean?"

Here are some of the reasons the children gave. Read them carefully and decide which are the best and which are the poorest.

———I heard someone say that they were neat and clean.

———I was in one Dutch home and it was clean.

———Our geography book said they were clean.

———I have been in many Dutch homes and all of them were neat and clean.

———I read in the story book that these houses were always neat and clean [3, 93].

Here the student is expected to judge the value of reasons in relation to a new question which is posed in the problem (2, 53–54).

Many teachers are using such measurements of learning outcomes in daily instruction rather than putting them in written tests. Also, test makers are increasingly trying to measure abilities by means like those described above. The Sequential Tests of Educational Progress, mentioned in Chapter 16, intend to measure more of these outcomes of education and less recall of factual information.

TESTS OF WORK SAMPLES

In many classes work samples rather than written tests are used by the teacher in evaluation. A few of the areas in which work samples are used will be discussed.

In business education the main tests are samples of typing, shorthand, and bookkeeping. The student simply hands in his work according to instructions of the teacher; this constitutes the test. In mathematics, students are assigned work to be performed; they turn it in and the teacher scores or otherwise marks it. In social studies, an outline map is given to the student on which he places names of countries, cities, rivers, products, and the like. If there are 30 entries the teacher may simply count each correct entry to arrive at a total score. In the natural sciences a variety of work samples is handled in the same manner. The work sample yields as useful evaluative information as any of the tests already discussed. When used for testing purposes, the work sample can be arranged to measure a variety of educational outcomes and may be scored objectively.

GUIDES FOR CONSTRUCTING OBJECTIVE TESTS

Stanley gives a meaningful group of guides for constructing classroom tests of achievement (8), most of them self-explanatory in terms of the previous discussion in this chapter and in Chapter 16:

A. *Planning the Test*
  1. Adequate provision should be made for evaluating all the important outcomes of instruction.
  2. The test should reflect the approximate proportion of emphasis in the course.
  3. The nature of the test must reflect its purpose.
  4. The nature of the test must reflect the conditions under which it will be administered.
B. *Preparing the Test*
  1. Begin the preliminary draft of the test as soon as possible.
  2. The test may include more than one type of item.
  3. Most of the items in the final test should be of approximately 50 percent difficulty.
  4. It is usually desirable to include more items in the first draft of the test than will be needed in the final form.
  5. After some time has elapsed, the test should be subjected to a critical revision.
  6. The item should be phrased so that the content, rather than the form of the statement, will determine the answer.
  7. An item should be so worded that its whole content functions in determining the answer, rather than only a part of it.

649

8. All the items of a particular type should be placed together in the test.
9. The items of any particular type in the test should be arranged in ascending order of difficulty.
10. A regular sequence in the pattern of correct responses should be avoided.
11. Provision should be made for a convenient written record of the pupil's responses.
12. The directions to the pupil should be as clear, complete, and concise as possible.

C. *Trying Out the Test*
1. Every reasonable precaution should be taken to insure excellent testing conditions.
2. The time allowance for the test should be generous.
3. The scoring procedure should be fairly simple.
4. Before the actual scoring begins, prepare answer keys and scoring rules.

D. *Evaluating the Test*
1. The difficulty of the test is a rough indication of its adequacy.
2. Individual items in the test should discriminate between pupils who rank high and those who rank low on the test as a whole.
3. It is a good practice to have the items interpreted and criticized by persons who have taken the test.
4. Whenever possible, the results on the test should be checked against an outside criterion.
5. It is sometimes desirable to estimate the reliability of the test.[1]

Three of the guides warrant further discussion. Number three under "preparing the test" implies that the average score made by all students who take the test should be about 50 percent. This is desirable if the intent is to devise a test which spreads the scores from very low to very high. In many cases, however, the teacher wants to find out how well the students have learned what has been taught, for example, 20 spelling words during the week. In this case, the test is comprised of the 20 words, and if every pupil scores 100 percent the teacher is satisfied with the test. If the average score is 50 percent, the teacher is properly dissatisfied with her teaching methods or with the performances of the pupils.

The same idea applies to number one under "evaluating the test." A test, of course, has a low reliability coefficient when students get most of the items correct. This in itself, however, is not adequate cause for selecting items that have not been taught or which the teacher thinks many students cannot for any other reason answer correctly.

[1] J. C. Stanley. *Measurement in today's schools.* (4th ed.) Englewood Cliffs, N.J.: Prentice-Hall, 1964. Reprinted by permission of the publisher.

Guide five under "evaluating the test" indicates the desirability of obtaining a reliability coefficient and procedures are outlined by Stanley for doing this (8, 341–359). Without computing a reliability coefficient, one can get a rough estimate of reliability by the following procedure. First, construct the best test possible and administer it. Second, score first the odd-numbered items and then the even-numbered items. Third, record the score on the odd-numbered items and then on the even-numbered items for each individual. Now, if the two scores for each individual are exactly the same, your test is 100 percent reliable. Suppose it is a 100-item test and many individuals have differences in scores of four or more on the two parts, some scoring higher and some lower on part two as compared with their part one scores. Your test is not highly reliable. Suppose a student made a score of 38 on the 50 odd-numbered items and a score of 33 on the 50 even-numbered items. The percent correct for each part test is 76 and 66 respectively. Suppose 70 percent is a passing mark. Which of the two scores should be used to decide whether the student passed? Your marking system should not have finer limits than the reliability limits of the tests used in arriving at the scores.

Teachers with access to a testing service tied in with electronic computers might investigate the possibilities for analyzing multiple-choice tests. A *Generalized Item and Test Analysis Program* for the 1604 Control Data Computer is useful for test analysis (1). The main information secured from computer analysis is:

1. Each individual's test score
2. The frequency distribution of the test scores, the number of pupils taking the test, the average pupil score, and the test's standard deviation
3. The reliability coefficient based on the internal consistency of the test
4. Item statistics that express the difficulty of each item and indicate whether or not the item is a "good" item; that is, did pupils who scored high on the test as a whole tend to get the item correct while others did not?

The preparation of the IBM cards for running the analysis is somewhat time consuming but much information is obtained.

Essay Tests

An essay test item may be responded to in a few minutes, during a class period, or during a longer period of time. If responded to in a few minutes, it is designated "short answer"; if during a class period, an "essay test"; and if during more than a regular class period, an "essay examination." These are arbitrary designations, of course, and are not equally applicable to third-grade children and high school seniors.

Whether shorter or longer items are included, essay tests may be used to appraise the student's ability to express himself clearly in written form, his ability to recall and organize relatively large amounts of material, and his ability to evaluate critically. If all three purposes are to be achieved with one test item, scoring must take all three factors into account. For example, the item "Evaluate the strengths and weaknesses of standardized tests" might be scored on the basis of how clearly the student expressed himself in written form, how many facts he cited, and how adequate his evaluation was. If only one mark were to be given for the entire answer, the teacher would have to decide how much weight to give each factor; this is difficult to do. It is perhaps wise to provide separate items for each factor, but this often destroys the usefulness of the test. In other words, a test with many short-answer items would make possible more reliable scoring but would not measure part of what it was intended to measure.

CLARITY OF EXPRESSION

Ability to express oneself clearly in written form is important in classes in creative writing, English composition, journalism, and business English. A teacher might use an essay test in summary evaluation or in preliminary appraisal of this ability. Appropriate items might be:

Outline the plot of *As You Like It*.
Write a theme on . . . .
Discuss the importance of form in business letters.
Summarize the important principles in writing a news story.

RECALL AND ORGANIZATION

An essay test may be constructed to measure the student's ability to recall a relatively large amount of material and to organize it into a meaningful pattern. This ability may be important in social studies, science, and literature. Here are samples of recall questions, frequently called "essay questions":

What are the provisions of the Eighteenth Amendment?
What nations are members of the United Nations?
List the Presidents of the United States since 1860.

Marking these items is fairly simple, but they do not measure ability to organize facts except at a very low level.

652

Items that appraise organizational ability must be more general. They might follow this pattern:

How did our tariff policies change from 1920 to 1940?
Discuss the growth of organized labor since 1880.
Describe how a federal revenue bill is enacted into law.

These questions require recall, longer answers, and more organization than the items in the first group, and they are more difficult to mark objectively.

CRITICAL EVALUATION

In many courses the teacher wants to develop the students' ability to evaluate critically. To some extent this ability may be measured by means of essay tests. Items intended for this purpose frequently begin with *How, Why, Compare, Contrast,* or some other term implying critical evaluation:

Why were the Articles of Confederation unsatisfactory? (A copy of the Articles may be provided.)
Compare the tariff policies of the Republican and Democratic parties, 1880 to 1948.
Contrast the editorial policy of the *Chicago Tribune* and of the *New York Times.* (The editorials may be supplied.)
Why does organized labor oppose the Taft-Hartley Act?

The emphasis in these questions is upon relationships, on the application of facts to broader problems, and on the evaluation of the facts and relationships.

In addition to the advantages already discussed, essay tests also may enable the student to acquire better methods of studying in preparing for an essay test than for an objective test. English teachers and teachers of other courses also use essay tests to encourage writing abilities and to gain insight into other cognitive abilities of children.

However, essay tests have certain weaknesses. Their validity may be low if they do not cover a comprehensive area of the subject field. There appears to be no way to correct for quality of handwriting and use of English, although these factors affect the tester's estimate of what is being measured. Essay tests may show low reliability, partly because only a few items can be answered during the test period and also because subjectivity enters into the scoring. Greater validity and reliability can be obtained when the teacher constructs test items carefully, defines the criteria for scoring the tests, and compares the marks given with those given by another competent teacher. Although essay tests take

653

considerably less time to produce, they are more time consuming to mark than objective tests.

SELF-REPORTING DEVICES

In Chapter 16, mention is made of published self-report inventories and check lists. Among other things, such instruments attempt to elicit information whereby interests, attitudes, values, problems, and a variety of personality traits of the student may be directly ascertained or inferred. The results of self-reports are best used to help the student understand himself, to help him make decisions about personal and educational matters, and to assist the teacher, psychologist, or other school personnel to provide optimal educational opportunities for him. The same purposes hold for teacher-made devices, including (1) questionnaire and check list as self-reports; (2) diary and autobiography; (3) conference and interview, (4) sociometric tests.

Questionnaire and Check List

The questionnaire and check list may be adapted to obtaining many kinds of information and may be planned to elicit general or specific responses. Here are questions intended to secure general responses:

1. Do you feel well and physically fit?
2. What do you like most about your home life?
3. What are your favorite recreational activities?
4. How do you get along with your classmates?
5. What are your plans after graduation?
6. What kinds of work do you think you are best suited for?
7. Are you getting from school what you need most?

Each of these questions may be made more specific and incorporate a checking feature. In this case interpreting the answers is less difficult, but considerably more time is needed to construct the questionnaire; also, the student's response is guided, not completely voluntary. Thus, the first question "Do you feel well and physically fit?" may be subdivided to include specifics, only one of which the student is to check:

a. All the time; never feel tired or ill.
b. Most of the time; feel tired once or twice each month.
c. Feel tired or unwell several times each month.
d. Feel tired or ill as many days as feel well.
e. Feel ill or tired most of the time.
f. Have not felt well for the past few months.

The student checks one of these choices but gives no reason for doing so. If the student's attitude toward his health as a whole is desired, it is better to use the general question without the specific choices.

Diary and Autobiography

The diary and autobiography, to be useful to the teacher in understanding the student, must be personal for the student. Because this is the case, the student should not be required to keep or to provide either one to the teacher unless it is understood that the purposes are as set forth previously for self-reporting devices. As a teacher, the senior author has not asked any elementary, high school, or college student in his classes to keep or to present to him a personal diary and does not plan to do so. Below is an outline for an educational autobiography which he uses in a first course in educational psychology.

EDUCATIONAL AUTOBIOGRAPHY

1. Review your formal and informal educational experiences up to this semester which you consider significant as a background for a teaching career. School, home, community, and church experiences may be included. You may wish to describe certain episodes or situations in detail. Other long periods of time may be dealt with in a sentence.
2. Give three to five of your main strengths for teaching, showing how they are related to the experiences above.
3. Discuss any doubts you may have about your qualifications for teaching or about teaching as a profession, showing how they are related to the experiences above.
4. Indicate what you will be doing five years after graduation and how well you will be satisfied with yourself and life generally at that time.

The student knows from the outset that the main purpose is to promote self-understanding and that no part of the autobiography will be revealed to any one else except with his consent (occasionally part of an autobiography is mimeographed without the student's name to illustrate style of writing, organization, type of significant incident, and the like). No information presented in the autobiography is communicated to any other person, including any one responsible for such decisions as encouraging the student to abandon a teacher-education program or to place him in a teaching position after he is graduated.

The autobiography is returned to the student at the time of the final interview between the student and instructor. Handled in this manner, the autobiography is useful in helping the student to understand himself better, to think about his lifetime goals, and to consider seriously the prospects for achieving his life goals through a career in teaching. Also, the student learns from first-hand experience some of the problems that may be encountered subsequently if he as a teacher invites pupils to reveal themselves accurately in an autobiography.

Conference and Interview

Conferences and interviews may be conducted like a prosecuting attorney examining a hostile witness or in an emotionally secure manner. The conference may be used to secure factual information of a nonemotional type, to discuss the results of a test or other evaluation procedure, to ascertain the causes of conflict between or among students, to appraise a student's personal problems, and the like. Though the conference must be planned for and conducted in terms of its purpose, the following guides are appropriate to many types:

1. Get to the purpose of the conference quickly, particularly if you initiated it.

2. Be courteous and friendly, regardless of the student's emotional state. For example, if the student is angry because he received a much lower grade than he expected, be calm and friendly as you ask him to tell you how he feels about the situation and what he thinks should be done about it.

3. Reflect the student's feelings in your comments and questions until the student gets his grievance "off his chest." Ask questions of the withdrawing or defensive student to keep him talking about his problem, but do not cross-examine. Unless severely upset, the student will give you all the information you need without much questioning if he trusts you.

4. Accept what the student says without contradicting him. If emotional, he will not accept contradiction from another person. If he is allowed to express his feelings, he himself will recognize when what he says is not factual.

5. Use words which the student understands, for a conference is basically a learning situation for him.

6. Reassure the student whose main problem is lack of assurance. A pat on the back and praise for what he has done well is all that is needed in some cases. But do not deceive a student by telling him that everything is all right when it is not.

7. Provide the student with the necessary information about any area in which he is in the process of making a decision-choice of courses,

cocurricular activities, friends, dating, and the like. Give him only enough information, however, to get him started securing information for himself if he can readily do so. In many places throughout his school life, the student needs information that is based upon adult experiences and he cannot readily get it except from adults. This is especially true in all situations involving conflicting values.

8. During the conference, summarize what has happened; do this yourself or ask the student to do it. For example, asking an emotionally upset student to summarize what has been said may help him to think more rationally about his problem. In discussing career choices, such a summary aids the student in clarifying his choice.

9. Encourage the student to propose a plan of action or to give a reasonable explanation of his problem. You may need to make suggestions to the student who apparently cannot bring himself to do this. You may find that such a student is severely disturbed emotionally or is faced with unfavorable conditions at home or in school which he cannot control.

10. Close the conference by summarizing what has happened, stating what apparently has been agreed upon concerning plans or arranging for another conference. Do this yourself or ask the student to do it.

After the conference, a written note might be made for the student's folder. If action by you is required, start it as soon as possible. For example, if some condition in the student's home or school life should be changed, initiate such changes yourself or go to the person who can. If the student is so severely disturbed that you cannot help him, begin referral procedures. After a series of conferences, further observation of the student is required for noting of any improvement; this followup helps in deciding whether future conferences may be helpful.

Most teachers, whether they want to or not, must confer with students at some time. It is rare to find a student who can solve his problems without individual guidance from adults. The student's success or failure in solving his problems and the help he receives from teachers and other adults are important in determining his success or failure as an adult. A little time spent with a student in an individual conference may save years of therapy later in his life or even years in a penal institution. Further, some students will provide information more reliably in a conference than in written form. Also, the teacher and student can make certain that the information desired and given is understood.

Sociometric Tests

Many teachers use a sociometric test for seating students in a classroom, for organizing students in work groups both in and outside the classroom, and for establishing effective relationships with the group soon after meeting them. Analysis of the results reveal to the teacher the interaction of the group as a whole, the patterns of friendship, and the kind and intensity of interaction among specific individuals within the group. The popular members of the group, the isolated and rejected members, and the cliques can be identified. When the teacher knows who the most popular members of the class are—there are usually from three to six in classes with 25 to 35 students—gaining their cooperation will assure him that most of the rest of the class will follow. When the isolated and rejected are located, the teacher knows who needs help first in making a good adjustment to the classroom.

ADMINISTRATION OF THE TEST

Depending on the purpose of the test and type of information desired, each student is asked to give the names of his best friends in the class, the students he would like to sit next to, those he would like to work with on a class project, or those he would like to work with in out-of-class activities. If the class is large, it is probably wise to ask each student to list three to five names. There is some advantage in placing no limit on the number of choices, for this will reveal more concerning the whole group.

The teacher makes sure that the students' choices are not revealed to other students, that they have no opportunity to discuss their choices before listing them, and that they do not see the pattern presented by their choices. The following are sample directions, using seating arrangement as the basis of choice:

You are now seated according to an alphabetical arrangement. Some of you have told me that you would like to change your seats. I want to give all of you an equal chance to sit near your friends. To help me do this, please write the names of those whom you would prefer sitting next to. Give your first, second, third, fourth, and fifth choices. I will use your choices to rearrange your seats. No one else will see your list of names.

To facilitate this, and especially to eliminate questions which would provide an opportunity for the discussion and comparison of choices, the teacher may give each student a slip of paper or 3 × 5 card like the following:

My name _____

Students I would like to sit next to:

First choice _____

Second choice _____

Third choice _____

Fourth choice _____

Fifth choice _____

It is imperative that the directions be specific and easily understood, that they be presented informally in a classroom situation, that they include the reason for administering the test, and that the data obtained lead to action by the teacher.

TABULATING AND DIAGRAMING

After the students have listed their choices, the teacher records them as shown in Figure 17.6. In the left margin are the names of the choosers. These same names are written across the top of the page in the same order under "chosen." Choices made by each student are placed in the proper column under "chosen." The number of choices received by each individual is obtained by totaling each vertical column. At the bottom of the chart are entered the total number of first, second, third, fourth, and fifth choices each student received.

A score for each individual may be arrived at by multiplying the total number of first choices by five, the total number of second choices by four, and so on down to one for the fifth choice. Thus, a student receiving three first choices, two seconds, and four thirds has a score of 35: $15 + 8 + 12$.

To seat the students according to their choices and to secure an overview of the patterning in the class, the choices are diagramed as shown in Figure 6.8 (p. 198). In a diagram, the teacher starts with the student who was chosen most frequently. Representing boys by a triangle and girls by a circle, he puts the most frequently chosen individual near the center of the paper and draws lines to all the other individuals chosen by him and from all the others who chose him. Arrows indicate the direction of choice; the order of the choice—first, second, etc.—is placed directly above the line and near the center. The teacher then plots the rest of the class, always grouping the most frequently chosen toward the center of the page and placing mutual choices near each other. Those who have received no choices are placed on the outer edge of the sociogram. Those who have neither received nor made choices are on the outside away from the group so they can be located readily.

CHOOSER

CHOSEN

	Alben	Anice	Briggs	Bush	Fabian	Fried	Gida	Gillet	Harms	Kay	Lee	Lester	Patmore	Prince	Ray	Ritter	Rusk	Smith	Stark	Towns
Alben	•			2			1			3					5				4	
Anice	5	•			2	4						1					3			
Briggs		4	•			1							3			5				2
Bush	1		5	•			2			4									3	
Fabian		3		2	•						5				4				1	
Fried			3			•	1			2							4			5
Gida	1	2		3		4	•			5										
Gillet							1	•							2					
Harms		1					3		•										2	
Kay		5		4						•		3					2			1
Lee	4			2							•				1					3
Lester		1										•								
Patmore		2								1			•							
Prince														•						
Ray	4			2		3					1				•		5			
Ritter			1						2							•				
Rusk		1			3												•			2
Smith				4		2						3			1	5		•		
Stark	2			5		1						3							•	4
Towns		4					3			1				5		2				•
1st choice	2	2	2			1	4			2	1	1			2				1	1
2nd choice	1	1	1	2	3		2		1	1					1	1	1		1	2
3rd choice		1	1	1		1	3				2	1	2				1		1	1
4th choice	2	2		1	1	1	1			1						1		1	1	1
5th choice	1	1	1		1					1	1			1	1	2		1		1
Score	19	22	18	13	15	10	39	0	4	17	12	8	6	1	17	6	9	1	14	19

Fig. 17.6.   Form for tabulating sociometric data. (Adapted from H. J. Klausmeier. *Teaching in the Secondary School* (2nd ed.) New York: Harper & Row, 1958, p. 53.)

Practice is needed to make sociograms. The first one may take two hours or longer and will require considerable experimentation in placing the symbols on the chart.

INTERPRETING SOCIOMETRIC DATA

The score indicates the intensity and amount of interaction. The students with the highest scores are the most accepted and desired members of the class; those with the lowest, the least desired.

The use of triangles for boys and circles for girls make it possible readily to determine the role of sex as the basis of choice. Except on the basis of sex, the sociogram does not reveal why choices were made as they were. Other information is necessary to determine why particular patterns are present.

The following will be found helpful in interpreting sociograms more fully: (1) Place intelligence or achievement scores in the triangles and circles to see if they were determining factors in choice. (2) Find out the racial or national background of the students and the location of their homes, for these may have been a contributing factor. (3) Determine whether a student's physical development or chronological age contributed. (4) Observe the group informally to see whether you can account for the pattern shown by the sociogram.

It should be noted that the results and interpretation apply only to a particular group and that scores are dependent upon the questions used to elicit the student's choices and upon other factors. For example, the total number of pupils in the class and the ratio of boys to girls in the class greatly affect the scores each individual receives and, therefore, the interpretation.

CAUTIONS IN SOCIOMETRIC TESTING

In the sociometric tests described thus far, the student is not asked to nominate those he does not like or least likes to be seated near, work with on a school activity, invite home, and the like. This can be done, however, and often is. Similarly, variations of sociometric test items used in research or by the teacher invite the student to make negative judgments about their classmates. In the "Guess Who" technique each student is asked to put in the name of the student who (guess who) fits such descriptions as:

Most talkative	_____	Least talkative	_____
Most liked	_____	Least liked	_____
Happy	_____	Unhappy	_____

Uses time well	_____	Wastes time	_____
Best in reading	_____	Poorest in reading	_____
Likes to recite	_____	Dislikes to recite	_____

To make the choices, the student is asked to make an unfavorable judgment, perhaps for the first time, about one or more of his classmates. Even when asked only to provide the names of friends or to guess who is happy, some incidental unfavorable comparing may be done. However, this is not deliberately encouraged by the administrator of the test.

Sociometric tests which elicit negative reactions to other students must be used with caution, if at all. They may provide useful information but also may initiate undesirable tensions and attitudes. Whoever administers such tests should assume full responsibility for possibly having encouraged a student for the first time to make an unfavorable judgment about a classmate with the approval of the administrator, and for having, perhaps unintentionally, encouraged the whole class in their out-of-class discussions of the test to categorize certain members of the class unfavorably. The giver of sociometric tests is obliged to use the information for constructive purposes and to answer any questions which parents of children rightfully raise after their children have informed them of the nature of the test. The latter applies, of course, to any information-gathering device.

Projective Techniques

Published projective tests were described briefly in Chapter 16. Also in that chapter the difficulties that school and clinical psychologists and psychiatrists have in inferring personality characteristics from the responses of the individual were mentioned. Though this difficulty is a real one, teachers uneducated in the theory and inexperienced in the interpretation of projective tests experiment at times with a number of devices such as paintings, play activities, and open-end statements.

Young children in the primary grades usually enjoy finger painting. In a 15-minute period, a child may produce several paintings. Occasionally, these paintings are examined to estimate such characteristics of the child as rigidity-flexibility, introversion-extroversion, and unhappy-happy. Also, the child may demonstrate his pleasant or unpleasant feelings toward self, classmates, teachers, or parents in his paintings.

In some clinical facilities, the child is given dolls of varying sizes and features to represent the persons in his immediate environment. On the basis of the child's reactions to the dolls and his responses to questions, the psychologist or psychiatrist infers the child's feelings to the people they represent. Children in school situations also may play with dolls and be observed and questioned by the teacher.

Open-end sentences, such as "I . . . ," "I like . . . ," "My teacher . . . ," "My school . . . ," "My parents . . . ," "The best . . . ," "The worst . . . ," "Sex . . . ," and the like are presented to the students with instructions to write whatever comes to mind as freely and fully as possible. On the basis of the responses, judgments are made about personal and social problems of the student, self-concept, and many other personality variables.

If the teacher who is with the child daily cannot make reasonably adequate judgments about the child through careful observing, interviewing, and other previously discussed informal procedures, it is doubtful that a projective device will be of much value. If the judgments are made reliably on other bases, the projective device is not needed. Therefore, published and informal projective devices should remain the responsibility of the school psychologist, clinical psychologist, and psychiatrist. Any teacher who has a strong need to experiment with the informal type might first administer it to himself and then turn the results over to a psychologist or psychiatrist for interpretation.

SUMMARY

Teachers' observations of students' performances and behavior and other observational information may be utilized advantageously to achieve the first three purposes of evaluation stated in Chapter 16. Rating scales and check lists are often constructed to summarize the results of observations. The anecdotal record is another means of securing observations of the performances and behavior of students. Developing criteria of good performances is essential to securing reliable and valid ratings of performance and behavior.

To achieve the many desirable outcomes that are possible, teacher-made tests must be carefully constructed and evaluated after being used. Objective and essay tests are generally used to ascertain how well students have learned. They also may be used to ascertain what the student knows or can perform before instruction begins.

Caution must be exercised in the classroom use of teacher-constructed self-reporting devices: the questionnaire, check list, diary, autobiography, interview, and sociometric tests. Useful evaluative information can be obtained with any of these; each also can be misused. The teacher or other person should know, before constructing and administering them, how the results will be used to improve the situation for those who respond.

With the widespread disagreement about interpretation of published projective tests, a person uneducated in the methods of personality appraisal should not attempt to devise projective tests, much less interpret the results. If the teacher cannot appraise the child's personality through daily observation and other informal techniques, it is doubtful that much insight will be gained through the teacher's attempting to use projective methods.

QUESTIONS AND ACTIVITIES

1. a. Discuss the number and types of evaluations the teacher makes about each student.
   b. For which of these might standardized tests be used advantageously?
   c. For which of these might teacher observations and other teacher-made devices be used advantageously?

2. Discuss the purposes of evaluation achieved through observation and evaluation of performance in a nontest situation.

3. Construct a rating scale of any performance or behavior which you consider important and applicable to your professional interests.

4. Construct a checklist for students' use in completing some project or other activity.

5. Construct a written objective test, based on the material in this chapter. In your test, use at least one item of each type listed in the chapter. If possible, administer the test to others who have studied the chapter and evaluate your test on the basis of the results obtained.

6. Construct at least two items, based on the material in this chapter, to measure the following: application, analysis, and evaluation.

7. a. Construct and, if possible, administer two essay items intended to measure the students' success in organizing and critically evaluating information presented in this chapter.
   b. Construct and, if possible, administer short-answer items intended to measure each of the following: recall of information, ability to organize information, and ability to evaluate information critically.

8. a. List types of information which you think teachers might ethically secure from all their students by use of self-reporting devices, other than sociometric tests.
   b. List the types of information you prefer not to supply to an instructor or other superior under any conditions.
   c. Of the types of information given in (b), which would you freely provide if you were certain constructive uses would be made of it? (Note that in responding to all parts of this question you are giving a self-report.)

9. Describe the conditions under which you would provide information freely about yourself in an interview.

10. Evaluate the guides proposed for conducting a conference or interview.

11. a. What types of useful information may be secured through sociometric testing?

b. What additional information is needed to interpret the results obtained from sociometric testing?

12. How can the results of sociometric testing be helpful to the isolated student? the members of cliques? the popular students?

SUGGESTIONS FOR FURTHER READING

Bloom, B. S. Quality control in education. In *Tomorrow's Teaching*, proceedings of a symposium held in January, 1961. Oklahoma City: Frontiers of Science Foundation, 1962, pp. 54–60. (In Page, 1964, 336–342.)

Bowden, B. V. Thought and machine processes. In B. V. Bowden (Ed.), *Faster than thought*. London: Pitman, 1953, pp. 311–337. (Portions reprinted in Cohen, 1964, 195–213.)

Council on Instruction. *Toward better evaluation on learning*. Washington, D.C.: National Education Association, 1962. (Portions reprinted under the title "Toward better evaluation of learning" in Seidman, 1965, 328–335.)

Ebel, R. L. Measurement and the teacher. *Educ. Leadership*, 1962, **20**, 20–24, 43. (In Ripple, 1964, 528–535.)

Educational Testing Service. *Multiple—choice questions: A close look*. Princeton: Educational Testing Service, 1963. (In Page, 1964, 343–356.)

Engelhart, M. D. Improving classroom testing. *What research says to the teacher*, No. 31. Washington, D.C.: National Education Association, 1964.

Findley, W. G. The complete testing program. *Theory into Practice*, 1963, **2**, 192–198. (In Seidman, 1965, 335–339.)

Glock, M. D., & J. Millman. The assignment of school marks. *Cornell miscell. Bull. 44*, 1963. (In Ripple, 1964, 558–566.)

Hastings, J. T. Tensions and school achievement examinations. *J. exp. Educ.*, 1944, **12**, 143–164.

Katz, M. Improving classroom tests by means of item analysis. *Clearing House*, 1961, **35**, 265–269. (In Seidman, 1965, 353–357.)

McLaughlin, K. F. *Interpretation of test results*. Washington, D.C.: U.S. Office of Education, 1964.

Stalnaker, J. M. The essay type of examination. In E. F. Lindquist (Ed.), *Educational Measurement*. Menasha, Wis.: Banta, 1951, pp. 495–532. (Portions reprinted under the title "Suggestions for improving essay questions" in Seidman, 1965, 339–346.)

Stanley, J. C. The ABCs of test construction. *NEA J.*, 1958, **47**, 224–226.

REFERENCES

1. Baker, F. B. *Generalized item and test analysis*. Madison: Univ. Wisconsin, 1963.

2. Bloom, B. S. (Ed.) *Taxonomy of educational objectives. Handbook I: Cognitive domain*. New York: McKay, 1956.

3. Henry, N. B. (Ed.) *The measurement of understanding*. Yearb. nat. Soc. Stud. Educ., 1946, **45**, Part I.

4. Klausmeier, H. J. *Teaching in the secondary school*. (2nd ed.) New York: Harper & Row, 1958.

5. Klausmeier, H. J. Effects of accelerating bright older elementary pupils: A follow-up. *J. educ. Psychol.*, 1963, **54**, 165–171.

6. Klausmeier, H. J., & R. Ripple. Effects of accelerating bright older pupils from second to fourth grade. *J. educ. Psychol.*, 1962, **53**, 93–100.

7. McCall, W. A. A new kind of school examination. *J. educ. Res.*, 1920, **1**, 33–46.

8. Stanley, J. C. *Measurement in today's schools*. (4th ed.) Englewood Cliffs, N.J.: Prentice-Hall, 1964.

CHAPTER 18

Statistics and
Research Design

T HE PURPOSE of this chapter is to
clarify the more common statistical terms and symbols frequently encountered in research reports so that the reader can interpret such reports meaningfully. Definitions are given, the symbols for common statistical terms are identified, and the computations needed to arrive at the statistic are shown. The computations are included to clarify statistical concepts, not to provide models of statistical analysis. Some of the information used for illustrative purposes was gathered by the senior author and his assistants on children of low intelligence enrolled in special classes for educable mentally retarded, and children of average and high intelligence in regular elementary school classes. Some of this comprehensive information about the same children is used throughout the chapter for illustrative purposes. Other information also is used for illustrative purposes.

The person who has had courses in descriptive and inference statistics may find it profitable to scan the chapter simply to identify any new ideas. The student with little previous work in statistics will find it necessary to read slowly and perhaps to perform the calculations. It is not necessary to be able to compute the statistic in order to understand the results of a study. However, it is helpful to understand such vocabulary and the use of statistics in: (1) tabulations and graphs; (2) measures of central tendency; (3) partition values; (4) measures of variability or dispersion; (5) standard scores; (6) measures of relationship; (7) sampling procedures; (8) significance of differences; and (9) factor analysis. Most introductory statistics books treat all of the above except factor analysis.

TABULATING AND GRAPHING DATA

In the Appendix are several tables of data to be used in conjunction with this chapter. Table A gives raw scores on 15 measures or variables for 40 boys. In the first column a number, from 1 to 40, is given to each boy. This series of numbers illustrates a *discrete* series; the total number of boys is obtained by counting each boy as a whole. Many other objects and events also can be counted as wholes and are not appropriately further divided into fractional parts.

The numbers in each of the other 15 columns are illustrative of a *continuous* series, although not arranged in sequential order. A continuous series of numbers implies gradations into fractional parts, with the whole number the midpoint. For example, boys number two and nine have IQs of 105 and 106, respectively. But the intelligence scores were already rounded off to the nearest whole number with the fractional parts eliminated; we therefore state that an IQ of 105 lies between 104.5 and 105.5, 106 is between 105.5 and 106.5, and so on. To be precise, 104.5 and 105.5 are the real limits of an IQ of 105. In all illustrations throughout this chapter, computations are based on series of continuous numbers.

Data that have been obtained on a group of subjects can be presented in a number of varied ways. Some of the more common means of tabulating and presenting data are discussed below, namely: the frequency distribution table, the histogram, the frequency polygon, and the cumulative percent curve.

Frequency Distribution Table

One way to present data is to consider each case individually and unaltered. For example, considering the IQ column in Table A, it could be said that of the 40 boys, one had an IQ of 52, one an IQ of 65, two an IQ of 70, etc. This is often the procedure followed in computing the mean of a number of scores (see the next major section on "Measures of Central Tendency").

Often, however, the data are grouped into a series of mutually exclusive, equal *class intervals* to reduce the results to a form more easily understood and graphed. The accuracy of the grouping method depends upon the number of class intervals and the number of cases. Although there is no fixed rule for deciding the number of class intervals into which to group scores, it is usually advisable to use no fewer than 10, nor more than 16. Also, computations are easier if the size of the interval is an odd number. For example, consider an interval of size four, with *class* limits from 103 to 106 (recall that the real, or true, limits of this interval are 102.5 to 106.5, a spread of four points). The midpoint of this interval is 104.5, a decimal, and would be used in all further computations. However if the interval size is an odd number, say five, the midpoint is a whole number (class limits 103 to 107, real limits 102.5 to 107.5, midpoint 105).

Consider the column of IQ scores in Table A. The scores vary from 52 to 146, a range of 95 points (146.5 minus 51.5). An interval of 7 points would yield 14 mutually exclusive categories. Table 18.1 gives the class intervals, the frequency (f) in each, the midpoints and real limits of the intervals, and also two other columns: cumulative frequency and cumulative percent.

TABLE 18.1.

Frequency Distribution of Boys' IQs

Class Interval	f	Cumulative f	Cumulative %	Real Limits	Mid-Point
143–149	1	40	100.0	142.5–149.5	146
136–142	1	39	97.5	135.5–142.5	139
129–135	1	38	95.0	128.5–135.5	132
122–128	6	37	92.5	121.5–128.5	125
115–121	3	31	77.5	114.5–121.5	118
108–114	8	28	70.0	107.5–114.5	111
101–107	9	20	50.0	100.5–107.5	104
94–100	1	11	27.5	93.5–100.5	97
87–93	0	10	25.0	86.5–93.5	90
80–86	2	10	25.0	79.5–86.5	83
73–79	3	8	20.0	72.5–79.5	76
66–72	3	5	12.5	65.5–72.5	69
59–65	1	2	5.0	58.5–65.5	62
52–58	1	1	2.5	51.5–58.5	55

The cumulative frequency is obviously the summation of the entries in the frequency column, beginning with the frequency in the lowest IQ interval. Entries in the cumulative percent column reflect the same information as in the cumulative frequency column. For example, the cumulative frequency up to and including the 101 to 107 class interval is 20, which represents a cumulative percent of 50.0 $\left(\text{i.e., } \dfrac{20}{40} \right)$.

Histogram

The information in Table 18.1 also may be graphically displayed by means of a histogram. The vertical axis of the histogram is marked off in frequency units; the horizontal axis can be marked off in either class or real limits. As a general rule, the vertical axis should begin at zero, but no such requirement exists for the horizontal axis. The histogram displayed in Fig. 18.1 uses real limits to partition the horizontal axis.

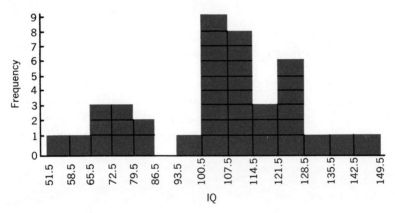

Fig. 18.1.   Histogram of boys' IQs.

In effect, each boy is represented by a small rectangle; a total of 40 such rectangles are located under the dark line that forms the shape of the histogram. This distribution is distinguished by its three peaks from 65.5 to 79.5, 100.5 to 114.5, and 121.5 to 128.5, that is, it is a trimodal distribution.

Frequency Polygon

A histogram is enlightening when a single distribution is being considered, but it is of limited use in comparing two or more distributions. More appropriate for the latter purpose is the frequency polygon.

The frequency polygon is laid out in exactly the same manner as was the histogram. However, the shape of the frequency polygon is determined by connecting the midpoints of each class interval at a height appropriate for the frequency in the class interval. The relationship between the frequency polygon and the histogram is readily seen in Fig. 18.2.

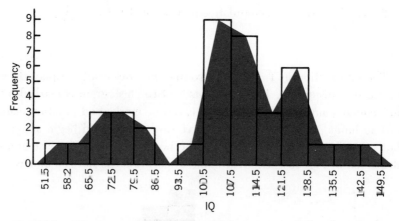

Fig. 18.2. Frequency polygon of boys' IQs superimposed on histogram.

It may be noted that the area under the two "curves," that is, under the frequency polygon and the histogram, is equal; each triangle of area included in the histogram but excluded from the frequency polygon is matched by a new triangular area found only under the frequency polygon.

Cumulative Percent Curve

The information on cumulative percent found in Table 18.1 can also be graphed. The vertical axis of the cumulative percent curve is marked off in cumulative percent, the horizontal axis in the *upper real limits* of the class intervals. Figure 18.3 depicts a cumulative percent curve based on the IQs of the 40 boys.

MEASURES OF CENTRAL TENDENCY

We often wish to describe a group of individuals in a classroom, school, or experimental situation by such terms as *typical* or *average,* and for this purpose we use a measure of central tendency which indicates where the scores are concentrated. Three measures of central tendency are the *mean, median,* and *mode.*

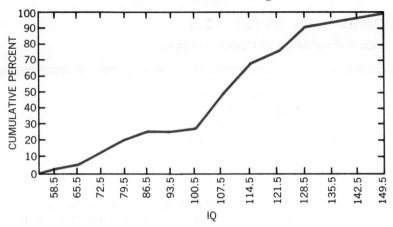

Fig. 18.3.   Cumulative percent curve of boys' IQs.

Mean

The mean is the arithmetic average of a set of scores, calculated by adding all the scores and dividing by the number of scores. In effect, the arithmetic mean is the balancing point for the distribution of scores. Let us demonstrate for a simple case of ungrouped data.

Suppose that you wished to find the mean of these five scores: 9, 8, 4, 3, and 1. Their sum is 25, which when divided by the number of scores (5), yields a mean of 5. For ungrouped data like this and like that presented in Table A, the formula for computing the mean is shown in Computing Guide 18.1.

Recall also that a set of scores can be grouped into a frequency table as was done in Table 18.1 for IQ for the 40 boys. When computing the mean from grouped data, it is assumed that all the scores in a class interval lie at the midpoint (M) of that interval. By multiplying each midpoint by the frequency, or number of scores in that interval, a product is determined that is used in computing the mean of the grouped data. This has been done in Table 18.2; note that the first three columns are taken directly from Table 18.1 and that the fourth column is the product of the second and third columns.

With this information, one is able to proceed to compute the mean for grouped data; this has been done in Computing Guide 18.2.

The fact that Computing Guides 18.1 and 18.2 produce slightly different mean IQs (104.1 and 104.0, respectively) should be no cause for alarm. Recall that an assumption was made in grouping the data; this has resulted in an approximate mean IQ which is .1 of an IQ point from the raw score mean IQ. By increasing the number of intervals, this

COMPUTING GUIDE 18.1

Computing the Mean of Ungrouped Data

Let: $\overline{X}$ (read *X bar*) = the mean
Σ (read *Sigma*) = the sum of
X = each score
N = the number of cases

Formula: $\overline{X} = \dfrac{\Sigma X}{N}$

Example: Find the mean of the 40 IQ scores shown in Table A.
Step 1: Add the 40 IQs; determine that the $\Sigma X = 4164$
Step 2: Substitute numbers in the formula and perform the indicated operations:

$$\overline{X} = \frac{4164}{40} = 104.1$$

TABLE 18.2.

*Multiplication of Frequency by Class–Interval Midpoints
for Boys' IQ, Grouped Data*

Class Interval	f	Midpoint (M)	fM
143–149	1	146	146
136–142	1	139	139
129–135	1	132	132
122–128	6	125	750
115–121	3	118	354
108–114	8	111	888
101–107	9	104	936
94–100	1	97	97
87–93	0	90	0
80–86	2	83	166
73–79	3	76	228
66–72	3	69	207
59–65	1	62	62
52–58	1	55	55
Total	40		4160

COMPUTING GUIDE 18.2

Computing the Mean of Grouped Data

Let: $\overline{X}$ = the mean
Σ = the sum of
f = the frequency in each class interval
M = the midpoint of each class interval
N = the number of cases

Formula: $\overline{X} = \dfrac{\Sigma f M}{N}$

Example: Find the mean of the 40 IQ scores as grouped in Table 18.2.

Step 1: Multiply each class interval's midpoint by the frequency in that interval.

Step 2: Add the products found in Step 1; determine that the $\Sigma fM = 4160$.

Step 3: Substitute numbers in the formula and perform the indicated operations:

$$\overline{X} = \frac{4160}{40} = 104.0$$

approximation would get closer to the true mean IQ. Once the number of intervals is great enough that each score is considered individually, the two quantities ΣX and ΣfM would be identical, and the two formulas would yield identical means.

Median

The median is the point in a set of continuous measurements on both sides of which there are an equal number of cases. If there is an odd number of cases, the median is the middle-most score. For example, given the scores 8, 10, 2, 6, and 5, 5 is the median as two cases lie both above it and below it. If there is an even number of cases, the median is the point that lies midway between the two middle-most scores. Given the scores 3, 6, 8, and 12, the median would be 7.

The computation of the median for grouped data is more complicated. Rather than burden the reader with extremely arbitrary symbols and formulas, Computing Guide 18.3 merely gives the steps necessary to determine the median of the 40 IQ scores presented in Table 18.1.

COMPUTING GUIDE 18.3

Computing the Median of Grouped Data

Example: Find the median of the 40 IQ scores as grouped in Table 18.1.

Step 1: Multiply the number of cases (N) by .5; $40 (.5) = 20$.

Step 2: Determine by inspection the real limits of the interval containing the median by counting up 20 cases from the lower end of the scores. Checking the cumulative percent column, the 20th case lies in the interval 100.5–107.5.

Step 3: Add to the lower real limit (100.5) an increment determined by multiplying the size of the class interval (7) times the quotient formed by dividing the frequency in the interval (9) into the quantity $.5N$ minus the frequency up to the interval (or $20 - 11$).

Therefore:

$$\text{Median} = 100.5 + 7\left(\frac{20 - 11}{9}\right)$$

$$= 100.5 + 7\left(\frac{9}{9}\right)$$

$$= 100.5 + 7 = 107.5$$

The mean is a better measure than the median if the value of all scores in a distribution is to be reflected in the measure of central tendency; the median is preferable where the value of the typical score is desired. For example, if five members of a bowling team scored 12, 14, 33, 51, and 300, the mean (82) is more appropriate for estimating how the team would place in a bowling tournament; the median (33) is better for estimating the standard bowling performance of the group members. In this case, no matter which measure of central tendency is used, the team appears headed for trouble.

Mode

The mode is the most frequently occurring X value, or score, in ungrouped data; or, in grouped data, it is the midpoint of the class interval which has the greatest frequency. For example, the mode number of permanent teeth of the boys shown in Table A is 12; 17 boys had 12 teeth. Again in Table A, the mode IQ scores are 101, 109, 123, and 128, 3 cases of each. For the grouped IQ data, the mode is the interval having real limits 100.5 to 107.5 (9 cases); this can be seen in either Table 18.1, Fig. 18.1, or Fig. 18.2. A unimodal distribution has scores clustering in one location (as in the case of the number of permanent teeth). Although not containing equal number of cases, the three clusters or humps in Fig. 18.1 result in a trimodal distribution, as was noted.

PARTITION VALUES

We often wish to know more about sets of scores than just the central tendency. If reading or intelligence scores are available for larger groups, we may wish to divide the scores into fourths, tenths, and so on; or we may wish to compare the relative standing of one individual on several measures. Quite analogous to the median in computation are the quartiles, deciles, and percentiles referred to as partition values.

The quartiles (Q_n) are the points in the distribution that divide the frequencies into four equal groups, the deciles (D_n) into ten, and the percentiles (P_n) into 100. The subscript n refers to the order of these values; for example, Q_3 is the third quartile and P_{10} is the tenth percentile. Q_1 has one-fourth of the cases below it; Q_3 has three-fourths of the cases below it; similarly P_{85} has 85 percent of the cases below it. Notice that the median $= Q_2$ (second quartile) $= D_5$ (fifth decile) $= P_{50}$ (fiftieth percentile). The fourth quartile, tenth decile, and one-hundredth percentile are not computed, for conceptualization of the point in the distribution below which 100 percent of the cases fall is difficult if not impossible.

Keep in mind that a partition value is a point in a distribution and is not necessarily equal to any score or case in the distribution. Computing Guide 18.4 can be used to calculate any partition value in a way similar to that used for the median (see Computing Guide 18.3).

MEASURES OF VARIABILITY
OR DISPERSION

Besides knowing the central tendency of a set of scores, we also often want to know the highest and lowest score, the extent to which the scores are dispersed about the mean or other measure of central tendency, and the like.

COMPUTING GUIDE 18.4

Computing Partition Values of Grouped Data

Example: Find the sixty-fifth percentile (P_{65}) of the 40 IQ scores as grouped in Table 18.1.

Step 1: Multiply the number of cases (N) by .65; $40 (.65) = 26$.

Step 2: Determine by inspection the real limits of the interval containing P_{65} by counting up 26 cases from the lower end of scores. Checking the cumulative frequency column, the twenty-sixth case lies in the interval 107.5–114.5.

Step 3: Add to the lower real limit (107.5) an increment determined by multiplying the size of the class interval (7) times the quotient formed by dividing the frequency in the interval (8) into the quantity $.65N$ minus the frequency up to the interval (or 26–20).

Therefore:

$$P_{65} = 107.5 + 7\left(\frac{26 - 20}{8}\right) = 107.5 + 7\left(\frac{3}{4}\right) =$$
$$107.5 + 5.25 = 112.75.$$

The *variability* of a series of scores is the extent to which the scores are spread out along the scale from an average value such as mean, median, or mode. No one partition value such as Q_1 or P_2 is a direct measure of variability, but certain comparisons of partition values such as P_1 and P_{99} or Q_1 and Q_3 yield a measure of variability.

Range

Discussed briefly above in the section on the frequency distribution table, the range is the simplest measure of variability. It is the difference between the highest and lowest real limits in the distribution, therefore the range alone provides little useful information. As an example, the range of arithmetic achievement, calculated from Table A $= 142 - 87 + 1 = 56$, or $142.5 - 86.5 = 56$. The 1 is added in the first computation to take care of the previously mentioned nature of continuous measures.

Quartile Deviation

The quartile deviation is used primarily with nonsymmetrical sets of scores in which the median rather than mean is the better measure of central tendency. Inspection of Table 18.1 should convince the reader that Q_1 or the twenty-fifth percentile is 86.5; applying Computing Guide 18.4, Q_3 or the seventy-fifth percentile is found to be 119.2, for example, $114.5 + 7 \left(\dfrac{30 - 28}{3} \right)$. With this information, Computing Guide 18.5 can be used to find the quartile deviation.

COMPUTING GUIDE 18.5

Computing the Quartile Deviation

Let: Q = the quartile deviation
Q_1 = the first quartile
Q_3 = the third quartile

Formula: $Q = \dfrac{Q_3 - Q_1}{2}$

Example: Find the quartile deviation of the 40 IQ scores as grouped in Table 18.1.
Step 1: Determine Q_1 and Q_3 using Computing Guide 18.4.
Determine that $Q_1 = 86.5$ and $Q_3 = 119.2$.
Step 2: Substitute numbers in the formula and perform the indicated operations:

$$Q = \frac{119.2 - 86.5}{2} = \frac{32.7}{2} = 16.35.$$

Variance and Standard Deviation

The variance and the standard deviation are widely used in describing the variation of a set of scores from the mean and also in testing hypotheses. The *variance* is defined as the average of the squares of the deviations of the scores from their mean; the standard deviation is simply the square root of the variance. Seldom is it now necessary to change all raw scores to deviation scores because of the availability of desk calculators and the advent of rapid electronic computers. These devices permit securing the variance, standard deviation, and many other measures described subsequently without grouping the scores. The raw scores are not put in rank order in most cases but appear as in Table A. Computing Guide 18.6 gives the formula (in raw-score units) and the procedure for computing the variance and the standard deviation.

COMPUTING GUIDE 18.6

Computing the Variance and the Standard Deviation of Ungrouped Data[a]

Let: s^2 = the variance

s = the standard deviation

N = the number of cases

ΣX^2 = the square of each score, subsequently added together

$(\Sigma X)^2$ = the sum of all scores, squared

Formulas: $s^2 = \dfrac{1}{N-1}\left[\Sigma X^2 - \dfrac{(\Sigma X)^2}{N}\right]$

$s = \sqrt{s^2}$

Example: Find the variance and standard deviation of the 40 IQ scores in Table A

Step 1: Add all the scores; determine that the $\Sigma X = 4164$.

Step 2: Square all scores and add them; determine that $\Sigma X^2 = 452{,}116$.

Step 3: Substitute numbers in the formula and perform the indicated operations:

$$s^2 = \frac{1}{40-1}\left[452{,}116 - \left(\frac{4164}{40}\right)^2\right] =$$

$$\frac{1}{39}\,(452{,}116 - 433{,}472.4) = 478.0410$$

Step 4: Take the square root of s^2 to determine s:

$$s = \sqrt{478.0410} = 21.86.$$

[a] This guide may be used for grouped data by substituting ΣfM (see Computing Guide 18.2) whenever ΣX now appears in the formula above.

The standard deviations of the 15 variables in Table A are calculated and listed in the row designated s. Recall that in raw score form, without grouping the data into a frequency table, the mean or $\overline{X} = \dfrac{\Sigma X}{N}$;

note that no new symbols are used in the formula for variance and standard deviation. It will be seen subsequently that N, $\overline{X}$, X, X^2, and $(\Sigma X)^2$ are also the basic data in computing standard scores and correlations from ungrouped data.

STANDARD SCORES

In Table A, a variety of measurements is given: height in inches, weight in pounds, strength of grip in kilograms, number of permanent teeth, carpal age in months, intelligence scores, reading, arithmetic, and language achievement in months, and ratings on six personality variables. To read across the rows for each boy is quite meaningless, because the numbers are not in comparable units. One means of getting more comparable scores is to change each set of scores to percentile scores as shown previously. A more precise method is to change each set of scores to standard scores. A standard score, usually called "sigma score" or "z-score," is a score derived from a set of raw scores by expressing each raw score as a deviation from the group mean in standard deviation units. Standard scores are useful in comparing measurements on unlike scales and with different variables as indicated above. Standard scores can be negative or positive. Most standard scores fall within the range of $+ 3.0$ to $- 3.0$ standard deviation units, and the algebraic sum of a set of standard scores is always zero. In other words, a distribution of standard scores has mean zero and standard deviation 1.

Computing Guide 18.7 shows how standard scores are computed and the resulting usefulness of the obtained standard scores.

In raw score units, Boy 29 had an arithmetic age of 140 months; his language age also is 140 months. These months of arithmetic and language age were obtained by looking up Boy 29's arithmetic and language raw scores in tables of norms. Though Boy 29 shows the same achievement level in the two subjects on the national level (140 months), how did he compare in arithmetic and language with the other 40 boys in this particular group? The z-scores computed in Computing Guide 18.7 show Boy 29 considerably above the average of the 40 boys in both subjects, but more so in arithmetic. In comparison with the other boys, he was above the mean in all except number of teeth. In relation to *himself,* he was highest in emotional adjustment, next high in IQ and so on.

By dividing deviation scores on a test or measure by the standard deviation for a particular group on that test or measure, one obtains

COMPUTING GUIDE 18.7

Computing Standard Scores

Let: $z =$ the standard score
  $X =$ the raw score
  $\overline{X} =$ the mean of a group of scores
  $s =$ the standard deviation of a group of scores

Formula: $z = \dfrac{X - \overline{X}}{s}$

Example: Compute the standard scores for Boy 29 in Table A for arithmetic, language, IQ, emotional adjustment and permanent teeth.

Step 1: Determine $\overline{X}$ and s for arithmetic achievement; in Table A they are given as 120.25 and 16.88 respectively.

Step 2: Substitute numbers in the formula and perform the indicated operations:

$$z \text{ (arithmetic)} = \frac{140 - 120.25}{16.88} = \frac{19.75}{16.88} = +1.17$$

Step 3: In similar manner, compute the other standard scores.

$$z \text{ (language)} = \frac{140 - 121.75}{23.86} = \frac{18.25}{23.86} = +0.76$$

$$z \text{ (IQ)} = \frac{139 - 104.10}{21.86} = \frac{34.90}{21.86} = +1.60$$

$$z \text{ (emotional adjustment)} = \frac{7.50 - 4.14}{1.39} = \frac{3.36}{1.39} = +2.42$$

$$z \text{ (permanent teeth)} = \frac{13 - 14.50}{4.10} = \frac{-1.50}{4.10} = -0.37$$

standard or z-scores. Although somewhat time consuming to compute, these standard scores allow meaningful comparisons among the scores of several tests, or measurements on several variables. This is true because they are expressed in a common unit, namely the standard deviation unit.

MEASURES OF RELATIONSHIP

One of the important problems facing psychologists and educators is to ascertain the relationships among sets of measurements of the same individual; for example, the relationship between IQ and achievement, between interest and achievement, between intellectual and psycho-motor abilities, between success in school and success in out-of-school activities.

In the study from which the information in this chapter was drawn, we were concerned, among other things, with the relationships among various physical, intellectual, social, and emotional measures. After ascertaining the relationships among 15 sets of measures for boys (and for girls), we were further concerned with ascertaining the extent to which growth during a period of one year is composed of general, group, or specific factors. After securing the measures on a stratified random sample (to be discussed later) of boys and girls from a larger child population, we computed correlations among the sets of measures.

The term *correlation* refers to the relationship between two or more variables such as height, weight, IQ, and the like. The *coefficient of correlation,* a number, indicates the magnitude and direction of the relationship. Which of several methods of computing correlation should be used depends on the type of numerical information obtained, the number of variables under consideration, and the method of treat-ing the variables. Product-moment and rank correlation will be dis-cussed here.

Product-Moment Correlation

The product-moment coefficient of correlation, usually designated by the symbol r, is a widely employed statistic, devised as a measure of relationship between two sets of measurements (variables) on the same subject, or between measurements on pairs of subjects. The r can range from -1.00 for a perfect inverse relationship, through 0 for no syste-matic relationship, to $+1.00$ for perfect direct relationship.

In interpreting a high correlation between two variables, it is incor-rect to conclude that one variable *causes* the other. Another alternative is that both variables may be influenced by some common factor or factors. Another caution is that r cannot be interpreted as a percentage; an r of .60 does not mean 60 percent relationship. Similarly, an r of .60 does not indicate twice the relationship shown by an r of .30. Also, r is entirely independent of the units in which the two variables are ex-pressed; for example, the boys' height in inches can be correlated with their weight in pounds or with carpal age in months. The meaning of correlation may be brought out more clearly by constructing a scatter-gram, a graph on which the two scores of the same individuals are plotted.

Figures 18.4, 18.5, and 18.6 are scattergrams which present the meaning of r's of varying size graphically. Figure 18.4 is for IQ and arithmetic, where $r = .94$; Fig. 18.5 is for IQ and strength of grip, where $r = .51$; and Fig. 18.6 is for carpal age and language achievement, where $r = .16$. To interpret Fig. 18.4, note that three boys had IQs between 66 and

IQ

	85-89	90-94	95-99	100-104	105-109	110-114	115-119	120-124	125-129	130-134	135-139	140-144
146-153											1	
138-145												1
130-137												1
122-129										1	2	3
114-121										1	2	1
106-113							1	2	4	3		
98-105							2	3	1	1		
90-97												
82-89		1	1									
74-81	1		1									
66-73	1		3									
58-65		1										
50-57	1											

Arithmetic

Fig. 18.4. Scattergram for boys' arithmetic achievement (X) and IQ (Y): r = .94.

73 and arithmetic ages of 95 to 99; similarly, three had IQs of 122 to 129 and arithmetic ages of 135 to 139; all other entries are interpreted in the same way. Figure 18.4 shows a high positive relationship between IQ and arithmetic; the higher the IQ, the higher the arithmetic achievement, and vice versa. Had the correlation been 1.00 instead of .94, every boy's set of two scores would more nearly have fallen in the 12 cells running diagonally from lower left to upper right. This scattergram is 13 by 12.

In Fig. 18.5 the r is .51. Notice that many cells with entries are quite distant from a diagonal line from lower left to upper right, and also that the six boys with strongest grip had IQs of 98 to 129 and that three

IQ	11.5-12.99	13-14.49	14.5-15.99	16-17.49	17.5-18.99	19-20.49	20.5-21.99	22-23.49	23.5-24.99	25-26.49	26.5-27.99	28-29.49
146-153					1							
138-145							1					
130-137							1					
122-129					1		1	2	1	1		
114-121								2	1			1
106-113			1			4	4					1
98-105			3				2	1		1		
90-97												
82-89					2							
74-81	1		1									
66-73		1	1		1		1					
58-65								1				
50-57					1							

Strength of grip

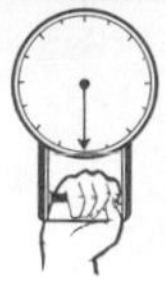

Fig. 18.5. Scattergram for boys' strength of grip (X) and IQ (Y) : r = .51.

with IQs above 130 were of about average strength. Figure 18.6 shows a correlation of .16 (near 0, or no relationship). Two boys of highest carpal age, 140 to 144, have the lowest and highest language scores— 70 to 75 and 148 to 153—respectively.

The size of negative correlations has the same meaning as that of positive correlations; however, the relationship is inverse. In a scattergram the scores would lie along a line going from upper left to lower right. The scattergram can be used directly for computing r, but the process is more laborious than using a desk calculator.

Several formulas exist for computing correlations. If the raw scores are already changed to deviation scores, for example, $x = X - \overline{X}$ and $y = Y - \overline{Y}$, the formula is $r = \dfrac{\Sigma xy}{\sqrt{(\Sigma x^2)\,(\Sigma y^2)}}$ where x and y are the deviation scores. If both the deviation scores and standard deviations are available, the formula is $r = N \dfrac{xy}{s_x\,s_y}$ where s_x and s_y are the standard deviations of the two sets of scores.

Ordinarily, raw scores are used in conjunction with a desk calculator to compute the correlation between two variables. Computing Guide

L.A.

L.A.	85-89	90-94	95-99	100-104	105-109	110-114	115-119	120-124	125-129	130-134	135-139	140-144
148-153					1		2					1
142-147					1	1		2				
136-141							1	2		1	1	
130-135			2				1	1				1
124-129				1	1	2			1			1
118-123	1					1	2	1				
112-117								1				
106-111												
100-105												
94-99										1		
88-93						1		1				
82-87			1	1	1	1	1					
76-81												
70-75					1							1

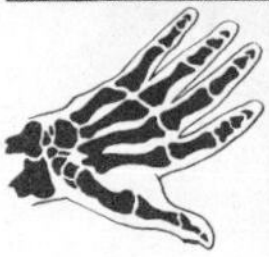

Carpal Age

Fig. 18.6. Scattergram for boys' carpal age (X) and language achievement (Y): $r = .16$.

18.8, when used in conjunction with columns 2 to 6 of Table B of the Appendix, provides the most common procedure for computing a correlation coefficient.

Thus the correlation between intelligence and reading achievement for the 40 boys is high and positive; the two variables are closely associated, yet neither necessarily *causes* the other. The correlations among the 15 variables given in Table A have been calculated and are presented in Table C in the Appendix. The r is .75 between height and weight, .33 between height and expression of emotion, and .69 between emotional adjustment and achievement in relation to expectancy. Other entries are read in the same way.

Rank Correlation

In our study each child was assessed on six personality variables, the last six, as shown in Table C. These ratings were subsequently treated as raw scores. But teachers often rank a classroom group from highest

COMPUTING GUIDE 18.8

Computing the Product-Moment Coefficient of Correlation between Two Variables

Let: r = the product-moment correlation coefficient

         N = the number of cases

     ΣXY = the sum of the cross products (a cross product is each person's X score multiplied by his Y score)

   $\Sigma X \Sigma Y$ = the sum of all the X scores multiplied by the sum of all the Y scores

     ΣX^2 = the square of each X score, subsequently added together

    $(\Sigma X)^2$ = the sum of all the X scores, squared

     ΣY^2 = the square of each Y score, subsequently added together

    $(\Sigma Y)^2$ = the sum of all the Y scores, squared

Formula: $$r = \frac{N \Sigma XY - \Sigma X \Sigma Y}{\sqrt{[N \Sigma X^2 - (\Sigma X)^2][N \Sigma Y^2 - (\Sigma Y)^2]}}$$

Example: Compute the product-moment correlation between IQ (X) and reading achievement (Y) for the 40 boys in Tables A and B.

       Step 1:   Add all the raw scores for X; add all the raw scores for Y. Determine that $\Sigma X = 4164$; $\Sigma Y = 5146$ (see columns 2 and 3, Table B).

       Step 2:   Square all X scores and add the products; square all Y scores and add the products. Determine that $\Sigma X^2 = 452{,}116$; $\Sigma Y^2 = 694{,}108$ (see columns 4 and 5, Table B).

       Step 3:   Multiply X by Y for each boy; add these to determine that the $\Sigma XY = 558{,}594$ (see column 6, Table B).

       Step 4:   Substitute numbers in the formula and perform the indicated operations:

$$r = \frac{(40 \times 558{,}594) - (4164 \times 5146)}{\sqrt{[(40 \times 452{,}116) - (4164)^2][(40 \times 694{,}108) - (5146)^2]}}$$

$$= \frac{915{,}816}{\sqrt{745{,}744 \times 1{,}283{,}004}} = \frac{915{,}816}{978{,}172} = .936$$

to lowest on these and other characteristics, such as originality and sociability, rather than attempting to give each child a rating. In turn when a group is ranked on any two characteristics, the relationship between the two sets of ranks is ascertained by computing the rank-difference correlation. A rank-difference correlation is sometimes computed because it can be done quickly and provides a rough approximation of *r*.

Computing Guide 18.9 gives the procedure for computing the rank-order correlation. It should be used in conjunction with Table B.

This *Rho* of .90 between IQ and reading compares favorably with an *r* of .94 obtained by the product-moment method. And well it should,

COMPUTING GUIDE 18.9
Computing the Rank Coefficient of Correlation
between Two Variables

Let: *Rho* = the rank correlation coefficient
        N = the number of cases
       $\Sigma\,d^2$ = the differences in rank for each pair of scores, squared
            and subsequently summed

Formula: $Rho = 1 - \dfrac{6\,\Sigma\,d^2}{N(N^2 - 1)}$

Example: Compute the rank order correlation between IQ (*X*) and reading achievement (*Y*) for the 40 boys in Tables A and B.

        Step 1:   Rank each set of scores in order of magnitude by giving 1 to the highest score, 2 to the next highest, and so on to the lowest score. The scores that have the same value take the mean of the ranks assigned to them as a common rank, for example, Boys 1 and 10 had an IQ of 107, the twenty-first and twenty-second scores from the top, and both are assigned a rank of 21.5 (see columns 7 and 8, Table B).

        Step 2:   Subtract to find the difference in rank (*d*) for each pair of scores (see column 9, Table B).

        Step 3:   Square each difference in rank to obtain d^2 (see column 10, Table B).

        Step 4:   Sum these d^2; find that $\Sigma\,d^2 = 1082$ (see Table B).

        Step 5:   Substitute numbers in the formula and perform the indicated operations:

$$Rho = 1 - \frac{6(1082)}{40(1600 - 1)} = 1 - \frac{6492}{63960} = .90$$

---

for the formula for *Rho* in Computing Guide 18.9 is in effect the product-moment correlation of the ranks; Rho's abbreviated nature merely results because of the simplifications possible when correlating two sets of ranks. The correlations obtained by the two methods, product-moment and rank-order, are not identical for some information is lost in transforming the raw scores to ranks.

SAMPLING PROCEDURES

Classroom teachers are most concerned with the characteristics of the pupils in their classes as are parents about their own children. Researchers, however, attempt to ascertain characteristics of children or of human beings generally, in the hope that generalizations may be found which have wide applicability. Assume that some researchers wanted to identify the cognitive abilities of children at each age level, 6 through 18. We already know such things as (1) cognitive abilities differ somewhat according to age, sex, rural–urban community, and subcultural groups (Chapter 4); (2) our present means of identifying known cognitive abilities range from crude to good (see Chapters 16 and 17); and (3) some cognitive abilities are not yet identified, as shown in Chapters 2, 7, and 8. Therefore, instead of trying to identify the cognitive abilities of 7-year-olds by attempting to test and assess every 7-year-old in the United States, we take samples of 7-year-olds from various locations in the United States in order to save time and money.

Population and Sample

A sample is a subset or subgroup of an entire group, called a "population." Sampling is used to save time and money, and may provide opportunities for better control than can be had when the whole population is used. Sampling is used in order to generalize from a sample to a population. But to generalize from any sample to a population involves uncertainty. The amount of uncertainty or risk of error can be determined if the sample used is a probability sample, that is, a sample in which every member of the population is ensured a known or determinable chance of being included in the sample. Among the many types of probability sampling, only simple random and stratified random sampling will be discussed.

Simple Random Sampling. A simple random sample is one in which the members of a defined population are drawn in such a way that each one of the population has an equal chance of being included in the sample, and every possible combination of members in the population has the same chance of being included. For example, if the entire population of 17-year-old girls in a city is 5000 and a sample of 500 is desired, each of the 5000 has an equal chance of being drawn into the sample of 500. This also permits every possible combination to be drawn into the sample. A table of random numbers is usually used for selecting a simple random sample.

Stratified Random Sampling. In this type, the population is divided into subgroups, called "strata," on the basis of some characteristic. Then, a simple random sample is selected from each stratum. In connection with the data presented in Table A, the population was first identified on the basis of chronological age, sex, and IQ level. Then, a simple stratified sample was drawn of 40 boys to include 10 of high IQ, 20 of average IQ, and 10 of low IQ. The intent was to secure a sample from the larger population of boys with IQs normally distributed.

The Normal Distribution

The normal curve is symmetrical about the mean and has its maximum height above the mean. Therefore, the mean, the median, and the mode coincide in the normal distribution. Figure 4.2 which presents the curve of the 2904 intelligence scores of the sample on which the 1937 Revised Stanford-Binet Scale was standardized, closely approximates a normal distribution. The idea of normality applies to the shape or form of the distribution but not to any other properties that the distribution may have, such as the mean and standard deviation. Thus, one normal distribution has a mean of 10 and a standard deviation of 3, whereas another has a mean of 80 and a standard deviation of 12. The scores in these two sets of data may be changed to standard scores, and in both cases the mean of the standard score equals 0 and the standard deviation 1, as noted before in this chapter. The various frequencies with which the values of a variable occur in the population can be expressed as proportions by dividing each frequency by the size of the population. Because the sum of all proportions must equal 1, the area under the normal curve can be made unity regardless of the number of cases involved. These two processes—changing raw scores to z or standard scores, and changing frequencies to proportions—illustrate that a normal distribution is independent of the number of cases, mean, and standard deviation.

688

For any amount of deviation from the mean that is expressed in standard deviation units, a normal probability table can be used to ascertain the proportion of the total area under the normal curve corresponding to that deviation. For example, about .34 of the area lies on each side of the mean up to a point of one standard deviation away; and thus about .68 of the area lies between $+ 1\sigma$ and $- 1\sigma$, as can be seen in Fig. 18.7. (Note that σ is used here for standard deviation

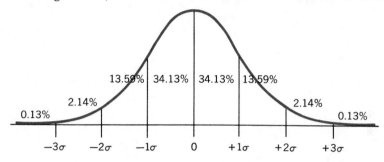

Fig. 18.7. Normal probability curve.

rather than s; the explanation of why this is done is involved, but suffice it to say that s represents the standard deviation for a sample, while σ represents the standard deviation for the population.) The area between $+1.96$ and -1.96 standard deviation units includes .95 of the area; thus .05 of the area lies beyond ± 1.96 standard deviation units. Moreover, .997 of the area of a probability curve lies between $+3\sigma$ and -3σ.

Scores Based on Normal Distribution

Many types of derived scores are based upon the assumption that the raw scores are normally distributed. Table 18.3 shows the relation of various scores derived from a large set of normally distributed raw scores or from a large set of raw scores "smoothed out" to fit a normal distribution.

SIGNIFICANCE OF DIFFERENCES

Hypotheses investigated in an experiment are often stated in the null form, that is, it is hypothesized that no significant difference exists between the results brought about by two experimental treatments. An example of a null hypothesis in an experiment involving team teaching

TABLE 18.3.

*Relations Among Various Scores When the Raw Scores Are
Normally Distributed*

Distance from Mean in σ Units (z Score)	Percentile Score	T Score when $\overline{X}=50, \sigma=10$	Deviation IQ when $\overline{X}=100, \sigma=15$
3.0	99.9	80	145
2.5	99.4	75	
2.0	98.0	70	130
1.5	93.0	65	
1.0	84.0	60	115
.5	69.0	55	
0	50.0	50	100
− .5	31.0	45	
−1.0	16.0	40	85
−1.5	7.0	35	
−2.0	2.0	30	70
−2.5	0.6	25	
−3.0	0.1	20	55

might be: "There is no significant difference in arithmetic achievement between children taught in self-contained classes and those taught in an instructional team arrangement."

The experimenter's task is either to reject or fail to reject the null hypothesis. Experimenters often accept some probability level (or level of significance), such as .05 (read point 0 5), or .01, for rejecting the null hypothesis. For example, if the difference is large enough to be significant at the .05 level, the researcher rejects the hypothesis at the .05 level and concludes that the difference is a true or real difference. However, the experimenter has taken a risk in making this conclusion; the .05 level means that a difference this large or larger would be found *by chance* 5 times out of 100. Therefore, the experimenter never "accepts" a hypothesis, he always rejects or fails to reject it. There is always some small probability (in our example a probability of 5 times in 100 or 1 time in 20) that a difference as large as that required for significance will occur by chance.

In testing the null hypothesis, two types of error are possible. A Type 1 error occurs when the null hypothesis is rejected when it is actually true (that is, the researcher erroneously concludes that the experimental treatments had an effect or did, in fact, produce significant differences). The probability with which the Type 1 error is risked is the same as the level of significance that is established in the study. For example, rejecting the null hypothesis when the level of significance equals .01 means that a difference that large would occur by chance only once if the experiment were repeated 100 times.

The Type 2 error occurs when the researcher fails to reject the null hypothesis even though it is, in reality, false. That is, even though the treatments are differentially effective, the difference found in the experiment is (because of faulty procedure or reason) too small to reach statistical significance. Thus, the researcher erroneously concludes that the treatments do not have different effects. Ascertaining the probabilities of a Type 2 error is much more complex and involves power calculations. Such a discussion is beyond the scope of this text.

The principal tests of significance are: between frequencies, the Chi-square test; between two means, the critical ratio and *t*-test; between three or more means, the analysis of variance and the *F*-test; and between three or more means of dependent or correlated measures, the analysis of covariance and the *F*-test. These tests are used in many of the references cited at the end of chapters in this book. All of these tests yield a numerical value; in turn, this numerical value is compared with computed values in lengthy statistical tables to ascertain the significance level of the obtained difference. One example of each test is given to show how to interpret the test.

Chi-Square Test

The fathers of 15 boys of average IQs and of 34 boys of high IQs were in professional, semiprofessional, managerial, and official occupations. On the other hand, the fathers of 25 boys of average IQ and of 6 boys of high IQ were in clerical, sales, service, and labor occupations. Figure 18.8 depicts the frequencies observed.

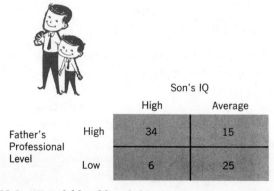

Fig. 18.8. Fourfold table of frequencies for computing Chi-square test.

Applying the Chi-square test to these frequencies (see McNemar, 1962, Chapter 13), it is found that the chances are less than one in 1000—.001—that the occupational categories of the fathers of the boys of average and high IQs were the same. Thus, the association between father's professional level and son's IQ in this sample is a close one, and could have occurred by chance only once in 1000 times.

Critical Ratio or z-Test

Table D in the Appendix gives the heights of two samples of 40 boys and 40 girls, with the means and standard deviations listed at the bottom. To what extent is the obtained difference in mean height between the boys and girls statistically significant? The critical ratio (CR) or z was computed in Computing Guide 18.10 and found to be $-.862$. The probability of getting a CR of $-.862$ by chance is .39. Had the researcher chosen a level of significance at the 5 percent level, he would conclude that the difference between the two means is not statistically significant; had he hypothesized that the mean heights of boys and girls is the same at a mean age of 125 months (null hypothesis), he would fail to reject the hypothesis.

t-Test

The t-test for significance of difference between means follows the same theoretical framework and interpretation as does the critical ratio. However, the t-test is a good test of the significance of difference with N's under 30, whereas the critical ratio is not. The t-test is commonly reported in the literature and is used when testing the significance of the difference between two means. (For a full discussion of the t-test, consult McNemar, 1962, Chapter 7.)

Analysis of Variance and F-Test

In many experiments, more than two samples are used or more than two treatments or methods are applied to the same sample. If five samples are used, the previous method of CR can be employed to ascertain the significance of difference between every set of two means, but this is an inefficient procedure; and to some extent it is not a good test of significance among the five means. The analysis of variance is a more efficient method and can be used to obtain a numerical value F which is interpreted much the same as the CR and t-test.

In the majority of research reports, the lengthy computations which

COMPUTING GUIDE 18.10
Computing the Critical-Ratio or Z-Test

Let: CR = the critical ratio
$\overline{X}_1$ = the mean of the first sample
$\overline{X}_2$ = the mean of the second sample
s_1 = the standard deviation of the first sample
s_2 = the standard deviation of the second sample
N_1 = the number of cases in the first sample
N_2 = the number of cases in the second sample

Formula: $$CR = \frac{\overline{X}_1 - \overline{X}_2}{\sqrt{\dfrac{(s_1)^2}{N_1} + \dfrac{(s_2)^2}{N_2}}}$$

Example: Compute the critical ratio for the two samples of heights (girls and boys) given in Table D.

Step 1: Determine $\overline{X}_1$, $\overline{X}_2$, s_1, and s_2.
From Table D, they are, respectively, 54.47, 55.00, 2.99, and 2.49.

Step 2: Substitute numbers in the formula and perform the indicated operations:

$$CR = \frac{54.47 - 55.00}{\sqrt{\dfrac{(2.99)^2}{40} + \dfrac{(2.49)^2}{40}}} = \frac{-.530}{.615} = -.862$$

are necessary to arrive at the value of F are not given nor are the raw scores. Consider an experiment involving 120 fifth-grade students. The students are randomly assigned to three experimental treatments, A, B, and C, for acquiring concepts in subtraction; the null hypothesis is that there is no significant difference in the ability to attain subtraction concepts between the pupils in the three experimental treatments. The test given at the end of the experiment yields the dependent variable (scores on a test of acquiring concepts in subtraction). Group A's mean score is 18.6, while B's mean is 13.2, and C's is 12.8. Table 18.4 shows the results of the analysis of variance and the F-value found for this study. Computation of the sum of squares is not shown, nor is the method for obtaining the degrees of freedom (df).

The mean squares are obtained by dividing the sum of squares by the corresponding degrees of freedom; for example, $\dfrac{29.02}{2}$. The F-ratio is obtained by dividing the mean square for between treatments by the

TABLE 18.4.

Results of Analysis of Variance
of Acquisition Scores in Subtraction

Source of Variance	Sum of Squares	df	Mean Squares	F-ratio
Between treatments	29.02	2	14.510	3.14
Within treatments	539.97	117	4.615	
Total	568.99	119		

mean square for within treatments; for example, $\dfrac{14.510}{4.615}$. Entering an F table with the proper degrees of freedom, 2 for the numerator and 117 for the denominator, we find that the obtained F of 3.14 is not significant at the .01 level but is at the .05 level (an F of 3.08 or larger is significant at the .05 level). If the .01 level of significance had been established for the study, the conclusion reached would be "no significant difference." However, if the .05 level had been set, the researcher would reject the null hypothesis at the .05 level.

The F-test applies to the difference among the three means; it does not answer which set(s) of two means is (are) different or the extent of the difference. Had the researcher accepted the .01 level, he does nothing further to clarify the differences. However, if the .05 level had been selected, the researcher must subsequently apply other tests to ascertain the significance of difference between each set of two means. By inspection of the means for treatments A, B, and C, it would appear that A is significantly higher than both B and C, but that B and C are not significantly different from each other. However, these impressions must be verified by subsequent rigorous tests.

The analysis of covariance is used to control a variable much the same as in partial correlation. Measures on a variable, the covariate, are taken *before* the experiment begins. The preexperimental differences existing on this variable are then "covaried out" of the final results. The F-test is applied and interpreted, however, in the same manner as the analysis of variance. (For complete discussions of the analyses of variance and covariance, see McNemar, 1962, Chapters 15, 16, and 18.)

Factor Analysis

Factor analysis, an extension of correlation techniques and analysis of variance, is widely used to identify human abilities and characteristics. The measures of the abilities or characteristics must be reduced to numbers whereby r's can be obtained among the various tests, ratings, and the like. We shall refer to all such measures as tests. Once a table of r's or correlation matrix is completed, such as the one in Table C, the data can be submitted to factor analysis with the possibility of identifying three types of factors—general, group, and specific. A general factor is one found in all the tests. A group factor is one found in more than one, but not in all the tests. A specific factor is present in one test but not in any other. Whether a general, group, or specific factor is identified depends partly on the measures originally selected and correlated. If we give only five vocabulary tests, we are likely to find a general vocabulary factor present in all five tests. Combine five numerical tests with the five vocabulary tests, and we are likely to identify two group factors—numerical and vocabulary. If all ten tests correlate highly, positively and significantly, we also will identify a general factor.

We now turn to a more specific problem for illustrative purposes. If it is desired to identify mentally retarded and academically talented boys in elementary school, how much weight should be given to the physical measures of height, weight, carpal age, and how much to IQ? Let us assume that high achievement in arithmetic, reading, and language are characteristic of the academically talented and that low achievement in the same subject-matter areas are characteristic of the mentally retarded.

The r's among height, weight, carpal age, IQ, reading, arithmetic, and language, as given previously in Table C, were analyzed to ascertain the extent to which there might be separate, group, or general factors present in the seven measures. By use of Thurstone's centroid method of factor analysis and a graphical rotation, two group factors were identified with loadings as shown in Table 18.5 (3). Because the method of factor analysis does not in itself lead to the naming of the factors, we shall call Factor I "physical development" and Factor II "scholastic development." Table 18.5 shows that the physical development factor, a group factor, is present in the three physical measures —with loadings of .85 on height, .87 on weight, and .78 on carpal age. One means of estimating the significance of a factor loading is to square it; for example, $(.85)^2 = .72$; $(.30)^2 = .09$. Many researchers ignore a loading of less than .50 because its square is only .25. Notice that the loadings of Factor I on the last four tests in Table 18.5 are small—.21, .30, .27, .25—and have been treated as nonsignificant.

The second group factor, scholastic development, is present in IQ

TABLE 18.5.

Factor Loadings Resulting from Analysis of Seven Measures

Variable	Factor I	Factor II
Height	.85	.23
Weight	.87	.00
Carpal Age	.78	.00
IQ	.21	.95
Arithmetic Achievement	.30	.94
Reading Achievement	.27	.96
Language Achievement	.25	.97

with a loading of .95, language achievement with a loading of .97, reading with .96, and arithmetic with .94. Had only these last four tests been included, we would classify the factor obtained as a general factor present in the four tests. Whether considered in the seven-battery test as a group factor or in a four-battery test as a general factor, our results show clearly that arithmetic, reading, language, and IQ are not specific factors. Also, the two physical measures, weight and carpal age, do not load at all on Factor II; while height is present to a very limited extent, with a loading of only .23. This tells us, among other things, that the physical development factor is almost totally independent of the scholastic, and vice versa.

From this factor-analytic study and others not reported in this chapter, one may safely give no attention to height, weight, and carpal age in attempting to identify gifted, average, and mentally retarded *boys in the elementary grades* when the purpose of identification is to provide differentiated instruction for the three groups in reading, arithmetic, and language.

As suggested earlier, factor analysis is done after correlations are computed, based on measurements of the same individuals. We cannot, therefore, identify general, group, or specific abilities or personality characteristics except as we can secure scores. Further, the researcher draws conclusions based upon the particular tests on which the correlations are based. Caution, a good theoretical framework, and judgment are therefore necessary in attempting to identify and name human abilities and characteristics.

Guilford, for example, described the tests he used, his theoretical framework, and also indicated that his subjects were male Air Force personnel (1). He subsequently listed many specific intellectual abilities which were identified in these males. One cannot generalize that the same abilities would be found in females of the same age and IQ, in the total male population of this age, or in younger people of school age. Therefore, the samples on which the measures are taken as well as the specific measures secured are of utmost importance in attempting to generalize about human abilities or other characteristics by use of factor analysis techniques.

SUMMARY

Experimentation, evaluation, and the use of published and other tests are increasing in school situations. Educational workers and psychologists in large numbers are participating in the collection and interpretation of information. Evaluating the outcomes of research requires tabulating and graphing data as well as knowledge of statistical and research terminology, including measures of central tendency, partition values, measures of variability or dispersion, standard scores, measures of relationship, sampling procedures, significance of differences, and factor analysis.

QUESTIONS AND ACTIVITIES

1. a. Make a frequency distribution for height or some other variable shown in Table A using 12 to 15 class intervals.
   b. Based on the frequency distribution, make a histogram.
   c. Based on the same distribution make a frequency polygon.
2. a. Define mean, median, and mode.
   b. Compute the mean, median, and mode reading achievement from Table A.
3. a. Define partition values, quartile, decile, and percentile.
   b. Arrange the ratings of emotional adjustment in Table A from high to low and compute the following: Q_2, median, D_5, and P_5.
4. Of what value is it to know the range, the mean, and standard deviation of a set of scores?

5. a. Define standard score.
   b. When might information stated in standard scores be helpful to the teacher?
   c. Change each rating of emotional adjustment into a standard score.
6. a. Define correlation.
   b. Construct a scattergram for IQ and reading achievement, drawn from Table A.
   c. Compute r and *Rho*.
7. a. Why is sampling used in modern experimentation?
   b. Define a normal distribution.
   c. Why is it helpful to have tables to convert scores of students into various equivalent derived scores as shown in Table 18.3?
8. Discuss the meaning and possible use of the following:
   a. Chi-square test;

697

b. Critical ratio;
c. *t*-Test;
d. *F*-Test with analysis of variance;
e. *F*-Test with analysis of co-variance.
9. a. Discuss the meaning and use of factor analysis.

b. Discuss the meaning of a general, a group, and a specific factor. Give an example of each.
c. What are some limitations of factor analysis?

SUGGESTIONS FOR FURTHER READING

Cronbach, L. J. *Essentials of psychological testing.* (2nd ed.) New York: Harper & Row, 1960. Ch. 9: Factor analysis: The sorting of abilities, pp. 247–268.

Kendler, H. H. *Basic psychology.* New York: Appleton-Century-Crofts, 1963 Ch. 4: Statistics—the description and interpretation of scientific data, 58–79.

Sanford, F. H. *Psychology: A scientific study of man.* Belmont, Calif: Wadsworth, 1961. Ch. 5: Experimental design and psychological statistics, 118–139.

Walker, Helen M., & J. Lev. *Elementary statistical methods.* New York: Holt, Rinehart and Winston, 1958.

REFERENCES

1. Guilford, J. P. The structure of intellect. *Psychol. Bull.,* 1956, **53**, 267–293.
2. McNemar, Q. *Psychological statistics.* (3rd ed.) New York: Wiley, 1962.
3. Thurstone, L. L. *Multiple-factor analysis: A development and expansion of the vectors of the mind.* Chicago: Univer. Chicago Press, 1947.

Appendix to Chapter 18

THE FOUR TABLES which comprise this appendix are to be used in conjunction with the computations presented and explained in Chapter 18. Table A shows the individual measurements for each of 40 boys for 15 variables, such as height, weight, etc. These data represent the raw scores for computing measures of central tendency and dispersion for the group, or sample, of 40 boys. Table B presents individual scores for two of these variables—IQ and reading achievement—and the individual computations required for arriving at correlation coefficients. The correlations between all possible paired combinations of the 15 variables are given in Table C. Finally, Table D provides individual data on height only for each of the 40 boys, along with data for a comparable sample of 40 girls.

TABLE A

Raw Scores for Fifteen Variables of a Random Sample of Forty Boys

No. of Boy	Height	Weight	Strength of Grip	Number of Permanent Teeth	Carpal Age	IQ	Reading Achievement	Arithmetic Achievement	Language Achievement	Emotional Adjustment	Achievement in Relation to Expectancy	Integration of Self Concept	Expression of Emotion	Behavior Pattern	Child's Estimate of Own Abilities
1	55.0	75.5	21.6	21	99	107	141	123	131	6.0	5.0	6.0	5.5	5.5	5.0
2	53.6	74.5	20.3	13	108	105	123	123	125	3.0	2.5	3.5	6.0	6.0	2.5
3	62.8	116.0	21.6	15	137	109	143	132	136	4.5	4.0	6.0	5.0	4.5	3.5
4	54.3	83.6	20.1	12	120	113	126	125	123	5.5	4.5	5.5	7.0	5.0	5.0
5	56.6	79.5	21.8	19	120	110	122	118	112	3.0	3.0	3.5	7.5	7.5	3.0
6	52.3	57.3	15.0	13	101	101	137	132	129	3.0	4.0	3.0	4.5	7.5	3.5
7	53.6	74.5	23.2	12	113	101	136	122	125	4.0	2.5	6.0	5.0	6.0	4.0
8	48.1	53.9	15.7	12	98	109	122	125	135	1.5	2.5	3.5	1.0	4.0	6.0
9	50.3	56.5	19.0	20	111	106	124	129	119	6.5	6.0	6.5	6.5	6.0	5.0
10	55.1	74.3	19.1	20	126	107	128	125	127	2.5	2.5	2.0	2.0	2.5	2.5
11	54.4	67.5	21.6	12	119	104	117	122	121	3.5	4.0	5.0	4.0	3.5	2.5
12	57.5	83.5	28.5	12	144	112	136	134	134	4.0	3.0	3.0	6.0	6.5	4.5
13	57.0	82.8	25.8	13	116	102	131	125	137	5.5	4.5	5.0	7.0	6.5	4.5
14	56.8	78.0	22.5	12	113	118	128	132	129	4.0	4.0	4.0	6.5	5.0	5.5
15	47.9	49.3	15.9	13	89	101	121	116	122	4.0	5.0	4.5	2.5	3.0	2.5
16	52.8	66.3	21.8	12	120	109	143	132	134	5.0	5.5	5.5	6.0	6.5	5.5
17	55.0	77.5	20.0	12	117	112	145	123	135	3.5	3.5	3.5	3.0	2.5	3.5

18	59.1	113.3	28.2	28	144	114	147	125	127	4.5	4.5	4.5	7.0	6.0	5.0
19	51.9	62.0	14.9	18	116	100	132	115	118	3.5	4.0	3.5	4.5	5.5	4.5
20	57.8	84.3	24.3	11	120	123	160	136	141	5.0	5.5	5.5	6.0	5.5	4.0
21	54.4	73.5	21.2	12	114	128	170	133	147	6.0	5.5	6.5	5.5	4.5	5.0
22	54.5	72.0	22.8	13	120	117	154	136	147	3.0	4.5	2.5	6.0	6.5	4.0
23	55.3	73.5	23.4	12	108	128	154	138	142	4.5	4.5	4.5	4.5	5.0	3.5
24	56.0	77.0	26.3	12	144	128	159	138	153	3.0	3.5	4.0	5.5	5.5	3.5
25	56.0	84.0	24.3	12	120	120	148	130	137	3.0	5.0	5.5	4.5	6.0	5.0
26	56.0	76.3	18.4	12	118	123	166	134	151	3.5	4.5	4.5	3.5	4.5	3.5
27	58.4	78.0	22.7	15	123	123	164	129	145	5.0	5.0	5.0	5.5	5.5	4.5
28	59.1	83.0	20.5	12	119	130	170	142	148	3.0	6.5	6.0	7.0	7.5	3.5
29	54.4	84.0	20.5	13	132	139	160	140	140	7.5	6.5	7.5	5.0	5.5	4.5
30	54.3	90.0	18.5	13	108	146	172	139	151	3.5	3.0	3.5	6.5	6.5	4.5
31	53.1	89.0	15.0	12	123	76	86	95	91	1.5	3.0	2.0	4.5	4.5	5.5
32	56.0	69.0	21.6	11	114	71	85	98	85	6.0	5.0	5.5	6.0	5.5	5.0
33	53.4	66.3	18.0	16	113	85	87	99	92	2.0	2.5	2.0	6.5	8.0	3.0
34	52.9	62.1	17.7	22	119	82	86	91	86	2.5	2.5	3.0	3.0	4.0	3.0
35	52.5	66.5	18.6	12	105	70	91	89	82	4.0	5.0	4.0	7.0	6.5	5.0
36	52.5	58.6	15.4	14	99	70	85	97	87	5.0	4.5	4.5	5.5	6.0	7.0
37	48.6	45.5	11.9	12	105	75	80	87	72	5.5	3.5	4.5	6.5	6.0	4.0
38	54.3	101.0	13.0	26	131	73	100	99	98	5.0	4.5	5.0	4.5	4.5	3.5
39	52.8	90.0	17.8	14	140	52	81	88	72	4.0	4.0	3.5	3.5	3.5	4.5
40	52.4	91.0	23.2	15	102	65	86	94	84	6.0	6.0	7.5	7.0	7.0	7.0
X̄	54.47	76.01	20.29	14.5	117.2	104.1	128.65	120.25	121.75	4.14	4.23	4.51	5.25	5.44	4.28
s	2.99	15.04	3.89	4.10	13.07	21.86	28.68	16.88	23.86	1.39	1.14	1.42	1.54	1.35	1.12

TABLE B

Computation of Product-Moment Correlation Between IQ (X) and Reading Achievement (Y) of Boys, and Rank Coefficient of Correlation for X and Y

No. of Boy	X	Y	X^2	Y^2	XY	Rank X	Rank Y	d	d^2
1	107	141	11449	19881	15087	21.5	16	5.5	30.25
2	105	123	11025	15129	12915	24	26	2.0	4.00
3	109	143	11881	20449	15587	19	14.5	4.5	20.25
4	113	126	12769	15876	14238	14	24	10.0	100.00
5	110	122	12100	14884	13420	17	27.5	10.5	110.25
6	101	137	10201	18769	13837	28	17	11.0	121.00
7	101	136	10201	18496	13736	28	18.5	9.5	90.25
8	109	122	11881	14884	13298	19	27.5	8.5	72.25
9	106	124	11236	15376	13144	23	25	2.0	4.00
10	107	128	11449	16384	13696	21.5	22.5	1.0	1.00
11	104	117	10816	13689	12168	25	30	5.0	25.00
12	112	136	12544	18496	15232	15.5	18.5	3.0	9.00
13	102	131	10404	17161	13362	26	21	5.0	25.00
14	118	128	13924	16384	15104	11	22.5	11.5	132.25
15	101	121	10201	14641	12221	28	29	1.0	1.00
16	109	143	11881	20449	15587	19	14.5	4.5	20.25
17	112	145	12544	21025	16240	15.5	13	2.5	6.25
18	114	147	12996	21609	16758	13	12	1.0	1.00
19	100	132	10000	17424	13200	30	20	10.0	100.00
20	123	160	15129	25600	19680	8	6.5	1.5	2.25

21	128	170	16384	28900	21760	5	2.5	2.5	6.25
22	117	154	13689	23716	18018	12	9.5	2.5	6.25
23	128	154	16384	23716	19712	5	9.5	4.5	20.25
24	128	159	16384	25281	20352	5	8	3.0	9.00
25	120	148	14400	21904	17760	10	11	1.0	1.00
26	123	166	15129	27556	20418	8	4	4.0	16.00
27	123	164	15129	26896	20172	8	5	3.0	9.00
28	130	170	16900	28900	22100	3	2.5	.5	.25
29	139	160	19321	25600	22240	2	6.5	4.5	20.25
30	146	172	21316	29584	25112	1	1	0.0	.00
31	76	86	5776	7396	6536	33	35	2.0	4.00
32	71	85	5041	7225	6035	36	37.5	1.5	2.25
33	85	87	7225	7569	7395	31	33	2.0	4.00
34	82	86	6724	7396	7052	32	35	3.0	9.00
35	70	91	4900	8281	6370	37.5	32	5.5	30.25
36	70	85	4900	7225	5950	37.5	37.5	0.0	.00
37	75	80	5625	6400	6000	34	40	6.0	36.00
38	73	100	5329	10000	7300	35	31	4.0	16.00
39	52	81	2704	6561	4212	40	39	1.0	1.00
40	65	86	4225	7396	5590	39	35	4.0	16.00
Σ	4164	5146	452116	694108	558594				1082.00

TABLE C

Matrix of Correlations Among the Fifteen Variables in Table A

Variable	Weight	Strength of Grip	No. of Permanent Teeth	Carpal Age	IQ (intelligence)	Reading Achievement	Arithmetic Achievement	Language Achievement	Emotional Adjustment	Achievement in Relation to Expectancy	Integration of Self Concept	Expression of Emotion	Behavior Pattern	Child's Estimate of Own Ability
Height	.75	.65	.08	.61	.40	.48	.44	.43	.07	.13	.15	.33	.13	-.14
Weight		.46	.28	.66	.16	.25	.19	.19	.10	.10	.20	.25	.01	.06
Strength of grip			-.07	.45	.45	.47	.51	.48	.18	.17	.26	.38	.22	.06
No. of permanent teeth				.23	-.18	-.16	-.21	-.20	.06	-.07	-.06	.00	-.04	-.10
Carpal age					.15	.21	.19	.16	-.02	-.06	-.06	.08	-.10	-.16
IQ (intelligence)						.94	.94	.94	.01	.15	.16	.05	.05	-.22
Reading achievement							.93	.96	.07	.27	.24	.04	.05	-.17
Arithmetic achievement								.97	.04	.21	.20	.04	.08	-.18
Language achievement									-.03	.16	.15	-.05	-.01	-.20
Emotional adjustment										.69	.79	.40	.09	.36
Achievement in relation to expectancy											.76	.32	.18	.35
Integration of self concept												.29	.11	.34
Expression of emotion													.78	.26
Behavior pattern														.22
Child's estimate of own ability														

TABLE D

Height in Inches of 40 Boys and 40 Girls at Mean Age of 125 Months

Height of Boys	Height of Girls	Height of Boys	Height of Girls
55.0	60.0	54.4	58.4
53.6	58.8	54.5	56.3
62.8	58.8	55.3	54.2
54.3	52.1	56.0	55.9
56.6	57.5	56.0	52.3
52.3	52.2	56.0	55.5
53.6	52.5	58.4	50.8
48.1	55.5	59.1	56.6
50.3	51.0	54.4	54.5
55.1	53.6	54.3	56.4
54.4	58.0	53.1	50.1
57.5	51.8	56.0	55.4
57.0	58.3	53.4	55.8
56.8	56.8	52.9	50.8
47.9	55.6	52.5	54.8
52.8	52.8	52.5	57.3
55.0	54.6	48.6	54.8
59.1	55.5	54.3	54.0
51.9	56.6	52.8	54.7
57.8	56.4	52.4	52.8
		$\overline{X}$ 54.47	55.00
		s 2.99	2.49

INDEXES

Index of Names

709

Index of Names

Index of Names

Index of Subjects

Ability, defined, 34
Acceleration, 507–512; effects of, 634–638
Accommodation, nature of, 69
Achievement: human need for, 430–433; tests of, 430–433
Affective characteristics: conditioning and, 76–77; effect of, on learning, 111–119; as objectives, 49–52; relationship of, to cognitive abilities, 51; in teaching, 143–151
Ages: attitude development at various, 348–356; concept development at various, 221–234; mental development at chronological, 119–120; personality integration at various, 397–403; psychomotor abilities at various, 307–314; and teacher behavior, 174; and teacher effectiveness, 151–154
Aggression, 388–390
Allport-Vernon-Lindzey Study of Values, 143, 150
Anxiety, 390–393; effect of, on learning, 118–119
    See also Emotional disturbance
Aptitude tests, see Tests
Arithmetic, attainment of objectives in, 630–631
Assimilation, nature of, 69
Attitudes: affective and informational components of, 344–346; developmental trends in, 348–356; extreme, 373–374; group, 346–347; nature of, 342–344; techniques for teaching, 347–348, 356–373
Autobiography, teacher's use of, 655–656
Autoinstruction, 549–559

Behavior: defined, 14; exploratory, 428–430; scientific study of, 15–17
Bell System Tele-Lecture, 534

Capacity, relationship of, to ability, 34

Character: effect of, on learning ability, 3–5; purposeful learning and, 67, 68; of teacher, 5
Characteristics: group, 7–8; and imitative learning, 81–82; and physical and psychomotor abilities, 107–111; pupil's, and learning ability, 94–131
Cheating, high school attitude toward, 350–354
Chi-Square Test, 691–692
Classes, 38; special section, 512–517
Closed-circuit Television, see Television
Coefficients of equivalence, internal consistency and stability, 585–586
Cognition, 39, 43
Cognitive abilities: characteristics and, 97–107; cognitive structure, 85–89 passim; and creativity, 288–291; as objectives, 35–46; and psychomotor skill development, 316–320; relationship of, to affective abilities, 51; relationship of, to psychomotor abilities, 49; in teaching, 139–142
College, see Higher education
Competition vs. cooperation, 443–445
Computer-Based Laboratory for Automated School Systems (CLASS), 558
Computers, in teaching, 558–559
Concepts: learning of, 221–234; properties of, 215–221; retention of, 464; techniques for teaching, 242–250
Conditioning, 70–77; and imitative responses, 82–83
Conferences with pupils, procedure in, 656–657
Correlation: defined, 681; product-moment, 681–684; rank, 684–687
Creativity: defined, 272–275; emphasis on, in education, 277–278; intelligence related to, 276–277; techniques for developing, 288–295; tests of, 602–605, 638–639
Critical ratio test, see z-Test
Cumulative percent curve, defined, 670

Format by Vincent Torre.
Set in Linotype Caledonia and Monotype Bulmer.
Composed and bound by The Haddon Craftsmen, Scranton, Penna.
Printed by Copifyer Lithographers, Cleveland, Ohio.
Harper & Row, Publishers, Incorporated.